P9-DMK-426

BALTIC
SEA

LATVIA

Riga

LITHUANIA

NIEMEN R. Kaunas

Memel

Wilno

Minsk

Gdynia
Danzig
Königsberg

POMERANIA

POLISH CORRIDOR

Marienwerder

EAST
PRUSSIA

Allenstein

Grodno

BELORUSSIA

Toruń

VISTULA R.

Białystok

RUSSIA (U.S.S.R.)

Poznań

Warsaw

BUG R.

Brest-Litovsk

P   O   L   A   N   D

Łódź

Lublin

Chełm

Łuck

Kiev

Breslau

ODER R.

SILESIA

Katowice

VISTULA R.

UKRAINE

Kraków

Lwów

C Z E C H O S L O V A K I A

Teschen

GALICIA

Tarnopol

Brno

DNIESTR R.

Bratislava

Cernauti

Vienna

RUMANIA

Budapest

POLAND
1921 – 1939

HUNGARY

DANUBE R.

|||||| To Poland as result of plebiscite

To Czechoslovakia as result of plebiscite

0   Miles   100

0   Km   100

palacios

BOOKS BY Richard M. Watt
Bitter Glory
The Kings Depart
Dare Call It Treason

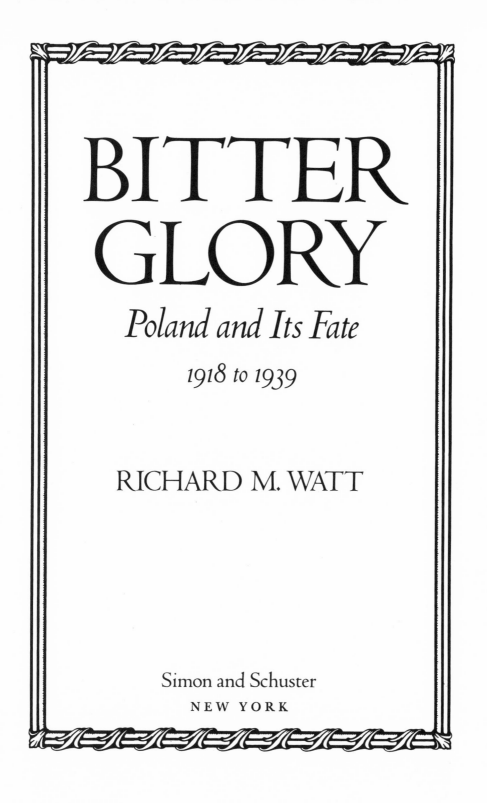

BITTER GLORY

Poland and Its Fate

1918 to 1939

RICHARD M. WATT

Simon and Schuster

NEW YORK

Designed by Slawomir S. Dratewka
Photo editor: Vincent Virga

Manufactured in the United States of America

1 2 3 4 5 6 7 8 9 10

Library of Congress Cataloging in Publication Data

Watt, Richard M   date.
Bitter glory.

Bibliography: p.
Includes index
1. Poland—History—1918-1939. I. Title.
DK4400.W37   943.8'04   79-12958

ISBN 0-671-22625-8

Contents

Preface

THE POLISH TOWN of Kuty possessed very little to lend it any sort of distinction or importance. It was just an ordinary community of about four hundred persons situated at the base of the Carpathian Mountains in the extreme south, where a little tongue of Poland projected into Rumania. Its only significance lay in the fact that it was a frontier crossing point; a half mile southeast of the town there was a two-lane steel-and-concrete bridge that spanned the Czeremosz River, which in 1939 marked the border between Poland and Rumania. On each end of the bridge was a hut housing customs officials and frontier police. The river itself was only about fifty feet wide. During the spring, when the snows melted in the Carpathians, the Czeremosz doubled in width and depth, and woodcutters floated logs down it from the mountains; but during the rest of the year, and particularly in the desperately dry September of 1939, the river was hardly more than a deep sluggish brook.

But on September 17, 1939, Kuty became a very important place; for a few hours it was the seat of the government of the Republic of Poland. The town was jammed with automobiles, trucks and horse-drawn carts inching their way slowly down the road to the bridge to Rumania. All these vehicles could proceed only slowly, because the Rumanian frontier police were examining passports and looking into luggage as if it were peacetime.

The Poles waiting to cross the Czeremosz were frantic at the delay. At four that morning the Soviet Union had invaded Poland. The Soviet border was only sixty miles east of Kuty, and there was little to stop the Red Army's advance. That afternoon Soviet tanks had entered Sniatyn, a town just twenty-five miles away. The bridge at Kuty was now the only point at which a Pole could cross into Rumania— the Red Army held all the others. The Russians would be in Kuty itself within hours. The only military force available to fight them was the personal guard of the president of the Polish Republic, Ignacy Mościcki, which numbered some fifty soldiers. The members of the presidential guard were not the only soldiers in Kuty. Thousands of Polish soldiers were tramping down the dusty road to the bridge to Rumania, but these men were no longer a cohesive fighting force. They were some of the hundreds of thousands of Polish soldiers whose units had been crushed in less than three weeks of fighting the German army and who had been ordered to make their own way south. These soldiers were crossing the border into Rumania; they would then be transported to France, where a new Polish army was being formed.

All day long the remnants of the Polish air force, now numbering no more than a hundred planes, had been flying over Kuty headed for internment at the Rumanian military airfield at Cernauti. They flew very low, because the Rumanian government insisted that they enter Rumanian air space at an altitude no higher than 200 feet.

The bulk of the traffic waiting to cross the bridge consisted of Polish soldiers and government officials, and wealthy Poles or foreigners with automobiles. Most of the foreign ambassadors and ministers accredited to Poland crossed over into Rumania during the day. Once there, they filed dispatches to their governments, stating that the battle for Poland had been lost. There had been little hope that the Polish Army could resist the Germans—and there was no hope whatever for the Poles, now that the Soviet Union had entered the war. The only course left to the leaders of the Polish government was to escape to Rumania. Then they would try to make their way through the still-neutral Balkans and Italy to Paris, where the Polish government would be reconstituted under the protection of its French ally. The Polish cabinet had adopted this plan at a meeting in Kuty that began at four in the afternoon. A proclamation had been issued, announcing that the government must flee in order to protect "the source of constitutional power from this temporary

deluge." At various times during the evening the Polish leaders, headed by President Mościcki, crossed over into Rumania. Prime Minister Sławoj-Składkowski and most of the rest of the Polish cabinet, including its most important member, Foreign Minister Józef Beck, had followed. And shortly before midnight, to the intense surprise of the cabinet members, they were joined in Rumania by Marshal Rydz-Śmigły, the commander in chief of the Polish Army.

By that time the Rumanian frontier police had stopped checking passports. Although those crossing the border were simply waved through, the area around the bridge on the Rumanian side of the Czeremosz filled up with Poles who had not, for the time being, any place to go. The fields around the bridge were crowded with cars and with refugees on foot. And still they came. But now they were mostly soldiers. On the Polish side of the bridge they were warned that the Rumanians would confiscate the rifles that they all dutifully carried. Rather than give them up, the Polish soldiers threw their weapons over the parapet of the bridge as they crossed. Soon thousands of Polish rifles filled up the shallow Czeremosz. Although neither these soldiers nor their government's leaders realized it, this night marked the end of an independent Poland. Almost none of the government leaders or officials who fled from the "temporary deluge" would ever return to Poland. Very few of the escaping soldiers would ever again set foot on Polish soil.

After only twenty-one years of resurrection and tormented independence, Poland again had been overwhelmed by its mighty neighbors.

I beg you to observe, gentlemen, that
I neither blame nor approve: I relate.
—TALLEYRAND

BITTER
GLORY

I

Piłsudski

JOZEF KIEMENS PIŁSUDSKI, the person who, more than anyone else, was responsible for the re-creation of an independent Poland in 1918, was born in December 1867 in the manor house of his father's estate at Zulow, Lithuania. Although the Piłsudski family was a noble one (in 1831 the Russian Herald's Office had required every family of the gentry class in the Empire to furnish proof of its claim, and the Piłsudskis amply satisfied the requirement by providing that they had owned the same lands for at least three hundred years) and although Józef Piłsudski's mother had inherited four large estates that totaled about 20,000 acres, the family had been reduced to genteel poverty. The senior Piłsudski was an appallingly poor businessman who had managed to lose most of his wife's money. When Józef Piłsudski was twelve years old, the manor house and barns at Zulow burned down. There was not enough capital to rebuild, so the entire family moved to Wilno, where the children were sent to school at the Wilno Gymnasium.

At this time the Russian government's efforts to Russify their minority peoples were at their most intense. Sons of the Lithuanian gentry were regarded as particularly hard cases. Not only did they reject Russification (reminding themselves that the Grand Duchy of Lithuania had once covered much of the Russian Empire), but the Lithuanian gentry, because of the ancient dynastic union between the Polish and Lithuanian houses, had historically chosen to regard themselves as members of the Polish aristocracy. They took fierce pride in this, and in many ways they were more Polish than the Poles themselves. They dreamed of the great days of the past, when the Polish nation and their class had been strong and independent. Józef Piłsudski was surely no exception.

Poland had been an enormous and powerful nation. In 1386 the thirteen-year-old Polish queen Jadwiga was married to the Grand Duke Jagiełło, the ruler of Lithuania. One result of this dynastic union was a coalition of forces that enabled Lithuania and Poland to crush the Knights of the Teutonic Order at the Battle of Grünwald (Tannenberg) in 1410. This victory over the greatest military power of the age marked the commencement of more than two hundred years of Polish growth and consolidation. By the sixteenth century the Polish Crown ruled over a federation that stretched from the Baltic Sea in the north to the Black Sea in the south. In the east the Polish lands extended almost to the gates of Moscow. In all of Europe, the Polish kingdom was second only to France in size of population.

But there were serious weaknesses in the Polish state. Poland lacked natural frontiers such as mountain ranges and major rivers, and as a result it was frequently invaded by Swedes, Tartars, Russians, Hungarians or Turks. Poland also was burdened with an extraordinarily quarrelsome and shortsighted aristocracy. The *szlachta*— gentry class—was huge; it is estimated that in the sixteenth century the gentry class totaled three quarters of a million persons, or 10 percent of the Polish population. The nobility ranged from the enormously wealthy Radziwills (who at one time owned almost all of Lithuania) to the "barefoot gentry" who existed precariously by farming their own little plots of land. But whatever their economic status, the Polish gentry were extremely jealous of the privileges they had extracted from their kings.

Difficulties with the Polish gentry had begun in the fifteenth century, when the Polish kings had been compelled to make certain concessions to their nobles in order to obtain military service from them. These privileges were gradually enlarged, and after 1573 it was established that the Polish Crown was not inherited but conferred by the gentry. All major laws had to be passed by a chamber of deputies, known as the Sejm, which usually met every two years for about six weeks and in which every member of the gentry could claim a seat and a vote. Any legislation in the Sejm could be vetoed by a single member, who had only to rise and declare, *"Nie pozwalam"* ("I disapprove"). This was the infamous *liberum veto,* which increasingly paralyzed Polish political life. Between 1652 and 1764 forty-eight of fifty-five sessions of the Sejm were dissolved through the use of the veto. Where a veto did not arise spontaneously, Poland's neighbors, anxious to promote Polish anarchy, found it easy to bribe a member of the gentry to exercise his right to veto. As a consequence, the Polish kingdom constantly verged on bankruptcy, because sufficient taxes could not be voted. The army was frequently in a state of mutiny because its soldiers were not paid. And in 1648, Poland's Cossack subjects in the Ukraine revolted and gave their allegiance to the Russian Tsar. This event abruptly changed the balance of power between Russia and Poland. Poland had been larger, richer, and better organized, but now suddenly Russia was dominant.

The mid-seventeenth century was a watershed in Polish history. Poland began to move into a period of turmoil, constant warfare and rapid decay. There was an endless succession of invasions by Poland's neighbors. For a time, in 1655, practically all of Poland was occupied by either Swedes or Russians. The general devastation caused by this and the subsequent Northern European wars was awful. In the first quarter of the eighteenth century, Poland's population, it is estimated, decreased by 25 percent.

Even after the end of wars in the early eighteenth century, Poland's neighbors—Austria, Prussia, and particularly Russia—continued to encourage the gradual disintegration of the Polish nation. From time to time they invaded the nation to intervene in the election of a king or to "support the Polish constitution," which, with its elective monarchy and *liberum veto,* did much to promote instability.

Throughout most of the eighteenth century Poland was virtually ruled by the Russian ambassador in Warsaw. Russian policy fluctuated between schemes to take over Poland outright and schemes to continue the indirect control that Russia presently enjoyed. But in 1776 the Russian ambassador in Warsaw demanded that the Sejm declare Polish adherents of the Russian Orthodox faith (most of whom were the poorest of peasants) to have all the privileges of Polish gentry. As the Russians obviously foresaw, the Sejm refused to do this. The Russians used this as an excuse to invade Poland, and after an extended campaign, the Poles were crushed.

Doubtless Poland would have been swallowed up by Russia much earlier had her other neighbors been able to agree on a common policy for her dismemberment. Austria and Prussia were not as covetous of Poland as was Russia, yet they did not want Russia to control all of Poland. So, in 1772 Poland's three powerful neighbors signed a treaty in St. Petersburg. Under its terms about 80,000 square miles of Poland (approximately 30 percent of the nation) were divided up. Austria obtained the large section of southwest Poland, known as Galicia. The Prussians got the territory known as Pomerania, which connected Prussia proper with East Prussia. The Russians were obliged to content themselves for the time with a belt of land taken from eastern Poland, although it was evident that this was not the last territorial demand they would make on Poland. After foreign bribery on an unprecedented scale, the Sejm was induced to approve this first of the Polish Partitions.

Incredible as it seems, for some years few Poles saw the danger of national extinction. A very small group of patriotic magnates and lesser gentry sought to reduce the anarchic condition of the political system through reforms in the Polish constitution. In 1791 the reform-minded members of the Sejm secretly drafted a new constitution and, at Easter time, when most of the other members were away from Warsaw, introduced it and demanded a vote. The document, known as the Constitution of May 3, was adopted that very day. Russia immediately demanded that the Constitution be revoked, and when this demand was defied the Russian army invaded Poland. After a spirited series of battles with the small Polish Army the Russians compelled Poland to sue for peace. The outcome was the Second Partition of Poland in 1793 in which the Russians took an enormous section of eastern Poland, comprising practically all of Lithuania, and Prussia obtained most of Poland west of Warsaw together with the port of Danzig and the city of Thorn. Poland was now a landlocked nation less than one third the size it had been before the Second Partition.

Now, at last, the most numerous group of the Polish gentry, the lesser landowners, became aware of their national peril. There was, to be sure, a degree of self-interest in their awakening. As Poland contracted, the various partitioning powers brought in their own laws and their own government administrations. The Polish gentry, who had been accustomed to filling various official positions, suddenly found themselves unemployed. They crowded into what was left of the Polish kingdom, where they sought employment in the only remaining arena for which their temperament and training fitted them—the Army. They filled the officer ranks and even accepted duty as noncommissioned officers. But shortly even these positions were to be denied them. As Poland shrank, the size of the army that it could support shrank too. After the Second Partition the foreign powers insisted that the Polish Army be reduced to 15,000 men.

Impoverished, unemployed and declassed, the lesser gentry suddenly realized how foolishly they had behaved in the past. They longed for the national freedom that they had so casually flung away. In 1794, led by Tadeusz Kościuszko, a hero in the American Revolution, they rose up against the partitioning powers. The Polish armies won several stunning victories, but the might of Russia, Prussia and Austria prevailed. After a heroic defense of Warsaw, the Poles were defeated in the fall of 1794.

The inevitable sequel was the Third Partition, which took place in 1795–96. Austria, Russia and Prussia divided up what was left of Poland. The lesser gentry, comprising most of the soldier class and the leaders of the insurrection of 1794, found themselves hunted and proscribed. In enormous numbers they fled their homeland, going principally to revolutionary France, which welcomed them. These Polish *émigrés* were superb publicists. They told of their nation's heroic struggles against the overwhelming forces of despotism and of the agonies that their countrymen were suffering in sundered Poland. They refused to accept the permanence of the Partitions and plotted endlessly for Poland's restoration.

The propaganda of the Polish *émigrés* created a ground swell of sympathy for Poland among the Western democratic nations. To postrevolutionary Frenchmen the spectacle of Poland writhing under Europe's most repressive monarchies seemed a horror almost beyond historical precedent. Thomas Jefferson wrote of the Third Partition as a "crime" and an "atrocity." In Britain, liberal thinkers composed poems in praise of Poland, and societies were formed to support the reestablishment of a united and independent Poland.

In 1797 a seemingly providential opportunity arose for the Polish *émigré* soldiers. France's young General Napoleon Bonaparte had defeated the Austrian army in Italy and needed troops to garrison France's new holdings. Several "Polish Legions" were recruited, and as the *émigrés* quickly proved to be superb soldiers, their numbers were constantly increased. They were far and away the most loyal of Napoleon's many foreign contingents. In the early summer of 1807 these Polish soldiers were rewarded. Napoleon met with Tsar Alexander I on a raft in the Neman river and at Tilsit concluded a sweeping, if temporary, peace settlement for Central and Eastern Europe. The map of Europe was redrawn, and most of Prussian Poland, Warsaw included, was taken from Prussia and declared to be the separate "Grand Duchy of Warsaw" to be ruled by Napoleon's loyal ally the King of Saxony. The creation of the Duchy was regarded by most Poles as the first step in their national resurrection. But they were mistaken. In 1814 Napoleon was defeated and abdicated. The victors sat down in Vienna to redraw the map of Europe.

At the Congress of Vienna, the first great international peace conference, it was found that no problem was more difficult to resolve than the Polish question—a situation that was to recur at every subsequent European peace conference for more than a hundred years. Finally, and after a great deal of compromise, it was decided to create a small, separate Kingdom of Poland, which became known as the "Congress Kingdom." Prussia gave up its holdings in central Poland, retaining the Poznań region and the province of Pomerania. The Austrians retained Galicia although they contributed one small district to the scheme and also declared Kraków a free city. Although the Russians contributed nothing, the Tsars were made the hereditary rulers of the Polish Kingdom. Under the constitution drawn up by the Congress of Vienna, the Poles were granted their own parliament and their own army, and they were given fairly broad guarantees of freedom of speech and the press. Additionally, all government positions were to be filled by Poles. In short, the Kingdom of Poland was to be pretty much independent—except that the Russian Tsar also carried the title of King of Poland.

In fact, however, the Tsars soon began to treat Poland as if it were nothing more than a province of Russia—and a troublesome and incorrigible one at that. The various guarantees of individual liberties were soon ignored. Whenever they found it expedient, Russians filled the Polish administration with their own officials.

Poland faced other difficulties too. The European price of grain, Poland's largest export, fell drastically in the 1820s. Polish wheat, rye and corn brought little or no profit. The Polish gentry, never wealthy, were soon almost ruined. Their peasantry was left grindingly poor. The kingdom seethed with hatred for the Russians, whom the Poles held to be responsible for all their woes.

From time to time there were desperate insurrections. In November 1830 the Poles rose up, gathered together a sizable army, and were crushed the next year by the forces of Tsar Nicholas I. In reprisal, the Russians suppressed the separate Polish army, closed Polish universities, and abolished the Polish parliament. In 1846 Polish nationalists prepared another revolution, but it was broken up before it even got started. In 1863 there was still another uprising, which survived into early 1864 before it too was put down. The Russians now determined to end their troubles with these difficult and stubborn people. Tsar Nicholas I had said that he knew only two kinds of Poles—those he hated and those he despised. His successor, Alexander II, came to adopt essentially the same outlook. He decided that the only way to eliminate the Polish problem was to eliminate the Poles as Poles. To achieve this, a policy of "Russification" was put into effect in 1864.

Henceforth, the Kingdom of Poland was referred to by the Russians as Vistulaland. Practically all official positions in the area were filled with Russians. An extremely repressive system of press censorship, police spies, and *agents provocateurs* was developed. The Polish language was replaced by Russian as the language of law and administration. The schools were staffed by Russian teachers, and study of the Russian language was mandatory. A complicated land-reform plan was put into effect to try to rivet the loyalty of the peasants to the Russian Tsars, while simultaneously punishing the Polish gentry. Once all this had been done, the Russians expected that the Polish problem would eventually settle itself.

During this period the government of Prussia adopted a somewhat similar plan for "de-Polonizing" its Polish population. Unlike Russia, Prussia had experienced practically no insurrectionary activity in its Polish provinces. But it was faced with an explosive increase in the size of its Polish population.

In a sense, the Prussians could blame themselves for this development. They had generally accorded to their Poles the same benefits that were granted to their own people in the Polish provinces. Much earlier than the Russians, the Prussians freed the peasants and allowed them to buy and own land. This drew Polish farm laborers into Prussia to work for both German and Polish freeholders. And once in the German provinces the Polish laborers tended to stay rather than return to Russian Poland. A similar situation was occurring in Silesia, a mining and industrialized province in southeastern Prussia. The Silesian economy was expanding rapidly and there were thousands of jobs to be filled, but the wage scales were low. To the Poles, however, the pay seemed generous enough, and they flocked across the border to take up these jobs.

The effect of Prussia upon the Poles who lived in it was indeed quite noticeable. They quickly took advantage of the opportunities available to them and became more "advanced" than their fellow Poles across the Russian border. Because of the superior Prussian school system, their children were better educated. The more industrialized Prussian economy offered many opportunities to enter trade, and a strong Polish middle class developed.

By the 1880s, the Prussian state government (and the German Imperial government) had begun to realize just how serious the situation was in their eastern provinces. With the exception of the port city of Danzig, where German capital and enterprise had practically eliminated the Polish presence, the Polish population was growing alarmingly; and these Poles refused to become Germanized. They persisted in speaking their own language, in attending Roman Catholic churches, and in forming their own political parties. In short, they continued to think of themselves as Poles and to expect the eventual restoration of a united and independent Poland. The Germans could not comprehend this. It seemed such gross ingratitude. Their Poles were obviously immeasurably better off as Germans than the Russian or Austrian Poles—why, then, did they not become de-Polonized? It seemed incomprehensible that these Slavs should resist the German "civilizing mission"; but there it was. For obvious military and political reasons the eastern provinces could not be permitted to fill up with unassimilated Poles. Something had to be done.

Finally, in 1886, a law establishing an Imperial Colonization Commission was passed. Its purpose was to buy up land held by Poles in Pomerania and Poznania and resell it on generous terms to German "settlers" brought in from other areas. Initially a hundred million marks were allocated for this purpose; in time, nearly a billion marks were spent. All for nothing. The price of land was driven up; the Poles who sold out reaped handsome profits and then moved into the Prussian cities and invested their money in trade. So, a separate program had to be established to buy out Polish small businesses.

Companion legislation aimed squarely at suppressing the Polish culture put into practice the techniques employed by the Russians. The German language was declared to be the only language acceptable in schools and courts. Eventually it became illegal to use a language other than German at any public meeting. Even Polish names of streets and villages were changed to German. German school teachers were brought in to fill every position. Every government job was filled by a German, who was paid a special subsidy for service in the eastern provinces. But none of these measures worked. In fact, they helped strengthen Polish national consciousness.

The German government was in a quandary. Everything that had been tried had failed. In 1861 in the Poznań region there were 801,000 Poles and 666,000 Germans. By 1911 there were 1,463,000 Poles and only 637,000 Germans—and this after every device had been tried to reverse the trend. The Poles did not presently constitute a physical danger to the regime; they did not murder non-Polish officials, rob banks, or raise insurrections, as they were doing in Russia's Polish provinces. But they did constitute a constantly increasing non-Germanic element within Germany. This was clearly seen as a future menace—but for the present it seemed that nothing could be done about it.

The problem of the Polish presence in Austrian Galicia was handled in the much more casual style that was characteristic of the Austrian government. To maintain the cohesion of its empire, Austria had long since decided to allow as much expression as possible of the nationalist sentiments of its various component peoples. Compared to the Russians and the Prussians, the Austrians took the easy way out in their relations with their Polish citizenry. Of course, there were not as many Poles in Austria as there were in the other nations. At the beginning of the twentieth century, there were about fifteen million Poles in the area that before the partitions had been Poland. Of these, nine million were subjects of Russia and three and one half million were subjects of Prussia. Only a little more than two million Poles lived under Austrian rule, and the Viennese bureaucracy felt that it could afford to be lenient with these people. The Austrians permitted Polish as the language of law and education wherever the inhabitants desired it. There was a provincial legislature to pass special laws that might be desired, and the governor of the province was almost always a Pole. The faculties of the Galician schools and universities were mostly Polish, and Poles were welcomed into the government service in Vienna. The police in Galicia (who were mostly Poles) took a tolerant view of the agitators and conspirators who had fled from Russian Poland. The police did not care much what plotting was done on their soil, as long as it was not too blatant and the conspiracy was directed at other nations.

It would seem that this easygoing attitude would have brought the Austrian government a great deal of trouble at the hands of Polish nationalists. But it did not. Every Pole recognized that the principal enemies of Polish independence were Russia and Prussia. Poland's freedom would have to be won from those powers. Once this occurred, there would be no difficulty with Austria. So, nothing was ever done by Polish nationalists to upset the *status quo* under Austria. Thus, Galicia drifted into the twentieth century as a placid political backwater.

A principal feature of Polish life during the latter part of the nineteenth century and the first decade of the twentieth was the physical mobility of the Polish peasantry. Free from plagues and wars, the Polish peasant population greatly increased. In a short time there was considerable overpopulation in Russian Poland and Austrian Galicia, and to a lesser extent in Germany's eastern provinces. Seeking a better life (and life was better almost everywhere west of Poland), the peasants emigrated by the millions. They created sizable colonies of Poles in Denmark, Switzerland and Belgium. Larger numbers went to Brazil and France. But the most, by far, went to the United States. During the years between 1870 and 1914, nearly two million Poles entered the United States (600,000 from Prussia, 595,000 from Austrian Galicia, and 750,000 from Russian Poland).

In the manner of immigrants with neither money nor training, they crowded together in the larger American cities, notably Pittsburgh and Chicago, where they worked at the hardest and most ill-paid jobs. Even so, life in the United States was better than that in Europe. Although they gradually became Americanized, they did not forget Poland or the fight for Polish independence. Their children attended parochial schools, where the Polish language and Polish history were taught. They formed societies to agitate for Polish freedom, and because they constituted a large voting bloc, their interests began to receive respectful attention in high places.

The Polish gentry, among them those now beginning to be known as the "intelligentsia" because they had some formal education, also went abroad. It became the accepted thing for ambitious Poles who were scientists, engineers, teachers, economists and artists—or who desired training in these fields—to leave their nation. They studied or taught in universities all over Europe. But they never lost their identity as Poles. They were inspired with the mission of Polish independence. They never ceased to dream of their nation's restoration. To the Europeans in whose countries these Poles lived, they seemed cultured and romantic figures who gave glamour to the cause of Polish independence.

The seedbed from which Polish independence was eventually to spring was the European socialist movement. The Polish socialist movement developed somewhat later than did the movement in Western Europe. One reason was that socialism had to await the development of an industrial proletariat of sufficient size to support it. This did not occur in Poland until the middle 1880s. And even then, of course, the bulk of Poles lived under Russian rule, and unlike the Western European states, Imperial Russia had made it illegal to belong to a socialist party.

However, eventually an organized Polish socialist movement came into being. At first there were two Polish socialist parties. One, called simply Proletariat, concentrated exclusively on socialist organizational work and preparation for the eventual proletarian revolution. The other party, The Polish People, had similar objectives, except that coupled with them was the demand for the restoration of an independent Polish nation.

The conflict between Proletariat and The Polish People was intense over the issue of national independence. It definitely retarded the growth of socialism in Poland—which was difficult enough, because of the necessity for both parties to operate in a clandestine manner in the face of constant danger from the Russian secret police. In time, the Russians temporarily solved the conflict between the two groups. Police spies infiltrated the organizations, arrested their leaders, and hanged them in the Warsaw Citadel. Numbers of other Polish socialists were sentenced to long prison terms at hard labor.

Faced with this disaster, Polish socialists of all persuasions decided to close ranks. In 1892 they met in Paris and founded a united Polish

Socialist Party—Polska Partia Socialistyczna (commonly referred to as the PPS). The stated objective of this party was a compromise between its nationalist and its internationalist predecessors—although the majority of its leaders were definitely nationalists who took the view that Poland could not possibly become socialist until it was first an independent nation.

The newly achieved "unity" of the PPS did not last long. A group of young Polish exiles, headed by Rosa Luxemburg, a brilliant young Jewish woman who had fled Poland in 1889, were living and studying in Switzerland. These people were violently opposed to making the achievement of Polish independence part of the PPS policy. They viewed Polish independence as being an archaic concept that was bound to cause error and deviation from the correct Marxist path. Under Luxemburg's direction, these Poles soon split away from the PPS and formed the Socjaldemokracja Królestwa Polskiego (Social Democracy of the Kingdom of Poland, or SDKP). In 1899 a Pole named Feliks Dzerzhinski,* who led a Lithuanian socialist movement, brought his following into the SDKP, which then became known as the Social Democracy of the Kingdom of Poland and Lithuania (SDKPiL).

The existence of two Polish socialist organizations was an enormous problem at every Congress of the Socialist International. The question of which group to recognize was an endless horror. Rosa Luxemburg was too important a theorist to be ignored or to be refused a place and a vote. On the other hand, her party was a relatively negligible factor within Poland itself, whereas the PPS were doing much dangerous work in the homeland. It had to be conceded that the nationalists within the PPS were brilliantly exploiting the elemental appeal of Polish independence to attract Polish workers to socialism. The party was growing very rapidly. So, when the PPS demanded that it be the exclusive voice of Polish socialism at the international socialist congresses, its claims were hard to deny. The whole business created such a turmoil (always-lengthy arguments were conducted in shrieking voices and were marked by great personal vituperation) that among European socialists an endless wrangle without a decision was called a *"Polendebatte"* ("Polish debate"). Most European socialists regarded their Polish colleagues as almost ludicrous.

* Dzerzhinski would later become head of the Soviet Union's Cheka.

However, there was at least one Polish socialist, a leader in the nationalist wing of the PPS, whom no one thought ludicrous. This was Józef Piłsudski—a man who was to become for many years a pivotal personality in Central Europe. Although the PPS was accustomed to having some rather diverse personalities within its ranks, it has to be conceded that Piłsudski—a member of the minor Lithuanian nobility and an ardent Polish patriot—was an unusual socialist.

Piłsudski's patriotism was clearly the result of his family upbringing. As a child he had been told again and again of the January Insurrection of 1863, in which members of the Piłsudski family had taken part and which had been put down with particular brutality in Lithuania. Piłsudski's mother, Maria, was practically a fanatic in the matter of Polish patriotism. She told her children endless tales of Polish heroism, and she kept portraits of Polish patriots locked in secret drawers, which she opened from time to time to show her children. An aunt, who lived with the family, told many stories of the November Insurrection of 1831–32. She was so militantly patriotic that she was referred to in the family as "The General."

If anything more was required to accentuate Józef Piłsudski's patriotic sentiments, it was provided by his schooling at the Wilno Gymnasium. The Russification program was at its peak, and all the teachers were Russians. Piłsudski later recalled that "their system was to crush as much as possible the independence and personal dignity of their pupils. . . . My pride was trampled upon listening to lies and scornful words about Poland, Poles and their history." No student could openly object to this procedure. If he did, he was expelled with what was known as a "wolf ticket"—a record that barred him from any educational institution in the Russian Empire. Piłsudski wrote, "I always count those years spent in the Gymnasium as among the most unpleasant years of my life."[1]

It was evident from his early youth that Piłsudski was an exceptional boy. He was extraordinarily handsome, with blond close-cropped hair, and eyes of a peculiar and intense shade of gray. He was an excellent athlete with a strong, slender frame. Piłsudski was, however, frequently unpopular with his brothers, sisters and classmates. In any relationship he demanded the right to dominate. Piłsudski was inordinately obstinate, and if he did not get his way he would burst into a rage that nothing would assuage. As he grew older, he realized that he must control his passions, and by his late teen-age years, he had become a young man of extreme self-restraint. He made himself become a silent, secretive sort of person; these traits were in contrast with the garrulous emotionalism characteristic of most of the sons of the Polish-Lithuanian gentry.

There was another reason for the development of Piłsudski's personality mask. He had joined an illegal party. He recalled that in 1884, when he was seventeen, "I first became a Socialist."[2] His interest in socialism was the result of his sympathetic, although rather cursory, observations of the misery of the Wilno industrial working class and the fact that becoming a socialist amounted to a sort of personal declaration of war against the Russian Empire. Piłsudski was not, and never became, a particularly well-informed socialist. He had arrived at his convictions as the result of an early and incomplete reading of certain of the Russian utopians. Piłsudski read Marx, but he rejected Marx's economic theory—which is to say that he rejected all of Marx.

Almost simultaneously with his becoming a "very superficial socialist,"[3] as he later described himself, young Piłsudski was forced to make a career decision. The two traditional occupations for the sons of the gentry of the Russian Empire were closed to him. His family had no land, so he could not farm. And to become a military officer, an idea he found most appealing, he would have to serve in a Russian regiment—which he would not do.

Finally it was decided that Piłsudski would go to the University of Kharkov to study medicine. It was a poor choice. He was very unsuited for medicine and spent most of his time with a primitive association of socialist students, of which his brother Bronislav was also a member. He became known to the police as a socialist sympathizer. After only a year at the university, Józef Piłsudski left Kharkov and returned to Wilno. He applied for admission at the University of Dorpat in Estonia, but was denied entrance because of his socialist record. About this time, on March 1, 1887, the Russian police picked up three young students who were lurking outside the Winter Palace in St. Petersburg with suspicious bulges under their overcoats. They were so obviously waiting for the appearance of Tsar Alexander II that their arrest was routine. It was found that the bulges under their overcoats were made by two Browning pistols that proved to be broken and a couple of bombs that were so poorly made they would not have exploded.

The Russian police promptly swept up seventy-four socialist students who were known to be friends of the would-be assassins—or friends of their friends. In this manner, Józef's brother Bronislav was arrested and put on trial with a number of others, including Lenin's older brother, Alexander Ulyanov. Lenin's brother, who had been closely involved with the plot, was executed. Bronislav Piłsudski, who had simply lent money to one of the conspirators, was sentenced to fifteen years at hard labor. Józef Piłsudski, who, it seems definite, had not even known of the plot, was never actually brought to trial but was sentenced by a Russian official to five years of "administrative relegation"—exile in Siberia—simply for having a socialist record and being Bronislav's brother.

"Administrative relegation" in Siberia was a form of punishment reserved for those whom the Russians thought to be "intellectual revolutionaries." The policy was simply to ship these troublemakers off to a remote Siberian village, give them a pittance to live on, and compel them to check in with the village police official from time to time. It was almost impossible for the exile to escape, because transportation was so poor and the few roads were watched by the police. The Russian authorities believed that intellectual socialists would be bored, chastened, and ultimately broken by the dreary life in a muddy little Siberian village. In addition, these socialists would be out of harm's way and would lose contact with their revolutionary comrades.

However, it frequently did not work out that way. For many of the socialist revolutionary intellectuals, administrative relegation to Siberia amounted to a combination vacation and graduate course in socialist studies. The exiles had all the time they wanted to read, write letters, and talk with other banished socialists in their village. They had time to think, observe, and arrive at conclusions. In their leisure time they hunted or fished or walked in the countryside. Many socialist exiles admitted to having thoroughly enjoyed the experience. It was a rare person who did not return as a more convinced and knowledgeable socialist as well as in improved health. Lenin, for example, gained so much weight during his Siberian exile that his family did not at first recognize him. Piłsudski was no exception. If he did not take the opportunity to improve his knowledge of socialist theory to the degree that others did, at least his banishment hardened his convictions. He was now completely convinced that no form of social change could ever come about in Poland until the nation was free and independent. To the Russians he was now actually what he had always been inherently—a formidable enemy.

Piłsudski returned to Wilno in 1892, shaved off his beard to disguise himself, and the following year went underground as a member of the newly formed PPS. To his fellow socialists he was known by the alias "Comrade Victor." As Piłsudski saw it, the immediate need of the newly formed PPS was for printed propaganda—socialist tracts, Polish translations of major socialist writers, and a newspaper directed at the Polish working class. He took charge of this area of PPS operations, set up a system of secret couriers, and smuggled in hundreds of tons of printed material during the next eight years. Beginning in 1894 he also wrote, edited and printed the party's illegal newspaper, *Robotnik* ("The Worker").

If Piłsudski was arrested again for illegal activity, he would certainly draw a long prison sentence. Therefore he had to operate in great secrecy. He cut himself off from party contacts as much as was possible. He had very little direct connection with the Polish workers—among whom, as a member of the nobility, he was not likely to have much influence anyhow. Piłsudski concentrated on the production of *Robotnik*. With only his wife and one assistant to help him, he got out an issue nearly every month. The mere printing of *Robotnik* was an exhausting job in itself. For security reasons Piłsudski was constantly changing addresses, and his printing press had to be small and light enough to permit it to be moved. The only machine that could serve was a small press designed for printing business cards. It ran so slowly that two thousand copies of one twelve-page issue of *Robotnik* took two weeks to print. The influence of *Robotnik* was far greater than its press run. Each copy was passed from hand to hand until it fell apart. The Russian secret police estimated that practically every literate industrial worker in Warsaw read the paper. The simple fact that it was published on a consistent basis was impressive to the Polish workers. *Robotnik*'s editor, Comrade Victor, soon became an almost legendary figure to the socialist workers—and to the Russian police. Most people did not know whether there really was such a person, and most of these few who did know Comrade Victor were ignorant of his true name.

It was too much to expect that this situation could last indefinitely. On February 22, 1900, two police agents following a suspect through the streets of Łódź arrested him as he was buying a suspiciously large quantity of printing paper. That evening the Russian police raided every building which the suspect had been seen to enter that day. In one apartment they found a man living under the name of Dombrowski, his wife, and a printing press. They had caught "Comrade Victor"—who, after a couple of months in the Łódź Prison, was put into a cell in the infamous Tenth Pavilion of the Warsaw Citadel.

The Warsaw Citadel was a stronghold of the Russian army in Poland. It was built after the 1831 Insurrection to give its Russian garrison a refuge against future uprisings. There were nine large soldiers' barracks, called "pavilions," inside the Citadel. After some years, a tenth pavilion was built to house political prisoners. Only the most important or the most dangerous persons were imprisoned in the Tenth Pavilion. Over the years every possible method was tried to escape from it, but no one ever succeeded.

For some months Piłsudski was a typical prisoner. He kept occupied by drawing a chessboard on the flyleaf of the Bible (a copy of which was placed in every cell) and playing chess with himself. He rearranged the furniture in his cell. He then succeeded in smuggling secret messages out to the PPS leadership—which had been thoroughly alarmed at the arrest of this major figure of the organization—and getting secret replies back. In particular, he received messages from a Polish doctor, a psychiatric specialist who was an expert in paranoia.

Gradually Piłsudski's personality changed. He began to talk animately to nonexistent persons—or to be alternately melancholy and despondent. He would not talk with his wardens; he would cringe in the corner of his cell when they entered. He began to rave that he was being poisoned and refused to eat anything except boiled eggs, shells and all, because, he babbled, they could not be poisoned.

After months of this bizarre behavior, a famous Russian doctor was brought in to examine the prisoner. He diagnosed him as a psychotic who was suffering from an almost textbook case of paranoia. The authorities gave instructions that this wretched lunatic was to be transferred to the prison hospital of St. Nicholas the Miracle Worker, in St. Petersburg.

Piłsudski, whose appearance had deteriorated shockingly, was put into a ward with fifty other madmen. He huddled in a corner while they shrieked and raved. His doctors professed to find him an interesting case. Particularly a newly arrived young Polish doctor who was doing research in the field of paranoia. On May 13, 1901, there was a great fair in St. Petersburg, and most of the hospital staff were given a holiday. On that day the Polish doctor appeared with his medical bag and asked to see the patient Piłsudski.

Ten minutes later the doctor, accompanied by a friend wearing civilian clothes, strolled out of the institution and hailed a droshky, and the pair drove off to disappear into the St. Petersburg traffic. The "friend," of course, was Piłsudski, whose lunacy had been a remarkable sham, and to whom the doctor had brought clothing in his medical bag.

Following his escape Piłsudski, using a succession of false papers supplied to him by the PPS, made an unhurried exit from Russia. He stopped briefly in Kiev for a sentimental look at his old printing press—which the PPS had recovered from the Russians and were again using to print socialist literature. He checked to see that *Robotnik* was continuing to be published (not an issue had been missed) and then coolly crossed the Russian border to safety in Kraków in Galicia.

Piłsudski's escape quickly became common knowledge. No censorship could keep it a secret in Poland, among whose workers he became a semilegendary figure of heroic dimensions. A whole series of anti-Russian exploits with which Piłsudski had nothing to do were popularly ascribed to him. The Russians, of course, were now utterly determined to recapture him. Through their increasingly active secret agents located abroad, they attempted to keep track of him when he was outside Russia, and his picture hung in every police station within Russian Poland.

Among officials of the PPS, however, Piłsudski did not enjoy the great popularity that he did with the masses. The PPS was gradually breaking up into nationalist and internationalist wings, with the latter choosing a program more closely allied to Rosa Luxemburg's SDKPiL. Piłsudski rarely bothered to become involved in argumentation with the Marxist purists. Indeed, there was no reason for him to do so. His reputation as a revolutionary activist overshadowed that of almost any other Polish socialist, and he was indifferent to the theoretical wrangles of people like Rosa Luxemburg. Piłsudski cared nothing for the fact that they regarded him as a potentially dangerous exponent of a bastard variant of socialism. They conducted their arguments in the safety of Switzerland and London. He *acted* in the field.

Commencing about this time, Piłsudski began gradually to revert to the gentry type. He became bored with doing socialist organization work among the masses. He gave poor speeches and made no effort to inform or convince his audiences. The authoritarian tendencies he had had as a child now manifested themselves again in a firmly in-grained habit of command. The central committee of the PPS, many of whose members regarded Piłsudski as a power-seeker, began to hold him at arm's length. He was sneered at as a "noble socialist." However, the central committee recognized that he must be given some responsibility and authority, so they put him in charge of organizing the party's covert military operations—which were at that time practically nonexistent. There was a general feeling in the central committee that it might be a good thing for the PPS to con-duct some terrorist activities, such as blowing up police stations, and Piłsudski seemed like just the man to direct this operation. He was authorized to form a group of gunmen which he called the Bojowka, or "Fighting Organization."

This was just the sort of undertaking that now appealed to Piłsudski—a military command that had to be shaped in an atmos-phere of conspiracy and danger. He adapted the socialist courier system that he had developed years ago, so that now it smuggled pistols and hand grenades instead of literature. He recruited and trained a group of men and women to use these weapons, and he flitted back and forth across the border from Austria directing op-erations. He defied the PPS central committee and refused to con-duct the sort of terrorism that they advocated. Piłsudski claimed that gunning down a Russian official, for example, brought no practical gain, only widespread reprisals. He insisted that the most worthwhile objective for his Bojowka was the simple demonstration to the Polish people that there was present on their soil a group, however small, of armed men and women who had, in effect, declared war on Russia and were prepared to give up their lives in this conflict. The activities of the Bojowka were directed into two broad fields—one was "ex-propriations," or raids on Russian banks or money shipments; the other was the rescue of socialist prisoners from the Russian author-ities. Although it never had more than a few hundred members, Piłsudski's organization was conspicuously successful in both fields.

In one year, 1904, the Bojowka pulled off dozens of sizable expropriations. They also developed considerable expertise in freeing socialist prisoners. On one occasion a police captain and a squad of soldiers appeared at the central prison in Warsaw with orders to transfer ten important socialist prisoners who were sentenced to be shot at the Citadel. The papers were found to be in perfect order, and the prisoners (who were roughed up a little and then handcuffed by the captain's soldiers) were put into a wagon provided by the prison authorities and driven off. They did not go far before the wagon driver was chloroformed and the prisoners' handcuffs were removed. The "captain" and his "soldiers" and the prisoners changed to civilian clothes, and the entire group disappeared into the Warsaw working-class districts. That night on twelve major street corners in Warsaw, other agents put up posters announcing "Bojowka has freed the ten Poles, sentenced to die, on the command of their leader Józef Piłsudski."[4]

But despite the Bojowka's successes, the year 1904 marked the beginning of a decline in Piłsudski's political fortunes. The Russo-Japanese War began, and Piłsudski, largely on his own initiative, traveled to Tokyo and attempted to interest the Japanese in supporting a free and independent Poland and in providing money and arms for a Polish insurrection that Piłsudski would lead. The Japanese refused Piłsudski's proposition. They doubted his ability to raise a revolution in Russian Poland and their doubts were well founded. The Russians mobilized their Polish troops without difficulty, and Piłsudski found that he could not raise a single ruble to obstruct the mobilization. An antiwar demonstration that Piłsudski encouraged took place in Warsaw in November 1904, and the Russian Cossacks broke it up with ease, killing eleven Poles in the process.

In the face of all this it was widely felt in Polish socialist circles that Piłsudski's methods were obsolete. It was not just that his Bojowka expropriations had never yielded enough money to cover the expenses of his organization. The more important issue was that Piłsudski's operations were frequently indistinguishable from simple banditry. The Russians had taken to countering the expropriations by selecting Polish hostages almost at random and shooting five men for every soldier or policemen who was killed in a holdup. It was undeniable that too many innocent Poles were being killed to justify the operation. The PPS central committee ceased its financial support and ordered the Bojowka dissolved. This action was, in a way, only an acknowledgment of what was already a fact. So many members of the Bojowka had been killed or arrested that it had ceased to operate effectively.

For a couple of years, Piłsudski practically withdrew from any active political role. A handsome and vigorous man, he was nearly forty years old. He now spent weeks at a time in a little house in the Galician mountains where he chain-smoked and read military manuals and histories of famous campaigns. In his studies, he imagined himself (in the romantic style of the Polish gentry) as the military dictator of a Poland that was free, but under attack from external enemies. He meticulously planned his campaigns of defense and reconquest against the invaders. For a long time he brooded over his frustrations—the failure of the Poles to rise up during the 1904 mobilization and the weakness (as he regarded it) of the socialist leadership. Then, finally, in late 1907 he roused himself. Acting on his own hook, Piłsudski gathered sixteen of the most devoted survivors of the Bojowka, without the sanction of the PPS, and led them on one last expropriation raid.

Shipments of gold, silver, cash and securities from Poland to St. Petersburg always followed the same pattern. They were first sent to a central collection point in Wilno. From there, with an escort of troops, they went by train over the only rail line between St. Petersburg and Wilno. In January 1908, Piłsudski went into Wilno to reconnoiter the area. It would be impossible to hold up a train in Wilno itself. The station was much too heavily guarded. But there was a small station at a place called Bezdany about an hour out of Wilno. Piłsudski determined that his raid would take place there. However, to make the attempt in winter proved out of the question. The snow was too deep for the raiders to get away. So, after posting one of his men in Bezdany to watch the trains passing through and discern the pattern of the military escort, Piłsudski put the attack off until late the following summer.

During the intervening months Piłsudski and his little group of Bojowka survivors all moved to Wilno. Among them were his most devoted adherents, such as Walery Sławek, Aleksander Prystor, and Aleksandra Szczerbinska. Each of the group traveled to Bezdany to reconnoiter the area under one pretext or another. Szczerbinska rented a small cottage in the forest near Bezdany. Another member of the gang, posing as a fisherman, rented a horse and wagon, ostensibly to carry his boat to the local lakes. The whole operation was run on a financial shoestring; the PPS refused to give this Bojowka remnant any support. Piłsudski and his followers had to pool all their money to live, and as the months passed, they had to borrow from friends.

By late September everything was ready. There was nothing more to do but wait for a train carrying a large cash shipment. Piłsudski's agents in the Wilno station were watching for this. In the meantime, Piłsudski occupied himself by writing an obituary, which he sent to a friend for publication in the event that he did not survive the attack. It was a remarkably clear (and remarkably enraged) statement of his objectives—

> I am not going to dictate to you what you shall write about my life and work. I only ask of you not to make me a "whiner and sentiment-alist." . . . I fight and I am ready to die simply because I cannot bear to live in this latrine which is what our life amounts to. . . . Let others play at throwing bouquets to Socialism or Polonism. . . . My latest idea, which I have not yet fully developed, is to create in all parties, and most of all our own, an organization of physical force, of brute force. I have already done much towards its fulfillment but not enough to rest on my laurels. So now I am staking everything on this last card. . . . I may die in this "expropriation" and I want to explain. . . . Money . . . may the devil take it! I prefer to win it in a fight than to beg for it from the Polish public which has become infantile through being chicken-hearted. I haven't got money and I must have it for the ends I pursue.[5]

Within a very short period Piłsudski was to have more money than he had ever dreamed of. On September 26 a money train with a military escort stopped at Bezdany. As soon as it halted, a number of the passengers produced pistols and broke into the escort compartment, killing one soldier and wounding five. Within the station other raiders cut the telegraph lines and held up the railroad employees. Piłsudski himself threw the bomb that blew open the mail car; he then entered the car and blew open the safes. The "fisherman's" wagon was brought alongside and filled with cash and bonds. The wagon was driven off, a few hand grenades were thrown to confuse the witnesses, and the raiders all dispersed into the forests.

The haul was so big that the horse that pulled the cart collapsed that night from exhaustion. The total value was 200,812 rubles—or approximately $100,000 in the exchange of that time. In Eastern Europe in 1908 this was an absolute fortune. The sheer weight of the stolen silver coinage created a problem. Most of it had to be hidden in a hole dug in the forest near the cottage that the raiders had rented. It was brought back to Galicia in small amounts during the following months. Piłsudski now had a fortune at his disposal.

Soon after Piłsudski's return to Galicia from the Bezdany raid, a new type of Polish military organization appeared. At first it was entirely secret, illegal, and open only to the PPS members who had been part of the Bojowka. Its name was the "Union for Active Resistance" and it was first formed in Lwów under the direct leadership of one of Piłsudski's closest disciples, a young man named Kasimierz Sosnkowski. The function of the organization was to secretly train Poles in guerrilla warfare. When the PPS refused to supply funds for such an operation, Piłsudski himself took over its direction and partly funded it with money from the Bezdany expropriation.

By 1910, however, the character of this secret military organization changed completely. Piłsudski shifted its orientation from guerrilla training to what appeared to be more conventional military drill—target practice, close-order drill, marching, and the like. He began to operate more openly and to accept recruits from outside the PPS. The tolerant Austrian government could not see anything very wrong in permitting a few Poles to enjoy some military exercise on weekends. Various national organizations were permitted in the Austro-Hungarian monarchy just as long as they did not agitate for the overthrow of the regime. The Czechs, for example, were positively mad about bicycling, and to the Austrians there seemed no great difference between the Czech bicycle clubs and these Poles with their enthusiasm for practicing shooting rifles at targets. Piłsudski changed the name of his organization to the Strzelcy—"Riflemen's Association"—and they were legalized in Galicia. There was now no need to operate secretly. In fact, inasmuch as it promoted the training of reservists, the Strzelcy were given a collection of used Austrian rifles to practice with. The Riflemen were even allowed to use the Austrian army's shooting ranges on their weekend drills.

Piłsudski, of course, had a much more sweeping program in mind for these Polish Riflemen's Associations. A member of the Strzelcy spent only a small part of his time in target practice. The bulk of his weekend and holidays was devoted to close-order drill and infantry tactics. Each member was expected to buy himself a blue-gray uniform and, while in uniform, to think of himself as a Polish soldier. There were weekday evening classes for all ranks—privates, non-commissioned officers and officers. Piłsudski created a staff school for senior officers, using as texts various military manuals that had been translated into Polish and mimeographed by other members of the organization.

By 1911, the Polish Riflemen's Association amounted to a small part-time army. Every weekend, all over Galicia there were Polish units making forced marches or practicing drill in camps owned by the Strzelcy. There was a Women's Division, which was trained for courier and intelligence operations—with special emphasis on the recognition of Russian military insignia and equipment. Branches of the Association were established among Polish emigrants in Switzerland, Belgium, France, and even the United States, where the Polish community contributed most of the money necessary for the operation of the parent organization. Secret sections were set up in Russian Poland. In Galicia alone, Piłsudski eventually had about seven thousand men in two hundred separate rifle units. This whole operation was so successful that other Polish leaders began to form more-or-less competing organizations.

Piłsudski himself and his personal staff worked on a full-time basis. (The Polish socialist cause had, by this time, clearly ceased to be of interest to Piłsudski, even though he was not to break with the PPS until the middle of World War I. As late as 1912 he was a PPS delegate at an Austrian Social Democratic Party congress. Even in 1914 he still held an official position in the PPS.) Within his organization Piłsudski was invariably referred to as the "Commandant." He wore the Strzelcy uniform, without any rank insignia, at all times. His followers were ardent and dedicated. Piłsudski and his movement seemed to have a special appeal to youth. His "soldiers" included many of the brightest young men from the emerging Polish intelligentsia. The Austrian authorities did not know quite what to make of all this. Obviously, the Riflemen's Association had blossomed into something distinctly more ambitious than simple shooting clubs. But, on the other hand, Piłsudski never spoke or acted against the Austrian regime. On the emperor's birthday, Piłsudski even sent a unit of his men for the birthday parade in Vienna. Eventually the authorities adopted the conviction that the Poles in Galicia had been so well treated that it was inconceivable that they could be disloyal and, anyhow, what threat could a few thousand partly trained Polish "soldiers" —all without artillery, machine guns, or horses for their "cavalry"— pose to the regime?

Many Poles saw it the same way. They regarded Piłsudski and his followers as deluded fanatics. By no means was there unanimity regarding the value of Piłsudski's little army. In Galicia a great many of the townspeople would turn out on Sundays and summer evenings to scoff at Piłsudski's earnest riflemen plodding through their drills. In Europe, where on the first day of mobilization for general war, more than ten million men would be called to arms, what possible weight could Piłsudski's men throw? Only one in twenty of them even had a rifle, and these were obsolete single-shot weapons.

There was, however, a down-to-earth reason for the formation of the Riflemen's Association. For three generations, Poles who longed for the reestablishment of a free and independent Poland had pondered the circumstances that might make it possible. The only hope, it seemed, was a general European war that would exhaust the partitioning powers, break up the ties among them, and dissolve the antipathy of the British government toward any Polish development that might disrupt the stability of Europe. The sequence of developments that would have to come to pass to enable this to happen was awesome—indeed so complex that it seemed impossible. There would have to be an enormous European war, in which Germany and Austria-Hungary would first beat Russia and then France would beat Germany. Great Britain would have to be on the side of France or, at least, adopt a benevolent neutrality.

Piłsudski was the foremost proponent of the idea that this wild and improbable series of events would actually come to pass. He truly believed it, and he devoted his life to preparing for it. The fundamental purpose of his Riflemen's Association was to create the nucleus of a Polish army that would support first one side then the other, to insure that the whole fantastic affair would come out the way that he had predicted. And then, when all this had transpired, his force would become the Polish national army.

Józef Piłsudski was not, of course, the only Polish political leader of stature. By about 1910, Polish political life was thoroughly polarized, and there were other leaders, whose methods and objectives

differed sharply from Piłsudski's. The most important of these men
was Roman Dmowski, who headed a party known as the National
Democrats.

Dmowski was born in 1864, in a small town near Warsaw, where
his father, who had started in life as a construction laborer, was a
modestly successful road-building contractor. Dmowski attended
Warsaw University, where he studied biology, although it was evident from the first that his main interest was politics. As a result of
a patriotic demonstration that he organized during his last year in
the University, Dmowski was forced to flee Russian Poland and live
for a while in Paris and Galicia.

In 1895 Dmowski established an influential magazine, the "All-
Polish Review," which discussed plans for Polish independence. It
was printed in Galicia and was smuggled into Poland. In 1897
Dmowski participated in the founding of the National Democratic
Party, whose political ideas he subsequently expounded in a widely
read book, *Thoughts of a Modern Pole*.

The membership of the National Democratic party consisted
mostly of Poles who lived in the Russian and German provinces. The
typical National Democrat was a conservative, a member of the middle class who generally owned property and who, although a staunch
advocate of Polish independence, would not join the PPS. He regarded himself as one of the "new men" of Poland—above all he
considered himself a *realist* who also possessed a sense of history.

Under Dmowski's guidance, the National Democrats made a close
analysis of the Polish past. What had gone wrong? What historic
defects in their national life had contributed to their loss of independence? Their conclusion was that Poland in years past had been
too heterogeneous. There had been too much religious toleration
and too many minorities who were not then, and who would never
be, assimilated into Poland. Groups such as the Belorussians, Ukrainians, and certainly Poland's numerous Jews, would never acquire the
national consciousness necessary for the restoration of Poland's independence. In order to pave the way for independence, the Poles
must be masters in their own house, neither seeking nor expecting
help from non-Polish elements. Before Poland could become a modern nation, it must develop the internal structure of a modern nation;
this meant both industrialization and a throwing-off of the habits of
the past. The descendants of the Polish gentry must abandon their
preoccupation with farming and the land. They must train them-

selves to be technicians— engineers, scientists, economists, and industrial managers. They must supplant the very large Jewish community as the mercantile class in Poland. When all this was done, then the Poles would be ready for independence.

But how was independence to be achieved? In the general manner of businessmen, property owners, or workers with families everywhere, the Polish National Democrats regarded themselves as being practical men—as opposed to persons like Piłsudski, whom they considered a hopeless romantic, dressing up as a soldier and playing at war. Their attitude was quite understandable. The typical National Democratic adherent lived and worked in Russian Poland. It was one thing for Poles in the security of Galicia or Switzerland to advocate expropriations or the development of a clandestine "Polish armed presence." It was quite another thing for a man whose family, job, career, or investments actually were in Russian Poland. The whole basis of the National Democratic Party was its attempt—in large part successful—to develop a program to make the best of the situation.

No one could really condemn Dmowski and his followers for lack of patriotism. In their own way, as Poles they were quite as good as anyone else; they were only trying to be practical. To begin with, they asked, was there *really* a prospect for a truly independent Poland? Most of Poland's industrial products were manufactured for sale in the larger Russian market, and it seemed certain that Polish industry could not survive without tariff-free access to Russia. Impressive statistical analyses seemed to prove that as a completely independent state, Poland would have to regress into practically a purely peasant economy.

To the National Democrats it was evident that the objective of their party must be the attainment of a semiautonomous (but really *no more* than a semiautonomous) status within the Russian Empire. They must preserve Poland's economic ties with Russia, and surely they must have Russian military protection against Germany, who they believed would rapidly gobble up an independent Poland. Once a semiautonomous status had been achieved, the National Democrats had many plans. They would gradually restore Polish culture and the Polish language to the international scene. They would redevelop the sense of pride in Polish history that the Russians had done their best to stamp out. They would have a democratic government and elect their own Polish leaders and officials to serve them. Finally, they had observed with a sense of envy the cultural and economic accomplishments of their fellow Poles in Germany's Polish provinces. They attributed this prosperity to the much better educational system of the Germans, and they were determined to offer the same benefits to their own children. Perhaps Poland would not be "free" in the strictest sense of the word, but under the National Democrats' plan it would be democratic, proud, educated and prosperous.

In order to achieve their objectives, Dmowski and his party adopted an attitude of "conciliationism" toward Russia. It consisted of demonstrating that they were friends of Russia—brother Slavs who, if permitted to form their own partly independent nation, could be depended upon always to be grateful and loyal to Russia. The National Democrats recognized that it was bound to take some time for the Russian government to become convinced of the essential friendship of the Polish people. From time to time the Russians would undoubtedly do things that were particularly offensive to the Poles. At these times, the National Democrats would turn the other cheek— a tactic that was called "superconciliationism." Conciliationism might be unpleasant—Dmowski himself had no love whatever for Russians —but this policy was seen as the only possible means to the end.

Against this context, the activities of Piłsudski seemed to be criminal follies. How could the Russians be conciliated when another group of Poles was robbing Russian army paymasters, holding up mail trains, and recruiting little armies that were training to fight Russia? Apart from the seeming pointlessness of his activities, Piłsudski's efforts obviously did an enormous amount to dissipate the good will that the National Democrats were so painfully building up. In fact, in 1904 Dmowski went to Japan at the same time that Piłsudski did, for the express purpose of convincing the Japanese that they should *not* support Piłsudski's scheme for a Polish insurrection. Dmowski prevailed.

As time went on, it seemed that Dmowski and his followers had so grown in strength and influence that they might ultimately find success. The Roman Catholic Church, seeing the National Democrats as the best political alternative to the mostly atheistic PPS, threw its considerable weight behind Dmowski's party. It is probable that the majority of Poles in Russia's Polish provinces chose to follow the National Democratic program, even though they might not actually be members of the party. Even in the face of an impending world war, which Dmowski predicted as early as 1912, it was widely accepted that Poles must assist Russia because a Russian defeat would mean the annexation of more Polish territory by Germany. On the other hand, should the Central Powers be defeated, then quite possibly the integrity of Poland would be restored, since a victorious Russia would demand and get the Polish provinces of Austria and Germany. Then, when semiautonomy came, Poland would indeed be united.

Thus it was that the Poles who followed Dmowski and the Poles who followed Piłsudski both regarded the advent of a general European war with considerable equanimity—even though the two parties chose to fight on opposite sides.

2

War and Peace
in Poland

THE HISTORY OF POLAND and the various Polish armies during World
War I is awesomely complex. There were usually three or four,
sometimes five, "committees," all claiming to be the "authentic"
voice of a future independent Poland. There were several Polish
Legions, a Polish Army Corps, a Polish Auxiliary Corps, and an
underground Polish Military Organization. At one time or another,
most of these organizations switched sides and fought against the
powers that they had originally supported. In addition, there were
sizable Polish contingents in the Russian, German, Austrian and
French armies. That it all ended up as well as it did for the cause of
a united and independent Poland is in large part due to the fact that
the Polish military and political effort was so spread out that some of
its forces could not help but be on the winning side.

The first and most important of the Polish Legions appeared
during that opening week in August 1914 when World War I began.
Entirely on his own hook and acting as if he were the head of an
independent nation, Piłsudski mobilized his Riflemen's Association
for service in the field. His tiny army took the name Polish Legion,
evoking memories of the Polish Legions of the Napoleonic wars.

The force with which Piłsudski "invaded" Russia's Polish provinces on the morning of August 6 consisted of about 170 men led by
eight cavalrymen. This was all the men that Piłsudski could quickly

scrape together in the vicinity of Kraków. The infantrymen each carried several old rifles with which to arm the recruits who were expected to flock to their banner. Only five of the cavalrymen, who had acquired their horses only the day before, were mounted. The other cavalrymen trudged across the border carrying their saddles.

The Austrian government did not restrain Piłsudski. In fact, Piłsudski's Legion crossed the border bearing a pass issued by an Austrian army captain. Nor had the Austrians protested when Piłsudski announced, on August 3, that an insurrectionary People's Government had been formed in Warsaw and that "Citizen Józef Piłsudski, whose orders must be obeyed by all, is appointed leader of all the military forces of Poland."[1] The Austrian government doubted that anyone would believe Piłsudski's announcement, but it raised no objection to anything that might create trouble for their Russian enemies.

Piłsudski's initial objective in his invasion of Russian Poland was the town of Kielce, the closest sizable city, about seventy-five miles northeast of Kraków. The weather was fine, there was no opposition, and there was a good road to Kielce. As they marched, Piłsudski's legionnaires tore down or painted over the road signs printed in Russian. Arriving in Kielce, they raised the historic white-eagle flag of Poland, and summoning reinforcements from the Riflemen's Association still mobilizing in Kraków, they awaited a Polish insurrection that would bring torrents of Polish volunteers to join them.

The insurrection never came. Hardly a man from Russian Poland took up arms in Piłsudski's Legion. The fact that no independent "People's Government" had actually been established by Piłsudski was evident to everyone. Rather than rush to join what might be a forlorn undertaking, most Poles in the Russian provinces preferred to await events. And in the meantime, the Imperial Russian Army swiftly mobilized practically all its Polish reservists—eventually there were about 600,000 Poles in the Russian army—and the German army called up all the 200,000 Polish reserves from its eastern provinces without any appreciable difficulty.

Only a few days after occupying Kielce, Piłsudski journeyed back to Kraków to investigate political developments. In his absence, the Russians pushed a small force toward Kielce and quickly forced the ill-trained Legion to retire behind the Austrian border.

The sequel to this inauspicious beginning was the decision by the

Austrians to bring Piłsudski's Polish Legion under some sort of control. It was decided in Vienna that Piłsudski's little army might be turned into a good thing for Austria. For all the Legion's defects and for all the problems it might pose, it was obvious that many Galician Poles would prefer to serve in a separate Polish force rather than in the Austrian army. This being the case, the Austrians encouraged the formation of a body called the Naczelny Komitet Narodowy (Supreme National Committee) or N.K.N. This body was established in Kraków, and it advised the Austrian government on Polish military and political affairs. The Committee included representatives of all the Polish political groups. Care was taken that there were enough of Piłsudski's political rivals on the Committee to prevent his dominating it.

As a result of negotiation between N.K.N. and the authorities in Vienna, the government announced the formation, within the framework of the Austrian army, of two brigades of the Polish Legion, each brigade having an initial strength of about 2,500 men. One of these, the First Brigade, was to be commanded by Piłsudski. The second Brigade was led at first by Austrian officers and then by Józef Haller, a Pole who until 1912 had been a captain in the Austrian army. Because these two brigades were composed of persons who were not politically compatible, it was decided that they would not serve together.

The war in the east did not begin well for the Austrians. During the summer of 1914 the Russians invaded Galicia, inflicting a series of sharp defeats on the Austro-Hungarian army. These eastern-front battles involved millions of men, and the small Polish Legion did not, of course, count for much. The Poles were part of the general Austrian debacle.

But in the spring of 1915, the German eastern armies joined with the Austrians to mount an offensive. They broke through the Russian front at Gorlice-Tarnów, and by the end of the year they had occupied Warsaw and had pushed the Russians almost entirely out of Russian Poland. The Polish Legion, marching in the Austrian army, abruptly found that, however small their part in the offensive, Poland was now "free"—at any rate, free from Russia.

The Polish Legion—particularly Piłsudski's First Brigade—had gradually become a rather formidable fighting force. In 1915 the Austrian government authorized the formation of a Third Brigade of the Polish Legion. It was recruited almost entirely from the occupied provinces of Russian Poland, and by the beginning of 1916 the combined strength of the three Polish Legion brigades was more than 12,000 men.

The Austrians had mixed views concerning the value of the Polish Legion. Under the right conditions these Poles could function as elite troops. Both the officers and enlisted men of the Legions were drawn mainly from the Polish intelligentsia. They were highly motivated and learned quickly. Frequently they were used as shock troops in an important assault or as the last-ditch defenders of positions that had to be held. Although the senior officers of the Austrian army admired the fighting qualities of the Legion's brigades, they also regarded them as unorthodox and ill-disciplined, and their officers as woefully inexperienced. These were valid charges, at least as seen from the Austrian point of view. The Legion, particularly Piłsudski's own First Brigade, did not conform to the prescribed practices of the Austrian army of which they were technically a part. The Legionnaires persisted in wearing their own uniforms, giving their own form of salute, and using "citizen" instead of conventional military titles. When awarded Austrian decorations for valor, as they frequently were, the Legionnaires refused to wear the medals. It was true that their officers were inexperienced—particularly in the First and Third Brigades. How could they be otherwise? All of them were very young men. Their only formal military training had been picked up in the primitive officers' schools of the Riflemen's Association. But it was not true that they were as ill-disciplined as the Austrians charged. They had all been selected on the basis of absolute loyalty to Piłsudski, whom they addressed as "Commandant," and they gave only grudging obedience to the Austrians. In this they reflected Piłsudski's own attitude. He had made it clear that his Legionnaires were never to forget that they were the nucleus of an eventual Polish army and were only temporarily allied with Austria.

Piłsudski was, as always, incapable of being a good subordinate. He persisted in following his own policies to the exclusion of all others. He would make only the barest political concessions to the Central Powers on whose side he was fighting. The Austrians and Germans, on their part, suspected that Piłsudski would switch sides just as soon as it served his purposes—and, of course, they were quite right. But the Central Powers could have no legitimate complaint regarding Polish duplicity. The Germans and Austrians, as well as the Russians, spent most of the war issuing a series of calculatedly vague pronouncements in which they half-promised future independence to the Poles. But none of these powers intended to fulfill these promises. Their object was simply to win the loyalty of the Poles and, more importantly, the military manpower that could be raised in the Polish provinces.

On August 14, 1914, the Grand Duke Nicholas, commander in chief of the Russian army and uncle of the Tsar, issued a proclamation—"Poles! The hour has come when the sacred dream of your fathers and forefathers can come true. . . . May the frontiers disappear that divide the Polish people, thus making of them a unity under the scepter of the Emperor of Russia! Under that scepter Poland will be born again, free in religion, in language, and in self-government. . . ."

Initially, this carefully drafted statement had an enormous impact in Russian Poland. It seemed to indicate victory for the policies of Roman Dmowski and the National Democratic Party. Polish newspapers congratulated Dmowski, and Warsaw students cheered the proclamation. The mobilization of troops in Russian Poland went off without a hitch. In fact, Piłsudski's invasion and occupation of Kielce was criticized in the Warsaw newspapers for introducing an unfortunate division among Poles.

In the face of what seemed to be a definite promise of future Polish autonomy, there occurred in Russian Poland a series of events that were remarkably similar to those that had occurred in Austrian Galicia. A Polish National Committee was formed in Warsaw under Dmowski's leadership to coordinate the relations between Poles and the Russian government. A body of Polish volunteers known as the Puławy Legion was recruited and commenced fighting on the Russian side.

However, as the months passed and the Russian army was driven from Poland, the Russian proclamation began to be regarded with suspicion. Rumors circulated that the Russians intended to take away the Polish territories of Austria and Germany, and make only those provinces into an autonomous Poland; Russia's Polish regions were to remain exactly as they were. Dmowski and his Polish National Committee (which had been forced to flee to St. Petersburg when the Central Powers invaded Poland in the summer of 1915) pressed the Russian government for definite commitments as to the future of Poland. Exactly what degree of autonomy would it be given? Exactly what territory would autonomous Poland comprise? They could obtain only evasive answers to these questions. It was clear that the Russian government was not acting in good faith. In 1915 Dmowski sailed for London to establish himself among the Western Allies, who he felt were more likely to make a commitment on the establishment of an independent Poland.

In the meantime, the Germans stuck their own oar into the matter of Polish independence. Their interest was dictated solely by military considerations. The German government estimated that there were as many as a million Poles of military age in the part of Russian Poland that Germany and Austria now occupied. General Ludendorff, in effect Germany's codictator at that time, observed: "My eye turns again to the Poles. . . . The Pole is a good soldier. Let us create a Grand Duchy of Poland and immediately after [this] a Polish Army under German command."[2] On November 5, 1916, the Germans and Austrians announced their intention to create a "self-governing" kingdom of Poland. But this kingdom was to consist only of territories taken from Russia. Germany and Austria would retain their Polish provinces as in the past. Pending the election of a king, Poland was to be ruled by a twenty-five–member Provisional Council of State. Its army, for which recruiting was to commence immediately, was to be commanded by German senior officers.

After an initial outburst of enthusiasm for the Central Powers' proposal, the transparency of this whole situation gradually became clear to the Poles. The Council of State, of which Piłsudski was a member, found that it had no authority or responsibilities—all decisions of importance were made by the German governor general in Warsaw, General Hans von Beseler. The only responsibility that the Germans gave the Poles was the awkward one of recruiting the proposed German-commanded Polish army, the Polnische Wehrmacht. But the Council of State refused to raise troops for this army until the Germans made some meaningful concessions in the matter of Polish independence. The Germans thereupon opened their own recruiting offices, but they succeeded in enlisting fewer than a thousand Poles. General von Beseler then decided to enroll in the Polnische Wehrmacht all those Poles serving in the Polish Legion. (Members of the Legion who were Austrian citizens were not required to join the Polnische Wehrmacht.) He ordered them to assemble in Warsaw for induction. For Piłsudski, this was the turning point. Imperial Russia was already greatly weakened by the war. Piłsudski now regarded the Central Powers as being the foremost enemies of an independent Poland. It was time to change sides. In fact, he had already begun to do so. On September 26, 1916, Piłsudski had re-signed his command of the First Brigade, although he instructed its officers, all of whom were loyal to him, to remain at their posts and await his orders.

In the late spring of 1917 the Germans announced that the mem-bers of the Polish Legions would be required to take an oath of loyalty upon their induction into the new Polish army. Included with this oath was to be a commitment to a "brotherhood-in-arms with the German and Austrian armies."

Piłsudski decided that he would not permit these troops, whom he still regarded as his own, to make such a pledge. He sent word to his Legionnaires to refuse to take the oath.

On July 9, 1917, all of those members of the First and Third Brigades of the Polish Legion who were not Austrian citizens were paraded in Warsaw for the administration of the oath. The matter had now become a *cause célèbre*. The oath was read, and those who refused to accept it were ordered to take two steps forward. More than five thousand of the approximately six thousand Legionnaires stepped forward. And their officers threw down their swords as a sign of refusal. All the Legionnaires who rejected the oath were arrested and marched off into internment. Shortly afterward, on July 22, the German authorities arrested Piłsudski himself and sent him off to a military prison at Magdeburg.

The cause of Polish independence was now in a most confused state. There now existed at least five more or less official Polish or-ganizations. One was the Supreme National Committee in Kraków, which was oriented toward accommodation with the Central Powers. A second was the Polish National Committee, which had been formed in Warsaw, moved to St. Petersburg, and then abandoned by its principal member Roman Dmowski when he went to London. Dmowski later settled in Paris, where he and a number of prominent Poles established the Polish Information Agency, which claimed to be the *official* voice of Poland. Eventually, Dmowski's organization changed its name to the Polish National Committee and was rec-ognized by the Western Allies as the authoritative Polish group. In Warsaw, there had been established a Central National Committee, which adopted Piłsudski's orientation. At the same time the Germans had established the Council of State for the Polish Kingdom, later changing this body into a smaller group known as the Regency Council.

The situation in the Polish armed forces was equally confused. In Paris, Dmowski's Polish National Committee was helping to raise a Polish army to serve under the French on the Western Front. The First and Third Brigades of the Polish Legion had been disbanded, but Józef Haller, the commander of the Second Brigade of the Legion, and several thousand of his men had continued in the service of the Central Powers and were now known as the Polish Auxiliary Corps. There were several Polish Legions in the Russian army. In Poland itself there was still another organization—the Polska Organizacja Wojskowa (Polish Military Organization), or P.O.W. Piłsudski had built up this secret paramilitary organization by diverting into it the excess of volunteers for his First Brigade. At the time of Piłsudski's arrest the P.O.W. was a sort of underground army, specializing in intelligence work and totaling some thirty thousand members. They were pledged to the strictest personal loyalty to Piłsudski, who was husbanding them against the day of Polish independence, when they would become the nucleus of the Polish Army. Just before his arrest, Piłsudski had entrusted the command of the P.O.W. to one of his most loyal subordinates—Edward Rydz-Śmigły. Rydz-Śmigły was to keep the P.O.W. intact, armed, and ready for orders from Piłsudski.

The Russian revolutions of March and November 1917 demolished several of these miscellaneous Polish armies. Haller and his Second Brigade of the Polish Legion, having lost faith in the promises of the Central Powers, abandoned their positions in the Austrian front and went over to the Russian side. From there they hoped to be transported to serve under the Wester Allies. But before this could be done, the Germans attacked. In a bitter battle with the Germans at Kaniev on the Dnieper River, Haller's brigade was defeated and dispersed. It could not be reassembled in Russia, where the Bolshevik Revolution had just taken place, and Haller's men were regarded as White Guardists. These soldiers made their way back through the German lines to Poland or, like Haller, found refuge at Murmansk with the British interventionary forces. After a while, the British shipped them to France, where they served in the Polish forces that the National Committee had raised.

With the war drawing to a close, the question of what was to be done with Poland became an important one to the Allies. Clearly, it was a matter that had to be resolved soon. In the early years of the war the matter of Polish independence had been treated very gingerly by France and Great Britain. Although unofficially sympathetic, they could not make statements regarding a people who were subjects of Imperial Russia, one of the Allied Powers. But the Bolshevik Revolution put an end to this awkward problem. The French, who viewed the Poles as a barrier against the westward spread of Bolshevism, became particularly anxious to declare Allied support for a free Poland. The British were considerably less enthusiastic, but in time they found that their hand was forced by the man who had become the world's most powerful statesman.

On January 8, 1918, President Woodrow Wilson appeared before a joint session of Congress to announce the war aims of the United States. These aims, which were set forth in fourteen numbered paragraphs and thus instantly became known as the "Fourteen Points," consisted of several rather general statements of intention coupled with a number of very specific promises. The Thirteenth Point promised that "an independent Polish State should be erected which should include the territories inhabited by indisputably Polish populations, which should be assured a free and secure access to the sea, and whose political and economic independence and territorial integrity should be guaranteed by international covenant."

The Fourteen Points were, of course, an enormous success. There is no question but that Woodrow Wilson was a master of English prose, and the simple clarity of the Fourteen Points at once attracted worldwide notice. The Fourteen Points were translated and publicized in practically every language as an example of the exalted objectives for which the United States was fighting. They were irresistible. The Allied governments found themselves with no option but to express concurrence—although in somewhat guarded terms on several of the objectives. But there was no equivocation about Polish independence. The French (enthusiastically) and the British (less enthusiastically) supported this goal.

Woodrow Wilson's support of a free Polish nation was not unexpected—certainly not by the Poles, who had worked long and hard for presidential favor.

In 1915 the Polish pianist Ignacy Jan Paderewski had gone to the United States for the double purpose of raising funds for Polish war relief and winning support for Polish independence. It is hard to conceive of a person better suited for these tasks. Paderewski was then fifty-five years old. He came from a family that had for several generations struggled for the cause of a free Poland. His grandfather had been exiled for anti-Russian agitation. As a boy, Paderewski had displayed a love for music. His parents, although not wealthy, arranged for him to study the piano under a series of well-known teachers. The teachers were not particularly impressed with this pupil. They regarded him as apt but not gifted. Paderewski compensated for this lack of youthful genius by enormously hard work. In his early twenties he went to Vienna and found a few students to give lessons to while he studied with the great pianist Theodor Leschetizky. After giving well-received recitals, he moved to Paris, where he became even more successful, and then he went on to London, where after initial setbacks his success was even greater. By the time that he was thirty he had captured Europe. Paderewski's phenomenal rise to fame was not dependent exclusively on his abilities as a pianist and composer. Without exception, contemporary descriptions of Paderewski emphasize his personal charm.

By the turn of the century, Paderewski was wealthy and famous. He was also a caricaturist's delight. He had a mane of curly red hair, which later turned white, on which a little black hat seemed to float. He was a flaming patriot, totally committed to the cause of Polish independence. Paderewski spoke English fluently, and his familiarity with the language was one reason for his going to the United States soon after the beginning of World War I.

In championing the cause of Polish independence in the United States, Paderewski was, of course, tilling a fertile field. There were more than a million Polish immigrants in the United States and three million second- or third-generation Polish-Americans. Their networks of organization—principally the Polish Roman Catholic Union and the Polish National Alliance—were extensive and vigorous. Paderewski, who eventually was recognized by Dmowski as the American representative of Dmowski's Polish National Committee, proved a superb propagandist. He virtually abandoned his musical career, except for Polish War Relief benefit recitals, and threw himself into the campaign for an independent Poland. Paderewski made more than three hundred speeches in the United States. He raised enormous sums of money; indeed, he almost single-handedly financed Dmowski's Polish National Committee, and in Chicago he helped establish a recruiting organization that eventually sent twenty thousand Polish-Americans to France to join the Polish army being raised there. But most importantly, Paderewski was successful in developing a close relationship with Woodrow Wilson's friend and confidential adviser, Colonel Edward M. House, who found Paderewski enormously impressive. If this charming, distinguished, and rational man represented the cause of free Poland, then it must be a cause worth supporting. Colonel House relayed Paderewski's arguments for Polish independence. House reported Paderewski's admiration, bordering upon reverence, for Wilson—particularly for Wilson's long-standing interest in the "self-determination" of peoples and their freedom to associate themselves into democratic governments on the basis of nationality.

All this had had its effect on Wilson. As early as January 1917, Wilson had told the Senate that "I take it for granted . . . that statesmen everywhere are agreed that there should be a united, independent and autonomous Poland."[3] This was indeed taking a very great deal for granted, because at that time the world's statesmen certainly had not so agreed. Nonetheless, the pressure of Wilson's Fourteen Points soon brought America's allies into line. On June 3, 1918, the prime ministers of Great Britain, France and Italy jointly declared that "the creation of a united and independent Poland with free access to the sea constitutes one of the conditions of a solid and just peace."[4]

But with the matter of Polish independence, as with several other of Wilson's Fourteen Points, there were a great many details that had yet to be worked out. In the case of Poland, the principal "detail" was to determine where Poland was. Wilson promised a free Polish nation that would "include the territories inhabited by indisputably Polish populations"—but exactly where were these territories? Even before the war ended it was foreseen that determining Poland's boundaries would present a thorny problem. To give guidance to its delegates at the peace conference that was to follow the end of the war, practically every Allied nation had set up its own more-or-less secret study group. In the United States this organization was set up under the general guidance of Colonel House and was unofficially called the "House Inquiry," later shortened to the Inquiry. The Inquiry staff consisted of 126 persons, mainly American university professors, who, beginning in November 1917, were given quarters in the American Geographical Society Building in New York City. They were to research the problems that might face the American delegation at a peace conference and to prepare recommendations where feasible. It soon became evident that Poland would be a major problem for the Inquiry. The scholars who were assigned to the Polish investigation produced forty-two separate reports. And the more reports they made, the more difficult was the formulation of definite recommendations.

Dmowski's Polish National Committee in Paris soon learned of the Inquiry's perplexity on the issue of Poland. Dmowski decided to present the Polish case directly, and just before the Armistice he arrived in the United States. With Paderewski, Dmowski called on Wilson. The President asked them what boundaries they had in mind for their future state. Dmowski pulled out a map on which was outlined Poland's vast 1772 prepartition frontiers plus the territory of Upper Silesia and all of East Prussia. Wilson later recalled that "they presented me with a map which claimed half the world."[5]

On November 11, 1918, the Armistice was signed, and shortly afterward the United States Peace Commission sailed to France to participate in the Paris Peace Conference. They had no agreed position on Poland, and their indecision was known to Poland's representatives in Paris. To guide them the American delegates had only the ominous assessment of the Inquiry's executive committee that "the subject of Poland is by far the most complex of all the problems to be considered."[6]

Events in Poland did not wait upon the deliberations of the Allies at Paris. On November 8, 1918, Germany had erupted in revolution. By that evening the Kaiser had fled for Holland, and a German delegation was in the forest of Compiègne receiving the Allies' armistice terms—which amounted to complete surrender by Germany. It was apparent to the German government that, like it or not, there would eventually be some sort of independent Poland. Resigned to this, they made a fitful attempt to come to early terms with this soon-to-be resurrected nation. To the Germans, the most readily accessible Polish leader was Józef Piłsudski, because at the moment he was still their prisoner in the German fortress at Magdeburg.

Piłsudski's imprisonment had not been harsh. The Germans had treated him as a prisoner of rank, and he had been kept in a small separate building called the Summer Officers' Arrest House. Piłsudski occupied the entire second floor, and the military guard (which called him "General" and whose members came to attention when in his presence) occupied the first floor. His food was sent in from a restaurant, and eventually the Germans moved in another prisoner, Colonel Kasimierz Sosnkowski, formerly Piłsudski's chief of staff in the First Brigade, to keep him company. The Germans gave Piłsudski writing materials and, under escort, even permitted Piłsudski and Sosnkowski to stroll about the town of Magdeburg.

Beginning in late 1918, the Germans began to make preparations for Piłsudski's probable role in an independent Poland. Count Harry von Kessler, a German army officer who had served as an attaché in several European capitals and was regarded as having a flair for diplomacy, was sent by the German Foreign Ministry to interview Piłsudski. He brought gifts of wine and chocolate (which Piłsudski gave to his guards) and attempted to draw out the Polish leader on his attitude toward postwar German-Polish relationships. Piłsudski refused to make any commitment.

On the morning of November 8, 1918, Kessler burst into the garden where Piłsudski and Sosnkowski were sitting. Kessler was dressed in a weird civilian outfit—an old hat that was much too small for him and a long, threadbare hunting cloak, beneath which his polished cavalry boots could be seen. Kessler was frantic. He announced that Piłsudski and Sosnkowski were being freed, and he was driving them to Berlin at once. There was no time for them to pack their clothes. Piłsudski put a toothbrush and a bar of soap into his pocket and got into Kessler's waiting automobile. They set out for the German capital, and on the way they were stopped at a rail crossing while a train passed going toward Berlin from the northeast. The train was filled with sailors waving red flags. Piłsudski realized that the German fleet had mutined, and it was now obvious to him why Kessler was in civilian clothes. An officer in uniform was clearly in danger.

In the late afternoon the party arrived in Berlin, where the two Poles were given a suite at a deluxe hotel. They were told that officials of the Foreign Ministry wanted to consult with Piłsudski and would meet with them at luncheon the next day. On the morning of November 9 Sosnkowski and Piłsudski dressed, and after the latter had borrowed a sword from Kessler (Piłsudski refused to appear in uniform without a sword), they walked out on the streets of Berlin. They had arrived on the first day of the German Revolution. Small bands of soldiers passed by offering their rifles for sale for a few marks.

The Berlin streets were beginning to fill up with marching workers on general strike from the factories. Piłsudski and Sosnkowski made their way to Hiller's, a famous Berlin restaurant on Unter den Linden; there they were shown into a private dining room where the Foreign Ministry representatives awaited them. The party sat down to a luxurious meal, but conversation was awkward. Piłsudski was taciturn and would reveal nothing about his plans. He saw no point in discussing anything with the representatives of the discredited regime of a nation in revolution. The Germans were attempting to be affable toward this somber man, who would, they believed, be head of a neighboring state. The noise of revolutionary workers could be heard from outside the restaurant. Only Sosnkowski enjoyed himself. He was amused by the spectacle of the distracted Germans trying to make small talk while their empire collapsed.

Finally the meal was over. Piłsudski, acting more every minute like a head of state, put it to the Germans that they must transport him back to Warsaw at once. With extreme difficulty, a private train was made ready, and that evening, with Sosnkowski and Piłsudski as the only passengers, it left Berlin for the Polish "capital."

There is a well-known photograph which, for some unknown reasons, is widely believed to show Piłsudski's arrival at the Warsaw railroad station on the morning of November 10, 1918. The photograph shows huge crowds, a band and an honor guard; surrounding Piłsudski are scores of uniformed well-wishers. On the basis of this photograph, many descriptions of Piłsudski's triumphant return to Poland have been written. But this photograph actually shows Piłsudski's arrival in Warsaw some two years earlier. When Piłsudski's train arrived in the Warsaw Station at seven in the morning on Sunday, November 10, there was no photographer, no honor guard, and no crowd. Only seven persons were on hand to greet him. The Warsaw P.O.W. had learned of Piłsudski's arrival only a few hours earlier. Waiting on the station platform was only Major Adam Koc of the P.O.W.; Prince Zdziław Lubomirski, one of the members of the Regency Council and Mayor of Warsaw; and five others.

From the railroad station Piłsudski went to Lubomirski's home for breakfast and a briefing on the political situation. He was then taken to a large pension, where rooms had been reserved for him. By noon the news of his arrival had spread through Warsaw, and the street outside the house was crowded with thousands of cheering people. In the afternoon Piłsudski visited Alexandra Szczerbinska,* his mistress, in an apartment in a suburb of Warsaw. There for the first time he saw their baby daughter, who had been born while he was in prison.

For several days Piłsudski lived at the pension, then moved to a private apartment, and on November 29 to an official residence at the Belvedere Palace.

During the fifteen months in which Piłsudski had been imprisoned, a very great deal had happened with Poland to further the cause of eventual independence. In fact, by fits and starts the Germans and the Austrians had actually done a lot to create a Polish government— although this progress had been reluctant and, in some cases, inadvertent.

The Polish Council of State, which the Germans and Austrians had formed in 1917 to help them administer Poland and enlist an army, had early proved to be troublesome. Not only had army recruits failed to materialize, but the Council members themselves had adopted an increasingly belligerent and independent manner toward the Central Powers. Piłsudski himself had resigned from it shortly before his arrest in July 1917. The rest of the Council had demanded additional Polish liberties, threatened to resign if these were not given, and eventually did resign in a body on August 25, 1917.

The Council's resignation forced the Central Powers to take a further step toward the creation of an increasingly independent Polish government. The German and Austrian governments consulted and reached an agreement by which a three-member Regency Council for the promised Polish kingdom was established. The Regents would act as the head of the Polish state pending the selection of an actual Polish king—a matter which was sure to be troublesome, since the Germans and the Austrians had their own candidates.

As the impending collapse of the Central Powers became more and more evident, the unrest within the Polish nation mounted.

---

* Piłsudski had separated from his first wife, Maria Piłsudska, many years previously. He then formed a liaison with Aleksandra Szczerbinska, who had been a member of the PPS's Bajowka. She had been one of the raiders at the Bezdany expropriation in 1908. Subsequently Mlle. Szczerbinska was a member of the secret intelligence section of the P.O.W. and was arrested and for a time imprisoned by the German authorities. Piłsudski's wife, who still loved him, refused to give him a divorce, and thus Piłsudski could not marry the mother of his child until 1921, after the death of Maria Piłsudska. Therefore, although his relationship with Mlle. Szczerbinska was well known, Piłsudski could not live with her at this time.

There were frequent general strikes and demonstrations for independence in the major cities—all of which the German and Austrian occupation authorities found themselves powerless to control. The Regency Council behaved in an ever more independent manner. Without consulting the Germans, they issued a "Call to the Polish People" announcing the formation of a national government and demanding the election of a constituent assembly. Bands of armed Ukrainians took over a large section of Galicia's eastern countryside in the name of a "Ukrainian People's Republic," and there was fighting between them and a little Polish corps which tried to hold the city of Lvov. The Socialist party leaders in Poland believed that Piłsudski was the only man who could bridge all gulfs and create national unity, and they demanded his release. Young Rydz-Śmigły was finding it difficult to restrain the P.O.W. forces under his command. This secret army now totaled fifty thousand men and women, many of whom now had arms and could scarcely be held back from rising up to take advantage of the chaos. The dispirited German occupation troops shut themselves up into their garrisons and made little effort to do more than simply protect themselves. By early November many of the Austrian occupation troops were deserting and handing over their arms to members of the P.O.W. On the night of November 6 a group of prominent Galician socialists led by Ignacy Daszyński, announced the formation of a Provisional Peoples Government of the Polish Republic. They established themselves at Lublin, a city southeast of Warsaw, which was the headquarters of the governor general of the Austrian occupation forces. The Provisional People's Government was "protected" by the P.O.W. (although there was no real need for any protection from the thoroughly demoralized Austrian military forces), and Rydz-Śmigły accepted the "command of all Polish troops" in the name of his still-imprisoned chief, General Piłsudski.

The arrival of Piłsudski in Warsaw on the morning of November 10 thus brought onto the scene the Pole who had every attribute for the hour. Stern, silent, having no close friends but many close followers, Piłsudski enjoyed the respect of practically every Pole. Above all, Piłsudski looked the part of a leader. He invariably wore a plain gray military uniform without insignia. He was a handsome man of medium height, close-cropped gray hair, heavy eyebrows, thick mustache, and piercing blue-gray eyes. His figure was sturdy without being too heavy. In Poland at a time when everybody talked too much and revealed everything about himself, Piłsudski was notably reserved and impenetrable. His prewar forecast of the course that events would take leading to Polish independence had proved remarkably accurate. The Central Powers *had* beaten the Russian Empire and then had been beaten by France and its allies. Everything had come to pass precisely as Piłsudski had predicted, and he had played his hand in exactly the manner that he had planned— first fighting on the side of the Central Powers and then, with his soldiers, refusing to be of service to them once they had effectively beaten the Russians.

Piłsudski was indisputably Poland's greatest military hero. Politically, he enjoyed many advantages—not the least of which was that his fifteen months' imprisonment had removed him from a confused scene in which many other Polish figures, even some very astute ones, had compromised themselves. Although Piłsudski possessed a base of power in his old PPS associates, he had ceased to consider himself a Socialist. (When some PPS leaders called on him and addressed him as "Comrade," he corrected them. "I rode on the red-painted trolley car of socialism as far as the stop called 'Independence,' but there I got off. You are free to drive on to the terminus if you can, but please address me as 'Sir!' "[7]) Even so, the Left considered Piłsudski an old friend, while the Right regarded him as an effective barrier against social revolution.

Piłsudski's position vis-à-vis his most important rival, Roman Dmowski, was very fortunate. He had the incomparable advantage of being physically present in Poland. On the day that Germany collapsed, Piłsudski was in Warsaw. Dmowski was in the United States and, in fact, had not been in Poland for three years. And Piłsudski was the commander of the P.O.W. Although this was only a paramilitary force and was poorly equipped, it was the best and largest armed organization in Poland.

So, when Piłsudski met with Prince Lubomirski in Warsaw on the morning of November 10, he was in every respect what his followers had consistently regarded him—the "Commandant." In the name of the Provisional Government in Lublin, Lubomirski offered Piłsudski full military powers. Piłsudski declined the offer. He would not accept any office from any self-proclaimed Polish provisional government (particularly an exclusively socialist one) and thus be beholden to it. He was determined that *he* would confer offices and positions on others—not they on him.

After considerable discussion, Prince Lubomirski offered Piłsudski the title of Supreme Commander. It was understood that the office carried with it much more than just the command of the Polish Army. The post of Supreme Commander was interpreted as being tantamount to dictatorship. The only proviso made by Lubomirski was that Piłsudski must transfer back all of his powers to the Polish parliament upon its election. Piłsudski agreed to accept the position and Lubomirski's condition. On November 11 he assumed office. Three days later the members of the Regency Council, recognizing that Piłsudski was the only leader capable of governing Poland, made over all their remaining powers to him and gave him the additional title of Chief of State. The Regency Council then dissolved itself. Simultaneously, the Lublin Provisional Government, accepting Piłsudski as the nation's *de facto* ruler, dissolved itself. Total authority over whatever political and military structure there was in Poland was now in the hands of Józef Piłsudski. He had been waiting all his life for this moment.

3

"No One Gave More Trouble Than the Poles"

WHEN THE VICTORS in the World War assembled for the Paris Peace Conference of 1919, they found themselves, to their surprise, engulfed by a cloud of persons representing practically every national, ethnic and religious group. There were special pleaders for the Sein Feiners, the Koreans, the Arabs and the Armenians; there were advocates for the Balts, the Aaland Islanders, the Kurds, the Hindus, and dozens of others. For all their pre-Conference preparation, the major allies had never contemplated dealing with the variety of problems that all these miscellaneous groups brought to them. Indeed, some of the would-be "nations" that sent representatives to Paris had never been heard of by any of the major Allied powers. This did not seem to discomfit or deter these suitors for independence. They all operated in about the same way. Having arrived in Paris, they set up offices and immediately commenced to churn out bulletins, announcements and historical studies, all aimed at convincing the important powers of the justness of their claims. Ceaselessly they made the rounds of the offices of every major power represented at Paris. They filled every anteroom, waited impatiently outside every meeting, and pestered everyone who might possibly have some influence.

The major allies did not quite know what to do with all these suppliants. Indeed, there was some question as to whether any notice at all should be paid to these people. After all, the principal business of the Peace Conference was supposed to be the drafting of a peace treaty to be presented to the Germans. But as the weeks went by, it became evident that some sort of recognition had to be given to many of these small nations—or would-be nations. This was particularly true of those states that bordered upon Germany and for which frontiers would obviously have to be defined. It quickly became clear that it was not enough to establish a new nation, to recognize it diplomatically, and to compel Germany to sign a treaty agreeing to the existence of a new neighbor. The new nations began to have internal problems, many of which they brought back to Paris for solution by the Allies. And beyond this, they frequently began fighting among themselves and thus forced the Allies to step in and settle their squabbles.

In the end, the major Allied delegates found themselves spending as much time solving the worrisome problems of various new or incipient nations as they did in dealing with the matter of peace with Germany. In this connection, as the British Prime Minister David Lloyd George observed, "No one gave more trouble than the Poles."[1] Given the extraordinarily contentious character of the new nations, this was saying a lot.

It is doubtful whether any of the persons who were to serve on the Polish delegation concerned himself much with the degree of exasperation that they would develop in Lloyd George and many others. In all their long history of aspiration to nationhood it had been amply demonstrated to the Poles that self-effacement was no virtue. Poland was on the brink of resurrection only because of years of single-minded perseverance on the part of Polish patriots. Their nation had not gotten to where it was now by its advocates' taking the low road. If the Poles had to be excessively troublesome, disputatious and aggressive, then they were prepared to be so. In all great affairs there was a time to be amiable (and they had surely demonstrated a capacity for this in the past), and there was a time to be assertive. The Poles would not have cared much if the Peace Conference had been forced to devote almost all of its time to Polish affairs; indeed, they would have regarded this as no more than Poland's due. It became apparent even to the friends of Poland in the United States delegation that the Poles had no sense of political proportion. They seemed to have an obsessive need to make every world issue revolve around Poland. The Western diplomats at Paris told one another an apocryphal story in which an Englishman, a German and a Pole prepared monographs on the subject of the elephant. The Englishman wrote on how to hunt an elephant. The German described the elephant's physiology. The Pole began his monograph with the words, *"L'éléphant, c'est une question polonaise."*

The Paris Peace Conference officially began on January 18, but by then the Polish delegation already had a fairly good idea how they stood with the most important of the Allies. They knew that the British government was only lukewarm in the matter of Polish independence. There was no particular animosity on the part of the British—only the definite sentiment that historically the Poles had been poor managers of their own political affairs. To be sure, Great Britain was definitely committed to the concept of Polish independence, but that did not mean that the British were going to support any exorbitant Polish demands. The Foreign Office had been careful to advise the British delegation that "for the sake of Poland's own future we must firmly oppose exaggerated Polish claims."[2]

The United States was much more sympathetic. It would not be too much to say that Woodrow Wilson was obsessed with the idea of independence for small nationalities. He had committed the United States to a program involving the redrawing of the frontiers of many nations "along clearly recognizable lines of nationality."

The strengths of Wilson's policies were their idealism and their utter lack of self-interest. Among their weaknesses were the failure to recognize that in Europe there were very few "clearly recognizable lines of nationality" along which frontiers could be drawn, and that various European nations, both old and "new," would not be able to overcome historic animosities. But as the Peace Conference convened, the weaknesses of Wilson's program were unsuspected. The president of the United States was the most admired, respected, and influential man in the world. No one could foresee, when the Peace Conference opened, just how rapidly his influence would wane. The Poles had concentrated their efforts on the United States, whom they regarded as their principal patron—until suddenly it became apparent to them that France was prepared to offer much more.

Although France had been historically sympathetic to Poland, she had fought most of the war under the definite assumption that Poland would remain what it had been—a province of France's ally

Józef Piłsudski (left) as a child, with his brother Bronislav.

Piłsudski's parents, Maria Piłsudska and Józef Piłsudski.

Piłsudski, aged nineteen, at the time of his first arrest by the Tsarist police.

The front page of the first issue of *Robotnik*, the socialist newspaper founded, written and printed by Piłsudski beginning in 1894. At one time it was estimated that practically every literate industrial worker in Warsaw read this clandestinely produced newspaper.

Warszawa.   Czerwiec 1894 r.   Nr. 1.

Proletaryusze wszystkich krajów, łączcie się!

ROBOTNIK

ORGAN POLSKIEJ PARTYI SOCYALISTYCZNEJ

Towarzysze, upraszamy Was o rozpowszechnianie „Robotnika".

OD REDAKCYI.

Spełniając obietnicę, wyrażoną w jednodniówce, gdzie uzasadniliśmy nasze stanowisko wobec rozwoju pracy robotniczej w Polsce, zakładamy obecnie pismo, którego zadaniem jest obrona interesów klasy robotniczej. Mając na uwadze, że pismo takie, jeżeli nie chce być oderwane od życia, nie może wychodzić za granicą, zakładamy je w kraju. Umieszczać w niem będziemy w jaknajdostępniejszej dla szerokiego ogółu formie wszystko, co tylko może interesować i pouczyć robotników, a ma bezpośredni związek ze sprawą robotniczą. Na pierwszym planie informować będziemy czytelników o wszelkich przejawach ruchu robotniczego u nas i w innych krajach; notować będziemy fakty, wypływające z nienormalnych stosunków politycznych i społecznych; krytykować każde rozporządzenie rządu, skierowane na krzywdę robotnikom; ujawniać wszelkiego rodzaju nadużycia władz administracyjnych; zdzierać maskę obłudy z naszych klas posiadających i obrońców obecnego porządku rzeczy i w ogóle stać zawsze będziemy na straży interesów klasy robotniczej i z tego punktu widzenia oświetlać wszystkie objawy społeczne.

Pismo to więc jest Waszem, towarzysze-robotnicy, Wam więc je poświęcamy, pragnąc aby ono stało się Waszym przyjacielem i doradcą w codziennej walce i w Waszej działalności agitacyjnej. Mamy nadzieję, że zaradzi ono bardzo ważnemu brakowi w ruchu socyalistycznym u nas i że przyczyni się ogromnie do rozszerzenia się świadomości wśród szerokich mas pracujących.

Już 10 lat mija, jak jesteśmy pozbawieni pisma robotniczego w kraju. 10 lat temu nasi bohaterscy poprzednicy założyli pismo «Proletaryat», którego wyszło zaledwie 5 numerów. Rozwścieczony rząd wytężył swoje siły, organizacyę ówczesną zgniótł, ale socyalizmu nie wytępił, bo tego żadne siły dokonać nie są w stanie. Od tego czasu wiele się zmieniło, ruch spotężniał i rozrósł się mając już 16 lat krwawej walki i swą męczeńską historyę za sobą. To co dla naszych dzielnych poprzedników okazało się niemożliwem, my podejmujemy z góry będąc przeświadczeni o trudnościach, jakie spotkamy i o prześladowaniach, jakie nas ścigać będą, ufni w to, że na swojem stanowisku wytrwać potrafimy.

Towarzysze! Oddając pismo do Waszego wyłącznie rozporządzenia, zwracamy się do wszystkich, komu sprawa robotnicza leży na sercu, z gorącą prośbą o poparcie i współpracownictwo. Jedynie wtedy tylko podołamy swemu zadaniu, jeżeli skąpić nam nie będziecie wiadomości i faktów, mających ogólniejszy charakter, a także udzielać nam będziecie swoich rad i wskazówek. Chcemy, aby czytelnicy nasi mieli pismo takiem, jakiem go mieć pragną.

Numer pierwszy poświęcamy przeważnie sprawozdaniom z obchodu święta majowego.

Piłsudski's cell in the Tenth Pavilion of the Warsaw Citadel. He was imprisoned here in 1900 after his arrest by Russian secret police.

Piłsudski's first wife, Maria Piłsudska.

Members of the Polish Riflemen's Association on a training march in Austrian Galicia, c. 1913.

Piłsudski in uniform as commander of the Strzelcy—the Polish Riflemen's Association —in 1914.

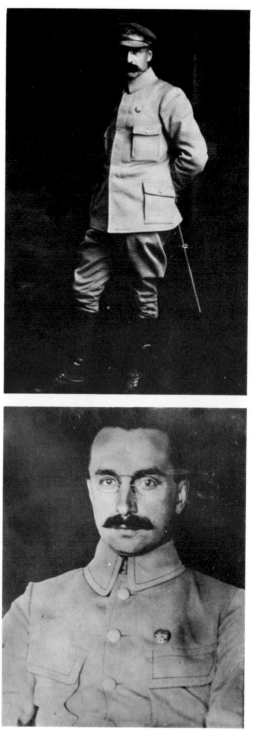

Kazimierz Sosnkowski, Piłsudski's principal aide in the Riflemen's Association and later in the Polish Legion. Sosnkowski was about 29 years old when this picture was taken sometime in 1914.

Józef Beck in the uniform of the First Brigade of the Polish Legion, c. 1915.

Walery Sławek, Piłsudski's devoted assistant in the Bojówka, the Riflemen's Association, and, in the photograph, as an officer in Piłsudski's First Brigade of the Polish Legion.

Roman Dmowski, Piłsudski's early rival for the leadership of independent Poland. (NATIONAL ARCHIVES)

General Józef Haller, commander of the Polish army raised in France in 1918, shown here presenting colors to one of his divisions. In 1919, Haller's "Blue Army" was repatriated to Poland, where it became an important part of the new Polish Army.

Ignacy Paderewski, Polish prime minister, 1919. (NATIONAL ARCHIVES)

Piłsudski, Polish chief of state, and Paderewski, Polish prime minister, on their way to the opening of the first Polish parliament, February 10, 1919.

Wojciech Korfanty, Polish plebiscite commissioner for Upper Silesia and leader of the Polish resistance in that region.

Parade in Warsaw in November 1918 celebrating Polish independence, just attained. The church on the left is the Church of the Holy Cross.

Józef Beck as a captain in the
Polish Army in 1919.

Piłsudski and General Rydz-Śmigły at the
front, May 1920. (NATIONAL ARCHIVES)

Polish cavalry entering Kiev, May 8, 1920.

The Allied Mission to Poland in
Warsaw, summer of 1920. In the
front row (l. to r.) are Lord
D'Abernon, Ambassador Jusser-
and, General Weygand, and Sir
Maurice Hankey.

Władyslaw Grabski, Polish
prime minister, 1920–22;
1923–25.

General Władyslaw Sikorski, Polish prime minister, 1922–23.

Gabriel Narutowicz, President of the Polish Republic, December 1922.

Stanisław Wojciechowski, President of the Polish Republic, 1922–26.

Piłsudski's home at Sulejówek where he was in "retirement" 1923–26.
It was from here that he left on the morning of May 12, 1926, for his
march on Warsaw.

Piłsudski starting across the Poniatowski Bridge for his meeting with
President Wojciechowski, approximately 5 P.M., May 12, 1926.

The Belvedere Palace.

Piłsudski's second wife, Aleksandra
Szczerbinska, and their two daughters,
Wanda and Jadwiga (c. 1925).

Kazimierz Bartel, Polish prime
minister, 1926; 1928–29; 1929–30.
(NATIONAL ARCHIVES)

Ignacy Mościcki, President of the
Polish Republic, 1926–39, at the time
of his first election to office.

Wincenty Witos, leader of the Piast
Peasant Party and Polish prime
minister, 1920–21; 1923; 1926.

Aleksander Prystor, Polish
prime minister, 1931–33.

Piłsudski in his office in the
Belvedere Palace, c. 1930.

Imperial Russia. A prominent French political figure later recalled "the prudence with which one had to talk in France about Polish independence."[3] French self-interest dictated that no effort at all should be made to assist the cause of Polish independence. But then the Imperial Russian government fell and in short order was replaced by a Bolshevik regime. The French now found that the whole basis of their postwar foreign policy had changed. To be sure, the essential objective remained—security against a resurgent Germany. But instead of a Russia allied to France and committed to support France against Germany, there was now a distinctly unfriendly Bolshevik Russia, which was doing its best to stir up revolution in Europe. The French made an abrupt alteration in policy.

France decided to support the creation of a group of "new" nations on Germany's eastern frontier to serve as a barrier against Russian Bolshevism as well as against German aggression. Thus France, which had not previously supported "liberation" of oppressed peoples, suddenly became a champion of this concept—at least in Eastern Europe. The French government wanted these new nations, which would be France's allies in the event of a war with Germany, to be as large and as heavily armed as possible. In December 1918 a Quai d'Orsay memorandum on preparations for the Peace Conference noted that "the more we aggrandize Poland at Germany's expense, the more certain shall we be that she [Poland] will remain Germany's enemy."[4] And when the French Foreign Minister Stéphen Pichon was asked what Poland should be, he instantly replied "big and strong—very, very strong."[5]

With the support of the Americans and the French the Poles should have been able to achieve a quick and complete diplomatic victory at the Paris Peace Conference. That they did not was largely because of the chaotic political situation that existed in Poland.

During the war none of the Allies had extended diplomatic recognition to Poland, because there was no Polish nation to recognize. As a practical matter, however, the Allies had tacitly recognized Dmowski's Polish National Committee as the voice of the Polish nation-to-be. But then, on November 16, each of the Allied governments received a telegram from Warsaw apprising them of the "existence of a Polish independent state, uniting all Polish territories." The telegram was signed by Piłsudski over the title "Commander in Chief of the Polish Army."

This announcement of the existence of a *de facto* Polish government created a dilemma. The diplomats of practically all the Allied Powers knew and respected the cultured and erudite Roman Dmowski. He was the man with whom Paderewski had now affiliated himself. In Western capitals it had generally been assumed that Dmowski would play the leading role in a resurrected Poland. Almost no one was acquainted with Piłsudski. He was known only by vague reputation—as a socialist, a one-time train robber, and an amateur general who had fought most of the war on the side of the Central Powers. Piłsudski, it seemed, had a revolutionary background that was disturbingly similar to that of most of the Russian Bolsheviks. And in the event that any Allied diplomats were unaware of this unflattering portrait of Piłsudski, Dmowski's associates on the Polish National Committee hastened to paint it for them.

Dmowski had had the ill luck to be away from Europe at the time of the Armistice. Immediately leaving the United States, he arrived in Paris on November 19 to take his place at the head of the Polish National Committee. Dmowski and his associates on the National Committee were understandably bitter about developments within Poland. They tried to persuade the Allies to ignore the Piłsudski government and deal solely with them, but the best that they could obtain was a wait-and-see attitude on the part of the major Western governments.

This situation could, perhaps, have continued for a long while if it had not been for the announcement that the Peace Conference would open on January 18. It was obvious that Poland could not have two separate delegations. Piłsudski wanted to break the deadlock, and he dispatched an emissary, Kazimierz Dłuski, to Paris to meet with Dmowski's National Committee and see if compromise was possible. At first Dmowski refused to make any concession whatever. There was a furious and bitter quarrel between Dłuski and Dmowski, with Dmowski refusing any sort of compromise. He was certain that he and his Polish National Committee would eventually be accepted by the Allies as the sole official Polish delegation to the Peace Conference. Why should he share representation at the peace conference with the Piłsudski forces? But gradually Dmowski came to accept the idea that compromise was necessary. Dłuski raised the argument that Poland could not possibly be represented in Paris by one political faction while being governed in Warsaw by another. Such a situation would expose the nation to ridicule. Eventually a bargain was struck. It was agreed that Dmowski would be in charge of the Polish representation at the Peace Conference. However, his staff would include a number of Poles of other political persuasions, and he would agree to give consideration to their views. Also, a Piłsudski nominee would serve along with Dmowski as one of the two official Polish delegates to the Conference.

Although much of the work of the Peace Conference was farmed out to committees and commissions, the principal organ of the conference was a group consisting of the heads of delegations of the five principal allied powers (United States, Great Britain, France, Italy and Japan) and their foreign ministers. Since this group consisted of ten persons it came to be known as the "Council of Ten." (Within a month it was found that ten members were too many for the discreet and efficient transaction of business, and a smaller group called the "Council of Four" began to meet. This body consisted of the heads of the delegations of the United States, Great Britain, France and Italy.) An appearance before the Council was, of course, a supremely important occasion for any small nation. Dmowski and his delegation prepared feverishly for their chance to present their case before the great ones of the Council.

For the Poles the case was, of course, the delineation of the Polish frontiers. There had been a serious dispute within the Polish delegation as to which territories they should claim at Paris. This dispute had its origins in a fundamental difference in political philosophy between Dmowski and his National Democrats on one hand and Piłsudski and his followers on the other. Dmowski had long held that an independent Poland could survive only as a centralized nation inhabited by persons who were Poles or who could be readily assimilated as Poles. Dmowski also regarded Germany as Poland's inevitable enemy. He believed that Russia, no matter what its political orientation, would probably be Poland's best ally against Germany. Dmowski's conviction was that Poland should claim as much German territory as she could get. Dmowski did not think that it would be difficult to achieve a Polish ethnic predominance in these areas. In the east, Poland should confine her acquisitions to those regions that had a large enough Polish population to make them assimilable and whose annexation would not cause a permanent dispute with Russia.

The Piłsudski followers held opposite opinions. They believed Russia, whether Bolshevik or Tsarist, to be a greater menace than Germany. They espoused a "Federalist" philosophy, the aim of which was to neutralize the Russian threat. The basis of Federalism was that Poland, as the largest and most advanced nation in East Central Europe, should associate itself with adjoining nationalities to the east, like the Lithuanians, Belorussians and Ukrainians. These peoples would have a semiautonomous status within the Polish nation. These acquisitions would weaken Russia while simultaneously strengthening Poland. Doubtless this would incur Russian animosity, but this was unimportant. It was foreseen that nothing would ever conciliate Russia or get her willingly to accept the existence of an independent Poland.

The Dmowski and Piłsudski factions were agreed on one thing. Situated between the great powers of Germany and Russia, Poland could not be a weak and insignificant nation. To survive, Poland must be strong—and strength would come with size. An agreement was worked out within the Polish delegation. In essence, it was decided simply to demand that the Allies award Poland the most generous frontiers for which an argument could be made. The problems of annexation or federalism were left to be solved later.

The first opportunity for the Poles to present their case to the Council of Ten came at 11 A.M. on January 29, 1919. The place was the large office of Stéphen Pichon, the French Foreign Minister, located in the Quai d'Orsay. Georges Clemenceau, the French premier, sat at one end of the room behind a small Louis XV table. Ranged on either side of this table in a semicircle were chairs for the senior members of the British, Italian, Japanese and American delegations. A wood fire blazed in a fireplace behind Clemenceau, and made the room hot and stuffy.

The Polish delegates—Roman Dmowski accompanied by Erazm Piltz—were ushered into the room with considerable ceremony and were greeted with cordiality—they were, after all, the protégés of the French and the beneficiaries of the sympathy and interests of the United States.

Dmowski began by asking the Council of Ten what area most interested them in Polish affairs. Clemenceau replied genially that he would like Dmowski simply to fill them in on the entire Polish situation.

Dmowski responded superbly to this agreeable invitation. He began a speech that, with a luncheon adjournment, lasted five hours. It was surely a tour de force. There were two official languages for the Peace Conference—English and French. Dmowski began his speech in perfect and idiomatic French and interrupted it from time to time, to translate his statements into faultless English. His listeners could not help but be enormously impressed, and at the conclusion of his presentation they broke into spontaneous applause.

Dmowski began with a survey of the military problems that Poland was then facing. The new nation was being attacked on all sides. Russian Bolsheviks were encroaching on the east. To the southeast, in Austrian Galicia, which Poland now claimed, she was fighting Ukrainians. In the southwest, Poland was fighting German irregulars for the possession of Silesia and the Czech army for the possession of parts of the Duchy of Teschen. Similar conflicts existed in the region of Poznań and in Danzig. Dmowski asked that the Allies provide Poland with arms, ammunition, and other military supplies.

Turning to Polish territorial aspirations, Dmowski advised the Council that "when reaching the settlement of the territory to belong to Poland, we should start from the date 1772, before the First Partition."[6] Dmowski's listeners were aware that Poland before the First Partition had been a very large territory. Dmowski now took his listeners on a *tour d'horizon.* He suggested that Lithuania and the Ukraine should be "united" to Poland inasmuch as they had "not yet reached the stage of nationhood."[7] Silesia in the southeast, even though it had not been Polish since the fourteenth century, was claimed by reason of its Polish majority—which Dmowski estimated at 90 percent of the population. Turning to what he described as "Eastern Germany," Dmowski adopted the attitude that the cession of a massive "Polish Corridor" to the sea was indisputable. He took a similar position on Danzig, Poland's only possible seaport, but a city that was overwhelmingly German in population. The only point on which Dmowski expressed uncertainty was the propriety of the Polish claim to East Prussia itself. He admitted that East Prussia was not Polish, but he suggested that the Allies remove it from Germany and make it into a small, separate "republic" over which Poland would have watch and ward.

At this point, it then being late afternoon, Dmowski concluded his presentation. Clemenceau rose and thanked him for "a masterly statement," and the Poles withdrew.

Of course, the members of the Council of Ten did not personally immerse themselves in the details of the Polish frontiers. As was the custom, a committee of five experts (the Commission on Polish Affairs) was established and instructed to prepare a report on "the question of the boundaries of the Polish State."[8] Generally speaking, the reports of expert subcommittees were accepted by the Council of Ten.

The Allied principals did not, at this early point, expect that they had heard the last of Poland at the Paris Peace Conference. But at the same time, considering the number of experts they had assigned to Poland's problems, they surely did not expect that they would have to spend as much of their own time on Polish matters as they found themselves compelled to do in the months to come.

The membership of the Commission on Polish Affairs had been happily selected—from the Polish point of view anyhow. The members were almost all Polonophiles. In deference to the unstated but general feeling at the Peace Conference that Poland was largely in the French sphere of influence, the chairman of the commission was a Frenchman—Jules Cambon.

Ideally, of course, all of Poland's frontiers—both east and west—should have been settled at the Peace Conference. But in point of fact, very little effort was expended in delineating Poland's eastern borders. The reasons for this neglect were various. An important one was that Bolshevik Russia was not represented at the Peace Conference—indeed, Clemenceau had announced that he would refuse to allow them in Paris. None of the major Allied powers had diplomatic ties with Lenin and his government. Thus there was no way to negotiate a Polish-Russian agreement.

The Poles themselves did not press the Allies in Paris to determine their eastern frontiers. In particular, the Piłsudski representatives in the delegation had plans for eastward expansion which overreached any territory that the Allies might consider appropriate. So, in the end, the matter was more or less swept under the carpet. The Polish delegation did submit a memorandum to the Commission on Polish Affairs entitled "A Note on the Eastern Frontiers of the Polish State," which suggested that Poland should be awarded Lithuania, East Prussia, and a generous border area running southward from Wilno. But when this was not acted upon, the Poles were content to let the matter rest. Thus, the Commission on Polish Affairs occupied itself mostly with Poland's border with Germany, a task that proved quite complex in itself.

At this point, the pivotal role of British Prime Minister David Lloyd George and his government in the matter of Poland at the Paris Peace Conference must be appraised. To put it baldly, Lloyd George (and the British Foreign Office) distrusted the ability of the Poles to govern themselves—and certainly their ability to govern others. The matter was complicated by Lloyd George's indifference to the legendary Polish charm. Saying no to what he regarded as extravagant Polish demands troubled Lloyd George not a bit. In fact, he seems to have relished it. He told the Council of Ten bluntly that the Poles "had no idea of organization . . . no capacity to direct or govern. The premier was a pianist, the president an idealist without any practical ideas."[9] Early in the conference, Lloyd George stated that he regarded Polish claims as "extravagant and inadmissible."[10]

Lloyd George's first opportunity to speak out on the Polish borderlands came on March 19, 1919, when the Commission on Polish Affairs presented its report entitled "Frontier Between Poland and Germany."[11] Jules Cambon, the chairman of the Commission, described his group's recommendation to the Council of Four. The Commission had cut down Dmowski's claims, but so slightly as to leave the Poles with small cause for complaint. Cambon's committee proposed to award Poland practically all of Upper Silesia, a wide corridor through German territory to the sea, a few districts of East Prussia, and outright ownership of Danzig. Concluding his report, Cambon asked if there were any questions from the members of the Council of Four.

Lloyd George at once spoke up. Flipping rapidly through the Commission's written report, he found the statistical table that indicated that 2,132,000 Germans would be included in the proposed Polish nation. This, Lloyd George observed, would be a source of "serious trouble for Poland in the future." He stated bluntly that the heavily German areas that the Commission proposed to assign to Poland would be "the seed of future war."[12] Lloyd George posed a frightening question: if the Germans in Poland rose against their Polish rulers, and if a future German government chose to go to their defense, "would France, Great Britain, and the United States go to war to maintain Polish rule over them?"[13]

Lloyd George's point was well taken. The report was referred back to the Commission for reconsideration. The Commission met on the following day, March 20, and decided to stand by its original recommendations with the explanation that "the large number of Germans assigned to Poland is primarily the result of the nature of the intimate racial distribution in this part of Europe, and not of any neglect on the part of the Commission to consider ethnographic facts."[14] A two-page memorandum dispatched to the Council of Ten concluded simply that "the Commission submits that their original proposals offer the best possible solution to the problem that they were called upon to solve."[15]

The news that the Commission on Polish Affairs had declined to revise its original recommendations naturally reached the Polish delegation almost at once. Encouraged, the Poles redoubled their efforts, particularly on the personal level. Paderewski, who was without question Poland's most attractive spokesman, came to Paris in early April, and a series of state dinners was given by his delegation. No opportunity was lost to display the legendary Paderewski charm, to which the American delegation was particularly susceptible. "Paddy was simply delightful," a young American diplomat, Charles Seymour, wrote to his family after having dined with the Poles. "He was all smiles and apparently delighted to be at a pure American dinner. He said he loved America more than anything else after his own Poland and had thought of becoming an American citizen often but had waited in the dim hope that some day he might have an independent country of his own. He was as cordial as could be, shaking hands with a very strong grip, joking and making pleasant speeches."[16]

Dmowski was incapable of making so good an impression and thus was reserved for the heavy work after the dinners had ended. Following one of these affairs, Seymour wrote, "I talked a long time with Dmowski, who is rather a cold politician, but I think, sincere. He says that Poland is now the only bulwark against Bolshevism. . . . He feels that England has not supported Poland as she should and that she will regret it later."[17]

But for all of this, the general image of the Poles was becoming tarnished. A number of problems had arisen, in the course of which the Polish government had not appeared to best advantage. One of these centered on the situation in the eastern part of Austrian Galicia, where the Poles were fighting a brisk war against an entity known as the "West Ukrainian People's Republic." The Poles claimed that it was a Bolshevik government, but the Allies in Paris very much doubted that it was. All that was definitely known was that in East

Galicia the majority of the population was Ukrainian. Only in the few cities, the largest of which was Lwów, were Poles in the majority. The Allies thought that a good case might be made for eastern Galicia being put under Ukrainian rule. In any event, they were not willing to concede that the Poles should take over the region. The fighting between the Poles and the Ukrainians grew very bitter, and the Allies in Paris reluctantly intervened. An armistice line was drawn, and a series of telegrams were sent by the Council of Four demanding that the Poles and Ukrainians stop fighting. But these demands were not met. It became evident that the Ukrainians could be compelled to stop, but not the Poles, who always had some excuse for resuming the attack. Woodrow Wilson now began to join Lloyd George in expressing disappointment with the Poles, particularly when he came to feel that the Allies had been actually hoodwinked in the matter of "Haller's Army."

Haller's Army (as it was generally referred to by the Allies) was indeed an important force. It will be recalled that General Józef Haller had commanded the Second Brigade of the Polish Legion, which late in the war deserted the Central Powers and went over to the Allies. Haller and some of his senior officers had been brought from Murmansk to France in July 1918. Here, Haller was put in command of the "Polish Army" that Dmowski's Polish National Committee was raising under French auspices. At the time of the Armistice, Haller's Army consisted of four divisions, with two more in the process of formation. It had a total of about 50,000 men. Although this force was formed too late to see much fighting on the Western Front, it was fully equipped by the French. Haller's men had been issued French horizon-blue uniforms and for this reason were frequently called the "Blue Army."

Haller and his senior officers were not popular with Piłsudski and his associates in Warsaw. The Piłsudski followers could not forget the wartime political differences that had existed between Piłsudski and Haller when Haller had commanded the Second Brigade of the Polish Legion. It was also well known that Haller was a supporter of Dmowski and a member of his National Democratic Party.

Political differences notwithstanding, Piłsudski's government was frantically anxious to have this army repatriated to Poland. By Western Front standards a force of fifty thousand men was not particularly impressive; but by the standards then prevailing in Poland, Haller's Army was an enormous and superbly equipped force. Regardless of the political orientation of their commander, the Warsaw government was determined to have these soldiers in Poland, and it demanded that these troops be repatriated.

The Allies had, of course, no further use for Haller's Army in France, but at the same time they were reluctant to let them go to Poland. Lloyd George was concerned that Haller's Army would end up fighting Ukrainians in East Galicia. The American delegation too was concerned, because a force the size of Haller's could easily turn the tide of battle in East Galicia. It was decided that before these soldiers were permitted to leave France, the Allies must be sure how the Poles would deploy them.

Like the other Polish problems, there seemed no end to the wrangles about Haller's Army. And as with so many other Polish matters, apparently only the Council of Ten could deal with it. They first came to grips with it on February 23, 1919, when they reviewed a formal request from Poland for the army. The next day they took it up again to discuss the problem of routes for the army's repatriation. The best way to send Haller's force to Poland was to ship the troops by sea, landing them at Danzig. But the Germans strongly objected. The matter was discussed again the following day. Additional questions regarding Haller's Army were debated by the Council on March 17, 19, 21, 22 and 24. In the end, the matter was resolved by transporting Haller's men, horses and equipment across Germany in three hundred railroad trains provided by the Allies. A guarantee was extracted from the Poles that they would not use this army to fight the Ukrainians.

But even after all this, it was shortly found that the matter was not closed. Allied officers in Poland soon reported that this blue-uniformed army had appeared in force in East Galicia and was fighting the Ukrainians. The Allies dispatched a telegram ordering Haller out of Galicia, but no answer was received. The Poles later claimed that they never received the message. Lloyd George made no secret of his suspicion that the telegram had been "mislaid" by the French member of an Allied mission in Warsaw. On May 21 a formal message was dispatched by the Council to the Polish government demanding to know whether Haller's troops were fighting in Galicia. There was no reply to this message either. But by May 27 the problem had more or less resolved when the reinforced Poles drove the Ukrainian army out of East Galicia.

As time passed it became apparent that it was impossible to draw a Polish frontier that would not leave substantial ethnic minorities within Poland. The size of these minority populations was still uncertain, but they would probably include substantial numbers of Ukrainians, Belorussians, Lithuanians and Germans as well as Jews, who, in the manner customary throughout Central Europe of the time, were generally considered to be a national group separate from the state within which they lived. Nearly 10 percent of the Polish population was estimated to be Jewish—the highest percentage by far of any nation in the world. The Allies, particularly Britain and the United States, became concerned that the Polish minorities might require special protection. In part, this concern was touched off by a series of reports published in *The Times* (of London) and other British newspapers. These articles, most of which were written by Israel Cohen, the "Special Commissioner of the Zionist Organization," described "The Pogroms in Poland." They were extensive accounts of Polish Jews being beaten by Polish soldiers, of contributions being extorted from the Jewish communities of several towns, and of Jewish women being stripped of shoes and compelled to march from one town to another along muddy roads in midwinter.[18]

These accounts, whether accurate or not, aroused general concern among the Allies. An American official, Stephen Bonsal, was assigned the task of sounding out Dmowski as to his position on the Jewish minorities. Dmowski was quite frank. His view for many years had been that Poland must develop its own ethnic—that is, non-Jewish—mercantile and professional class. He stated that Poland's Jews "form at least ten percent of our population, and in my judgment this is at least eight percent too much. When there is only a small group of Jews in our villages, even when they are grasping storekeepers or avaricious moneylenders, as they often are, everything moves along smoothly; but when more come, and they generally do come, there is trouble and at times small pogroms. . . . Unless restrictions are imposed upon them soon, all our lawyers, doctors and small merchants will be Jews."[19]

The Council of Four decided that Poland must be compelled to sign an agreement to protect its Jews and other minorities, and the Council of Ten gave instructions to that effect to a drafting subcommittee. (The Czechoslovak government too was compelled to sign a minorities-protection treaty.)

The port city of Danzig was a continuing and constant problem for the Allies at the Paris Peace Conference. Since Wilson's Thirteenth Point had promised them "free and secure access to the sea," the Poles assumed that they would be awarded Danzig (which was the only suitable Baltic port) together, of course, with the "corridor" through German Pomerania. The Commission on Polish Affairs agreed with this assumption and recommended that Danzig be given to Poland outright.

But Lloyd George led a fight for a different settlement of this question. He pointed out that the Commission's own figures indicated that Danzig had 324,000 inhabitants of whom all except 16,000 were German. He called the attention of the Council to the fact that the Poles had never been promised that they would *possess* Danzig, only that they would have *access* to a seaport, which he agreed must be Danzig.

At the Council of Four meetings on March 27 and April 1, Lloyd George proposed that Danzig should be given the status of a "free city" allied to Poland by a customs union and under the control of a High Commissioner appointed by the League of Nations. All Danzigers were to give up their present nationalities and become citizens of the Free City. This plan was supported by historical precedent. During most of its period as Poland's principal port (the fifteenth to the eighteenth century), the city had been the property of independent dukes who had merely attached themselves to the Polish kings by a conditional personal union. During those years the city had coined its own currency, raised its own army and navy, and maintained its own legations abroad. Thus, the Poles would have difficulty claiming that Danzig's status as a free city would be much different from the position it had had in the past. Perhaps because this proposal involved his pet scheme, the League of Nations, Woodrow Wilson gave it his support.

In the end, Lloyd George's scheme was adopted over the vociferous objections of the Poles and the French. Paderewski, appearing before the Council of Four, complained bitterly of the treatment that his nation was receiving from the Allies. He made the threat that if the Polish people did not get what they wanted, they would succumb in despair to Bolshevism. "My people," Paderewski declared, "have belief in no one now, because they were told by me, and most emphatically, that these things promised to them would be given to them. Well, now if something is taken away from them, they will lose all faith in my leadership. They will lose faith in your leadership of humanity and there will be revolution."[20]

To this reproach Lloyd George instantly responded in kind. It was time for plain speaking. Who were the Poles to castigate the Allies? During the war the Poles were fighting ("insofar as they were fighting at all") mostly on the German side. In any case, the British Prime Minister pointed out, no wartime promises of specific frontiers had ever been made to Poland by the Allies. Nor was there any reason why there should have been.

> Only five years earlier the Poles had been a subject nation with no human prospect of recovering its liberty: certainly without the slightest chance of recovering it by its own exertions. . . . [They] have only got their freedom because there are a million and a half dead Frenchmen, very nearly a million British, half a million Italians, and I forget how many Americans. . . . Poland has won her freedom, not by her own exertions, but by the blood of others; and not only has she no gratitude, but she says she loses faith in the people who have won her freedom!

Lloyd George then alluded to the matter of Polish greed. This nation which had always claimed to want only independence was now "claiming three millions and a half of Galicians," and this led him to the acid complaint that Poland, like the other new Central Europe states, was treating the Allies to the sorry spectacle of "annexing the territory of other nations and imposing on them the very tyranny which they have themselves endured for years. . . . It fills me with despair," he cried.[21]

There was nothing left for the flustered Paderewski to do but accept the Allies' decision and withdraw "with profound respect but with deep sorrow."[22]

Only a portion of Poland's frontiers were definitely established in the Treaty of Versailles when it was signed on June 28, 1919. The Peace Conference made no determination of Poland's borders with Russia, although in Article 87 of the Treaty the Allies specifically reserved the right to determine Poland's eastern frontier at a later date. In practice what this meant was that the Poles were left to fight it out with Russia.

Even the boundaries with Germany were somewhat indefinite. Plebiscites were to be held in Allenstein, Marienwerder and Upper Silesia. What was definite was that Poland was awarded the Poznań region, the "corridor" through Pomerania, and most of Galicia. Poland was compelled to accept the free-city scheme for Danzig, and it agreed to a plebiscite in the Duchy of Teschen to determine its division with Czechoslovakia. But however these plebiscites went— or however the eastern frontier matter was settled—it was certain that Poland would be a large nation having at least thirty million citizens.

The general Polish feeling was that the Allies had been ungenerous in their determination of the Polish-German frontiers. The Poles, in particular Dmowski and his supporters, were grateful only to the French. As Dmowski observed, "All that we realized . . . we owe primarily to the French."[23] Despite the attitude of bravura that the Poles maintained over the outcome of the various plebiscites, they were intensely concerned about them. The minorities treaty was viewed as an affront, and the Poles signed it only when it was made clear to them that the whole Polish settlement must be viewed as a "package." Poland could take it or leave it. But if the package was rejected, the Allies would wash their hands of the Poles, who would then have to negotiate with the Germans on their own. Faced with this risky prospect, the Poles signed.

4

Organizing
the New Poland

ALL OF THE MANY "new" nations that were born or reborn in the wake of World War I experienced considerable birth pain. But none of these so-called successor states was faced with the variety and enormity of problems that Poland encountered during its first months of existence. Here was a nation with no national boundaries as yet agreed upon—not even that with Germany—inasmuch as the Treaty of Versailles would not be signed until Poland had been in existence for nearly eight months. At least seven different currencies circulated in the area that would eventually be declared Poland. Four different legal systems operated. The first Polish national budget, drawn up for the first six months of 1919, anticipated an income of six hundred million Polish marks and expenditures of one billion seven hundred million marks. Since there was virtually no state treasury, the deficit had to be made up by printing money and accepting the resulting inflation.

The Polish industrial plant had been looted or demolished during the war. In 1918 only about 15 percent of the nation's industrial workers were employed. Poland's railroad system—actually three different systems, which had been built and operated by the three partitioning powers—was not designed to link together this new nation, and about half of its rolling stock, bridges and workshops had been destroyed.

Devastation in the Polish countryside paralleled that of industry. Six million acres of forest land had been sawed down to provide lumber for trench systems. More than a third of the livestock had been taken by the occupying armies. Well over half of Poland's agricultural acreage lay uncultivated.[1]

Every aspect of life in Poland had been disrupted by the war. Seven hundred thousand Poles had been driven eastward into Russia during the German offensive of 1915 and had not yet made their way back. Nearly a half million Poles had been killed while serving in the armies of Austria, Russia and Germany. Another million had been wounded. Pandemic Spanish influenza was sweeping through the nation, and there were serious outbreaks of typhus. Starvation was widespread and was relieved only by massive relief shipments from the United States. Whatever governmental machinery existed was primitive. Most of the normal administrative departments of a modern state either did not exist or had only recently been established, and very few Poles had any experience in government administration.

Finally, to complicate matters even further, there were 80,000 German occupation troops in Poland at the time of the Armistice. There were an additional half million German soldiers stationed to the east of Poland, in the Ukraine and in the Baltic countries. Thus Poland was both occupied and almost entirely surrounded by German armies.

The officers of the German occupation force in Poland had not displayed a very high standard of responsibility or personal discipline. Upon receiving news of the Armistice, General von Beseler, the German governor general of Poland, had put on a disguise and fled to Germany. His senior officers too abandoned their posts. Without commanders, the German occupation forces began to loot Polish shops. In retaliation, German soldiers were being attacked by armed Poles.

When Piłsudski arrived in Warsaw on the morning of November 10, it was evident to him that one of his first tasks must be to get these German occupation troops out of Poland. In the absence of any other German military authority, he summoned a large group of soldier delegates from the German Warsaw garrison. They met at 8 A.M. on November 11 in the great hall of a Warsaw palace that had once housed the administrative offices of the Russian governors general. There were several thousand German soldiers present, and Piłsudski spoke to them in their own tongue. He told them that he would arrange for their immediate repatriation and that their personal safety would be assured by the P.O.W., which was now openly mobilizing. Piłsudski laid down one condition: the Germans must leave all their military equipment behind.

The German soldiers agreed at once. They had no interest other than getting home and being demobilized. Starting the very next day, November 12, the trains began to roll. One week later all of the 80,000 German occupation troops were out of Poland, and the P.O.W. had their weapons. This was, however, practically the only event that came off smoothly in the early days of Polish independence. Everything else was confusion and controversy.

As "Chief of State," once the title of the revered Tadeusz Kościuszko, Piłsudski was Poland's dictator. But Piłsudski regarded his position as a temporary condition. He believed that the Polish people must govern themselves through a democratically elected parliamentary system. Until elections could be held, Piłsudski wanted the responsibility for the government's day-to-day operations to be assumed by a prime minister and a cabinet. He had no desire to occupy himself with endless administrative details. His main interest was the army, and as commander in chief, he supervised every phase of its development. He had neither the time nor the interest for further service. A prime minister had to be appointed who would serve under the chief of state. Jay Pierrepont Moffat, one of the first American diplomats to arrive in Warsaw, thought that there was more to Piłsudski's desire to appoint a prime minister than simple lack of time to handle the job himself. "To Piłsudski the words 'Prime Minister' meant the equivalent of a Grand Vizier who took orders from the Chief of State, and by assuming nominal responsibility protected him from the consequences of a mistake."[2] But regardless of his motives, Piłsudski found that appointing a prime minister and cabinet was a much more difficult task than he had anticipated.

Polish politics had rapidly polarized in the few days following Piłsudski's return to Warsaw. On the Right were the National Democrats and several smaller parties. They viewed the socialization of Poland as an imminent threat, and they were determined to prevent it. The Polish Left was dominated by the PPS and its counterpart among the peasantry, the Left wing of the Populist Party. Although the Left exhibited various degrees of extremism, in general its leaders were agreed in their determination to enact a number of basic reforms—notably the nationalization of major industries and the distribution of land to the peasants.

On the extreme Left stood the SDKPiL, Rosa Luxemburg's old group, which was in the process of transforming itself into the "Communist Workers' Party of Poland." They demanded, of course, a complete revolution on the Russian pattern. But the Communists were a negligible force in Polish politics and for the moment could safely be ignored.

The center of Polish political life was dominated by the Piast Peasant Party, the moderate wing of the Populist Party, and various smaller groups representing the Polish intelligentsia. Piłsudski had originally hoped to select Poland's first government from among these moderates, but the Center parties failed to exert the force that the Right and the Left displayed. In establishing an interim government, Piłsudski, therefore, was forced to select ministers from the extremes of Polish politics.

The task of serving as a moderator among contending politicians was not one for which Piłsudski was well suited, and certainly not one that he enjoyed. He had not anticipated the acrimony that would develop in Polish politics. He was not prepared for the job-seeking, the favoritism, and the greed that quickly became characteristics of Polish political life. In later years Piłsudski spoke often of his original optimistic expectations—"I thought that together with her physical resurrection Poland would also achieve a spiritual rebirth."[3] A romantic and an idealist where Poland was concerned, Piłsudski had hoped to encounter "an element of moral strength, heretofore missing in our country. It was with this dream and with this illusion that I returned to Poland."[4]

Piłsudski's first two nominees for the prime ministership were not successes. The first to be named, the prominent Galician socialist Ignacy Daszyński, never got a chance to serve; the Polish Right reacted against his appointment so strongly that it had to be withdrawn. On November 18, Piłsudski succeeded in appointing Jedrzej Moraczewski as Poland's first prime minister. Although he was a member of the PPS, Moraczewski was reputed to be a moderate socialist. The parties of the Right made little protest over his appointment. They were confident that the elections would give them control of the government, and they believed that the stop-gap ministry of Moraczewski and his socialist colleagues could not do much harm and might act as a deterrent to any revolution from the extreme Left.

Both the PPS and the National Democrats claimed to represent the majority of the Polish people. Piłsudski considered it essential that elections be held as soon as possible to discover which group—the Left or the Right—was dominant and should be given the responsibility of governing Poland. His first instructions to Moraczewski concerned elections. They were in the form of a military order, which came easily because Moraczewski had been a captain of engineers under Piłsudski in the First Brigade of the Polish Legion. Piłsudski had summoned Moraczewski and told him, "Captain, you are to become Prime Minister, but under two conditions: First, in your decrees you are not to tamper with social conditions; second, [and here Piłsudski raised his voice] in the course of one week you will produce an electoral law, just as if you had a trench to dig."[5] Moraczewski managed to complete the second assignment in three days, but he was less obedient in other matters. His ambition and determination had been underestimated. He was not content to be just an interim prime minister. Despite Piłsudski's original orders that the government was "not to tamper with social conditions," Moraczewski and his colleagues from the Left quickly began to prepare a number of sweeping social reforms.

The reaction of the Right to Moraczewski's unexpectedly militant program was to boycott the purchase of Polish bonds, to refuse to pay taxes, and to sabotage any of the government's attempts at social reform. Faced with such formidable opposition, the Moraczewski government could not survive for long. The cabinet had been in office for only six weeks when it was apparent that it must be replaced. Rumors of a forthcoming coup from the Right began to circulate in Warsaw.

At that point Ignacy Paderewski appeared on the scene. Arriving at Danzig on Christmas Day 1918, he did not go directly to Warsaw, but went first to the city of Poznań, which, although overwhelmingly Polish, was still part of Germany and was still garrisoned by units of the German army. Dmowski's National Democratic Party had always been very strong in Poznań, and thus a warm welcome for his ally Paderewski was anticipated. But no one had anticipated the extraordinary reception that Paderewski received from the Poznań populace. There was an enormous parade in his honor and other popular demonstrations of affection for the pianist. In fact, the welcome for Paderewski turned into a citywide uprising, in the course of which the German garrison was driven out and a *de facto* Polish administration was installed.

When Paderewski arrived in Warsaw on January 3, 1919, he received a public welcome fully as warm as that in Poznań. It was clear that Paderewski's popular reputation as a leader in the struggle for Polish independence was close to that of Piłsudski himself. In his few days in Poland it had been established that Paderewski was a major Polish political figure. On the night that Paderewski arrived in Warsaw he was called on by several old friends who advised him that a *coup d'état* against Piłsudski and the Moraczewski government was being planned. The leaders of the plot were Prince Eustachy Sapieha and Colonel Marian Januszajtis. Although this coup was not directly connected with the National Democratic Party, it was certainly a Rightist plot, and many of Dmowski's National Democrats were expected to take office if the attempt were successful. Paderewski was asked to join the plot, but he refused.

The next day, Sunday, January 4, Paderewski was invited to meet with Piłsudski. This was a sounding-out interview; the two men had never met before. Paderewski was nervous and ill at ease by reason of his knowledge of the impending coup, but he said nothing of it to Piłsudski. Paderewski would not betray his old friends. As soon as the meeting between the two men was over, Paderewski departed for Kraków in order to be out of the way during the coup, which was planned for that very night.

In the event, the coup attempt was not distinguished by any commendable degree of organization or resolution. Piłsudski was then living at the Belvedere Palace. Two conspirators carrying pistols and accompanied only by a chauffeur drove up to the palace, where they were promptly disarmed. Another group of conspirators succeeded in seizing a few cabinet ministers and held them prisoner in a garage for a few hours. Meanwhile, another small group of dissident junior officers proceeded to the Hotel Bristol, where they planned to seize General Stanisław Szeptycki, Chief of the Polish General Staff. They knocked on his bedroom door. Szeptycki, dressed in pajamas, opened the door and grasped the situation in a glance. He drew himself up, ordered the officers to come to attention and then to right face, and he marched them off to be arrested. That was the end of the coup. Piłsudski chose to regard it almost as a joke, which in its execution it certainly was. He apparently held no ill will against any of the conspirators. In fact, within a short time he appointed Prince Sapieha minister to Great Britain. And the day after the attempted coup, Piłsudski dispatched representatives to invite Paderewski back from Kraków to discuss the prospect of the pianist's forming a government and becoming prime minister. Piłsudski realized that Paderewski had been aware of the prospective coup, but the matter was never mentioned between the two men. In the end, Paderewski became Poland's second prime minister. His government took office on January 16, 1919.

Since Paderewski was allied with Piłsudski's opponents, his appointment might seem to have been a defeat for Piłsudski. In point of fact, Piłsudski was probably lucky to have been able to strike a bargain with Paderewski, who at least brought with him a cabinet consisting mostly of nonparty experts and even a couple of Socialists. The Moraczewski government was dead in the water, immobilized by the enmity of the Right, and it was high time to make a compromise that brought into office a government that could function.

Paderewski had additional commanding assets—his international prestige and his friendships with many of the most powerful people in the United States and Western Europe. A Polish government headed by Paderewski was bound to have much more influence abroad than one led by Moraczewski, a relatively unknown Socialist.

Piłsudski fully realized all this and refused to tolerate any criticism of his appointment. When he was visited by two onetime Socialist comrades who accused him of handing the "people's government" over to the Right, Piłsudski flew into a rage:

> You don't understand my situation at all. . . . I care nothing about "Rightists" or "Leftists"; I already have them up my ass. I'm for everyone. . . . [Right now] it's the army which matters, the army that I still don't have. . . . [Haller's divisions were then in France, and their release to Poland was still a matter of dispute]. . . . Who is able to talk to Foch about this matter? Not Moraczewski! Don't you understand? Paderewski speaks the same language as these people [i.e., the Allied leaders then in Paris]. . . . I'm in accord with him on practically every question, he's even more Federalist than I am, and he'll moderate Dmowski. You talk to me about a "people's government"—I don't care about your "people" at this moment. I care only about a government which can give Poland what she requires.[6]

The first major political event to occur under the Paderewski government was the election of January 26, 1919. The purpose of the election was the selection of deputies for a "Constitutional Sejm," the Polish legislature that was to perform the double task of enacting legislation and, simultaneously, drafting a Polish constitution. The Sejm first convened on February 10, 1919. For the moment there were 340 deputies to the Sejm. Eventually there would be a hundred more, but these would come from Pomerania, Upper Silesia and East Galicia, where no elections had been held because those areas were not presently under Polish control.

The election revealed that a remarkably coherent political party structure had developed in Poland. (At least it was remarkable considering that the nation had existed independently for only eleven weeks.) The parties of the Right consisted of the National Democrats, the National Christian Party and the Christian Socialists. The last two were quite small, and the Polish Right was dominated, as was the entire Sejm, by the National Democrats, who had elected 116 deputies. This spectacular showing gave them 34 percent of the seats in the Sejm.

The Center was dominated by the Piast Peasant Party, which won 44 seats. This party was the outgrowth of a strong peasant movement that had developed in various parts of prewar Poland. Eventually the movement had become a political party, which split into two wings. One was the Piast Peasant Party which advocated moderate land reform and was under the leadership of an effective politician named Wincenty Witos. The other peasant party advocated a more radical system of land redistribution and was known as the Populist (Liberation) Peasant Party. This latter group won 58 seats and was usually, although not always, considered to be part of the Polish Left.

Another party of the Left was the PPS, which won only 32 seats. As was customary in European Socialist parties of the day, the PPS contained persons of various degrees of socialist convictions. Some were quite moderate in their views. Others were more radical and more ardent. The electoral showing of the PPS was surprisingly poor for this party, which before the war had probably been Poland's biggest. This was apparently due to the fact that the prewar PPS had been the leader in the struggle for Polish independence and had thus attracted a number of adherents who would not otherwise have joined a socialist party. But now, with independence a fact, these persons drifted to the center.

The balance of the Left in the Polish Sejm consisted of two Communists (elected under other labels because the Polish Communist Party had boycotted the voting) and a scattering of other radicals. All told, the entire Left occupied about a hundred seats in the Sejm. But this included the delegates of the Populist (Liberation) Peasant Party, which could not always be counted upon to vote with the Left. So, because the National Democratic representatives alone almost equaled the Leftist delegates, Poland's first legislative assembly was dominated by a Right-Center coalition that could easily defeat any radical proposals from the Left. And, naturally, this Right-oriented majority was most interested in circumscribing the power of Piłsudski, who, as they liked to remind everyone, had been a socialist since he was nineteen years old.

By February 20, 1919, the Sejm had established itself along customary parliamentary lines, had elected its own officers, and was meeting regularly to enact legislation and start work on a constitution. On this day Piłsudski honored the commitment he made when he accepted the office of Chief of State from the Regency Council in November. "Power and responsibility," he had been told then, "we put in your hands, Supreme Commander, to be handed over to the national government."[7] Now, three months later, Piłsudski handed over his dictatorial authority to the Sejm for its disposition. But there being no constitution as yet, the Sejm had no realistic option but to hand back much of this authority to Piłsudski. Even Piłsudski's political enemies conceded that the nation must have a strong political and executive head. The deputies of the Sejm passed a resolution that was both a message to Piłsudski and an outline of their intentions regarding the governance of Poland. It was anticipated that this brief declaration would be a temporary working guide during the presumably short period of time before a formal Polish constitution was promulgated and a complete government structure established.

As it turned out, nearly three years was to elapse before the Polish constitution was written, approved in a general referendum, and put into effect. In the meantime, the Sejm declaration of February 20, together with certain minor amendments and amplifications, became known as the "Little Constitution" of Poland. It began with an acknowledgment of Piłsudski's transfer of authority to parliament, but immediately handed much of it back to him with the words, "The Sejm entrusts Józef Piłsudski with the further execution of the function of Chief of State until the constitution shall be enacted." There were definite conditions, however. The declaration stipulated that the Sejm "embodies the sovereign and legislative authority of the State of Poland."[8] Piłsudski as Chief of State was empowered to appoint the prime minister and his cabinet ministers, but this required the previous consent of the Sejm, and further, the prime minister and his cabinet could be dismissed at any time by parliament.

For a declaration of such brevity, less than 250 words, the "Little Constitution" did a remarkable job of spelling out the rights and privileges of parliament. In fact, these were virtually the only matters to which the document addressed itself. Everything else awaited the drafting and ratification of a complete constitution, which in the end had to await the conclusion of a much more pressing matter— Poland's war with the Soviet Union.

5

History of Hatred

Relations between Soviet Russia and the newly independent Poland started as they would end twenty-five years later—in an atmosphere of distrust and distaste. Neither nation expected that it would be able to avoid going to war with the other; and considering the policies that each pursued, war was indeed almost inevitable.

As is well known, in the period immediately following the Russian Revolution, Lenin and his associates assumed that similar revolutions would soon take place in all the industrialized nations of Europe. This was a hallowed Marxist theorem. The proletariat of the world, seeing that the workers' revolution had succeeded in one nation, would be persuaded that their hour too had struck. The Russian Communists did not intend to remain passive through the revolutionary agonies of their European neighbors. They conceived it to be a duty, as well as a matter of self-preservation, for them to promote, support, and if necessary intervene in the revolutionary struggles of other nations. They were prepared for the most awful sacrifices, for, as Lenin had warned in early 1918, it was "inconceivable that the Soviet republic could continue to exist for a long period side by side with imperialist states."[1]

But, while Lenin and his associates awaited the worldwide revolution, they were faced with an enormous array of problems of their own. For several years after the Revolution, Bolshevik control over

Russia itself was tenuous. There were internal political enemies to be suppressed, both on the Left and on the Right. There were Allied interventionary armies to stave off, a civil war to fight, and a ruined economy to reconstruct.

It was therefore obvious to the Soviet leaders in 1918–19 that they could not carry the social revolution into Europe by force of arms. The best that they could do for the time being was to assist (or actually direct, if necessary) the subversion of European capitalist governments. The Soviets quickly worked out a number of techniques to accomplish this. The most promising course was the reestablishment of diplomatic relations with capitalist nations. Virtually every European government had broken off relations with Russia after the Revolution took place and the Soviets made peace with Germany. The Soviet government was anxious to regain diplomatic recognition and to open embassies or legations in Europe's capitals. These would be staffed by trained revolutionaries who would develop propaganda campaigns and supervise agitation among the workers. They would oversee the development of native Communist parties. And all of this would be done by agents who enjoyed diplomatic immunity.

Theoretically, a major weapon in the breakdown of the capitalist nations would be the activities of their domestic Communist parties, which at that time were newly founded and functioning openly in most European states. There were exceptions, however, and the Communist Party of Poland was one of them.

The Communist Workers' Party of Poland (CPP) was founded in December 1918 as the result of a merger of the orthodox Marxist SDKPiL and a breakaway Left wing of the PPS. The first of many problems that would bedevil this party throughout its brief and harried life was its extreme Marxist orthodoxy, which was a legacy from its SDKPiL past. The Polish Communists rarely made a tactical concession to anyone or anything. Their positions sometimes verged on idiocy, as when they took the line that an independent Polish state was unnecessary and indeed undesirable. "The Polish proletariat," the Communists claimed in their party's platform, "rejects every political solution that is to be connected with the evolution of a capitalist world, solutions like autonomy, independence, and self-determination. . . . It will oppose every war for national frontiers."[2]

This was nice theory, but it failed to recognize that almost all

Poles, including the members of the proletariat, were intensely proud of Poland's independence. Almost no one would support a party that rejected the concept of a Polish nation. Another tactical error was the CPP's repudiation of the concept of private ownership of farmland. In a peasant nation whose citizens were, as Engels had warned, "passionate property owners," this was enough to set almost every man's hand against Communism. The existing Polish peasant political parties, which had no intention of losing their adherents to the Communists, were quick to exploit this weakness in the CPP position.

Lenin, who was a superb tactician, again and again warned the Polish Communists that they must be more flexible. But they ignored him. Eventually Lenin became quite disgusted with them; he thought they were very stupid.

Probably at the core of the CPP problem was, as has been observed, the fact that "they had no Lenin."[3] They had no Trotsky either. This lack of leadership does not mean that there were no capable Poles who were Communists. Actually there were a great many, but practically all were in Russia, where many held high-ranking posts in the Soviet government. Feliks Dzerzhinski and Karl Radek were native Poles who would have been towering figures in the Polish party had they been in Poland. However, they had no time for Polish party work, because, as they explained in a message to the Polish workers, "they were overburdened with Russian affairs."[4]

The result of all this was that the Polish Communist Workers' Party presented a rigid approach to every issue. They succeeded in alienating many of those whom they might have won over from the proletariat and the peasantry. Believing that it was their duty to provoke a constant conflict between themselves and the Polish government, the party boycotted the elections of January 1919 and retreated into name calling from the sidelines. They called the Sejm a collection of "National Democratic hooligans, dumb peasants, and socialist traitors." They claimed that the Army was a gang of "mercenaries" and that the Polish state was itself "the incarnation of counterrevolution."[5]

It did not take long for the Communists to reap the fruits of such dogmatism. The Polish government came up with a clever scheme. In mid-January 1919 it required all political parties and associations to register with the government. The Communist Party—firmly committed to a policy of noncooperation with a government whose

members, it claimed, were "agents of the French stock exchange"[6]—
refused to register, as the government had foreseen, and on February
7 was declared to be an illegal party. Having been in existence for
about seven weeks, the CPP was forced to go underground, where it
remained for the rest of its tormented existence.

The story of Russo-Polish relations during 1919 and 1920 is essentially the account of the contest between the two nations for the
control of a broad band of territory that lay east of "ethnic" Poland.
This region was inhabited mostly by certain "nationalities" of the
former Russian Empire—Lithuanians, Belorussians, and Ukrainians
—none of whom welcomed the domination of either Soviet Russia
or the newly independent Poland.

In the end the matter was settled (or at any rate, papered-over for
twenty years) by the Polish-Soviet War of 1919–20. But during the
months before the outbreak of full-scale warfare, the two nations
conducted a prolonged military and political skirmish. This preliminary period was characterized mainly by constant attempts of
Soviet Russia to establish diplomatic relations with Poland, while,
on their part, the Poles resisted Communist penetration by holding
the Soviet government at arm's length.

The Soviets' view of independent Poland was not complex. They
regarded Poland as nothing more than an embryonic reactionary
nation ruled by a landlord-and-officer class. Piłsudski, whom many of
the Russian Bolshevik leaders had known during their prerevolu-
tionary socialist days, was thought of as a traitor to socialism and a
lackey who was probably in the pay of the major Western capitalist
governments. Poland itself was regarded as important primarily for
its geographical position as a "bridge" to Germany and Central
Europe.

The Polish view of Soviet Russia was equally straightforward.
Most Poles simply hated the Russians. It made little difference to
them whether Russia was Bolshevik or Tsarist. Practically every Pole
believed that any Russian government, no matter what its political
orientation, would be the enemy of Polish independence. Were the
Soviet leadership to be supplanted by a restored Russian monarchy,
the new Russian government, the Poles suspected, would at once
march on Warsaw. (This Polish suspicion was almost certainly correct. The slogan of the White armies was "Russia—One and Undivided." Had they prevailed over the Soviets, it is most unlikely that

they would have accepted Polish independence.) As the Poles viewed it, the principal task of their foreign policy was to prevent Russia from snuffing out Poland's national life—either sooner or later.

The Polish government realized that it did not have long to find a solution. Russia was weak now, but that would not last; Poland must make its moves in the east quickly, while the Soviet government was absorbed in internal problems and before the Western Allies could intervene to restrain Poland's actions on its eastern border.

Through most of 1919, Britain and France showed little interest in Russo-Polish relations. At no time during the Paris Peace Conference did the major Allied powers indicate to Poland how far to the east it would be permitted to expand. The Treaty of Versailles had been fairly explicit about Poland's western frontiers, but it made no mention of the eastern borders. The Allies intended to rule eventually on the matter of Poland's frontier with Russia, but they had not yet gotten around to determining where this frontier should be established. Even well into 1920, the major Allied powers had no official policy regarding Russian affairs; they had little or no diplomatic contact with Moscow, and they did not want to have any. They hoped that the Bolshevik government would collapse or that the opposing White Russian armies would triumph. In fact, the Allies had decided to let the Russians fight it out among themselves, but they never made this decision clear to other European nations. So, the Poles decided that, at least for the moment, they were free to expand their borders eastward. Some of the Allies might disapprove, but for the present none of them would do much about it.

Piłsudski held that Poland must expand and thus become "a power equal to the great powers of the world." If it did not enlarge itself it would always remain "a small country requiring the protection of others."[7] Among the Poles, eastward expansion—even beyond the point where the majority of the population was Polish—was generally desired.

The two major approaches to eastward expansion were federalism and incorporation. The federalist position, which was advocated by Piłsudski and supported by the PPS and other Leftist parties (excepting the Communists), was that Poland should encourage and assist such nationalities as the Lithuanians, the Ukrainians, and possibly even the Belorussians, in achieving their independence from Russia. It was expected that, once free, these new nations would be grateful to Poland and would recognize that they must have power-

ful assistance to maintain their independence. They would seek to
become closely allied, in one way or another, with Poland. The relationship between Poland and these nations was never precisely
defined, but it was assumed that they would be joined economically,
would have a common foreign policy, and would maintain a common military staff. This federation, which was Piłsudski's objective,
would obviously be led by Poland. Federalism was, to a great degree,
a calculated effort to pick apart the former Russian Empire and
attach its western nationalities, thus weakening Russia and strengthening Poland. This whole scheme came to be known as Piłsudski's
Great Design.

However, federalism was opposed by the National Democrats and
other members of the Polish Right, who viewed this policy as risky
and problematical. They believed that Poland should simply expel
the Bolsheviks from such eastern territories as could conveniently be
invaded and annex them to Poland. This "incorporationist" approach
was strongly supported by the many Polish landowners in Lithuania,
the Ukraine and Belorussia.

For the time being, however, it made no difference whether
Poland's eastern aspirations were federalist or incorporationist. The
area in dispute was blocked off both to Soviet Russia and to Poland
by some 500,000 troops of the German Oberkommando-Ostfront,
commonly called the Ober-Ost. The territory controlled by these
German soldiers was nearly 1,500 miles long, stretching from the
Baltic Sea to the Black Sea, and its width ranged from only fifty miles
in certain places to several hundred miles. Under the provisions of
the Armistice, Germany was required to maintain this force temporarily, as a barrier against Bolshevism.

During the four months following the end of the war, the presence
of the German troops of the Ober-Ost was sufficient to keep apart the
Soviet Red Army and Piłsudski's emerging Polish Army. But then,
gradually, and by means of various local agreements with local forces,
the German commander succeeded in withdrawing his forces northward into East Prussia. By February 1919 the Germans had left most
of the Ukraine, Belorussia and Lithuania. The Polish Army and the
Red Army both moved into the evacuated region. At seven o'clock
on the morning of February 14, a Polish captain led a patrol into
Bereza Kartuska, a small town about sixty miles northeast of Brest
Litovsk. He found it occupied by a reconnaissance force of the Red
Army. There was a sharp fight, and the Poles took eight Bolshevik

prisoners. This skirmish proved to be the beginning of the Polish-Soviet War. For some months, however, the war was confined to small border skirmishes, while each side sought to increase its forces and Soviet Russia sought to outmaneuver Poland diplomatically.

The Polish government had decided that it must have as little diplomatic contact with Soviet Russia as possible. There were two reasons for this. First, a Soviet legation in Warsaw would in all likelihood be a subversive force. Secondly, since all the major Western powers had refused diplomatic recognition to Soviet Russia, it would hardly be politic for the new Polish government to do so. In fact, the Polish Foreign Minister Leon Wasilewski took special pains to assure the French and British governments that Poland "will not recognize any Bolshevik representatives or allow them to enter the capital."[8]

But the Poles found it impossible to completely ignore Russian diplomatic overtures. The Soviets held at least one trump card. Because of the evacuation of Poland during the German advance of 1915, approximately 700,000 Poles had moved eastward into Russia. In addition, a substantial number of Poles had been members of the Russian Imperial Army and were still in Russia. Most of these soldiers and refugees wanted to return to their homeland. The Soviets were not holding them hostage, but neither were they making it easy for them to return to Poland. Moscow realized that the Polish government would always be willing to discuss the repatriation of these marooned Poles.

The first exchanges between the Soviet government and the government of independent Poland consisted of a series of radio messages between Moscow and Warsaw. (There could not be any direct personal contact between representatives of these two governments because at that time the German Ober-Ost barred the way.) This radio communication continued for nearly a month. The Soviet government, ever agreeable, pointed out that there was so much to discuss that face-to-face negotiation was necessary. This would involve mutual diplomatic recognition, followed, of course, by the opening of embassies. The Poles evaded this request. They continued to protest the treatment of the Polish nationals in Russia and stated that any consideration of diplomatic recognition must await the return of those refugees.

The Soviet government saw that nothing was being accomplished by this exchange of radiograms and thereupon took more direct action. On December 20, to the astonishment of the Polish government, a group of five prominent Russian Communists suddenly appeared in Warsaw, having secretly made their way from Moscow through the German lines. These persons described themselves as a delegation from the Russian Red Cross and that they had come to discuss the repatriation of Polish refugees. It did not take the Polish government more than a few hours to determine that this was a very unusual group of Red Cross representatives. Most of the mission's members had been prominent in the SDKPiL, and the leader of the group was Bronislaw Wesolowski, chairman of the Highest Revolutionary Tribunal. He was therefore a prominent Soviet official who was used to dealing with espionage and counterespionage. It could not be established that any of the members of the mission had ever demonstrated any previous interest in Red Cross affairs. They had brought with them more than one million rubles which was a startlingly large amount for a group whose ostensible purpose was arranging for the repatriation of Polish refugees. It became known that there were one or two other Russian "Red Cross" missions either on their way to Warsaw or perhaps already secretly present in the city.*

The Polish government swiftly came to the not unreasonable conclusion that the real objective of Wesolowski and his delegation was to force diplomatic contact and subsequent recognition. And the makeup of the present "Red Cross delegation" gave a clear indication of the type of diplomatic representation that the Soviets would send to Warsaw. So, only a day after the mission's arrival the Polish government arrested the "Red Cross" delegates and ordered them expelled from Poland. The Russians were spirited out of Warsaw and taken to the Polish frontier. There, for reasons that are unknown to this day, they were dragged from the cart in which they were traveling and taken into the woods, where four of them were murdered by their Polish police escort; the fifth member, Leon Alter, was wounded and left for dead. But he did not die; eventually he made his way back to Moscow with an account of the whole business.

These murders introduced a major grievance into the already tense Soviet-Polish relations. A series of telegrams and radio messages

---

* The technique of sending abroad teams of political agents in the guise of Red Cross missions was a favorite Soviet device. Béla Kun, for example, was returned to Hungary in early 1919 as part of a Russian Red Cross mission. He and his mission associates promptly directed a Hungarian revolution and led the short-lived Hungarian Soviet Republic.

between Moscow and Warsaw ensued, with the Soviets protesting the murders and the Poles promising that they would investigate the affair and punish the guilty. There were other imbroglios too, and they served to further exacerbate relations between the Soviets and the Poles. Among these, the matter of Lithuania predominated.

Lithuania had declared its national independence in December 1917. The Germans, who then occupied all of Lithuania, had encouraged this as part of a plan that they had for dismembering Russia. But then Germany collapsed, the war ended, and the German occupiers (and protectors) of Lithuania gradually withdrew. The feeble Lithuanian government found itself menaced by adversaries within and without. Most Lithuanian aristocrats and landowners were ethnically Polish or chose to regard themselves as Polish. Piłsudski himself had been born in Lithuania. The two nations had been joined in a dynastic union for four hundred years. Wilno, the capital of Lithuania, contained far more Poles than Lithuanians. It also contained a number of religious shrines and was considered a holy city by most Poles. There were therefore considerable grounds for restoring the historic ties between Poland and Lithuania. The Soviet government, however, regarded Lithuania as part of prewar Russia. Although theoretically Lithuania had the right to secede from Russia, any "nationality" that did so was automatically subject to invasion by the Red Army. And, in fact, Lithuania was invaded in January 1919. At this time, the Red Army that invaded Lithuania was undermanned and poorly organized, but even so, it was incomparably superior to the almost nonexistent forces of Lithuania and adjoining Belorussia. Within a few weeks, the Bolsheviks had occupied practically all of Belorussia as well as the eastern part of Lithuania, including Wilno. The Lithuanian government, chased out of its capital, set itself up in the city of Kaunas, fifty miles to the west. Meanwhile, Moscow set up an "independent" government known as the Soviet Socialist Republic of Lithuania-Belorussia to administer the two countries.

The capture of Wilno infuriated the Poles. It frightened them even more. It meant that the Red Army was advancing in some strength just to the northeast of ethnic Poland. And the Poles, of course, had had their own designs on Lithuania. To have Wilno, with its large Polish population, declared the capital of the Soviet Socialist Republic of Lithuania-Belorussia was utterly unacceptable. However, Piłsudski had no intention of allowing Lithuania to remain a part of

Soviet Russia. The capture of Wilno had touched a nerve within the Polish Chief of State. Wilno was his native city; he loved it. Assisted by only a few officers, Piłsudski commenced in great secrecy to plan the liberation of Wilno by the Polish Army.

The recapture of Wilno, which occurred on Easter Sunday, April 20, 1919, was a triumph for the Polish Army. Covered by a diversionary attack on the Red Army's positions well to the south of Wilno, Piłsudski had infiltrated a mixed force of infantry and cavalry through the Soviet lines. Moving by night, they traveled cross-country and attacked Wilno from the rear. The Red Army forces in the city were either sabered in the streets or put to flight by the Polish cavalry. Within a day or two the Polish Army cleared the Soviets from a wide area surrounding the city.

The swiftness, ease and totality of the Polish victory over the Red forces in and around Wilno came as a stunning surprise to the Russians. Probably it astonished the Poles almost as much. The Red Army and the appeal of Communism in the region, it was now established, were much weaker than the Poles had thought. To the Poles there seemed to be no point in stopping with the capture of Wilno and its environs. Obviously now was the time to push the Red Army deeper east, out of Lithuania and Belorussia altogether. So the Polish forces assembled in this region were formed into a front and commenced to advance slowly but steadily eastward.

The reaction in Moscow to these developments was a combination of embarrassment, outrage and frustration. The Soviets were humiliated by the ease with which the Poles had seized Wilno. But the Soviet government could not launch a counteroffensive against the Poles—it was the summer of 1919, and the Russian Civil War was at its height.

The Red Army was under so much pressure in 1919 that the Poles were able to gain easy victories in Lithuania and Belorussia. Almost simultaneously with the Polish offensive, a White army under Nikolai Yudenich was advancing on Petrograd. In the south another White general, Anton Denikin, was commencing a major offensive. In the east, Aleksandr Kolchak's White army had begun its spring offensive and had almost broken through the Red Army front in the Urals. Even the Ukraine was not secure. Although the Red Army had earlier captured the capital city of Kiev, it had not succeeded in destroying the anti-Communist Ukrainian People's forces under

Simon Petlyura, which were still holding out in the east. Additionally, large guerrilla forces led by the anarchist Nestor Makhno denied the Red Army control over wide sections of the Ukraine.

Assaulted from all sides, the beleaguered Soviet government could muster neither the military forces nor the attention necessary to contest the Poles. Compared with the immediate threats posed by Kolchak and Denikin, the Polish advance was a side-show. So, against almost negligible resistance by the Red Army, the Polish Army moved eastward by fits and starts through the summer of 1919. The territorial gains soon became impressive. By September, the Poles occupied Minsk and even beyond; they captured Borisov and occupied a series of river lines that extended roughly southward from Borisov through the Pripet Marshes and then bent slightly back to the west as the front skirted that part of the Ukraine held by Petlyura. This was quite an advance indeed. The Russo-Polish front was now located almost halfway between Moscow and Warsaw. In their advance they had much earlier left ethnic Poland. In fact, in the easternmost areas that the army had captured, the Polish population was less than 5 percent of the total.

But the very success of this offensive created great political problems within Poland. How long was this "semiwar" to go on? The government had given no explanations of Polish war aims to its people. In fact, even senior government officials were unsure of Piłsudski's direction. Michael Kossakowski, the chief of the eastern department of the Polish foreign ministry, noted in his diary, "Where are we going? This question intrigues everybody. . . . To the Dnieper? To the Dvina? And then?"[9]

A great many Poles, including most of the members of the foreign affairs committee of the Sejm, believed that Poland had gone far enough. They favored stopping the Polish Army, annexing the territories in hand, and concluding a peace agreement with the Soviet government. But there were serious problems posed by this approach. No one knew what the attitude of the major Allied powers would be. Article 87 of the Treaty of Versailles had reserved to the Allies the power to delineate Poland's eastern frontiers. Would they confer their blessing on Poland's recent captures, and thus in effect guarantee the Polish border against a future Soviet attack? And how about Soviet Russia itself? It was not known whether it would sign a peace treaty that would allow Poland to keep the very large gains it had recently made. And even if such a treaty was signed, could the

Bolsheviks be trusted to honor it? Piłsudski did not think so. "Let us imagine for a moment," he said to an official of the foreign ministry, "that I have concluded peace with them. I must then demobilize the army. . . . And then I will become powerless at the border. Lenin will be able to do what he wants, because he will not hesitate to break even the most solemn word."[10]

In the simplest terms, the question in Poland was whether the Polish Army had gone too far or not far enough. Piłsudski believed that the army must continue eastward. He was adamant in his view that it was too soon to make peace with Soviet Russia. He believed that federalism was Poland's only hope for survival. The Polish advance must continue in order to liberate enough territory from Soviet Russia to put together the federation. There could be no turning back now. Of course, even Piłsudski realized that he was embarked on a risky business. Poland's neighbors might elect not to join a Polish-led federation, leaving Poland alone and exposed until such time as the Red Army could gather enough strength to turn upon the Poles in great force. But this was a risk that Piłsudski believed had to be taken—and his views carried the day.

In the months that followed, Polish diplomatic activity intensified greatly. Extensive discussions were entered into with Rumania, Latvia, Estonia, and Finland in the hopes that they could be induced to join Poland in an anti-Bolshevik crusade. A Polish mission was sent to the headquarters of General Denikin to see if the Whites could be persuaded to reverse their view that the Poles were nothing more than dissident subjects of the Tsar and that their temporary independence would end with the restoration of the monarchy.

Another Polish mission was sent to open conversation with the Ukrainian People's Republic, a rather ramshackle organization that had been driven from Kiev, the capital of the Ukraine, and was now pressed against the western rim of the Ukraine. This Ukrainian "government" was led by Simon Vasilievich Petlyura, a forty-two-year-old former bookkeeper. It was questionable just how much actual support could be obtained from Petlyura's regime, whose popularity with the Ukrainian people was dubious. For many months Petlyura and his entourage had been forced to live a sort of gypsy life in a railroad train pulled around the western Ukrainian countryside. They disposed of very little in the way of armed force. In fact, a member of its government recalled, "There were times when the only territory over which the Ukrainian government exercised any authority was the few miles of trackage on which its cars were temporarily located."[11] Nonetheless, Petlyura was known to be open to negotiation, and a Polish military delegation was sent to his headquarters to determine whether some support could be extracted from him.

As a final part of their diplomatic efforts, the Poles made an energetic attempt to enlist the support of the British and the French. In September 1919 Paderewski visited Paris to appear before the Heads of Delegations of the Five Great Powers—a sort of continuation of the Paris Peace Conference. The United States was represented by an official without plenary powers, but Lloyd George and Clemenceau were in attendance on the afternoon of September 15 to hear Paderewski announce that Poland was prepared to provide the principal interventionary army in an invasion of Bolshevik Russia. However, there was a condition. Poland must have the positive support of the Allies. Paderewski announced that the Polish Army then consisted of 545,000 men, and if necessary an additional 480,000 troops could be raised in a few months. However, on its own, Poland could not afford to enlarge its army; indeed, it could not afford to maintain its army at the present level indefinitely. If the Allies wanted Poland to undertake the invasion of Russia, then they would have to contribute the cost involved. The Polish estimate was that 500,000 men would be needed, and the charge for their services would be approximately ten million francs per day (then equal to $1.5 million).[12]

This indeed put the whole matter of what the Allies intended to do about Russia squarely on the line. While Paderewski sat back and listened, the representatives of the most powerful governments of Europe debated the matter. Finally, summing up the feelings of the Allied governments, Clemenceau stated that they "did not desire that the Poles should march on Moscow." As for suggesting to the Poles what they should do in their present circumstances, the best suggestion that Clemenceau could make was that if he were a Pole "he would not make peace nor would he make war."[13] This was all the advice or guidance that the Allies were prepared to give.

The Poles took this as a statement of the Allied attitude toward Soviet Russia. Obviously the great European powers were not going to spend either money or lives in an anti-Bolshevik crusade. They were simply going to try to contain Soviet Russia behind a barrier of East European nations, which the French, borrowing a term from the medical vocabulary, called the *cordon sanitaire* (literally, quarantine line). Poland, as the largest and most exposed of these nations, was in what the French referred to as the "place of honor." All well and good, observed the Poles, but henceforth they would continue to be guided only by their own interests and would cease to concern themselves with the opinions or desires of the Western powers. The Poles now assumed that they had carte blanche from the Allies to do whatever they wished in the matter of their eastern frontier.

By the winter of 1919–20 a lot had happened in the endlessly fluid Russian Civil War. As 1919 ended, the Soviet government rightly felt that it had defeated most of its opponents. Having faced mortal danger during the previous summer, the Communists now found themselves delivered on almost every front. The anti-Bolshevik Czech Legion was retreating from Russia and would soon turn over Admiral Kolchak to the Reds, who would execute him. The White General Yudenich had failed at the gates of Petrograd, and his forces had been driven back into Estonia. General Denikin's army, so successful in the south during the spring and summer of 1919, had now been beaten decisively and was being forced back into the Caucasus. It would seem that now was the time for the Red Army to go against the Poles.

But although the Red Army had prevailed almost everywhere, the struggle had left Russia a virtual industrial desert. The workers in the cities were exhausted from hunger. The railway system had practically collapsed. Typhus and syphilis were rampant. Almost every aspect of civilized life seemed to have broken down. No longer did the leaders of the Soviet government have the heady feeling that a general proletarian revolution was just around the corner. Capitalism was proving more resilient than expected, and it was evident that the world revolution would take somewhat longer than had once been thought. Of course, the Soviets did not waver from their goal of worldwide revolution, but right now nothing seemed more necessary than a prolonged breathing space. So the Soviets made every effort to arrive at some sort—any sort—of peace settlement with their enemies. If the Soviets had not been serious about peace with their neighbors before, they most definitely were at the end of 1919. They were willing to make almost any kind of concession, recognize any kind of government, make any kind of promise, if only they could get peace.

During the fall of 1919 the Soviet government made generous and apparently sincere offers of peace and recognition of frontiers to Estonia, Finland, Latvia and Lithuania. Despite great pressure from Polish diplomats to prevent these settlements, the Baltic nations began to sign treaties with Soviet Russia. The prospects for the Polish-led federation began to dim as Poland's neighbors to the north reached accommodation with the Soviets. There is no question but that Moscow would have been glad to reach some sort of agreement with Poland. A number of overtures were made to Warsaw, and on several occasions there were informal meetings between Polish and Russian representatives. But the Polish government could not believe that the Soviet peace efforts were sincere. The Poles found ominous motives in the Russian negotiation with the Baltic nations. Is seemed to them that Moscow's objective was to isolate Poland in preparation for a Soviet attack. Not only did Poland find it impossible to trust the Soviet peace overtures, but also the Polish government was not sure that it wanted peace with Soviet Russia. Piłsudski had not given up his dream of a Polish-led federation that required the liberation of the Ukraine and probably also of Belorussia. So, the Polish Army continued to advance slowly against desultory Soviet resistance. No one knew exactly what Piłsudski's objective was. His enemies claimed that the war was nothing more than his private adventure, but there was no one capable of opposing him. By the end of 1919 Poland did not even possess a prime minister of independent stature, because Paderewski, having been a conspicuous failure both as prime minister and as minister for foreign affairs, had resigned.

Paderewski had brought to his offices a set of personal idiosyncrasies that had led to his downfall.

His fundamental problem was that he was a highly emotional man who had had no experience in directing a bureaucratic organization. As an administrator, he was absolutely hopeless. He came to his office, located in his official residence at the Royal Palace, at any hour that suited him—usually too late in the day for effective direction of a working ministry. Paderewski found the tone produced by a telephone offensive, and he refused to use the instrument. He would not allow his secretaries to touch his desk, which was an alp of papers. He could not concentrate on one task at a time and see it to completion. His appointment calendar listed a jumble of friends, office-seekers, and official callers on whose visits he set no time limit.

Paderewski's wife, Helena, was an additional complication. She had handled all of Paderewski's business affairs when he was a concert pianist, and it did not seem to her that she should behave any differently now. She acted as if the official visitors to Paderewski's offices at the Royal Palace were also her guests. She felt free to join in her husband's official conversations, to read confidential state documents, and to advocate the appointment to office of persons she knew and liked. She meddled in state affairs and felt quite free to openly debate Paderewski's decisions with him, in the presence of his colleagues.

The chaotic organization of Paderewski's office and the meddlesomeness of his wife soon became well known in Warsaw. There was considerable public criticism of Paderewski's methods, and public criticism was something that Paderewski could not tolerate. Most of his life he had been a beloved and respected figure who had been above criticism. Under the strain of not being universally adored, Paderewski quickly cracked. He became incapable of decision. He did not know whether he wanted to resign or remain in office. Finally, toward the end of 1919, opposition within the Sejm overwhelmed Paderewski. The Left had always regarded him as an adversary, and now the deputies on the Right turned against him, claiming that he was failing to resist Piłsudski. With this, Paderewski resigned.

Paderewski's departure from Warsaw to his prewar home in Switzerland approached the pathetic. Although he resigned on December 9, 1919, he did not actually leave Warsaw until February 1920. His departure was announced many times, and on each occasion the foreign diplomatic corps turned out at the station to bid farewell, only to find that Paderewski had not yet decided to leave. The United States Minister, Hugh Gibson, visited Paderewski in his suite at the Hotel Bristol. Gibson found Paderewski to be an emotional wreck—sobbing and distraught by the strain of packing for his journey. Important letters had been lost, and trunks were being torn apart to find them. Paderewski had not slept for a day and a half. "Oh me, oh my, I don't know where I am," Paderewski told Gibson.[14]

The next day the former prime minister did finally appear at the station and boarded his private train. At the last moment a group of persons got aboard the train, having been invited by Madame Paderewski to join them in the journey. But she had forgotten they were coming and there were not enough sleeping berths in the car. With Paderewski announcing his intention to sleep on the floor and his guests insisting that *they* would sleep on the floor, the train steamed off. It did not get very far, because it was soon discovered that all of the Paderewski's baggage had been left at the Warsaw station. A separate locomotive had to return to get it.

Paderewski's successor as prime minister was Leopold Skulski, a forty-two-year-old former chemical engineer who had once been mayor of Łódź and a founder of the Rightist National Peasant Union. Skulski was a colorless person whose appointment as prime minister would not have been confirmed by the Sejm except that his ties to the Right were so strong that he could not be denied by the National Democrats. Skulski brought with him, as foreign minister, Stanislaw Patek, a PPS lawyer who had been one of Piłsudski's nominees to the Polish delegation at the Paris Peace Conference. Neither of these men was greatly gifted. The forceless Skulski was incapable of resisting Piłsudski, and Patek was an old and loyal associate of Piłsudski. These men knew their places. So now, without any appreciable opposition, Piłsudski commanded Poland's army and conducted Poland's foreign affairs. He kept his own counsel and made his own plans, paying no great attention to the desires of the Sejm, the majority of whose members, both on the Left and on the Right, wanted peace with Soviet Russia. And, in the meantime, the Polish Army continued to slowly advance.

Actually, Piłsudski's attitude regarding the war with Soviet Russia had gone beyond the desire to put together the dreamed-of Polish-led federation. Toward the end of 1919, Piłsudski apparently became convinced that regardless of whether Poland now made peace with Moscow, the Soviets would launch a full-scale attack on Poland in the following spring—probably in April 1920. The exact processes by which Piłsudski came to this conclusion are not clear, but Polish diplomatic and military policies were turned from attempts to achieve federalism toward preparations for meeting the Red Army in an all-out war. Belief in a Red Army attack in the spring became the *idée fixe* of Polish policy, and throughout the winter of 1919–20 the Polish government bent every effort to prepare itself militarily and diplomatically for war. The Polish Army was feverishly expanded to 700,000 men, of whom 300,000 were soon actively serving on the eastern front.

From the Soviet government there came a barrage of peace proposals which they made public for their propaganda effect on both
Polish and world opinion. Over the signatures of Lenin, Trotsky,
and Chicherin these documents promised categorically and without
reservation that the Soviets would recognize the sovereignty and independence of Poland. The Soviets pledged that the Red Army
would not cross the present front lines, and they declared solemnly
that "insofar as the real interests of Poland and Russia are concerned,
there is no single question . . . which could not be decided in a
peaceful way."[15]

In subsequent messages or announcements, all of which were made
public, the Soviet government swore to the Polish people that "our
enemies and yours deceive you when they say that the Russian Soviet
government wishes to plant communism in Polish soil with the
bayonets of Russian Red Army men. . . . The communists of Russia
are at present striving only to defend their own soil, their own
peaceful constructive work. . . ."[16]

The Soviet pleas for peace had an undeniable effect on Polish
opinion. A great many Poles were bewildered and asked why there
must be war between Poland and Russia. The Russians seemed to be
willing to grant every concession and to make every promise, and
therefore it was pointless to continue down the road to full-scale war.
The Polish Army was occupying eastern territories exceeding by a
wide margin the hopes of most Poles. The Polish Sejm reflected this
popular anxiety for the war to end. On the Left the PPS deputies
demanded peace, and the PPS held large peace rallies in Warsaw.
Their principal newspaper openly questioned the government's motives, asking, "Will Poland be the Lackey of Reaction?"[17]

On the Right, the National Democrats too could see little reason
for the continuation of hostilities. If the Russians were willing to
give up the extensive areas that Poland now occupied, then all was
well and good. These territories should be annexed by Poland, a
peace treaty with Soviet Russia should be negotiated, and then each
nation should go about its business.

The Foreign Affairs Committee of the Sejm demanded that the
government make clear its position. If there were facts that had not
been revealed to the committee, then let the government now make
them known.

Meanwhile, France and Britain were becoming nervous about
Polish intentions. The Allied ministers in Warsaw were reporting

Polish preparations for an all-out war that neither the French nor the British wanted to occur. The Allies could not determine whether the Poles were simply preparing to defend themselves or whether they intended to try to crush the Red Army before they themselves were attacked. The suspicion was growing, however, that Piłsudski intended to strike first.

The French and British governments began to regret that they had not been more specific in their earlier advice to the Poles at the time of Paderewski's visit to Paris in September 1919. Lloyd George resolved to put the matter straight, and so, when Polish Foreign Minister Patek visited London in January 1920, there was no ambiguity. Lloyd George had told Patek bluntly that the day of British intervention in Russia and its support of the White armies was over. If Poland made war on Bolshevik Russia, then it was on its own. Britain "did not wish to give Poland the slightest encouragement to pursue her policy of war, because if it were to give that advice it would incur responsibilities which it could not discharge."[18] Poland, Lloyd George suggested, should propose reasonable terms to the Soviets and negotiate a peace settlement. Patek thereupon asked an important question. Would Great Britain recognize such a treaty and would she support Poland if the Soviets broke it? In other words, if Poland did as Britain asked, would Britain then guarantee the safety of Poland? Lloyd George would make no such guarantee, although he indicated that both France and Britain would surely give some sort of unspecified support to Poland.

The French government told Patek much the same thing when he appeared in Paris. But the French were not as explicit. They suggested that in its relationships with Soviet Russia, Poland emulate a barbed-wire fence, and they left it at that.

Upon his return to Warsaw, Patek informed the Polish General Staff of the outcome of his visits: "In one word, we can count only on our forces and, according to that, conduct our policy towards Russia."[19]

Hugh Gibson, the United States minister to Poland, agreed. Poland had been isolated by the Western Allies, and Washington was not willing to give the Poles any advice. "Poland has been cast adrift politically," Gibson wrote, "and must shift for herself."[20]

Piłsudski was of the same opinion, and he made no secret of it. On February 12 he told the Warsaw correspondent of the *Echo de Paris* that "Poland is left alone to face the eastern problems because

Europe does not know what to do. France and England can afford
to wait, watch events and procrastinate. We are immediate neighbors
of Russia. We cannot wait."[21]

As a matter of fact, Piłsudski now believed that Poland was in
almost mortal danger. Soviet Russia had survived the most critical
period of its civil war. Piłsudski was convinced that if he now made
peace with Russia, the Soviets would break the treaty and crush
Poland as soon as the Red Army had been revived. At the same time,
the Polish Chief of State recognized that the present situation of
semiwar could not continue. There was, in Piłsudski's view, only one
answer to this dilemma. There must be a showdown. Before Poland
could make peace with Soviet Russia, *it must inflict such a shattering
defeat upon the Red Army that Russia would for many years be
deterred from resuming war with Poland.* Piłsudski concluded that
Poland's only hope for avoiding eventual destruction was for the
Polish Army to launch a full-scale preemptive attack on the Red
Army. And this Polish offensive must come early in the spring of
1920, before the anticipated assault by the Red Army, which was
being rapidly reinforced on the Polish front.

Piłsudski had secretly been planning the Polish attack since January. An early priority had been to gather allies from among Poland's
neighbors to join in an attack on the Red Army, regardless of
whether they were interested in joining a Polish federation. This
quest for allies had been fruitless. All the Baltic nations had been
approached. But the Finns and Latvians, although friendly toward
Poland, had only recently concluded wars of their own with Soviet
Russia, and they were not willing to start again. The Estonians had
just signed a peace treaty with Russia and would not break it.
Rumania would have liked to assist, but was frightened of eventual
Soviet retaliation. Hungary was anxious to aid Poland, but the two
nations had no common frontiers. Poland's relations with Lithuania
and Czechoslovakia were so poisoned by frontier disputes that it was
pointless even to propose an alliance with them.

The only possible ally left was Petlyura's Ukrainian People's Republic, but this alliance would add little strength to the Polish
offensive. Petlyura's Ukrainians had been virtually chased out of
their homeland by Denikin and later the Red Army. During the
early months of 1920 Petlyura's government was, in fact, sheltering
itself behind Polish lines on the western rim of the Ukraine. But the
support of this group was better than nothing at all, and on April

21, 1920, Poland signed a secret treaty with Petlyura's Ukrainians, which spelled out the agreement between the two governments in such matters as diplomatic recognition, frontiers, and reciprocal rights for each nation's minorities. Three days later the two governments signed a secret military convention in which they agreed upon the manner in which they would jointly conduct war against Soviet Russia. Piłsudski assumed personal command over the combined Polish-Ukrainian forces. On April 25, as soon as the roads were dry, the two armies launched a full-scale attack in the Ukraine. Within a few days the Soviet force facing the Poles and Ukrainians was scattered. By May 7, having done remarkably little fighting and having suffered very few casualties, Piłsudski's army captured Kiev, the ancient capital of the Ukraine.

Without allies, other than the negligible support of the government of the Ukrainian People's Republic, Poland had embarked upon a supremely ambitious undertaking. Piłsudski's objective was to crush the Red Army and, as a result, reestablish Poland as the major European power it had been nearly three hundred years before. This adventure began easily and gloriously with the capture of Kiev, the first great victory of Polish arms since the eighteenth century. But the end of the tale had yet to be told.

6
From Kiev to Riga

THE TWO ARMIES that fought the Polish-Soviet War in 1920 were military improvisations, not complete conventional armies. Both had enormous defects, both had terrible supply problems, and both were commanded by leaders who had had very little formal military training. Neither army had existed for very long.

The army of Soviet Russia—the Red Army—was essentially the creation of one man, Leon Trotsky. In 1918 Trotsky had been made chairman of the Supreme Military Soviet and Commissar for War. It was a superb appointment. Trotsky possessed fantastic energy, awesome determination and great administrative gifts. During the darkest days of the civil war he constantly demonstrated his remarkable ability to come up with unorthodox solutions to desperate problems. Probably the most innovative of these was his successful use, over the objections of almost every member of the Soviet government, of former officers of the Imperial Russian Army to remedy the Red Army's desperate shortage of trained military leaders. By 1920 thirty thousand of these "enemies" were serving in the Red Army. Although they were closely watched by Communist commissars, these Tsarist "specialists"—as Trotsky named them—ended up holding most of the senior Soviet commands.

In the end, of course, Trotsky's improvised army defeated its opponents—or, at least, defeated such enemies as appeared on the field in 1918 and 1919. It was an army that lived off the land or off supplies captured from its enemies, for despite Trotsky's efforts, the Soviet war industry never approached the capacity necessary to supply the Red Army. And, although a considerable amount of organizational work had been done, the Red Army still resembled a horde that had been broken into divisions and upon which the refinements of military administration lay very lightly. But the Red Army triumphed during the desperate civil war days of 1919. In 1920, however, there was a real question about the Red Army's ability to mount another major effort. Could these divisions be relied upon to suffer another campaign? Or would the soldiers just disappear to find their way back to the villages where their starving families waited for them to put in the spring planting? No one knew. Lenin and the other top members of the Soviet government were quite confident and looked with equanimity on the prospect of a 1920 war with Poland. They predicted that such a war would immediately trigger a Polish revolution. Trotsky, on the other hand, was nowhere near as optimistic. He knew how exhausted the Red Army was. And the idea that the Polish workers would rise up and overthrow their government was, to Trotsky, only nice theory; in practice it would not happen quickly enough. He later observed that "the events of war and those of the revolutionary mass movement are measured by different yardsticks. Where the action of arms is measured in days and weeks, the movement of masses of people is usually reckoned in months and years."[1] But Trotsky's warnings had no weight in the spring of 1920; the Soviet government believed that they had little choice but to fight Poland—and in this light, preparations were made.

At the outbreak of full-scale war with Poland, Trotsky was Commisar of War and thus head of the Red Army. But so much of his time was taken up with administrative and political concerns that he rarely appeared on the western front. The military commander in chief of the Red Army was General Sergei Kamenev, formerly a colonel in the Tsarist army and once a member of the Imperial General Staff.*

---

* At this time the Red Army did not use conventional military titles. Instead they used functional contractions, as "comdiv" for divisional commander; "commankor" for corps commander; "commandarm" for commander of an army. The military ranks given in this work are the conventional equivalents. The Red Army ultimately reverted to standard military nomenclature in 1940.

The Russian front facing Poland was divided into two major commands. The southern half, which consisted principally of the Ukraine, was defended by a Soviet force known as the Army of the Southwest, under the command of General Alexander Yegorov, also a former Tsarist specialist, whose political commissar was Joseph Stalin.

The commander of the larger Red Army force holding the northern part of the Russian front was General Mikhail Nikolaevich Tukhachevsky, a tall, thin young man who was one of the strangest figures in a war in which strange figures abounded. In 1920 Tukhachevsky, the son of an impecunious Russian nobleman and an Italian mother of peasant stock, was only twenty-nine years old. He had joined the Imperial Russian Army in which, in 1914, he was commissioned a lieutenant in an elite regiment, the Semyonovsky Life Guards. In 1915 Tukhachevsky was taken prisoner by the Germans but escaped and made his way back to Russia just in time for the Bolshevik Revolution.

Tukhachevsky was an intelligent man, and an ambitious one. During his German imprisonment he had told fellow prisoners, "War is everything to me! At thirty I will either be a general or I will be dead."[2]

The Russian civil war gave Tukhachevsky ample opportunity to satisfy his military ambitions. He had joined the Red Army as a specialist and rose with extraordinary rapidity. He had directed the Red Army's pursuit of Kolchak into Siberia. This operation was a military masterpiece: the army had covered 2,000 miles in only 250 days. Tukhachevsky professed himself a Communist, and despite his aristocratic background, the Soviets believed in his conversion and accepted him, although Trotsky thought that Tukhachevsky had perhaps made "an over-rapid leap from the ranks of the Guards Officers to the Bolshevist camp."[3] This was the man who commanded the northern part of the front with Poland, known as the Army of the West.

At the end of April 1920 the Red Army facing the Polish front consisted of twenty divisions and five cavalry brigades. Most of these had just arrived on the front and some were considerably under-strength. But merely to have them present represented a herculean effort, because as recently as February there had been only five infantry divisions and five cavalry brigades on this front. The Soviet high command was not sure of the size of the enemy forces present, but for the time being they had given all they had to the front. It remained to be seen how the Polish Army would fight.

Although the Polish Army was less unorthodox than the Red Army, they nonetheless had great similarities. The Polish Army too had been put together in a great hurry. And, somewhat like the Red Army, it was largely the creation of one man. It would be incorrect to say that the Polish Army was Piłsudski's only interest—but it would surely be right to say that nothing interested him more than his army. To command the Polish Army had been his lifelong dream, and no one dared to interfere with him in its creation.

Piłsudski's role as the military commander of the Polish Army was confirmed, if it was ever in doubt, during the spring of 1920, when he was visited at the Belvedere Palace by a group of Polish generals. On behalf of the Polish Army they offered to create the rank of First Marshal of Poland and award it to Piłsudski. There would be no rank in the Polish Army senior to First Marshal. Piłsudski at first professed reluctance, but on March 19, 1920, with full-scale war with Soviet Russia about to start, he announced that he would accept. On April 3 the appointment order was signed by the Minister of War. For the first time in history there was a Marshal of the Polish Army.

When Piłsudski had returned to Warsaw in November 1918, the only force that could be considered a "Polish Army" was the Polonische Wehrmacht. It consisted of only six battalions of infantry and three squadrons of cavalry. From this pitifully small nucleus, Piłsudski had managed to build a rather sizable army in only eighteen months. It had been done by sweeping together the bits and pieces of Polish armed forces that had been created during the World War. About forty thousand former members of the Polish Legion had volunteered for service. The mobilization of the P.O.W. added more. Haller's Army brought another fifty thousand troops. The Polish regiments of the Austrian Army declared themselves to be part of the Polish Army and were absorbed into it. A separate Polish division that had been organized by the French for anti-Bolshevik service at Odessa made its way through the Balkans to join the homeland army. Similar detachments stranded in Murmansk and Vladivostok eventually straggled in. And supplementing all this was a nationwide conscription, which began in March 1919. By the spring of 1920 the Polish Army consisted of twenty-one infantry divisions and seven cavalry brigades—a total of 740,000 men.

However, the size of the Polish Army was not a true indication of its efficiency. It was burdened with enormous defects, which would take a great deal of time to remedy. The greatest problem was in logistics. A single Polish division might be equipped with four different rifles—the French Lebel, the Austrian Mannlicher, the Russian Berdan, and the German Mauser. Each of these used a different ammunition, a matter that created endless resupply problems.

As for artillery, the Poles found themselves almost entirely dependent upon the French and their 75mm cannon. Stocks of these guns were sold to the Poles, but obtaining the cannon themselves proved to be the easy part. Building up an ammunition supply in Poland was more difficult and costly, and this stockpiling had scarcely begun when full-time war broke out in 1920.

When it came to uniforms, it was inevitable that the Polish Army should present a motley and ragtag appearance. The Haller battalions wore the French blue uniform. The elite "legionnaire" division of the army wore the Austrian blue-gray. The rest of the army was clothed in cast-off German field-gray uniforms. Only a relatively few troops wore the greenish-khaki uniforms that Poland was just beginning to produce itself.

In the highly technical area of aviation, the Poles were almost helpless. In the end, they sent emissaries to London and Paris, where they recruited a couple of dozen demobilized British and American pilots who had fought in the World War in France. They brought the group to Warsaw, named them the Kościuszko Squadron, and outfitted them with captured German Albatross fighters. This was the Polish Air Service.

There was only one commodity that the Polish Army had in abundance—senior officers. The army was overloaded with colonels and generals of every grade. And since these officers had come from different armies, there was no way of evaluating their seniorities vis-à-vis other senior officers. Many officers, mostly protégés of Piłsudski, were very young men who had served in the Polish Legion or the P.O.W. and had been abruptly elevated to senior ranks. This created endless jealousies and rivalries, which were only partly solved by creating a number of more or less independent commands and overstaffing them with senior grades.

Second only to supply, the biggest problem that faced the Polish Army was training. With the exception of the few elite units, the entire army was in the process of training, and most of its formations were presently capable of only the simplest kinds of manuevers. The problem of training this army-in-formation was not solved before the beginning of the Polish-Soviet War in 1920, although a vigorous effort was made by a large French military mission to Poland. In a sense, the French "adopted" the Polish Army and supplied most of its officer-training cadres. The post-World War French Army had plenty of officers to spare, and France sent an enormous number of officer-instructors to Poland.* At its peak, the French military mission consisted of nine generals, twenty-nine colonels, sixty-three majors, nearly two hundred captains, and more than four hundred lieutenants. But, despite this intense effort, no one, least of all the French, thought that the job of training the Polish Army had much more than barely begun.

In sum, then, the Polish Army was riven with problems. When measured against the forces that had fought in France during the World War, it was, in no sense, a modern army. But, then, neither was its Soviet opponent.

In early 1920 the steppes of the Ukraine were sparsely populated by a very independent people who regarded themselves as a distinct nationality. The only large cities were Kharkov, Odessa, and the ancient Ukrainian capital of Kiev. The Ukrainian economy was almost exclusively agricultural, dominated by large estates, a sizable percentage of which were owned by Poles or by people of Polish descent. Among Ukrainians, Poles were identified with the landowner class and were therefore not popular.

The Ukraine had recently and repeatedly been fought over. During the last three years the Ukrainian city of Berdichev had changed hands fourteen times. At various intervals it had been occupied by Galicians, Petlyurists, Bolsheviks, Whites, and several irregular forces who were close to being bandits. Kiev had had roughly the same experience. In 1919, the city and the surrounding countryside had been controlled by the Bolsheviks, the Petlyurists, Denikin's forces and, since December 1919, once more by the Bol-

---

* One of the French officers was a captain named Charles de Gaulle, who had come to Poland with Haller's Army. He had served in East Galicia and had then become an instructor at the Polish training camp at Rembertow, about six miles from Warsaw. In the summer of 1920 he went into the field with a Polish division. In 1921 he was offered, but declined, a commission as a major in the Polish Army.

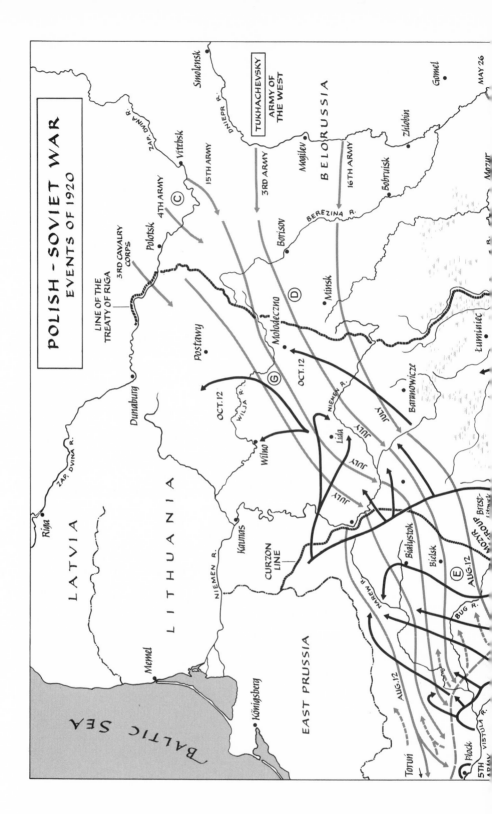

POLISH – SOVIET WAR
EVENTS OF 1920

LINE OF THE
TREATY OF RIGA

3RD CAVALRY
CORPS

TUKHACHEVSKY
ARMY OF
THE WEST

BALTIC SEA

LATVIA

LITHUANIA

EAST PRUSSIA

BELORUSSIA

Riga
Memel
Königsberg
Dunaburg
Postawy
Kaunas
Wilno
Lida
Białystok
Bielsk
Płock
Toruń

Smolensk
Vitebsk
Polotsk
Borisov
Mogilev
Minsk
Molodeczno
Baranowicze
Bobruisk
Zlobin
Gomel
Łuniniec
Mozyr

ZAP. DVINA R.
ZAP. DVINA R.
DNIEPR R.
BEREZINA R.
NIEMEN R.
NIEMEN R.
WILJA R.
NAREW R.
BUG R.
VISTULA R.

15TH ARMY
4TH ARMY
3RD ARMY
16TH ARMY
5TH ARMY

CURZON LINE

MOZYR GROUP

Brest-Litovsk

OCT. 12
OCT. 12
JULY
JULY
JULY
AUG. 12
AUG. 12
AUG. 12

MAY 26

©C
©D
©E
©G

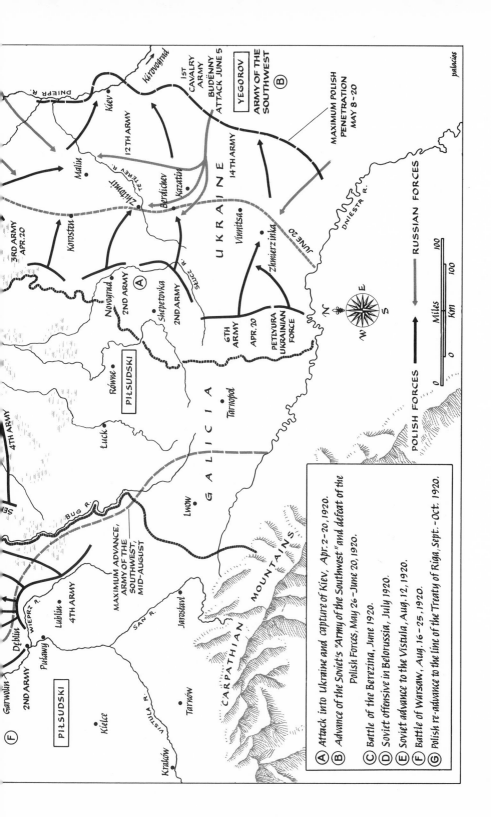

PILSUDSKI ⒡

Kielce•

Kraków•

Tarnów•

VISTULA R.

SAN R.

Jarosław•

CARPATHIAN MOUNTAINS

Puławy• Dęblin•
Lublin•   WIEPRZ R.
4TH ARMY

MAXIMUM ADVANCE,
ARMY OF THE
SOUTHWEST,
MID-AUGUST

BUG R.

Garwolin
2ND ARMY

SE

4TH ARMY

Łuck•

Równe•

PILSUDSKI

Tarnopol•

Lwów•

G A L I C I A

Novograd•

Shepetovka•
2ND ARMY

2ND ARMY

3RD ARMY
APR. 20

Korosten•

⒜

Malin•

Berdichev•
Zhitomir•
TETEREV R.

SŁUCZ R.

Kazatin•

6TH ARMY
APR. 20

Zhmierzinka•

Vinnitsa•

PETLYURA
UKRAINIAN
FORCE

JUNE 20

DNIESTR R.

DNIEPR R.

Kiev•

Kirovograd

1ST
CAVALRY
ARMY
BUDËNNY
ATTACK JUNE 5

12TH ARMY

U K R A I N E

14TH ARMY

MAXIMUM POLISH
PENETRATION
MAY 8–20

YEGOROV
ARMY OF THE
SOUTHWEST

⒝

N
W E
S

Miles
0   100
0   Km   100

POLISH FORCES

RUSSIAN FORCES

⒜ Attack into Ukraine and capture of Kiev, Apr. 2–20, 1920.
⒝ Advance of the Soviet's "Army of the Southwest" and defeat of the
    Polish Forces, May 26–June 20, 1920.
ⓒ Battle of the Berezina, June 1920.
ⓓ Soviet offensive in Belorussia, July 1920.
ⓔ Soviet advance to the Vistula, Aug. 12, 1920.
⒡ Battle of Warsaw, Aug. 16–25, 1920.
ⓖ Polish re-advance to the line of the Treaty of Riga, Sept.–Oct. 1920.

palacios

sheviks. The Red Army now occupied all the Ukrainian cities and most of the larger villages. It dispatched forces to search the farms and small settlements for guerrillas. But the peasants were sullen and uncooperative. The Ukrainians had learned to be wary and suspicious. Their loyalties were confused—they had seen too many political movements come and go. They did not want to become involved. It was into this situation that the Polish Army marched, supported by approximately twenty-thousand of Petlyura's troops.

In the early spring of 1920 the Polish-Soviet front ran roughly north and south for about three hundred miles. In almost the center of this front were the Pripet Marshes, an enormous swampy area, which separated the front into two halves. The southern half of the front (i.e., the part that was held by Yegorov's Soviet Army of the Southwest and which defended the Ukraine) bulged toward the west, and then, at its southern extremity, curved back eastward. Within this large arc were two small Ukrainian cities—Zhitomir and Berdichev, each about fifty miles from the front. About one hundred miles east of them was Kiev.

Along this southern front the Poles had assembled nine infantry divisions, four cavalry brigades, one Ukrainian division, and an additional Ukrainian operational group. These Polish forces were divided into three "armies"—from north to south the Third, Second and Sixth armies respectively. The total of the Polish-Ukrainian forces on this front amounted to perhaps 65,000 fighting troops (i.e., rifles and sabers). The entire Polish southern front was under the personal command of Marshal Piłsudski, who had left Warsaw on April 21 to establish his field headquarters in Rowne.

The Soviet forces under General Yegorov were also subdivided into "armies"—in this case the Soviet Twelfth and Fourteenth Armies. When the Polish and Ukrainian forces struck on April 25, 1920, they caught Yegorov's Army of the Southwest in the process of concentration. The first Polish attack was delivered in the south, for military and political reasons. Piłsudski believed that he could crush Yegorov's Army of the Southwest more easily than Tukhachevsky's Army of the West. And after the Soviet forces in the Ukraine had been scattered, Piłsudski foresaw that native Ukrainians would flock to join Petlyura's troops. The Polish forces would then be free to move to the north to deal with Tukhachevsky.

The outstanding feature of this early phase of the Polish-Soviet

War was the almost incredible speed of the Polish advance. It was particularly remarkable because the Poles had hardly any mechanical transport and barely enough horses to draw their ammunition and artillery. The Polish infantry divisions simply marched, and they marched enormous distances. The original plan was that the Polish army would make a fighting advance of fifteen miles per day, but frequently this rate was exceeded. Sometimes Polish battalions made forced marches as great as forty miles in a day.

At the very beginning of the Ukrainian campaign, the Poles established a definite ascendancy over the opposing Red armies. The Polish Second and Third Armies crashed down from the north and in a matter of only a day captured the cities of Malin and Zhitomir. Berdichev fell to them on the following day, April 27. Meanwhile, in the south of the Ukrainian bulge, the Polish Sixth Army and Petlyura's troops stormed forward against the Soviet Fourteenth Army, which retreated as fast as it could march.

It was just the sort of campaign that suited a semitrained army. In battalion-sized groups the Polish invaders trudged along the dirt and gravel roads that crossed the flat Ukrainian countryside. At night they bivouacked in the fields. Sometimes in the course of their advance, the Polish battalions would come across a strong point of Red Army defenders crouched behind a line of rude trenches. When this occurred, the Polish battalion commander would send out a company or two to work their way around the enemy's flank. On the open Ukrainian plain any strong point could be outflanked. This process would usually dislodge the Soviet defenders. In the case of an exceptionally stubborn strong point, the Poles would await the arrival of a few pieces of horse-drawn artillery, which would reduce the position. The tactics were all very rudimentary.

Piłsudski continued to direct the entire operation. In an open Cadillac touring car that had been obtained from the United States Army, he constantly roamed along the front. On the spot he resolved conflicts between commanders, ordered up supplies, and made decisions of every sort.

Within a week of the opening of the offensive, the Soviet Twelfth Army, which had borne the brunt of the attack, was close to being destroyed. It had broken up into small groups of frightened men who were making their way eastward deeper into the Ukraine. The neighboring Soviet Fourteenth Army allowed itself to be pushed south and east, and thus out of the battle.

On May 8 the combined Polish-Ukrainian armies marched into Kiev, the most important city in the Ukraine and the ancient crossing point of the Dnieper River. There was no resistance from Yegorov's Army of the Southwest, which had retreated across the river, deeper into the Ukraine. At this point the Polish Army stopped its offensive. The Poles established a bridgehead a few miles east of Kiev and quickly extended their line north along the Dnieper, which straightened out their front so that it ran north and joined the Polish troops facing Tukhachevsky's Army of the West.

The Polish invasion of the Ukraine had succeeded with incredible swiftness. In less than two weeks Yegorov's Army of the Southwest had been knocked back almost two hundred miles in places, and its component Twelfth Army had been nearly broken up. The casualties in the Polish Army were surprisingly light—about one hundred and fifty men had been killed and three hundred wounded. It was the first great victory for Polish arms since the Battle of Vienna in 1683. The Polish people were ecstatic. The Marshal (already Piłsudski was known only by his title) was acclaimed by his people as one of history's great military geniuses.

On May 18 Piłsudski returned to Warsaw, where he received a hero's greeting. In a carriage drawn by four white horses he was driven from the railroad station to St. Alexander's Church for a celebratory mass. Crowds stood outside the church, the outer columns of which were garlanded with flowers. As Piłsudski left the church for the parliament building to receive the thanks of the Sejm, students unhitched the horses from his carriage and pulled him through Warsaw in triumph.

Even Piłsudski's political enemies were adulatory. Wojciech Trąmpczyński, the marshal of the Sejm and a National Democrat, compared Piłsudski to the greatest of Poland's warrior kings and declared, "Your march on Kiev gave the nation a feeling of strength, renewed its faith in the future, reinforced its spiritual courage, and, above all, created the basis for a successful and lasting peace."[4]

It was generally assumed that the Polish Army in the Ukraine could now be transferred north to deal similar blows to Tukhachevsky's forces. In the meantime, Petlyura and his government would rapidly take over the defense of the Ukraine against the battered Red Army. In a proclamation to the Ukrainian people Piłsudski promised that Poland had no design upon their independence—"From the moment that a national government of the Ukrainian

Republic has established its authority . . . and the free nation is strong enough to settle its own fortunes, the Polish soldier will return beyond the frontier, having fulfilled his honorable task in the struggle for freedom of nations.''[5]

These were heady days for Poland. It was easy to overlook two ominous facts: that Petlyura's government had little support; and that the Red Army, whatever its defects, had a demonstrated capacity for swift reorganization in the face of defeat. This war was far from over. For Poland it had only started well.

There had been very little fighting on the northern part of the Polish-Soviet front during the lightning offensive in the Ukraine. This inactivity was caused in large part by lack of troops. The Poles were awaiting reinforcements from the south. And Tukhachevsky's Army of the West was still in the process of being formed. This force consisted of five subsidiary armies—from north to south the Fourth, Fifteenth, Third and Sixteenth Red armies plus the 3rd Cavalry Corps. However, these armies were understaffed and desperately needed the soldiers who were on their way from the interior.

Organizational difficulties aside, the strategic problem that the Red Army of the West faced was the possibility of being thrown out of their areas of concentration by sudden Polish attack. The consequences of this would be very serious, and for this reason Tukhachevsky took a daring gamble. On May 14, before his army was concentrated, reinforced, or supplied, he launched an attack on the Poles. This offensive did not go well for the Red Army. The Poles counterattacked in the region of Postawy and beat back the Soviet forces. In short order, the entire Red Army of the West was forced into a poorly organized retreat, stopping only in back of the line that they had held two weeks before. A month-long period of inactivity now descended upon the northern front. To the Poles this was most welcome, because in the south they now found themselves in desperate trouble.

A principal instrument in the war of the Red Army against the White forces of Denikin and, subsequently, Wrangel was the famous "cavalry army" commanded by General Budënny.

The organization of this force, known officially as the First Cavalry Army, had given the Soviets a great deal of trouble. An early attempt to recruit industrial workers who were reliable Communists and teach them enough horsemanship to serve as cavalry troops had ended in failure. It took too much training to transform a city-bred worker into a passable cavalryman. So the Red Army scraped up miscellaneous Cossacks and peasants without much inquiry into their political leanings, formed them into cavalry regiments, and hoped for the best. By 1920 the experiment had come off pretty well. The First Cavalry Army had been formed, and for a cavalry force it was extremely large. It consisted of nearly 17,000 horsemen, some artillery, five armored trains and a few dozen armored cars. It was under the command of Semyön Mikhailovich Budënny, a tall, enterprising former sergeant major in the 18th Seversky Dragoons of the Imperial Army's cavalry. Budënny was a roughhewn leader who, if he was not actually illiterate, certainly could not read or write to any significant degree. But he had a good deal of dash and daring, as well as cavalry experience.

The First Cavalry Army always operated as a unit. Thus, when this great mass of horsemen came up against an enemy front, they simply rode right through it "like a ship of the line driving through a fleet of fishing smacks."[6] Having burst through the front, Budënny's cavalry would devastate the enemy's rear—burning, killing and looting as they went. These Red cavalrymen inspired an almost numbing sense of terror in their opponents. Most of Budënny's troopers were Cossacks—and Cossacks were generally regarded as unthinking, primitive, and very violent. They had no sense of "Socialist discipline." They plundered, raped and murdered in the notorious Cossack style. Their enemies learned that Budënny's cavalry customarily shot captured enemy officers (or sometimes literally nailed an officer's epaulets to his shoulders). Before a group of opponents surrendered to the Red Cavalry, they discarded their uniforms so that the officers could not be recognized.

Trotsky did not completely trust these cruel and dangerous people. He thought that they were less loyal to the Revolution than they were to Budënny. "Where he leads his gang they will go," Trotsky said. "For the Reds today, tomorrow for the Whites."[7]

When the Polish offensive in the Ukraine began in late April 1920, Budënny's cavalrymen were fighting the remnants of Denikin's Whites in the Caucasus. But upon the Polish breakthrough, the First Cavalry Army was instructed to head northwest and breach the Polish lines south of Kiev. Budënny's troopers had a thousand miles to cover, but they moved quickly. By the end of May, the First

Cavalry Army was concentrated in Zinovievsk (now Kirovograd), about 150 miles southeast of Kiev and, shortly afterward, set out for the front.

On the day before it made contact with the Polish front, Budënny's cavalry was spotted by an American pilot of the Kościuszko Squadron. The Red force was advancing in thick columns and the American flier estimated its speed of advance at a phenomenal seventy-five miles a day.[8] Clearly, Budënny's troops could pierce the Polish front at any point they pleased, and on June 5, near Kazatin, they burst through the Polish defenses in a compact torrent. Budënny's entire force came through the Polish front at one time and then, spreading out, swept through the Polish rear. This attack took the Poles completely by surprise. They had not expected that they would have to fight the First Cavalry Army. They had not thought that Budënny's force could be spared from the Don front or that it could reach the Ukraine so rapidly. As Piłsudski admitted later, "I will confess that I left it out of account."[9]

Wherever a Polish force could concentrate and entrench, it was safe. But Budënny's cavalry, leaving the roads at will, simply flowed around Polish strong points. They cut the telegraph wires, blew up the railways, and fell upon Polish supply depots. They raided towns and villages, hung any suspected enemies on the spot, swept off and then returned the next day to raid again. They split up into small independent groups that seemed to be every place at once. There were not enough Polish cavalrymen to deal with Budënny's force. The very names "Budënny" and "Cossack" terrified the Ukrainian population, and they moved into a state of neutrality or even hostility toward Petlyura and the Poles.

Most of the Ukrainian towns had large Jewish populations. The terrorization of Jews had long been a Cossack specialty and in the memoirs of one of Budënny's troopers he tells how in a Ukrainian village an elderly Jew was pulled from his shuttered home and accused of spying. A group of Red Army soldiers were about to shoot him but the old man put up a dreadful row. This upset the soldiers and they dithered about, unable to kill their prisoner. A disgusted Cossack walked over to them, took hold of the old man's hair and tucked his head under his arm. The elderly Jew straddled his legs. The Cossack pulled out a knife and carefully, so as not to splash blood on his own clothes, slit the old man's throat. Dropping the body in the road, the Cossack pounded his fist on the door of the dead man's house. "Anyone who cares may come and fetch him," he shouted at the shuttered windows, "You're free to do so."

Meanwhile, in the same village, a Bolshevik political officer had herded together a number of townspeople, mostly Jewish, who had that day been plundered and terrorized by the Cossack cavalry. "You are in power here," the Red commissar assured them. "Everything is yours. . . . I now proceed to the election of the Revolutionary Committee."[10]

Various attempts were made to create lines of defense against the infiltrating Red cavalry but none was successful. Only two days after their breakthrough, Budënny's men raided the important cities of Berdichev and Zhitomir. They blew up the Polish military warehouses, opened the prisons, burned down a Polish military hospital that housed six hundred wounded and freed five thousand Red Army prisoners of war. Now the Soviet Fourteenth Army and the recently mauled Twelfth Army launched their own offensives. With its front under infantry assault and its rear a shambles from cavalry depredations, the Polish Army began a rapid retreat from the Ukraine. A Polish veteran later reminisced: "We ran all the way to Kiev, and we ran all the way back."[11]

The First Legion Division and other troops under Rydz-Śmigły held out in Kiev until June 10, when they were practically cut off. At noon on that day, there was a single bugle call, the Polish flag was hauled down from above the Kiev Citadel, and the division marched out. It was to be a very long march to safety and was made possible only by the good discipline of the Legionnaires, who forced open the roads as they went.

This was the picture by the end of June. Within only three weeks the Polish armies in the south had been infiltrated, outmaneuvered, and forced into full retreat. Several of the Polish divisions were thoroughly demoralized. All were utterly exhausted. Pressed by the Red Fourteenth Army and the remnant of the Red Twelfth Army in their front and harried by Budënny's cavalry in their rear, the Poles were compelled to retire westward as fast as they could march until somehow, somewhere, a line might be found where they could make a firm stand against the Red infantry while simultaneously concentrating enough of their own cavalry to deal with Budënny. But such a position had yet to be found, and fear grew that the oncoming Reds would capture Lwów and then turn north toward Warsaw.

The sudden catastrophe that had befallen the Poles on the southern front touched off a political panic in Warsaw. The fervent eulogies to Piłsudski that had been delivered only a few weeks before were forgotten. The members of the Sejm howled with rage, disappointment and fear. They recalled that they had wanted peace, but Piłsudski had insisted upon war. He had concluded an alliance with Petlyura, whose "government" had proved so lackluster that it attracted the support of scarcely a single Ukrainian. The Marshal's military "genius" (which the National Democrats now claimed always to have doubted) was seen to be rank amateurism. He had, it was charged, led the Polish army into disaster.

The government of Prime Minister Leopold Skulski, who was a cat's-paw for Piłsudski, was incapable of resisting the outcry. On June 9 the Skulski government resigned, and for more than two weeks no replacement could be found for it. Finally, on June 24, a coalition government was formed headed by Władysław Grabski, a prominent economist but not a member of any political party. There was no pretense that Grabski and his cabinet were anything more than a stopgap administration. Neither Grabski nor the National Democratic Party that had supported his nomination as prime minister wanted to assume responsibility for the war at such a late date and in such a critical situation. Grabski proposed that the defense of the nation at this critical hour should not be directed by the government but by a specially created executive body that would draw its members from the Sejm and the military. Grabski was prepared to subordinate himself to such a group, and Piłsudski agreed that in these extraordinary circumstances an extraordinary group to be named the State Defense Council should be organized. On July 1 the Sejm gave its approval, and the new body came into existence. It consisted of the speaker of the Sejm and ten representatives drawn from the leading parties in the Sejm (Piłsudski's old adversary Roman Dmowski among them), three cabinet ministers, and three delegates from the General Staff. Piłsudski was the chairman of the Council. It was agreed that this group would have complete discretion in waging war and making peace. The Sejm in effect signed over its powers to this Council and ceased to meet during the period of its existence. It was fortunate that the State Defense Council was created when it was, because only four days later Tukhachevsky's army crashed through the Polish northern defense system like an avalanche.

The topography of western Russia, Lithuania and Poland in the regions north of the Pripet Marshes is notably flat. The only military obstacles are the rivers that meander across the countryside. An army fighting its way from Smolensk to Warsaw, for example, must cross in succession the Berezina, the Niemen, the Narew, the Bug and finally the Vistula (on which, of course, Warsaw itself is located and which flows north to Danzig).

In early July 1920 Tukhachevsky's Army of the West was concentrated in the region of Vitebsk—an area that Tukhachevsky rather theatrically called the "Gates of Smolensk."

Facing these Red Army forces were the Polish First, Fourth and Seventh armies. These armies, that is to say the entire Polish front north of the Pripet Marshes, were under the command of General Stanisław Szeptycki. He had extended his First and Fourth armies along the length of his front, which was the Berezina River, leaving the Seventh Army (which consisted of only one weak division and was still in the process of formation) in reserve.

The size of the respective forces involved in this theater of war has been the subject of endless debate. The best estimates indicate that the Soviets had 160,000 fighting troops compared to 120,000 Polish front-line infantry and cavalry. This numerical superiority was most evident at the point where Tukhachevsky attacked in the region just south of the Dvina River along the Smolensk–Brest-Litovsk railway. In this relatively narrow area Tukhachevsky concentrated his Fourth, Fifteenth and Third armies, which were faced only by part of the Polish forces that extended along the entire front.

It is frequently remarked that, in attitude, Tukhachevsky resembled Genghis Khan or, perhaps, Attila. To be sure, his order of the day for his troops just prior to beginning his offensive does have a wild, antique ring—"The fate of world revolution is being decided in the west: the way leads over the corpse of Poland to a universal conflagration. . . . On to Wilno, Minsk and Warsaw—forward!"[12] With this exhortation, on July 4, 1920, the Soviet Army of the West attacked.

For two days the Polish First and Fourth armies put up a sturdy defense. The Soviet divisional commanders did not in this fighting make good use of their superiority in manpower. They were probing too delicately at the Polish lines. Tukhachevsky thereupon intervened and suddenly a wide hole was punched in the Polish lines. By July 7 the Polish Army was in full retreat—and it was not a very well-organized retreat. Various Polish divisions retired the wrong way or, sometimes, never even received orders to fall back and found themselves defending an isolated stretch of river line with Red Army patrols in their rear.

Tukhachevsky seems also to have suffered from some initial confusion. As early as the first day of his offensive he thought that he had pulled off a victory as sweeping as that of the Prussians at Sedan and needed only to chase down a beaten and pulverized enemy. Surprisingly, however, Tukhachevsky's misconception was exactly what was needed at that hour. As Piłsudski observed, "Tukhachevsky understood the art of communicating to his subordinates his own energy and well-directed activity."[13] The Soviet army, galvanized by the retreat of the Polish forces, suddenly abandoned its tentative manner and began to act as if they actually were pursuing a scattered and beaten foe. They ceased to worry about their flanks or their rear and concentrated all their energies on remorselessly harrying, chivvying, and unbalancing the Polish divisions as they retreated westward. And the Poles, who had not been badly beaten at all in a military sense, responded by behaving as if they had been utterly defeated.

Tukhachevsky had failed in his original tactical conception, which was to smash the Polish Army on the Berezina River front, but everything else was succeeding for him. Without a great deal of heavy fighting—certainly without major pitched battles—the Polish divisions were chased inexorably westward. At each successive river line the Polish Army attempted to dig in and construct a line of defenses. Each time they were either outflanked or a key bridgehead city was captured, and they were abruptly uprooted. Even when, on July 11, the retreat had reached the old German trench system before Wilno, the Poles failed to hold. This trench system was all that even the most cautious and conservative general could wish for. It ran for more than two hundred miles from Daugavpils in the north to Luck in the south. It had been constructed during the World War as the principal German line of defense against the Russians; it could have been made practically impregnable. And yet Tukhachevsky's Fourth Army at once flowed around it, captured Wilno (in the rear of the trench system) on July 14, and the Polish Army resumed its retreat.

The Red Army was now advancing just about as fast as its tide of commandeered peasant carts could carry it. On July 19 the Soviet cavalry galloped into the city of Grodno and, after several days of heavy fighting, captured it. The defensive line offered by the Niemen River was lost to the Poles. On August 1 the city of Brest-Litovsk fell, and with it went the barrier of the Bug River.

The boldness of Tukhachevsky's drive westward was the key to his success. The Soviet High Command dispatched 60,000 men as reinforcements, but Tukhachevsky never stopped to let them catch up with him. His onrushing armies were leaving behind greater numbers of stragglers every day, but Tukhachevsky ignored these losses. His supply services were in chaos and his rear scarcely existed as an organized entity, but Tukhachevsky was unconcerned; his men would live off the land. On the day his troops captured Minsk, a new cry arose—"Give us Warsaw!" Tukhachevsky was determined to give them what they wanted. All things considered, Tukhachevsky's performance was a virtuoso display of energy, determination and, indeed, rashness.

General Szeptycki, unfortunately for him, had tidier instincts than his adversary. Szeptycki seemed unable to see that he must stop and fight. Instead, he continued to seek the security of a *line*—a river front, a fortress, or a trench system—where there would be orderly attacks and counterattacks, where there would be no Red cavalry roaming about in his rear and his flanks would not be in the air. But Tukhachevsky moved much too fast to allow Szeptycki to establish a front. The Soviet cavalry and Fourth Army poured around the northern flank of the retreating Poles and thereafter the whole Polish front was constantly outflanked and in serious danger of being enveloped.

By late July the Polish northern front was beginning to break up. The troops had marched so far that they were completely exhausted. The confusion produced by the retreat, combined with the petty jealousies and lack of discipline of the senior Polish officers, had caused various units to split up. There were groups of fewer than 300 troops, commanded in person by a general officer, wandering about the battlefield. No one on the Polish General Staff knew where many of these independent groups were, and some of their commanders would not respond to orders when they were finally located.

"This uninterrupted mass movement," Piłsudski said of the Russian advance, "broken from time to time by a series of forward leaps . . . lasting for weeks, gives an impression of something irresistible, advancing like a monstrous storm cloud which nothing can hinder. There is something in it that engenders despair and breaks the internal resistance of the individual and of the mass."[14] By late July the morale of the Polish Army had been seriously eroded, as had that of their commander of the northern front, the hapless General Szeptycki. But Szeptycki had never had much confidence. He was a sick man; he had had an attack of influenza earlier in the year and had not fully recovered. In late June, even before Tukhachevsky's offensive had started, Szeptycki had traveled to Warsaw, gone to the Belvedere Palace and told Piłsudski that the war was as good as lost and peace should be concluded.[15]

Szeptycki had not been alone in this opinion. There were many people in Warsaw in July 1920 who wanted to make peace with Russia on almost any terms. It was well known that the supply situation was desperate. In preparation for the war, the Polish government had purchased large quantities of munitions abroad. But now it was found that they could not be brought into the country. Every avenue of transportation into Poland had suddenly been blocked off. Germany, almost gleeful at the prospect of Poland's destruction, would not permit weapons for Poland to cross its borders. The Chief of Staff of the German army observed, "I refuse to support Poland, even in the face of the danger that she may be swallowed up. In fact, I count on that."[16] The dockworkers at Danzig, whether because of their Communist sympathies or because they were Germans, refused to unload military cargoes for Poland. The Czechs, who were embroiled in a bitter dispute with Poland about the Duchy of Teschen, would not allow Polish shipments to travel through their territory. British dockworkers, who were in the midst of a "Hands off Russia" campaign protesting foreign intervention against the Bolsheviks, refused to load supplies for Poland.

Given these circumstances the Polish State Defense Council was dominated by thoroughly frightened men. Piłsudski attempted to interject a note of confidence and spoke of "ringing the great bell of war,"[17] and he counseled them to be of good heart and firm conviction. But this was asking more of the Council's members than they could do. The Russians were advancing everywhere. The Polish Army was crumbling. Over Piłsudski's objections, the Defense Council decided to appeal to Britain and France for help.

By what seemed to be a fortunate coincidence, Britain and France together with the rest of the victorious Allies were already meeting at Spa, in Belgium, to discuss German war reparations. British Prime Minister Lloyd George and French Premier Alexandre Millerand headed their nations' delegations. There was a Polish delegation present led by Stanisław Patek, the foreign minister in the previous Skulski government.

On July 6 Patek was instructed by his government to request an immediate interview with Lloyd George to acquaint him with the Polish situation. It was to be an exploratory session. It was anticipated that a meeting of this type with Lloyd George would be an unpleasant occasion—which proved correct. Lloyd George opened by reminding Patek that when they had met, in the previous January in London, he had warned that Poland would have to make war entirely on its own and would have to bear all the consequences. Now, with the record set straight, he asked what Poland wanted.

Patek said that Poland was ready "to discuss peace terms with the Bolsheviks," but "the moment was inopportune as the Polish Army was retreating." Lloyd George replied coldly that "there was nothing the Allies could do for Poland."

In this manner and in this tone the conversation wallowed for a brief time and finally concluded with Patek's appealing for "the sympathy and friendship of Great Britain." Lloyd George observed that to obtain this Poland must "accept true nationalism and not imperialism as the basis of its policy," and on this note Patek was dismissed.[18]

On July 6, the same day that Patek met with Lloyd George at Spa, the Polish Minister for Foreign Affairs, Prince Eustachy Sapieha, drafted a message to the Allies which was approved and dispatched by the Polish State Defense Council. This message was a formal appeal for Allied intercession with the Soviet government to obtain peace, which "would be immediately accepted by the Polish Government and nation." Should this fail, the Poles asked for "the moral and material aid of the Allies." The note made no stipulations about Poland's border with Soviet Russia except for the proviso that "populations inhabiting territories situated between Poland and Russia must be permitted to determine their own fate."[19] That night Prime Minister Grabski boarded a train for Spa to present his nation's case to the Allies. At three o'clock in the afternoon of July 9 Grabski was received in a villa at Spa by Lloyd George, Lord Curzon (the British foreign minister), Millerand, Marshal Foch, and Foch's chief of staff General Maxime Weygand.

Grabski had anticipated that the Allies would be difficult to deal with. They were very busy with the matter of reparations, and the unlooked-for intrusion of this Polish business would be an annoying burden. It must have seemed to Grabski that this was no time for halfway measures. Poland had come to Canossa to do penance. Grabski was prepared to humble himself before the Allies in whatever manner might be required of him. With his first words, Grabski announced that "Poland was in a very dangerous condition. . . . [She] understood that it was her own fault that she was in this condition and that she had to change her policy both toward her neighbors and the Allies. She recognized that she had to leave the decision of her vital interests, even in the matter of her own frontiers, to the Allied Powers."[20]

Grabski then sketched the present military situation. On the southern front, the Polish Army was being driven back into Eastern Galicia. On the northern front the Polish Army still stood considerably outside Poland, but it was greatly outnumbered by the Red Army and was in mortal danger. Poland now wanted peace. Grabski conceded that "Poland had certainly missed good opportunities [for peace] in the past."[21] But he asked that the Allies undertake to support Poland in the event that the Russians continued their advance and refused to make peace.

Lloyd George then took the floor. Certainly, he said, "there was no use in recrimination." And thereupon he proceeded to recriminate at considerable length on the theme of Polish greed—"She had quarrelled with Lithuania, and seized Lithuanian territory. She had marched into Russia and occupied territories containing between 20,000,000 and 30,000,000 Russians. She had insisted on incorporating 3,500,000 Ruthenians [i.e., Ukrainians who lived in East Galicia] against their vehement protest. She had failed to agree with the Czechs. She had made difficulties over Danzig."[22] And now Poland wanted the help of the Allies, but Lloyd George "was not sure that the Allies could do very much."[23]

The French, from whom the Poles had hoped for some support, heard all this in silence, contributing nothing to the Polish case. Grabski, desperate, promised that Poland would do anything the Allies required. There was no abasement or admission he would not make—"M. Piłsudski the head of the state, now acknowledged his mistake,"[24] and "Poland now only wanted agreement and not domination."[25] Finally the session came to an end, and Grabski was advised that the Allies would receive him again the following afternoon and would then tell him their decision.

When Grabski appeared the next day, he was informed that the Allies had reached agreement among themselves on a course of action. The British, on behalf of all the Allies, would propose to the Soviet government that the Polish Army retire behind a line that the Allied Commission on Polish Affairs had laid down on December 8, 1919.* The Red Army would be permitted to approach no closer than 50 kilometers of this line. There would then be an armistice. Delegations from Poland, Soviet Russia, Finland, Latvia, Lithuania and East Galicia would be summoned to London for a peace conference. If the Soviet government refused this offer and crossed the proposed armistice line, then the Allies promised to "give Poland all the assistance, especially in war matériel, which is possible . . . to enable the Polish people to defend their independence and national existence."[26]

As the price for the services of the Allies in procuring an armistice, the Poles must agree to accept the decision of the Allied Supreme Council on all presently outstanding frontier issues such as Lithuanian boundaries, Teschen, East Galicia and Danzig. Grabski protested. It seemed that the Poles were being required to give up too much. Why should the Bolsheviks be given all this territory? Why not just make them stop where they were? And exactly what military assistance could Poland expect from the Allies in the event of Russia's rejection of the armistice plan?

---

* This line had been drawn up by the Commission as a minimum frontier which the Poles could count upon for the purpose of internal organization. It was conservatively drawn to include only those areas whose population was overwhelmingly Polish. This line generally corresponds to the present (i.e., post–World War II) eastern frontier of Poland. But at the time of its issuance the Polish government had not accepted it as its eastern frontier because it already occupied territory considerably east of the Commission line, and this territory contained a great many Poles. Indeed, in December 1919 the Allies themselves had regarded the line as preliminary and negotiable and anticipated awarding additional eastern territory to Poland.

Lloyd George replied quite sharply. The Poles had to understand that they were in very parlous circumstances. The Allies were not completely confident that the Soviet government would accept the December 8 line proposed for the armistice. This was no time for the Poles to haggle. "The difficulty," Lloyd George said, "was that the Polish government refused to recognize facts and, until they did, there was no basis for discussion."[27] Regarding Allied military assistance, Lloyd George was vague. It might take the form of war matériel or officers or perhaps airplanes. He was not prepared to say exactly what it might be—but certainly no Allied troops would be sent.

In the end Grabski capitulated. Every possible concession and admission having been wrung from him, he agreed to the Allied demands and departed for Poland. The next day, July 11, the British dispatched the Allied proposition to the Soviet government. Because the message was signed by the Foreign Secretary Lord Curzon, the proposed armistice line immediately and for all time became known as the "Curzon Line," even though Curzon himself had had nothing to do with its creation. It was now up to the Soviets to make the next move.

On his return to Warsaw, Grabski was roundly abused by the State Defense Council. The military members of the Council attacked him for defeatism. The politicians assailed him for sacrificing Polish negotiating positions in the matters of Teschen, Lithuania, *et al.* Piłsudski made no secret of the fact that he hoped the Russians would refuse the British armistice proposal and thus release Poland from its agreement with the Allies. Everyone castigated Grabski for having abased Poland before the Allies and getting, in the end, only some very vague promises of support in return. It was apparent that the days of the Grabski government were numbered.

Grabski was furious at all this. It was easy for these armchair diplomats to criticize him, but if they had gone to Lloyd George, they would have seen that the Poles had nothing to bargain with— nothing to offer and no counterthreats to impose. And that, in the end, was exactly the way the Soviets saw it too.

On July 12, the Soviet government received Lord Curzon's note proposing an armistice. The Soviet Politburo did not, at first, know exactly what to do about it. Curzon's note was passed around among the Soviet leaders for general comment. They knew they had to reach a decision quickly because Tukhachevsky was roaring westward and, if not halted by orders from Moscow, would soon burst across Curzon's proposed armistice line.

Opinions varied among the Russian leaders as to what should be done. The Red Army High Command reported that the war was nearly won. They anticipated the capture of Warsaw and the surrender of the Polish Army within two months—perhaps sooner. Trotsky, on the other hand, was not so sure that the war was as good as won; doubts nagged in his mind. During nearly three years of civil war in Russia, he had seen a number of swift Red Army advances that were followed by equally swift retreats. And, too, Trotsky worried about taking Warsaw. It was one thing to seize a small city like Minsk. It was quite a different thing to storm a major European capital like Warsaw. Other prominent Bolsheviks were also disturbed. They were deeply concerned that there was no evidence of an imminent revolution among the Polish proletariat. These doubters, who included prominent Poles serving in the Soviet government, such as Radek and Marchlewski, found the Curzon offer attractive. They counseled its acceptance.

But Lenin would hear none of this. The prospect of crushing Piłsudski, of creating a "Red" Warsaw and, above all, of linking up with the German proletariat (which he considered to be teetering on the edge of revolution) was intoxicating. He intended to "probe Europe with the bayonet of the Red Army."[28]

It took Lenin only five days to convince, coerce, or command his associates into agreement. He telegraphed Stalin his opinion of Curzon's proposal—"I personally think it is a complete swindle. . . . They want to snatch victory from our hands."[29] Stalin agreed. It was decided that the Red Army would cross the Curzon Line, capture Warsaw, oust the "White" Polish government, and bring the revolution to Poland. Then, depending upon circumstances, the Red Army would either withdraw from a "Sovietized" Poland or else pass beyond it to assist the German proletariat. Instructions were issued to the Red Army to speed up its already swift advance so that invasion of Poland would become a *fait accompli* before France and Britain had a chance to intervene. The Soviet High Command ordered its armies in the field to disregard the Curzon Line and to capture Warsaw no later than August 12—which, at this juncture, seemed well within the scope of the possible.

All this having been decided, the next step was to answer Curzon's note of July 11. The Soviet reply, dispatched on July 17, was evasive, calculatedly confusing, and propagandistic. The Soviet government declared that it would be happy to make peace with Poland, but in doing so it would consider only "the interest and aspiration of the Polish proletariat." Accordingly, they felt obliged to "categorically reject" the idea of a conference in London at which the Allies would "take on themselves the part of supreme arbiters of the fate of other peoples."

The Soviets stated that they would make peace with Poland only by direct, private negotiations; and "if the Polish government makes such a proposal . . . [the Soviet government] will not reject such a proposal." In fact, the Soviets promised, they would give the Poles a frontier line more advantageous (i.e., farther eastward) than the Curzon Line, which, Chicherin claimed, had been drawn up by the Allies "under the influence of counterrevolutionary Russian elements."[30]

Apart from the very crucial fact that the Soviet note made no promise that the invading Red Army would stop at the Curzon Line, there was not much that the Allies could take exception to. That, of course, was the Soviet intention. The note, which was transmitted to London in the form of an *en clair* radio message, was received on the evening of Sunday, July 18, and its contents were telephoned to Lloyd George, who was spending the weekend in the country. He put down the receiver and told a friend that all the Poles had to do was to ask for an armistice and they would get it—surely an over-simplification of the Soviet message. "I don't call that unreasonable, do you?" Lloyd George inquired.[31]

The British immediately exerted pressure on the Poles to respond to the Soviet note and request an armistice. Sir Horace Rumbold, British Minister to Poland, was instructed to appear before the State Defense Council sitting in Belvedere Palace and virtually demand that they send a dispatch to the Soviet government at once. The British felt they had done their part; now it was up to the Poles. Developments in the field lent emphasis to Rumbold's urgings. On July 19, Tukhachevsky's cavalry galloped into the city of Grodno, only 150 miles from Warsaw. With this went the line of resistance that had been expected to develop on the Niemen River. The forcing of the Niemen also meant that the Soviets had crossed the Curzon Line. In these circumstances, the Polish State Defense

Council (Piłsudski, of course, excepted) could not resist the pressure to appeal for an armistice. But first there had to be a new government to replace that of the discredited Grabski.

In the course of several days the British Minister spent hours fidgeting in an anteroom, while the State Defense Council haggled over who would serve in the cabinet. On July 24 it was decided: the new government would be headed by the forty-six-year-old leader of the Piast Peasant Party, Wincenty Witos, and there would be a coalition cabinet. The vice-premier was to be the Left-wing socialist Ignacy Daszyński and the minister for foreign affairs was to be, again, Prince Sapieha.

With the political preliminaries out of the way, the Polish government dispatched radio messages to the Soviets. It announced its desire for peace, requested an armistice, and asked where and when Polish emissaries would be received for the negotiation of an armistice. In response, the Poles received three different replies from three different agencies of the Soviet government, and the resulting confusion took a few days to get straightened out—which undoubtedly was the way the Russians had planned it. Finally it was settled that on July 30 Polish representatives would be permitted through the Soviet lines and that an armistice conference would be held in the city of Baranovichi. On July 29 the Polish armistice delegation left Warsaw.

While these armistice developments were taking place, the French and British governments were trying to decide exactly how they were obligated to support Poland in the event of a Soviet refusal of an armistice. It was a very difficult situation to resolve. The French agreed to put pressure on the Czechs to allow military supplies to cross their territory into Poland. The British agreed to perform the same function at Danzig, even if the supplies had to be unloaded by their own troops stationed in the city. Clearly they had to be prepared to do more than this to help the Poles. But what? In a quandary, the French and British cabinets took refuge in the time-honored procrastinatory technique for governments that cannot make up their minds: they dispatched a mission of distinguished diplomats to the scene with orders to investigate and send back advice.

Actually, the British government's instructions to the head of its mission were somewhat more encompassing than simply surveying the situation and advising. He was charged also with explaining to the Poles what was required of them and, if possible, engineering the replacement of Piłsudski with a Polish leader more acceptable to the Allies. Very little was to be mentioned to the Poles regarding Allied assistance. It became quite apparent that British policy—and to only a slightly lesser degree, French policy—was to force the Poles to accept an armistice.

At the head of the British group was Viscount Edgar Vincent D'Abernon. At the time, D'Abernon was sixty-three years old and had only recently been appointed ambassador to Germany. Assisting him was a general from the War Office, Sir Percy Radcliffe, and the secretary to the cabinet, Sir Maurice Hankey. The French mission was nominally headed by Jules Jusserand, the ambassador to the United States, who had happened to be in Paris at the time. The dominant figure, however, was General Maxime Weygand, a slender, dapper man, who had served as chief of staff to Marshal Foch throughout the World War, and in the course of this had picked up some of the charisma of Foch himself. Certainly he impressed D'Abernon and Jusserand, who regarded Weygand with undisguised admiration and thought him a military genius.

The Allied mission met in Paris on July 21 and conferred with Paderewski, then living in France. Paderewski's gloom was frightening. He suggested that Dmowski should become prime minister, and he provided a list of officers who could replace Piłsudski as commander in chief. Paderewski urged the Allied mission to keep airplanes ready in Warsaw in order that they might escape from the city when it fell to the Red Army, an eventuality that Paderewski deemed "almost certain."[32] The members of the mission were not convinced that Paderewski's pessimism was justified, but for safety's sake they decided to live on board their train (with an engine always attached) after they arrived in Warsaw on July 25.

It is clear that the Allied representatives did not understand the Poles. On the day they arrived, the mission was taken to Piłsudski (of whom they subsequently saw very little), who told them that the principal service they could render was to open up the port of Danzig to the passage of supplies. This relatively modest task did not seem enough to the members of the Allied mission. They had apparently expected to be consulted, and deferred to, in all matters of Polish policy. The members of the mission, especially Lord D'Abernon, began to urge the Polish leaders to "take advantage of General Weygand's . . . unrivaled experience and capacity for military organization."[33] There was, obviously, some idea that Weygand would and could take complete charge of the Polish Army, instantly reorganize it, and immediately repel the Soviet advance. The response of the Polish government was that while it did not wish to seem unappreciative, it was certain that Piłsudski would tolerate no such interference.

As the days went by and as the Red Army drew relentlessly closer to the capital, the members of the Allied mission became alarmed. To them, the most frightening aspect of the whole affair was the absence of any apparent fright on the part of the Poles. The Allied delegates expected the roads leading from the front to be choked with refugees. There were practically none. They expected to see some signs of panic among the Warsaw population. There was none. They expected to attend nonstop meetings with anxious government leaders. Instead, they found that on July 27 Prime Minister Witos took the day off to travel to his country property to help get in his harvest. Such government meetings as were held proceeded on a much less formal and organized basis than the French and British were accustomed to. The Prime Minister never wore a tie, and Sir Maurice Hankey reported to Lloyd George that Witos was a "stage peasant."[34] It was not unusual for an important government meeting to begin an hour or two late and to be interrupted constantly by subordinates bearing trivial messages. It appeared to the Allies that the Polish government did not have much poise or administrative experience when dealing with matters of great moment.

So the members of the Allied mission found themselves reduced to wandering about attempting to impress the Poles with the necessity of making use of the talents of General Weygand. And, of course, they never ceased to counsel or pressure the Polish government on the advisability of concluding an armistice with the Soviets. At least they did so until, finally, they received information regarding the terms which the Soviet government demanded in exchange for an armistice.

On July 30, the Polish armistice delegation had appeared at the front and had been escorted through the Russian lines to Baranovichi. There they presented their credentials and, after a day or two, were told by the Soviets that their credentials were not in order. The Poles had authority only to discuss an armistice, not a peace treaty. The Russians announced that they would not do business with such a mission. The Polish delegation thereupon returned to Warsaw.

The Soviet government was obviously stalling. Its armies had now crossed the Curzon Line at almost every point, and the capture of Warsaw was expected within two weeks. The Soviets procrastinated in setting a new date for peace talks. Eventually it was announced a Polish delegation would be received at Minsk on August 14.

In the meantime, Moscow attempted to further confuse the issue. The Bolsheviks believed, certainly with good reason, that the British government greatly desired an armistice between Poland and Soviet Russia and would urge the Poles to accept practically any armistice conditions. The British, it was assumed, could get the Poles to sign anything. And so, on August 10, a Soviet representative in London presented Lloyd George with a note that gave a preview of the Soviet terms for an armistice with Poland. If accepted, these terms would amount to a Polish surrender. The Soviets demanded that the Polish Army immediately be demobilized and subsequently be restricted to only 50,000 men. All weaponry above that required for this small army must be turned over to the Red Army; all Polish war industries must be dismantled; and importation of war matériel would be prohibited. Certain important Polish railroads would be placed under Soviet control. When all this had been accomplished, the Red Army would withdraw to the Curzon Line, and the Soviet terms for a final peace treaty would be presented.

Lloyd George did not find these requirements to be objectionable. He had Lord Curzon telegraph Sir Horace Rumbold in Warsaw that Britain would not endeavor to force the Soviets to grant better terms. However, the British officials in Poland vehemently disagreed with the policy set in London. Rumbold thought that the Allies had "been flouted by the Bolsheviks [and] eaten more dirt than is good for anybody and ought to declare war."[35] D'Abernon regarded the Soviet armistice proposals as "incredible."[36] He wrote in his diary that "these terms were so extravagant that I cannot conceive any Polish government taking them into consideration. I should have expected London to have refused them without further parley."[37]

The French government shared the sentiments of the British representatives in Warsaw. They refused to advise the Poles to accept such terms, no matter how desperate the military situation. All of this support was welcome in Warsaw, but it really made no difference in the attitude of the Polish government. As long as Piłsudski was chief of state, there was not the slightest chance that Poland would accept the Russian terms—although it was decided that a Polish delegation would be sent to Minsk on August 14 to see if the Soviet terms would be moderated in the course of negotiation. But in the meantime, the Poles now knew that they must defeat the Red Army or Poland would simply disappear. Were the Soviet terms accepted, the Soviets would quickly engineer a revolution and take over a virtually defenseless Poland.

As a matter of fact, the Soviet government had already appointed the Provisional Polish Revolutionary Committee, which, given the Soviet fondness for contractions, was called the Polrevkom. The announced purpose of the Polrevkom was the takeover of the political administration of all captured Polish territory. But, obviously, the Polrevkom was waiting in the wings to become the government of the future Soviet Poland that the armistice would bring.

The Polrevkom had formed on July 23 in Moscow. Its members were Poles who already occupied senior posts in the Soviet Russian administration. The nominal head of the commission was Julian Marchlewski, who had been the principal Soviet representative in the prewar negotiations with Poland. But the actual leader of the Polrevkom was Feliks Dzerzhinski, who was also the head of the Soviet political police—the Cheka. Dzerzhinski had pioneered the use of torture and terror against the enemies of Bolshevism and quickly became the most feared man in Soviet Russia. He was well acquainted with many of the members of the Polish government, who had known him from their preindependence socialist days. There was no doubt in any Pole's mind as to why this terrifying figure had been made the *de facto* head of the intended government of Soviet Poland.

For the time being, the Polrevkom waited aboard a special train in Białystok. The train had its own printing presses, office facilities, security services, and a direct telephone line to Lenin in Moscow. Expecting a Polish collapse, the Polrevkom staff made administrative preparations for the conversion of Poland into a Bolshevik state. Recruiting was even commenced for a Polish Red Army.

By early August the military situation was, for Poland, truly desperate. In the north the Polish Army had been retreating for six weeks at an average and exhausting rate of ten miles a day. There were no more river lines on which a defense of the capital could be constructed—only the Vistula, on which Warsaw itself lay. The left wing of the Polish Army had been outflanked and was in process of being enveloped. A Polish line of defense had been established on a semicircle facing north and eastward about a dozen miles from Warsaw and the Polish First Army had been brought into it; but it was by no means sure that this line could be held. Tukhachevsky had dispatched the Fourth Army to march deep into northern Poland, skirting the East Prussian border with the aim of capturing Płock and Toruń. The fall of either of these cities would mean that the Vistula would be blocked above Warsaw, and both rail and water communications with Danzig would then be cut off. Since the main Polish forces had been forced southward, there would be virtually no opposition to this Red Army thrust led by the 3rd Cavalry Corps. The early capture of Toruń—and with it most of northern Poland— seemed certain.

In the south, the advance of Yegorov's Army of the Southwest had been slowed down but not stopped. Although this army's direction of advance was presently toward Lwów, it seemed certain that it would shortly veer to its right and advance upon Warsaw from the south, rolling up the Polish Army's right flank.

In the course of the series of military disasters that Poland had suffered, the nerve of the State Defense Council had been seriously shaken. On July 19 several members of the Council had strongly criticized Piłsudski's leadership. Roman Dmowski proposed a change in the Army's command, replacing Piłsudski with the Rightist General Josef Dowbor-Musnicki. There was much additional criticism. In the course of the meeting Piłsudski was called from the room briefly to receive a delegation from Poznań led by a priest, Father Stanislas Adamski, who was Sejm deputy. Adamski launched into a prepared address that stated that the people of Poznań did not comprehend how Poland could have come to such a desperate condition in the war. They suspected treason, Adamski announced, and they believed that the treasonous activities originated "right here" in the Belvedere Palace. With this, Adamski pointed his finger at Piłsudski.

Without replying, the Marshal spun around and left the room. Returning to the meeting of the State Defense Coucil, Piłsudski demanded a vote of confidence. The balloting was secret. Only one vote was negative. It was obviously that of Roman Dmowski, the National Democratic Party leader, who thereafter ceased to attend Council meetings and was regarded as having resigned. But even Piłsudski experienced qualms. On August 10, temporarily "exhausted by the absence of moral strength among us . . ." and desiring "to be partly relieved of the responsibility,"[38] as Piłsudski afterward explained it, he offered General Weygand the position of chief of staff of the Polish Army. It was never made clear exactly what this proposal involved. Piłsudski described it as "a share in command."[39] Presumably it was the post for which Weygand had been sent to Warsaw. But Weygand consulted Paris and then turned the offer down with the excuse that he was insufficiently familiar with the Polish Army and its officers.

This probably was not the real reason for Weygand's refusal. The French Army had no desire to involve its senior officers in the last act of a lost war. And by August 12 it was clear to most observers in Warsaw that the last desperate week of the resurrected Poland had arrived.

At 2 A.M. on the night of August 13–14, to the sound of artillery fire at close range, a special train carrying almost the entire foreign diplomatic corps left Warsaw for the safety of Poznań. Of the Franco-British mission only Generals Weygand and Radcliffe remained in the city—and they had been provided with automobiles for flight when it became necessary.

A nine-man Polish delegation left the capital for Minsk, where they expected to start armistice or peace negotiation with the Soviets. It did not seem that they would arrive in time to do much good. Warsaw was under martial law, and a general attack by the Red Army was expected for 5 A.M. on August 14. Dzerzhinski and the Polrevkom were en route to Wyszków, a town only thirty miles from Warsaw, from which they planned to enter the capital on August 17, the date on which the city was expected to fall.

Piłsudski, too, had left the capital—but not in flight. On August 12, he went to Puławy, a city on the Vistula seventy miles south east of Warsaw. It was the place from which he intended to take personal command of the Polish forces in a counterattack that he himself had conceived in the Belvedere Palace on the night of August 5–6.

The Polish situation was grim, but Piłsudski had seen hope. During the last weeks many of the Polish Army's weaknesses had been remedied. Piłsudski had replaced General Stanisław Haller with the more dynamic General Tadeusz Rozwadowski as chief of staff. The command of the entire northern front had been taken from the demoralized and defeated Szeptycki and given to General Józef Haller. A new Polish Army, designated the Fifth Army, had been created and placed under the command of the brilliant thirty-nine-year-old General Wladyslaw Sikorski. A tall, slender, ramrod-straight man, Sikorski had just been promoted to general rank. He was extremely energetic and imaginative. His new army was placed on the Polish left flank and immediately began to fiercely contest the Red Army's envelopment.

In the south, the thirty-four-year-old General Rydz-Śmigły and his Third Army had at last succeeded in dealing with Budënny's Red Cavalry. Rydz-Śmigły had put well-supplied garrisons of a thousand men each into the important towns and rail junctions in the line of Budënny's advance. It was found that the Cossack cavalry was very good at surprise raids but not well suited for pitched infantry battle. When faced with a determined, heavily armed force which had fortified a town, Budënny's troopers could not do much more than harass the defenders and then withdraw. Meanwhile, Rydz-Śmigły had pulled together his cavalry, so that now, operating in mass formation, the Poles proved at least a match for the Soviet First Cavalry Army. The advance of the Red Army of the Southwest was now going slowly. The Polish effort had also been helped by a mathematically gifted Polish Army captain, Jan Kowalewski, who was attached to the cryptographic section of the Polish General Staff. He had broken the codes of the Red Army, and the Poles were now reading much of the Soviet coded radio traffic.

The Polish armies had suffered a series of demoralizing and exhausting setbacks, but they had not been smashed. The Red Army had taken fewer than 20,000 Polish prisoners—not a very great number, considering that the Polish Army had been in full retreat for six weeks. And, in one sense, the retreat had worked to the Polish advantage. As the Polish supply lines shortened, more Polish troops could be brought to the front. By the beginning of August the Polish Army for the first time actually outnumbered the Red Army in terms of fighting men (rifles and sabers) at the front. It has been estimated that about 191,000 Poles now faced 177,000 Soviet troops.[40] And the rapid advance of the Red Army had created great problems for the attackers. Tukhachevsky's supply line scarcely existed, and the rear of the Red Army had almost no organization. It was impossible to bring up reinforcements rapidly, a critical problem, because the Red Army badly needed fresh troops. And, too, the Soviets had expected that a Polish revolution would take place as soon as the Red Army entered Poland, but there was not any sign of a Polish Communist uprising. In fact, the invading Red Army soldiers found the Polish peasantry to be thoroughly hostile to them.

The failure of the Soviet invasion to provoke the slightest revolutionary support from the Polish masses was a crucial feature of the war. The moribund Polish Communist Party was incapable of assisting the advancing Red Army. There were no general strikes of the workers. The Polish Army found it unnecessary to waste men guarding its interior communication systems against sabotage. And of the 20,000 or so Polish prisoners taken by the Soviets only 123 joined the Communist Party.[41] The Polrevkom attempted to raise a Polish Volunteer Regiment but attracted only 175 men. It had become clear that a Soviet Poland would be established only by military conquest, and this finding was profoundly discouraging to the Red Army.

Problems of ideology and morale aside, the invaders had committed a serious strategic blunder. Once the two separate Red Army commands (Tukhachevsky's Army of the West and Yegorov's Army of the Southwest) had emerged beyond the Pripet Marshes which had separated them, they were to have swung together. Thus they would have caught the bulk of the Polish forces in a pincers in the region of Warsaw. Instead, Yegorov's army, the principal commissar for which was Joseph Stalin, declined to play a contributory role and, disregarding orders from the Soviet Supreme Headquarters, went careering off toward its own prize, the city of Lwów. The consequence was a gap between the two armies, and Tukhachevsky could fill it only with a scratch force known as the Mozyr Group. In failing to fill this gap with something more than a light screening force, the Red Army was obviously taking a chance. But reinforcing the Mozyr Group would have taken troops away from the assault on Warsaw. And considering that the Polish Army seemed either semi-shattered or else fully engaged, the Soviet High Command took the gamble.

To his great credit, Piłsudski saw the existence of this gap and, on the night of August 5–6, determined that this juncture of the two enemy armies was the point at which he must strike—and that he personally must direct the attack. This was not an easy decision to make. Piłsudski had no idea that the Mozyr Group was as weak as it actually was. And the idea of leaving Warsaw, in the immediate region of which were ten Polish divisions (almost half the Polish Army), gave Piłsudski great pause. He believed that the Polish Army and the Polish government would fight much more effectively wherever he was on the spot, and he feared that Warsaw might fall should he leave it to direct a battle in the south.

A second concern for Piłsudski was that in order to strike at the Mozyr Group a number of the best Polish divisions would have to be secretly concentrated opposite it. These divisions were at present heavily engaged on other parts of the front. They would have to break loose, retreat, and then march or be railroaded to the area of concentration. This operation, a difficult one for any army, would have to be accomplished with much greater speed, secrecy and efficiency than the Polish Army had heretofore demonstrated. And the temporary withdrawal of even a few of the best divisions from the line might well precipitate the collapse of the entire Polish front. Nonetheless, on August 6 orders went out for the Polish concentration.

The area chosen for this Polish concentration was along the south bank of the Wieprz River, which after its northwestward passage through Lublin province, flows almost due westward for about forty miles to join the Vistula about fifty miles southeast of Warsaw. At Dęblin, approximately fifty miles south and slightly east of the Polish capital, the Vistula is joined by the Wieprz River, which runs eastward for about forty miles before bending to the south. It was beneath the defensive barrier offered by this west-east leg of the Wieprz that the Polish attacking force was to be assembled. The troops involved were the 14th, 16th, and 21st Divisions, which made up the Polish Fourth Army. They were to be supplemented by two crack divisions, the 1st and 3rd Legionary Divisions, which were taken from the Polish Third Army. Once these divisions, each bolstered by an additional infantry brigade, were gathered behind the Wieprz, they would be facing north. Directly across the river in front of them would be the Red Army's Mozyr Group and behind that would be the rear of the biggest of the Soviet armies—the Sixteenth Army, which was then besieging Warsaw.

If all went well in the offensive, which was scheduled for August 17, the Polish divisions would cut behind the Soviet Sixteenth Army and catch it from the rear. Either the Sixteenth Army would be crushed or, to save itself, it would retreat to the north, stumbling over the rears of the adjacent Soviet Third, Fifteenth, and Fourth Armies. If all went *very* well, Tukhachevsky's entire Army of the West would be cut off and destroyed. This was, however, a very big *if*, particularly since the Polish attacking force consisted only of a few divisions. And as Piłsudski himself observed, they were expected to take the offensive "in the face of any enemy who up till now, had constantly broken the resistance of the great part of our army."[42]

Because the whole operation was so risky and was being conducted with such a small force, Piłsudski decided that he must direct the offensive in person. "It seemed only right," he said, "that I should assume responsibility for the carrying-out of the most absurd part of the plan, and, as a matter of principle, I decided that the troops for the counterattack should be commanded by me in person."[43]

On August 12 Piłsudski left Warsaw, and the next day, with only five staff officers, he established his headquarters at Puławy. That day he inspected his troops and spoke with as many of them as he could. There was not much that was encouraging. The familiar problems were still in evidence; the wrong rifle ammunition had been sent to certain units, and others were so poorly equipped that Piłsudski wrote that "never in the whole course of the campaign had I seen such ragamuffins as I saw now."[44] When he inspected the 21st Infantry Division, he found that more than half the men were barefoot. The 3rd Legionary Division, which was to form the right flank of the Polish attack, had not yet arrived. And the city of Kock, which was a bridgehead on the Wieprz, had been lost by the 21st Division to a weak Russian force of the Mozyr Group. Piłsudski had stressed the importance of holding this city, and its loss was ominous. The entire Mozyr Group was a frightening entity. Polish intelligence knew almost nothing about its composition except that it contained the Soviet 57th Infantry Division. But at this point they had no idea as to what other forces were present on the north side of the Wieprz.

Then, on August 14, came desperate appeals from Warsaw. The Soviet Sixteenth Army had commenced an all-out attack on the city, and the defensive perimeter was beginning to crumble. Piłsudski had planned to launch an attack on August 17, but the Warsaw commander pleaded with him to act sooner. Could it not be launched at once? Piłsudski made a compromise of sorts and moved his attack up one day, to August 16, by which time the supply chaos would have been sorted out a little, the 3rd Legionary Division would have arrived, and Polish intelligence might have found out more about the size and composition of the Mozyr Group.

In the end, they were able to find out about the Mozyr Group only by attacking it. On the morning of August 16, along a front of about forty miles, the Polish divisions crossed the Wieprz, skirmished with various small Red forces, and then broke completely into the clear as they headed north. By evening, each division had advanced nearly twenty miles. Piłsudski, who had spent the day in his car in the field, found this easy advance incredible—and very frightening. With the exception of various elements of the Soviet 57th Infantry Division, the attacking Poles could not find an enemy. Piłsudski later wrote that "the divisions advanced and encountered practically no enemy at all, save that they had one or two small skirmishes here and there with small groups which, as soon as contact was made, disappeared in flight. . . . And yet it was before this legendary monster [the Mozyr Group] that many of our divisions had been retiring for a whole month. It seemed like a dream. The conclusion at which I arrived was that somewhere or other an ambush was being laid for us."[45]

On the next day, August 17, the Poles resumed their offensive. By that night, they had covered an additional twenty miles and were now due east of Warsaw and squarely in the rear of the Soviet Sixteenth Army. Piłsudski still could not believe it—"I thought that I was dreaming or was in a world of fairyland. . . . No, pleasant as this fancy might be, it could not possibly be real."[46] It *had* to be a trap. The Red Army's rear simply could not be that empty.

Finally, later that night, in his field headquarters in Garwolin, Piłsudski's fears were allayed. As he was drinking a glass of tea before going to bed, he heard the sound of guns from the north. He was profoundly relieved—"So there was an enemy after all! . . . The enemy really existed, and the proof was the battle music from the north."[47]

And so it was. Piłsudski's 14th Infantry Division had brushed the rear of the Red Sixteenth Army and had, at the price of fewer than two hundred casualties, turned this Soviet force in a horde of panicky refugees.

It is difficult to think of another battle (assuming that this operation was really a "battle") that so profoundly changed a strategic situation as did the so-called Battle of Warsaw. On the morning of August 16 the Red Army was besieging Warsaw with every prospect of success. By the morning of August 18, only forty-eight hours later, it was in disorganized retreat to the northeast seeking desperately to outmarch the Poles and keep from being cut off. The Soviet Third and Fifteenth Armies were also forced into panicky retreat. The Soviet Fourth Army and 3rd Cavalry Corps, both of which had ad-

vanced deeply into northern Poland, found themselves in desperate
danger. All of these forces—which, with the exception of the Communist armies fighting Wrangel in the Crimea, represented the bulk
of the Red Army's fighting capability—abandoned their artillery and
their stores, and gave up hordes of prisoners. Tukhachevsky, at his
headquarters in Minsk, was in an absolute quandary. It was not until
August 18, two days after the onset of the Polish offensive, that he
learned that it had begun. The headquarters of the Mozyr Group
had never gotten off a message to him. The commander of the adjacent Sixteenth Army found himself forced to flee for his life from his
field headquarters and could only manage a sketchy report. There
was so little opportunity for coordination or assessment that Tukhachevsky could do little more than direct his surviving forces out of
Poland. In fact, within only a few weeks Tukhachevsky was compelled to abandon his own headquarters at Minsk just before the
city's capture by the Poles.

Piłsudski returned to Warsaw on August 18 to organize additional
assaults by the forces defending Warsaw. He found a curious state of
affairs. Practically no one in the Polish government, and not even
very many senior army officers, were convinced of the awesome totality of the Polish victory. They could not conceive that the night-
mare was over so abruptly. It is hard to blame them—the victory had
been achieved without any real fighting. Away to the north and east
of the capital there were reports of Red forces attacking Plock, which
seemed to indicate that the Soviets were about to gain control of the
Vistula and with it the vital water traffic to Danzig. Piłsudski had
great difficulty in getting his compatriots to understand that these
Soviet raids, mostly by the Red Fourth Army and Ghai's 3rd Cavalry
Corps, now posed no threat. In fact, the farther west they went, the
more certain they were to be cut off.

At this juncture, when bold initiative was needed, the Polish General Staff and the Polish government were cautious; they retained a
large number of troops protecting Warsaw when, in fact, there was
no enemy left to attack the capital. The Polish General Staff was dis-
oriented and confused by the almost overnight change in the military
situation. In retrospect, Piłsudski blamed himself for this. "I have
always come to the conclusion," he said, "that I did not take sufficient
advantage of the situation. I did not immediately take full control
of the situation and put an end to the general chaos."[48]

The Polish pursuit of the fleeing Red Army of the West was not as aggressive as it could have been; certainly it was not as vigorous as it would have been had Piłsudski taken personal charge of practically every detail, as he had done in the original attack across the Wieprz. But the Polish victory was enormous nonetheless. The Soviet forces in the northeast were cut off and captured or were forced over the German border into East Prussia, where they were disarmed and interned by the German Army. Those of Tukhachevsky's troops that got away did it only by abandoning their equipment and fleeing. By August 25, when the Polish attackers paused to reorganize, they had captured nearly 70,000 prisoners (with another 70,000 Russians interned by the Germans), 231 artillery pieces, 1,000 machine guns, and 10,000 carts or wagons.

The Red Army that had invaded Poland from the north was, for all operational purposes, destroyed. Tukhachevsky could make a new front on the Niemen River only with the reinforcements that he had been unable to bring forward earlier in the campaign. They were not sufficient. In mid-September Piłsudski resumed the Polish attack. Just enough troops were launched against the Red Army on the Niemen to pin it down. Then, from the north emerged two brigades of Polish cavalry leading two especially strong infantry divisions. These swept behind the Red Army's defenses and came close to cutting off Tukhachevsky's troops, who were forced into another precipitate retreat, losing an additional 50,000 prisoners.

Events in the south were equally fortunate for the Poles. Between August 30 and September 2 General Sikorski managed to inveigle Budënny's four divisions of cavalry into a twelve-mile-long, four-mile-wide valley surrounded by Polish infantry and cavalry. In a prolonged battle that included the last great European cavalry charge, the Red First Cavalry Army was broken. The remnant of this once awesome force burst through the Polish encirclement and escaped to the east as rapidly as it could. The remainder of the Army of the Southwest was forced to follow suit. The Polrevkom was quietly disbanded and its members returned to their former duties.

Few Allied leaders could comprehend how the Poles had put together this sudden series of victories that came close to annihilating the fighting potential of the Soviet army. The Allies could not believe that Piłsudski, the untrained soldier with his ridiculous title of marshal, could possibly have brought off these battles. It was assumed in Western capitals that Weygand must, of course, have done it. But Weygand himself never made that claim; in fact, he specifically denied it, stating that "the victory was completely Polish; the plan was Polish; the army was Polish."[49]

Undeniably Piłsudski had enjoyed a certain amount of luck in the Battle of Warsaw when, upon attacking the Red Army's Mozyr Group, he found that it was only the thinnest of screens and tore at his touch. But the Polish attack would probably have been successful even if the Mozyr Group had been more formidable. As a military commander, Piłsudski had displayed admirable imagination and audacity in launching his attack when and where he did, rather than simply waiting to slug it out with the massed forces of the Red Army besieging Warsaw. And in the major battles following the Battle of Warsaw, Piłsudski continued to exhibit exceptional military agility. Each of his victories was decisive and was obtained with a minimum of Polish losses.

The Red Army was forced to commit its premier forces and its best commanders to its war with Poland. During the summer of 1920 the Polish forces saw action against eight of the sixteen "armies" that comprised the Red Army. The Poles defeated them all.

Piłsudski was not a military genius but, certainly, he must be considered to have been an extremely competent commander who had proved completely capable of leading his nation's forces successfully in a war against a great power.

A Polish delegation, sent to the Soviet-held city of Minsk, had begun discussions with the Soviets on August 17, the very day that the Piłsudski's five attacking divisions were slicing their way through the Red Army's Mozyr Group. But this event was unknown to the isolated Poles. The Soviet representatives presented their peace demands, which were virtually identical to those that they had previously made and again amounted to a Polish disarmament and virtual surrender. For several days the Polish delegates squirmed under Soviet pressure. They tried to send radio reports to Warsaw and were told by their Soviet hosts that atmospheric conditions were too poor for transmission. Very little information from Warsaw reached the Polish delegation, but on August 21 they finally got word of the Battle of Warsaw, which the Soviets had, of course, been attempting to keep from them. The attitude of the Polish delegation underwent an abrupt alteration. They now made demands of their own—one of which was that the site of these armistice–peace treaty talks be moved to a neutral location. So, in mid-September, the talks were transferred to Riga, Latvia. The strength of the Polish position, based on the continuing successes of the Polish Army in the field, was partly offset by the fact that the head of the Polish mission, Deputy Minister for Foreign Affairs Jan Dabski, was a member of the Piast Peasant Party and had had little experience in diplomatic negotiation. The Soviet delegation, on the other hand, was headed by Adolf Joffe, who had had a great deal of diplomatic experience. But both delegations had one thing in common: They wanted peace. The Soviets were exhausted and, in addition, were fighting an intense war in the Crimea with Baron Wrangel's White Army. The Polish delegation was made up of tired men representing a debilitated nation which had a number of other border problems to worry about.*

After a relatively brief period of negotiation at Riga, the negotiators reached an agreement that resulted in an armistice commencing on October 18, 1920. The final Treaty of Riga was not signed until March 18, 1921, but in the meantime all the major issues had been settled. The most important of these matters was, of course, Poland's eastern frontier. In the final treaty Poland agreed to recognize the "independence" of the Ukraine and Belorussia—or, anyhow, the part of Belorussia that was not awarded to Poland. It was understood by the Poles that for all the treaty talk about "self-determination" and "independence," both the Ukraine and eastern Belorussia would quickly be absorbed in one manner or another by the Soviets. This clearly meant the end of Piłsudski's federalist dream, and Piłsudski severely criticized the Polish delegation at Riga. But the eastern border that the treaty allotted to Poland was not ungenerous. It greatly exceeded that which would have been awarded Poland if the Curzon Line had been accepted. The territory given Poland contained very large Ukrainian and Belorussian populations and the new frontier failed only by an average depth of about fifty miles to reach as far east as the historic 1772 borders of prepartition Poland.

The balance of the Treaty of Riga dealt with economic matters, the repatriation of prisoners, the return of historic archives and objects, et cetera. The treaty also specified that Poland was free to

---

* When the British government reminded the Poles that Grabski at Spa had signed an agreement leaving the settlement of all of Poland's other border disputes to the Allies, the Poles reminded the British that the Allies had agreed to protect Poland against Soviet invasion. Since the Allies had not done this, the Poles announced that they considered the Grabski agreement to be void.

work out the details of its frontier with Lithuania without Soviet interference.

Despite Piłsudski's disappointment with many aspects of the Treaty of Riga, the Polish-Soviet War did have certain positive results for the Polish Republic. Most importantly, it taught the Soviet government that it was dealing with a tough, patriotic people who were unready for a revolution with a Russian flavor. Lenin himself admitted that the war had been a serious mistake. Poland had been probed with the bayonets of the Red Army and the bayonets had been blunted. The Soviets would not attack Poland again for nearly a generation.

7

Finalizing the Frontiers

THE WAR WITH SOVIET RUSSIA was only one, although certainly the most serious and hard-fought, of Poland's conflicts with its neighbors. From 1919 through 1921 Poland established its borders with six separate nations (Soviet Russia, Germany, Rumania, Czechoslovakia, Latvia and Lithuania) and the Free City of Danzig. With the exceptions of Latvia and Rumania, Poland experienced conflict with each of its neighbors. Almost all of these conflicts eventually degenerated into military operations. And all of these wars—some little, some sizable—were fought at about the same time.

Apart from the war with Soviet Russia, the most violent and probably the most important of these armed conflicts took place in Upper Silesia, an area at the extreme southwest of Poland.

The question of which nation should be the legitimate sovereign of Upper Silesia has historically been disputed. When the Polish kingdom was first organized, in about 960 A.D., Silesia was part of it. But soon the region fell into the hands of various petty Polish princes and dukes who subdivided it. Thus weakened, in the early fourteenth century Silesia was taken from the Poles by Bohemia, who lost it to the Hapsburgs, who in turn gave it up to Prussia under Frederick the Great in the eighteenth century.

But through all of these changes in rule, one thing remained the same. The clear majority of the population of Upper Silesia—about

two thirds in fact—were Roman Catholic, spoke Polish, and thought
of themselves as Poles. Not even Prussia's vigorous attempts to col-
onize the region had had any significant effect. Frederick's dictum
regarding Silesian colonization ("Populate, mix up, Germanize!")[1]
simply failed to work in Upper Silesia.

At bottom, the reason for the persistence of this Polish predominance was economic. Upper Silesia rested on an enormous bed of
coal; it was the second-largest coal field in continental Europe. And
interspersed with the coal were extensive deposits of iron and zinc.
This natural wealth, combined with the cheap transportation offered
by the Oder River, early made Silesia into an enormous industrial
basin employing hundreds of thousands of miners and factory workers. But these jobs did not pay well. Silesia had the reputation of
offering the lowest industrial wages in all of Germany. As a result,
the jobs were filled with Poles who would work for less pay than
would the Germans. The population of Silesia grew from 670,000 in
1828 to nearly two million in 1905, and the increase was made up
largely of Poles who immigrated there to find employment.

When the World War ended and an independent Poland was
created, most of the Poles of Upper Silesia wanted to rejoin the resurrected nation. There was more to this than simple national pride. In
Upper Silesia the better-paying and more responsible jobs had historically gone to Germans. The Poles were the common laborers, the
landless peasants, and the poorest class of industrial workers. Their
only avenue for betterment seemed to be the annexation of Upper
Silesia by Poland. The Polish government held that Upper Silesia
should be placed under Polish sovereignty. At the Paris Peace Conference the Polish delegates stressed again and again that the majority
of the region's people were Poles, that the area had once belongd to
Poland, and that Poland badly needed the mines and factories of
Upper Silesia.

The Germans were, of course, prepared to refute this claim. They
viewed the ancient Polish title to the area as no longer in force, and
after six hundred years the title was surely in doubt. The Germans
stressed that everything of value in Upper Silesia—the mines, factories, railroad, and so on—had been developed or created by German capital and technology; the Polish contribution had been only
the meanest type of industrial labor. The Germans believed that these
Polish immigrants and their descendants had no right to challenge
German sovereignty. Every level of German society—the govern-

ment, the army, the industrialists and the common people—cried out against the transfer of Upper Silesia to Poland.

The Allies had decided to award Upper Silesia to Poland when they first met in Paris to draft their peace terms for Germany. But the German reaction to this was so violent (and the logic of their objections so compelling) that it was decided to permit the fate of Upper Silesia to be determined by a plebiscite. If the majority of the population of Upper Silesia wanted the region to become part of Poland, then the plebiscite vote would show it.

The Poles, however, preferred not to put the matter to the hazards of a plebiscite. Upper Silesia was not ethnically homogeneous. There were large pockets of Germans scattered through it. In fact, in areas containing some of the most desirable mines and factories, the Germans were in a majority. It would be difficult to draw a plebiscite line through Upper Silesia and be certain that it would include both a Polish majority and the bulk of the most valuable mines and industrial properties.

In August 1919, units of the P.O.W. led an insurrection in Upper Silesia, with the obvious purpose of presenting to the Allies a *fait accompli*—that is, attaching the territory to Poland before a plebiscite could be held. Of course, this objective could scarcely be made public. So the P.O.W. leaders announced that the insurrection was a "spontaneous uprising" of Poles who had been the victims of German terrorism. Nonetheless, for a spontaneous uprising it was suspiciously well organized. Arms in considerable quantity had been smuggled in from Poland. Commanders and staffs had been selected for all the more important towns and cities in eastern Upper Silesia. On the night of August 16–17 more than twenty thousand armed Poles appeared in the streets and occupied the major public buildings in the predominantly Polish eastern part of Upper Silesia.

The German response was swift. From Breslau in Lower Silesia, a Reichswehr infantry brigade moved into the region. It was accompanied by several units of the *Freikorps*, a volunteer infantry force. By August 24 they had recaptured everything that the Poles had taken over, had killed or wounded several hundred members of the P.O.W., and had restored order. The surviving Polish insurrectionaries buried their weapons in the forests and melted into the population to await another day.

The German military occupation of Upper Silesia did not last

long. Under the terms of the Treaty of Versailles, Germany was prohibited from sending troops into the region. Acting on Polish requests, the Allies assumed all military authority in Upper Silesia. On
February 11, 1920, an inter-Allied commission arrived in the region
with 2,000 Italian troops and 11,500 French soldiers. For the day-to-
day police work, a special force, known as the *Abstimmungspolizei*,
or APO, was organized. Most of its members had previously belonged
to police forces in the territory, and thus the APO was almost entirely
German.

These German police were a predictable source of controversy.
When the APO was formed, both Germans and Poles in Upper Silesia
were preparing for the plebiscite that was to take place in the spring
of 1921. The Poles found themselves at a serious disadvantage. Armed
German terrorist gangs, clandestinely subsidized partly by local German industrial interests and partly by the German Ministry of Defense, roamed through the region. They broke up Polish rallies, tore
down Polish posters, and murdered several Polish leaders. Although
the German Army was not permitted to enter Upper Silesia, there was
no way to prevent independent German *Freikorps* units from doing
so, and their presence precipitated almost constant uproar and violence. The German APO did little to curb the German terrorist
gangs. The French and Italian occupation forces, their commanders
confused by a conflict they did not understand in a region they did
not know, were simply confined to barracks most of the time.

In August 1920, during the most desperate moments of the Polish-
Soviet War, a German newspaper in Upper Silesia printed an announcement of the fall of Warsaw to the Red Army. The streets of
Silesian towns were soon filled with thousands of Germans celebrating what they assumed to be the end of an independent Poland.
Polish citizens and their homes and businesses were attacked by the
jubilant German crowds. And these attacks did not cease even when
it was learned that Warsaw had not fallen. A Polish insurrection led
by the P.O.W. was only hours in coming—and this second uprising,
unlike that of 1919, was truly spontaneous. It began on August 19,
with the Poles seizing all government offices in the eastern part of the
region and ended in September 1920, after protracted counterterror-
ism against the German gangs, and after an agreement had been negotiated under which half of Upper Silesia's police would be Poles.

Both sides spent the next six months preparing for the plebiscite,
which was to take place in March 1921. The Polish Plebiscite com-

missioner was Wojciech Korfanty, a dynamic forty-seven-year-old lawyer. He directed a widespread propaganda campaign as well as organizing trade unions and farmers' cooperatives. Protected by the now-half-Polish police force and under the now-benevolent eyes of the Allied occupation troops, who were commanded by a French general, the Poles used many of the same terrorist tactics that had so embittered them against the Germans in previous months. Throughout Upper Silesia the level of Polish-German hostility rose dramatically.

The Germans intensified their propaganda efforts. German school teachers (and practically all teachers in Upper Silesia were German) were set to work influencing their Polish students. German employers warned their Polish employees that should Upper Silesia become Polish, Germany would erect a customs barrier, whereupon Upper Silesian industry and employment would virtually cease. Simultaneously, the German government made a thorough search for people who had been born in Upper Silesia and now lived in other areas of Germany. These persons, almost all of whom were the children of German officials or employers, were eligible to vote in the plebiscite. In the end nearly 200,000 of these "migrants" were tracked down, given free railway transportation, and were persuaded to return to Upper Silesia for the voting.

When the plebiscite finally took place on March 20, 1921, the results astonished Korfanty and his followers. They could scarcely believe what had happened. Of a total of 1,186,234 votes, only 479,414 were cast for Poland as opposed to 706,820 for Germany. This meant that 60 percent of the voters had opted to remain with Germany. Polish cries of fraud went up at once. There had been 192,000 "migrant" votes of which only 5 percent had been for Poland. This, it was claimed, was grossly unfair, because few of these persons had any intention of returning to Upper Silesia to live. On a map of Upper Silesia, Korfanty drew a line that, he claimed, marked the boundary of an area in which the majority of the population was Polish, despite the evidence of the plebiscite. The area set off by the "Korfanty Line," as it was called thereafter, also included two thirds of Upper Silesia and most of its industrial wealth.

The Allies, who under the Versailles Treaty had the right to determine the fate of Upper Silesia, at first gave no indication as to what their decision would be. But it gradually became known that they contemplated a division of the province. When they learned this, the Germans were enraged. The plebiscite had been held, and its outcome was clear—and they had won, had they not? Obviously they had convinced a very large number of Upper Silesian Poles that they would be better off as German citizens. Upper Silesia, the Germans argued, was an industrial entity that could not be divided without collapsing economically. And anyhow, the Poles would never be able to operate the technologically advanced Silesian economy. "One might as well give a clock to a monkey as give Upper Silesia to the Poles," they said.[2] No one knew what the eventual Allied decision would be, but Korfanty and the Upper Silesian P.O.W., with whom he had now been forced into a close alliance, decided not to await events. Acting without the authorization of the Polish government, Korfanty attempted a military solution.

On May 3 Korfanty established a general headquarters in Bytom. He issued a proclamation announcing that he was at the head of an armed uprising, and that the Third Silesian Insurrection began. It was obviously well prepared. Within twelve hours P.O.W. formations had seized control of most of the cities in the eastern part of Upper Silesia. The P.O.W. put sixty to seventy thousand irregular soldiers in the field. By May 5 they had occupied all of the province as far west as the Korfanty Line, which they began to fortify against antici-pated German counterattacks. The French commander of the Allied occupation forces turned a blind eye to the Polish uprising.

The German counteroffensive was not long in coming, although it had to take an irregular form. Even though the province was ob-viously in a state of war, the German government feared to use its regular troops. The Allied occupation forces might be reluctant to fire upon Polish insurrectionaries, but they would show no such reluctance to shoot at Germans. And if the Germans used regular troops, the Polish Army might enter the fighting, and the whole affair could easily end up in a general war with Poland. But, fortunately for the Germans, they had other options. There were the *Freikorps*— tough, independent military units that were actually private armies, secretly subsidized by the German government for anti-Communist service in 1919. These troops were not technically members of the German army, but they were thoroughly professional and in some cases as good as, or even better than, the regular German army itself. A secret call went out for certain of these units to assemble at Breslau in Lower Silesia.

These men were the elite of the *Freikorps* and were very good soldiers indeed. For the German government they had the advantage of being technically private persons whose activities had no manifest official sanction. There were only about 25,000 *Freikorps* fighters in Silesia, and thus they were considerably outnumbered. But they more than made up for this disadvantage in experience, fighting ability, and sense of mission. After beating off Polish attacks on May 12, the German forces took the offensive on May 21. The center of the Polish defense system was buttressed by Mount Annaberg, which rises nearly one thousand feet above the surrounding flatlands. The Poles had heavily fortified this mountain, and they used it as an observation point. The main weight of the German assault was directed against Annaberg, whose capture was regarded as important both as a symbol and as a military objective. The German central columns broke through the Polish defenses and on the night of May 23–24, after a good deal of hard fighting, the *Freikorps* battalions captured Annaberg.

The conquest of this little mountain changed the whole picture in Upper Silesia. Although the fighting continued, Korfanty now announced that "the Poles recognize the authority of the Interallied [occupation-army] Commission under whom they ask for protection and whom they will obey without reservation in any decision they think best."[3]

Within a few days, fighting died down as Allied troops, reinforced by four British infantry battalions, now asserted their authority in all areas still held by Korfanty's forces. Although the *Freikorps* were not permitted to advance any further, they were not forced out of the areas they had captured. The war in Upper Silesia having thus been brought to a standstill, all parties concerned were anxious for a rapid determination of the final line of demarcation between Poland and Germany. The matter was referred to the Conference of Ambassadors of the principal Allies. After debating for several months, the conference declared that they could not reach a decision in this complex matter and referred the matter to the League of Nations, which rendered a judgment in October 1921. Their decision left the Poles without grounds for legitimate complaint (although they did protest it violently). Poland got less than one third of the territory in which the plebiscite had been held, but their area contained more than 40 percent of the population. More importantly, Poland got all the zinc mines, and more than three fourths of the coal mines and iron-ore works. The Geneva Convention on Upper Silesia, a complex economic and minorities-protection treaty, was worked out to protect the individual rights of persons left on the "wrong side" of the borders and to cushion the impact of tariff barriers on the economy of the region.

But the Upper Silesian problem did not end there. In the minds of most Germans, this settlement ranked with those of Danzig and the Polish Corridor as a humiliating swindle. Almost to a man, the Germans believed that they had been cheated and that their temporary postwar weakness had been callously exploited by the Poles. Germany had won the plebiscite, but much of Upper Silesia and most of its wealth had gone to Poland. In the years to come the *Freikorps'* Silesian Campaign and the storming of Annaberg were viewed as stirring patriotic deeds by almost every German. The name of Korfanty became synonymous with Polish treachery. The Upper Silesian settlement was a permanent source of German animus and was not to be forgotten or forgiven.

The story of the struggle for the Duchy of Teschen is remarkably similar to that of Upper Silesia—although in the case of Teschen it was the Poles who ended up believing themselves the victims of treachery. The Duchy of Teschen was not much of a place. Its total area was only 850 square miles, and in 1919 its population was only about 400,000. The town of Teschen, from which the area took its name, contained only about 15,000 people. Lloyd George complained to the British House of Commons on April 16, 1919, "How many members have ever heard of Teschen? I do not mind saying that I have not."[4] And certainly Lloyd George had some justice to his complaint—who, indeed, *had* ever heard of Teschen? The name is rendered even less identifiable for Westerners by the fact that Teschen was always referred to by the Poles as Cieszyn and the Czechs as Těšin.

The Duchy of Teschen derived its only importance from the fact that it is geologically the southern extension of Upper Silesia. For the three centuries before World War I, the region had belonged to the Hapsburgs and was thus, of course, Austrian. But geological features know no political boundaries, and the extensive coal fields of Upper Silesia reached under the prewar borders into the duchy. These fields were extensive and well developed. At their production peak in 1916 the Teschen mines were producing nearly eight million tons of coal a year and were a vital source of fuel supply for Vienna, Budapest and Prague. In addition, an important international railway ran through the region.

Under Austrian rule, the duchy had been subdivided into four districts. One of the four, called Frýdek, had a population that was mostly Czech. The other three districts, those in which most of the coal was to be found, were inhabited by Poles in overwhelming percentages. (The Austrian census figures of 1910 had set the ethnic divisions of the entire duchy at 54.8 percent Polish; 27.1 percent Czech; and 18.0 percent German.)[5]

The major Allies had devoted little time to Teschen before the end of the war. However, the Czechs (and to a lesser extent the Poles) had given it a lot of thought. Better by far than the other "successor states" that came into being at the end of World War I, the Czechs had prepared for their eventual independence. Under the leadership of Beneš and Masaryk, they had acquired a reputation for moderation, reliability, and attention to detail that made them favorites in every Allied capital. Moreover, the Czech leaders were so wonderfully likable that the Allied leaders found it difficult to say no to the always tactful requests of the provisional Czech government.

With their customary thoroughness, the Czechs foresaw that Teschen might become a source of conflict between themselves and Poland. It came as no surprise to the Allies to learn that before the end of the war the Czech leaders had reached an agreement with certain prominent Poles, potential leaders of an independent Poland, regarding the partition of Teschen on an ethnic basis. The Allies found nothing objectionable about this and were pleased to learn that when, on November 5, 1918, the Poles and Czechs in the region disarmed the Austrian garrison in the duchy and took over the region, the two parties concluded an on-the-spot provisional agreement to divide the area along its obvious ethnic lines. The Poles had immediately taken over the areas that appeared to be theirs, just as the Czechs had assumed administration of theirs. Nobody objected to this friendly arrangement, and the conciliatory attitude of the Czechs was widely admired.

Then came second thoughts in Prague. It was observed that under the agreement of November 5 the Poles now controlled about a third of the duchy's coal mines and held all the important railway lines. The Czechs suddenly realized that they had given away rather a lot. And although the November 5 agreement was "provisional," history has proved that provisional agreements tend to become permanent. As weeks passed, the newly established Czech government reflected on how best to acquire the Polish-held areas of Teschen. It was, of course, recognized that any takeover in Teschen would have to be accomplished in a manner acceptable to the victorious Allies, who were at that moment assembling for the Peace Conference of Paris. The Czechs were much too wise to push the Poles out of Teschen on the simple grounds that they wanted all of the duchy. This would certainly be viewed by the Allies as unbecoming greed. So, instead, the Czechs cooked up a tale to the effect that the Teschen area was becoming Bolshevik. While this story was circulating, the Czechs put together a substantial body of infantry—about 15,000 men—and on January 23, 1919, they invaded the Polish-held areas of Teschen. To confuse the Poles, the Czechs recruited some Allied officers of Czech background and put these men in their respective wartime uniforms at the head of the invasion forces. After only a little skirmishing, the tiny Polish defense force in Teschen was nearly driven out of the duchy. But at this point the Czech offensive was stopped dead by an international howl of rage. The Allies had not been fooled by the Czech claims of Bolshevism in the duchy. The subterfuge of having Allied officers at the head of the offensive was viewed in Paris as being positively insulting. The Allies in Paris sent a peremptory demand that the Czechs cease firing and evacuate most of the territory they had siezed. An inter-Allied military commission was sent to Teschen to make sure that the Czechs did as they were told. Even Lloyd George was on the Polish side in this affair.

For most of 1919 the Teschen matter was studied by an Allied commision in order to draw a permanent frontier line between Poland and Czechoslovakia. Each nation was invited to Paris to give its views. The Poles based their claim on Teschen on the fact that Poles were the overwhelming majority in three of its four districts; let the territory simply be split up on an ethnic basis in the same manner that the Allies were demanding elsewhere, and the Poles would be content. It was a good case.

The Czechs had a more difficult concept to sell, although in Beneš they had probably the best salesman in Paris. The Czechs stated that they needed the Teschen coal in order to influence, for the best, the actions of Austria and Hungary, whose capitals were fueled by coal from the duchy. The Czechs held that the large Polish population in

Teschen should not influence its partition. They claimed that these Poles were only relatively recent arrivals in a territory that was historically Bohemian.

For months the Allied commission had been debating the Teschen border question without coming to a conclusion. At one time they drew a tentative line that would give the Czechs 60 percent of the coal fields, while the Poles got most of the people and the railroad. Just as the Allies were about to adopt this boundary, Beneš asked that the affair be settled by a plebiscite. The Allies in Paris were astonished. The British warned Beneš that every population survey indicated that the Poles would win a plebiscite. But Beneš was insistent, and in September 1919 the Allies announced that the future of Teschen would be decided by vote of its inhabitants.

As it turned out, Beneš knew what he was doing. A plebiscite would take some time to set up, and a lot could happen in that time—particularly when a nation's affairs were conducted as cleverly as were Czechoslovakia's. Perhaps events would work in Czechoslovakia's favor; perhaps the plebiscite would not actually be held— and eventually that was exactly what happened.

It will be recalled that in July 1920 the major Allies were meeting in conference at Spa in Belgium when Polish Prime Minister Grabski suddenly arrived to plead for assistance in Poland's war with Soviet Russia. It will also be recalled that the price stipulated for such aid was that Poland must accept the dictates of the Allies in the matter of Poland's frontiers. One of these frontiers was the Duchy of Teschen, where a plebiscite had yet to be held.

This was the moment that Beneš, who was also present at Spa, had been waiting for. Over the dinner table he convinced the British and French that the plebiscite should not be held and that the Allies should simply impose their own decision in the Teschen matter. More than that, Beneš persuaded the French and the British to draw a frontier line that gave Czechoslovakia most of the territory of Teschen, the vital railroad, and all of the important coal fields. With this frontier, 139,000 Poles were to be left in Czech territory, whereas only 2,000 Czechs were left on the Polish side.

The next morning Beneš visited the Polish delegation at Spa. By giving the impression that the Czechs would accept a settlement favorable to the Poles without a plebiscite, Beneš got the Poles to sign an agreement that Poland would abide by any Allied decision regarding Teschen. The Poles, of course, had no way of knowing that Beneš had already persuaded the Allies to make a decision on Teschen.

After a brief interval, to make it appear that due deliberation had taken place, the Allied Council of Ambassadors in Paris imposed its "decision." Only then did it dawn on the Poles that at Spa they had signed a blank check. To them, Beneš' stunning triumph was not diplomacy; it was a swindle. The Polish parliament eventually felt compelled to ratify the agreement, under which the Teschen frontier was imposed on them. But as Polish Prime Minister Wincenty Witos warned, "The Polish nation has received a blow which will play an important role in our relations with the Czechoslovak Republic. The decision of the Council of Ambassadors has given the Czechs a piece of Polish land containing a population which is mostly Polish. . . . The decision has caused a rift between these two nations, which are ordinarily politically and economically united."[6]

The Teschen affair was, indeed, a tragedy. It poisoned relations between two nations that had every reason to act in concert. The Poles could never forget how they had been duped. They swore that the day would come when the Czechs would find themselves in the same desperate position as the Poles had been in at Spa. Then there would be a different end to the story of Teschen. And, of course, eventually that day did come.

The port city of Danzig (or, in Polish, Gdansk) lies on the southern edge of the Bay of Danzig, which opens onto the Baltic. It was known as one of Germany's most beautiful seacoast cities; the bay was clear and gray-green, the beaches had fine, white sand, and the trees extended to the coastline. The center of the city was a well-preserved and romantic reminder of Danzig's medieval greatness.

During most of its existence Danzig had been a wealthy and flourishing port—practically an independent nation. Although under the protection of the Polish kings, Danzig had once possessed its own army and navy, dispatched its own ambassadors, and minted its own currency. In the seventeenth century, Danzig had a population of 80,000, which made it a large city for the time. During the Partitions, the city became part of Prussia and was subsequently cut off by tariff barriers from its natural role as the principal port for central Poland. Danzig thereupon sank in population to the point where, in 1817, it had only 48,000 inhabitants. But, with the extraordinary industrial development of Prussia and the German Empire the city began to make good its population losses. In the twenty years before the World War Danzig's harbor facilities had been greatly improved—almost entirely rebuilt, in fact—and its shipbuilding industry had become very large. All of this was due to German energy and German capital investment.

In the course of this economic rebirth, the city had become populated almost exclusively by Germans. In 1918 almost 96 percent of its inhabitants were German. Poland claimed that there had been some falsification of the census figures to improve the German percentage, but even making the most generous allowance for frauds, there is no doubt that almost everyone in Danzig was German and wanted to remain German.

Because of this overwhelming preponderance of Germans in Danzig, the Allies decided not to award the city to Poland but to make Danzig a "free city"—a semi-independent state under League of Nations control. The Poles were desperately unhappy over this decision. They claimed that they had been promised a "free and secure access to the sea" and that the Polish Corridor, which had been created to give them possession of the Vistula and the railroads running south from Danzig, should have been capped with possession of Danzig.

"Free city" status did not please the German Danzigers any more than it did the Poles. They made their opposition clear by a series of riots and violent demonstrations in the months before the Peace Treaty's signing. Under the terms of the Peace Treaty, all Germans in the city would lose their German nationality and become citizens of the "Free City of Danzig" under the protection of the League of Nations. The League was charged with appointing a high commissioner who would oversee the government of the city in its early stages and would supervise the city's relations with the League. Poland was awarded free customs transit through the port, and it was stipulated that the foreign affairs of the city were to be handled by Poland. A Convention between the Free City and Poland was to spell out the details of the relationship between the two parties.

On January 10, 1920, when the Treaty of Versailles came into effect; all was in readiness for Danzig's transition. The populace of the city itself and some of the surrounding districts, a total of 357,000 persons, became citizens of the Free City of Danzig, and a British diplomat, Sir Reginald Tower, arrived in the city to begin his tenure as League of Nations High Commissioner. Assisting him in the early stages of his incumbency were two battalions of British troops. Tower's first move was to establish an administrative organization, the Staatsrat, which he charged with the daily operation of the city's affairs. This organization was staffed almost exclusively with former German civil servants who had been officials in Danzig before the turnover. They were all highly experienced and efficient. The Staatsrat was headed by Heinrich Sahm, an exceptionally able man who had been mayor of Danzig. This body administered the city so well that there was almost nothing in the area of internal government for Tower to do.

Tower, however, was kept very busy negotiating the Convention as required by the Treaty of Versailles. The first meeting between the two parties was held on May 26, 1920. Both the Poles and the Danzigers submitted drafts for the Convention. As could be expected, they were very far apart in their thinking.

The Poles took the position that Danzig should be Poland's in everything but name. To be sure, nominal sovereignty would rest with the League of Nations, but this would be only a legal technicality. The Poles wanted Polish law to be in force, Polish currency to circulate, Polish officials to govern, and Polish army and navy contingents to be stationed in Danzig. In short, if the Poles had their way, the city would be Polish.

The Danzigers, of course, had continued to regard themselves as German and had quite another view of things. They offered a plan that would preserve the city's German character and prevent incursions by the Poles. Their draft proposed that the citizens of the city determine questions of currency, police, language and law. The Danzigers insisted that the city should be demilitarized. They offered to guarantee Polish access to Danzig's port facilities on a customs-free basis, and they agreed to protect the rights of the Polish minority in Danzig. Apart from these few concessions, however, the city would remain German. Sir Reginald Tower made it clear that he was in general agreement with the Danzigers' position.

Negotiation for the Danzig Convention dragged on for several months, much to the distress of the Allies, who had hoped to see this important treaty concluded in rapid order. The feeling grew in the western capitals that the Poles were being recalcitrant and were asking too much. The German government did nothing to reduce tensions. It wanted the Danzigers to know that they had not been forgotten by their homeland, and it did everything it could to preserve the ties between Germany and Danzig. Germany made large, and sometimes secret, loans to the city and to its German industries. Germany and Danzig exchanged civil servants; Danzigers were frequently transferred to important civil-service posts in Germany where they were given temporary German citizenship. German ministries signed generous supply contracts with German firms in Danzig. The German government continued to pay pensions to its retired civil servants and military officers living in Danzig, even though such payments were technically illegal under German law.

The Convention was eventually drafted by the Allies at a conference of their ambassadors in Paris. It was signed by both Danzig and Poland on November 15, 1920. But there were still points of conflict, and these were ultimately resolved in a detailed treaty known as the Warsaw Agreement, which was signed in October 1921. And even then, all the details had not been worked out; conflicts continually came up and had to be resolved by supplementary negotiation that seemed to drag on endlessly.

In essence, though, the settlement was the one that had been advocated by the Danzigers. The administration of customs, regulations, port activities, railways and certain communications systems was placed under the joint supervision of Poles and Danzigers. Danzig guaranteed civil liberties to Poles within the Free City and established a customs union with Poland. The city was demilitarized and its sovereignty guaranteed by the League of Nations. Polish soldiers and naval vessels were refused the right to be based at Danzig. Danzig was free to elect its own government, which would be supervised by the League of Nations' High Commissioner, whose duties included the arbitration of Polish-Danzig disputes.

The Poles were very disappointed by this settlement. As early as 1920 they started a costly project—the construction of a competing port at the fishing town of Gdynia, which was located on a small strip of Polish coastline ten miles north of Danzig. The Poles regarded the Free City as incorrigibly German. They foresaw great trouble at Danzig at any moment of stress between Poland and Germany—and eventually they were proved right.

Of all of the disputes concerning Poland's frontiers, that involving Lithuania was the most prolonged. This was partly because the Lithuanian-Polish embroilment was really a sort of civil war. For four hundred years, from 1386 when the Lithuanian Grand Duke Jagiełło married the Polish Queen Jadwiga until the Partition of 1795, the two nations had been joined together in a dynastic union. Many Lithuanians, particularly members of the gentry, came to think of themselves as Poles. In large numbers these Polonized Lithuanians were found in the higher echelons of Polish life— politics, the Army, the professions and the arts. Piłsudski had been born a Lithuanian, and so had Gabriel Narutowicz, who was soon to become Poland's first president. The list of Lithuanians in the service of independent Poland was practically endless.

Although Piłsudski regarded Lithuania as the prime candidate for "federalization" with Poland, many Poles believed that the federalization of Lithuania would raise that nation to too high a status. They regarded Lithuania as simply a Polish province in which the few towns and cities were mostly inhabited by Poles while the countryside was largely populated by backward persons—mostly peasants—who happened to speak a different language. Quite a few Poles believed that Lithuania should simply be annexed to Poland without any special status being given to it.

The government of Lithuania, of course, was determined that the nation remain completely independent. This government was made up mainly of persons who had risen from the peasantry and viewed the Polonophile Lithuanian gentry as traitors who had abandoned their national heritage and identity. They regarded Poland as the foremost enemy of Lithuanian independence—and it is difficult to fault their judgment.

The population of Lithuania was not large. Depending upon what areas were considered Lithuanian, there were only some 3 to 4 million persons. Similarly, there were only two important cities that could be considered Lithuanian. They were Wilno in the east and Kaunas in the center. Although Kaunas was the smaller of the two cities, it was the capital of Lithuania. However, this was not by choice. The Lithuanian government had first established itself at Wilno, but in December 1919 it was forced to flee to Kaunas upon the approach of the Red Army to Wilno. Kaunas was in the heart of ethnic Lithuania, but even so, it had a large Polish population. This reflected the basic Lithuanian problem—in all of the territory claimed by Lithuania probably fewer than half the population were ethnic Lithuanians. Wilno was an even more extreme case. Of its population of approximately 200,000 persons, almost 60 percent were

Poles. The remainder was polyglot, and Lithuanians probably comprised less than 3 percent of the city's population.[7] In the surrounding countryside, particularly in the areas to the north and east of the city, the bulk of the population was Belorussian. Thus, although Wilno was the historic capital of the Grand Duchy of Lithuania and although the Lithuanian government called it the "Lithuanian Jerusalem," it was neither populated nor surrounded by ethnic Lithuanians. Moreover, the city had an enormous sentimental and symbolic significance for many Poles. As Piłsudski said to a British diplomat in 1919, "I am never really happy except there [in Wilno]. So strong was this feeling with me that when I was a fugitive proscribed by the Russian police, I could never let a year go without seeing my homeland, though of course, the risk of capture was infinitely greater because they were always on the lookout for me."[8] Leon Wasilewski, Piłsudski's close associate, saw Piłsudski weep only once—when Wilno fell to the Red Army.

The special place that Wilno occupied in both Polish and Lithuanian thought, coupled with its geographic position and ethnic mélange, quickly brought it great difficulties. Throughout 1919 and 1920 the city passed through a harrowing and confusing series of occupations, invasions and coups. The Lithuanian government was too weak to hold the city or to recover it once lost. The only opportunity afforded the Lithuanian government to return to Wilno came in August 1920, when the Red Army, retreating pell-mell from Poland after its defeat at the Battle of Warsaw, turned over Wilno to the tiny Lithuanian Army.

It was obvious, however, that Poland was not going to leave Wilno in Lithuanian hands simply because Soviet Russia had chosen to transfer it to the Kaunas government. On October 8, 1920, the Poles struck. At that time, the Polish Army had just beaten Tukhachevsky at the Battle of the Niemen. A general pursuit of the Red Army had ensued, and the Polish forces had pushed as far east as their government wanted to go. An armistice was about to be signed. During these days the Polish Army's 1st Lithuanian-Belorussian Division was encamped at Bieniankonie, just twenty-five miles south of Wilno. This division had been recruited from among the Lithuanians and Belorussians in the Wilno area. Its commander was the redoubtable General Lucian Zeligowski, a Lithuanian-born officer whose exploits had already made him famous. On the morning of October 8, Zeligowski led his division, accompanied by a few support squadrons of cavalry and an extra battalion of infantry, northward toward Wilno. There was a short skirmish with the Lithuanian Army, but Zeligowski brushed it aside. "We are not going to fight you," Zeligowski told the Lithuanian officers. "We are simply returning home."[9] The next day he marched into Wilno. To the acclamation of the city's largely Polish population, Zeligowski claimed that he and his men had acted without orders from his Polish superiors. He announced that he had led his men in a "revolt" in which they had simply "gone home" to Lithuania, where most of them had come from. Zeligowski thereupon expanded the territory under his control so that it ran north to the Latvian border. In all, he controlled a strip of land measuring about 175 miles from north to south and 70 miles from east to west. Zeligowski announced the establishment of a new government for the region to be known as the "Government of Central Lithuania." Although Zeligowski's "revolt" was a transparent fraud and had obviously occurred on direct orders from Piłsudski himself, for some time the Polish government steadfastly maintained that the "mutiny" had been authentic. More to the point, the Polish government quickly recognized Central Lithuania as a sovereign government, lent it money, and exchanged diplomatic representatives with Wilno. No conventional formality was overlooked.

The League of Nations then stepped in. In an attempt to resolve the situation, the League turned the matter over to a mediator, the Belgian diplomat Paul Hymans. In 1921 he came up with several plans under which Lithuania would be divided, Swiss style, into two autonomous cantons united with Poland in the manner of a federation. The Kaunas government rejected this proposal and all negotiation collapsed.

In early 1922 Zeligowski's government held an election to determine the future of Central Lithuania. About two thirds of those who voted agreed that the area controlled by Zeligowski's forces should be unified with Poland. The Polish Sejm wasted no time and on March 24, 1922, passed an Act of Unification under which Wilno and the territory of Central Lithuania became an integral part of Poland. With this one act, Poland gained about 15,000 square miles and an additional million persons. There were those, however, who thought the affair had been clumsily handled—and the most important among them was Piłsudski. He believed that Central Lithuania should have been attached to Poland only on a semiautonomous, federalist basis. He believed that the Sejm's insistence on a "clear-cut solution" to the matter had demonstrated to every adjacent nationality (including the Kaunas Lithuanian government) that affiliation with Poland meant annexation. Piłsudski made a sensitive and sorrowful speech directed at the Lithuanian government; in it he said that "On this day of Polish triumph, I cannot help stretching my hand across the boundary dividing us from those over there, in Kaunas, who may consider this, the day of our triumph, a day of disaster and mourning. I cannot help but think of them as brothers."[10]

Piłsudski's sympathy had no effect on the Kaunas government. They would never believe or trust the Poles again. Although their army was too small to do anything about it, the Lithuanians continued to regard themselves as being, in a sense, at war with Poland. They blew up the railroad bridges between Poland and Lithuania, and cut the telephone and telegraph lines. They closed their boarders with Poland and refused to have any diplomatic relations with Warsaw. There was not even any mail service between Poland and Lithuania. The Lithuanian government refused to sign most treaties to which Poland was also a signatory. This, of course, worked a great hardship on the small Lithuanian nation, which thus cut itself off from a great neighbor and natural trading partner. But it was a sacrifice that most ethnic Lithuanians were willing to make. And, in time, it also proved to be a source of the greatest irritation and inconvenience to Poland.

However, with the stabilization of the Lithuanian borders, the creation of the Polish republic was complete. The German territory in the Poznań region had, of course, gone to the Poles much earlier. First it had been taken over by them in a series of uprisings organized by the P.O.W., and then, when the German Army attempted to put the insurrection down, the Allies had intervened to bar German military activity in most of the province. Under the terms of the Versailles Treaty, Poland had been awarded almost all of the Poznań region. Without doubt, the Poles had a very strong case for their having the province. Certainly they did predominate in population, just as they did in those formerly German areas of West Prussia and the eastern part of Pomerania which were also awarded to Poland and became the Polish Corridor to Danzig. All of these areas were relatively lightly populated agricultural regions. Although these regions were large, they had no real industrial or commercial significance for Germany. But nobody could tell the German people any of this. They burned with an implacable conviction of injustice.

They swore that they would never reconcile themselves to the loss of the Polish Corridor. They would never forget and would never stop hating Poland for it.

Few Germans believed that the Versailles System, which had forced these concessions upon them, would last or that the Poles would survive as a nation. The Germans regarded Poland as a *Saisonstaat*, a nation that would last only a season or two. For most of the next twenty years the German government behaved as if its territorial losses to Poland were only temporary and provisional. In 1920 the German Army's Chief of Staff General Hans von Seeckt wrote, "Poland's existence is intolerable, incompatible with the survival of Germany. It must disappear, and it will disappear through its own internal weakness and through Russia—with our assistance. For Russia, Poland is even more intolerable than for us: no Russian can allow Poland to exist. . . ."[11]

There were endless opportunities to fan the flames of hate. Under the provisions of the Versailles Treaty any German who lived in a region transferred to Poland could opt for German citizenship and move himself and all his property unhindered to German territory. Poles in Germany were guaranteed reciprocal rights. But as it worked out, these optants frequently were evicted or found their property seized or, upon temporarily leaving their place of residence, were denied the right to return. There were about 150,000 German optants who had returned to Germany from Poland. Many of these had tales of woe about their treatment by the Polish government, and the German press saw that nothing was lost in the recounting.

On March 14, 1923, to the accompaniment of great rejoicing in Poland, an Allied Ambassadors Conference confirmed the eastern frontiers of Poland as they were presently constituted. This action was made in accordance with Article 87 of the Treaty of Versailles under which the Allies reserved the right to determine Poland's eastern border. By recognizing the *de facto* frontiers, the Allies accepted the Treaty of Riga and, very reluctantly, the Polish incorporation of Wilno and Central Lithuania. This recognition also had the effect of confirming Polish sovereignty over Eastern Galicia.

The net result of Poland's protracted struggles was a state of about 150,000 square miles, with a population of twenty-seven million people. In terms of both population and area, Poland was the sixth-largest nation in Europe.

The Poles were proud of themselves and their accomplishments. They had confronted all their neighbors and in most cases had prevailed. Poland had fought a war with mighty Russia and had crushed the enemy's army. Poland's frontiers had been recognized by international covenants bearing either the outright or the implied guarantees of the victor nations of the World War. But even in the general Polish euphoria of the time, it was difficult to overlook the dangerous defects in the nation's geographical and ethnic makeup. Poland had no easily defensible frontiers and was surrounded by seven nations, the most powerful of which—Soviet Russia and Germany—would concede no permanence to Poland. The Polish border was 3,437 miles long. Only 8 percent of that frontier was held in common with nations—Rumania and Latvia—that could be described as friendly. All of the rest was shared by nations or territories with which Poland lived in a state of barely submerged hostility. Most of Poland's neighbors believed that they had actually been robbed of territory by Poland—either by coup or at the point of a bayonet.

Fewer than 70 percent of Poland's population could be considered ethnic Poles. Only in the historic core of Poland, an area about two hundred miles in diameter centered on a point halfway between Kraków and Warsaw, was the population almost exclusively Polish. To the east, along the 600-mile edge of the Polish heartland, ran a broad strip of territory that was known as the Eastern Kresy. In the northern half of the Kresy, the region called Polesie, were about a million Belorussians, a people whose kin lived in much larger numbers across the border in Soviet Belorussia. The Belorussians possessed some vague separatist aspirations, but their level of national consciousness was still quite low. They dwelled on the poorest land in Poland and were aware that they were regarded as the most backward, economically and intellectually, of the Polish minorities.

To the south of these Belorussians, in Volhynia and East Galicia, dwelled the Ukrainian population. There were nearly four million Polish Ukrainians, making them the most numerous of the Polish minority peoples. The Ukrainians had a national history of their own, and they deeply resented being submerged in the Polish nation. Although the rights of Ukrainians were protected under the Polish

Minority Treaty, which the Allies had forced the Polish government
to sign at the time of drafting of the Treaty of Versailles, nothing
could convince the Ukrainians that they would be equitably dealt
with by the Polish government. They blamed Poland for the fact
that there was no separate Ukrainian nation, although this was clearly
beyond Poland's control, because the bulk of the Ukrainian people,
some thirty million of them, were Soviet citizens. Poland's Ukrainians wanted national autonomy, and pending its attainment, they
were a large, reluctant and recalcitrant element within the Polish
nation.

The German minority within Poland, apart from the optants, consisted of about three quarters of a million persons. They dwelled
mostly in the Polish Corridor, in Upper Silesia, and around the city
of Łódz to which they had come at the end of the nineteenth century
to build the enormous Polish textile works. In general, the German
Pole enjoyed a better standard of living than any other group in the
nation. Many Germans were successful farmers; others held positions
in manufacturing as engineers, managers or owners. From the very
beginning it was evident that the German minority would create a
problem in Poland. They displayed a stubborn refusal to assimilate
or to give any degree of loyalty to the Polish state. Their economic
contribution to Poland was substantial, but the Germans' sense of
superiority and their emotional detachment from the state created
serious internal difficulties for the new nation.

Poland's problems with its minorities were predictable from the
time that its frontiers were finalized. As a consequence of its desire
to become as large and as populous as possible, Poland had added a
very large body of minorities, which were at best disaffected and at
worst openly hostile. Compounding the problem was the fact that
these Polish minorities were tied by blood and language to powerful
neighboring nations.

The Polish Republic had thus incorporated into itself a covey of
actual or potential enemies who nursed rich grievances against it.
And it was a nation that, to a very great extent, owed its rebirth to
the assistance of certain Western powers with whom Poland had no
direct geographic contact. A great many informed Europeans believed that Poland could not survive in its present form for more
than a very short time.

8
Sejmocracy

THE POLISH GOVERNMENT was, of course, very well aware of the many enemies that it had made and the menaces that it faced. However, it seemed to the Poles that most of its dangers could be dealt with very simply: Poland had only to enter into an alliance with France in order to achieve complete security against its principal enemies.

At this time France had enormous influence on the nations of Eastern Europe. There were many reasons for this, but in the end they boiled down to one salient fact: France had an important interest in supporting the East European states against a resurgent Germany. It was evident that the other Allied Powers, among them Great Britain and Italy, had agreed that Eastern Europe would be considered France's particular sphere of interest. France was prepared to sign treaties of alliance and military assistance with the larger nations on Germany's eastern borders. To such nations, a treaty with France seemed to offer almost complete security, inasmuch as it allied them with Europe's largest army, which was commanded by an officer corps that was widely believed to possess almost a monopoly on the world's military wisdom. The French Army was thought to be supported by a resolute nation that burned with hatred for Germany.

The prestige of France stood particularly high in Poland. There were historic reasons for this admiration. Poles generally regarded France as a traditional supporter of Polish independence. Portraits

of Napoleon, who was given credit for the creation of the Duchy of
Warsaw out of partitioned Poland, still hung in many Polish homes.
The important role of the Polish Legions and the Polish cavalry in
the Napoleonic armies was still recalled. The French influence was
found in almost every area of Polish life. In fact, the Polish Constitution of 1921 was patterned on an old French constitution draft. The
Polish political parties modeled themselves on French counterparts
and generally conducted themselves in a manner that they thought
similar to that of the French. And, of course, there was the pervasive
element of French culture. Every Pole with any pretension to education spoke French. To an even greater degree than in other eastern
European nations, the Polish bourgeoisie dressed in French fashions,
ate food prepared in the French manner, read French literature, saw
French plays, and visited Paris whenever possible.

In the military area, the Polish Army was being trained by a
French military mission. Diplomatically, France was represented in
Warsaw by Hector de Panafieu, a highly intelligent man, who had
been sent as minister to Poland in February 1920. In short order,
Panafieu won the esteem and friendship of the Poles. He was able
to repair almost completely the earlier French-Polish diplomatic
misunderstandings that had been caused by the French support of
Dmowski rather than Piłsudski.

To a considerable degree, the French government reciprocated the
Polish regard. Poland had something very material to offer in any
military alliance—it was by far the largest nation on Germany's
eastern frontier. Poland had proved itself to be a militarily robust,
aggressive nation that would tolerate no interference with what it
regarded as its rights. The French admired this and had frequently
demonstrated their willingness to assist their potential ally. As
Raymond Poincaré observed at the time of the Upper Silesian dispute, "Everything orders us to support Poland: The [Versailles]
Treaty, the plebiscite, loyalty, the present and future interest of
France, and the permanence of peace."[1]

For many months prior to 1921, the French government had considered offering a treaty of alliance to Poland. There was no doubt
that Poland would leap at the opportunity. The Polish Foreign
Minister Prince Sapieha had, in fact, already made several inquiries
about such a pact, and the Polish Army's General Staff had drafted
a Franco-Polish military pact, which was presented to the chief of
the French Military Mission in Warsaw. The only thing that had

held the French government back was its desire to let the dust settle after the Polish-Soviet conflict to be sure that Poland would survive this war. But by the end of 1920 the Quai d'Orsay thought it quite possible that Poland would endure. So, on December 28, 1920, the French extended a formal invitation to Marshal Piłsudski to pay a state visit to Paris. It was understood that the purpose of this visit would be to negotiate a treaty of alliance. The French invitation was immediately accepted, and although the visit was delayed by a French government crisis that brought Aristide Briand to office as prime minister, Piłsudski went to Paris in early February 1921.

The visit was regarded by the Poles as a great success. Certainly they could not find the slightest fault with the hospitality extended by the French government to its Polish guests. Piłsudski, Sosnkowski and Sapieha arrived on February 3 and were lodged in magnificent suites at the Hotel Crillon. That evening the Polish delegation was honored at a state banquet at the Élysée Palace. During the following days, while Sapieha met with French foreign-office officials and Sosnkowski held discussions with the French General Staff, Piłsudski visited World War I battlefields. On February 5 he visited Saint-Cyr, where he decorated Marshal Foch with Poland's highest military medal, the *Virtuti Militari*, taken from Piłsudski's own uniform. That night he was the guest of the city of Paris at a splendid reception at the Hôtel de Ville. The next day Piłsudski visited Verdun, where he decorated Marshal Pétain. That evening he departed for Warsaw.

The Polish press, reflecting popular pride and gratitude for the honors that the French had shown the Polish delegation, greeted Piłsudski's return with lavish praise. The assembled members of the Sejm gave three cries of "Vive la France!" followed by extensive thanks to the French nation for the respect that its officials had shown to Poland.

Piłsudski's role in the visit had not been exclusively ceremonial. During the first days of meetings, little progress had been made. It became apparent that Sosnkowski and Sapieha and their French opposite numbers required more definite instructions. Too much time was being wasted in trying to define the scope of the treaty. So, on February 5, after a luncheon at the Hôtel de Ville, Piłsudski and the French President, Alexandre Millerand, withdrew to an adjoining room and quickly worked out guidelines for an alliance. Things went very rapidly after that. On February 19 a political alliance was signed by Sapieha and Briand. A secret military agreement between the two nations followed on February 21.

The political agreement—which was to be the cornerstone of Polish foreign policy for nearly twenty years—committed each nation to consult and act together on all foreign matters of mutual interest; to conclude a separate economic agreement; and most importantly, to act together in the event of unprovoked attack on either. This agreement was quite short and not very specific.

The military agreement was secret, longer, and far more specific. Article One of the agreement committed each party to mutual aid in the event of German aggression. Article Two discussed the eventuality of a renewed Polish-Soviet war. In this case, France promised to help prevent Germany from simultaneously attacking Poland and to "aid in [Poland's] defense against the Soviet Army." This agreement, it was understood, did not necessarily commit France to intervene militarily against Soviet Russia.

Subsequent articles in the agreement dealt with such matters as staff talks for the purpose of drafting war plans, a scheme for the exchange of military attachés and instructors, and a promise of French assistance in developing a Polish arms industry. Poland agreed to organize its army on the same basis as the French—"it is understood that the infantry divisions will consist of three regiments of three battalions, each battalion having a machine-gun company, and two regiments of divisional artillery comprising three groups of three batteries of four pieces of field artillery and one group of three batteries of four pieces of heavy artillery."[2] Most importantly, Poland was required to maintain a regular army of thirty divisions. This was quite large for a nation of Poland's size. Even the Polish General Staff, which thought in rather extravagant terms, had previously planned for only twenty-six divisions. To support this undertaking the French agreed to lend Poland 400,000,000 francs, approximately $60,000,000 in the currency of the time.

Neither the political agreement nor the military convention was to come into force until the conclusion of a separate economic-commercial pact. But the drafting of this pact took much longer than had been anticipated. The delay was caused by an unattractive feature of French diplomacy —France's invariable insistence on extracting generous economic concessions as a sort of "bonus" for signing alliances. The French could be quite predatory, and smaller nations that signed treaties with France usually found that they lost an appreciable degree of control over their own economies. In this case the French extracted a "most favored nation" agreement from Poland, obtained substantial tariff reductions for French goods, and were granted extensive oil concessions in Galicia. The French insisted, of course, that all military supplies purchased abroad by Poland must come from France.

The economic demands of the French dampened to some extent the Polish elation at the conclusion of the political alliance. The Poles felt that they had been exploited, and to an extent they had been. But eventually they went along. Although the economic agreement took a full year to conclude and, technically, the political alliance and military convention would not take effect until the economic agreement was signed, both France and Poland during the interim acted as if they were in force. The Polish people, including the Right-wing majority in the Sejm, were overjoyed with the alliance; they believed that the French alliance practically guaranteed Poland's safety against Germany, regarded by most Poles as their most dangerous potential enemy.

The one neighbor with which Poland enjoyed a completely cordial relationship was Rumania. The two countries had no border disputes and no economic rivalries. Both nations had long borders with Soviet Russia and both felt menaced by the Soviets. This community of interest was heightened by the fact that Rumania occupied Bessarabia, which the Russians claimed. Rumania viewed Poland as a large and aggressive neighbor that could be counted upon to honor any treaty obligations in the event of a Soviet attack upon Rumania. Poland viewed Rumania in much the same way.

The outcome of this mutual regard was a treaty that was signed in Bucharest on March 3, 1921. It was a short agreement, consisting of only eight articles. The essence of the agreement was spelled out in the first article, which read: "Poland and Rumania undertake to assist each other in the event of their being the object of an unprovoked attack on their present eastern frontiers. Accordingly, if either State is the object of an unprovoked attack, the other shall consider itself in a state of war and shall render armed assistance."[3]

The combination of the treaty with France and the almost simultaneous agreement with Rumania, potentially the strongest nation in southeastern Europe, was generally regarded by Poles as a diplomatic triumph. Two powerful nations had sought Poland out and, as it was viewed in Poland, had asked it to enter into alliances that contributed greatly toward guaranteeing its borders against its most powerful enemies.

In this heady atmosphere of diplomatic success Poland went so far as to attempt to negotiate a treaty with Czechoslovakia. The matter was initiated in the summer of 1921 by the Czechs, who at French insistence were making a modest effort at a rapprochement with Poland. The fact that the Czech overtures got any hearing at all in Warsaw was astonishing, because the Poles had not forgotten their grievance in the matter of Teschen nor had they forgotten how the Czechs had choked off the transit of munitions to Poland during the Polish-Soviet War only the year before.

But now in Warsaw there was a new face at the foreign ministry and a new approach in Polish diplomacy. In June 1921 Konstanty Skirmunt, a diplomat and politician of the moderate Right, succeeded Prince Sapieha as Polish foreign minister. Skirmunt had been Polish minister to Italy, and there he had observed how foreign diplomats regarded Poland. He had been disturbed by what he had learned. He saw that such episodes as the Polish seizure of Wilno, the incorporation of Central Lithuania, the Upper Silesian Insurrections and, indeed, the events leading to the outbreak of the Polish-Soviet War had all combined to give Poland an unfortunate international reputation. In the foreign offices of the major powers of the world, Poland was regarded as being adventurist, imperialistic, and prone to point-of-the-bayonet conduct of its affairs. Skirmunt was determined to improve the Polish international image. Poland was now an established nation and must behave like one. Nothing would demonstrate this new Polish moderation like the conclusion of a pact with Czechoslovakia. In the end Skirmunt nearly pulled it off. During the summer and fall of 1921 he succeeded in negotiating a rather detailed commercial treaty with Czechoslovakia, followed by a rather vague but significant political agreement that was known as the Beneš-Skirmunt Pact. In foreign capitals the treaty was acclaimed as the harbinger of a new day in international relations in which leaders of good will could calm inflamed national prejudices. But this elation was premature. The treaty still had to be ratified by both parliaments, and the Polish Sejm was hostile to it. Piłsudski himself was absolutely opposed to the treaty; he regarded it as a repudiation of his policies and an insult to Polish honor. He pointed out that the clause in the treaty under which each nation guaranteed the other's frontiers had the effect of confirming Czechoslovakia's title to Teschen—a condition that very few Poles were willing to concede. Realizing that he had underestimated opposition to his treaty, Skirmunt delayed submitting the treaty for ratification until a more propitious moment. The Czechs, who could have created a favorable climate by handing over a little village of four hundred persons, mostly Polish, on the frontier in the Tatra Mountains, refused to make this absurdly small concession. In the meantime, however, the Treaty of Rapallo was signed, and as its Polish sequel Skirmunt was removed as foreign minister. As a result the Beneš-Skirmunt Pact, which might have been the most important treaty that independent Poland could have concluded, was never submitted for parliamentary ratification. Relations between the two neighbors simply drifted along in an atmosphere of dislike and distrust, with Poland awaiting the moment that it could retaliate for the Teschen affair.

The Treaty of Rapallo of 1922 was really only an accident that took place during a theoretically more important treaty meeting— the European Economic Conference at Genoa. This Conference had been called by the major Allied powers to normalize relations between themselves and the "outcast" nations of Europe—Germany and Soviet Russia. A secondary objective of the Conference was the final determination of the amount of reparations payments that Germany would be required to make. The British, who were the principal sponsors of the Conference, let it be known that they hoped to lead the conferees into sweeping agreements in the general matters of reconstruction and security. Almost every European nation was invited to attend the Conference, which convened on April 10, 1922.

The principal Polish objective at Genoa was to obtain the blessing of the major Allies on Poland's Treaty of Riga frontiers. This was a very important matter to the Poles, and Foreign Minister Skirmunt made careful preparation for the presentation of the Polish case. All the preparation was wasted, however. During the first four days of the Conference the Germans and Russians, both of whom had been promised that they would be greeted on terms of friendship and equality, found that they were in fact being held at arm's length, while the wartime victors closeted themselves for extended private discussions. The Germans, in particular, suspected that the Allies intended to offer Russia a special treaty under which the Allies would compel Germany to make extensive reparations payments to Russia. The Soviets expected that if this occurred, the Allies would set various unacceptable requirements of them. The result of the suspicion and hostility thus engendered was that the Germans and Russians met privately on Easter Sunday, April 16, 1922, in Rapallo, a pleasant village on the coast about sixteen miles southeast of Genoa.

The next day, the Allies learned to their stupefaction that Germany and Soviet Russia had signed an agreement of their own at Rapallo. Under its terms, Russia renounced all reparations claims upon Germany. In return, Germany waived all claims for repayment for German property nationalized by the Communists in Russia. The two nations agreed to enter into commercial relations and to commence full-scale diplomatic exchange. On the face of it, the Treaty of Rapallo (which, incidentally, broke up the Genoa Conference) was not particularly menacing. But it was suspected that a secret military alliance was part of this pact. To the Allies, it came as an absolute bombshell. To the rage of the Allies, Germany and Russia had shown that they had a certain community of interest that they intended to explore and exploit. The French were infuriated at what was regarded as the duplicity of Russia and Germany. In Paris there was serious discussion regarding the possibility of military mobilization. Lloyd George, who had personally promoted the Genoa meeting, was profoundly embarrassed.

But to the Poles, Rapallo represented much more than a loss of face. This rapprochement between Poland's two powerful neighbors was terrifying. The Polish fear was not simply the result of national self-absorption or paranoia. Even if there were no secret clause written into the Rapallo Treaty, it was obvious that the agreement opened the way to future German-Soviet cooperation in economic, military and political fields. Most of the other nations in Central Europe regarded the treaty as being in large part directed at Poland. One nation, Finland, viewed Poland's post-Rapallo future as so doubtful that it declined to ratify a Baltic nations treaty that included Poland.

Reaction in Poland was divided. The press noted that Foreign Minister Skirmunt had made an extremely favorable impression upon the major Allied powers at Genoa. His charm, tact and gentility were everywhere remarked. But there were other Poles, and Piłsudski was foremost among them, who observed that for all of Skirmunt's affability, Allied confirmation of Poland's eastern frontiers had not been discussed at Genoa. In certain quarters the conviction hardened that Skirmunt was not nearly tough enough for his job—and that the cabinet of Prime Minister Antoni Ponikowski in which Skirmunt served shared responsibility for this diplomatic defeat. Therefore the Ponikowski government was induced to resign in June 1922.

The departure of the Ponikowski cabinet meant that Poland had experienced more than a half dozen governments in less than four years. Although Poland had a number of national successes to its credit during the brief period since independence, its political life was not one of them. Basic to the whole problem was the disorderly, selfish and frequently corrupt manner in which Polish politics of this period were conducted. Perhaps little more could be expected of a nation whose only previous experiences in self-government had been the riotous Sejms of the pre-Partition era. To an extent, the parliament of the new Poland conducted itself in a manner similar to that of its predecessors. There was the same inability to compromise. There was the same refusal to share authority that had historically resulted in the crippling of the Polish monarchy. There was the same reluctance to unite, even in the face of near catastrophe, and there was the same selfishness that, although joined with other nobler qualities, had been a notable characteristic of the old Polish gentry. These political failings should not, probably, have been surprising, because the majority of the members of the new Sejm sprang from the old gentry. Like flies in amber, their political attitudes and habits had been preserved, to the detriment of the new Poland.

It would certainly not be correct to say that all Polish politicians were corrupt, but it would surely be fair to say that there was a high degree of corruption in Polish political life. Poland had been ruled for so long by other nations that the Poles had come to consider any government a hostile and alien body, the cheating of which was patriotic duty. This attitude did not disappear with the creation of an independent Poland; rather it seemed to be reinforced by the extraordinary number of opportunities for corrupt practices.

The easiest way for enrichment at public expense was through import licenses. Almost from the beginning of Polish independence, the government had attempted to control the entire national economy. Licenses were required to import and to export goods. The number of such licenses was, of course, limited. The result was that the possessor of one of these authorizations, particularly an import license, was practically guaranteed a substantial profit. The political party in control of a government ministry that issued such licenses could reward its friends in a most tangible manner. In any Polish cabinet, each major political party clamored for the right to control one or more ministries, which promptly became bastions for patronage and the issuance of export and import licenses. All too often the cabinet members who headed these ministries regarded themselves less as parts of a national government than as defenders of their party's privileges.

Some of the political parties could be surprisingly sophisticated in their peculations. For example, in 1921, the Piast Peasant Party succeeded in placing one of its officials as chairman of a government commission on land-reform administration. In the course of his duties, the chairman supervised the purchase by the Polish state of the extensive Dojlidy estates in Pomerania. Soon afterward, in August 1921, he authorized their resale to the Bank Ludowy for the bargain price of seventy-five million marks. The bank, which was owned by the Piast Peasant Party, immediately resold the Dojlidy estates for a windfall profit of five times what it had paid the government. When the circumstances of this fraudulent undervaluation of the Dojlidy properties became known, they were considered remarkable chiefly for the fact that the scheme had been engineered by the Piast Peasant Party, which was generally thought not to possess persons technically competent to pull off a complicated financial swindle. Very few Poles were surprised by the swindle itself.

Land sales and import licenses were not the only avenues of reward for the Pole with good political connections. Similar opportunities were found in government land and forest leases, military supply contracts, and licenses for the sale of tobacco and alcohol. Bribes to obtain these contracts and concessions were so widespread that investigation was impossible. Every political party was guilty to some degree and a situation arose whereby no party could even demand the housecleaning of a ministry controlled by another party, lest that party retaliate in kind. In fact, members of the Sjem frequently extorted favors from cabinet ministers in exchange for their *not* asking questions in parliament which the minister would find embarrassing.

Much of Poland's political corruption could have been prevented by a well-trained civil service. But only in Austrian Galicia had Poles served at management levels in the civil administrations of prewar

Poland. Therefore there was no Polish tradition of integrity and efficiency in public office. Instead, every government operation such as the railroads, postal service, and arms factories quickly became choked with an excess of workers at every level. The state bureaucracy swelled with persons whose jobs were the result of political connections. Wire-pulling and jobbery were constant features of the immature Polish political system. The average Polish citizen, and certainly Polish businessmen, believed that political connections, and consequently payoffs, were absolutely necessary if one were to do business with any government ministry. There was an almost total lack of public confidence in the willingness of the Polish courts to mete out impartial justice when a well-connected defendant was on trial. The Polish press, as partisan and vociferous as the politicians, fell viciously on each fresh instance of opposition malfeasance and thereby enlarged the public impression of corruption.

General confidence in the Polish political system was also diminished by the frequent and confusing changes of government. In the first three and a half years of Polish independence there were seven separate cabinets, and few of them were capable of withstanding the most modest crisis. The government of Jedrzej Moraczewski, which had taken office in November 1918, was replaced in January 1919 by the generally nonparty cabinet led by Paderewski. This government fell in December 1919, because of the Sejm's disappointment with Paderewski's leadership. The Leopold Skulski ministry, which followed, was another nonparty government. In practical terms, "nonparty" meant that enough reluctant votes could be scraped together in the Sejm to establish the government, but not enough could be found to maintain it once there was any real crisis or once a large enough block of deputies began to believe that they might be able to replace the government with one dominated by their own party. This was the essential weakness of Polish politics. There was not any single party, or even any group of closely allied parties, that could create and maintain a sufficient working majority in the Sejm. As a result, Skulski's ministry fell in June 1920 and was replaced by the cabinet headed by Władisław Grabski, which lasted only one month.

Grabski's successor, Wincenty Witos, created the Government of National Union, which weathered the critical moments of the Polish-Soviet War but collapsed after a financial crisis in September 1921. The cabinet which followed was headed by Antoni Ponikowski, a distinguished educator, who put together a nonparty government after it became evident that none of the political parties in the Sejm was willing to undertake ministerial responsibility for raising taxes—an obvious necessity at the time. Not unnaturally, a cabinet established on such a negative foundation could not survive very long, and it was brought down in March 1922.

But at this point, the Sejm was like the dog that has chased a moving train and caught up with it. The Ponikowski ministry had been voted out, but what were they going to do to replace it? Five days were spent in debate before the Sejm returned the Ponikowski ministry to office. Since this "new" cabinet contained practically the same persons, it could not be anticipated that it would survive much longer than before. During its second tenure there occurred the frightening Rapallo affair, a prolonged conflict over army pay, and a continuing wrangle with the Sejm over a new election law. Finally, on June 2, 1922, Piłsudski summoned Ponikowski and his cabinet. He spoke to them and made no secret of his displeasure with Foreign Minister Skirmunt's tactics of moderation and conciliation. Piłsudski obliquely suggested that the government should resign. That very afternoon Ponikowski and his cabinet submitted their resignations.

This was a landmark occasion in the political history of Poland. Never before had Piłsudski as Chief of State suggested a government's resignation. Never before had it been suggested that a cabinet served at the pleasure of the Chief of State. The Sejm deputies from the Right and Center parties were enraged at these developments. Seeking to assert their authority over Piłsudski, they voted in a third Ponikowski ministry, but then found that Ponikowski, apparently intimidated by the Chief of State, refused to take office. In great confusion, the Sejm was unable to agree upon a candidate, and it was finally left up to Piłsudski to select a new prime minister. He appointed a friend, Artur Śliwiński, who was accepted by a very close vote in the Sejm. Śliwiński's ministry lasted less than two weeks, falling on July 7, 1922. For nearly three weeks the Sejm debated the matter of Śliwiński's successor. At one time it appeared that they might vote in Wojciech Korfanty, the hero of the Upper Silesian insurrections. But Piłsudski intervened with enough strength to block his election.

Poland was now in a political turmoil. The Left declared a general strike. The Right mounted a vicious newspaper attack on Piłsudski and proposed a motion of no-confidence in the Chief of State; it failed by a vote of 205 to 187. Eventually, in late July, the Sejm permitted Piłsudski to take the initiative in selecting a ministry. He proposed Julian Nowak, a professor at Kraków University, who formed the usual nonparty government with the usual lack of support in the Sejm. And there the matter rested for the time. The whole political passage at arms commencing with the fall of the Ponikowski ministry had been a victory for Piłsudski. The deputies of the Sejm were enraged at the Chief of State's successful incursion into their area of authority. But they consoled themselves with the belief that the powers that Piłsudski had assumed would revert to them when the new Polish Constitution came into effect.

It will be recalled that in February 1919 the Sejm voted a brief declaration in which it established itself as the "sovereign and legislative authority of the State of Poland" and entrusted to Piłsudski the office of Chief of State. This declaration, known as the Little Constitution, was intended to be a stopgap instrument pending the imminent creation of a constitution. But, because of the war and domestic turmoil of the following months, the new constitution was not completed until early 1921. It was approved by the Sejm on March 17, 1921, having been pushed through by the Right and Center against the opposition of the Left. Under the new constitution the Polish parliament became bicameral. The lower house was the Sejm and the upper house the Senate. The number of senators was fixed at 111. There were to be 444 deputies to the Sejm. Senators and Deputies were to be elected for a period of five years. Only the Sejm had the power to initiate legislation. The Senate's authority was confined to a limited veto power, and its powers were so circumscribed that its duties could be considered mostly ceremonial.

The actual administration of the Polish state was to be handled by a cabinet, which was referred to as "the government" or, more formally, the Council of Ministers. The cabinet was headed by a prime minister, formally known as the President of the Council of Ministers.

The prime minister and his cabinet were to be appointed by the President of the Republic, but the Sejm could refuse to accept a prime minister or any member of his cabinet by simple majority vote and thus prevent the President's nominees from taking office.

Similarly, by simple majority vote the Sejm could at any time dismiss from office either an entire incumbent government or any individual cabinet minister.

The various other powers of the Polish parliament were extensive and clearly spelled out. Only the parliament had the power to make laws, approve the national budget, fix the size of the armed forces, control the currency and authorize borrowing. The judiciary system was denied the right "to challenge the validity of Statutes legally promulgated"—which, of course, meant that the courts could not strike down any legislation as unconstitutional.

The Polish constitution had been written by two men who were both prominent members of Right-wing parties. One was Edward Dubanowicz, a lawyer, professor, and National Christian Party Sejm deputy. The other was Kazimierz Lutosławski, a Dominican priest, who was a National Democratic Sejm deputy. Their parties were, of course, Piłsudski's adversaries.

The Right's fear of Piłsudski showed most clearly in the constitutional provisions dealing with the duties and privileges of the President of the Polish Republic. Dubanowicz and Lutosławski had drafted the constitution under the assumption that Piłsudski would be elected president. Therefore their constitution made this office almost entirely ceremonial. To begin with, the President was not to be popularly elected. He was voted into office by the Sejm and the Senate, meeting jointly as a National Assembly for the occasion. Although the president appointed the Council of Ministers, this gave him little power in the government, since these ministers served at the pleasure of the Sejm. And although the President promulgated legislation and signed executive decrees, these duties were mostly just formalities. All legislation emanated from the Sejm, and all executive decrees had to be countersigned by a minister who could be removed from office at any time by the Sejm. The President possessed no veto power and no power of legislative initiative. Even the President's power to dissolve the Sejm for new elections, a customary feature of parliamentary governments, was severely limited. The President could only dissolve the Sejm with the concurrence of three fifths of the Senate, which thereupon had to dissolve itself. In practice, this meant that the President had virtually no dissolution authority. Finally, in a provision aimed directly at Piłsudski, the President was specifically prohibited from taking command of the Army in time of war.

Polish politicians were fond of saying that the Constitution of March 17, 1921, had the best features of both Western European parliamentarianism and American democracy. But this was nonsense. There was no authentic separation of powers in the Polish government. All authority flowed from the Sejm. The deputies of the Sejm had seen to it that they were virtually omnipotent. Even the Senate was practically powerless. Under the best of political circumstances, the Polish constitution of 1912 would have been a poor one. And given the jobbery, partisanship, fractionalization and corruption that characterized the Sejm at this stage of Polish political development, this constitution was clearly a deeply flawed document.

The Constitution was approved in the spring of 1921, but it did not go into effect until November 1923. This delay occurred because the new Constitution required that the present Sejm dissolve itself. Elections then had to be held for the Sejm as well as for the newly created Senate. A large number of existing deputies were reluctant to submit to the hazard of an election, and so the process was almost scandalously delayed on one pretext or another. When the elections finally did take place, the results did not significantly alter the political makeup of the previous Sejm. The National Democrats,* running in combination with the smaller parties of the Right, elected nearly 40 percent of the deputies. The parties of the Center, dominated by Witos's Left-Centrist Piast Peasant Party, received nearly 20 percent of the vote. The Left, consisting in the main of the Populist (Liberation) Peasant Party and the Socialist Party, also won about 20 percent of the seats. Thus the Sejm would continue to be dominated by the Right in alliance with certain Centrist elements. The Left, which was much more fractionalized and loosely organized than its opposition, could prevail only in exceptional circumstances when it was able to offer a program that attracted the support of all of the Center as well as of the various new political groups that appeared for the first time in this Sejm. These new parties were the so-called "minorities clubs" that had come into existence to represent the nation's principal non-Polish ethnic groups—Ukrainians, Belorussians, Germans and Jews. These clubs

* In early 1919 the National Democratic Party was renamed the National Populist Party. This name never captured the public imagination, and the party changed its title several times in subsequent years. For the purpose of clarity in this work, the party and its members will be referred to as the National Democrats, which is what most Poles called them.

had succeeded in electing more than eightly deputies, 20 percent of
the Sejm membership, and they frequently voted as a bloc. The support of these minority parties was to become essential in the making of any ministry or the passage of any significant legislation. As
this came to be recognized, the minorities commanded a higher and
higher price for their support.

The makeup of the Polish Senate was similar to that of the Sejm.
Out of the one hundred and eleven senatorial seats, the Right won
forty-nine. The Center held twenty and the Left fifteen. The National
Minorities elected twenty-seven senators, which gave them a swing-
vote position of even greater strength than that which they enjoyed
in the lower house.

Apart from the appearance of the National Minorities parties, the
election of November 1922 contained another novelty, the importance of which was not appreciated at the time. In this election,
no fewer than seventeen separate political parties had succeeded in
winning seats in the Sejm or the Senate. The difficulties inherent in
this fractionalization of the Polish political system, a trend that was
increasing, were not generally recognized. Most of these newer parties
were presently small and inconsequential. But it would not take
long for this multiplication of parties, programs, and leaders to sap
the strength of the major groups. By 1926 there would be ninety-two
registered political parties in Poland, and thirty of them were represented in the Sejm.

The newly elected Polish parliament met in its opening session on
November 28, 1922. Within ten days it had completed its internal
organization and was prepared to turn its attention to the task of
electing a president of the Polish Republic. A number of candidates
had been mentioned in the Warsaw press, but no one doubted that
Piłsudski would be elected. The parties of the Right might consider him an enemy, but there was no possibility that the parliament
could refuse to elect this towering figure in Polish life to the presidency. After all, he was the man who had established and then saved
the nation, the First Marshal of the Army, the nation's first chief of
state, and the "grandfather" of the common people. For Piłsudski
not to have been elected president would have been considered a
national scandal.

But, in the last days of November, rumors were reported in the
press that Piłsudski would refuse to run. At first these were regarded
as absurd. The general view was that Piłsudski could no more refuse

to run than parliament could refuse to elect him. But on December 4 it became known that the stories of Piłsudski's refusal to stand for election were more than just rumors. Piłsudski thanked his supporters but he refused to become what he regarded as being the figleaf of the Sejm. He declined to be a candidate for a virtually powerless office that he called a "gilded cage."[4] He would retain only the post of chairman of the Inner War Council, which carried with it the designation of commander in chief in time of war.

Piłsudski's announcement threw the election into a turmoil. On December 9, when parliament met to elect the president of the Republic, there were five candidates. The most prominent of these were Count Maurycy Zamojski, a wealthy National Democrat diplomat, and Gabriel Narutowicz. Narutowicz was fifty-seven years old, a former professor and more lately a minister of public works and then foreign minister in the short-lived Śliwiński and Nowak cabinets. He was a sympathizer (although not a member) of the Populist (Liberation) Peasant Party, the more radical of the peasant parties, and thus he was considered a Leftist candidate. Narutowicz was known to be a close friend of Marshal Piłsudski.

Zamojski led in the first round of balloting but did not receive the necessary majority. The election gradually resolved itself into a day-long contest between Zamojski and Narutowicz. Finally, on the fifth ballot, the crucial minorities parties swung over to Narutowicz. At this the Piast Peasant Party indicated its unwillingness to support Zamojski, Poland's largest landowner, and the combination of the Left, the peasants and the minorities prevailed. Narutowicz was elected president of the Polish Republic by a vote of 289 to 227.

Very few events illustrate so well the viciously partisan character of Polish politics as the treatment given to Gabriel Narutowicz upon his accession to the presidency. The bitterness that the Right bore him was most intense. It was one thing for them to have to accept Piłsudski; it was quite another to have to accept Narutowicz, whom they regarded as Piłsudski's puppet. In particular, the National Democrats and their friends were enraged at the fact that Narutowicz had been elected with the support of the non-Polish nationalities parties. The day following Narutowicz's election the National Democrats announced that in the future they would give no support to any government "created by a President imposed by foreign nationalities: Jews, Germans and Ukrainians."[5] Father Lutosławski demanded in a party newspaper, "How could the Jews dare to impose their

President upon us?"[6] The Right took up a new cry—"Narutowicz, the President of the Jews."[7]

On December 11, Narutowicz took his oath of fidelity to the constitution. Although this was a major state event, most of the deputies and senators from the Right refused to attend it. Stones were thrown at Narutowicz's automobile as he was on his way to his inauguration. The fury of the Right was heightened by Narutowicz's inaugural speech, in which he announced a certain fealty to his "illustrious predecessor Marshal Piłsudski" and stated that he intended to "follow faithfully Piłsudski's policy of peace, justice and impartiality toward all Polish citizens, without distinction of origin or opinion."[8] Threats were made on Narutowicz's life, and Minister of the Interior Antoni Kamienski resigned, claiming that the police at his disposal were insufficient for him to accept the responsibility of protecting the President. Apart from Kamienski, however, very few people expressed concern about the President's safety. Assassinations of Poles by Poles were thought to be alien to the national character.

On December 16, only five days after his inauguration, Gabriel Narutowicz made one of his first ceremonial appearances as President of the Polish Republic—the official opening of the annual winter exhibition of paintings at Warsaw's Palace of Fine Arts. Accompanied only by a couple of aides, the President arrived at the institution punctually at noon. Narutowicz was greeted at the entrance by the institute's president and in his company formally opened the exhibition. There were already a number of invited dignitaries present in the hall.

Narutowicz spent a few minutes viewing the paintings and sculptures. He was standing in front of a large winterscape by a Polish artist when Sir William Max-Miller, the British minister to Poland, strode up to pay his respects. This was the first opportunity that Max-Miller had had to compliment Narutowicz upon his election to the Polish presidency. "My congratulations, Excellency," Max-Miller said. With a smile, Narutowicz replied, "You should offer me your condolences instead." There was now a group of perhaps a half dozen persons gathered before the painting. Three loud popping noises were heard. The source of the sounds was obscured by the acoustics of the large gallery. Without a moan or cry, the President fell to the marble floor. He had been hit by three pistol bullets. The British minister collapsed in a faint. The astounded bystanders looked up and, about twelve feet away, saw a conventionally dressed man in his middle fifties. He held a pistol in his right hand. He pointed it at the ceiling and announced, "I won't shoot anymore." Guards grabbed his weapon and seized him. All of this took only a moment or two, but Narutowicz, shot in the heart, lay dead on the marble floor.[9]

The man who had killed Narutowicz was quickly identified as Eligiusz Niewiadomski, a fairly well-known Polish painter, art professor and critic. Although not a member of the National Democratic Party, Niewiadomski was an extreme nationalist and an anti-Semite. He had shot Narutowicz because he had been elected president with the help of Jewish minority party votes and because Niewiadomski regarded Narutowicz as being a tool of Piłsudski, whom Niewiadomski hated.

Niewiadomski, who was not mentally sound, had acted entirely alone in murdering the Polish President. But at first no one knew that. In the hours immediately following the assassination it was suspected that this might be the commencement of a widespread series of political murders that would culminate in an attempted coup by the Right. Most of Poland's important political figures quickly gathered at the official residence of Prime Minister Nowak to discuss what should be done to suppress any unrest. Political assassination had been virtually unknown in Polish history, and this act had left everyone in a state of shock. Maciej Rataj, who as Marshal of the Sejm became provisional President under the terms of the constitution, strode about the ministerial offices, with clenched fists pressed to his head. Piłsudski was asked to come to the meeting, and when he arrived his appearance shocked everyone present. Even those who had served under him in every kind of wartime trial had never seen him so grief-torn or horror-struck.

The assassination had occurred at an awkward political moment. Under the Polish constitution, the prime minister and his cabinet were required to present their resignations to a newly elected President, and Nowak and his government had done so two days before. But no new cabinet had yet been selected, and so the Nowak government remained, serving in a caretaker capacity. It was clearly a matter of extreme urgency for Poland to have a government, and at Piłsudski's suggestion Rataj immediately named as prime minister the forty-one-year-old General Władysław Sikorski. Piłsudski was given Sikorski's previous office as army chief of staff. This willing collaboration between these two men who disliked each other intensely is testimony to the atmosphere of crisis that existed at this moment. Nonetheless, at this moment Piłsudski supported the young general whom he disliked but recognized as one of the most brilliant men of his generation in Poland. Sikorski at once took over the government, assumed the office of minister of the interior, moved detachments of troops into Warsaw, and declared a state of martial law. Sikorski met with the leaders of every political party and did not hesitate to warn the National Democrats that in the event of any public disturbance he would use troops to suppress it, "not distinguishing between guilty and innocent."[10] These rapid, decisive actions had their intended effect. There was no further assassination, no demonstration, and no riot. Official spokesmen for every political party denounced the assassination. Only four days after the murder, parliament was able to hold a new election for the presidency. The same coalition of Left, Center and minority parties that had elected Narutowicz now elected Stanisław Wojciechowski, a moderate Peasant Party leader, as president. He was elected on the first vote and was sworn in without incident.

However, this tranquillity was only skin-deep. The antagonisms and tensions that had indirectly produced the assassination of Narutowicz still remained. And they all came to the surface again when, on December 29, 1922, Niewiadomski was put on trial for the murder. The assassin exploited every opportunity to make lengthy statements extolling nationalism and accusing Piłsudski of having arranged the election of Narutowicz with the help of decadent and disloyal minorities. As the trial developed, and it lasted for two weeks, the political atmosphere changed. Standing in court before his judges, Niewiadowski contrived to cut a lonely, proud and courageous figure. Instead of regarding him as a fanatic and a murderer, a number of Poles began to view the assassin as a man of honor who was sacrificing his life for the ideal of Polish nationalism. These sympathizers were, of course, almost exclusively members of the Right-wing parties. But there were many of them, and their numbers seemed to grow every day. The Right-wing newspapers ran lengthy and generally favorable biographies of the accused.

By the time Niewiadomski was found guilty and sentenced to death, a very considerable segment of the Polish public had managed to forget that he had murdered an admirable man in cold blood. He had become a kind of hero. It did no good for Piłsudski, appalled at this development, to issue a moving eulogy of the assassinated Narutowicz. Likewise, President Wojciechowski could not still this disgraceful phenomenon by his statement when he received the trial transcript and was asked for clemency. "I have examined the files," Wojciechowski announced, "and I cannot find either in them or in my soul any reason to alter the court's verdict."

On January 31, 1923, Eligiusz Niewiadomski was shot by an army firing squad at the Citadel in Warsaw. Dramatic to the end, he carried a single rose in his hand and refused the blindfold, saying, "I will remain quiet. Shoot me in the head and heart. I am dying for Poland which Piłsudski has destroyed."[11]

The Right wing made Niewiadomski's funeral a political event, complete with speeches and flags. Expressions of respect for Niewiadomski by some members of the Right did not end with the assassin's funeral. In the space of only a few months, more than three hundred babies baptized in Warsaw were given the uncommon name Eligiusz, in honor of the assassin. His grave became a sort of nationalist shrine. The majority of Poles found this to be disgusting and disgraceful. It had a particularly forceful effect upon Piłsudski. During Niewiadomski's trial it had become clear from testimony that the assassin would have preferred to have shot Piłsudski himself. It was equally evident that substantial portions of the membership of the National Democratic Party and its associated parties would have been pleased at such an event. If there had been a gulf between Piłsudski and the Right-wing parties, there was now a chasm. As Piłsudski viewed it, the Right had supported the murder of his friend, and they would have applauded his own assassination. The Marshal's close associates now detected a subtle but definite alteration in his view of Poland's people and their future. Piłsudski had begun to speculate—what manner of people were these?

9

Land and Money

THE BULK OF POLAND'S POPULATION lived on the land. Scattered about the Polish countryside were countless small farming villages and random groups of houses assembled into remote settlements that had no names. All of these hamlets had a certain similarity. The houses were one-story wooden structures with thatch or wood-shingle roofs. Typically, each house had three rooms, one of which was a kitchen with a brick stove; the other two rooms were for sleeping. The furniture was sparse. The beds for the family were generally broad wooden seats that jutted out from the walls. The floors were made of planks and, to save the cost of glass, there were few windows. The only adornment, generally, was religious pictures that hung on the walls. Behind or alongside these little houses were cottage gardens in which the occupants grew much of their own produce. A well, a pig pen, and a small barn for a horse and one or two cows usually completed the establishment.

In the early 1920s probably about 70 percent of the nation's people could be classified as being dependent on agriculture for their livelihood, and most of these were members of the peasant class. There was nothing pretty about peasant life in Poland. The peasants had little education. (Official figures put the level of illiteracy among rural Poles in 1921 at almost 40 percent.)[1] A peasant community usually had no school, only a small store, and perhaps a little church. In the winter many peasants came close to starvation in their remote, muddy villages. Whether they worked as laborers for large landowners or owned land themselves, the peasants lived a life of the most ferocious economy. The peasants who worked for landowners on a regular basis could not earn enough to survive. Peasant families supplemented their incomes in countless additional ways: they collected nuts in the forests, picked mushrooms, fished, cut firewood, and collected honey. But despite the harsh conditions of their lives, the Polish peasants clung to the soil with a sort of gluelike adhesion, stoically enduring the most awful privations.

Either the peasants worked cruelly long hours for little reward or they did not work at all, for one of the curses of peasant life was overpopulation. There were simply far too many peasants. Poland's birth rate was the highest in Europe. During the years 1922–1926 the population increased at an explosive annual rate of sixteen per thousand. Most of this increase was attributable to the large peasant families, and these rural children were largely uneducated and without technical skills. If young peasant men went to the cities to seek work, they were the last to be hired and the first to be let go. So they came back to the land and married early, and their children were born into a still bleaker world. It is estimated that in the 1920s the rural population of Poland was about 15 million, and of this number between four and five million could be termed surplus. In other words, the same amount of agricultural produce could have been raised by about a third fewer persons.[2]

But this overpopulation problem did not deter the peasants in their consuming ambition—to own land. "Land hunger" obsessed the peasants and frequently led them further into their morass. The desire to possess their own land was so great that peasants would pay almost anything to obtain it, including prices far higher than the land's economic value. And then they did very foolish things with it, particularly in Eastern Europe. As opposed to the custom in, say, England, where land was usually inherited entirely by the oldest son, the Polish peasant left his land to be divided up among his children. It did not take long for this practice to fractionalize even a sizable farmstead into a series of unconnected strips of land scattered here and there or else a single plot too small to support a family.

The end result of land fragmentation through inheritance is known as "dwarf holdings." A dwarf holding was a property of less than five acres. Given the conditions of Polish agriculture—poor soil and backward agricultural methods—it was impossible for a family to make a living from such a plot. In fact, a Polish peasant family probably could not support itself on a plot of less than twelve acres—although among more efficient farmers, as for example, in Denmark, a plot of that size would have made its owner prosperous.

Polish agriculture was dominated by farms that were too small. In 1921 there were about 3.3 million separate farmsteads in Poland. Of these, approximately 2.1 million were less than twelve acres and therefore capable of providing only a subsistence, if that, for their owners. About a million more farms ranged from twelve to thirty acres, and their owners were just getting by. About 75,000 farms were from 50 to 125 acres, while only 30,000 farms were more than 125 acres.[3]

The combination of these factors—land hunger, overpopulation, dwarf holdings, and agricultural inefficiency—conspired to create an atmosphere of constant rural discontent. The Polish peasants were politically unsophisticated and inclined to give their support to the politician or party that made the most extravagant promises. If the peasants had not been by nature so conservative, they might have become a revolutionary menace. But socialism had no attraction for these people, dedicated as they were to the principle of personal land ownership. They were, however, recognized as a huge voting bloc whose desires ought to be satisfied and who, if they could be made to prosper, would lead the way to general prosperity in the nation.

There were a number of ways to attempt to solve the problems of the East European peasants: attracting them off the land by increased industrialization or emigration; improving their productivity by teaching them more advanced farming technology; or giving them extra income through the development of cottage industries. Poland tried these strategies but met with little success. The peasants' main interest remained the acquisition of land. The peasant political parties demanded the passage of land-reform laws that would redistribute the land among their supporters. And because the peasant parties occupied much of the vital Center of the Sejm, their wishes had to be taken into account. The pressure was so intense that almost the first item of business to come before the first Polish parliament in 1919 was land reform. It was an awesome and complicated task. To make more land available to the peasant, there had to be plans and legislation covering the sale of government lands, the improvement of existing nonarable land, methods for compelling the sale of dwarf holdings so that farmsteads could be consolidated and, finally, the breaking-up of large estates and compulsory sale of their land to the peasants. It was this last that was the crucial issue. Depending on the locality, somewhere between 20 and 30 percent of the arable land in Poland was the property of a small number of large estate owners. Only by forcing the estate owners to sell off a good part of their lands could the peasants' land hunger be even partly satisfied.

The large landowners, most of whom were members of the Right-wing parties, vehemently protested the redistribution of their lands. Wealthy Poles were, by inclination and tradition, farmers. If most of their land was taken from them, how would they occupy themselves? Indeed, how would they be paid for their lands, since it was obvious that few peasant families had enough money to buy land outright. The major landowners had a good case: The problem of Polish agriculture was not that there were too many large farms, but that there were too many small ones. To further divide the land might assuage the peasants' land hunger, but only temporarily. They would remain inefficient farmers, and in the course of a couple of generations the land would be refractionalized and the peasantry would be back where they started. In any event, it was evident that there was not enough arable land in all of Poland to give a viable farm to every peasant family that wanted one.

But as logical a case as the large landowners presented, it was not good enough to prevent land redistribution—and it never would be. In a nation where about two and one-half million ballots, a quarter of the total vote, were cast for the peasant parties, the arguments of some sixteen thousand major proprietors could not possibly prevail. Land reform was *the* political issue in Poland. Gradually the great landowners came to realize this. The story of land redistribution in Poland became a series of hard-fought delaying actions by the major estate owners, who possessed political influence far greater than their numbers. They were powerful enough to stave off land reform for a while, but the time would come, and did come, when it was politically imperative that the parties of the Right have the support of the peasant parties. And the price of this support would be land reform. So the estate owners sought to delay the inevitable, while seeking to improve the terms under which they would eventually be compelled to give up their land. Their general tactic was to allow a series of ostensible land-reform measures that gave the appearance of progress without compelling actual distribution.

In July 1919 the Sejm passed an Agrarian Reform Resolution that declared land redistribution to be the policy of the state and generally set 250 acres as the maximum amount of land that could be held by a single owner. But there was no companion legislation passed to implement this resolution, and thus it remained an ineffective declaration of future intention. A year later, at the height of the Polish-Soviet War, the Sejm again addressed itself to land reform. To stimulate the peasants' support of the war, the Sejm now declared its previous resolution to have the force of a law. But still there was no legislation to determine exactly how and when the large estates were to be cut up and distributed.

The Polish Constitution of 1921 gave further lip service to land reform, but there still was no actual redistribution. Another two years passed during which the Right continued to block any real change. But by 1923 the peasants' insistence on land reform could not be resisted. It was this imperative demand of his followers that eventually drove Wincenty Witos, leader of the Piast Peasant Party, into accepting a compromise with the Right. In the spring of 1923 Witos and the National Democrats worked out the Lanckorona Pact, under which he agreed to accept a very modest program of land redistribution in return for National Democratic support. With this agreement, the way was cleared for the overthrow of the incumbent Sikorski government and the installation on May 28, 1923, of a coalition cabinet headed by Witos in his second appearance as prime minister.

But this cabinet did not last long. Witos created a ministry for agrarian reform and passed some minor legislation aimed at a feeble implementation of the Agrarian Reform Law of 1920. This was all the land reform that Witos's National Democratic cabinet associates would permit, and it was clearly not enough. The more radical Populist (Liberation) Peasant Party went into violent opposition. Even Witos's own Piast Peasants began to desert him, some seventeen of them going off in a bloc into opposition under the leadership of Dabski. By the end of 1923 Witos's personal support had become so eroded that he was forced to resign. His successor was Władysław Grabski, who was also forming his second cabinet.

During his two years in office, Grabski did as little as possible to implement land reform, but owing to constant prodding from the peasants and the Left, a start was made. In 1924 the State Agrarian Bank was established to finance peasants' land purchases, whenever legislation should be passed enabling them to do so. Finally, in late

1925 a new Agrarian Reform Law, this one with teeth in it, was drafted. It did not pass until December 1925, by which time Grabski was out of office. It is certainly the most debated, amended, and disputed piece of legislation ever to go through the Sejm. The large landowners fought it every step of the way, and when the fight was finished, the act was a crazy quilt of compromises. But it was workable. The law now provided that a landowner could retain a maximum of 450 acres, with exceptions made for lakes, forests, and certain regions in eastern Poland. The landowners themselves could determine which sections of their excess land they would sell to the peasantry, whose purchases were to be financed by the State Agrarian Bank. The peasants were required to pay 5 percent down and the rest over a forty-one–year period. An equitable repayment scheme was worked out to indemnify the owners, and the amount of land to be redistributed annually was limited to 500,000 acres.

Under this law, which was passed six years after the Sejm's first resolution, land redistribution gradually became a fact. In the years to come, about six and one half million acres were bought from large estates and formed into about 750,000 separate farms for sale to peasants. Under a companion program some 13.5 million acres of strip holdings and dwarf farms were bought up, consolidated into viable properties, and resold. A separate program of draining swamps and improving previously barren land produced an additional 1.5 million arable acres for distribution.

But these efforts did not solve the problems of Polish agriculture. Overpopulation on the land continued, and the large estate owners were proved correct in their claim that they were more efficient producers than any peasant farmer could ever be. The peasant proprietors had no money for fertilizers or for improvement of their land. They lacked advanced farming skills. Polish agricultural produce was only marginally competitive on the international market. The new peasant landowners found it as difficult as ever to make a living. The service on their debt was yet one more item added to the crushing burden of poverty they already carried. In fact, the ownership of land probably caused the progressive pauperization of the Polish peasantry. Nonetheless, given the situation, there was no other way to quiet the desperate land hunger of the majority of Poland's population. If they owned land, the Polish peasants were content, no matter what else might happen to them. And, at least they usually had enough to feed

themselves—which, during the difficult economic times of the early
1920s, made them better off than many of Poland's industrial workers.

Throughout the early 1920s, the economy of Poland was in an
appalling state. In fact, at times it seemed that the nation might collapse financially. From the outset there had been a ramshackle quality
to the Polish fiscal system. At the time of Poland's rebirth there was
no national currency. Seven different kinds of money, each depreciat-
ing rapidly, circulated in the new nation. (The currencies were German occupation marks, Polish paper marks, Austrian paper crowns,
and four kinds of rubles—Russian Imperial, Ober-Ost, Russian Provisional, and Soviet.) The closest approximation to a national bank
was the Polish State Loan Bank, which had been established by the
Germans in 1917. But the bank had no gold reserve, the Germans having taken it away with them, and its assets consisted of the bank's own
paper currency, loans of doubtful collectability, and advances to the
Polish government. The nation had no credit standing abroad, and
its commercial banking system was in such an administrative shambles that for some time it was not even possible for Polish Americans
to send money to their relatives in Poland.

The basis of the Polish economic problem lay, of course, in the
damage done during the World War. Although Poland was an agricultural nation that had historically been a food exporter, the farms
were so war-ravaged and the means of distribution so disorganized
that the nation was actually starving. Eleven million acres of previously cultivated land lay unused at the end of the war. As late as
1921 seven million tons of foodstuffs had to be imported to feed the
nation.

The manufacturing segment of the Polish economy was even more
dislocated. The wartime occupying nations had dismantled the huge
textile works at Łódz and Białystok and shipped the machinery to
their homelands. Similar treatment had been given to the foundries
and the oil industry in Galicia. The capital to rebuild these industries
did not exist in Poland, and so in 1920 Polish industrial activity had
sunk to 35 percent of its 1913 level. Nor did the complications end
with the wartime damage. The region that was now Poland had not
functioned as an economic unit before the war. Even though the
whole area was the basin of the Vistula River, and thus naturally unified, the partitioning powers had made sure that it did not operate as
a discrete entity. To be sure, the Polish regions had imported and

exported, but less than 10 percent of these imports and exports were *between* the Polish regions. Thus, an integrated "Polish economy" had to be organized.

The first step in developing a financial system in Poland was obviously to establish a currency and print money. It was decided that the monetary unit would be the Polish mark, the value of which was pegged to the German mark. The next step was to draw up a national budget. The first Polish full-year budget, for mid-1919 through mid-1920, called for an expenditure of 12 billion marks. But try as the finance ministry might, it could only come up with income of 1.6 billion marks. This set the pattern for budgets to come. Poland's expenses—including reconstruction costs, military costs, and the special costs of the Polish-Soviet War—continued to be enormous. Enough revenue could not be extracted from the economy to cover these costs. In the first years the gross imbalance in the Polish national budget was obscured and partly relieved by various windfalls. The American Relief Administration shipped vast quantities of food to Poland, and the U.S. Liquidation Board sent in a large part of the supplies left in France by the American Expeditionary Force.

By the middle of 1920 American aid ended and, in fact, none of it had been an outright gift. All the shipments had been sold to Poland on credit, with the result that the Polish government now owed the United States $160 million in 5 percent notes. Almost at once it was discovered that Poland could not pay even the interest, much less repay any part of the capital.

Every attempt to increase revenue to cover expenditures failed. The Polish government levied taxes on everything in sight—imports, exports, luxuries, necessities and incomes. But there was great difficulty in collecting these taxes, partly because tax evasion had historically seemed a patriotic duty to Poles, who did not much alter their habits now that their nation was independent.

There were a host of other financial problems. Although successive governments made sporadic attempts to manage the economy at every level, they lacked the ability to do much more than confuse things. In 1918 there had been too few commercial banks, but by 1921 there were suddenly too many, almost all inadequately capitalized. So, too, was the Polish State Loan Bank, which remained the closest approximation to a national bank that the nation had.

Germany contributed to the continuing Polish financial crisis. Beginning in 1920 and accelerating after 1924, Germany implemented a

policy of economic harassment aimed at Poland. It was effective because, whereas the Polish market was not particularly important to
Germany, the German market was vital to the Poles. In 1923 more
than half of Poland's exports went to Germany, while less than 3.5
percent of Germany's total exports went into Polish markets. Thus,
Germany could harass Poland by raising tariffs on Polish goods or
requiring special licenses to import Polish items without worrying
about any Polish retaliation. The impact upon Poland of this German economic warfare was considerable. And when, in 1925, Germany abruptly ceased to buy Upper Silesian coal, the effect was
almost catastrophic.

All of this combined to unbalance every Polish budget from 1919
through 1923, at which time the nation was obviously facing financial
collapse. To close the gap between income and expenditure—in 1922
the state's income covered only 51 percent of Poland's expenses—
successive governments sought to borrow everywhere they could. As
time went on, Polish credit, always regarded with suspicion, became
virtually unavailable. Attempts made to float loans through international bankers were disappointing, and an internal capital levy attempted in 1922 brought inadequate results.

The easiest way for a chronic budget imbalance to be covered is
for the nation to print more currency. This the Polish government
did. In early 1919 there had been about one billion Polish marks in
circulation; two years later there were 229 billion marks. By December 1923 a total of 125 *trillion* marks were circulating. The inevitable
economic companions of increased money supply are, of course, inflation and currency depreciation, which is exactly what happened in
Poland. In early 1919 one United States dollar bought twelve Polish
marks. In January 1920 the rate was one dollar to 120 marks. At the
end of that year a dollar was worth five hundred marks. By September
1921 it took 6,500 marks to buy a dollar. The Polish mark was now
hopelessly compromised as an international currency and, indeed, as
a domestic one.

An almost daily increase in prices, starting slowly at first, gathered
momentum in 1922–23. Savings evaporated, and bank deposits ceased
as everyone rushed to purchase goods before the mark fell further. No
one, except currency speculators, could win at this game. Industrial
workers' wages could not keep up with the price increases. Manufac-
turers' income fell below cost of production while their accounts were

in the process of being collected. The government's receipts, based on established rates expressed in marks, were ludicrously insufficient to cover expenses. Government employees appealed for wage increases but were told by Prime Minister Witos, "I will not give you anything. It would only make things still worse."[4]

In the fall of 1923 a wave of strikes swept through the nation. Among the strikers were the railway and postal workers. The Witos government ordered the Army to take over these services, draft the strikers, and compel them to work. The PPS retaliated by proclaiming a general strike for November 5. This call was observed by most of the workers, and when the Army attempted to arrest striking railwaymen, there were extensive riots. In Tarnów and Borysław the workers held off the Army in bloody fighting. In Kraków the workers disarmed an entire infantry battalion, beat off a cavalry charge, and captured five thousand rifles together with some machine guns and armored cars. Thirty-two persons were dead. The strikers held the town for a day and a night. On December 14, 1923, the Witos government, unable to deal either with land reform or the disintegrating Polish economy, resigned.

At this juncture, it was generally acknowledged that Poland was facing its most serious crisis since the most desperate moments of the Polish-Soviet War. The value of Polish currency had now dropped to the point where one United States dollar was worth more than six million Polish marks. The Polish economy was clearly on the brink of collapse. President Wojciechowski cast about for political leaders who could command support in the Sejm to establish a new government. A couple of days were spent in this exercise until it became generally realized that the situation was far too critical to permit the conventional political reshuffling. The President called in Władysław Grabski, the Centrist politician who had been prime minister in 1920, and asked him to form a government. Grabski was a logical choice. An economist and a university professor, he was not a member of any political party, although he was generally considered to be an ally of the National Democrats. Grabski had served as minister of finance in several recent governments and was known to have decided views on measures that had to be taken to avoid economic collapse. He told Wojciechowski that he would form a government only if parliament would agree to give him special, virtually dictatorial powers in the financial sphere. Grabski had seen too often in the past how economic programs had failed because parliament refused to pass implementing legislation.

The Sejm, by now thoroughly frightened, agreed to Grabski's demands. On December 19, 1923, Grabski took office as prime minister and finance minister in a strong, nonparty cabinet. The Sejm virtually abdicated its financial powers and permitted Grabski to rule by decree for a period of six months. He attacked Poland's problems with energy and ruthlessness. His first step was to draw up a government budget, not for a year but for only a month at a time. Working in such a small time period he found it possible to monitor almost every item. To increase the government income he decreed that such items as customs duties, postal and telegraph fees, and railway charges must be paid in marks but calculated on a gold price basis. On each day Grabski published the price of gold in Polish marks on the London market, and it was at this rate that government charges were assessed. This at least had the advantage of keeping part of the government's income in step with inflation and currency depreciation.

Grabski reduced the government's expenditures by wholesale firings in the overstaffed Polish bureaucracies. Eventually, some forty thousand persons were cut off the government payroll. He sold off a number of business enterprises that the government had operated. He increased taxes and greatly improved tax collections. Within two months of his taking office, Grabski announced that he had brought national expenditure and income into balance. But eliminating the chronic government deficit had solved only part of the problem. The next step had to be the reconstitution of the Polish banking system and the issue of new currency to replace the ridiculously inflated mark. In April 1924 Grabski established the Bank of Poland, which replaced the moribund Polish State Loan Bank. This new institution was privately owned with shares of its stock being offered on a proportionate basis to industry, private individuals, cooperative societies, et cetera. All bank stock purchases were required to be made in gold or foreign currency. The stock offering was immediately oversubscribed and the Bank of Poland opened for business on April 15, 1924 as the national bank of Poland and the sole bank of issue for Poland's money.

This coincided with the issuance of a new Polish currency, based on the *zloty* (pronounced "swoty"), which would replace the mark. The zloty, backed by the reserves of the Bank of Poland, was tied to the value of the Swiss gold franc, considered to be Europe's most stable currency. Based on this valuation, about 5.18 zlotys equaled one American dollar. The old Polish marks were exchangeable into zlotys at the rate of 1.8 million marks to the zloty.

The credit of the Polish government, both internally and on the world money market, immediately improved. Grabski was able to float loans in Italy, guaranteed by the income from the government's tobacco monopoly. Polish bonds and treasury notes sold well in the spring of 1924. Unemployment dropped, prices stabilized, and business improved. Poland's postwar debts to the United States and Great Britain were renegotiated; they were extended, and at lower interest rates. When Grabski's authorization to run government finances by decree ended in July, the Sejm extended it for another six months. His accomplishments seemed almost miraculous, and he was decorated with Poland's highest civil award, the Order of the White Eagle. For a man who was not a member of any party, Grabski displayed extraordinary political acumen; he carefully structured his cabinet to include members of every group. From time to time he changed ministers so as to give recognition to various factions within each political group. Recognizing the realities of the time, Grabski was not above ensuring support for his policies by handing out extralegal favors, or even cash bribes, to Sejm deputies. On the failure of a motion to censure Grabski, a member of parliament candidly observed, "Why should we vote against Grabski when we have all received money from him?"[5]

In January 1925 Grabski appeared before the Sejm committee on finance to make the encouraging statement that the entire 1924 national budget had been balanced. Even more than that, it appeared that there was actually a budgetary surplus. Additionally, there had been a great increase in bank savings deposits, a definite sign that public confidence in the Polish economy had been restored. The general feeling was that the Polish financial crisis had passed. Without question, almost every Pole had suffered, in particular the industrial workers, who had experienced high levels of unemployment and frequently actual hunger. But now, it seemed, this suffering was at an end.

There were, however, a number of profoundly disturbing economic indications of which little notice was taken at this time. First, there was a real question about whether the 1924 budget was actually balanced. A substantial amount of the government's income was scheduled to have come in the form of payments on the capital levy of 1922. Grabski had carried this receivable at the full estimate. It now appeared that a large part of this revenue would never be collected, and without this income the budget was unbalanced to a significant degree.

A second portent of trouble was a serious failure of the Polish farm crop of 1924. It was evident that, instead of exporting grain, Poland would be importing, with consequent loss of foreign exchange.

Finally, the erosion of capital through inflation had resulted in a serious shortage of funds for industry. Competition for borrowable funds had driven interest rates in Poland up to uneconomic levels. The obvious answer would have been to borrow from abroad, but the latest attempt to float a loan in New York was not meeting success. Only $28 million out of an expected $50 million would eventually be realized, and even that would command an extraordinary high interest rate.

In early 1925 little notice was taken of all these adverse factors. But by the summer of 1925 a number of additional problems had emerged, and it was suddenly revealed that the Polish economy was in serious trouble. In June, Germany ceased to purchase Upper Silesian coal, an economic catastrophe that abruptly cut Polish coal exports in half. There were sudden drops in the world prices of timber, coal and sugar, all of which were Poland's major exports. Polish banks began to fail as it became evident that their loans could not be repaid. The corollary to this was a sudden fall in the value of the zloty, the supposed stability of which was the symbol of Polish recovery.

It was 1923–24 all over again. As inflation recommenced, unemployment rose. Foreign Minister Skrzyński was sent to New York and London to negotiate loans, but found that there was no confidence in the Polish financial system. The Sejm, which until only a few months before had regarded Grabski as a financial genius, now began to heap abuse on the prime minister. The Socialist deputies, unwilling to have their supporters suffer through another bout of inflation and unemployment, demanded an enormous public-works program, which the government rejected on the grounds that it would further imperil the zloty.

On November 12, 1925, the Bank of Poland refused to sell any more of its dwindling gold or foreign-exchange reserves to support the parity of the zloty with the Swiss mark. Grabski, whose policy had been founded on a secure zloty, immediately resigned, thus ending the longest Polish government since independence had been achieved.

Grabski's successor in this difficult situation was Count Aleksander Skrzyński, who accepted the task of forming a coalition government after many others had refused. Skrzyński, the former foreign minister, who did not pretend to any financial expertise, agreed to serve only after he was convinced that the most important role for the next Polish prime minister would be appealing for loans in foreign capitals. By now, however, public confidence was completely at an end. Unemployment among industrial workers had risen to at least 400,000, about a third of the labor force. The unemployed on the farms were uncounted and uncountable. The only remedy that the government seemed able to offer was a draconian version of Grabski's 1924 program: a budget balanced by increased taxes, further wholesale dismissals of public servants, and price increases in government-controlled commodities—tobacco, alcohol, matches, electricity, salt, et cetera. The Socialists, disgusted at a plan that would only increase the suffering of their supporters, resigned from Skrzyński's government.

In late March and early April of 1926 the Polish zloty broke on the world market. Its value, which had dropped steadily since mid-1925 from its official rate of 5.18 to the dollar to eight to the dollar, suddenly sank in two weeks to nearly ten to the dollar. The dislocation of the Polish economy was now profound. These were balmy economic days for the rest of Europe, while Poland was gripped in a depression that its leaders were unable to control. The spectacle of politicians (many of whom had somehow become rich during all this general suffering) squabbling among themselves disgusted the average Pole. Most Poles cared nothing for politicians, respected almost none of them, distrusted almost all of them.

In early April 1926, riots occurred throughout Poland. The Army was called out and there were strikers killed in the streets. On May 5 Skrzyński and his cabinet resigned. Wincenty Witos returned to form his third cabinet on May 10. Two days later, Piłsudski was leading regiments of troops into Warsaw, more than a thousand men were dead or wounded, and the Witos government had evaporated.

10
Piłsudski's Intervention

IN EARLY 1926 Jósef Piłsudski was fifty-eight years old and was living as a private citizen at Sulejówek, a town about fifteen miles east of Warsaw. Together with his wife and two young daughters, then nine and seven years old, he lived an unpretentious life.* Piłsudski's home was a large country cottage that had been built and given him as the result of donations made by soldiers and officers of the Army. Parliament had awarded him a pension, but Piłsudski had declined it. All that he would accept from public funds was the service of two aides-de-camp, his prerogative as a Marshal of the Army. He chose to live quite simply in order to serve as an example to the nation.

During the nearly three years that he had lived at Sulejówek, Piłsudski's personality and outlook had changed almost as radically as his life style. The murder of Narutowicz and the events following it were horrors that he brooded on constantly. His aides observed that Piłsudski, once a relaxed and genial person, now rarely laughed and never joked. He had become embittered, depressed and distrustful. The circle of persons with whom the Marshal would consult had gradually contracted so that it included only those whose loyalty had

---

* In 1921 the wife from whom Piłsudski had long been estranged died, and Piłsudski was able to marry Aleksandra Szczerbinska, the mother of his two children. The marriage was performed on October 25, 1921, by an army chaplain in the military chapel of the Lazienki Palace in Warsaw.

been proved—mostly members of the wartime First Brigade. Even
these persons were distressed by the changes in their Commandant's
manner. One of the most notable changes was in his language. In discussions with his followers, Piłsudski shocked them by his frequent
use of the coarsest words and the crudest obscenities. This mannerism
became especially evident when he talked about Poland's parliament.
Politicians, whom Piłsudski neither liked nor made any attempt to
understand, seemed to him to be crooked, money-grubbing adven-
turers. He regarded the Sejm with absolute disgust, publicly calling
it the "prostitute Sejm."[1] Even worse than the politicians' corruption,
to Piłsudski, was evidence of similar graft by the Army officers responsible for awarding military contracts. The Marshal attributed this to
the pernicious influence of the politicians, who he thought were
spreading a moral rot throughout Polish life.

Piłsudski was generally described as "living in retirement" during
this period. But, in fact, he was intensely busy. He supported himself
by lecturing (he was an excellent speaker, and his discourse on the
Polish Revolution of 1863 was extremely popular), as well as by writing newspaper articles and a book, *The Year 1920*, which was his history of the Polish-Soviet War. So Piłsudski was in retirement only in
a comparative sense. His departure from public life had been by his
own choice. He had, of course, served as Chief of the General Staff in
the Sikorski government, which took office after Narutowicz's assassination. At the same time he had served as Chairman of the Inner
War Council, which meant that he was commander in chief designate
in the event of war. But only six months after Piłsudski had taken
these offices, the Sikorski government fell and was replaced by Witos's
second cabinet—a coalition of Right and Center. Piłsudski, who regarded the Rightists as virtually the murderers of Narutowicz, refused
to continue in his official posts. "Serve under such people?" he said
"Never!"[2] Abruptly resigning, he went off to Sulejówek. Parliament
richly reciprocated Piłsudski's hatred. It was only with difficulty that
enough members of the Sejm could be persuaded to vote a modest
farewell resolution in June 1923, stating that "Jósef Piłsudski, both
as Chief of State and as Commander in Chief, has rendered merito-
rious service to the Nation."[3] The ballot was 162 to 88 with the balance of the 444 deputies either abstaining or absenting themselves.

Animosity toward Piłsudski was not confined solely to the politicians. Now that the Marshal was out of power, there were those
whose dislike of him could at last be openly revealed. Almost to a

man, Piłsudski's enemies were senior officers whose preindependence careers had been made in the Austrian Imperial Army and who had always been jealous of the officers who rose through the Legion and the P.O.W. They regarded these generally much younger men as fundamentally untrained and believed their principal qualification was their personal loyalty to Piłsudski. The former Austrian senior officers, often referred to collectively as the "Viennese War Academy," tended to be politically Rightist and to prefer duty stations in Galicia or Poznania, where the National Democrats were strongest.

Piłsudski's resignation gave his enemies the opportunity to strike back at him by dismantling the military command structure that he had established. In January 1921, while he was Chief of State, Piłsudski had established an army command system consisting of two principal institutions—the Full War Council and the Inner War Council. The first included the president of the Republic, the minister of war and his deputy, and the most senior officers of the Army. It was an advisory body that suggested plans and made decisions in the areas of training, supply, fortifications, et cetera. But the actual *operational* authority under the Piłsudski system was reserved for the smaller Inner War Council, which was made up only of the wartime commander in chief designate, the various wartime corps commanders designate and the Army chief of staff. The minister of war was allowed to attend meetings, but he had neither a vote nor any authority over the others. The Inner War Council also controlled the selection for promotion of all officers from colonel upward. Under the Piłsudski plan, parliamentary authority over the Army had been effectively limited, if not actually eliminated.

Piłsudski justified this command arrangement on the grounds that it eliminated political interference, improved security, and allowed for fast action in the event of war. Parliament was unimpressed by these arguments. The Sejm saw clearly that the whole command structure was designed by Piłsudski on the assumption that he would be the wartime commander in chief and that he therefore had removed this post as far as possible from parliamentary observation and control.

No sooner had Piłsudski resigned than two former Austrian officers, Generals Stanisław Haller and Stanisław Szeptycki were appointed to the positions that the Marshal had occupied. Within six months the Witos government prepared a new organizational plan that provided for much more control over the Army by the civilian government. It had been drawn up by General Sikorski who at that juncture (March 1924) was serving as minister of war. As a courtesy, Sikorski submitted to Piłsudski, for his review, his draft plan together with the proposal that the Marshal return to active service as the Army's inspector general, which in Sikorski's plan was the title for the wartime commander in chief designate.

This was a sincere offer. The incumbent prime minister, Władysław Grabski, was anxious to placate Piłsudski's supporters. Although not formally organized into a party, Piłsudski's friends and admirers constituted a very important faction in the nation. They could not understand why the Marshal held no active post in the Army, and they were extremely critical of the Prime Minister for permitting this situation to continue. So, Grabski was anxious to have Piłsudski accept an official position in his government. But the Marshal would have nothing to do with the government's offer. Piłsudski scoffed at Sikorski's organization plan and flatly refused to accept the inspector general post on the grounds that its powers were unclear and that the inspector general would serve under the war minister. Under no circumstances would Piłsudski accept a post in which he would be responsible to a cabinet minister who, under the Polish constitution, served at the pleasure of the Sejm. At a meeting with prominent government officials who asked him to reconsider, Piłsudski was so insulting and abusive that Deputy Prime Minister Stanisłas Thugutt walked out in the middle of the conference. Increasingly suspicious, Piłsudski regarded the entire affair as a cheap attempt to pacify his supporters by offering him an emasculated position that he would be unwilling to accept. And there it lay. Piłsudski was without an Army post and the Army was without a permanent organizational plan because Piłsudski's opposition to the Sikorski draft was enough to prevent its being adopted by the Sejm.

Within the Army itself Piłsudski's personal influence was enormous. His enemies among the senior officers constituted only a very small segment of the Polish Army. The remainder of the Army was devoutly pro-Piłsudski. The Marshal was the idol of most of the middle-grade and junior officers. They regarded him as the founder of the Army, and they considered that his military genius had been proved by his direction of the Polish-Soviet War. Even in retirement, Piłsudski remained the First Marshal of the Army, its most senior officer in terms of rank.

In short, Piłsudski was too important to be kept out of the Army, but at the same time he regarded himself as too senior and too experienced to accept anything but absolute and unhindered control over military affairs—which, of course, no opposition government would give to him. And even though he occupied no official position, Piłsudski continued to meddle with the Army—criticizing officers he disliked, forecasting dire tragedies, complaining about morale or equipment or training. He would not go back into the Army, but then again, he would not stay out of it.

The government, deeply desiring tranquillity in the Army, sought at various times to mollify Piłsudski by appointing close associates of his to the office of minister of war. But nothing could placate him. Piłsudski chose to regard the elevation of his friends as an attempt to buy his silence, and he refused to be bought. He continued his direct and emotional relationship with the Army, and most of the Army continued its equally emotional relationship with him. He was the invariable guest of honor at Army reunions, where he spoke pointedly of the need for "moral renewal" in Polish life. The Army reciprocated Piłsudski's devotion by dispatching mass delegations of officers to the Marshal's home every March 19, the Feast of St. Joseph and therefore Piłsudski's name day. They filled the Marshal's home with gifts of flowers and fruit. Hundreds of officers sent telegrams offering their congratulations and assuring Piłsudski of their personal devotion.

Sometimes these demonstrations of fidelity to the Marshal took on an aspect that the government found ominous. For example, on November 15, 1925, a large number of officers, including twenty generals, went to Piłsudski's cottage to celebrate the seventh anniversary of his return from imprisonment at Magdeburg. The delegation was headed by General Gustaw Orlicz-Dresser, an old comrade from the earliest days of the First Brigade. Orlicz-Dresser now commanded the Second Cavalry Division, an important post with headquarters in Warsaw. On this occasion Orlicz-Dresser made a speech. After dwelling upon the Army's gratitude to Piłsudski and its "ardent desire to have you among us again," the general concluded with the statement that "in addition to our grateful hearts we are also bringing you our sure, battle-tested swords."[4] Not surprisingly, the government believed that this speech bordered on sedition. The next day General Sikorski relieved Orlicz-Dresser of his command and posted him to a job in distant Poznan.

Against the background of recurring Polish financial crises, strikes, riots and unemployment, Piłsudski increased the number of his speeches, articles and Army appearances. The Marshal's tone had become increasingly critical, increasingly abrupt, and increasingly demanding. He now spoke constantly of "moral rot" and the need for public discipline and self-sacrifice. He did not hesitate to summon supporters from the Sejm to Sulejówek, where he instructed them in their duties. When the parliament was considering reduction of the Army to help balance the budget, the Marshal's personal intervention was sufficient to kill the proposal. In November 1925 Piłsudski even went so far as to visit President Wojciechowski, hand him a memorandum protesting alleged government assaults on the honor of the Army, and demand a written receipt for the memorandum.

No one knew what Piłsudski's plans were during these difficult last months of 1925 and early months of 1926. In fact he himself had no clear-cut plan of action. However, he was certainly readying himself for assuming again the task of governing Poland. As early as September 1925, he had secretly summoned Kazimierz Bartel, a mathematics professor and Sejm deputy, whose administrative ability as minister of railways had impressed the Marshal during the Polish-Soviet War. Piłsudski told Bartel to prepare himself for the day when he would be called upon to become prime minister in a Piłsudski-sponsored government. At the same time the Marshal ordered his close associate, General Orlicz-Dresser, to make certain clandestine military preparations.

The times favored such preparations. On November 27, 1925, General Lucian Zeligowski, a long-time Piłsudski intimate who had led the 1920 "mutiny" that seized Wilno, was appointed minister of war in the government of Prime Minister Skrzyński. Zeligowski had plenty of experience in conspiratorial activity and was personally devoted to Piłsudski. Practically his first orders involved bringing Orlicz-Dresser back into Warsaw to his former cavalry command. Other staunch Piłsudski adherents, such as Colonels Wieniawa-Dlugoszowski, Beck and Sciezynski, were placed in key General Staff positions. Simultaneously, a number of the Marshal's old enemies were weeded out of the Army. Various members of the Viennese War Academy were retired, dispatched to obscure commands, or sent on lengthy and unimportant missions.

It is not certain what Piłsudski was preparing for. But he was probably *not* readying himself for an actual coup. A coup meant civil war, fighting within the Army (an eventuality almost too horrifying for

Piłsudski to contemplate), and the thrusting of an unwanted regime upon an unwilling people. Piłsudski certainly did not want this and surely did not think a coup was necessary. He apparently anticipated that he would take over the government at a point when the entire Polish political system had already collapsed.

The problem with adopting such a course of action is that the political system of an organized nation never actually "collapses." No matter how desperate the situation, someone can always be found to form another government, and others can always be persuaded to serve in a new cabinet. The civil servants in, for example, the Ministry of Posts and Telegraphs do not simply abandon their jobs. But a national government can gradually deteriorate to the point where it can solve no problems and resist no outside pressures. The government can then be said to be in a state of collapse, even though it is still in office and most of the services of the state continue. It staggers on until some outside force declares it has indeed "collapsed," bloodlessly sweeps out the wreckage, and becomes a sort of receiver in bankruptcy. The key question is: When has the point of collapse actually arrived? In the early spring of 1926, Piłsudski believed that this moment was at hand. The method by which he had arrived at this determination is instructive and illustrates a problem frequently encountered by great men.

During the nearly three years that Piłsudski was a private person he saw a large number of people, but only on his terms and in circumstances that made it difficult for him to arrive at dispassionate judgments. To live a life in which all others stand when one enters a room can be unbalancing. The Marshal received visitors at Sulejówek exclusively by his invitation, which was regarded as a very great distinction. Those welcomed to Sulejówek were almost always Piłsudski adherents, and they were overwhelmed by the honor accorded them. Under these circumstances, it is not surprising that the visitors expressed nothing but admiration, respect and loyalty to the Marshal.

This adulatory attitude was not confined to Piłsudski's visitors. When he lectured publicly, it was almost inevitable that the audiences should consist of rapt and enthusiastic well-wishers. When Piłsudski appeared at an Army reunion, it was certain to be a gathering of cheering comrades. When he received his daily mail, it was sure to contain scores of letters imploring him to return to public life.

Thus, although Piłsudski rightly regarded himself as being in touch with a great number of Polish citizens, he either did not admit or did not realize that this seeming multitude was actually a select group comprised almost entirely of his admirers. Everyone with whom Piłsudski spoke assured him that the government was in a state of collapse and that the nation longed for the Marshal's return to leadership.

When the Skryzński cabinet fell on May 5, 1926, and was succeeded five days later by the third Witos government, it was evident that the Polish government was in crisis. Piłsudski and Witos had long been bitter enemies, and the incoming prime minister, on the day before his assumption of office, made no effort to conceal this. Witos took the view that his two predecessors in office had attempted to mollify Piłsudski but had received nothing but scorn and abuse for their trouble. Witos resolved not to subject his government to the same humiliation. He gave a newspaper interview in which he threw down the gauntlet. He intended, he said, to govern vigorously, and he demanded that the Marshal cease his behind-the-scenes maneuvers and take an open political stance. Let Piłsudski rally whatever political support he had in the Sejm and go into outspoken opposition.

It became known that Witos was planning to fire Piłsudski-ite prefects in various administrative districts of the country. And in his new cabinet Witos was dropping Piłsudski's old friend Zeligowski as minister of war and replacing him with General Juliusz Malczewski, an officer from the old Austrian Army.

Piłsudski responded at once with a newspaper interview in which he denounced Witos (and his predecessors) as corrupt, inefficient, and guilty of calculated attempts to destroy the morale of the Polish Army, presumably as a way of attacking Piłsudski personally. Indeed, he charged that under the previous Witos government "I was surrounded by paid spies and they [the government] bribed with money or promotions everyone who betrayed me—the former commander in chief!"[5] Piłsudski concluded the interview with a promise—"I am going to attack the main evil of this country which is its domination by political parties which care nothing for the nation and whose members are only intent upon graft."[6]

This interview was so explosive that Witos ordered the newspaper confiscated when it appeared on May 11. It was clear that the suppression of this interview would eliminate any possibility of repairing relations between the government and the Marshal. Witos therefore gave instructions that precautions be taken against a possible insurrectionary attempt by Piłsudski.

Events were now moving very fast. During that day and the next, Minister of War Malczewski issued a torrent of orders designed to prevent an armed coup. Generals Tadeusz Rozwadowski and Stanisław Haller, both former Austrian officers, were summoned to Warsaw to take command of troops in the capital military district. Live ammunition was given to the tightly disciplined students at the Infantry Officers School in Warsaw. Several infantry regiments, commanded by officers known to be loyal to the government (or at least believed opposed to Piłsudski) were ordered to entrain for the capital. All other troop movements were forbidden except by Malczewski's direct order.

Piłsudski's supporters were equally active. During the afternoon and evening of May 11 bands of civilians led by officers entered cafés in Warsaw, compelled the orchestras to play the marching song of the Polish Legion, "We, the First Brigade," and led patrons into the streets for a series of Piłsudski-ite demonstrations. That night a rumor was spread by Piłsudski's supporters; it was said that the Marshal's home had been attacked and fired upon by hoodlums in the pay of the Witos government. The rumor had its hoped-for effect. The Warsaw populace was shocked and indignant. More importantly, on the morning of May 12, the officers of several nearby Army regiments ordered their troops to arms and rushed detachments to Sulejówek to protect the Marshal. These units, together with cavalry already on hand, made up the force with which Piłsudski began his coup later that same morning.

The situation in Warsaw on the morning of May 12 was this. The newly constituted Witos cabinet, seeing clearly that an attempted coup was imminent, was meeting in emergency session. The attention of the government was directed to the east of Warsaw, toward the large Army training camp at Rembertow close to Piłsudski's home at Sulejówek. Only a few hours before the cabinet meeting, Minister of War Malczewski had discovered that his predecessor, Piłsudski supporter Zeligowski, had secretly ordered a crack cavalry regiment, the 7th Uhlans, to Rembertow. These troops, commanded by Piłsudski's former aide Colonel Kazimierz Stamirowski, had arrived in Rembertow on May 11. Their movement to Rembertow had been personally directed by Zeligowski on May 8, his last day as minister of war.

Zeligowski had instructed the commanding officer of the regiment that he was to take orders directly from Marshal Piłsudski, who had asked to be provided with troops in order to personally conduct some maneuvers. Since every attempt had been made to keep this movement secret and since Piłsudski had not conducted any maneuvers since his retirement, the cabinet realized that the 7th Uhlans were to be the shock troops of a Piłsudski coup.

Throughout Wednesday morning, May 12, the Witos government continued to issue counterinsurrectionary orders, instructions and decrees. Civil rights were suspended in the capital district. The entire Warsaw garrison was placed on full alert. A proclamation was drafted and telegraphed to every Army command demanding that officers and men preserve the Army's honor and discipline by keeping their oath of allegiance to the government. Clearly the government intended to rally military support not on the basis of its own questionable popularity, but on the grounds of simple legitimacy. At the time of his enlistment every man in the Polish Army had sworn an oath "to obey the law and the President of the Republic." This vow was simple, clear-cut and certainly binding. (Ironically, Piłsudski himself had participated in its drafting.) The officer corps of the Army was mostly professional and exclusively volunteer. They had sworn this oath freely, and now the duly constituted government expected them to honor it.

In adopting a legitimist approach, the Witos cabinet received astonishingly strong support from a quarter they had first distrusted. Stanisław Wojciechowski, the President of the Republic, had left Warsaw early in the morning of May 12 for a visit to the presidential summer residence at Spala, some twenty miles southwest of the city. This excursion may seem inexplicable in view of the ominous situation, but Wojciechowski knew practically nothing about the Piłsudski-ite troop movements of which the government had become aware. In fact, it is likely that Witos had deliberately failed to inform Wojciechowski of the probability of a coup attempt. Wojciechowski did not like Witos, and Witos knew it. Moreover, Wojciechowski was known to be a very dear friend of Piłsudski. Piłsudski had proposed Wojciechowski for the presidency, and Wojciechowski was one of perhaps only a dozen persons in the world with whom Piłsudski used the familiar, second-person form of address. Indeed, there were some grounds for the government to question the President's determination in opposing Piłsudski coup. And so, it was not until nearly noon

of May 12 (and after a coup attempt was clearly underway) that Witos
sent word to Wojciechowski informing him of events and requesting
his presence in Warsaw. The President arrived back in the city by
midafternoon, and it was at once evident that he would be a tower of
strength to the government. Old friendships notwithstanding, it was
clear that Wojciechowski intended to honor his presidential oath to
the letter and was prepared to insist that everyone else honor his commitment to the legitimate government. Wojciechowski believed that
he had been hoodwinked by Piłsudski. Witos had approached Wojciechowski only a few days before and told the President that he suspected a coup to be in the wind. Wojciechowski had replied, quite
honestly, that he did not believe Piłsudski to "be capable of such a
crime." Only recently Piłsudski had "given him his word of honor
that he was not contemplating any coup." The President reminded
Witos that "Piłsudski always kept his word."[7] To the surprise of the
cabinet, who knew him as a kindly, unaggressive person with no military experience, Wojciechowski proved to be a man of great physical
courage and personal toughness. He insisted that any coup attempt
must be resisted by force of arms and announced that he would not
shrink from bloodshed if it came to that. In fact, it was Wojciechowski who, alone, first confronted Piłsudski on the afternoon of May 12
and denied him admittance to Warsaw.

The First Marshal had left his home at Sulejówek at about 7 A.M.
on May 12. With a few aides, he had driven the short distance to the
Army camp at Rembertow, where troops under the command of
Orlicz-Dresser awaited him. This force was made up of units of the
7th Uhlan Regiment, some troops from the 22nd Infantry Regiment,
and a few smaller groups. These soldiers were immediately ordered
to march westward toward the capital, which lay six miles away.

All told, at this point Piłsudski had only two thousand men—an
absurdly small force to attempt the overthrow of an established government in a major European capital. But Piłsudski was utterly confident that his forces would be more than ample. Although his men
had been given live ammunition, he was convinced that there would
be no fighting of any consequence. Piłsudski could surely have put
together a much larger force, but that seemed to him to be totally
unnecessary. All that he needed was sufficient troops to put on, in
Piłsudski's words, an armed "demonstration."[8] The only force capable of stopping him was other units of the Polish Army, and it was

unthinkable to Piłsudski that any contingent of the Polish Army would fire upon their First Marshal. He anticipated a rapid triumphal march into Warsaw, where he would occupy General Staff headquarters, announce his return to the leadership of the Army, and then in the following days proceed to sort things out politically. He anticipated no military opposition, and he foresaw no serious difficulty with the civil government. He sized Witos up as a coward who was incapable of ordering a military showdown. He knew Wojciechowski to be an old friend. Piłsudski was certain that the Witos cabinet would resign at once, leaving the way clear for the installation of the Marshal's nominee, Bartel.

So confident was Piłsudski of immediate success that when he left his home that morning, he told his wife to expect him for dinner at two-thirty in the afternoon. This schedule allowed barely enough time to drive to Rembertow, march west into Warsaw, and return directly home.

The Vistula River flows along the eastern edge of Warsaw where in 1926 it was spanned by two conventional bridges and one railway bridge. The principal bridge was, and still is, the long Poniatowski Bridge, which leads directly onto Jerozolimski Avenue, on which the railroad station and many banks and office buildings were located. On the eastern side of the Poniatowski Bridge is the suburb of Praga, which on the afternoon of May 12 was filling up with insurrectionary soldiers under Piłsudski's command.

Piłsudski's troops had marched from Rembertow and occupied Praga without encountering any resistance. But this situation ended abruptly at the Poniatowski Bridge, where a company of about two hundred students from the Infantry Officers School was blocking the Warsaw side of the bridge. These soldiers were the flower of the Polish Army. Absolutely under the control of their superior officers and inculcated with the concepts of discipline, honor and courage, they were adversaries of the most elite type. There was not the slightest doubt that these young soldiers would fire upon any one when their superiors ordered them to do so. Nor was there any doubt that their rifle fire would massacre any cavalry or infantry force that attempted to cross the bridge.

The deployment of these officer candidates had been a shrewd stroke. It was an eventuality for which Piłsudski was totally unprepared. The appearance of troops who would fire upon him had apparently never entered his thinking. He was absolutely confounded. The very last thing that Piłsudski had intended to do was to precipitate fighting between opposing units of the Army. After all, the preservation of the cohesiveness of the Army had been one of Piłsudski's principal objectives in commencing his coup.

Faced with this unexpected opposition, the insurrectionary troops milled about at the eastern (Praga) end of the bridge. There was now quite a large force in Praga, because the 1st Light Cavalry Regiment had, earlier in the day, marched out from the Warsaw garrison to join the insurrection. The streets of Praga were choked with soldiers and horsemen, all brought to a standstill by the single company of infantry at the other end of the bridge.

It was now late afternoon. An automobile approached the bridge from the Warsaw side, was passed through the government troops, and drove out onto the center span of the bridge. President Wojciechowski got out and handed a note to Colonel Stamirowski, the commander of the 7th Uhlan Regiment. The note contained a demand to see Piłsudski. The Marshal quickly came forward. He thrust out his hand, but Wojciechowski refused to take it. Piłsudski thereupon grasped the president by the arm and drew him to one side of the bridge, where, standing alongside the balustrade, the two men talked animatedly.

Their conversation did not last long. Piłsudski demanded that the president dismiss the Witos government, a demand that Wojciechowski refused. Wojciechowski ordered Piłsudski to return his troops to their barracks and desist in his attempts at insurrection. Piłsudski refused. "For me." he said, "the legal road is closed."[9] The conversation grew very heated. Piłsudski seized the lapels of Wojciechowski's coat and swore to him that he intended to do no harm to the president. Wojciechowski pulled himself free, got into his automobile, and drove off—pausing only to reaffirm the orders to the commander of the Infantry Officers School troops that Piłsudski's soldiers were not to be permitted to cross the bridge. The President drove directly to the Namiestnikowski Palace, where the Witos cabinet was in continuous session. He told them of his interview with Piłsudski, and his obduracy appears to have stiffened the backbones of Witos and his ministers, who had been discussing the possibility of some sort of compromise.

Piłsudski, left at the Poniatowski Bridge, was almost numb with shock. Coming on top of opposition from the Army was this second blow, the obvious willingness of his good friend Wojciechowski to commence a civil war. Piłsudski walked up to Major Marian Porwit, the commander of the opposing troops from the Infantry Officers School, who was standing nearby. Putting his arm about Porwit's shoulders, he appealed to the major to ignore Wojciechowski's orders and permit his troops to cross the bridge. Porwit was a much-decorated soldier from the wartime Polish Legion. But he had served in the Second Brigade, and Piłsudski did not know him personally. Porwit replied, with great respect, that his orders were to open fire on any insurrectionary force that attempted to cross the bridge. These were legal orders from his legal superiors. Porwit intended to carry them out.

Stunned, Piłsudski walked back to the Praga side of the bridge. For perhaps the only time in his career he was completely unnerved and lost the capacity for decision. He gave a perfunctory order that the 22nd Infantry Regiment be sent about a half mile north to see if the Kierbedz Bridge was as strongly held as the Poniatowski Bridge. But obviously he had little hope that it would not be. He retired to the barracks of the 36th Infantry Regiment in Praga, where, as evening fell, he spent the time in reminiscences about the old days in the Polish Legion. Meanwhile, Piłsudski's troops backed away from their end of the Poniatowski Bridge. A detachment of soldiers from the Infantry Officers School which had been on maneuvers outside the capital marched firmly through Praga and swung across the bridge on their way to join the government forces. Piłsudski's regiments let them pass without opposition. The Marshal himself lay on a couch in the barracks. In despair he told an associate, "The Poniatowski Bridge is lost. Do you understand, lost . . . lost . . . lost. . . ."[10]

Events now suddenly changed in Piłsudski's favor. The troops dispatched to the Kierbedz Bridge found it blocked by a unit of infantry loyal to the government. But these soldiers were not of the caliber of those defending the Poniatowski Bridge. After only a few minutes of argument, their officers were persuaded to change sides. Within minutes Piłsudski's cavalry was cantering across the bridge and spreading through the northern center of the capital. When the news reached Piłsudski, he could not believe it. "You are wrong, boys," he said, "that is not so. There is no entry into Warsaw."[11] But it was true. However, Piłsudski's forces had not gotten into the city without fighting. As the troops crossed the Kierbedz Bridge, they brushed past a unit of the 30th Infantry Regiment. It was commanded by officers who refused to go over to the Marshal. The 30th Regiment troops opened fire, and before they were pushed back, they had killed eleven soldiers of the Piłsudski-ite 36th Infantry Regiment and wounded twenty-eight others. Piłsudski himself was not far away in Praga. He could hear the firing, but he could scarcely believe that his beloved army was fighting among itself. "So it has started after all," he said in horror to Colonel Kasimierz Sawicki, commander of the 36th Infantry Regiment. "I never thought that it would come to this."[12]

By midnight of May 12–13, Piłsudski's forces occupied an important sector of inner Warsaw. After having repelled the troops of the 30th Infantry Regiment, which had fired upon them, Piłsudski's soldiers had spread south and had captured the principal railroad stations, the railroad ministry offices, the war ministry, and the central telephone and telegraph exchange. Most of these important buildings were taken with practically no fighting. The defenders had evacuated them almost as soon as the Piłsudski forces appeared. Piłsudski himself had driven into the city at nine in the evening and set up headquarters in the captured offices of the Warsaw garrison on Saxon Square. Had he been willing to further force the issue and risk the possibility of a sharp battle, his troops would surely have overwhelmed the government's defenders and probably captured Witos, Wojciechowski, and the entire cabinet. But the Marshal, horrified and distraught by the fighting that was taking place, refused to precipitate combat on any sizable scale, and so the government forces had been permitted to retreat south into the extensive park and grounds of the Belvedere Palace, in front of which they were beginning to dig shallow trenches. Witos and his cabinet had moved into the Palace, thus joining Wojciechowski in his official residence.

To the north of the area controlled by Piłsudski's troops was the Warsaw Citadel, an immensely strong fortress built by the Russians as a bastion against a city in revolt. This too was occupied by loyal government forces of the 30th Infantry Regiment.

During the early hours of May 13, there was extensive skirmishing as each side probed the other, and Piłsudski's troops established the perimeters of their advance. In terms of military position, manpower and equipment, Piłsudski's forces had an early advantage. Their occupation of the main railroad station and the telephone exchange gave them virtual control of communications into and out of the capital. Their troops were more numerous and were increasing as various units of the Warsaw garrison defected. Piłsudski was extremely popular in Warsaw—probably more than in any other city in Poland. Many hundreds of civilians, most of them former soldiers, came to the Piłsudski headquarters and asked to be armed for the fight against the government. Even though they were turned away, the moral support of the Warsaw populace was valuable to Piłsudski in these critical hours.

The government defenders were not discouraged, however. Their forces in Warsaw were small, but their core, the troops of the Presidential Guard and the Infantry Officers School, was of exceptionally high quality and was proving very loyal. The redoubt being built around the Belvedere had no food or military supplies, and none of the communications systems possessed by Piłsudski's forces, but as the official residence of the Polish president, the Belvedere had enormous legitimist symbolic value. The fact that they were presently outnumbered in Warsaw did not particularly dismay the government defenders. They controlled the air force, the nearby airport and the roads to it. They were in radio communication with Army regiments in other parts of the country, particularly those stationed in Poznania, where National Democratic (hence anti-Piłsudski) sentiment was very strong. These regiments were ordered to entrain for Warsaw to defend the government. There was little doubt that the commanders of these units would obey their orders. In fact, on the night of May 12–13, contingents from three infantry regiments (the 10th, 57th and 58th) arrived just outside Warsaw, detrained at a freight station, marched around the Piłsudski troops, and entered the Belvedere Park from the south. More loyalist troops were expected imminently.

In terms of military leadership, the government believed itself fully the equal of its enemies. A government disadvantage—uncertainty about which of the Army's officers would remain loyal—seemed outweighed by the presence of many senior, former Austrian Army officers in the Belvedere Palace. Men such as Rozwadowski and Stanisław Haller were given senior command positions. There was no doubt as to their allegiance, based as it was on their animosity toward Piłsudski.

In the vital matter of simple determination, the government was not in the least deficient. Although neither Witos nor his cabinet could be described as bellicose or even especially resolved to prevail in a civil war, President Wojciechowski more than made up for their deficiencies in this regard. He flatly rejected any thoughts of mediation or compromise and firmly held that the government must use every means at its disposal to stamp out the rebellion. The fact that one part of the Polish Army would be forced to fight another did not in the least deter him. Without doubt, it was Wojciechowski, the former close friend of Piłsudski, who animated the government's defense—which on May 13 became an offensive.

Piłsudski's position was less categorical. Upon his arrival at the Warsaw Garrison headquarters on the night of May 12, he had summoned representatives of the press and confessed to them that he was at the end of his emotional tether. It seemed that Piłsudski was also uncertain of his objectives. His old friend and colleague, Ignacy Daszynski, asked him, "Where are you going to, Józef?" and the only reply that Piłsudski could make was, "I do not know."[13] He made no secret of his personal horror of civil war among the Poles, and particularly within the Army. He issued invitations for mediation to the Witos government, sent well-known envoys with compromise offers to Wojciechowski, and refused to use artillery against the opposing forces in the fear that it would cause extensive casualties.

As the hours passed, Piłsudski recovered his composure. It became clear to him that he had crossed his Rubicon. He had no choice but to press on with the coup. Piłsudski spent the early hours of May 13 establishing a command structure for his operation—something that had not been done before because the military phase of the coup was expected to end almost as soon as it began. General Orlicz-Dresser, the thirty-seven-year-old Legion veteran who had organized the armed support for the coup, was appointed to command the forces fighting in Warsaw. Another young former Legionnaire, thirty-two-year-old Lieutenant Colonel Józef Beck, was appointed Orlicz-Dresser's chief of staff. Beck was an artillery specialist and had in the past frequently been used by Piłsudski for duties of a confidential character. Only a few other appointments were made, the principal ones being the designation of officers as "commissars" for the key railroad centers of Lublin and Łódz, through which almost all troops responding to the government's call for reinforcements would have to pass.

The creation of a command structure for the insurrectionary force came none too soon. All of Piłsudski's proposals for negotiation had been abruptly rejected, and the government had made some impressive military gains. After some probing attacks in the early morning of May 13, the government committed the bulk of its forces to an assault, and by midday its troops had succeeded in storming and capturing the ministry of war building and the Light Cavalry barracks. Both buildings were fought through floor by floor and room by room.

When they had finally been taken, the government had captured about five hundred prisoners and, more importantly, found the way open to move northward into central Warsaw. During the late afternoon, government patrols moved toward Piłsudski's headquarters. Eventually they were driven off, but they had come close to retaking the railroad station, telephone exchange and Railroad Ministry Building—all of which were key positions for the Piłsudski forces.

This sharp series of successes had an immediate and considerable effect on the government. The cabinet issued a forceful proclamation demanding the support of every citizen in suppressing the "criminal revolt." In the proclamation they claimed that large, loyal forces were hastening to the government's defense and that many misguided persons who had defected to Piłsudski were now returning, conscience-stricken, to the support of the legal government. This bellicose confidence was based on the predictions of the government's generals, who strolled about the Belvedere radiating optimism. Apart from the Minister of War, General Malczewski, who was visibly affected by the strain, the government generals were buoyant. They had attacked Piłsudski, and he had proved to be vulnerable. Large numbers of reinforcements, they claimed, were responding to their orders and hurrying to Warsaw. Soon they would direct these fresh troops to put down the revolt completely. Instructions had already been given that Piłsudski himself was not to escape. His headquarters was to be overrun, and the Marshal was to be captured or killed.[13]

Actually, Piłsudski's troops, although roughly handled on May 13, had achieved some success. The officers commanding the government troops in the Citadel had had second thoughts about their personal loyalties. There was considerable confusion, and one of the gates of the fortress was left open. One of Piłsudski's generals audaciously drove his automobile into the stronghold, announced that he was relieving the commanding officer, and led the garrison over to Piłsudski. The Citadel episode illustrates two characteristics of the Army's reactions throughout the coup. One was that the enlisted men and junior officers almost invariably followed the orders of their superiors. Whether a regiment fought for Piłsudski, remained neutral, or fought against him, its stance was determined almost exclusively by the attitudes of its higher-ranking officers, usually the colonel and his senior aides. The other was the understandable vacillation of many of the senior officers. They were torn between the loyalties they had sworn to the legal government and the respect and fidelity that they felt

toward Piłsudski. These senior officers knew that any commander who
failed to support Piłsudski would suffer should the Marshal be successful; whereas, if the government prevailed, an officer who had declared for Piłsudski might be shot. Faced with this harrowing decision, most senior officers delayed in responding to government orders
to march on Warsaw. Several generals, Sikorski among them, sent
excuses explaining why they could not march to the government's
defense—the Ukrainian elements in this military district were restive;
the Russian border had to be watched; and so on. General Sosnkowski, once perhaps Piłsudski's closest friend, attempted suicide in his
office at Poznań when he received orders to march his command to
Warsaw.* Other officers, who could not bring themselves to refuse an
order from legitimate authority, accompanied their troops on trains
to the capital but gratefully and passively accepted any blockage of
the railway lines engineered by pro-Piłsudski forces.

By the evening of May 13 the conflict between Piłsudski and the
government had entered another phase, often called the Race for
Reinforcements. The government's small infantry force in Warsaw
was exhausted by its efforts during the day. It was essential that these
soldiers be augmented with fresh troops. Piłsudski also needed fresh
troops. At this point, the Socialists joined the battle.

Although Piłsudski had long since abandoned socialism, the socialist parties had never abandoned him. The PPS remained especially
loyal, partly because the Marshal had been an early hero of the party
and partly because he was the only real barrier to the complete dominance of the Right in Polish political life. Of course, many PPS
members had qualms about Piłsudski at this juncture. They pointed
out that it would be ridiculous for a European socialist party to
support a man who had disavowed socialism, had become a military
leader, and was presently engaged in a Bonaparte-like adventure
against the lawful government. Yet, on the other hand, the Polish

---

* Sosnkowski, at one time Piłsudski's principal associate and most uncritical devotee,
was, in May 1926, commander of the Poznań Military District. For various reasons,
Sosnkowski's relationship with Piłsudski had cooled somewhat. Sosnkowski had been in
Warsaw only two days before the coup began, but no one from Piłsudski's staff had
approached him to ask his support, which he would unquestionably have given. Tormented by the thought that the Marshal did not trust him, he apparently attempted
suicide but succeeded only in wounding himself in the chest.

socialists simply could not continue to lend support to the series of essentially Rightist governments that had presided over the economic catastrophes wrought upon the Polish proletariat. The railroad workers, whose ranks had been severely thinned and whose pay had been cut by previous governments, were particularly pro-Piłsudski.

On May 13 the Central Executive Committee of the PPS met in Warsaw in a session that lasted all day and deep into the night. There was endless debate as each faction of the party stated its case. The ardent Piłsudski-ites proposed calling a general strike in support of the Marshal; other party members were not so sure. They could not bring themselves to collaborate in an armed coup against the legal government. Toward evening the matter was suddenly resolved by an announcement from the railroad workers that they would strike—that, in fact, they were already on strike, regardless of the Central Executive Committee's decision. This did it. A general strike announcement by the PPS went out at 8 P.M., and it was instantly effective. Even the tiny and illegal Polish Communist Party announced its support for what they termed Piłsudski's "revolutionary armies"[14] and endorsed the general strike. The most important role in the strike was played by the railroad workers. Acting on instructions telegraphed from Bartel's staff in the Railroad Ministry, the strikers shunted Warsaw-bound government troop trains onto sidings, uncoupled the engines and abandoned them. The railroad men also tore up tracks or destroyed switches along lines where government reinforcements were expected. Trains carrying Piłsudski-ite reinforcements were rushed straight through to Warsaw's central station. In this manner, the 1st Legionary Division dispatched from Wilno by Rydz-Śmigły and parts of the 2nd and 3rd Infantry Divisions sent from Lublin and Kielce arrived in the capital early on the morning of May 14.

The general strike called by the PPS, as helpful as it was to his cause, was personally distressing to Piłsudski. He felt it demeaning to have to depend upon the PPS for such obviously vital support; he was concerned about future claims on him from the Leftists based on their help in his hour of need; and he feared that a socialist general strike, declared during a period of revolutionary ferment, might snowball into a revolution. When a worker's militia was proposed, Piłsudski was reluctant to arm it. "The Army," he said, "will stop shooting at my command. I do not know if the civilians will stop."[15] But whether he liked it or not, the railroad workers' assistance proved vital for Piłsudski and he won the Race for Reinforcements. By the morning of May 14 he commanded more than fifteen regiments of infantry in Warsaw and could bring in reinforcements at will. The government had fewer than five regiments, all tired and undersupplied, and could not expect that significant reinforcements would reach Warsaw for some time.

At 5 A.M. on the morning of May 14, the insurgent forces began a full-scale attack. Piłsudski had put his qualms behind him. He was determined to put an end to the government's resistance before the Left's support became even more obligating or the conflict spread beyond Warsaw. Piłsudski took personal command of the operation. His troops launched a concentric attack upon the government's positions. By noon they had driven their enemies back about three blocks and had recaptured the ministry of war building lost the previous day. From its windows they looked down upon the Belvedere park and the white neoclassic façade of the Belvedere Palace.

Within the Belvedere, the government was beginning to panic. The plethora of general officers in the palace was proving to be a problem. The chain of command was breaking down as counterorder succeeded order. The government troops, exhausted by nearly two days of constant fighting, were confused and uncertain. Those generals who had been so confident and optimistic the day before now began to lose their nerve and suddenly started to make alarming and pessimistic predictions. President Wojciechowski, disgusted by the generals' vacillations, virtually took command himself. He ordered Witos and his cabinet, who were becoming unnerved as the fighting drew closer, to retire to the upper floors of the Belvedere while he directed the defense of the building. Wojciechowski proposed a rather theatrical scheme—the government troops would escape to the south to fight another day while the president and the cabinet covered their escape with volleys of shots from the palace's stock of revolvers.

In the end it did not come to this. Early in the afternoon the government's principal link with the rest of Poland, the airport, fell to Piłsudski's forces. They were massing for a direct assault on the Belvedere. Wojciechowski consulted with Colonel Władysław Anders, chief of staff to General Rozwadowski and the man who struck the president as being the most intelligent and level-headed officer in the Belvedere. Anders advised that they all flee Warsaw while the road to the south was still open. The government could establish itself, temporarily at least, in the suburb of Wilanow, where there was an old palace built by King John III Sobieski. They could take refuge there and loyalist troops that were known to be assembling south of Warsaw could join them.

The president took Anders's advice. At about 4 P.M. Wojciechowski, Witos, the cabinet, and the remaining troops, about two thousand men in all, marched out the back gates of the Belvedere. The entire party went on foot in a long column. With some difficulty they avoided Piłsudski's troops and, using back roads, made their way to Wilanow, four miles away. The party lost some stragglers and most of the loyalist 10th Infantry Regiment, which, while serving as a rear guard, was cut off and captured. So, when they arrived at Wilanow, there were only about one hundred soldiers present with the government. By 5:30 P.M. they were all established in one wing of the palace.

Immediately upon their arrival at Wilanow, the cabinet went into session to decide on their next move. President Wojciechowski joined the discussions. The flight from Warsaw had had a profoundly unsettling effect on the government members. No one could discern the practical alternatives left to them. The troops that the government's generals had claimed would rally to them at Wilanow had not arrived. Piłsudski's forces were closing in and would soon capture them. Their only chance for survival lay in flight to the south, where they could try to rally support, but they were not sure that they wanted to do this. Witos believed that if the fighting continued, Poland would either be destroyed in a civil war or would be overrun by the Soviet Union, which, according to a recent dispatch sent by General Sikorski from Lwów, was preparing for an invasion.

It is not clear who was responsible for the government's eventual decision to resign. In later years, everyone who had been at Wilanow blamed everyone else for stampeding the government. It is clear that all those present concluded that the only way Piłsudski's coup could be crushed was for the government to rally whatever forces it could and commence a long, bloody civil war on a nationwide scale. In the course of this war, it was probable that independent Poland would cease to exist. The government was unwilling to risk the nation's life. By 7 P.M. the government decided to ask for a cease-fire. Witos and his cabinet had determined that they would resign, and Wojciechowski announced his intention to resign, thus allowing the presidency constitutionally to devolve upon Maciej Rataj, the Marshal of the Sejm. The government was throwing in its hand, and no one knew what the next deal would bring.

The government's capitulation was accomplished quickly. Wojcie-chowski dispatched his personal chaplain to make contact with Rataj in Warsaw and apprise him of the situation. By 10 P.M. Rataj had notified Piłsudski, who immediately ordered a cease-fire. By midnight Rataj, accompanied by Colonel Beck, had arrived at Wilanow, where he received the resignations of Wojciechowski, Witos, and the entire cabinet. Rataj, now legally the president of the Polish Republic, ordered a cease-fire, announced his intention to consult with Piłsudski regarding a future government, and drove back to Warsaw.

In rather less than three days, and at the price of 371 dead, Piłsud-ski had overthrown the government and become the focal point of all power in Poland. (Casualty figures vary slightly depending on the source, but the most widely accepted figures are 371 killed, of which 176 were civilians, and 918 wounded, of which 313 were civilians.)[16]

The problem that faced Poland was the immediate establishment of a functioning government. This was urgent; it was obvious that the Witos cabinet could not stay on in a caretaker capacity. It had been expected that Piłsudski would simply announce his own assumption of the office of prime minister. But it became clear that he was going to permit the constitutional process to function, and it was therefore the duty of Acting-President Rataj to nominate a government. Rataj acted with admirable dispatch. Starting in the early hours of May 15, Rataj began to interview various political leaders and solicit their advice as to who should serve in a new cabinet. Rataj was, however, laboring under a misconception. Just because Piłsudski had as yet made no outright demands did not mean that he would tolerate the formation of a government that was not Piłsudski-ite. So when, at 8 A.M. on May 15, Rataj announced that he had selected Jan Debski, an important peasant party leader, to head a new government, Piłsudski acted promptly to set things straight. Within a half-hour he appeared at Rataj's offices and made it quite clear that his own nominee, Kazimierz Bartel, was to be prime minister. Rataj, although surprised at this abrupt demand, immediately agreed. By 7 P.M. Bartel had submitted to Rataj a list of his cabinet members, who at once assumed their offices.

The Bartel cabinet was essentially a government of experts. It was regarded as politically Centrist. All Right-wing leaders had been excluded, as had any prominent persons from the Left. The PPS leaders were both angered and embarrassed by this. They recognized that Piłsudski was telling them that he felt no particular obligation for the Socialists' support during his coup.

In addition to Prime Minister Bartel, who also took the portfolio of his specialty, the Ministry of Railways, the new cabinet consisted mostly of former professors and experienced civil servants. Four of them had previously been members of cabinets. The foreign minister was August Zaleski, a forty-three-year-old diplomat who had just served as Polish minister in Rome. For himself, Piłsudski chose only the office of minister of war.

On the morning of May 16 the new cabinet gathered for the customary group photograph. Piłsudski's appearance in this picture reveals the distress he had experienced during the preceding days. Alone among the cabinet members, the distressed Piłsudski does not look at the camera. He appears ashen and looks years older than photographs of him taken only a short time before.

Later that day Piłsudski returned to the Warsaw apartment to which he had moved his family from Sulejówek. His wife later wrote, "I was appalled at the change in him. In three days he had aged ten years. . . . Only on one other occasion did I ever see him look so ill, and that was within a few hours of his death."[17]

The Bartel government, having assumed office, quickly displayed a moderate approach that surprised both its friends and its enemies. Witos and his cabinet ministers, who had been placed in "protective custody" by Piłsudski's troops following their resignations at Wilanow, were quickly released and allowed to go about their business. Wojciechowski, who had been permitted to go home to his family on the night he handed over his office to Rataj, was not harassed in any way. There were no political arrests, no martial law, and no press censorship—although the new government strongly intimated that it expected cooperation from the press.

On May 16, the day after taking office, Bartel issued a lengthy statement that emphasized the legality of his cabinet's accession to power. Ignoring the circumstances under which his predecessor had resigned, Bartel stressed the constitutional character of his government. He called for domestic calm and asked the Polish people for hard work and patriotic dedication. Bartel promised that the Polish state would be purified of incompetent and corrupt elements and that its decayed political life would be regenerated. He implied that all this would be possible under the general leadership of Poland's First Marshal, who would provide a moral example as well as more specific guidance, which he left undefined. Bartel promised that upon the election of a president of the Republic to replace Acting-President Rataj—an event expected to take place within a few weeks—his cabinet would resign and place itself in the hands of the constitutional process. No one believed that this promise to resign meant that there would actually be a change in government. It seemed obvious that the new president would be Piłsudski, who would reappoint Bartel.

The rapidity with which calm now descended upon Poland was impressive. Even in Poznania and Pomerania, where the dominant National Democrats had been mobilizing paramilitary forces for a countercoup, overt opposition gradually died away. The press did as it had been warned to do, and comment on the new government was generally favorable. The parties of the Right, seeing that Piłsudski proposed no revolutionary changes and no vengeful reprisals, found little to complain about. Their members did not like Piłsudski any more than before, but they could scarcely object to the new government's call for domestic tranquillity and the elimination of corruption and incompetence. In fact, a few Rightist-dominated business groups were soon issuing public statements cautiously praising the Bartel cabinet's moderation and efficiency.

Ironically, it was the parties of the Left who had the most to complain about. As if to demonstrate that he recognized no obligations to the Left, Piłsudski's government rejected demands from the Left more frequently, it seemed, than it did those from the Right. For example, upon Piłsudski's expected election to the presidency, the PPS wanted parliament dissolved and new elections held. They were certain that new parliamentary elections would give them a commanding majority over the discredited Right. Piłsudski absolutely refused to discuss the matter. There were other issues, too. The Left-wing politicians resented being lumped together with the Right and Center in Bartel's condemnations of corrupt politicians. And certainly the Left was offended by its exclusion from the Bartel cabinet. But for the moment the Leftists suffered in silence. They awaited the presidential elections, now scheduled for May 31, at which time they would again support Piłsudski, hoping that this fresh expression of their devotion would finally win them the Marshal's favor. The PPS members could not believe that Piłsudski, who had sprung from their ranks, would continue to ignore them. They were certain that he would veer to the Left following the presidential election, and they looked forward to being strongly represented in the new cabinet that would be formed following the election.

All the parties of the Left came to believe in the imminence of a rapprochement with Piłsudski. The Polish Communist Party, which was illegal but was operating fairly openly through a variety of fronts, scarcely expected to be brought into a Piłsudski-ite government, but the Commnunists did not at this time regret their support of Piłsudski's coup. In fact, the CPP was even prepared to use its meager resources to help elect Piłsudski to the presidency. The CPP was supporting the Marshal because he seemed to represent a lesser evil than a coup by the Polish Right. And the CPP hoped to be able eventually to infiltrate the Piłsudski government, which would have been ideologically softened by the expected inclusion of the PPS.

The Polish Communists would soon come to regret their backing of Piłsudski. Within only a few weeks they were sharply criticized by Stalin for supporting Piłsudski's coup. By the end of the year the CPP was violently assailed by the Comintern in Moscow for this mistake, and the Polish party split into "left" and "right" wings because of it. Eventually the "May Error" of the CPP would become famous in the litany of Communist deviations.

On May 29, two days before the presidential elections, a large group of senators and deputies gathered at the Prime Minister's offices to listen to a lengthy speech by Piłsudski. They had come at Bartel's invitation to hear the Marshal's views on the Polish presidency. Very few members of the Right had accepted Bartel's invitation, and none of the national minorities had even been invited. So the majority of those present were from the Left or Center and could thus be expected to support a Piłsudski candidacy.

Given the composition of this audience, Piłsudski's speech was startling. Dressed as usual in an Army uniform, the Marshal hectored his listeners in a belligerent and threatening manner. He opened with an abrupt refusal to either explain or apologize for his recent coup. He claimed that his conscience did not trouble him, and he regarded the matter as closed. Piłsudski reminded his listeners that, at the time of Poland's rebirth in 1918, he could easily have become the nation's dictator. But the idea had been repugnant to him, and he had given the power of governing to the Polish people as represented by their politicians in the parliament. But these politicians, Piłsudski declared, had permitted Poland to sink into a swamp of corruption. They had been responsible for Narutowicz's murder. Their greed and stupidity had forced him to initiate his successful coup. And now, Piłsudski continued, he again had the opportunity to become Poland's dictator. But as before, the idea was repugnant to him, and in permitting presidential elections, he was again returning power to the people. "I do not want to govern Poland with a whip," he said. However, he warned that this was the politicians' last chance. They were free to elect whomever they wished, but they must elect a strong president. He must be a man who would be a national leader and totally above their parliamentary squabbles and politicking. And once they had elected him, then parliament must recess. The senators and deputies must go away for a time and let the president appoint a government and permit the government to govern. If they again proved incapable or faithless, he would "no longer protect them from the anger of the street when the next revolutionary wave burst."[18] With this he dismissed his audience.

Piłsudski had made himself very clear, and his listeners were sure that they understood him. They believed he had given the parliament little choice. It could elect Piłsudski and then adjourn until he called it into session, or it could refuse to elect him, and the Marshal would then foment a revolution and ride in to total power on the shields of the Army. The members of the parliament dispersed to carry this threatening message to their colleagues.

To most persons, Piłsudski's warnings were unnecessary. He was, of course, the nominee of the Left for the presidency. Without doubt he would be elected. In fact, until the very day of the election the Right was not able to find a candidate to oppose him. Finally, on the morning of May 31, the day of the election, a second-rank National Democratic official, Count Adolf Bniński, was persuaded to stand for the Right. Only one ballot was needed. The result was 292 for Piłsudski and 193 for Bniński. Piłsudski swept the Left and Center, even gaining a scattering of votes from the Right.

The outcome of the election created immediate excitement and enthusiasm in Warsaw. The PPS, still determined to regard Piłsudski as one of their own, commenced a huge parade. The Army dispatched an honor guard to "report" the Marshal's election to the Tomb of the Unknown Soldier. Then, with this rather theatrical business out of the way, the news of the election was officially conveyed to Piłsudski himself who was waiting in his apartment. It was now Piłsudski's turn to be theatrical. On the stationery of the Ministry of War, he wrote a brief note flatly declining to serve as president of the Polish Republic.

This was a bombshell. Everyone had assumed that his speech of May 29 had indirectly announced his candidacy. Certainly he had never once hinted that he, the most obvious candidate for the office, would refuse it. Indeed, he had gone out of his way to give the impression that if he was not elected to the office, then he would seize it. But Piłsudski did not want to be president. He had allowed himself to be elected to legitimize his coup and to display his contempt for the parliament. As he observed in his letter of refusal, "For the second time in my life my deeds and historical works are legalized."[19] Poland's politicians had given him the highest office they had in their power to award, and he had thrown it back in their faces.

A new presidential election was promptly scheduled by the parliament for June 1, the very day after Piłsudski's election and refusal. By this haste, the humiliated senators and deputies hoped to embarrass Piłsudski, who presumably would propose a candidate to act as his stand-in. Such rapid new elections were expected to catch Piłsudski unready, and this would redress to some extent the affront given the parliament.

This plan nearly worked. Piłsudski had indeed made no definite decision regarding his presidential nominee. He wanted a widely respected, nonparty figure who would make a strong president. But there were not many such persons available, particularly in view of the fact that any nominee of Piłsudski's would obviously have to function to some degree as the Marshal's mouthpiece. In the few hours available between his rejection of the presidency and the commencement of new balloting, Piłsudski and his aides hastily considered a number of candidates. One of them, Prince Lubomirski, refused. Several other possible candidates were rejected as too old or too out-of-touch. Finally, haste being imperative, Bartel suggested the name of Ignacy Mościcki. Piłsudski instantly approved.

Mościcki, like so many other Polish political figures, had been a university professor—in fact, he was a renowned chemist. Born in 1867, he had been active in his youth in the PPS, where he knew Piłsudski well. As a young chemistry instructor, Mościcki had made bombs for the activist section of the PPS. But he became increasingly involved in his profession and gradually drifted away from political activities. He moved to Switzerland, where he became a professor at the University of Fribourg and became famous for several technical inventions. Shortly before World War I Mościcki returned to his homeland, where he distinguished himself as the superbly effective manager of a large government-owned Silesian nitrate works. Without question he was a competent organizer and internationally famous in scientific circles; he had the additional advantage of being to some degree a man of the Left. This last was particularly important, because the Leftists could not be counted on to support a Piłsudski candidate in the new elections. Piłsudski's rejection of the presidency had been a terrible blow to them. Moreover, the Leftists were affronted by the fact that Piłsudski apparently expected and took for granted their support. The general feeling among them was that they had shown Piłsudski vastly more loyalty than he had shown them—which was true. So, ignoring Mościcki, the rank-and-file PPS deputies supported their own candidate, a fellow deputy named Zygmunt Marek.

The first ballot on June was indecisive. There were 211 votes for Bniński, who was again the candidate of the Right, and Marek got 56. Mościcki got 215 votes. On a second ballot the PPS, having made their gesture of defiance, withdrew Marek's candidacy. Mościcki received 281 votes, just barely enough for election to the office that he would hold for thirteen years.

The outcome was all that Piłsudski could have asked. He had splintered and degraded the parliament. He had forced the election of a man who would prove his obedient and reliable supporter. The two men exchanged immediate and warm salutations, Piłsudski praising Mościcki for his "clear and methodical mind, which would be brought to bear in a salutary manner on all questions." Mościcki responded in kind, stating that the Marshal "as no other man in no other country, incarnated his nation."[20]

Piłsudski rejected proposals for dissolving the parliament, even though new elections would have swept out of office many of the discredited politicians who had opposed him. He rather liked the confusion and divisions that now developed among the legislators. He told a friend who had asked him about the holding of elections in the near future, "It is not clear what tomorrow [i.e., new elections] would bring, so I will not hurry. . . . Moreover, at present they vote as I like, resolve as I command, because they are afraid."[21]

The Bartel government, fulfilling its promise, resigned immediately after the election of a new president. Mościcki asked Bartel to form a new government, and after three days' delay—presumably to avoid the appearance of unseemly haste—Bartel agreed. His new cabinet was virtually identical with the previous one. Piłsudski again served as minister of war. Immediate matters of government having thus been satisfactorily disposed of, Piłsudski was now free to turn his attention to the Army.

Piłsudski's obsessive concern for the Polish Army, *his* army as he regarded it, has often been remarked. Following his coup Piłsudski could hardly wait to divest himself of political affairs so that he might throw himself into reconstructing the Army. In fact, he had acted almost at once to begin the process of reconciliation within the Army. On May 22 he had issued an eloquent Order of the Day, which was read to every unit in the Army. The Marshal's message was that it had been its soldiers that had won Poland its independence, and it had been Poland's soldiers, all of them, that had recently rescued the nation from political strife. Piłsudski attempted to avoid even mentioning that the Polish Army had ever been divided. Certainly he repudiated the idea that any conflict would ever be perpetuated within the Army. Piłsudski, anguished by the loss of life caused by the coup, concluded his Order with an appeal: "May God who is merciful forgive our sins and withhold his avenging arm; and as for us, let us set about our work to strengthen and rejuvenate our land."[22]

There were a number of Army matters that Piłsudski believed needed his attention. One was the command structure, the organization of which had been a factor in precipitating his coup. After this was the restoration of the Army's morale, which Piłsudski regarded as having suffered in unwholesome hands during the period that he had been out of power. Finally, and perhaps most importantly, the profound division caused by the coup had to be healed. This last was crucial, and because Piłsudski had been responsible for the combat within the Army, he undertook to remedy its aftermath.

This was no mean task. The Polish Army was very large for its time—nearly 300,000 men, with an officer corps of 18,000. Although most of these troops had taken no part in the actual fighting, a large percentage of the senior officers had been compelled by force of circumstances to give some indication as to where their loyalties lay; and many of these officers now found that they had chosen the "wrong" side.

Piłsudski did his best to ignore the question of which side an officer had been on. He was not by nature a vindictive person. He regarded most of the officers who had fought against him as honorable men who simply obeyed orders. Piłsudski even complimented certain units for the skill with which they had fought his own forces. Otherwise, he behaved as if the intra-Army combat had never taken place. He refused to award any medals for valor or service during the coup. Insofar as possible he continued to promote officers who had been on the "wrong" side. For example, he retained Major Marian Porwit, the resolute officer who had refused to permit the insurgent forces to cross the Poniatowski Bridge, as commander of the Infantry Officers School.

In short, Piłsudski refused to authorize a purge of the officer corps. The only exceptions to this were his old enemies at the general-officer level. These men he regarded as having fought him for personal reasons. It did not prove difficult to eliminate the Viennese War Academy from the Army. Most were older men, such as Generals Haller and Szeptycki, who at once retired. A few others were jailed on charges of corruption, although most of these were freed without being brought to trial. Those valuable senior officers whose loyalty to Piłsudski was suspect (such as Sikorski) were assigned ardent Piłsudski-ites as chiefs of staff.

Although Piłsudski rarely sanctioned any retaliatory action against an officer, particularly one of middle or junior grade, this did not mean that such reprisals did not occur. Even though the Marshal generally refused to punish those who had opposed him, he did reward those whose support had been conspicuous—and these favored ones frequently made subtle reprisals on fellow officers who had been on the other side. Thus, well below the Marshal's level of attention and generally unknown to him, a purge of sorts actually did take place. Medical review boards were extraordinarily quick to find certain officers unfit for further service, and promotion boards were suspiciously slow in passing upon the upgrading of many others. Sometimes Piłsudski would notice a particular case of this kind and intervene to rectify it, as when he spied Colonel Władysław Anders at a diplomatic reception in 1930. Anders had, of course, ended up as the virtual commander of the government forces just before the cease-fire on May 14. He had been a colonel then, and although his talent and dedication were well known, he held the same rank four years later. "Oh, still a colonel, Anders?" Piłsudski asked, seeming surprised. "Of course, Marshal," Anders replied. Piłsudski said nothing more, but when the next list of promotions to brigadier general was announced, Anders's name was on it.[23]

Nonetheless, Piłsudski could not be everywhere or see everything. Although the divisions produced by the coup were gradually healed, the most fortunate officers were those who had served under the Commandant in the P.O.W. or the Legion and had taken a strong Piłsudski-ite stand during the coup. For men with this background, there were clearly great opportunities in the Polish state.

Although deeply involved in Army affairs, Piłsudski found time to encourage the passage of amendments to the constitution. In mid-June 1926, the Bartel government presented to the Sejm drafts of a number of amendments. The government simultaneously began a press campaign designed to develop public support and to pressure the parliament into adopting these amendments. And a month later they were approved by the Sejm by an impressive majority of 246 to 95. They went into effect on August 2, 1926. Most of the amendments had been passed exactly as submitted by Bartel. Most Poles now accepted the idea that the 1921 constitution needed alteration, and the changes suggested by the government did not seem excessive.

All of these "August Amendments," as they came to be called, added to the powers of the presidency, while diminishing those of the Sejm. There were four principal amendments. The most important permitted the President, upon recommendation of the cabinet, to adjourn the parliament for thirty days. Another amendment gave the cabinet the power to promulgate the annual national budget by decree in the event that the parliament failed to pass one. This was a valuable weapon for a Polish cabinet. In the past, the parliament had held a whip hand over the cabinet by its power to refuse to authorize a national budget.

A third amendment enabled the President in the case of "urgent state necessity" to enact laws in many areas simply by his own decree during any period that the parliament was not in session. The final major constitutional change was a provision that limited the parliament's power to compel the ouster of a government or an individual minister. A minimum one-day "cooling off" period was now required between the introduction of a motion to censure and the vote upon it. This amendment, which seemed like inconsequential tinkering with the constitutional process, had far-reaching consequences. The "cooling-off" day gave the President, with the concurrence of the cabinet, the opportunity to adjourn the parliament before it could force the cabinet's fall. This provision was expected to curb the parliamentary capriciousness that led to frequent changes of government.

There were several other amendments, but those were of a relatively minor nature. All in all, though, the fact was that the parliament had voted through a series of constitutional changes that reduced its powers by transferring them to the President and cabinet. These amendments could have been passed only by a parliament that was splintered and, moreover, was frightened of Piłsudski.

In fact, the parliament gave up even more than a number of its constitutional privileges. The senators and deputies had also passed a separate but companion piece of legislation. Known as the "Act Conferring Full Powers," its authority ran until 1928. It gave the president very sweeping powers to "harmonize existing laws with the constitution and enforce those of its provisions that call for . . . special laws, reorganize and simplify the state administration and put in order the legal system of the country . . . ensure budgetary equilibrium, stabilize the currency and the economic reconstruction of the state."[24] In effect, this act enabled the President to rule by decree over an enormous range of the nation's activities. While this law was in force, the presidential powers clearly outweighed those of the parliament.

Practically the first of the presidential decrees dealt with Piłsudski's obsession, the reorganization of the command structure of the Army. This decree, having the force of law, was practically a copy of that which Piłsudski had promulgated while chief of state in 1921. The president was authorized to appoint the inspector-general of the Army, who was to be the commander in chief in time of war. The inspector-general's powers over the Army, in both war and peace, were almost absolute. The Polish General Staff was subordinate to him and he was virtually immune from parliamentary interference. Piłsudski, of course, was appointed inspector-general in addition to continuing as minister of war.

The improvement in the administration of the Polish government in the months following Piłsudski's coup was immediate and dramatic. This improvement was chiefly due to the fact that Prime Minister Bartel turned out to be a brilliant and innovative executive with a passion for organization and a determination to govern unimpeded by parliament.

Kazimierz Bartel had started out in life as a locksmith's apprentice, but, by dint of enormous effort, he had gotten a university education and had subsequently become professor of mathematics at Lwów Polytechnic University. Surprisingly, for a man who had become so close to Piłsudski, Bartel had not been a member of either the Legion or the P.O.W. He had not even been in the PPS, but he had at one time been a member of the Left-wing peasant party, the Populist (Liberation) Party. However, Bartel had broken with it over its attitude toward expropriation of estates, and now he belonged to no party and was regarded as a Centrist.

Although Bartel was only forty-four years old, he suffered from a kidney ailment that kept him in almost constant pain. Despite this, he almost always maintained a pleasant demeanor, and even his parliamentary enemies found it difficult to dislike Bartel on a personal level. As prime minister, he went out of his way to do small favors for any member of parliament. He saw no point in being unnecessarily offensive to anyone. In short order, many Polish legislators found themselves supporting the Prime Minister in matters that they would not ordinarily back. They had become victims of the Prime Minister's unusual conciliatory style, which became known as "Bartelisme." But all this did not mean that Bartel lacked convictions. From the very beginning of his ministry he adopted the attitude, unusual in Polish politics, that Poland's senators and deputies had only one right—that of making laws. It was the right of his ministry to implement these laws, and he refused to permit parliamentary interference. For example, the practice of questioning government ministers from the floor of the Sejm chamber was scandalously misused in Poland. Deputies and senators had virtually blackmailed various ministries by threatening to raise questions on embarrassing or sensitive matters. Bartel put an end to this by refusing to permit his cabinet ministers to answer questions from the floor. He also formed special committees of experts in agriculture, economics, education and labor to work within the prime minister's office. Members of the parliament quickly found that the Bartel government was better informed than they were and could therefore defuse most parliamentary criticism through public rebuttal by experts.

Bartel's committees of experts drafted legislation for submission to the parliament. Members of Bartel's staff worked to ensure the draft's passage exactly as written by the government. These procedures, as politically rudimentary as they now seem, were impressive innovations in Polish government of the time.

In dealing with his own cabinet, Bartel showed similar expertise and determination. Under most previous governments, each cabinet minister had acted as the semi-independent ruler of his own ministry, which all too frequently became a cornucopia of patronage for the minister's political party. Bartel's cabinet ministers, however, were expected to function efficiently and without reference to any political friendships or loyalties they might have. The budget for every ministry had to be audited and approved by Bartel's own staff. Bartel held his cabinet members strictly accountable for their ministries. They were not permitted to have extensive separate political careers. They were required to submit any speeches before the parliament to the Prime Minister's office for clearance. Bartel required each of his cabinet members, before taking office, to give him a signed but undated letter of resignation. Bartel could simply fill in the date and "accept" this resignation whenever he wished. Interestingly, even Piłsudski gave Bartel such a letter.

Bartel himself prepared the entire agenda for every cabinet meeting and would not permit any subject to be brought up without his prior approval.

At the Prime Minister's instruction, positive evidence of loyalty to the Bartel government was required of all senior personnel. Any senior civil servant, particularly a provincial governor, prefect or subprefect, who was not prepared to display scrupulous dedication and enthusiasm for the government's policies was instantly dismissed.

Piłsudski was more than content to allow Bartel to function mostly on his own. The Marshal had no desire to be involved in the day-to-day functions of government. He asked only that the cabinet be strong, honest, and efficient, and that it allow him to devote himself to the Army and foreign affairs. In fact, Piłsudski was so disinterested in the daily details of Bartel's ministry that he attended only about one third of the cabinet meetings, and even then he often stayed for only part of the session.

Coincidentally with Bartel's improvements in Polish government administration came dramatic improvements in the Polish economy. Very little of this economic recovery can be credited to Piłsudski or his coup. Piłsudski himself had only the haziest knowledge of economics and had proposed no plan whatsoever for the improvement of the deteriorated Polish economy. Piłsudski's interest in government finance extended only to insuring that public funds were not stolen. He viewed the minister of finance as a high-level bookkeeper whose duty it was to make sure that no money was embezzled from the treasury. Even Bartel had little expertise in the critical area of fiscal policy. His government had pledged that it would not undertake any radical economic experiments, and their attempts to improve the economy differed little from the unsuccessful efforts of previous governments.

Most of the sudden improvement in Polish economic affairs was the result of amazing good fortune. Before Piłsudski's coup the Polish coal-mining industry had been severely depressed. There was work for less than half the miners. But practically simultaneously with the coup came a three-month strike by British coal miners. Suddenly, the Polish mines in Upper Silesia were deluged with orders from all over Europe. There was employment for every miner, and the export price of coal soared.

At the same time, ironically, many of the economic efforts of previous governments came to fruition. Only two weeks after the coup, the Polish textile industry received a large British loan. A month later a large American investment in the Silesian zinc industry was announced. Other foreign loans, all of which had been in negotiation for months or years, suddenly came through in a cluster. They stimulated business, and the rate of unemployment among industrial workers dropped rapidly while wages rose. Even agricultural export prices increased as the result of a worldwide rise in food prices.

The sensational increase in coal exports produced, for the first time in independent Poland, a surplus of exports over imports. The industrial revival produced an increase in internal tax revenue for the fiscal year from April 1, 1926, to March 31, 1927, and this produced the first surplus of receipts over expenditures in independent Poland's national budget. In turn, the confidence that this over-all economic recovery generated resulted in a sevenfold increase in the reserves of the Bank of Poland. And this was accompanied by a dramatic increase in the value of the Polish zloty, which rose from 11 to the American dollar to 9.15 to the dollar in the two months following Piłsudski's coup.

The government took advantage of the fortunate economic climate to put into effect an ambitious package of loans and monetary reforms known as the Stabilization Plan. Although this entire plan had been developed several years before by the Grabski government, only now were circumstances favorable for its implementation. During late 1926 and extending into 1927, a number of measures were taken with the objective of "stabilizing the zloty, on a good basis, establishing Poland's credit at home and abroad, and measuring a solid foundation for the economic development of the country."[25] Small-denomination paper currency was called in and reissued in silver coinage. Certain short-term treasury debts were paid off and the capital of the Bank of Poland was increased by 50 percent. The culmination of this and the capstone of the Stabilization Plan was the successful floating in October 1927 of a long-term loan from a syndicate, most of whose members were United States investment bankers. With this so-called Stabilization Loan, Poland's currency was considered among the world's most solid. Within a few months the Polish treasury reserves exceeded a half-billion zlotys, a surplus of a size that was almost embarrassing. Quite naturally, the Bartel government took full credit for all these happy economic developments.

As 1926 ended it was possible to put Piłsudski's "intervention" (he preferred this word to *coup*) into some sort of perspective. Piłsudski had ridden back into power almost on a whim and surely on a misconception.

Unlike most men who seize power, he had little in the way of a definite and detailed plan for what he would do when he got it. He was also unusual in that he headed no political party. The only ideology that Piłsudski brought with him was the intense conviction that Poland's affairs had been terribly mismanaged, but that they could somehow be put right by a man of integrity and dedication. His followers had already coined a word to describe the movement that the Marshal personified—*Sanacja*, which can be roughly translated as a "movement of cleansing change." Piłsudski conceived of his own role in Polish life as being that of a vastly respected, almost infallible figure towering above the everyday business of politics. He intended to personally direct only foreign affairs and the Army, which he hoped to make a bastion of purity from which his devoted young officers would go forth to serve the nation in many fields. Otherwise he would rule mostly by personal example, and under his leadership the Polish people would reconcile their differences and move forward in unity.

Without doubt, Piłsudski had had a good deal of sheer luck. His success in pulling off his coup without having it devolve into a full-fledged civil war was based, to a great extent, on luck. His economic successes were either good fortune of the harvest of the fruits of the work of others. At this point Piłsudski was safe from political attack simply because the Right viewed him as the only alternative to the domination of the Left, while the Left viewed him as their savior against the Right.

Opposition to Piłsudski was rare at the end of 1926, when every aspect of Polish life seemed to be improving. Piłsudski's political opponents had been badly disorganized by the coup and were still regrouping. Few people realized that Piłsudski had no detailed plans for Poland's future. It was assumed that he had come to power with a definite program to right all wrongs and remedy all ills, and it was supposed that he would reveal his plans at the appropriate moment.

II

Friends and Enemies

PIŁSUDSKI BELIEVED HE HAD a "feel" for diplomacy, and he was probably right. For as long as he lived, Poland's foreign policy was Piłsudski's foreign policy. While there could be, and very frequently were,
enormous divisions within Poland on domestic matters, there was
practically never any public dispute about foreign affairs. All parties
and all persons closed ranks in support of the Marshal and his policies.

Piłsudski had chosen August Zaleski to serve as foreign minister in
the government formed after the coup. For a relatively young man in
a virtually new diplomatic service, Zaleski had had a good deal of
experience. During World War I he had been chief of the Polish
Information Committee in London. He was independent Poland's
first minister to Greece, and later he served as minister to Italy. But
he was known as a supporter of Piłsuski, and the precoup government
had been about to make him pay for this. In May 1926, Zaleski was
in Warsaw on his way from Rome to Tokyo, where he was being
shuffled into a dead-end job as Polish minister to Japan. After the
coup Piłsudski selected Zaleski because he was on the spot and because he was a known quantity. It turned out that Zaleski's temperament precisely suited the requirements of the hour. Plodding, pleasant and patient, he was content to follow without complaint the
instructions of the Marshal. At first these orders were so detailed that
Zaleski gained the reputation—with the United States minister at

least—of being "an office boy doing the bidding of Piłsudski."[1] But the Marshal soon lost interest in the petty details, and Zaleski's authority expanded slightly. Even so, no decision of any importance was made without Piłsudski's approval.

Within days after the coup, Piłsudski was asked whether any of Poland's powerful neighbors posed an immediate threat to the country. He foresaw no acute problem developing in the very near future and said, "We have at least five years of calm."[2] He believed that the coming half-decade had to be years of consolidation and preparation. Poland had to solidify its relations with its allies, reduce tensions with its smaller neighbors, and build up its strength against potential enemies, while remaining on the best of terms with them.

Polish foreign policy was to be essentially defensive. Poland had no significant territorial ambitions; all it desired was to preserve its independence and to maintain its present frontiers. As the French ambassador reported to his government, Piłsudski had advised the Rumanian government, "I don't want to annoy the Soviet Union. I only want to live in peace with the whole world and be satisfied with our boundaries which are already stretched too far and which I have to guard."[3] The keystone of Polish foreign policy was, of course, the nation's alliance with France. (In 1924 Poland was gratified when the French legation in Warsaw was raised to the status of an embassy. The British government elevated its Warsaw legation to an embassy in September 1929, an action taken shortly thereafter by the United States and Italy. Today virtually every nation exchanges ambassadors with even the smallest and most inconsequential countries, and it is difficult to comprehend the importance that was once attached to the exchange of ambassadors. France, for example, maintained embassies in only ten capitals in 1925. To exchange ambassadors in this period was a signal of exceptional respect or recognition of mutual importance between two nations.)

The special relationship between France and Poland explains why the Locarno Pact, which was signed seven months before Piłsudski's return to power, was such a frightening event for Poland. This pact, concluded on October 16, 1925, was named after its place of signature, a very small, charming Swiss health resort on the northern shore of Lake Maggiore. It was not a single pact, but rather a series of seven interlocking agreements among France, Britain, Italy, Belgium, Germany, Czechoslovakia and Poland. At the time, it seemed that these agreements marked the dawn of a new age in European diplomacy.

In Locarno's village square, bands played and peasants danced. Even cynical newsmen were crying with joy. The next day's headline in *The New York Times* read, "France and Germany Bar War Forever." Italy's premier, Benito Mussolini, had sailed dramatically across the lake, signed the treaties, and sailed back. British Foreign Secretary Austen Chamberlain was made a Knight of the Garter for his role in the conclusion of the treaties. Most of the other statesmen involved were rewarded in similar fashion by their grateful nations; they all viewed Locarno as the most important event in European diplomacy since the Treaty of Versailles.

The Locarno events had all started with Germany's Minister of Foreign Affairs Gustav Stresemann, who had a rather simple objective in mind. Under the provisions of the Treaty of Versailles, France and Britain were still occupying the German Rhineland. Stresemann wanted to terminate this occupation before it precipitated a separatist movement among the Rhinelanders.

Early in 1925, the German ambassadors in Paris and London communicated Germany's willingness to make sweeping concessions in the interests of a permanent European peace. In particular, Germany indicated its willingness to agree to the permanence of its present frontiers with France and Belgium, a matter that had been in dispute ever since the borders had been drawn in the Treaty of Versailles. The Germans let it be known that an integral part of the plan was the ending of the Allied occupation of the Rhineland. For the next eight months, the British and the French consulted each other and then consulted the Germans. A rather broad preliminary agreement was worked out, and it was decided that the three nations would meet at Locarno for final discussions. The British and French had kept Belgium and Italy closely informed of their plans. The Poles and the Czechs had been kept advised too, but not in very great detail.

The Czechs and Poles were upset by what they learned of these discussions, which to them smelled suspiciously like a sellout by their French allies or an extremely clever German stratagem to break up France's treaty structure with its eastern allies. The French tried to allay Czech and Polish fears, but their anxiety was heightened when neither received formal invitations to participate in the conference at Locarno. In great embarrassment, the foreign ministers of the two nations were forced to travel to Locarno to play almost the role of high-class gate crashers. To the chagrin of the Polish Foreign Minister Count Aleksander Skrzyński, and to the private glee of

Germany's Stresemann, the Poles were kept waiting for a week before being admitted to the councils of the senior nations. Even then, the various suggestions and treaty drafts that the Poles had brought with them were largely ignored or rejected. It was little consolation to the Poles that the Czechs were dealt with in similarly cavalier fashion.

After the briefest possible consultation with the smaller nations, the great powers announced and signed a series of treaties. The most important of these was the Treaty of Mutual Guarantee by which Germany, France, and Belgium mutually guaranteed their common borders and agreed to submit any border disputes to the League of Nations. Under this treaty, Britain and Italy also agreed to come to the assistance of any of the signatories whose frontiers with one another were violated without provocation. This treaty was widely called a document that made war impossible. It was expected that the climate of mutual trust that this treaty produced would hasten the evacuation of Allied troops from the Rhineland (which it did) and would enable Germany to join the League of Nations promptly (which it also did).

But to Poland and Czechoslovakia, who were not signatories to the Treaty of Mutual Guarantee, this agreement gave grounds for the greatest concern. While Germany had declared its recognition and acceptance of its western borders (and the great powers had, in turn, guaranteed their inviolability), Germany had said nothing about its eastern frontiers, and no mention had been made about guaranteeing them. Moreover, it appeared that by this treaty, France had renounced its right to go to war with Germany unless the League of Nations agreed that it had been attacked, clearly a cumbersome and uncertain process. Obviously France's commitment to obtain the League's approval before going to war meant that France's treaties with Poland and Czechoslovakia would greatly decline in value.

The only compensation that the two eastern states were given were separate "arbitration-of-differences" treaties between Germany on one hand and Poland and Czechoslovakia on the other. This did not seem like very much, so France single-handedly concluded at Locarno separate treaties with its two eastern allies. In these, France promised to go to their defense in the event that they were attacked by Germany and the League of Nations agreed they were attacked without provocation.

This was a rather complicated deal for Foreign Minister Skrzyński to take back to Warsaw. Although he tried to put a good face on it, it was clear that Germany, by refusing to guarantee its eastern frontiers, had served notice that it refused to accept the permanency of its borders with Poland. Equally disturbing was the fact that France had seemingly bargained away much of its ability to give military aid to Poland in the event of a Polish-German war. Certainly France could no longer play the role of Poland's staunch, uncritical ally. All that Poland had gotten was a couple of meaningless treaties. For all of the relaxation of West European tensions that the "Locarno Spirit" produced, it could not be ignored that Locarno had been a serious diplomatic defeat for Poland. No one was quicker to point this out than Piłsudski, then, prior to his coup, living at Sulejówek. He scoffed at the manner in which the Polish government had allowed itself to be treated, the lack of a formal invitation to Locarno, and the refusal of the great powers to permit Poland to enter their councils. He believed that Poland had been hoodwinked and that France might well be preparing to renege on its alliance with Poland. Piłsudski referred to Locarno as a "notoriously brutal attempt"[4] by Germany to break up Poland's alliance with France and said that "every good Pole spits with disgust at the name [of Locarno]."[5]

After Piłsudski came to power, the French gave indications that they would welcome conferences to "clarify" the meaning of the 1921 Franco-Polish Alliance in light of the events of Locarno. Upon Piłsudski's instructions, the Polish government refused to entertain any discussion whatever on the matter. Piłsudski foresaw that by "clarification" the French actually meant modifications and limitations of their commitment to Poland. The Polish government declined to admit that there could be any modifications or limitations to the 1921 treaty and adopted the position that Locarno had no effect whatever on the Polish alliance with France. The Poles cited various official statements made after Locarno in which the French had assured them that there was no change in their mutual relationship. So what was there to talk about? This stance intensely annoyed the French, but they could do nothing about it, and the alliance remained as written.

The Locarno Pact, or really the imminence of the pact, had driven Poland and Czechoslovakia into a modest rapprochement. As Germany, France and Great Britain were conducting preparatory negotiations for Locarno during the spring and summer of 1925, the alarmed governments of Czechoslovakia and Poland realized that they had a community of interest. Both stood to lose under the Locarno arrangement. At a League of Nations meeting in March 1925, Polish Foreign Minister Skrzyński met with his Czechoslovakian opposite number, Eduard Beneš. After a discussion of the Beneš-Skirmunt Pact of 1921, which, as we have seen, was not ratified, the two men decided that the time had come for another attempt at reconcilation. Rapprochement was made doubly appealing by the knowledge that the German Foreign Office believed that the enmity between Czechoslovakia and Poland was so deep that any understanding between the two could be, in the words of the German minister at Prague, "completely ruled out."[6]

In mid-April, Skrzyński traveled to Prague, where he was treated with the greatest cordiality. A few days later Beneš came to Warsaw, where, following a series of lavish official receptions, treaties were signed on April 23.

Unfortunately, these treaties were limited. The serious animosity between the two nations generated by the Teschen dispute and the Czech embargo on arms shipped to Poland during the Polish-Soviet War was still too fresh too allow a free and trusting relationship. It should also be noted that there has been a historic antipathy between these two nationalities, an aversion that is difficult to explain since both are western Slavs and speak remarkably similiar languages. In any event, the Czechoslovak-Polish treaties of 1925 did not produce anything remotely close to a major alliance. But there was a treaty of arbitration and conciliation, another treaty regulating the treatment of each other's minorities, and a commercial treaty. There was certainly nothing very earth-shaking about these treaties, although Warsaw and Prague, in preparation for Locarno, tried to make these treaties seem like more than they were. The Germans were surprised but unimpressed. Only the French, happy to display a benevolent attitude toward its two protégés, responded with official huzzahs.

The Polish government, humiliated at Locarno and able to claim only the faintest of successes in its treaties with Czechoslovakia, now believed it essential to achieve some sort of diplomatic victory. Happily, there was an opportunity at hand. The Polish-Rumanian alliance signed in 1921 was about to expire. Renegotiating a treaty with Rumania posed no problems for Poland. The occasion was, in truth, a pleasure for both parties. There existed between these two nations a strong bond of compatibility and friendship, and on March 26, 1926, they renewed their treaty of alliance. Actually, the new treaty went

further than the previous one. The 1921 treaty had promised mutual
support only in the event of an attack on either nation's eastern frontiers—in other words, each would support the other in the event of
war with Soviet Russia. In the new treaty the two signatories undertook to guarantee each other's borders against attack from any quarter. For Poland this was a worthwhile accomplishment. A close
alliance with a nation of nearly twenty million headed by a strong
king was a valuable asset. The Polish government made the most of
this diplomatic achievement.

Another sequel to Locarno was the alteration of Poland's status
in the League of Nations. The League was divided into two member
bodies—the Assembly, in which every nation was represented, and the
smaller Council, on which, at its inception, only eight nations held
seats. There were two types of seats on the Council. Permanent seats
were held by the larger, more important nations. The nonpermanent
seats were rotated among smaller nations, which held them for short
periods of time. Apart from the very significant matter of prestige,
permanent membership on the Council had important procedural
values. The members of the Council controlled the League's agenda
and had various veto privileges over decisions of the League.

Poland had not held a seat on the Council since the organization
of the League of Nations in 1919. Polish appeals for permanent Council membership were constant, particularly because the continuous
imbroglios over Danzig and the German "optants" problem had been
brought before the League for solution. Poland had thus become the
League's "best customer," and consequently the Council was an important forum for Poland.

In 1926, under the terms of the Locarno agreements, Germany
became a member of the League and was immediately elected to a
permanent seat on the Council. It now seemed more important than
ever for Poland to obtain a Council seat and thus achieve international acceptance as a "great power." To the fury of the Poles, Germany opposed this. The issue quickly became more than a matter of
national prestige. To the Poles, obtaining a permanent Council seat
seemed almost a question of national survival. In September 1926,
the matter was finally resolved. Poland was voted a nonpermanent
Council seat for a three-year term and with eligibility for reelection
at the end of the term. This "semipermanent seat" was made possible
by a special amendment to the Locarno agreement, and Poland's elec-

tion to it was hailed by the Poles as a great diplomatic triumph, and perhaps it was.

Shortly after Poland's elevation to a Council seat, the League of Nations became the site of a dramatic personal confrontation between Piłsudski and Lithuanian Premier Augustinas Voldemaras. It will be recalled that the Lithuanian government had never reconciled itself to the loss of Wilno to Poland. As a consequence, Lithuania had severed diplomatic relations with Poland and had closed its borders with Poland. In December 1926 a coup in Lithuania brought Voldemaras into office. While virtually all Lithuanian political figures were anti-Polish, Voldemaras was noted for the extravagance of his anti-Polish bias. Immediately upon assuming office, Voldemaras moved against the Poles in Lithuania. Many Poles were arrested, Polish schools were closed, and the Polish press was placed under strict censorship. Voldemaras announced that as far as he was concerned Poland and Lithuania would be in a state of war until such time as Wilno was returned to Lithuania.

For about a year this situation dragged on. Indignation within Poland became intense when it was learned that Polish teachers were being held in Lithuanian prisons. The Poles in Wilno retaliated by closing thirty Lithuanian schools. For a time it appeared that Piłsudski might order the Polish Army into Lithuania to overthrow the Voldemaras government, an action that the French and the Soviet Russian governments earnestly warned Poland against. The Polish government then requested the Council of the League of Nations first to direct Lithuania to rescind its declaration that a state of war existed between the two nations, and secondly, to recommend methods for smoothing out the existing tension.

The confrontation between Lithuania and Poland took place on December 10, 1927, before the Council of the League in Geneva. Both Voldemaras and Piłsudski were present. Voldemaras, a poor speaker, began a long-winded presentation of his case. Suddenly Piłsudski pounded on the table before him. "I didn't come all the way from Warsaw to Geneva just to listen to your long speeches. There's only one thing I want to know: do you want war or peace?" Startled, Voldemaras replied that he wanted peace. "In that case," Piłsudski answered, "I have nothing more to do here."[7] The Council promptly declared that no state of war existed between the two nations and suggested that the countries begin direct talks leading to the establishment of normal relations. The Poles were careful to honor the Council's recommendation, and they proposed several conferences with Lithuanians. Meetings were held, but they led to no satisfactory conclusion. Lithuania declined Polish offers of a treaty, refused to reopen its frontier to Poland, and, in short, closed the door to any sort of relationship with Poland for as long as Poland held Wilno.

Apart from the League of Nations, there was one other supranational entity with which it was important for Poland to establish itself. This was the Vatican. The special position of the Roman Catholic Church in Poland had always been recognized by the Polish government. The level of devotion of the mass of the population to the Roman Catholic faith was equaled nowhere else in the world, except possibly in Ireland. Ninety-five percent of the people of Poland, the minorities excluded, professed themselves to be Roman Catholic. The Church controlled enormous amounts of property, and apart only from the Army officer corps, the priesthood was the largest organized group of educated persons in the nation. Article 114 of the Polish Constitution confirmed the importance of the Church—"The Roman Catholic religion, being that of the great majority of the nation, occupies the chief position among the religions accepted as such by the State. The Roman Catholic Church governs itself under its own laws. The relations of the State and the Church will be determined on the basis of an arrangement with the Holy See, which shall be ratified by the Sejm."

Despite the importance of an understanding with the Vatican, several disputes delayed the signing of a concordat. The Vatican proved to be a hard bargainer. Most importantly, it refused to allow Church lands to be subject to the Land Reform laws. After a good deal of haggling, and after what many Poles believed were excessive concessions, a concordat was ratified in March 1925.

Without question the Church had made a good deal. Apart from giving the Church full freedom in the conduct of its affairs and the right to own property, the government agreed to pay the salaries of Polish priests and make religious instruction mandatory. The only major concessions made by the Church were the agreements to sell some of its farm holdings for land reform and to submit the names of bishops proposed for Poland to the Polish President for his approval or disapproval. All in all, this was a far better arrangement than the

Vatican then had in concordats with most other nations. Relations between Rome and Warsaw were thoroughly cordial. Then came Piłsudski's coup in May 1925.

Most of the Roman Catholic clergy were National Democrats or otherwise staunch Rightists and thus politically opposed to Piłsudski, the former Socialist. It was well known that Piłsudski, President Mościcki, Prime Minister Bartel, and most of their intimates could scarcely be described as devout, or even practicing, Catholics. The immediate reaction of the Church in Poland was to do anything it could to express its opposition to Piłsudski and support of his enemies.

Outright opposition by the Church to a Piłsudski government, if it had been allowed to continue, could have created a most serious problem in church-state relations. However, at that time, Pius XI was Pope. Prior to his elevation to the papacy, Pius had served for two years as Papal Nuncio in Warsaw and had an accurate knowledge of Polish life and politics. During the darkest days of the Polish-Soviet War in August 1920, at a time when almost every diplomat had left Warsaw, he remained in the capital. It was known that Piłsudski had admired and appreciated his bravery. Although most of Pius's Polish friends had been prominent Right-wing figures, and although he had been decorated with the Order of the White Eagle by a Right-wing Polish government, the Pope would not endanger the favorable position of the Church in Poland by political conflict with the new government. Only two weeks after Piłsudski's coup, the Pope sent a special papal blessing to Piłsudski—an act that made a signal impression upon the Polish clergy. In filling prominent Church offices in Poland, Pius made a point of bypassing senior Rightist churchmen in favor of men who would be more acceptable to the Piłsudski regime. By a number of discreet additional favors, he clearly indicated that the policy of the Church would be conciliatory toward the new Polish government. His disciplined priests and bishops in Poland, whatever their private views might be, fell in with the papal wishes.

On the government's side, the desire to achieve friendly relations with the Church was equally evident. While religion provided little personal solace to Piłsudski, he had no intention of provoking an unnecessary conflict with a force as powerful as the Catholic Church. President Mościcki attended a four-day Catholic Congress in August 1926, and in a number of other official ways made plain the government's sympathetic attitude toward the Church. In this manner,

entirely based upon the political interests of both parties, the Piłsudski government and the Catholic Church achieved a solidarity that
did much to strengthen the cohesion of the Polish state.

During the 1920s Germany could offer no physical threat to Poland. The Treaty of Versailles had, of course, compelled Germany to
reduce its army to only one hundred thousand troops. But this military weakness did not prevent Germany from displaying a consistently hostile attitude toward Poland. Many elements poisoned Polish-
German relations, but the underlying cause of tension was Germany's
refusal to consider its borders with Poland as permanent. The German government carried on a relentless campaign for the revision of
the Treaty of Versailles provisions that had created the Polish Corridor and made Danzig a free city. An enormous quantity of secret
German government funds was channeled into propaganda designed
to convince foreigners (no German required any convincing) of the
horrible injustice of the Versailles settlement. The Versailles Treaty
was a constantly boiling pot, which practically every German government and almost every German politician kept stirring.

Given this situation, it was expecting too much for Polish-German
relations to achieve any real tranquillity. Piłsudski, for one, very
much regretted this. Certainly he did not trust Germany but he then
believed, as he always had, that Poland's most dangerous enemy was
Russia. The Marshal would have given a lot for an acceptance by
Gemany of its eastern borders, as Germany had accepted its western
frontiers at Locarno. But for the time being this was clearly impossible, so the best that Poland could do was to strive for a workable,
however cool, relationship with Germany. There were many obstacles
to attaining even this modest goal, principal among them being the
problem of Danzig.

The Danzig dispute was a constant abrasive in the German-Polish
relationship. The tedious wrangles between Poland and the thoroughly Germanic free city never stopped. And there was no pettiness
to which the parties would not descend. An example of this sort of
thing was the defacement of the Polish mailboxes in January 1925.
These mailboxes bore a representation of the Polish eagle, and on
the night of January 6, 1925, each box was painted red, black and
white, the German Imperial colors. In short order this incident led
to Polish demands for compensation for the insult, followed by
threats of military intervention. The matter finally ended up before

the Council of the League of Nations, which eventually referred it to the Permanent Court of International Justice.

The "mailbox episode" was typical of the constant, silly, tiresome disputes that were a permanent feature of life in Danzig. Each side jealously guarded the most trifling of its privileges and prerogatives, with the German government assisting the Danzig Senate with whatever intervention it found possible. Germany never accepted the free-city status of Danzig. Millions of marks were poured into a semi-official German agency that produced a continuing torrent of propaganda designed to publicize the "injustice" that had been perpetrated at Danzig. The Polish government responded with boycotts of Danzig-manufactured goods and a propaganda campaign of its own.

As early as 1920, the Polish government had foreseen extensive problems with Danzig. A government committee had been sent to look for a possible alternative Baltic port site, and it had found one. About ten miles north of Danzig, but still within the limits of the Polish Corridor, was a fishing village called Gdynia. To develop this town, which was nothing more than a few hundred houses fronting on a sandbank, into a port capable of competing with Danzig was obviously a monumental task. Apart from the docks, cranes, and warehouses that would be necessary, an entire railroad system would have to be constructed to connect the new port with the Polish heartland. A complete city would have to be constructed to house the workers and officials. Everything would have to be built from scratch from the slim resources of an impoverished nation. And even when the new port was finally finished, it would not contribute any special economic benefit to Poland. It would only duplicate facilities that already existed at Danzig. The creation of a port at Gdynia would be mostly a political exercise. Nonetheless, in 1922 the Polish government decided to go ahead with the project. Contracts were signed with a French construction consortium in 1924, and work went rapidly forward.

The construction of a port-city at Gdynia proved to be popular with all Poles. It became a national goal and a symbol of national pride. Photographs documenting the progress of construction ran in every Polish newspaper.

The Danzigers scoffed at the whole business, considering it impossible that the Poles could construct a facility competitive to long-established Danzig. But they did. At the cost of tremendous capital investment, the port became operative in 1926. In that year its shipping volume was less than 6 percent of that of Danzig. But as new facilities were completed, Gdynia's share steadily increased. By 1930 Gdynia enjoyed a freight turnover equal to half of that handled by Danzig.

Gdynia now became a serious economic threat to the Free City. Poland offered many economic concessions to divert shippers from Danzig to Gdynia. The Danzigers could not match these incentives, and they claimed that they were being ruined by this Polish competition. But there was nothing they could do about it. The German government protested that the Poles had an obligation to use Danzig. The Poles claimed that they were free to use any port facilities, and this whole issue remained a constant source of friction between the two nations.

There were other conflicts with Germany, too—particularly after the Upper Silesian economic agreement terminated in 1925. A whipsaw of economic warfare broke out. Germany cut its coal imports from Poland in half. Until other markets were found, this cutback was a disaster for Polish Upper Silesia. The Poles retaliated by prohibiting the importation from Germany of a wide variety of manufactured goods, a policy that proved to be much more of a hardship to Poland than to Germany. The Germans reciprocated by limiting the importation of Polish agricultural products and withdrawing German deposits from Polish banks.

This economic war would continue for ten years, until the Polish-German Trade Agreement of 1935 was signed. Clearly, Germany "won" the battle in the sense that it hurt Poland more than it was hurt by Poland. But Germany did not achieve its real objective—the economic destruction of Poland. The Poles succeeded in developing their own facilities to produce essential products usually imported from Germany—or they simply bought from other nations. And eventually the German government concluded that, while Poland could be seriously inconvenienced by Germany, it could not be brought to a state of collapse. When this was realized in Berlin, and when Warsaw was willing to make sufficient political concessions, the trade war gradually came to an end.

For all the tensions with Germany, it was Soviet Russia that proved most menacing to Poland during the middle 1920s. This was peculiar because, during this time, the Russians truly wanted peace. In 1925 Stalin had made his famous proclamation of "Socialism in One

Nation," and in the same year Soviet Commissar for Foreign Affairs Grigori Chicherin came to Warsaw to offer a nonaggression pact. The suspicious Poles turned down the offer, but it had been a sincere one. So, although Soviet Russia really wanted peace, two years later it nearly went to war with Poland as a consequence of what is now called the "Soviet War Scare of 1927."

The periodic war scares that swept the Soviet Union with all their attendant ballyhoo and venomous propaganda were usually regarded by the Western capitalist nations as nothing more than an inventive attempt by the Soviet government to distract its peoples' attention from some domestic difficulty. So when, in 1927, Moscow suddenly announced extensive preparations for a Soviet defense against foreign invasion, it was assumed in other capitals that this was simply another trumped-up diversion. But in 1927 this was not the case. The Soviet government had convinced itself that war was imminent and that Russia would shortly be attacked by a consortium of capitalist nations directed by Great Britain, with the Polish Army in the vanguard. The Russian fears were acute and absolutely genuine. They were also completely groundless.

As has been frequently observed, the Soviet government tended to have a different view of reality from that of most other nations. The Soviet rulers were isolated and intensely suspicious. They were also egocentric in the sense that they believed every capitalist government was obsessed with the single objective of destroying Soviet Russia. These factors, combined with a coincidental series of international events, in 1925–1927 produced in Moscow an attitude that bordered on hysteria.

The Soviet War Scare started with Locarno, which the Soviets viewed as an attempt by Britain and France to woo Germany away from its Rapallo-born relationship with the Soviet Union. Then, only seven months later, came Piłsudski's coup.

There was no question in Moscow as to how this coup had taken place. It had been engineered by the British Foreign Office and the British Secret Service. Clearly, they had reinstalled Russia's archfoe in order that he might lead the military offensive. The Soviets awaited the capitalist nations' next move with great apprehension.

The immediate prelude to the Soviet war mania of 1927, it is generally agreed, was the "Arcos Raid." *Arcos* was the name of the official Soviet trade organization that had opened export-import headquarters in London. In May 1927, the British police raided the Arcos offices, occupied them for four days, seized a large quantity of propaganda, and announced that some members of the Arcos staff were espionage agents. The British government promptly broke off diplomatic relations with Soviet Russia.

The Soviet government was now thoroughly frightened. They believed that the British intended to use the Arcos affair as an excuse for an early declaration of war. Reviewing the recent past, the Russians found much to support this theory. A British naval squadron was now cruising in the Baltic. Chiang Kai-shek, whom Moscow had supported, had just captured Shanghai, whereupon his new regime put thousands of his Communist allies to death. This severe setback in China was explained as another British machination.

The Russians began to discern other ominous signs. The Soviet security apparatus was catching an increasing number of spies and terrorists trying to cross the Russian borders. These persons, most of whom were part of the pathetically weak anti-Soviet campaign mounted by certain White Russian émigré groups, aroused enormous dread within the Soviet government. These officials viewed the White infiltration of the Soviet frontiers as the start of an Allied program of terror and sabotage within Russia, an obvious prelude to invasion. Every fire, every industrial mishap of any kind was ascribed to the sinister forces of the legendary British Secret Service, which the Soviets believed to be of incredible size and efficiency. Orders were given to the OGPU to intensify its security efforts, and this had the effect of producing a large number of arrests which, of course, only increased the war hysteria.

Then, on June 7, 1927, Pavel Voikov, the Soviet ambassador to Poland, was murdered in Warsaw. He was an emotionally important figure in Soviet Russia—and out of it. He had been a member of the small execution squad that in 1918 had shot Tsar Nicholas II and his family in the cellar of the house in Ekaterinburg. A man with this background would naturally have mortal enemies among the White Russian refugees, who could now be found all over Europe. The Polish government had been reluctant to accept Voikov as ambassador because of the security problems he presented. But the Soviet government had insisted, and so Voikov had been received. The Polish government had several times offered a police bodyguard to Voikov, but the offers had been refused.

On June 7, while standing on a platform in the main Warsaw railway station, Voikov was shot to death by eighteen-year-old Boris

Koverda. The assassin, who was immediately apprehended, was the son of a Russian monarchist, one of many then living in Warsaw. Coincidentally, on that very day, there were minor terrorist raids on Communist Party offices in Leningrad and Moscow. All these events were interpreted by the Soviet government as the final steps before an actual declaration of war by Britain and Poland. Military leaves were canceled. Senior Red Army officers were ordered to return to their units. A news blackout was instituted. The Russian people began to hoard food. Every step toward military readiness was taken short of outright mobilization.

The Polish government appreciated the necessity for the most profuse apologies to Soviet Russia, and it was prepared to make them. But what the Polish government was not prepared for was the violent and accusatory tone of Soviet notes to Warsaw. The Poles did not at first realize that the Russians honestly believed themselves to be on the brink of war, and their messages were appropriate to such a perilous situation. The Soviet government denounced Voikov's assassination as an "unprecedented and criminal act" connected with "the provocative suspension of diplomatic relations by England."[8]

Poland replied with a series of soothing and apologetic messages, the burden of which was that Voikov's assassin was a madman. The Soviets refused to be placated. In another note they charged that the young murderer was a member of a terrorist group secretly supported by the Polish government. And Stalin, in a newspaper interview, charged that Voikov's assassination was a calculated attempt by Poland to provoke a war.

These were very serious charges from what Poland now perceived as a genuinely frightened nation. Piłsudski understood this Russian fear, and Poland made extreme efforts to placate the Soviet Union. The Polish envoy in Moscow, Stanislaw Patek, was a lawyer who, years before, had specialized in defending revolutionaries in Tsarist courts. Many important Soviet leaders had once been his clients. Patek was given the task of convincing Moscow that Poland was guiltless of Voikov's murder and that the Poles desired peace with the Soviet Union. Offers of financial compensation to Voikov's family were made and rejected. The Polish government expelled a number of Russian émigrés who, it appeared, might have terrorist connections. Voikov's murderer was speedily tried and sentenced to imprisonment for life. But still the Soviet government was unsatisfied. They demanded that the Poles expel all émigrés who held anti-

Soviet views. Tension increased to a level unknown since 1920. Finally, Piłsudski sent Patek a message to be transmitted privately in the most explicit manner to the Soviet government. "In attempting to humiliate Poland," the message read, "you only incur the risk of humiliating yourself, since you have not sufficient force behind your threats, which you know as well as we do. We have done everything that is reasonable to give you satisfaction, and now we must courteously urge you to let the matter drop, because if regrettable incidents follow, you alone will be responsible."[9]

The Soviet government was moved by Piłsudski's warning, and tensions gradually eased. As months passed, the Soviets became convinced that Poland and Britain were not going to attack them, and Soviet relations with Warsaw thawed considerably. And in 1928 the Soviet diplomat Maxim Litvinov was able to propose a treaty that would outlaw war between the two nations. This "Litvinov Protocol" would be signed in 1929, but, despite a superficial cordiality that eventually developed, there was never any real trust between Poland and Soviet Russia.

12
"With or Without Piłsudski?"

THE ACCOUNT OF POLISH domestic politics in the critical years from 1926 through 1930 is a tale of constant strife between the government and the parliament. This conflict subsided only with the elections of November 1930, and these years are often described as a time of emerging dictatorship.

Although the Polish government eventually did devolve into an authoritarian regime of sorts, Piłsudski had not planned this from the very beginning; he did not regard himself as an enemy of democracy. The Marshal had not come to power with a carefully prepared plan for the subversion of parliamentary democracy in Poland, any more than he had a carefully prepared plan for Poland's economic growth. If he had wanted, Piłsudski could have abolished the parliament by decree after his May 1926 coup, but he did not do so. Piłsudski cannot be compared with Mussolini or Hitler or any of the dictators who had emerged or were about to emerge during this period in Europe. Unlike those leaders, he had no antidemocratic philosophy. Indeed, he was astonished and angered whenever he was accused of being the foe of democracy in Poland. He constantly professed to believe that democracy was the correct form of government for Poland, and he considered that he was its champion. Only a month after his coup he told an associate that he had "every intention of maintaining 'parliamentarianism' in Poland because it is the basis of democracy. There is always a place for parliament in Poland."[1] But despite Piłsudski's avowals, his prolonged conflict with the parliament undeniably had the effect of gradually stifling democracy in Poland and converting the government into an authoritarian regime, which, after Piłsudski's death, acquired some of the trappings of fascism.

Piłsudski's admirers claim that at the core of the struggle between him and the Sejm was his almost obsessive fear that Poland would slide into political anarchy. He believed that a basic flaw in the Polish national character was its people's inability to achieve agreement in political matters. His study of Polish history had proved to him that again and again the Polish people had precipitated the destruction of their government by a suicidal urge toward political anarchy. Piłsudski believed that from 1919 to 1926 the Polish parliament had demonstrated this historic tendency. Its members seemed to have perpetuated the ancient *szlachta* heritage in which the gentry members of the Sejm maintained their personal privileges at the expense of the strength of the Polish republic, an attitude and habit that led directly to anarchy and the Polish partitions. Polish politicians tended to criticize rather than act, to be in opposition rather than accept responsibility.

Piłsudski was convinced that the events of the years 1921–26 had established that the present Polish constitution was unsuitable for the nation. None of Poland's political institutions—the parliament, the politicians, and the welter of political parties—strengthened the nation. Quite the reverse. Their rancor and squabbling had demonstrably weakened the nation. Piłsudski believed that the Polish political situation was especially disastrous, since, according to him, Poland was a special case among the larger European states. It was economically weaker than these nations and, unlike them, was surrounded by potential enemies. More than other nations, Poland had to be strong and united internally. It simply could not, in Piłsudski's view, afford the luxury of political divisiveness.

To Piłsudski it seemed that the problems of Polish democracy could be remedied in a simple way. He never completely articulated his philosophy of government, but its essence was this: Poland's politicians had to go about their business in a responsible, quiet, and honest way. They must cease their noisy partisan vituperation and their relentless criticism of the government of the hour. They must be ready to sacrifice their private interests for the public good. In

short, they must do for Poland in their small way what Piłsudski
believed he had done in a larger manner. In one of his first interviews after the coup, Piłsudski told a prominent French journalist
(the Polish government regarded interviews with French newspaper-
men as important events, and great care was taken as to what was
said) that

> I do not believe that Poland can be governed by the rod . . . I am not
> in favor of a dictatorship in Poland. I conceive the role of the chief of
> state in a different fashion; it is necessary that he should have the right
> to make quick decisions on questions of national interest. The chicanery
> of parliament retards urgent action. We live in a legislative chaos. . . .
> I have friends in the Right and in the Left, but Poland cannot recover
> with the party system.[2]

Piłsudski was utterly confident that he knew far better than anyone else what was best for Poland and what was best for its people.
One had only to look around to see what had been accomplished
since his return to power. The nation's economy was greatly improved. The currency had been stabilized. Corruption was being
rooted out. The efficiency and quality of government services had
been significantly improved under Bartel's administration. Piłsudski's
foreign policy seemed successful. All of these were accomplishments
of the most solid kind. So, when opposing politicians criticized the
government, Piłsudski became enraged. He was certain that their
criticism stemmed from only the basest motives.

Those opposed to the Piłsudski government viewed the political
scene differently, of course. Both the corrupt ones (there were plenty
of these) and the honest ones (and there were many of these too) saw
Piłsudski as a present and future menace to democracy in Poland.
Most persons, even those in opposition to Piłsudski, agreed that the
1921 Constitution had serious flaws, but many questioned the necessity of a military coup to alter it. Similarly, many people, while they
agreed that there were serious faults in the Polish political process,
questioned whether overthrowing the legal government was the appropriate way to improve things. The opposition rejected Piłsudski's
opinion that he alone had been responsible for Polish independence.
Many others had played leading parts in the struggle for freedom.

Piłsudski was fond of stating that he was "only a soldier" in the
service of Poland and that all Poles, politicians included, were also
soldiers who must obey and serve. But Piłsudski could not or would

not realize that, although he was indeed a "soldier," he had never in his life been a subordinate. He had always been the Commandant or the First Marshal. When he stated that Polish politicians should also be "soldiers," he was demanding that they should be his loyal and obedient subordinates. But the opposition leaders disdained the opportunity to become common soldiers under Piłsudski. They believed that they had higher duties, and they would not concede that the Marshal had infallible and exclusive knowledge of what was best for Poland.

For many members of the opposition, Piłsudski was simply an egocentric who was accumulating personal power at the expense of his political opponents and the parliamentary system. The example of fascism was already abroad. Mussolini had taken power in Italy, and his dictatorial "experiment" was attracting attention. The parallel between the march of Mussolini's Black Shirts on Rome in 1922 and Piłsudski's coup of 1926 was striking. In short, the majority of Piłsudski's opponents regarded themselves as honorable patriots who, at some considerable danger to themselves, were defending Polish democracy against authoritarianism.

Interestingly enough, however, the mass of the Polish population took very little part in the political conflict. Universal public education had been introduced at the time of independence and was being promoted vigorously. But the mass of the Polish voters were still poorly educated peasants who were interested in little besides their struggle for existence in their own villages. If agricultural prices were high and if land was available for purchase, then all was well. The intelligentsia and the people in the cities were free to worry about what seemed to the peasants merely like abstract political problems. The peasants themselves generally did not care to become involved.

Piłsudski and his family lived in the Belvedere Palace which he had caused to be designated the official residence of the minister of war. His second marriage had not proved completely happy. To be sure, although he adored his two children, Piłsudski could scarcely be described as a devoted husband. The Marshal's life was completely dominated by his work. Madame Piłsudska herself was thoroughly involved in her work in numerous Polish social and humanitarian organizations. Gradually, Piłsudski and his wife drifted apart. The

Marshal's office in the Armed Forces Building, only a block from the Belvedere Palace, contained a small apartment where he frequently spent the night. Sometimes he lived there for weeks at a time without returning to the Belvedere.

In his work Piłsudski was assisted by a large number of relatively youthful aides, all of whom had served him more or less continually for many years and had originally been members of the Riflemen's Association, the Polish Legion, the P.O.W. or, quite frequently, all three. These men were now officers in the Army or were reserve officers who now served as the Marshal's eyes and ears in various civilian ministries. Most of those who were active officers were colonels or lieutenant colonels. They were now in their middle thirties and included such men as Colonel Józef Beck, Colonel Walery Sławek, Colonel Bolesław Wieniawa-Długoszowski, Colonel Aleksander Prystor, General Felicjan Sławoj-Składkowski, and Kazimierz Switalski. To his staff, Piłsudski was always "the Commandant"; they worshiped him and gladly gave him instant, unquestioning obedience.

Their loyalty was thoroughly tested, because Piłsudski was, and became increasingly, an extremely difficult person to work for. His style was unorthodox—particularly for a person who was the *de facto* head of a large European nation. Piłsudski was extremely secretive. He kept no diary nor did he keep any one person informed of his plans. Instead, he discussed bits and pieces of various programs with a number of aides, who were then left to try to put the whole together in conversations among themselves. Piłsudski made no attempt to coalesce his ideas of govenment into a rational philosophy that could be implemented by his associates. As a result, all that was then known (and all that we now know) about Piłsudski's theories and objectives was based on the day-to-day comments that he made in a relatively offhand manner to one associate or another.

Piłsudski preferred to start his working day around noon and then continue work until very late, frequently until three in the morning. The best hour for meeting with him was eleven in the evening, the hour that he reserved for his most important interviews. He would rarely see anyone whom he had not sent for—his visitors presented reports that had been requested and received orders that were given; they were rarely allowed to initiate discussions. His accessibility was further limited by the fact that in conference he discussed only those matters that he himself raised or had approved for inclusion on the agenda. It was very difficult for his associates to engage Piłsudski in any form of wide-ranging discussion.

The persons who functioned as Piłsudski's secretariat had an almost insuperable task. The Marshal was a "messy-desk" worker who refused to permit anyone to put his papers in order. Piłsudski abhorred paperwork and loathed reading reports. He disliked writing them even more. He virtually never wrote out, or even dictated, the precise wording of any document. Whenever Piłsudski met with major figures—particularly foreign diplomats—someone from his staff was present to take down the substance of the conversation. If this were not done, there would have been no record of the interview on the Polish side because Piłsudski never bothered to dictate a minute of any meeting. In fact, he usually did not give any of his aides a complete account of any interview.

In essence, Piłsudski's work practices were those of a man who expected to live forever and therefore to direct Poland's affairs forever. From 1926 through 1930, Piłsudski experienced no serious physical problems, although there were frequent rumors that he was in poor health. In April 1928, he suffered a minor stroke, which temporarily paralyzed his right hand, but he made a rapid recovery and suffered no permanent aftereffects. Although he took little exercise, chain-smoked cigarettes, and drank countless glasses of tea every day, Piłsudski remained in good physical condition, except for a chronic bronchitis, which was undoubtedly exacerbated by his smoking. His emotional health was a different matter. During these years Piłsudski was in his early sixties. It is apparent from many accounts that the Marshal was no longer the person he had been during the Polish-Soviet War in 1920. Piłsudski had always loathed detail, despised political conflict, and deeply disliked dealing with people whose duty it was to bring these matters before him. Over the years the necessity of performing distasteful bureaucratic tasks had made him extremely nervous, impatient, and sometimes very unreasonable. He was not emotionally equipped to deal with the demands of the day-to-day business of government. Piłsudski had realized this, which was why he had made Bartel his first prime minister.

It was not that Piłsudski had simply lost the ability to withstand stress. He probably could have fought another war with decisiveness and equanimity. He had a demonstrated ability to handle foreign relations with great poise. But he could not abide being involved in the detailed activities of government and politics. Under the stress of dealing with these, Piłsudski developed a rigidity of thought and became intolerant of opposition. With each passing year his temper grew increasingly quick, and when he grew angry he sometimes was almost out of control. His closest associates were frequently frightened of him. Extended political discussions at cabinet meetings sometimes drove Piłsudski into such a nervous state that he exploded, cursing and shouting obscene abuse. Piłsudski himself recognized that his presence at cabinet meetings made the transaction of political business almost impossible, so he generally avoided these sessions. When he did attend, he stayed only while military matters were being discussed.

All of Piłsudski's aides and associates paid the closest attention to the manner in which he addressed them. His attitude toward them at any given moment was substantially indicated by the first words from his mouth. If he addressed an aide in the formal form of the second person, then all was well. If the Marshal addressed a man by his title or rank (for example, "Colonel"), then he was displeased with him. However, a salutation of "my dear child" or the use of the intimate form of the second person was a mark of signal favor and indicated that the person addressed had recently performed a duty in a manner that had particularly pleased the Marshal. When an aide had completed a complex task—parts of which in Piłsudski's view he had done well, parts satisfactorily, and parts poorly—the Marshal was quite capable of commenting on the aide's performance using a mixture of all three types of address. His associates were never confused by this. They knew exactly what Piłsudski meant.

Despite his eccentricities, Piłsudski was no incompetent petty tyrant. For all his defects—and they were many and substantial—he towered over any potential rival in the public estimation. His reputation for absolute honesty contrasted sharply with the view that most Poles had of their politicians. Piłsudski's patriotism and his selfless dedication to his work persuaded the public to overlook those of his idiosyncrasies that were generally known. Piłsudski was bluff and blunt, but most Poles expected these traits in a man of his age and aristocratic background. If he was impatient and irritable with politicians, the Polish populace found it easy to forgive these "faults." One thing was certain: Piłsudski's stature as the founder of his country and the victor in its wars of independence could not be

undermined by petty personal failings. Piłsudski stood for a strong
Army, an efficient administration, and a government that commanded
respect abroad. Most Poles found these objectives admirable and
correct, and they revered Piłsudski and believed that he was the
best man to lead their nation.

It is significant that, on his frequent trips from the Belvedere
Palace to the Inspector General's office, Piłsudski usually walked the
block that separated them. On these walks he was accompanied only
by an aide or two. He did not like to be followed by a bodyguard,
and no special security measures were taken to prevent an attack on
him. It would have been simple for an assassin to have killed him,
but no attempt on his life was ever made.

As much as he disliked dealing with political matters, Piłsudski
found that he could not completely avoid doing so. His government
(technically, usually Bartel's government) had, of course, to deal with
parliament, which meant perforce that it must deal with politicians. Bartel's task was made difficult by the fact that the only
parliamentary support that his government could usually count on
was the grudging backing of the parties of the Left. Piłsudski refused
to be dependent solely upon the sullen support of the PPS. Shortly
after his coup, Piłsudski began trying to build bridges to various
other political groups. His first effort was directed toward the large
landowners, a class with which Piłsudski identified himself and which
he thought of as representing certain old Polish virtues such as
patriotism and personal integrity. At a formal visit to the Radziwill
family estate at Nieswiez in October 1926, Piłsudski met with the
heads of the great magnate families. This reception was magnificent.
Piłsudski radiated charm and displayed great sympathy toward the
landowners' political positions. Piłsudski had seen to it that two members of the aristocracy had recently been given cabinet positions.
Very soon he captured the support of the conservative magnates.
Obviously, the Polish aristocracy represented very few votes but,
directly or indirectly, they controlled banks, newspapers and industries. These could all be used for political ends. Moreover, the
landowners' alliance with Piłsudski weakened the National Democrats, with whom they had formerly affiliated themselves.

At the same time Piłsudski also made inroads into the Center
parties. The prestige of association with the Marshal was considerable. And, of course, Bartel made sure that the government hand-

somely rewarded any support given it by politicians from the Center. Soon, important segments of the Center as well as the nationalities' parties were recognized as supporters of the Piłsudski government.

However, while Piłsudski was developing these alliances, his opponents were equally active. And as the shock of the coup subsided, they grew more outspoken and better organized. His alliance with the conservative landowners estranged many of his Left-wing supporters. By the fall of 1926 Piłsudski probably had more opponents than allies in the parliament. The first clash between the Sejm and the government began in September 1926, only four months after the coup. At that time the Sejm, for rather arbitrary reasons, passed a vote of no confidence in two members of the Bartel cabinet. Piłsudski viewed this as the start of a trial of strength between the Sejm and his government. Instead of simply having the two cabinet ministers resign, as Article 57 of the constitution required, Piłsudski instructed the entire Bartel cabinet to submit their resignations. Then President Mościcki promptly reappointed the same ministers. The opposition members of parliament were dumbfounded. They claimed that this was illegal, but the government had been counseled by Stanisław Car, a shrewd constitutional lawyer. Since the whole government had resigned en masse, the ministers constituted a "new" government. It was clear that if the parliament attempted to peck apart a pro-Piłsudski government with a vote of no confidence, this device would again be used. The Piłsudski government simply would not allow parliamentary removal of any of its cabinet ministers. Piłsudski's opponents had not anticipated this ingenious tactic; it was indeed perfectly legal, and it put an end to the parliamentary practice of harassing a government by the removal of individual cabinet ministers.

Confrontations between the parliament and the government did not end, however. On September 30, 1926, only a few days after the return of the Bartel cabinet, the Senate voted a cut in a budget proposed by the government. Bartel declared that this constituted a vote of no confidence, and he and his entire cabinet at once resigned. A new government, with Piłsudski himself serving as prime minister, was immediately appointed by President Mościcki. The parliament, stunned by this riposte, did not dare to reject a government headed by Piłsudski, even though Bartel was serving as deputy prime minister and was known to be performing all the routine administrative tasks.

It did not take long for Piłsudski's parliamentary enemies to regroup. If they could not throw Piłsudski from office, they could at least create all kinds of difficulties for him. The parliament's principal weapon was its power over the purse strings. The opposition succeeded in making the passage of the quarterly and annual budgets a great ordeal for the government. For reasons often capricious and arbitrary, the opposition cut certain government appropriations and increased others. Again and again the government would propose various constitutional amendments, and every time the parliament, seeing that these amendments were designed to reduce its power, refused to consider them.

Of course, Piłsudski did not enjoy these endless petty skirmishes with the parliament, even though as prime minister he kept himself remarkably free of administrative details. It was apparent that he found this office irksome. He attended fewer than a third of the cabinet meetings, and the government continued to be run by Bartel. But the endless uncertainties, obstructions, and vituperations involved in dealing with parliament enraged Piłsudski. He saw clearly a major weakness in his position. He did not have what every other European prime minister had—a political party personally loyal to him and strongly represented in parliament. Beginning in January 1927, he moved to remedy this situation.

Colonel Walery Sławek was forty-eight years old at this time and was a long-time intimate of Piłsudski. Sławek had served in the First Brigade of the Polish Legion, but his association with the Marshal extended even further back. He had joined the PPS as a young man, had met Piłsudski at a Socialist conference in 1902, and had later joined him in the organization of the Riflemen's Association in Galicia. Sławek had had a good deal of experience in the terrorist wing of the PPS before the World War. He had been an extraordinarily handsome young man, but in 1906 a bomb he was assembling blew up. The accident seriously scarred the right side of his face and left him with a drooping right eyelid, which gave him a decided leer. He was a poor writer and a mediocre public speaker, but he was respected as being honest and upright almost to the point of naïveté. Piłsudski admired Sławek's ability to get things done, and shortly after the war Sławek became his personal aide for political affairs. Even on a staff noted for its members' devotion to Piłsudski, Sławek was known for his fanatical dedication to the Marshal. He was Piłsudski's creature, and he filled a necessary function for him. The Marshal would never demean himself or place himself under a personal obligation by asking for a politician's support or for his vote. Obviously, someone had to do this for him—and this person was Sławek. Everyone with whom Sławek discussed political affairs knew, of course, of his intimacy with the Marshal. A conversation with Sławek was generally considered to be the practical equivalent of a discussion with the Marshal.

In January 1927, Piłsudski instructed Sławek to put together a pro-government political organization in preparation for parliamentary elections to take place at some unspecified future date. Having issued this order, Piłsudski disengaged himself from all the details of the undertaking. The matter was left entirely in Sławek's hands, and he undertook the task with his customary zeal.

The creation of a Piłsudski-ite political organization was not an easy task. The only program at that point was the rather vague philosophy of *sanacja*. It was difficult to explain precisely what this meant and even more difficult to build a political platform on it. On the other hand, the very vagueness of *sanacja* had some advantages. Theoretically, at least, all Poles were in favor of patriotism, selfless public service, and morality in political life. So, it was possible for Sławek to unite a number of persons with widely disparate political philosophies into one organization, which was called Bezpartyjny Blok Wspolpracy Z Rzadem (Non-Party Bloc for Cooperation with the Government). This group was soon universally referred to as the BBWR. It was not a political party in the ordinary sense; it was simply an association of persons pledged to support Piłsudski. A member of the BBWR could also retain his membership in another party. The only political commitments that BBWR adherents were required to make were that they would back Piłsudski's ideals and objectives and that they would favor constitutional reform.

Although the BBWR did not immediately become the powerful force that Piłsudski and his intimates had hoped for, Sławek achieved an impressive amount in quite a short time. He very quickly lined up the support of the large landowners and their industrialist allies. At the same time, on the other end of the political spectrum, Sławek brought some important members of the PPS into the BBWR camp. He used a number of techniques to persuade individual members of the PPS to dissent from their party's increasingly substantial opposition to Piłsudski. He would ask, for example, who would head a government that might supersede the Marshal's? The certain answer was that the cabinet would be dominated by the PPS's old foes, the National Democrats. Sławek emphasized that affiliation with the BBWR would give a politician the support of Piłsudski's name, and this could be an important consideration.

From among the ranks of the other major political parties, the BBWR drew scattered but considerable support, particularly from the Piast Peasant Party and the national minorities parties.

Of course, many of those who joined the BBWR were simply persons who saw alliance with the government as the quickest road to power or fortune. These people found it convenient to claim that they had been Piłsudski-ites for many years. Of course, wartime service in one of the three brigades of the Polish Legion, particularly the First Brigade, was evidence of established devotion to the Marshal. After the coup of May 1926, many people clambered aboard the bandwagon and claimed old ties with Piłsudski. These opportunists were sarcastically referred to as members of the "Fourth Brigade."

By the fall of 1927, nine months after Sławek had begun organizing the BBWR, the government felt ready for a showdown with the parliamentary opposition. On October 21, 1927, parliament reconvened after a recess. Within an hour after the session's opening, a presidential decree suspended the parliament for one month. Since the five-year terms of the deputies and senators expired in the following month, the decree meant, in effect, the dissolution of the parliament and the holding of new elections—which then were scheduled for March 1928. The government looked forward to the elections with the expectation that its troubles with the parliament would soon be ended and that a stunning victory for the pro-Piłsudski forces would further confirm the legitimacy of the May 1926 coup and would prepare the way for extensive constitutional reform.

The opposition parties, of course, began intense preparations of their own for the elections. They had certain advantages over the BBWR. They had historic roots and well-defined philosophies and platforms. And now they were able to raise the additional issue of Piłsudski's encroachments upon parliamentary rights and liberties. The opposition stigmatized Piłsudski's ultimate intentions as fascist.

Indeed, some of the government's actions at this time could be termed fascist. Certainly the government permitted itself a number of extralegal liberties in the course of the campaign. Full use was made of its control over the national administrative apparatus. According to Polish law, elections were to be supervised by an Electoral Commission appointed by the president. Mościcki named the ingenious legal expert Stanislaw Car head of this commission, thus giving the government control of the administration of the election.

The cabinet ministers made their own contributions to the BBWR cause. The Minister of the Interior summoned his provincial governors before him to demand their active support of the BBWR slate of candidates. The governors, in turn, passed this directive on to their subordinates. Special attention was given to creating a public climate favorable to the government. Tax officials were instructed to settle outstanding claims in a generous manner, and many other official concessions were made.

The police were also helpful to the BBWR. At times they stood by when opposition political rallies were broken up by BBWR supporters. A few opposition leaders were taken into custody or were harassed by conspicuous police surveillance. National Democratic newspapers were occasionally confiscated. These acts did not occur every day, but they did happen often enough to have an unsettling effect on the opposition's campaigns.

Probably the greatest advantage the government enjoyed in its campaign was the amount of money available to it. Some of its funds came from legitimate sources; the BBWR was, after all, supported by many of the wealthiest families in Poland. But added to these legal contributions was a secret transfer of eight million zlotys (the equivalent of about a million United States dollars) from the Polish Treasury to the BBWR. This was an enormous sum by Polish electoral campaign standards, and the transfer was made on the direct order of Piłsudski.

The BBWR used this money like a bludgeon. Its candidates were able to fund campaigns of dimensions previously unknown in Polish politics. Money was available to buy off certain opponents, and still there were funds left over. The BBWR nominees lacked nothing in their campaigns that money could buy.

All of the government's extralegal activities were helpful to the BBWR candidates, but they had far less of an impact than had been anticipated. When the March 1928 elections were over, it was found that the BBWR and its affiliated parties had won just 130 out of the 444 seats in the Sejm. The Leftist opposition, led by the PPS, had done almost exactly as well, winning 129 seats, although they had gotten about 100,000 more votes. By contrast the National Democrats and the other Rightist parties had done poorly. They had won only 37 seats, sixty-one fewer than they had previously held. This electoral disaster for the Right was caused more by the prevailing political climate than by governmental harassment at election time. The Center parties were equally hard-hit, getting only 54 seats. The various national minorities parties ended up with sixty-five deputies in the Sejm.

In the Senate the BBWR did even better. They won 46 of the 111 seats. The Right and the Center elected only 9 senators each, the Left elected 20 and the national minorities elected 23.

Which side "won" the elections of 1928 depends upon how the outcome is viewed. On the Left, the PPS was well satisfied with the result. The party had increased its number of deputies by more than 50 percent above the total in 1922. And the PPS argued that having received the largest popular vote of any party, it had been given a mandate by the Polish people.

The government, on the other hand, took the position that it had actually received the mandate of the people. After all, the BBWR had elected more deputies and senators than any other party. Piłsudski believed that he had been the victor in this election. He could not conceive that the results could be regarded in any other light. Piłsudski also believed that the opposition ought to acknowledge his victory by adopting a restrained and deferential attitude. His enemies should recognize that they had been repudiated by the electorate and were now obliged to cease obstructing the government's policies. As one of Piłsudski's cabinet ministers stated, the parties of the Right and Center were "defeated parties . . . whose public role should now end."[3] The government anticipated no difficulty in obtaining the support of the PPS in the new parliament. The result would be an absolute majority acting at the Marshal's direction.

As it turned out, the Piłsudski government experienced fully as many difficulties with the opposition in the new parliament as it had faced in the previous parliament. On May 27, 1928, Piłsudski appeared at the opening session of the newly elected parliament to read a message from President Mościcki. No sooner had the Marshal begun his address than fifteen deputies elected by a Communist-front party began to heckle him. There were no parliamentary officials to maintain order. (Since parliament had just convened, the senators and deputies had not yet elected their officers.) Piłsudski ordered, "Silence, or I will have you turned out."[4] There was more clamor, and Piłsudski called in police and had the Communist deputies ejected. At this point the PPS deputies grew restive. Piłsudski turned on them with the warning that unless they contained themselves, he would have Mościcki adjourn the parliament. This unpleasant scene set the tone for the government's future relations with the parliament.

The balloting for the office of marshal, or leader, of the Sejm took place on the following day. Piłsudski, in the belief that the Sejm was under a moral, if not actually a legal, obligation to elect a representative of the majority party to this important post, had proposed the election of Kazimierz Bartel. Instead, the Sejm elected Ignacy Daszyński, the veteran PPS leader. Piłsudski was enraged. He regarded it as an indictment of the Polish parliamentary system when the party holding the most seats in the Sejm could not name the leader of that body. The entire BBWR membership walked out of the Sejm chamber in protest and remained out for several days.

In the coming months it became evident that having 30 percent of the Sejm seats did not enable the BBWR to dominate parliament. The opposition parties, even if they did not always unite on issues, were sufficiently numerous to create many difficulties. They made the passage of the quarterly and annual budgets an extremely troublesome exercise for the government. The opposition constantly accused the cabinet of fascist inclinations. They made a particular point of reducing or eliminating proposed expenditures for the secret police of the ministry of the interior. The opposition created a commission in the Sejm to look into abuses in the recent elections—a subject on which the government could not help but be very sensitive. And at all times the opposition fought off any attempt at constitutional reform, which they saw as an effort by the government to emasculate parliament.

The opposition made no secret of the fact that they were playing a waiting game. It was widely rumored that Piłsudski's health was not good, and there was even speculation that he was dying of cancer. The opposition was certain that the BBWR would not long survive, if Piłsudski should die or be forced into retirement. The conviction that they had only to hang on for a while undoubtedly was responsible for many of the opposition's obstructionist actions.

In late June 1928, to general surprise, Piłsudski himself seemed
to confirm the opposition's speculations about his failing health. He
abruptly resigned as prime minister, keeping only his customary post
as minister of war. Piłsudski announced that his resignation had
been made necessary by poor health, and he deeded over the post of
prime minister to Bartel. However, the Marshal made it clear that
he was not retiring from public life. He was frustrated by the heavy
load of responsibilities that the prime minister was required to carry
without, as Piłsudski saw it, sufficient constitutional power to implement his decisions. In an intemperate newspaper interview he
described the Sejm as "a sterile, jabbering, howling thing that engendered such boredom as made the very flies die of disgust."[5] It was
obvious that the parliament's obstinacy had driven Piłsudski into an
absolute fury. He demanded extensive constitutional changes to
prevent the political disaster that he claimed was impending.

And, indeed, it did seem apparent that a period of violent political
strife was looming. The government had been unable to obtain the
support of the bulk of the PPS in the parliament. Only a small wing
of that party known as the PPS-Frakcja had split off to support
Piłsudski. The balance of the PPS was now completely in opposition
and in a position to frustrate most of the government's programs. In
response, the government began to take actions that increasingly
verged on the illegal. For example, in January 1929 the government
removed scores of opposition judges. This action was taken on the
basis of a legal "interpretation" by Stanislaw Car, but the government's own minister of justice considered it such an abuse that he
resigned in protest.

In late 1928 and early 1929 the Sejm met to consider the budget
for the forthcoming fiscal year. This presented a perfect opportunity
to closely examine the government's previous fiscal practices, a task
that the opposition deputies did with a will. During the budget
hearings, it developed that the government had overspent the previous budget by 560 million zlotys. Included in this sum was, of
course, the 8 million zlotys that had been transferred from the
Treasury to the BBWR for its election campaign. The money spent
on the secret police was well above the amount authorized by the
parliament.

There was nothing very new about a Polish government's over-
spending its budget. And in the present case most of the funds had
been used to expand the new port at Gdynia—a universally popular

project. In the past the government would always deal with over-spending by having its minister of finance appear before the Sejm, explain specific deficits, and ask for supplementary appropriations to cover them. Now the Sejm demanded the present finance minister, Gabriel Czechowicz, appear before it and explain the overspending.

Piłsudski refused to permit this. Czechowicz's testimony would have led to questions concerning the Treasury funds given to the BBWR, and these could seriously embarrass a government dedicated to *sanacja*. For the sake of consistency, Piłsudski himself also refused to appear in his capacity of minister of war to answer parliamentary questions about Army appropriations.

Eventually, the Sejm did pass the budget for the next year, but only after the Army's funds were cut somewhat, and the Secret Police appropriation was eliminated. However, the Sejm had not forgotten the matter of supplementary appropriations for the previous deficits. The opposition threatened to impeach Minister of Finance Czechowicz unless he appeared before the Sejm. Piłsudski announced that anything Czechowicz had done was done on Piłsudski's own orders, and Piłsudski refused to permit him to appear. In a newspaper interview the Marshal said that Czechowicz himself desired to appear before the Sejm in order to defend his honor, but Piłsudski forbade it—"Where can one find honor among such apes?"[6] Such insults only hardened the opposition's determination to bring Czechowicz before the Sejm and get at the truth regarding the Treasury funds that, it was now widely known, had been given to the BBWR. Piłsudski's refusal to permit Czechowicz to testify soon developed into a constitutional crisis, in the course of which the unlucky Czechowicz resigned as minister of finance and then, in March 1929, was impeached by the Sejm. A month later, in a complicated effort to arouse support for Czechowicz, Bartel resigned as prime minister. He was replaced by another of Piłsudski's confidants, Kazimierz Switalski, a forty-three-year-old veteran of the Polish Legion and an officer in the Army following independence. He had gone into "retirement" with Piłsudski at Sulejówek, where he served as an aide to the Marshal. Switalski had played an important role in planning the May 1926 coup. Subsequently he had served as minister of education.

The Switalski cabinet was the first post-coup government in which Piłsudski's real intimates, younger Army officers, held a number of cabinet-level offices. Most of the cabinet members in the three previous Piłsudski governments had been experienced civil servants or civilians with technical expertise in their respective fields. Piłsudski's military aides, while playing important roles as members of the Marshal's personal staff or in filling temporary assignments in various ministries, had not heretofore been given senior ministerial positions. Bartel had convinced Piłsudski that giving cabinet posts to these young military men would be offensive to the Sejm. Now Piłsudski no longer cared about the Sejm's reaction. In Switalski's cabinet Colonel Aleksander Prystor was appointed minister of labor; Colonel Ignacy Matuszewski, minister of finance; and Colonel Ignacy Boerner, minister of posts. Opposition newspapers called the new cabinet a "government of colonels," a name that stuck.

With so many cabinet posts held by Piłsudski's long-time associates, there was less and less need for formal cabinet meetings. Most of the ministries were headed by men who were so close to the Marshal and who knew one another so well that they needed little day-to-day guidance from either Switalski or Piłsudski. These officer-ministers either knew what was expected of them or could quickly find out by telephoning old friends in the Marshal's office. Consequently, the number of cabinet meetings dropped off sharply. In 1929 there were only sixteen full cabinet meetings, and Piłsudski attended only five of them.

As it turned out, Bartel's resignation had not succeeded in quashing the impeachment of Czechowicz. There was nothing that the Switalski government could do to prevent the trial of Czechowicz before a Sejm tribunal. This procedure began in June 1929, and Piłsudski regarded it as an indirect attack on him by the Sejm opposition—which, of course, it was. It was now common knowledge that Czechowicz had transferred the Treasury funds to the BBWR on Piłsudski's direct order. As the trial progressed, it became apparent that the Czechowicz affair could develop into a showdown between the parliament and the Piłsudski government. Many politicians, even those who were Piłsudski's enemies, began to fear that this whole business had gone too far. No one knew what Piłsudski might do if Czechowicz was to be found guilty. He might declare himself dictator and abolish the parliament. Marshal of the Sejm Daszyński secretly visited Piłsudski on June 24 and attempted to work out a compromise that would save face for all concerned. It is evidence of the seriousness of the crisis that Piłsudski was willing to discuss a settlement with Daszyński. But it was too late—the Sejm opposition had taken the bit in their teeth. Piłsudski himself appeared before the Sejm tribunal to testify in Czechowicz's defense. He told the deputies that he was proud of his accomplishments since his coup—"For only I had the courage to curb the sovereignty of the Sejm and destroy its omnipotence."[7] Turning toward his accusers, Piłsudski charged that it was "a ridiculous situation" when a minister of a government "led by the greatest man in Poland [himself] whose hands do not stink like yours can be impeached."[8] After two days of testimony, the tribunal's deputy-judges retired to consider their verdict.

On June 29 the tribunal returned its judgment. It was obvious that its members had been apprehensive of the consequences of an outright verdict of guilty. So, in a complicated and evasive decision they declared that they could not find Czechowicz guilty unless the Sejm, in full session, should decide that the money had been misappropriated. (This had never been formally determined.) In other words, Czechowicz could not be found guilty until the Sejm first stipulated that a crime had been committed. The Sejm was not then in session to consider the matter, so no final verdict could be reached.

The final resolution of the Czechowicz business now awaited the convening of the parliament in October 1929. Piłsudski was determined that the matter of misappropriated funds should not be brought to a vote and that the Sejm must confine itself to only two issues—the passage of the national budget and the initiation of constitutional reform. The BBWR made every effort to limit the agenda to these two items. But the opposition members would have none of this. For the first time since May 1926, they believed that they had Piłsudski on the run. The government appeared to be weakening, and Piłsudski had admitted to ill-health. This was no time to bow to the Marshal's wishes. The opposition made it clear that it would bring the Czechowicz matter to a vote and would then propose a motion of no confidence in the government. It anticipated success in both undertakings.

The government, for its part, made preparations to try to frustrate the opposition's plans. It was announced that Piłsudski himself would deliver the opening message from the President of the Republic to the Sejm on October 31, 1929. Ordinarily, Prime Minister Switalski would have read the presidential address, but it was announced that he had been "taken ill." It was evident that the government hoped that the formidable figure of the First Marshal would intimidate its enemies.

At the hour designated for the opening of the parliament, four in the afternoon, Piłsudski arrived at the Sejm building. He strode into the lobby to considerable applause. About one hundred Army officers had gathered to cheer the First Marshal. It was obvious that this was not a spontaneous welcome. Colonel Józef Beck, the chief of Piłsudski's War Ministry staff, was on the scene and in charge. At first the parliamentary opposition could not figure out what this demonstration was all about. Marshal of the Sejm Daszyński sent aides to see what was going on. They reported back that it appeared to be a calculated effort to intimidate the deputies. Ushers had asked the officers to leave, but they had refused to do so. In his office, Daszyński had a violent interview with Piłsudski; it ended with Daszyński refusing to open the session of the Sejm. "Is that your last word?" Piłsudski demanded. "Yes," said Daszyński, "I refuse to open the session under the menace of swords, bayonets, carbines and revolvers."[9] This reply became famous, although in actuality the officers were carrying no weapons other than the customary dress swords. Daszyński postponed the opening of the parliament until November 5—whereupon, in retaliation, President Mościcki prorogued it for an additional month, until December 5. The net effect of this "Affair of the Officers in the Lobby" aroused the parliamentary opposition into more determined hostility. When the Sejm finally convened, a formidable coalition of the Center and Left (known as the Centrolew) had been created, and it was found that it could dominate parliamentary affairs. As practically its first order of business, the Centrolew succeeded in passing a no-confidence vote in Prime Minister Switalski. He and his cabinet promptly resigned. This was, of course, the first time since the coup of 1926 that an entire government had been discharged by the parliament.

For several weeks Piłsudski hesitated about what should now be done. Finally, he persuaded Bartel that he should again serve as prime minister. President Mościcki called in the parliamentary leadership and persuaded them to accept Bartel, who was probably the most liberal and independent of Piłsudski's close supporters.

In typical Bartel style, this new cabinet, technically Bartel's fifth government since 1926, was put together with some thought toward assuaging the parliament. A couple of the "colonels" were dropped, and the new Ministers of the Interior and of Justice were men who were serious about upholding the letter of the law. Otherwise, the cabinet remained about the same—including, of course, Piłsudski as minister of war. Another holdover was Colonel Aleksander Prystor, an intimate of Piłsudski's who held the post of minister of labor. In his youth, Prystor had been a member of the PPS, but now he was a leading opponent of his old party. Bartel had wanted to drop Prystor from his new cabinet, but Piłsudski insisted that he remain.

For the first few months, relations between government and parliament were surprisingly good. The budget was passed promptly, and the Sejm made no effort to pursue the Czechowicz affair. Both sides were trying to be conciliatory, but this comfortable situation did not last long. It was now the turn of the Sejm opposition, pleased at its gains in the recent months, to overplay its hand. In March 1930, the PPS turned on Colonel Prystor and voted a motion of no confidence in the Minister of Labor. The Sejm certainly did not intend to precipitate the resignation of the entire Bartel government. But for Piłsudski, as well as the ill and reluctantly serving Bartel, this opportunity to show up the opposition was too good to miss. Bartel made a violent speech to a shocked Sejm, stating that this body was behaving in the same irresponsible manner that it had manifested before May 1926. He then resigned with all his cabinet.

For a time Piłsudski again hesitated. He was tempted to stand aside and let the opposition flounder about and prove that it was too weak to create a government. The Centrolew submitted the names of several possible prime ministers to the President; but, without the Marshal's strong personal support, it was clear that no government could be formed. Then, after two weeks, Piłsudski proposed the name of Walery Sławek, the officer and intimate who had formed the BBWR. With Piłsudski's backing, Sławek and his cabinet were nominated and took office.

The Sławek government was quickly seen for what it was—a throwing-down of the gauntlet to the Sejm. Sławek was among the most unbending of Piłsudski's supporters. Unlike Bartel, who consistently offered minor concessions to the parliament, Sławek would concede nothing. He named to his cabinet all the colonels, including Prystor, whom parliament had previously found so objectionable.

Now there was no compromise by either side—and few holds were barred. The opposition openly stigmatized Piłsudski as a "dictator." The Centrolew thirsted to revive the Czechowicz affair and finally have it out with Piłsudski and the BBWR. Parliament was not presently in session, but in May 1930, the Centrolew was able to put together a petition signed by 149 deputies, which compelled President Mościcki to call the parliament back into an extraordinary session. But he did not have to *keep* it in session, and the very day that the deputies reconvened, they received a message from Mościcki adjourning the parliament.

Having been blocked from meeting officially, the Centrolew called a "Congress for the Defense of Law and the Freedom of the People" to be held in Kraków. It convened at the end of June 1930, with about 1,500 official delegates and 30,000 supporters present. The size of the crowd impressed everyone, particularly members of the government. The delegates made it clear that they believed democracy in Poland was moribund. They were very militant in their opposition to Piłsudski and displayed posters which read "To the Gallows with Piłsudski" and "Down with the Puppet President." In a number of speeches, fervent hopes were expressed that Piłsudski health was deteriorating. The Centrolew announced plans for twenty-eight mass meetings to take place throughout Poland and they challenged the government to dissolve the parliament and call new elections, which, they believed, the Center-Left coalition would surely win.

At the conclusion of the meeting the chairman bade farewell to the cheering crowd: "Good-bye, until we meet again in Warsaw for the formation of a worker-peasant government."[10]

This congress at Kraków was a distinct surprise to the members of the Piłsudski government. They were astonished at the size of the meeting. They were frightened by the militancy, the radicalism and the enthusiasm of the participants. The government regarded this Centrolew congress in the same light that the congress's organizers apparently did—as a preliminary step to a possible Leftist coup.

Piłsudski reacted with dispatch. The Minister of the Interior was ordered to assemble the police dossiers on the Centrolew leaders. Piłsudski informed his ministers that he intended to have Mościcki dissolve the parliament and that they must prepare for new elections. Events began to move rapidly. Sławek resigned as prime minister on August 23, to make way for Piłsudski, who took over the next day, bringing in Colonel Jósef Beck as his deputy prime minister. On August 30, Mościcki announced the dissolution of parliament, and a few days later it was announced that elections would be held on November 17, 1930, for the Sejm and on November 23 for the Senate. On September 1 the minister of the interior gave Piłsudski a list of opposition deputies and senators. With a green pencil the Marshal checked off a number of names—those of persons to be arrested.

The seizure of opposition politicians began on the night of September 9. Eighteen senators and deputies were taken into custody on various charges, generally involving preparation of a *coup d'état*. The arrests were technically illegal in that all of those arrested enjoyed parliamentary immunity under Article 21 of the Polish constitution. However, the government held that since the parliament had been dissolved for elections, parliamentary immunity was not in force.

During the following nights, some sixty-odd more opposition leaders were arrested. Most of them were taken to an Army fortress, the Citadel in Brest Litovsk, where they were held incommunicado.

Because these arrests were made without public announcement, it took a little while for the opposition parties to determine which of their members were being held. But when a list of those arrested was put together, it was found that the government had virtually decapitated the Center and Left opposition. Six of the top PPS leaders had been jailed. The two most important members of the Piast Peasant Party had been seized—including Wincenty Witos, who had been three times prime minister of Poland. Virtually all the Ukrainian minority party leaders were in custody.

It was not for some months, certainly not until well after the November 1930 elections, that the Polish public learned what happened to the prisoners at Brest Litovsk. They were put in the custody of Colonel Kostek-Biernacki, an officer who had served in the French Foreign Legion and had adopted that service's policies of prisoner treatment. Kostek-Biernacki was instructed to make the opposition leaders "know they were in prison."[11] The colonel carried out his instructions. Senators and deputies at Brest Litovsk were underfed, regularly beaten, forced to clean latrines with their bare hands, and constantly insulted. Several of the arrested deputies were subjected to the horror of a mock execution.

Meanwhile the government set out to win the November elections —legally if it could, illegally if it must. Given the current circumstances, it was difficult for the BBWR to campaign on the *sanacja* concept, so its platform simply stressed the need for constitutional reform and support of the Marshal. For the first time, Piłsudski's own name appeared on the election ballots. The slogan of the BBWR was a challenge: "With or Without Piłsudski?" And the presence of the Marshal's name on the ballot made this question impossible to avoid. The enthusiastic support of civil-service officials was demanded and to a large degree gotten. Many political arrests at a level lower than deputy or senator were made, and by election time there were probably two to three thousand opposition politicians languishing in prison. Many others, not arrested, were subjected to severe beatings. Rowdies were permitted to break up opposition rallies without hindrance from the police—indeed, the police themselves sometimes led the assaults. The Electoral Commission invalidated certain registration lists known to include a large number of anti-government voters. This tactic probably cost Piłsudski's opponents nearly a million votes. The government launched a campaign encouraging voters to mark their ballots in the open, implying that anyone who chose to vote secretly must have something to hide. Money in substantial amounts was available for the BBWR campaign, while the opposition was starved for funds and their offices were frequently broken into by police, who carried away their contributors' lists.

The surviving (unarrested) leadership of the Centrolew parties called upon the public to resist official repression with a torrent of antigovernment votes. They sought to create a ground swell of outrage against the government's actions, and they threatened a general strike. But the ground swell never materialized. The Polish public was apathetic. The general belief—and probably a correct one—was that even if the Piłsudski forces lost the election, they would not step down. Many of the Polish intelligentsia were apalled at Piłsudski's arrest of the opposition leaders, and a number of his important supporters began to defect. But, of course, the intelligentsia represented only a small segment of the vote. For the workers and peasants, Piłsudski still possessed great charisma. If unpleasant things were vaguely rumored to be happening to some members of the parliament, their general reputation was such that the public could not bring itself to be greatly concerned.

The result of the November balloting was that the BBWR and its allies won an outright majority—55 percent of the seats in the Sejm and sixty-eight percent in the Senate. The Center and Left parties were practically demolished. Among the six of them, they elected only 21 percent of the Sejm's deputies. The National Democrats, who had run on a thoroughly nationalist platform, did surprisingly well, electing 14 percent of the deputies. They had been left alone by the government, which regarded these old enemies as now being unimportant. The national minorities parties, on the other hand, did poorly and lost half of their strength in the Sejm—dropping to only 7 percent of the deputies elected.

So Piłsudski and his government had won decisively. Quietly the government began to release on bail the arrested opposition leaders. By December almost all of them were free. If it was not quite the victory that the BBWR had hoped for—they had wanted to elect two thirds of the Sejm so that constitutional reform could be pushed through at once—it was not hard to settle for a simple majority. A lot could be done with that. In fact, it made constitutional change seem a lot less imperative.

The government's victory had, however, been purchased at a great price for democracy in Poland, and there could be no turning back now.

13

Good Times and Bad

ALTHOUGH THE YEARS from 1927 through 1929 were marked by great political turmoil, they were generally pleasant ones for most Poles. It was a time of considerable economic growth in virtually every European nation, and Poland was not exempt. Even though its gains were far more modest than those enjoyed in many other countries, a faint glow of prosperity shone upon most classes and occupations in Poland.

For the peasantry, the nearly two thirds of Poland's population that lived on the land, there had never been a period in history that could truly be termed "prosperous," and the late 1920s were no exception. However, because of land reform there was farm land for sale, and thus many peasants were able to satisfy their most ardent desire. And although the Polish peasants were among Europe's least efficient farmers, the worldwide prices of rye, barley and hogs had increased to the point where even they could sell their crops for export at a modest profit. Increased employment opportunities in the cities reduced the surplus population in the countryside. The percentage of Poles who lived on the land dropped from about 70 percent to near 60 percent. Work abroad was so plentiful that a half million peasants could sell their labor in France or Germany, thus reducing the number of mouths that had to be fed from Polish crops. And these emigrants almost always sent a little money home. So, each year a little more cash trickled through the Polish villages. And in a nation as poor as Poland, even the slightest economic improvement had a great impact on the lives of the peasantry. The small rural stores stocked and sold more goods. It was no longer necessary for the peasant farmers to sell almost everything they produced, and so the peasants' diet became better. Granted, the peasants could scarcely be called prosperous, but their poverty had become a little less oppressive. In the Polish countryside, it took no more than that to make the people hopeful and happy.

A somewhat similar economic improvement took place among the industrial workers in the cities. During the late 1920s nearly a million Poles were working in commerce or industry. The textile industry was the largest employer, followed by mining and metalworking. Polish industry was very thinly capitalized, and still quite small in scale—fewer than one out of every thirty Poles was an industrial worker. But during the late 1920s a good deal of foreign capital, mostly French and American, was flowing into Poland. Soon a third of the capital of Polish business had been provided by foreigners.

One attraction that brought foreign investment to Poland was the very low prevailing wage scale. A typical Warsaw industrial worker's family consisting of the worker, his wife and two children earned an annual income of only 2,600 zlotys (approximately 300 dollars). This was so close to subsistence that 60 percent of this income had to be spent just for food. In most areas of industrial activity, the Polish workers were the most poorly paid in Europe. Even so, members of the Polish working class were far from dissatisfied. They were protected by extensive government-subsidized programs for sick pay and unemployment insurance. Under law, each worker received a two-week paid vacation annually, and each year wages went up a little. There was full employment for skilled workers. General economic progress was evident, and it was thought that the imminent completion of the port of Gdynia would bring further industrial development. Wages might be low but times were better than they ever had been, and the workers' contentment was reflected in the very low number of strikes during 1927–29.

The government, of course, claimed most of the credit for these favorable economic developments. They were certain that foreign investors found Poland attractive because of the stability of its government under Piłsudski and because of the soundness of the zloty. (The Stabilization Loan of 1927 had provided the Bank of Poland with sufficient gold and foreign exchange to support the zloty firmly, a matter that the government took great pride in and considered as being of the greatest importance in maintaining Poland's financial stability.)

The relatively small Polish middle class, customarily referred to as the intelligentsia, fared even better during these years than did the workers or peasants. To be considered a member of this class, one was expected to possess a university degree or to be an artist or writer. The intelligentsia probably made up about 5 percent of the Polish population. As a class, they were the descendants of the Polish gentry and continued to embody some of the old *szlachta* attitudes—although many of them had overcome the gentry's historic aversion to employment in commerce. For the rest, there was ample employment available in the government bureaucracy, the field in which most members of this class wanted to work. Although the pay of civil servants was low, the prestige was considerable. With careful economy the civil servant and his family could afford a pleasant five-room apartment and could employ a maidservant. They could spend their four weeks of summer vacation in the mountains or in a rented manor house on some small country estate. They could enjoy the cultural events that all middle-class Poles dearly loved—lectures, the opera and the theater.

The increased prosperity could be seen in every field. By 1929 more than 95 percent of Polish children were attending school; fifty thousand young people were enrolled in Polish universities. A growing number of modern buildings were being built in Polish cities. Warsaw, in particular, became both charming and impressive. The Royal Castle and parts of the Old City were restored. The broad avenues were repaved. Large theaters, sports stadiums, museums, and schools were built. If the architecture of these buildings was often distinguished, the interior design and decoration were outstanding, since these were fields in which Poles have traditionally excelled.

The Polish cities were warm and alive, and the Poles themselves had many charming customs. One's name day—the feast day of the saint for whom one was named—was celebrated rather than one's birthday. On days like May 15, the name day for Saint Sophia, whose name was a popular one among Polish women, the streets of every city were filled with people carrying flowers—the traditional name-day gift—to various Sophias. The main avenues of the principal Polish cities were lined with pleasant restaurants and sidewalk cafés, where one could buy a cup of coffee for one zloty and sit in the sun all morning. The café owners reserved tables for groups of poets, writers and artists, and competed for their patronage. Foreign diplomats liked to be posted to Warsaw. It was considered a gay and cosmopolitan city with a friendly intelligentsia, whose members were noted for their wide cultural interests and command of a number of languages. Polish women, blessed with a happy combination of Slavic features, were considered among the most beautiful in Europe.

These were years of political conflict, but an observer of the Polish people would be most struck by their comfortable stability. During the late 1920s, life in Poland was better and happier than it had ever been.

The worldwide Depression of the 1930s started as a slightly different time in each nation. For Poland it began during the first quarter of 1929. There was a sudden reduction of activity in practically every industry. During the course of 1929, Polish coal output dropped by about 25 percent, and steel mills cut their production by 20 percent. Building construction declined, and textile shipments dropped about a third. By December 1929, the number of persons employed in Polish industry had declined about 10 percent from the level of the previous December.

Accompanying this recession, and even more ominous, was an abrupt worldwide drop in the price of agricultural products. For the bulk of the Polish population, who, of course, made their living from agriculture, this caused an extremely serious crisis. The Polish peasants' costs of production were so close to the selling price of their produce that any drop in prices was bound to cause real suffering. The peasants could not afford to store their crops and wait for better prices. They had to sell their produce—usually to pay the loans they had taken out to raise it. If they had to sell at a loss, the only way that they could make up this loss was to reduce their already minuscule expenditures.

For the Polish peasant faced with disastrous market conditions and for the Polish industrial worker faced with layoffs and shortened hours, life suddenly became grim and frightening. At first, it was not perceived that these developments were only the start of a worldwide economic catastrophe that would last for years and would get much worse. In 1929–30 it was thought that these were only temporary problems that would soon right themselves. In the meantime, the

Polish people hoped that the government could find some way to reduce the nation's distress.

It is usual to condemn the Polish government's handling of the nation's fiscal affairs during the Depression. And it is true that in retrospect the government's policies were excessively conservative and were dominated by an almost obsessive determination to maintain the stability of the zloty. It is also true that the Polish government had very few economic experts and that no government dominated by Piłsudski ever introduced innovative economic policies. To them, this seemed somehow to smack of juggling the books. The leaders in the Piłsudski regime viewed finance in a very orthodox and unimaginative manner. They believed that the value of the zloty, which had been established and maintained with heroic effort, had to be preserved at any cost.*

The fiscal policy of the Polish government was simply to meet bad times by reducing expenditures. The concept of "spending one's way out of a depression" was too sophisticated for the Polish government, and in any event, this Keynesian concept had not yet been generally accepted, even in nations much larger than Poland. As the Depression deepened in the early 1930s, the Polish government chased the downward spiral of its income by progressive decreases in public spending. The Polish policy was to balance the national budget at almost any cost. During the fiscal year ending in March 1930, the government reduced its expenditures in midyear and succeeded in showing a small surplus. During the following year, government revenues dropped even more sharply, and after again cutting its expenditures severely, the government showed only a small deficit. But for the next several years, even the most drastic cost-cutting efforts could not offset the drastic fall in government income from customs, railroad receipts, and all types of tax. The deficit was 245 million zlotys in the fiscal year 1932–33; 371 million in 1933–34; and 108 million in 1934–35.

Every conceivable orthodox expedient was attempted to lessen

---

* In fact, the zloty eventually *rose* in value against such major currencies as the dollar. In the spring of 1933, the dollar fell against the zloty from nine zlotys to the dollar to five zlotys to the dollar. Although this made it easier for the Polish government to pay off its obligations to the United States, it had the much more serious effect of making Polish exports more expensive on the world market. And the devaluation of the dollar without a parallel devaluation of the Polish zloty was catastrophic for many Polish families whose modest savings were in United States dollars, which circulated as a second currency in the Polish countryside.

these deficits. In retrospect it is evident that many of these measures only worsened the situation. The government-owned railways were losing money, so the government increased railway fees and fares—which, of course, further reduced railway use and revenue. The pay of civil servants was cut by 15 percent, and the salaries of the Army officers, the favored sons of Piłsudski-ite Poland, were cut by 5 percent. Many civil servants were discharged, which saved the government money but compounded the increasingly severe unemployment problem. Import duties were increased sharply, which brought in income but also raised prices for the raw materials that most Polish industries had to import.

Even Poland's heroic effort to maintain its credit standing abroad by paying foreign loans as they fell due, while many other nations defaulted, created great problems. During the first five years of the Depression, Poland spent 1.5 billion zlotys in payments of interest and capital on foreign loans. This enormous sum could be raised only by a transfer of gold from the Bank of Poland. The Polish gold reserve dropped sharply; this weakening of the Polish monetary system caused foreign capital to be withdrawn frm Poland, further exacerbating Poland's economic woes.

To arrest the gold outflow (and thus maintain the value of the zloty), the Polish government had to reverse its adverse balance of payments. This it attempted to do by stimulating the sale of Polish goods abroad, but given the worldwide depression, this was much more easily said than done. Most Polish goods were salable abroad only if they were "dumped"—that is, sold at prices close to or actually below the cost of production. The losses on this kind of sale could only be recouped by charging higher than normal prices at home. To the Polish government there seemed no help for it. Foreign currency had to be obtained in order to staunch the gold outflow and thus maintain the value of the zloty—therefore the Polish population must be forced to pay indirectly for the losses on the dumped goods.

Every class of Polish society suffered acutely during the Depression. But, as is usual in economic crises, the peasantry suffered the most. The prices of agricultural products dropped so far and so fast that life in the villages became indescribably wretched. In 1928 the peasants could sell 100 pounds of wheat for 23 zlotys. In 1933–34 they could get only 8 zlotys for the same wheat. Similarly the price of 100 pounds of rye dropped from 19 to 6 zlotys, while barley fell from 18 to 5 zlotys. While farm prices were plummeting an average of more than 60 percent, the prices of industrial items that the peasant used declined only about 30 percent.

In 1932 the average net income of Polish farms of 1 to 20 acres was three zlotys per acre—that is, the owners were getting less than one United States dollar per acre over the cost of producing their crops. On smaller farms net income simply did not exist. Everything was grown and sold at a loss. It is estimated that in 1934 the cash income of the average Polish peasant farming family was less than two (U.S.) cents per day.

The peasant problem did not end there. The villages were filling up with extra mouths. Unemployed industrial workers who had nowhere else to go went back to their native villages to live with relatives who had no use for their services. Emigration abroad was shut off, and various European countries repatriated the Polish immigrants who were taking work from their own people. Remittances from abroad, the invisible cash income on which many Polish villages had subsisted for years, practically stopped.

At the depth of the Depression, money virtually ceased to circulate in the Polish countryside. There was not even enough money to buy ordinary salt for cooking purposes. The peasants used a grayish rock salt, and the cooking water was saved for reuse. Most peasant men owned only one shirt, one pair of boots, one pair of pants—the rest having been cut up to make their children's clothes. During the winter there were no coats for the children, and many wore cotton sacks filled with straw.

The situation was scarcely much better for the Polish industrial workers, although at least some of them received unemployment-insurance benefits, which cushioned the blow for a period of time. Between 1929 and 1932 the number of Polish workers employed in large- and medium-size industries fell from 844,000 to 534,000. But this was only part of the story. Those who remained employed went on short hours (the total number of hours worked in Polish industry dropped by nearly 50 percent between 1929 and 1933), and the average wage rates dropped by about 15 percent.

When the Depression came, it was found that many of the privately held industries in Poland, including some very large ones, were so thinly capitalized that they could not withstand a period of prolonged unprofitability. It was obvious that Polish industry could not be permitted to slide into general bankruptcy. So, one by one, (and often dozen by dozen), insolvent manufacturing firms were taken over by the government. Within only a few years the Polish government came to own 70 percent of the facilities for iron and steel production, 30 percent of the coal mines, and 80 percent of the chemical industry; and it was writing half the insurance coverage issued in Poland.

Not only did these extensive government holdings require an' enormous investment of public capital to rescue them from insolvency, but along with ownership came the problem of managing these new national enterprises. Like many other nations, the Polish government had never been notably effective in showing a profit in the operation of a business. When this sudden flood of industries came under government management, their efficiency undoubtedly suffered. The cost of production in these industries rose to the point where they could be operated only at a loss.

It was estimated that there was a total of 1,200,000 industrial workers who customarily worked in mines or factories having twenty or more employees. In 1936 nearly a half million of these workers were unemployed and about 150,000 more were employed only two to four days a week. The typical hourly wage for an employed industrial worker was .71 zlotys, which worked out to about 12 United States cents per hour.

The end result of the Depression in Poland and the government's attempts to combat it was that the Polish economy was put through a deflationary wringer. The total of national income dropped from 28 billion zlotys in 1929 to 15 billion in 1933. The Polish standard of living, already low, of course, fell with the decline in national income. The per capita consumption of electricity dropped by 21 percent between 1929 and 1934 and had not regained the 1929 level even by 1937. Between 1929 and 1934 Polish consumption of such basic items as matches declined by 60 percent, sugar by 20 percent, tobacco by 30 percent, textile fabrics by 20 percent, iron by 46 percent, and steel by 41 percent. Consumption fell dramatically in virtually all of the items that people need for sustaining life or making it tolerable.

In almost every European nation, the Depression caused the political radicalization of the workers and peasants. But, as usual, the Polish Communist Party (CPP) was its own worst enemy. The party was technically illegal and had been so since February 1919. Nonetheless, it had displayed such abysmal political ineptitude that the Polish government apparently decided that it suited its interests to permit the CPP to operate more or less openly. Throughout the 1920s the CPP worked hard to lose its reputation as an agent of Russian imperialism and therefore the opponent of Polish independence. But nothing ever went right for the CPP. When it supported Piłsudski in the 1926 coup the party was lambasted by Stalin, an attack that nearly wrecked the CPP. But with the Depression, the CPP anticipated that better days were in store for it. Not so. Now wholly intimidated by Moscow, and acting on Comintern instructions, the CPP adopted the line that its mortal enemies were not the parties of the Right but the other Left-wing parties. What little energy Polish Communism could muster was squandered in attacking the PPS and the rest of the non-Communist Left. Involved in this misconceived crusade, the party virtually ignored the boundless opportunities presented by agitation among the millions of Polish peasants and unemployed workers.

The Depression in Poland did not markedly ease until 1937. By then the government had adopted a number of less orthodox economic policies designed to pull the nation out of its slump. Export-import agreements and quotas were agreed on with various other nations, and it was then possible to obtain higher prices for Polish agricultural products abroad. Poland's foreign debt was refinanced, and massive internal loans were floated to provide industrial-development capital. Factory output gradually increased, and employment went up. But the Polish recovery from the Depression was never complete. Even by 1938 such important trade indicators as rail freight moved, coal mined, foreign trade, and total corporate profits all stood below the 1929 levels. Very few nations have endured sufferings as great as that experienced by Poland during its Depression.

14

A "New Course"

THE ELECTIONS OF NOVEMBER 1930 had given the Piłsudski government a reliable working majority in the Sejm and the Senate. Piłsudski, who promptly turned the office of prime minister over to Walery
Sławek, could now compel the passage of almost any piece of legislation through the parliament. And, in the years that followed the
Piłsudski government made full use of this happy circumstance.

Curiously, though, the government never lost its distrust of the
politicians in the parliament, even when most of them were loyal
government supporters and the parliament itself functioned virtually
as a rubber stamp. From the first sessions of the parliament elected
in November 1930, the government made calculated efforts to emphasize the impotence of the Sejm and the Senate. Piłsudski himself chose
the new marshal of the Sejm, his old friend and former Prime Minister Kazimierz Switalski. Promptly confirmed by the BBWR majority, Switalski made it clear that he had been sent to parliament to
"keep order."[1] He quickly proposed and had passed a new set of by-
laws that greatly reduced the opportunities for independent action by
the Sejm. Meanwhile, Prime Minister Sławek suggested to his BBWR
followers in the Sejm that they "should pursue the tactic of ignoring
the opposition, of refusing to debate with them at length, thus demoralizing them by showing that their arguments have no significance and that everything is done without any regard for their

views."[2] Piłsudski instructed his supporters "to outvote the opposition mercilessly from the start."[3]

These were exactly the tactics that were employed. The government drafted practically all legislation and sent it to the parliament, where it was generally passed as submitted, down to the last comma. This system was not entirely without merit. The government was able to rapidly pass some admirable legislation in such fields as educational improvements and local government reforms. And in 1932 legislation submitted by the government created the first uniform legal system to operate throughout Poland. But a good many potentially repressive measures also sailed through the Sejm and the Senate. The government passed laws requiring the approval of the ministry of the interior for any outdoor meetings or rallies. A law authorized the conscription of railway workers if they should strike during a time of "insecurity threatening the State"; another law permitted the minister of education to retire university professors whose antigovernment stances had made them objectionable. Certain matters embarrassing to the government were also quickly eliminated through parliamentary action. The Czechowicz affair, for example, was finally swept under the carpet for good simply by having parliament declare that all the supplementary credits for the 1927–28 budget had been legally allocated.

The preelection arrests and the imprisonments at Brest Litovsk were dealt with in similar fashion. The opposition demanded that an inquiry into these arrests be held by parliament. The government was of two minds in the matter—should it refuse to allow any debate on the subject and thus appear guilty of all the opposition's charges, or should it permit open parliamentary discussion on the matter and bring the matter to an end? Eventually it was decided to permit a short debate from midnight to 4:20 A.M. on January 26, 1931. (The designation of these early morning hours for the debate was not quite as malicious as it may appear. The Sejm began its sessions at noon, and it was not unusual for it to sit until well past midnight. But, obviously, these very late hours were not the most desirable time for debate.) At the conclusion, Sławek read a government statement denying that any brutality had occurred. The BBWR majority voted to accept this statement, and the inquiry was closed.

The only item that the government could not ram through parliament was constitutional reform. This was an obsession of Piłsudski and his adherents. They had bested the parliament and put it in its place, but no one knew how long this state of affairs might last. The Polish government was determined to prevent members of parliament and their political parties from regaining the preponderance of power which they had formerly enjoyed. The best way that this could be done was through constitutional reform so sweeping that it would amount to the drafting of an entirely new document. But passage of a new constitution required a two-thirds vote of parliament, and the government did not presently possess this majority. So, for the time being the Piłsudski government had to content itself with alternately humiliating and scorning parliament.

As it turned out, the government's policy had a double-edged effect. It was demeaning to the opposition to have its parliamentary role ignored. But this tactic could not be applied without equally ignoring the BBWR majority. The BBWR members came to feel almost as distrusted and helpless as their opponents; there is nothing very stimulating about being a rubber stamp. The BBWR deputies and senators did their duty, but in a cheerless and unenthusiastic manner. A slow dribble of demoralized government supporters in parliament began to resign their seats.

But, at least, the BBWR senators and deputies were not subjected to the legal harassment that some of the opposition members suffered. In 1931 the government brought to trial some of the men who had been imprisoned at Brest Litovsk. They were charged with conspiring to stage a *coup d'état*. Obviously, any Piłsudski government was on shaky grounds when accusing any group of plotting a coup. Probably the government would have preferred to forget about the trial, but this would have constituted an admission that there had been no grounds for the Brest Litovsk arrests. So, eleven of those who had been imprisoned in 1930 were brought to trial in December 1931. Ten were found guilty and given sentences of from three to five years. After a lengthy appeal process, half of them were pardoned. The other five, including Witos, fled into exile in Czechoslovakia rather than serve sentences.

There were a few other trials of persons accused of one sort of anti-government activity or another during this period, but none resulted in a long sentence, although in 1934 the government established a concentration camp for political prisoners at Bereza Kartuska near the eastern border of Poland.

In fairness, it must be said that the Piłsudski government's repressive actions toward its opponents were not very extensive nor very violent. The Bereza Kartuska concentration camp was opened only after a Ukrainian terrorist assassinated the Polish minister of the interior on June 15, 1934. The total number of people who passed through the concentration camp during the five years of its existence did not exceed five hundred- - and most of these were either Ukrainian nationalists or currency-exchange offenders against whom the government may well have had fairly strong cases, but cases that could not be proved in court. Although the Piłsudski regime had certainly become authoritative, its counteropposition activities could not be compared to those of many other European governments during this decade of emerging fascism. The government's enemies were not often persecuted; they were just ignored and reduced to the role of bystanders in the political process.

In fact, Piłsudski regarded fascism as a menace and some of his government's most immoderate attacks were directed against it. These antifascist moves came to a head in 1934, when the government dissolved several crypto-fascist parties that had arisen out of the Right-wing National Democratic Party. One of these groups, the National Radical Camp (ONR), patterned itself closely after the German Nazis, complete with anti-Semitic extremism. Perhaps because of the frustrations caused by the Depression, these fascists-type parties quicky developed a following among Polish university students, most of whom were very conservative. But in 1934, the Piłsudski government moved against these groups. It declared them illegal and flung some of the ONR leaders into the concentration camp at Bereza Kartuska. This did not do away with fascism in Poland, however. Nor did it eliminate anti-Semitism. But for the time being, it eliminated any openly fascist activities from the Polish political scene.

In the early 1930s Piłsudski's health began to deteriorate. His chronic bronchitis became more severe. The attacks of influenza that he had suffered every year since his youthful exile in Siberia became more frequent and more debilitating. In March 1931 he told Sławek and Mościcki that he no longer had the energy to interest himself in matters other than the Army and foreign affairs. Although the Marshal never discussed his ailments, even with his closest associates, the effects of his illnesses can be seen in the successive formal photographs taken from 1930 onward. Piłsudski, always in uniform and seated at the left of President Mościcki, appears progressively wasted and worn.

Piłsudski now took frequent and lengthy vacations for his health. With a very small entourage, usually only his doctor and an adjutant, he visited Madeira, Rumania and Egypt. He stayed in rented villas and occupied himself by writing short works on military history. When he was in Warsaw, he no longer attended cabinet meetings. It became increasingly difficult for his subordinates to meet with him, and when they actually met with him, the conversation usually consisted mainly of a series of laconic orders from the Marshal, who sat hunched over a table and played endless games of solitaire. Despite Piłsudski's increasing disinvolvement in governmental affairs, many of his cabinet ministers found it difficult to take any major step without his instructions. They generally lacked initiative—they were terrified of inadvertently displeasing the Marshal. Many of them simply took refuge in craven subservience. General Sławoj-Składkowski was typical of these persons. In 1930, Piłsudski had summoned Składkowski, who found the Marshal playing solitaire in an empty drawing room in the Belvedere. Without any preliminaries Piłsudski said, "Now then, you will become Minister of the Interior."

Składkowski modestly observed that he had no experience of politics. Piłsudski laughed, "Politics is not necessary for that post. Everyone makes such a fuss about you being an organizer. For that reason you shall become Minister. Present yourself to the Prime Minister. Good-bye." Piłsudski resumed his game and Składkowski departed to find his new offices.

After some months of service as minister of the interior, Składkowski was called back to the Belvedere. Piłsudski asked him if he wanted to stay on as minister or return to the Army. Składkowski replied, "Marshal, I shall work as you order."

Piłsudski was irritated by this servility and snapped, "You are tedious."

But Składkowski demurred, "I cannot judge, Commandant, for which service I am better fitted. . . . In my service for you I have long since forgotten what I should prefer. I am altogether at your disposal and whatever decision you make is certainly the correct one."[4]

Although few of Piłsudski's entourage were as excessively deferential as Składkowski, nothing of any great importance—especially in the fields of foreign affairs and the military—was done without his approval. Everything revolved around him. Piłsudski recognized this and recognized the dangers inherent in it. In 1931 he told several of his closest associates that he "cast too big a shadow on Polish life.

Everything hinged on him and he was the deciding element, which was not a healthy situation."[5] But this situation had been created by Piłsudski himself, and he did nothing to alter it. He kept everyone off balance by his secretiveness, arbitrary decisions, and capricious favoritism. An unpleasant interview with Piłsudski could be a most formidable experience—one that few cared to undergo. No one coming into his presence knew exactly how he would be received and prayed only to find the Marshal in a good mood. No one could fathom the Marshal's abrupt changes in attitude toward his associates. Colonel Aleksander Prystor, for example, had been one of his closest and most highly valued disciples. Piłsudski made him prime minister in 1931. Then, suddenly, two years later Piłsudski turned against Prystor, accusing him of relying "on his 'own men,' "[6] surely not an unreasonable thing for the prime minister to do. Prystor at once lost his office, and subsequently Piłsudski would scarcely even speak to him. In 1933, as the term of office of President Mościcki neared its end, no one knew whether Piłsudski wanted him reelected. Not until a week before the election did the Marshal reveal his desire that Mościcki be returned to office. This was promptly accomplished, but the incident reveals much about the political climate of the time.

In earlier years Piłsudski, encouraged by Bartel, had made an effort to fill most government positions with civilian experts. But as time went by, more military men were brought into the cabinet. This policy created a thorny problem. For their subordinates, these Army officers naturally selected men they knew and trusted. Obviously these persons tended to be friends from the Army. And these people, in turn, frequently selected old military associates for the subordinate positions that they had to fill.

This process came to be called the "Exodus from the Army." In the Prystor cabinet (May 1931 to May 1933) there were as many military officers as civilians. In the cabinet of Janusz Jedrzejewicz, which followed (May 1933 to May 1934), the situation was exactly duplicated. Army officers were appointed to numerous senior management positions in government-operated industries. Most provincial governors and senior provincial officials were, or until recently had been, Army officers. The ministry of the Interior and the Ministry of Foreign Affairs were rapidly flooded with officers. The "Exodus from the Army" had adverse effects on both the Army and the government. The Army's officer corps was picked over, and many of its best men were plucked out for nonmilitary jobs. And the members of the Po-

lish civil service were demoralized by constantly being passed over in
favor of officers.

Few of these Army officers had experience of managing civil enterprises, and this problem led to a phenomenon known as the "Changing of the Guard." Every year or so, there would be a wholesale
shuffling-about of cabinet ministers, deputy ministers, prefects, and
so on. After each shuffle the same faces would emerge—but in different posts as the government sought to improve efficiency by finding
the right spot for each favored person.

Jedrezejewicz (an educator who had been a member of the Polish
Legion, and P.O.W. officer) succeeded Colonel Prystor as prime min-
ister in May 1933 and was in turn succeeded a year later by Leon
Kozłowski, a civilian, but a former member of the Polish Legion. Less
than a year later, Kozłowski was succeeded by former Colonel Sławek.
And amidst all this the same faces appeared and reappeared.

Apart from approving, or disapproving, the various shuffles of ministerial offices Piłsudski now devoted most of his waning energies to
foreign affairs. There is no question but that Piłsudski was a master
in European diplomatic relations. Divorcing himself from the bur-
dens of day-to-day governmental detail, but in a position to familiar-
ize himself with every significant fact turned up by Polish diplomats
abroad, he spent most of his time brooding over foreign affairs. Probably no other person in authority in Europe possessed Piłsudski's exceptional grasp of international developments. No detail or nuance
eluded him. He had a remarkable ability to forecast events. And he
had imagination and courage. His associates were awed by his pro-
ficiency and his intuition. As a matter of course, nothing of consequence in Polish foreign policy was done without having been
cleared with the Marshal. Indeed, most foreign policy initiatives came
from Piłsudski himself.

European diplomatic affairs during the early 1930s were a jumble
of treaties, pacts, conferences, declarations and conventions. The
"Spirit of Locarno" had died, and the ability of the League of Nations to compel peace was dubious. So, within the space of only
months, one nation would ally itself with another, then with another,
then with still another. Relationships between particular nations
warmed, cooled, dissolved, then warmed once again. At the root of
all this was the central tension of the time—the fear of a resurgent
Germany, wherein momentous changes were taking place. Coupled

with this fear was the knowledge that very soon Germany would compel revision of the constraints imposed upon it by the Treaty of Versailles. These constraints were numerous, and they affected practically every European nation. The remilitarization of the Rhineland was opposed by France. A union of Germany and Austria was opposed by Italy. The return of Danzig and the Corridor was opposed by Poland. Restoration of the German colonies was opposed by Great Britain, while German rearmament was objected to by practically every nation. And yet no one European government had both the strength and the will to single-handedly deny Germany what it was demanding. So, the alternative was a series of alliances and realliances as each nation sought in collectivism what it could not achieve alone.

It is necessary to review Poland's relations with its neighbors and allies at the beginning of the thirties. There had been little change in the relations between Poland and Lithuania since the dramatic affair of December 1927, when Piłsudski had challenged the Lithuanian strong man Voldemaras with the question, "Do you want peace or war?" Voldemaras had opted for peace, but this had not restored diplomatic relations between the two nations.

Nor had Polish-Czechoslovak relations improved much. Piłsudski persisted in regarding Czechoslovakia as a doomed and unnatural hybrid nation that would collapse in a time of stress. The Teschen affair continued to rankle and prevented any real warmth between the two nations. The Polish government was constantly protesting the Czech treatment of the Polish minority in Teschen, which the Poles alleged to be harsh and discriminatory. Relations between the two nations were further strained by the Czech government's benevolent attitude toward the dissident nationalist faction of Poland's Ukrainian minority. Ukrainian terrorists escaping from Poland could flee across the Czech border and count upon Czechoslovakia's refusing to extradite them.

A particular irritant to Piłsudski was the consistent propaganda successes of the Czechs. It seemed easy for the Czechs to marshal European opinion in their favor. Prague possessed a superb diplomatic propaganda service, and the image that it projected of the Czech Foreign Minister Éduard Beneš was excellent. The Poles, by comparison, did poorly in this regard, and the international reputation of the Polish leadership compared unfavorably to that of the Czechs. Piłsudski found this infuriating.

Rumania, on the other hand, remained the ally and ever faithful friend of Poland. Nothing was ever permitted to disturb the warmth of relations between Warsaw and Bucharest.

The situation with Soviet Russia was complicated and beset with constant fluctuations. The Soviet War Scare of 1927 had given way to a period during which Moscow desired nothing so much as an assurance of peace. In January 1929, Stalin expelled Trotsky from the Soviet Union, and it was evident that a period of tranquillity was necessary to permit internal political consolidation. Moscow proposed to Poland that the two nations sign the Kellog-Briand Pact as an instrument of national policy. The Poles were not averse to this action, provided that Rumania and the Baltic states neighboring the Soviet Union were included. This condition was promptly agreed to by the Soviet negotiator Maxim Litvinov, and in January 1929 the document known as the Litvinov Protocol was signed. But after a brief period of good feelings the Soviets began to cool toward the Poles as their own internal problems seemed to be on the way toward solution. There was a resumption of minor Soviet raids across the Polish frontier accompanied by an increase in Russian espionage and sabotage activity. But then in 1931 the Japanese occupied Manchuria. Alarmed, the Soviet government moved much of the Red Army eastward to meet the potential threat at its border. Simultaneously, Soviet-German relations, which had been cooling ever since Locarno, took a decided turn for the worse. The Soviets were also experiencing internal problems—meeting the goals of the first Five-Year Plan was proving difficult. Suddenly the Soviet government became sincerely interested in concluding some kind of very definite nonaggression agreement with its immediate Western neighbors—the most important of which was, of course, Poland.

The sudden interest of the Soviets meshed precisely with that of the Poles. Although Piłsudski did not put much value on nonaggression treaties as such—"all those useless pacts, short-lived and worthless"[7]—he attached great importance to the generally friendly atmosphere that they could create—a friendliness that was surely missing from Russo-Polish relations at that time. There were other advantages for Poland. The conclusion of a treaty with Russia could do much to strengthen the Polish position vis à vis Germany. It would also make Poland more important and durable in the eyes of France and Britain. As the Polish Foreign Minister Stanislaw Patek observed, "The West is of the opinion that we are caught in the pincers of two enemies. . . . We must prove that we can tear the pincers apart."[8]

Despite the obvious interest of both sides, the negotiations for the treaty proceeded tortuously. The Poles, as was customary, attempted to make the treaty multinational, including the Baltic States and Rumania. The Soviets became reluctant and suspicious. They viewed the Polish demands for a multinational treaty as an attempt to coerce Russia into recognizing Poland as the leader of the Baltic group of nations. Finally, Piłsudski instructed the Polish minister in Moscow to cease haggling and bring things to a conclusion. On January 25, 1932, a nonaggression pact was signed between the two countries. It reiterated the renunciation of war as an instrument of policy between the two countries and incorporated a mutual pledge to refrain from indirect participation in any aggressive act directed at the other by a third party. There was a separate conciliation agreement under which the two nations agreed to arbitrate any disputes.

Relations between the two nations rapidly thawed. There were cultural exchanges, a series of official visits (at which men who had played prominent roles in the Polish-Soviet War were discreetly absent), and exchanges of political prisoners. Considering the fundamental differences in political ideology between the two nations, the interplay that developed was quite astonishing. The Poles even went so far as to present to the Soviet government a collection of Lenin's personal papers that he had left in the Polish provinces in 1914. In return, Stalin sent Piłsudski the Imperial Russian secret police dossier on the Marshal.

Through all of this, Piłsudski maintained a most realistic attitude. He did not expect the atmosphere of cordiality would last forever; nor did he expect that the Soviet government would necessarily abide by the nonaggression pact itself. What was important to Piłsudski, however, was that the German government could never be certain of whether the Russians would honor the treaty. At this time Germany had supplanted Soviet Russia as Poland's most menacing enemy.

It is widely thought that Germany did not start to behave in a menacing manner toward its neighbors until after Adolf Hitler came into power in January 1933. But this is untrue, at least as far as Poland was concerned. No German government had ever resigned itself to the existence of the Polish Corridor or Danzig's status as a free city. Beginning in mid-1930, the government of Chancellor Heinrich Brüning became more outspoken about these grievances, and for a time at least it appeared that Germany might precipitate a military action to recover its lost territory. Although the Brüning government was a middle-of-the-road coalition, it found itself under great pressure from the nationalist parties of the extreme Right—most notably, of course, Hitler's National Socialists. When elections to the German Reichstag were held in September 1930, the National Socialists' representation jumped from twelve seats to 107. This phenomenal increase had messages for the Brüning government, which continued (barely) in power. Certainly one message was that the German people were increasingly and ardently nationalist and were demanding revision of the Treaty of Versailles. So, commencing in 1930, the government felt compelled to vie with the Nazis in displaying ardor for undoing the "Versailles Humiliation." Gottfried Treviranus, a member of the Brüning cabinet, made violent speeches in which he demanded the return of the Corridor and Danzig. The Polish government took these inflammatory attacks to be an official, or at the very least a semiofficial, expression of government policy. The Polish protests drew only veiled and evasive explanations from Berlin. Border incidents began to occur. The Polish Ministry of Foreign Affairs became concerned that the German propaganda assault was the prelude to direct military action by Germany against the Corridor, once world opinion had been prepared.

Logically, of course, the Poles should have looked to Paris for support. Under the terms of the Franco-Polish Political Agreement of 1921 and the secret military convention that had accompanied it, the French were obliged to come to the aid of Poland in the event of unprovoked aggression—which a German seizure of the Polish Corridor certainly would have been. But Piłsudski was unconvinced that the French would fulfill this obligation, and he had good cause for his suspicions. Since Locarno in 1925, the French had been attempting to inveigle Poland into amending their agreements to conform with the Locarno treaties under which France had agreed not to go to war with any nation unless the League of Nations had first branded that nation an aggressor. On several occasions the French had dispatched important personages to Warsaw with the objective of altering the 1921 agreements. But Piłsudski had refused to discuss the matter. As far as he was concerned, France had bound itself to Poland, and he would not permit the French to modify this alliance.

Nonetheless, Poland could not close its eyes to the fact that France was wavering. It was no longer the reliable, determined, and heavily armed power of the early 1920s. It was now apparent that French diplomacy tended to look over its shoulder to assure itself of support from Britain. It was evident that France desired to placate Germany, even to the point of allowing the revision of sections of the Treaty of Versailles. Warsaw, of course, found this profoundly disturbing. Polish foreign policy had been almost entirely constructed around the Franco-Polish alliance. The Poles had consulted Paris on most matters of importance and had generally been responsive to French advice. Now it appeared that this procedure was no longer useful to Poland. Piłsudski became disillusioned with France. He was coming to the conclusion that henceforth Poland must follow a much more independent policy. While still preserving the Franco-Polish alliance and, above all maintaining the *appearance* of the alliance, Poland would carve out a much more independent and aggressive foreign policy of its own. Much more than in the past, Poland would behave as a great power in its own right. Poland would henceforth demand to be consulted as an equal by the important nations of Europe—and if it was not consulted, then it would adopt a haughty and intransigent attitude. To emphasize its importance, Poland would throw its weight around or act in a touchy and abrasive manner whenever it chose. Poland would not hesitate to test the waters or to probe for reaction by creating an incident. Poland would keep its friends and potential enemies a little off balance by behaving in an unpredictable manner. It would not seek to be liked—only respected or feared. And, obviously, to implement this rather brutal "new course" in Polish diplomacy there had to be a new face at the Foreign Ministry. The affable but colorless August Zaleski, who had been Poland's minister of foreign affairs since 1926, was clearly not an appropriate personality; so, on November 2, 1932, Zaleski was succeeded by a much tougher leader, Colonel Józef Beck.

At the time of his appointment Beck was only thirty-eight, but he had the right credentials for advancement in the Polish government. In 1914 he had enlisted in the First Brigade of the Polish Legion. When the First Brigade was interned by the Germans, Beck escaped and went underground with the P.O.W. in the Ukraine. After the achievement of independence Beck served first as an artillery battery commander in the Army and then was posted to the General Staff. From that point on, Beck made his career in a series of staff and quasi-diplomatic positions. In 1922–23 he was military attaché in Paris. Recalled from France, he was sent to the Polish War College, from which he graduated with distinction. By this time he was a lieutenant colonel. Always closely identified with Piłsudski, Beck played an important part in the May 1926 coup. He later served in the War Ministry as the Marshal's personal *chef de cabinet*. In 1930, when Piłsudski briefly assumed the office of Prime Minister, he brought Beck into the cabinet with him as his deputy prime minister.

So, it surprised no one in the Polish government that in December 1930 Beck was sent to the ministry of foreign affairs as deputy minister. Years before, Piłsudski had told officials in the ministry of war that the Army should not "count on Beck. You will never have him. Beck will not make his career in the Army. Beck will go to Foreign Affairs to be charged with responsibilities of high importance."[9]

Beck was a tall, good-looking man who dressed in elegant fashion and was thought to be both very intelligent and intensely ambitious. He was capable of being arrogant and unpleasant, and he struck some foreign observers as being devious or deliberately obscure. The French ambassador even claimed that "whenever Beck told the truth, one noticed it at once."[10] However, French accounts of Józef Beck are always critical. For reasons that will presently become apparent, the French disliked Beck intensely and constantly strove to blacken his reputation. They floated lies about Beck—such as stories that Madame Beck had unusual sexual appetites or that Beck had been recalled after only brief service as military attaché in Paris at the request of the French government because he (a) had stolen secret French documents or (b) had offended the French Army by adopting a harsh and abrasive manner toward its officers or (c) was involved in some sort of sexual scandal. Actually, the circumstances of his recall from Paris are very simple and straightforward. In late 1923 Roman Dmowski became foreign minister in the second Witos government. At this time Piłsudski was out of power and in retirement in Sulejówek. The then-major Józef Beck, Polish attaché in Paris, was known to be extremely close to Piłsudski. The post of military attaché, being quasi-diplomatic, was at the disposal of the foreign minister. Dmowski preferred not to employ a disciple of his old enemy Piłsudski, and thus Beck was recalled.

But the constant French intrigue against Beck notwithstanding, it is a fact that he was disliked and sometimes distrusted by many of the foreign diplomats who were in contact with him. Unlike August Zaleski, the genial and popular foreign minister whom he replaced, Beck seemed to be a young man who had risen too fast and too easily with his only known qualification being his Piłsudski connection. Beck considered himself intellectually superior to many of his fellow cabinet members, some of whom were offended by his manner toward them. His personality earned him the antipathy, almost at first meeting, of a surprising number of persons who subsequently found it impossible to have a kind word for the Polish Foreign Minister. Count Galeazzo Ciano, in his diaries, quotes the Italian Princess of Piedmont as remarking that Beck (frequently described as handsome) had a face that was "equivocal, the sort of face you might well see in a French newspaper as that of the ravisher of little girls."[11] A man who exudes this sort of unfortunate aura labors under a decided and positive handicap. But whatever foreign diplomats might think of Beck personally, it was generally understood that his appointment was a signal that the Marshal had decided upon a new direction for Polish diplomacy.

Actually, the risky *Wicher* affair, which Beck, who was then deputy minister for foreign affairs, planned and carried out was the first signal of Piłsudski's "new course" in Polish policy. The *Wicher* was a Polish destroyer usually based at Gdynia. Throughout 1931 and 1932 Poland's relations with Danzig had worsened markedly. The Depression had caused Poland to rescind certain favorable customs agreements that had been made with the Free City. In addition, the new Polish port facilities at adjacent Gydnia had drained away an increasing amount of Danzig's trade with the Polish interior. The Free City, steadily being deprived of its *raison d'être*, was experiencing something very close to an economic catastrophe. More than 20 percent of the labor force was unemployed. The only thing that kept the city from plunging into insolvency was a series of emergency loans from Germany, itself suffering severely from the Depression.

The Danzig Senate appealed to the League of Nations for help. The senators claimed that, although Poland was obliged to make the fullest use of the Danzig harbor facilities, in fact, the Polish government was diverting trade to Gdynia. This constituted a *de facto* boycott, and when the matter was referred to various League authorities for a ruling, most of them came up with the decision that Poland was indeed required to use the Danzig harbor to its fullest extent. While Poland was appealing these rulings, the Free City's Senate refused to renew certain agreements with the Polish government that were expiring. One of these was a delicate arrangement under which Polish naval vessels were allowed to visit Danzig without requesting permission from the Free City, as was required for the warships of other nations.

In June 1932, it was announced that three British destroyers would shortly visit Danzig on the invitation of the city's Senate. The Poles suggested to London that the visit was inopportune. The suggestion was ignored. Piłsudski thereupon ordered the Polish destroyer *Wicher* to enter the Danzig harbor on the day the British squadron arrived. The *Wicher* was not to request permission from the Free City to enter the port, and its captain was to exchange courtesy calls only with the Royal Navy vessels; further the captain of the *Wicher* was secretly instructed that in the event the Polish flag was in any way insulted by Danzigers while he was in the harbor, he was immediately to open fire upon the closest public building.

As it turned out the visit of the *Wicher* went off without incident—except for the furor it caused in Danzig and, of course, in Germany. The Free State protested to the League of Nations that its sovereignty had been violated by the *Wicher*'s uninvited intrusion into the port, and relations between Danzig and Poland worsened. Obviously, this had been a reckless adventure on Poland's part. Zaleski, who was at that time still foreign minister, was horrified. But Piłsudski had made his point. He had challenged Danzig and Germany. He had shown that Poland would not tolerate even a minor transgression of what it regarded as its rights, and it was prepared to take extreme measures to protect these rights. Poland was a power to be feared.

This was the warning that had been given and the atmosphere that existed when Beck became foreign minister.

During the last half of 1932 three successive German cabinets collapsed as they found it impossible to put together a coalition that could dominate Hitler's Nazis, now the nation's strongest party. Finally, it was realized that Hitler could not be denied and that no German government could be established without Nazi support. On January 30, 1933, President Hindenburg sent for Hitler and appointed him chancellor. Hitler promptly announced that a new Reichstag would be elected on March 5. It was anticipated that such an election, coming close upon Hitler's elevation to the chancellorship, could only result in a dramatic increase in Nazi strength in the Reichstag.

On February 27, 1933, the Reichstag Fire occurred. The next day Hitler persuaded President Hindenburg to sign a special decree "For the Protection of the People and the State," which suspended most individual liberties guaranteed by the constitution.

On March 5 the elections returned enough Nazi deputies to the Reichstag so that, in combination with deputies of the National Party, they were able to pass the Enabling Act on March 23, 1933. Under this law practically all normal legislative power was taken from the parliament and given to the cabinet and its chancellor for a period of five years. In only two months, Hitler had thus succeeded in having himself awarded virtually complete dictatorial powers— and in an entirely legal manner.

The foreign ministers of other European nations were stunned by the speed and success of Hitler's actions. No one knew what Hitler might do with the great power he now wielded—the situation was particularly confusing because Hitler at this time was making a calculated display of moderation, which was considerably at variance from his previous declarations.

Of course, no nation was more concerned with the developments in Germany than Poland. Relations between the two nations had almost reached a crisis point even before Hitler's accession to power, Judging from Hitler's previous statements, it was assumed that he would be violently nationalistic and aggressive. Many persons expected that he would rearm Germany and, at gunpoint, demand the revision of the Treaty of Versailles and the return of the Polish Corridor.

Piłsudski, however, believed that Poland was not in any immediate danger. Hitler could not do everything at once. Before he embarked upon any anti-Polish adventures, Hitler would first have to consolidate his internal position, complete his "revolution," and deal with a host of domestic problems. Even given the extraordinary energy and ruthlessness that Hitler had displayed to date, all this would take some time. Then, too, Piłsudski believed, there was a good chance that Hitler might not regard Poland as an authentic enemy. The Marshal set great value on the fact that Hitler was not a Prussian and thus would be free of the virulent anti-Polish sentiment traditional in Prussia. Also, comment had reached Warsaw through diplomatic circles that Hitler admired and respected Piłsudski, whom he thought to be a man of his own type.

Piłsudski decided that the best course for Poland would be to determine quickly if his assessment of Hitler was correct. Poland must probe for Hitler's reaction while simultaneously giving him a sharp warning. The place selected for this test was again, as in the *Wicher* incident, Danzig. The date selected was March 6, 1933—the day after the Reichstag elections. The Poles intended to force a direct confrontation with the Danzig Harbor Police Force. This agency had been established in 1925 as a security service solely for the waterfront area. Its officers reported to the Danzig Harbor Board which was a mixed-nationality body. The Free City itself was patrolled by city police who were German and were responsible to the city's Senate. In 1927 the special agreement between Poland and the Free City that had established the Harbor Police Force expired. But the arrangement continued as before—until February 1933, when the Danzig Senate announced that the Harbor Police would henceforth be under the command of the city police. This announcement came almost simultaneously with Hitler's accession to power and with a number of anti-Polish provocations by a large Nazi SA group which had been assembled within Danzig. Piłsudski seized upon the affair of the Harbor Police to make what Beck later described as "a new energetic move"—a "psychological test [of Hitler] which would have a preventive character."[12]

Extending out from Danzig is a sandy hook of land known as the Westerplatte, which is the northern promontory of the harbor. By virtue of a special agreement made in 1921 with the Danzig Senate, Poland had been permitted to store naval ammunition on the Westerplatte. The dump was guarded by eighty-two Polish soldiers, a number that had been agreed upon as a maximum and was not to be increased except by express permission of the League of Nations High Commissioner for Danzig.

At dawn on March 6, 1933, the Polish naval transport *Wilja* appeared off the Westerplatte and disembarked 120 Polish troops to reinforce the garrison. This was done without consultation with the League of Nations High Commissioner for Danzig. The Polish Foreign Ministry gave it out that the additional soldiers were required by Danzig's change in the status of the Harbor Police and the threat of attack by German nationalist elements. So, Poland's act instantly became an international incident of surprising magnitude. The violence of public reaction in Germany was equaled only by the indignation in Geneva, where the League of Nations regarded Poland's behavior as an insult to its authority—which it certainly was. Great Britain led the cry for instant action at Geneva. The Danzig question was quickly considered by the League's Council, which demanded withdrawal of the excess troops. As a *quid pro quo*, the Danzig Senate agreed to restore the old Harbor Police system. Not a single European nation rose to Poland's defense. With this, Poland withdrew its troops, and the incident was at an end.

The questions who had prevailed in the Westerplatte affair and what it had established were difficult to answer. The storm of unfavorable reaction it had drawn from Poland's nominal friends and allies surely surpassed any Polish expectations, and diplomatically isolated, the Poles had been compelled to withdraw their troops. On the other hand, Piłsudski and Beck believed that they had accomplished what they had set out to do. They had pulled off a display of military defiance to which Germany had not responded in kind. They had shown that Poland was unpredictable, aggressive and alert. They had thrown down the glove, and Hitler had not picked it up. The feeling in Warsaw was that Poland had given the Germans a lesson. The Poles were well pleased with themselves.

But almost simultaneously with the Westerplatte incident came another international development that Poland did not initiate and that was an authentically frightening experience for it. In early 1932 an International Disarmament Conference had begun meeting in Geneva. Although the conference was to last until 1934, it was evident from the start that it would not be successful. The French refused to discuss their disarming until a plan had developed for guaranteeing their security against potential aggressors—which, of course, meant Germany. Germany, on the other hand, noted that it was the only nation that was at that moment actually disarmed. It refused to enter into serious discussions until the provisions of the Treaty of Versailles which had disarmed Germany were revised. Another major stumbling block was posed by the horde of smaller nations that were participating. Each demanded that consideration be given to its own individual problems. Each had a complicated draft of a disarmament scheme of its own. These plans had a common element—the classes of weapons to be banned were those that the proposing nation did not itself possess.

Mussolini, among others, grew impatient with the lack of progress at the Disarmament Conference. An ardent advocate of the principle of "great-power diplomacy" (now that Italy was generally agreed to be a "great power"), the Duce believed that there were far too many small nations at the Disarmament Conference, as well as in the League of Nations. If European peace was the objective, this goal could be reached much more simply if the four major European powers (Britain, France, Germany, and Italy) met and decided what must be done. The other European nations would then have to acquiesce.

The Duce's views met with general favor in the capitals of the four powers involved. So with the speed that characterized Mussolini's diplomacy, the Italian Foreign Office drafted a "Four Power Pact" dated March 18, 1933. Inasmuch as Great Britain's Prime Minister Ramsay MacDonald and Foreign Secretary Sir John Simon were in Rome at the time, it was generally assumed by the diplomatic community that they had been consulted by the Italians and that the draft pact met with British approval. It appeared quite certain that Britain, France, and Germany would soon sign it.

The release of the Italian draft came as a bombshell to Poland. It was obvious that one purpose of the pact was to pave the way to appeasing Germany by enabling important revisions of the Treaty of Versailles to be made. The second article of the Italian draft stated bluntly, "The Four Powers confirm the principle of the revision of treaties . . . in cases in which there is a possibility that they will lead to conflict among the States."

It was apparent to the Poles that the most convenient and painless way to assuage Germany would be to give it something that directly affected none of the other three Powers—specifically, the Polish Corridor. It took the Poles next to no time to calculate what the attitude of each of the Four Powers would be toward such a proposition. Mussolini, who considered himself the founder of Fascism, would be anxious to indulge the Hitler government. The British, whose consistently critical attitude toward Poland had most recently been evident in their actions at the League in the Westerplatte matter, would probably be pleased to vote away the Corridor. Everyone recalled Austen Chamberlain's famous remark in 1925, when, as British foreign secretary, he said that "for the Polish Corridor no British government will or ever can risk the bones of a British grenadier." It went without saying that the Germans would be enthusiastic. This left only the French to protect Polish interests—and the Poles had little confidence in them. They would knuckle under and later excuse themselves on the grounds that they had been outvoted.

Panic seized the Polish Foreign Ministry when the Italian draft of the pact became known. The apprehension was so acute that Beck went so far as to make plans for a visit to Prague for consultations with the Czechs—previously an unthinkable action. But then it appeared that the Czechs might be wavering in their opposition to the Pact. Coincidentally, Piłsudski was confined to bed with a high fever, so Beck's visit was canceled with the excuse that no major move could be made when the Marshal was not available for consultation.

There is still a question as to whether there could have been a meaningful rapprochement between Poland and Czechoslovakia at this time. Had there been one, it might subsequently have had the greatest importance. Beck consistently stated that the Czechs never made any offers of alliance. Czech President Éduard Beneš claims in his memoirs to have offered Beck "a political agreement which was to pave the way for a military treaty"[13] as early as 1932. Beneš later—in 1933—told the British that Beck had offered him an alliance but he had refused to accept it because he did not want "to give Germany clear cause for fearing encirclement."[14] But a few days later Beneš told the French ambassador to Poland that he had offered Beck a "pact of eternal friendship,"[15] which Beck had refused.

The answer to this whole business is clearly that Beck and Piłsudski viewed Czechoslovakia as a doomed nation, while the Czechs believed that Poland was certain to be dragged into a war with Germany over the Polish Corridor. Neither nation wanted to undertake a commitment to the other.

In opposing the Four Power Pact, the Poles worked to raise the hue and cry against it in every capital in Eastern Europe. The Little Entente nations were quickly made to see that revision of the Treaty of Versailles would certainly not stop with the Polish Corridor. Their protests, particularly those of the outraged Czechs, carried substantial weight in Paris. The Poles did all they could to point out the inequity of a directorate of four nations banding together to dictate the affairs of many. Count Jerzy Potocki, newly appointed Polish ambassador to Italy, resigned his post before even going to Rome. Poland threatened to leave the League of Nations if the Four Power Pact was signed in the present draft. The culmination of these Polish "demonstrations," as Beck called them,[16] was a dramatic direct approach to Hitler, which was as stunning as it was effective.

On April 4, 1933, a personal and most secret instruction went out from Beck to the Polish minister in Berlin, Dr. Alfred Wysocki. Apart from Beck himself, even the most senior officials of the Polish Ministry of Foreign Affairs knew nothing of this message. In it,

Wysocki was instructed to seek to arrange an interview between Polish Under Secretary of Foreign Affairs Count Jan Szembek and Adolf Hitler. If possible, Wysocki was to make the appointment directly with the German Chancellor's office, bypassing the German Foreign Office, which was known to be rabidly anti-Polish. Wysocki was informed that Count Szembek was prepared to hold with Hitler "and only with him in person, a conversation of utmost importance."[17] In this meeting Szembek would demand that Hitler publicly announce that Germany would not violate Polish rights in Danzig. Should Hitler refuse, Poland was prepared to take the most extreme measures. Although Wysocki was not informed of this, Piłsudski made detailed plans for the reorganization of the Polish government into a wartime administration. It seems certain that Poland was prepared either to go to war with Germany or, at the very least, to mobilize its army as the ultimate threat.

On April 6, after discreet inquiries, Wysocki replied that he found it impossible to request an audience for Szembek through any channel other than the German Foreign Office. Additionally, he expressed doubt that Hitler would agree to a private interview with a Polish official, such was the degree of anti-Polish feeling in Germany.

Piłsudski and Beck believed otherwise—and they were proved correct. They gave Wysocki new instructions. Instead of Szembek going to Berlin, Wysocki was to seek the interview with Hitler himself. Assuming that it would be granted, Beck instructed Wysocki "to limit your conversation to a single topic, namely, Danzig"[18] Wysocki was to explain that the Polish populace was alarmed by German statements that had been interpreted as threats of German intervention in Danzig. Wysocki, speaking in a most definite tone, was to request (in fact, virtually demand) that Hitler allay those Polish fears by issuing a press communiqué stating that "the Chancellor is against any action directed against Polish rights and legal interests in the Free City of Danzig."[19]

This was a very great deal to ask of any German chancellor—and particularly of Adolf Hitler. But to his astonishment, Wysocki found that he was given a forty-minute audience with Hitler on May 2. Moreover, at the conclusion of this interview, Hitler expressed his willingness to issue the statement that the Poles requested. There were a few hours of haggling, while the astounded German Foreign Office attempted to substitute a watered-down version, but by the next day both Berlin and Warsaw issued communiqués declaring that in their relations with each other they intended to act "strictly within the limits of existing treaties."[20]

These statements, which gave the appearance of a détente between the two nations, created intense surprise throughout Europe. The Poles had surely pulled off something of a coup. The stunned foreign offices of London, Paris and Rome could not at first take the event at face value. They feared that there had been some sort of secret deal between Hitler and Piłsudski—possibly an agreement by the Poles to tolerate a German *Anschluss* with Austria.

It is, in fact, not easy to determine exactly why Hitler agreed to the Polish request. Certainly the communiqué made domestic difficulties for him with German nationalists and caused the greatest dismay in Danzig. But Hitler viewed these as only short-term problems. Hitler was much more sophisticated than his alarmed supporters. At this point he was preparing for Germany's rearmament. The thing that he feared above all was a determined alliance—particularly of France and Poland—whose interference might prevent any expansion of the German armed forces. In 1933, Poland alone had an active army of more than a quarter million men, as compared to the German Reichswehr of only 100,000. Rumors of a "preventive war" by Poland and France abounded. Germany's international image under Hitler was that of a bellicose and dangerous nation. So, undoubtedly it served Hitler's purposes to give peaceful assurances to Poland while at the same time driving a slender wedge into the Polish-French alliance.

But the subtlety of Hitler's strategy was not generally understood at this time. The German communiqué was widely viewed as a triumph of Polish diplomacy. Poland's importance was greatly enhanced in major European capitals. It was noted that the German press had adopted a much more friendly tone toward Poland. The Polish minister to Germany, Józef Lipski, who had succeeded Alfred Wysocki in October 1933, reported numerous displays of official amiability—a marked contrast to previous years, when Polish diplomats had been treated as pariahs. The Poles took advantage of this new-found warmth to conclude a bundle of minor treaties and conventions of a consular character. Even in Danzig, where the Nazi Party now dominated the city's Senate, there was a marked alteration in the official attitude toward Poland. Hitler had personally instructed the Nazi officials in the Free City that in the future their struggle against Poland could proceed only "silently and secretly."[21]

The Sławek government of 1930–31. Sławek is seated third from left; President Mościcki at center; Piłsudski, occupying his customary post as minister of war, is seated third from right.

The Kozłowski government of 1933–34. Piłsudski, ill and aging, is second from right. Beck sits next to him on extreme right.

August Zaleski, Polish foreign minister, 1926–32.

General Felicjan Sławoj-Składkowski, an army doctor and old Piłsudski associate from the pre-World War PPS, Polish prime minister 1936–39.

Józef Beck, Polish foreign minister, 1932–39.

The Polish destroyer *Wicher* which figured in the Danzig incident of
June 1932.

Piłsudski in a frequently observed relaxation, playing patience in a
drawing room of the Belvedere.

Walery Sławek, perhaps Piłsudski's closest associate. Founder and leader of the BBWR; Polish prime minister, 1930, 1930–31, 1935. His face was badly scarred when, while a member of the pre-World War PPS, a bomb he was assembling blew up. Sławek committed suicide in April 1939, using the pistol he carried in the Bezdany raid of 1908 which Piłsudski led.

The Polish Sejm, the lower house of the parliament, in session, March 1938.

French foreign minister
Louis Barthou in Warsaw
in 1934 to attempt to
interest the Poles in his
Eastern Pact scheme. Left
to right are French ambassador to Poland Jules
Laroche, Piłsudski, Bar-
thou, Beck and Polish
deputy foreign minister
Szembek. (NATIONAL
ARCHIVES)

Józef Lipski, Polish
ambassador to Germany,
1933–39.
(NATIONAL ARCHIVES)

German propaganda minister Joseph Goebbels' visit to Poland of June 1934. Left to right are German ambassador to Poland Hans von Moltke, Piłsudski, Goebbels, and Beck. (NATIONAL ARCHIVES)

Colonel Adam Koc, head of the government OZON movement, 1937–38. (NATIONAL ARCHIVES)

RIGHT: The body of Marshal Piłsudski lying in state, May 13–14, 1935. (NATIONAL ARCHIVES)

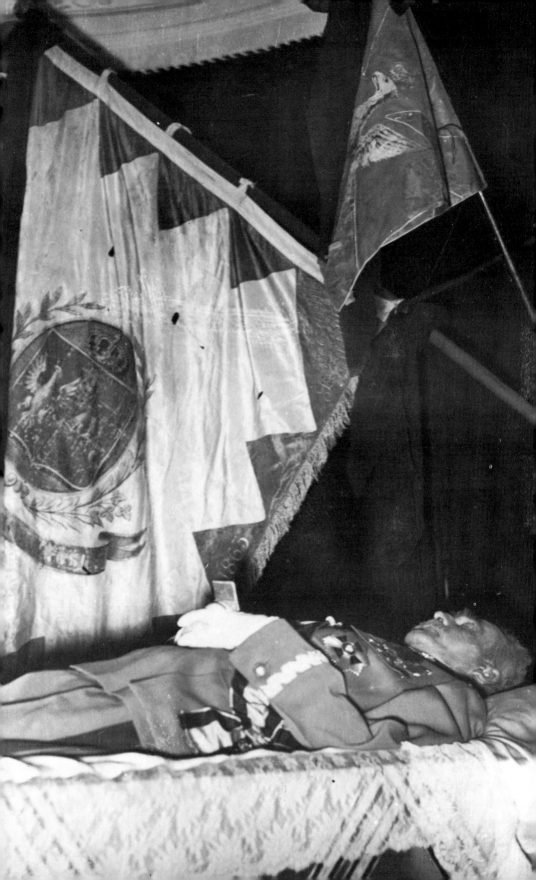

Piłsudski's death mask.

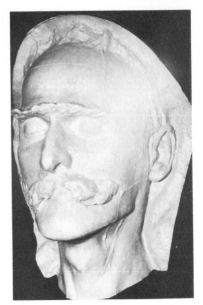

The casket containing Piłsudski's body, borne on an artillery piece, was placed on a mound at the Mokotov parade ground, May 17, 1935.

Units from every regiment of the Polish Army parade past Piłsudski's casket in a final salute. The march past was led by the army's generals, with Rydz-Śmigły at their head; May 17, 1935.

Piłsudski's casket was placed aboard a flatbed railroad car and drawn slowly to Krakow. Many thousands of persons stood along the rail tracks to watch the Marshal's body pass during the night of May 17–18, 1935.

The embalmed body of Piłsudski in a windowed casket was placed in the crypt of Wawel Castle, Krakow. Madame Piłsudska is shown seated. May 18, 1935.

Rydz-Śmigły in mid-1936 at which time he was Inspector-General of the Army but still held the two-star rank of General of Division. By November 1936 he had been made first a full general and then Marshal of the Army. (NATIONAL ARCHIVES)

Marshal Rydz-Śmigły at a review in 1938. His saber is an eighteenth century Polish weapon.

A flight of Polish P.Z.L.11 fighter planes. When introduced in 1931
this aircraft was one of the world's most advanced. But by 1939, when
it was still the standard Polish fighter, the P.Z.L.11 was hopelessly
outmoded and could not match the modern German aircraft.

Polish infantry, although lightly armed by German standards of 1939, were considered extremely tough and brave.

For centuries the Polish cavalryman had been classed as among the world's best. The Polish Army of 1939 had large quantities of cavalry which proved to be of little value in modern war.

Polish prisoners of war are marched off to German stockades. More than 100,000 Polish soldiers escaped through Rumania to fight again in France. (U.S. ARMY)

The German flag is raised over the last Polish bastion, the fortifications of the Hel Peninsula, which fell on October 2, 1939, after a protracted resistance that the Germans found astonishing. (UPI)

Beck escorts Italian foreign
minister Ciano on an inspection
of a Polish guard of honor
during a 1939 visit by Ciano.

Anthony J. Drexel Biddle, U.S.
ambassador to Poland, 1938–39.

Josef Stalin and Joachim von Ribbentrop shake hands after signing the
Soviet-German Non-Aggression Pact, August 23, 1939. (UPI)

Adolf Hitler reviews his victorious armies at a massive parade in
Warsaw on October 5, 1939. (U.S. ARMY)

As a result, the Danzig Senate quickly concluded a number of agreements with Poland that resolved many outstanding grievances.

All of this was carefully observed, especially by the French. They had been surprised by the decisiveness and independence that Poland had displayed in this affair. Such an important approach by Warsaw to Berlin, without having previously consulted Paris, would have been unthinkable only a year before. It emphasized to the French how much they had allowed their relations with the Poles to deteriorate. They hastened to make amends. At French behest, the revisionism section of the Italian draft of the Four Power Pact, which was still in negotiation, was dropped. The Italian version was discarded and replaced with one that did not contain the offending sentences regarding treaty revision. The Poles were somewhat mollified, but the whole Four Power Pact affair had ominous overtones for them. Increasingly, it seemed that their old alliances were wobbly and that their decision to pursue an aggressive foreign policy of great independence had been the correct one. They were enormously flattered by the new and respectful German attitude. Perhaps Poland's allies failed to regard it as a "great power," but it seemed that Germany did. This was all most gratifying.

The affair of Piłsudski's proposal for a preventive war against Germany has always had an air of mystery about it. Although the event cannot be documented, there are good reasons to believe that it actually occurred, and this is accepted by a great many authorities having contemporary knowledge.[22] Certainly, it was quite in character with the Polish diplomatic style of the time, and if the whole scheme was never put into writing, there were obvious good reasons for this.

According to various accounts, at some time in March 1933, and again a few months later, Piłsudski dispatched certain private persons to France to make the "unofficial" suggestion that the time to stop Hitler was now, and that this could be done very easily by a preventive war. The plan seems to have been that the French would occupy the Rhineland, while the Poles seized Danzig and East Prussia. The bearers of these overtures, who were at liberty to reveal that their messages came directly from the Marshal, met with old friends with excellent connections in the French government. Nothing was done through conventional diplomatic channels. In fact, even the Polish ambassador in Paris knew nothing of these soundings.

When no response was made by the French, Piłsudski concluded that his message had not been received or not been understood. It was decided to take a new approach and determine whether France would come to the support of Poland if Poland initiated a preventive war attack upon Germany. Piłsudski resolved this time to insure that this matter would be brought to the attention of the highest French authorities. And so, in October 1933 the Marshal summoned Ludwik Morstin, an old associate and Polish Army Reserve officer. In 1920, Morstin had been the Polish liaison officer to the French General Staff. In the course of this assignment, he had become very friendly with General Weygand, who was now chief of the French General Staff. On the Marshal's instructions, Morstin immediately left for France. Such was his friendship with Weygand that Morstin stayed at Weygand's home as the general's guest. Morstin had been ordered to ask two questions in the name of the Marshal: First, "If Poland were attacked by Germany at any point of her frontier, would France react by a general mobilization of all her armed forces?" Second, "Would France, in this event, poise all of her available forces on the German frontier?"[23] It was understood by Weygand that the hypothetical German attack might be provoked in some manner by the Poles in order to initiate a preventive war. According to Morstin, the answers he received, after Weygand had referred the matter to his government, were negative in each case. The best the French would do was to promise to aid Poland by supplying ammunition, arms and military staff, and by arousing world opinion in Polish favor.

Piłsudski probably made his veiled proposal of a preventive war simply to test French opinion. Probably, too, he knew what the French answer would be, but simply wanted to force them to give him their answer so that he could gain latitude for future actions. The French had now demonstrated their timidity and indecision. They could not subsequently reproach Poland for any objectionable unilateral moves it might make.

The French had been put in a very difficult position by Piłsudski's overtures and had probably given the only reply that it was possible for them to make. If they had responded affirmatively, then they would have given Piłsudski carte blanche to create a border incident with Germany and claim that Poland had been invaded. The current Polish diplomatic style surely gave little assurance that Warsaw would exhibit much restraint. The French and Polish armies, when mobilized, would have totaled several million men compared to the 1933 German Army's 100,000 men. Obviously, Germany could easily be invaded, but for the French government there were other considerations—would the French people support such an adventure, would world opinion tolerate such an affair, and what would they do with Germany after they had crushed the German Army? The French could not possibly go along with Piłsudski, and he must surely have suspected that they would not. He had asked his questions principally to free himself for his next major diplomatic move.

On October 14, 1933, Germany abruptly withdrew from both the League of Nations and the Geneva Disarmament Conference. Hitler made no secret of the fact that these withdrawals cleared the way for German rearmament. These diplomatic moves, of course, caused great shock and concern throughout Europe. The Poles were probably less surprised by Germany's actions than were most other European nations. Only a few weeks before the German withdrawals, Beck had traveled to Geneva for the League's General Assembly session. While there he received an unexpected luncheon invitation from Joseph Goebbels. The two men talked for some time. Goebbels did not conceal his distrust of the League of Nations. In the course of his conversation he threw open a window that looked down upon the new building being constructed for the League. "In this modern Tower of Babel we shall find no solution,"[24] he declared. Goebbels went on to state that Hitler believed that there was more to be gained by direct negotiation between two nations than any general understanding reached through the League. Beck replied that Poland's experiences in dealing through the League had also been disappointing. He also expressed interest in direct understandings. On this note, the luncheon ended. Germany having made the exploratory move, it was up to the Poles to follow it up.

On November 5, 1933, Polish Minister Lipski was summoned from Berlin to Warsaw to consult with Piłsudski. They met, with Beck, in a small drawing room in the Belvedere Palace. Piłsudski asked for Lipski's appraisal of Hitlerite Germany. Lipski replied that Hitler was firmly in control although he had many domestic problems to resolve. He added that he had heard that Germany was considering offering Poland a nonaggression treaty. Piłsudski did not believe this—the rumor was only "a Czech intrigue,"[25] an attempt to discredit Poland in the eyes of the French. The Marshal, however, remarked to Beck, "We will make a test."[26] Piłsudski instructed Lipski to ask for an interview with Hitler. When this audience had been granted, Lipski was to present Piłsudski's personal compliments and advise Hitler that Poland was concerned about Germany's withdrawal from the League of Nations. Germany's previous adherence to the League had provided Poland with a certain degree of security—Piłsudski described it as a sort of reinsurance against a German move against Poland. Lipski was to ask Hitler "whether he is willing to compensate for this loss of a security factor in Polish-German relations."[27]

What Piłsudski expected Hitler to offer for this is not certain. Possibly Lipski's interview was to be only a fishing expedition. But it was certain that a direct treaty of nonaggression between Germany and Poland, should Hitler propose it, would receive serious consideration in Warsaw.

On November 15 Lipski was given his audience with the German Chancellor. Lipski explained his government's position. Hitler replied in generalities, except to observe that in the relationship between Germany and Poland "the very idea of a possibility of war should be excluded."[28] He paid tribute to Piłsudski as "a great personality"[29] and left the impression that he would do something quickly to accommodate Polish desires. A German communiqué was issued advising of Lipski's visit with Hitler and stating that the two governments had decided to "deal with the questions affecting both countries by way of direct negotiation, and further to renounce all application of force in their mutual relations."[30] For nearly two weeks the Poles heard nothing more from the Germans.

On November 27, Hans von Moltke, the German minister to Poland, asked for and received an immediate interview with Piłsudski. He presented to the Marshal a proposed draft of a document eventually to be known as the Declaration of Nonaggression and Understanding between Germany and Poland. Piłsudski accepted the draft for study and shortly afterward left for Wilno for an extended vacation. The Polish Foreign Office advised the Germans that nothing further could be done until the Marshal's return to Warsaw. This delaying tactic would give the Poles time to consider all the implications of signing such a declaration with Germany.

In the interim, however, many revisions of the draft were requested by the Poles. They insisted that the document take cognizance of Poland's existing treaties with Rumania and France, and they asked for various legal and technical changes. The Germans were accommodating. All the requested changes were quickly made. It was an unusual document. It was not drafted in a conventional diplomatic form. It was not subdivided into "articles" and was not called a pact or a treaty—although it was, in fact, a treaty of sorts, since it required ratification by the parliament of each nation.

The gist of the declaration was that all disputes between the two nations would be resolved by arbitration and "in no circumstances . . . will [Germany and Poland] proceed to the application of force for the purpose of reaching a decision in such disputes."[31] On January 26, 1934, the declaration was signed in Berlin by Lipski and German Foreign Minister Konstantin von Neurath, and it was formally ratified by the two nations' parliaments the following month. It would remain in effect for ten years.

This German-Polish Declaration was, indeed, a great surprise when it was announced. The French had suspected that something was afoot, but in response to their inquiries the Poles had lied and said that they were negotiating only economic agreements with Berlin. A torrent of ambassadors and ministers descended upon the Polish Foreign Office to request explanations and demand clarifications.

The Russians were particularly upset and suspicious. They undoubtedly believed that there were secret codicils to the declaration in which the two parties had agreed to combine against Russia. To assuage the Soviets, Colonel Beck went to Moscow in February 1934, during the period between the signing and the ratification of the German-Polish declaration. His visit was a success. It was the first official visit of a Western foreign minister to Moscow since the Revolution, and the Soviets were anxious to have it come off well. The pomp and entertainments rivaled those of Tsarist days. Beck offered to extend the expiration date of the Soviet-Polish Treaty of Nonaggression to ten years—to coincide with the expiration date of the Polish-German agreement. The Soviet government was apparently mollified and seemed convinced that the German-Polish declaration was not directed at them.

It was more difficult for the Poles to placate the French. The French government was indignant and resentful over the German-Polish Declaration. The fact that they had in no way been consulted by Warsaw simply heightened their suspicions of Beck, whom the Quai d'Orsay blamed for the whole event and now distrusted deeply. It was necessary for Piłsudski himself to assure French Ambassador

Jules Laroche that the German-Polish Declaration would have no effect upon Poland's existing alliance with France. The French were dubious, but their only option was to develop a more dynamic policy of their own. This was not long in coming.

In February 1934, Jean Louis Barthou became the French foreign minister in the government of Gaston Doumergue. An energetic and not unintelligent man, Barthou conceived the idea of an Eastern Pact of Mutual Guarantee, which was intended to be a sort of eastern version of the Locarno treaties. The French object was to avoid being dragged into war with Germany as the end result of an East European dispute. The plan was very complicated, and was subjected to a number of alterations. In brief, the first step projected was to be a collective nonagression and mutual assistance pact between Soviet Russia, Latvia, Lithuania, Estonia, Poland, Czechoslovakia and Germany. After this had been signed, the Soviet Union was to guarantee the pact, pretty much on the same basis as that on which Britain and Italy had guaranteed the Locarno Pact. It would intervene to support any nation that the League of Nations labeled an aggressor.

On April 22, 1934, Barthou visited Warsaw to explain his plan to the Poles. This was the first visit of a French foreign minister to Warsaw. All previous ministerial visits had been unilateral—the Polish foreign minister had been obliged to go to Paris. And on occasion the Poles had been treated rather shabbily there. When Beck visited Paris in 1933, he had not been greeted at the railroad station by his French opposite number. Now, in April 1934, Beck repaid the discourtesy by dispatching his deputy foreign minister to greet Barthou at the station. But ignoring this calculated snub, Barthou was determinedly friendly. It was apparent that he desired to clear up past misunderstandings as well as to perform some salesmanship on behalf of his Eastern Pact plan. In the new style of Polish diplomacy, Piłsudski and Beck were very direct with him. A meeting between Beck, Barthou, the French ambassador, and the Marshal did not go well. Barthou tried to convince the Poles that France was determined to resist Hitler.

"I have had enough of these concessions," he declared, "The Germans must feel that we will not yield one step more."

Piłsudski replied, "You will yield, gentlemen, you will yield. You would not be what you are if you did not."

Offended, Barthou responded, "Marshal, how can you suspect us of such a thing?"

"Maybe you yourself will not wish to yield," said Piłsudski, "but then either you would withdraw from the Cabinet or you would be outvoted."[32]

The conversation turned to the old Franco-Polish military agreement. Piłsudski stated that the French had never made any real effort to assist the Polish Army with the improvement of its armament. This was an old complaint of the Marshal's. Barthou offered to help. He would send the French military attaché in Rumania to discuss requirements with the Poles. Piłsudski replied that sending a second-rank French officer to Warsaw showed that the French were not very serious about helping the Poles or that Barthou was afraid of international repercussions.

However, the talks concluded on a friendly enough note, and Barthou went on to other East European capitals to promote his plan. In the end, the French scheme fell apart. The Poles were not interested in it. Under the French plan they might well find the Red Army marching across Poland to defend one of the signatory nations—a wholly unacceptable prospect. Nor did Poland have any interest in guaranteeing the territory of Czechoslovakia or Lithuania. Finally, Barthou's plan excluded Rumania, Poland's only ally in Eastern Europe.

The Germans were similarly disinterested in the French idea. The Polish minister to Germany was called to the Chancellor's office for an interview with Hitler, who expounded on the menace of Russia. He asked for and received the Poles' support against the French plan. Although their scheme could not succeed in the face of combined German-Polish opposition, the French did not stop trying. Even after Barthou's death in October 1934, the new French foreign minister, Pierre Laval, continued to press the concept of an Eastern defensive alliance. The best that the French were able to do was to put together a complicated and unstable relationship between Czechoslovakia, Russia and themselves. In May 1935, France and the Soviet Union signed a treaty of mutual assistance in the event that either was attacked. Two weeks later the Soviets signed a similar treaty with Czechoslovakia. However, the Soviets would not be bound by this latter treaty unless France also intervened on Czechoslovakia's behalf.

The net effect of the failure of the Barthou plan was to draw Germany and Poland closer together, while simultaneously cooling off the Polish relationship with Russia. Obviously, the affair had done nothing whatever to strengthen ties between France and Poland. The Poles accepted this as inevitable result of their opposing the French plan.

Poland was now treated to many evidences of German favor. In June 1934, Joseph Goebbels visited Warsaw for the purpose of putting some warmth into the Polish-German relationship. The visit was a success, marred only at the end of Goebbels's visit by the assassination in Warsaw of Polish Minister of the Interior Bronislaw Pieracki by a Ukrainian terrorist. The assassin was a member of the Organization of Ukrainian Nationalists, a group that made its headquarters in Berlin and had, until recently, been subsidized by the German Foreign Office. In fact, the assassin fled to Germany after the killing. Horrified at this development and desperately anxious to prove their new good faith, the Germans arrested the Ukrainian terrorist who had planned the killing and flew him to Warsaw for the Poles to do with as they wished.

Six months later, in January 1935, it was Hermann Göring's turn to visit Poland. Although this visit was announced as a private hunting trip, Göring had come to sound out the Polish leaders regarding the possibility of their participating in a joint "crusade" against Communist Russia. There was nothing delicate about Göring's method. He simply ignored the fact that Poland had signed a non-aggression treaty with the Soviet Union and thus could be expected to be very sensitive concerning such a discussion. Göring as good as offered an anti-Soviet alliance to the Poles and indicated that when the defeated Soviet Union was divided up, Poland's share would be the entire Ukraine. The Polish ambassador to Germany had to warn Göring to be more subtle when he met with Piłsudski, as he did toward the end of the "hunting trip," to avoid "overdefinite proposals."[33] Even so, Göring got his message across to the Marshal, who promptly dismissed the idea with a "stiffened gesture," as Göring later recalled. [34] Piłsudski had been willing to sign a pledge of nonaggression with Germany, but under no present circumstances would Poland consider joining an alliance with either of its great neighbors against the other.

The Germans apparently took no offense at this rebuff and continued to show Poland frequent signs of esteem. In May 1935, in a Reichstag speech, Hitler stated, "We recognize with the understanding and the heartfelt friendship of true Nationalists, the Polish State as the home of a great, nationally conscious people."[35] In June 1935, the two nations initiated talks that led, in November, to the signing of a German-Polish Trade Agreement. This treaty was extremely important to Poland inasmuch as Germany was by far Poland's most important export market. In the past, Germany had been able to work considerable havoc on the Polish economy by implementing arbitrary changes in tariffs or quotas on imports from Poland. This new agreement gave Poland most-favored-nation status and cleared up a number of economic disputes between the two nations.

It was only a matter of time before the new Polish diplomatic stance of bristling independence would lead to a refusal to honor the Polish Minority Treaty. Poland had, of course, signed this agreement with great reluctance in 1919. But the Allies had forced it to accept the treaty as the price of independence. If the treaty had been repugnant then, it was infinitely more so fifteen years later, when Poland was committed to a policy of refusing to accept inferior status to any other power. This particular treaty was enforced by the League of Nations, and at various times almost all of Poland's neighbors had gone to the League to protest real or imagined Polish abuses perpetrated on their countrymen who were one of the Polish minorities.

Poland found it galling to be brought before the Council of the League and to be compelled to explain its actions. It was particularly irritating because Germany, which in years past had frequently complained to the League over alleged Polish injustices to Germans in Poland, had not itself been required to sign a minorities-protection treaty. The situation became intolerable to Polish pride when, in September 1934, the Soviet Union was admitted to the League and given a seat on the Council. Now Poland's other mighty neighbor, also uncommitted to any minorities-protection treaty, would be allowed to peek into Poland's pockets, as it were, and to complain about Poland's treatment of its Ukrainian and Belorussian minorities.

On September 13, 1934, Józef Beck was in Geneva to announce to the Assembly of the League of Nations that "pending the introduction of a general and uniform system for the protection of minorities, my government is compelled to refuse, as from today, all cooperation with the international organizations in the matter of supervision of the application by Poland of the system of minority protection."[36] Of course, there was no prospect of any international "general and uniform system" for minority protection, so the Polish declaration amounted to a unilateral abrogation of the treaty. As was foreseen by Poland, the League of Nations neither could nor would do anything about this. Of course, having renounced this treaty, the Poles were in a poor position to complain when other nations abrogated treaties, as Germany did beginning in March 1935.

For at least a year prior to March 1935, the German government had been directing the surreptitious rearmament. In fact, much rearming had already been secretly accomplished. In clear violation of the Treaty of Versailles, a German air force had been created. Various Nazi SA and SS formations had been incorporated into the Army. The French and British, as well as the Poles, certainly knew that Germany was rearming. Yet they made no protest. As long as the German buildup was modest and Hitler did not fling it in their faces, these governments were tolerant. The Poles, having signed their nonaggression agreement with Germany and having become, in effect, Germany's partner in opposing the Barthou Plan, found themselves in an awkward position. They could not protest German rearmament strongly. If they did, Berlin would surely ask them what they feared. Did they doubt Germany's sincerity in signing the nonaggression declaration? Nor could Poland, which had unilaterally renounced its minorities treaty on the grounds that it had been unfairly imposed by the Allies at Versailles, complain when Germany renounced treaties for the same reason.

On March 9, 1935, Hitler officially informed the governments of Europe that a German air force existed. No marked outcry having resulted, on March 16 the German government announced that military conscription would commence immediately. The peacetime strength of the German Army was set at thirty-six divisions, or about 550,000 men. Hitler kept the British and French off balance by simultaneously continuing negotiations on disarmament, making amiable declarations, and giving general reassurances of peaceful intent.

It all worked. The French and British protests were suitably subdued and restrained. Polish protests were nonexistent. Ambassador Lipski (Poland and Germany had elevated their legations in each other's capital to embassy status in October 1934) visited the German Foreign Minister and advised him that Warsaw had instructed him "to call the attention of the German government—in quite a friendly way—to the fact that the situation created by . . . the Reich government might result in complications in international relations."[37] This was certainly not much of a protest, and the Germans quickly waved it aside with a variety of gracious genialities.

By 1935 the "new course" of Polish foreign policy seemed to have yielded conspicuous benefits. Piłsudski and Beck had been almost startlingly successful in realizing a series of complex goals. While preserving Poland's alliance with France, they had simultaneously engineered a détente with Germany and Russia. Poland had brought itself, as Beck described it, into a state of "equilibrium" between its two powerful neighbors whom it believed to be ideologically and irreconcilably enemies of each other. Poland was friendly to both and was allied to neither. Then, too, there had been other successes—the renunciation of the repellent Minorities Treaty and the conclusion of a series of accommodations with the Free City of Danzig.

In the pursuit of these complicated goals, the new Polish tactic of brutally direct, independent action had had the impact that had been hoped for. Poland was now beginning to be regarded as a "great power" in many circles. It had demonstrated that it was not willing to allow itself to be woven into a lesser corner of a treaty tapestry. Poland had seemingly proved that it could confront the largest European powers on terms of equality. Other nations now treated Poland with an exhilarating new respect. The French, for example, no longer took Polish support for granted. As Beck subsequently observed, "It was obvious that whether people liked our system or not, it was regarded in the world with general repect."[38]

The Poles, however, had paid a price for their diplomatic coups. Their defiance of the League of Nations in the Westerplatte affair and the Minorities Treaty renunciation had certainly contributed toward a gradual weakening of the League's authority. The Polish diplomatic approaches to Germany had been exactly what Adolf Hitler wanted. The Poles had provided him with his first opportunity for significant, direct negotiation with one of Germany's armed neighbors. In the past, Germany had always been confronted by a number of World War victors (and their allies) acting in concert. The German-Polish Nonagression Declaration broke this unity. It destroyed the solidarity of Germany's neighbors and allowed Germany to rearm.

And German rearmament would be crucial for Poland. It was one thing for a Polish envoy to speak to Hitler in a threatening tone in 1933 and extract a friendly communiqué. It was roughly the same thing to be able to obtain a nonaggression declaration from Germany in 1934. But it would be quite another thing a few years hence, when Germany had rearmed and some of Hitler's other objectives been achieved. Would the Chancellor's interviews with Polish ambassadors then be so pleasant? Would Germany then remain supine in the face of a Westerplatte-type incident at Danzig?

All this, however, lay in the future and everything remained to be seen.

15

The Commandant Departs

Jozef Piłsudski probably began to suffer from cancer of the stomach during the second half of 1934. A malignancy of this type generally proceeds swiftly and is profoundly debilitating. It is still relatively rare for a patient to be cured of this type of malignancy. In the 1930s the prognosis was absolutely hopeless.

For some time after the malignancy had developed no one, not even Piłsudski himself, realized that he was suffering from cancer. Not only was cancer of this type difficult to diagnose at that time, but in this case the effects of the disease were masked by chronic bronchitis, arteriosclerosis, and recurrent attacks of influenza. Piłsudski's personal physician, an Army doctor and an old friend, but a man who possessed only mediocre medical talents, was out of his depth with a disease like this. During the winter of 1934–35 it was noticed that Piłsudski tired more easily than he had ever done before. He now spent most of his time sitting in an easy chair playing endless games of solitaire. Whenever he went to work at the offices of the inspector general, the one-block walk from the Belvedere was enough to exhaust him. In November 1934 it was observed that at a public function that included a review of troops on parade, for which Piłsudski had invariably stood at attention, he was now compelled to sit in a chair. Finally in April 1935, it was decided that the Marshal was seriously ill with a malady far graver than those he had previously been known to suffer. A renowned Viennese doctor was sent for. The doctor correctly diagnosed Piłsudski's disease, declared the cancer inoperable, and gave the opinion that the Polish leader's death was imminent. The only persons who were told of this, apart from Piłsudski's doctors, were President Mościcki, Prime Minister Sławek, and subsequently Józef Beck. They told no one else—not even Madame Piłsudska or Piłsudski himself.

It was easy to conceal the gravity of the Marshal's illness. The members of the Polish government had become accustomed to seeing him rarely. Only Beck was received with regularity. Piłsudski had become almost inaccessible to the rest of his colleagues during the past few years.

It is ironic that at precisely the point when Piłsudski's death was imminent, a new Polish constitution was finally about to be passed. This new constitution had been drafted by Piłsudski's supporters and it created a political system in which Piłsudski would either become president of the republic or would choose the president from his closest supporters. By 1935 it was known that Piłsudski did not want the office himself but that he expected to name Walery Sławek as president when the new constitution was adopted.

Since 1930 a parliamentary drafting committee, dominated by Piłsudski-ites and assisted by the government's legal expert Stanislaw Car, had been engaged in drawing up a new constitution. The outcome of these years of labor was a document that greatly strengthened the powers of the presidency. The privileges and prerogatives of that office seemed boundless. Under the proposed constitution the president appointed the prime minister and all cabinet ministers. These persons could be removed only by the president or a joint resolution of the Sejm and Senate, but the president could intervene and prevent dismissal by suspending or dissolving parliament. The president enjoyed a sort of veto power over legislation passed by the Sejm; he could refuse to sign any law and return it to parliament for "reconsideration."

The Polish president held the unhindered right to appoint the president of the supreme court, the officers of the Army and Navy (including the inspector general), and an extensive variety of other officials. He could suspend the parliament at any time for any reason. The president even enjoyed the privilege of appointing one third of the members of the Senate—a power that gave him great influence in the legislative process, because any law sent back to the Sejm for reconsideration had to be approved also by the Senate before resubmission to the president. And at the conclusion of his seven-year term the president could nominate his successor, who would then either be declared president or would face election opposed by no more then one candidate proposed by an "Assembly of Electors." (This assembly had eighty members. Five were government leaders; seventy-five were "worthy citizens," of whom fifty were named by the Sejm and twenty-five by the Senate.) In time of war the president could simply appoint his own successor.

Just in case there might be any lingering misunderstanding, Article 31 stated positively that "the functions of governing the State do not belong to the Sejm." The president, on the other hand, enjoyed the most generous privileges and immunities. He was responsible and answerable for his acts to no man—only to "God and history" (Article 2).

There was no question but that this constitution would have the effect of drastically reducing the influence of both the Polish parliament and Poland's political parties. Opponents of this draft constitution denounced it as a document under which Piłsudski, either acting as president himself or through a nominee serving as president, would become the "uncrowned king" of Poland. Viewing the election prospects realistically, the Piłsudski opposition had to concede that in the event the new constitution was adopted, it was almost certain that any nominee personally supported by Piłsudski would be elected president. The only way for the Piłsudski opposition to prevent all this from occurring was to vote in the Sejm against the adoption of the new constitution. Only in that body did they command sufficient strength to prevent a constitutional revision—which had to pass each house of parliament by a two-thirds vote. Piłsudski's adherents held enough Senate seats to insure the new constitution's passage, but first they had to get it through the Sejm.

As time passed, it became increasingly important to the Marshal's supporters that the proposed new constitution be enacted. It seems not to have occurred to them that it might be irresponsible, or at least unwise, to pass a constitution that had the structural defect of being specifically tailored to a unique regime headed by a unique man in his late sixties. The Marshal's followers did not even consider this factor. They believed that the new constitution would always serve as a sort of testament to Piłsudski's life's work. Through this constitu-

tion the Marshal would always be with them. And it would be their
gift to Piłsudski for all that he had done for Poland. Their frustrating
failure to have it passed by the Sejm made them desperate. Finally, in
early 1934 Stanislaw Car suddenly came up with a legal stratagem to
enact the new constitution.

It had been arranged that on January 26, 1934, various draft sections of the proposed new constitution would be submitted to the
Sejm for debate. For this purpose, the drafts were printed and arranged in the form of sixty-three separate articles. It was not generally
observed that when all of these articles were put together, they formed
an entire constitution. The opposition deputies had been informed
that the only purpose of the January 26 debate was to discuss and
modify the various articles, which were only thought to be a rough
draft. At no time was it even suggested that any one of the sixty-three
articles was being presented for a vote as an actual section of the
proposed new constitution. Polish law required fifteen days' notice to
be given before parliamentary voting on constitutional revision, and
no such notice had been given.

To indicate their complete rejection of the proposed constitution,
the opposition deputies decided to boycott this debate. Most of the
opposition simply stayed away from the parliament building. Others
milled about in the lobbies or sat in the parliament's restaurant. Only
one opposition member, S. Stronski, a National Democrat, was detailed to remain in the Sejm chamber to watch developments.

Stanislaw Car suddenly observed that at this moment the circumstances uniquely favored the adoption of a new constitution. Thanks
to the opposition's boycott, the government could now meet the requirement for the passage of any constitutional revision, that it be
approved by a two-thirds vote of the deputies present, with at least
one half of the statutory number of deputies attending. But the provision that fifteen days' notice be given to all the deputies prior to balloting on a constitutional revision had not been met. Car consulted
with some of his colleagues and gave the opinion that inasmuch as the
Sejm had been the scene of debate on constitutional revisions for
many months, this prolonged debate in itself constituted the necessary notification. Car rose and made the motion that the sixty-three
draft articles now being discussed by the Sejm be brought to a vote at
once as *actual constitutional amendments*. The astounded Stronski
objected violently, but, as the only opposition member in the chamber, he was quickly overruled. As Stronski ran frantically from the

chamber to summon his friends, the government's supporters quickly proceeded to vote on each of the sixty-three articles. Each article was, of course, accepted almost unanimously. The entire process took perhaps two hours. Whatever opposition deputies could be rounded up rushed into the chamber, but they were too few and too late. The balloting finished, the triumphant BBWR deputies stood and sang "We, the First Brigade"—the old marching song of the Polish Legion.

Kazimierz Switalski, marshal of the Sejm, ran to a telephone and gave Piłsudski the news that the constitution had passed the Sejm. To Switalski's surprise, the Marshal was not pleased. He had not been privy to Car's plan, and he apparently thought it unseemly that the Polish constitution should be brought to a vote in such a manner. As Piłsudski later told Sławek and Switalski, "It was not healthy that a Constitutional Law should be adopted by a trick or a joke."[1] Piłsudski was willing to go along with it, inasmuch as it was a *fait accompli*, but he insisted that the Constitution be deliberated at appropriate length and with fitting formality by the Senate. But this was only a formality; more than two thirds of the senators were government supporters.

The Senate did as it was instructed. Its debate on the new constitution was suitably lengthy, as befitted such an important document. Finally, it was approved, as was obvious it would be all along. On April 23, 1935, the new Polish constitution, a document embodying the personality and methods of Józef Piłsudski, went into effect. But by then Piłsudski had less than a month to live.

Piłsudski's last days were not very painful. He had, however, grown very weak. He could no longer lay out his games of solitaire, and aides did this for him. By early May 1935, Piłsudski evidently realized that he was close to death. He wrote out a one-page will that expressed his wishes relative to his burial. Most of the time he was confined to his bed in the Belvedere Palace, to which he would occasionally summon important officials for brief conversations. Insofar as he could, Piłsudski kept himself current, through Beck, with major developments in foreign affairs.

In May 1935, the French foreign minister, Pierre Laval, visited Warsaw. He was on his way to Moscow, to attend the ceremonies attendant upon the conclusion of the Franco-Soviet pact. The Poles had, of course, opposed this treaty and had refused to enter into it.

Laval sought an interview with Piłsudski. Beck had explained that this was impossible. The French, always distrustful of Beck, had suspected that Laval was being kept from seeing Piłsudski for some devious reason connected with the pact. Finally, Beck simply told Laval that "the days of the Marshal's life are numbered, and you understand what that means for us."[2]

On the night of May 10, Beck was the host at an elaborate formal dinner given in Laval's honor. During the course of the meal, Beck received a message that he must come to the Marshal immediately. Dressed in evening clothes will full decorations, he drove to the Belvedere Palace and was immediately admitted to the Marshal's bedside.

Piłsudski looked Beck up and down and then, with a smile, observed, "Aren't you *chic*, my boy. And how are you?"

After a little conversation, Piłsudski asked "Well, my boy, are you afraid?"

Beck replied, "Commandant, men whom you have honored with your confidence are never afraid."

The two men talked for an hour about Laval's visit. Piłsudski gave some instructions. Beck replied that he would carry them out. "Thank you," Piłsudski replied, "then everything is all right. Myself I don't think that I can do anything more."[3]

This was the last time Beck was to see the Marshal alive.

At 8:45 P.M. on Sunday, May 12, 1935, Piłsudski died at the age of sixty-seven. His death was peaceful—he had been in a coma, and his death mask and the photograph taken after his death show a face that is tranquil and unravaged.

The Marshal's death came, of course, as a great shock to the Polish people, who had not been in any way prepared for it. The reaction of the world press was one of similar surprise, but usually coupled with respectful comment. *The New York Times* of May 13 commented that there was "no other such human rock to dominate and direct the Polish tide."

The first effort of the Polish government was to prepare a funeral worthy of Piłsudski's place in the life of the nation. It was a monumental task, particularly when it was discovered that no plan for the Marshal's funeral had been developed.

Piłsudski's body was treated in accordance with his own expressed wishes. Conscious of the fact that he had been an exceptional person, the Marshal had instructed that his brain be given for study to the

Institute for Neurology at the University of Wilno. His heart was removed, placed in a casket, and taken to Wilno, to be entombed with his mother. The body was embalmed, dressed in full uniform, and carried into the Cathedral of St. John's, where it lay atop an enormously tall catafalque. A small painting of the "Holy Mother of Wilno" was placed in his hands. For two days, May 13 and 14, the public was admitted, and they came in enormous numbers.

On Friday, May 17, the funeral service took place. Dignitaries from almost every nation were present, including Göring at the head of the German delegation. Laval, who had not foreseen that he would return to Warsaw so soon, came from Moscow to head the French representation jointly with Marshal Henri Pétain. Only the Soviet Union alone refused to send a special representative to Piłsudski's funeral. They could not bring themselves to send anyone more important than their ambassador in Warsaw to the last rites for the victor of the Battle of the Vistula. However, Karl Radek wrote a respectful and friendly article in the Soviet press, and Litvinov gave a eulogy of sorts at the League of Nations the next week.

After the cathedral service the casket was carried outside and placed on an artillery carriage drawn by six horses. A continuous cordon of troops lined the streets to hold back the crowds while the carriage was pulled slowly through Warsaw. A double file of troops escorted the carriage and the several thousand mourning officials and dignitaries who followed it.

That afternoon the casket was placed at the edge of the vast Mokotov parade ground, where units from every Army division passed by in final salute. The scene was made even more somber by an extraordinary and unexpected thunderstorm that put the field into an eerie semidarkness for a half-hour during the march past. Then, in late afternoon, Piłsudski's casket was placed on a railway flatcar hooked up to a train and, surrounded by an honor guard of generals, was drawn slowly through the night along the two hundred miles of track to Kraków. Spotlights illuminated the casket, and hundreds of thousands of Poles stood in the fields by the railroad to see the body pass. The next morning, May 18, the casket was drawn through the streets of Kraków, past the enormous equestrian statute of Kościuszko, and placed in the crypt of the Wawel Castle. There Piłsudski's body was transferred to a silver casket with glass panels on the sides, permitting a view of his face within.

Wawel Castle was the historic burying place of Polish kings. Before its gates, President Mościcki gave a eulogy. "Here, in the shadow of our kings, comes a new companion in their eternal sleep. There is no crown on his head, and he holds no scepter in his hand. However, he was the king of our hearts and the ruler of our will. . . . With the boldness of his mind, the bravery of his plans and the force of his deeds, he burst our shackles and forged the sword which armed us. . . . He gave Poland freedom, territory, might, and the respect of others."[4]

16
Without Piłsudski

It goes without saying that Piłsudski's death tore an immense hole in practically every part of Polish political life. Even though at the time of his death he occupied only two official posts—minister of war and inspector general of the armed forces—Piłsudski had provided a sort of supreme moral authority that was basic to the organization of the government of independent Poland. Regardless of how great or how little a role he played in day-to-day affairs, Piłsudski was the cement that held the whole structure of government together. Now he was gone, and the Polish leaders he left behind were devastated.

Such was Piłsudski's influence over them, even after death, they could only think in terms of how the Commandant would have wanted affairs handled. Like faithful executors of an estate (for in a sense that was the way they thought of themselves) they rummaged about seeking a political testament that the Marshal might have left them. But there was none. All there was to guide them was a few very general (and very terse) instructions that Piłsudski had given in the months before his death. And it was not known whether they were instructions he had given in anticipation of his early death. Were they still operative? It was understood that Piłsudski wanted Walery Sławek to become president of the republic under the new constitution. The incumbent president, Ignacy Mościski, still had

five years of his seven-year term to serve. Did the Marshal's wishes
still apply? Was Mościcki expected to resign his office in favor of
Sławek? Then there was the crucial matter of the Army. Piłsudski
had indicated that his old associate Rydz-Śmigły should become Inspector General of the Armed Forces, although Sosnkowski clearly
seemed more able. Why had Piłsudski designated Rydz-Śmigły? No
one knew exactly, because the Marshal had rarely explained why
he chose any course of action. And what was to happen to Beck and
the others in the inner circle of Piłsudski intimates?

At first they all turned for answers to Walery Sławek. He was the
prime minister. He had been the Marshal's closest friend. Piłsudski
referred to him as "Faithful Walery." But Sławek had no answers to
give. In fact, for some months after the marshal's death, Sławek was
very depressed and could scarcely perform his official functions. This
was profoundly disturbing to his colleagues in the government.
Apart from being the prime minister and the official leader of the
BBWR, Sławek was expected soon to be the next president of the
republic. He, more than anyone else, could be called Piłsudski's heir.
It was difficult not to like and respect Sławek, for he was utterly
honest. He was invariably truthful, reliable, idealistic. He had not
the slightest capacity for intrigue and, now devastated by the Marshal's death, he displayed himself completely devoid of political
acumen.

Several persons quickly stepped into the vacuum thus produced.
One was the sixty-eight-year-old Mościcki. Prior to Piłsudski's death,
he had been preparing to step down from his office in favor of
Sławek. He would still have done so immediately after the Marshal's
death, but then Sławek's incapacity manifested itself. Sławek did not
reach out to claim the presidency, and Mościcki quickly convinced
himself that his continued presence in office was necessary.

During the years that he had been president, Mościcki had never
displayed the slightest degree of independence. No one had deferred
to Piłsudski with greater alacrity than he. But it now developed that
Mościki was shrewder and more ambitious than had been thought.
Mościcki presently indicated that he had no intention of stepping
aside in favor of Sławek, and he commenced certain political intrigues designed to consolidate his position. The other members of
the ruling circle, such as Prystor and Beck, found this unattractive.
After all, Sławek's succession to the presidency had been decided by
the Marshal himself. But Mościcki now claimed that Piłsudski's plan

to have Sławek replace him as president had been made before Piłsudski realized that he was mortally ill. Mościcki no longer regarded the plan as binding. He announced that he intended to stay on as president but suggested certain divisions of authority; Beck, for example, was to continue as foreign minister with full control of that field. And eventually Mościcki consolidated his position by means of an alliance with the new Inspector General of the armed forces, Rydz-Śmigły.

General Eduard Rdyz-Śmigły was forty-nine years old. He was undoubtedly Piłsudski's heir-designate as inspector general and had been appointed to this post by President Mościcki on the very night of the Marshal's death.

Rydz-Śmigły had been born as Eduard Rydz, of Polish peasant stock near Lwów in Austrian Galicia. He was the son of a noncommissional cavalry officer in the Austrian army. When he was nine years old both of his parents died, leaving Rydz a penniless orphan. In the ordinary course of events it would have been impossible for a boy in such circumstances to obtain any higher education. But even as a child, he possessed two extraordinary qualities: great charm and a definite gift for painting and drawing. The boy was taken in and raised by a family of impoverished Polish nobility. The parish priest, greatly impressed by Rydz's artistic ability, paid for his education at academies of fine arts in Kraków and Munich. Young Rydz rose considerably in the world. He became a reserve lieutenant in the Austrian army, and returning to Galicia, he joined Piłsudski's Riflemen's Association. During 1913–14 he was a lecturer at the Association's officers school. At this time most members of the organization used a cover name. Rydz's was "Śmigły," which is an antique Polish word that was used to describe an eagle in flight and had connotations of bravery, loftiness and speed. During World War I, Rydz served in the First Brigade of the Polish Legion. When Piłsudski was interned by the Germans, he designated Rydz as commander of the underground P.O.W., an office that Rydz filled ably. By the time of independence, Rydz had lived for so many years under his cover name and was so well known by it that he decided to couple it with his own. He usually wrote his name Rydz-Śmigły, although many persons and many official documents referred to him as Śmigły-Rydz. The general had no objection to this.

After the war Rydz-Śmigły decided to make his career in the

Polish Army. He rose to hold the most senior commands during the
Polish-Soviet War. It was Rydz-Śmigły whose troops captured Kiev,
and in the last extremity, Piłsudski had put Rydz-Śmigły in command
at Warsaw in August 1920 at the time of the crucial battle. He had
contributed strong support in the 1926 coup. It was said that Rydz-
Śmigły had never lost a battle. He was always extremely popular
with the troops under his command.

At the time of his elevation to Inspector General, Rydz-Śmigły
was known as a modest man, indeed he was thought rather shy. He
had always been content to work in backwater areas, such as Wilno,
where he had served for many years. Rydz-Śmigły's talents included
a certain oratorical ability, a wide knowledge of philosophy and
literature, definite artistic ability, an excellent seat on a horse (every
biographer mentions this), an engaging personality, and an encyclo-
pedic knowledge of the campaigns of Napoleon. He was generally
regarded as an extremely cultured person.

On the other hand, many of those in the inner circle of Poland
at that time were surprised at the selection of Rydz-Śmigły as Inspector General. While they agreed that he was a very good commander of an army corps, they did not believe him to be suitable
as the wartime chief of the entire Polish Army. Most of Piłsudski's
intimates had been puzzled by the favor that the Marshal had shown
to this pleasant general, who seemed to them to be clearly out of his
depth. But Piłsudski had known Rydz-Śmigły for many years, and it
was generally assumed that the Marshal had seen in him some significant ability that others failed to perceive. Quite possibly he valued
Rydz- Śmigły's total disinterest in politics. When Piłsudski designated
Rydz-Śmigły as his military heir, there was only one other likely
candidate for the job, General Kazimierz Sosnkowski. The rest of
the Polish generals of stature were either too young or too junior.
It was speculated that Piłsudski might have selected Rydz-Śmigły because he was completely apolitical. He had not the slightest experience in political matters, nor had he shown any interest in them—
whereas Sosnkowski had. It was therefore thought that this choice
of Rydz-Śmigły indicated the Marshal's determination to exclude
politics from the Army.

While all the intrigue attendant upon the succession of power was
going on, the government was compelled to deal with a very pressing
political matter—elections. The recently adopted constitution had

altered many of the institutions of Polish government, and new elections were required to fill newly defined positions. Just before Piłsudski's death, Sławek and others had drafted a new law under which these elections were to be conducted, and in July 1935 this law was enacted by parliament.

Under this new electoral law, the number of Sejm deputies was reduced to 208 from the previous 444. The new law prescribed how these 208 deputies were to be selected: Poland was divided into 104 voting districts, each of which was to send two deputies to the Sejm. Nobody had any particular objection to this. But there were plenty of objections regarding the manner in which candidates were to be *nominated* for election. Sławek's electoral law (which, of course, was the government's creation) specified that an "electoral assembly" was to be convened in each district to nominate a maximum of four candidates for the elections. Under the law, the members of each of the electoral assemblies consisted almost exclusively of the representatives of various recognized local organizations—professional organizations of lawyers and doctors, municipal officeholders, chambers of commerce, and the like. Each assembly met under the chairmanship of a commissioner appointed by the government. It was instantly pointed out by the government's opposition that their people would have very little chance to be nominated by such an elite group, which, in the natural course of events, would be packed with persons who were BBWR supporters.

The situation was similar regarding the nomination of men for Senate seats. The new electoral law cut the number of senators from 111 to ninety-six. Of these, one-third were appointed by the president of the republic. The remaining sixty-four were to be elected not by popular vote but by senatorial electoral assemblies in each of the Polish provinces. And the members of these local senatorial electoral assemblies were drawn, if anything, from a more government-dominated group than the electoral assemblies for the Sejm. Senatorial electors were all senior government officials, holders of official decorations, or presidents of local professional groups.

The opposition's objection to these electoral procedures was so intense that most of the opposition parties refused even to attempt to nominate candidates. The government professed to be astonished by the opposition's objections. The BBWR denied that there had been any intention to rig the elections. Sławek, who was probably sincere, explained that the objective of the new electoral law, as he had conceived it, was only to reduce the role of political parties in the selection of candidates while simultaneously broadening the representation of the general population in the nominating process. The opposition scoffed at this explanation, and most of the opposition parties planned to boycott the elections.

The elections were held on September 8 and 15, 1935. The BBWR elected three-quarters of the Sejm deputies and almost the same percentage of senators—in addition to obtaining the thirty-two additional senate seats which President Mościcki appointed. But the government party members' elation was considerably dampened by the impact of the opposition's boycott. In the 1930 elections, nearly 75 percent of those eligible to vote had done so. In this election well under 50 percent had voted—and many of these had cast blank ballots in protest. Nonetheless, the government unquestionably had a plenitude of support in parliament, and it was assumed that henceforth the Piłsudski-ite heirs could cease to concern themselves with opposition from that quarter.

With the elections out of the way, a new cabinet had to be formed, and a struggle for power began among the members of the governing circle. Under the new constitution, it was the president's duty to appoint the prime minister. It was evident that Mościcki was searching for an excuse not to reappoint the incumbent, Walery Sławek. Sławek was still Mościcki's foremost rival, still possessed great numbers of important friends, and had at last begun quietly to inquire as to when Mościcki intended to step aside as president.

Mościcki now offered to reappoint Sławek as prime minister but only on the condition that Eugeniusz Kwiatkowski, a close associate of Mościcki's who had been minister of commerce in previous governments, should be brought into the cabinet to serve as a sort of "economic czar" as well as deputy prime minister. Sławek, as was probably foreseen, refused to form a government in which he was required to include, in a key post, the protégé of his rival. He claimed that under the Polish constitution the prime minister alone enjoyed the prerogative of naming his cabinet. The president should not interfere. Mościcki therefore adopted the position that Sławek had refused his offer and turned to another man, Marian Zyndram-Koscialkowski.

Koscialkowski had been a long-time supporter of Piłsudski, although he had never been an intimate of his or a member of the

governing circle. He was obviously flattered by Mościcki's unexpected offer of the prime ministry and was perfectly agreeable to
including Kwiatkowski in his cabinet and giving him carte blanche.

When the imminence of Koscialkowski's appointment became
known, several important Piłsudski-ite leaders visited Mościcki to
protest. They still felt a certain loyalty toward Sławek, and they distrusted what they had heard of Kwiatkowski's economic policies. But
each protester was either fobbed off or placated by the president. In
the case of Beck, this took a lot of doing. Beck announced that he
would not serve in a Koscialkowski government, but in the end he
was persuaded that only he could maintain the continuity of Piłsudski's foreign policy. He agreed to stay on in his old post as foreign
minister with the promise of a more-or-less free hand in foreign
affairs. As for the other members of the old ruling circle, there proved
enough jobs to go around. Prystor become marshal of the Sejm. Car
was made marshal of the senate. Koscialkowski became prime minister on October 13, 1935. Only for Sławek was there nothing. Except
for his duties as a deputy in the Sejm, he went into retirement—but
not before announcing that he was dissolving the BBWR, of which
he was the founder and present leader.

Sławek's motives for destroying the BBWR have never been clear.
It is certain, however, that he did not do it because he felt betrayed
or was vindictive. Possibly, Sławek believed that the new electoral
law had made political parties as unnecessary as he felt them to be
undesirable. Or, possibly, Sławek had simply lost his bearings now
that the Marshal was no longer alive to guide him. At any rate,
without consulting anyone, "Faithful Walery" broke up the BBWR
organization which had served the Piłsudski-ite cause for the past
eight years.

With the demise of the BBWR, its adherents now dissolved into
smallish cliques, each led by a major figure from Piłsudski days. Some
former BBWR members clustered about Prystor; some followed
Beck or Switalski. Probably the largest group of BBWR senators and
deputies transferred their loyalty to Mościcki, and they were regarded as "the president's men." But, even so, they were a minority.
The other groupings, in combination, were far larger than Mościcki's
band, and the leaders of these factions regarded themselves as having
legitimate grievances against the President. They were angry at

Mościcki for what he had done to Sławek, and they deeply distrusted the Koscialkowski government, which Mościcki had installed.

The President was, of course, aware of this increasing animosity. He was also aware that within the parliament there was growing support for a vote of no confidence against the Koscialkowski cabinet. It was known that Rydz-Śmigły had expressed opposition to Koscialkowski. Mościcki realized that these were all manifestations of a power struggle that could be resolved only by the elevation of someone to a symbolic position of authority roughly similar to that which Piłsudski had enjoyed. But who should this man be? Mościcki would have liked it to be himself, but he was a realist. He was, after all, sixty-nine years old, and this conflict was tiring him rapidly. At prolonged meetings it was noticed that Mościcki had difficulty following the discussion and tended to lose his chain of thought when speaking. Mościcki knew that he could not now hope to achieve the prodigious stature that Piłsudski had had in the eyes of the Polish people. He must be content with suppressing political strife and ensuring his position as president. To achieve these ends he must tolerate a rival who would, while inheriting the aura and some of the moral authority of Piłsudski, still be content to be second in command. The obvious candidate for this position was General Rydz-Śmigły.

In December 1935, the two men apparently reached some sort of agreement. Rydz-Śmigły, while technically occupying only the military position of Inspector General, would also be awarded a substantial share of political power, and every effort would be made to enhance his prestige. Mościcki would remain as President. The Koscialkowski government would be dismissed as soon as convenient (actually this did not occur until May 1936) and replaced with one more suitable to Rydz-Śmigły.

In the ensuing months no effort was spared to build up the stature of Rydz-Śmigły. At first this was not an easy task. The general was not a vain man—not, at least, in these early days. He did not especially enjoy the adulation that the government publicists heaped on him. But gradually his attitude toward publicity changed. Rydz-Śmigły's staff officers had their own ambitions. His entourage was greedy for the increase in power that would come with their general's elevation in importance. Rydz-Śmigły's wife was an intensely ambitious woman and was determined to push her husband ahead. Rydz-Śmigły could not withstand the pressures of his staff and family. In particular he deferred to his wife's wishes. Rydz entered into the spirit of the promotional effort on his behalf—and soon began to enjoy it.

The essence of the government's publicity campaign was the revelation to the Polish nation that Rydz-Śmigły had been designated as Piłsudski's military successor by the Marshal himself. This fact was first asserted in February 1936 by a government speaker in the Sejm who announced that Rydz-Śmigły had been named inspector general in accordance with "the will of the Marshal."[1] A few weeks later, President Mościcki in a radio address to the nation claimed that as long as two years before his death Piłsudski had confided to him that Rydz-Śmigły was his chosen successor and had urged the President to rely on him. A series of posters in which Rydz-Śmigły's picture was superimposed over a drawing of Piłsudski were released by the government to further hammer home the theme of designated succession.

The government's publicists quickly made Rydz-Śmigły's name day a major public occasion. In 1935 the event had been completely ignored in the press. But on March 18, 1936, the general was the subject of long, laudatory articles, accompanied by large photographs, in the major Polish newspapers. Government press officers saw to it that ample supplies of photographs of Rydz-Śmigły (on horseback, looking through binoculars into the distance, and so forth) were made available to the press and were frequently printed. Posters with Rydz-Śmigły's photograph and with such exhortations as "Supreme Commander, lead us!" were placed in post offices and government buildings. Government publicists constantly stressed Rydz-Śmigły's position as the "legitimate successor" to Piłsudski, the executor of the Marshal's policies, and the guardian of the "soul" of the Polish nation.

After this drum beating had been going on for nearly a year, it was judged that the public had been prepared for the final step in Rydz-Śmigły's transformation into a Piłsudski-like leader—his promotion to the ranks of marshal. At the time of Piłsudski's death there had, of course, only been one First Marshal, Piłsudski himself. The only other marshal ever created in the Polish Army had been Foch of France, but this was obviously an honorary appointment. The general-officer ranks in the Polish Army were, from the most junior upward, general of brigade (one star), general of division (two stars), and general of the army (three stars). Rydz-Śmigły, when appointed inspector general on the night of Piłsudski's death, had been only a general of division. Obviously something had to be done about that.

So, in November 1936, he was made a general of the army. And only a few days later, President Mościcki announced elevation to the rank of marshal.

Although the Polish public may have been prepared for his promotion, a great many important persons in the old Piłsudski-ite ruling circle found it extremely offensive. Beck, in particular, thought Rydz-Śmigły's elevation to the rank of marshal to be premature, unnecessary, and a major political blunder. Others of importance in the old *sanacja* hierarchy agreed. They felt that it was a tasteless attempt to fill Piłsudski's shoes only a year and a half after his death. A great many of the old Piłsudski-ites objected to Rydz-Śmigły's trying to replace their irreplaceable Marshal. Sławek described the event as "the saddest day of my life."[2] It was a final blow to the unity of the once enormously cohesive Sanacja-BBWR group that had governed Poland under Piłsudski for the best part of fifteen years. From this point onward a number of the old Piłsudski-ites disassociated themselves from the government of Mościcki and Rydz-Śmigły.

Well before Rydz-Śmigły's promotion, Mościcki had fulfilled his part of his political bargain with Rydz. In May 1936 Prime Minister Koscialkowski, whom Rydz found objectionable, had been removed and his government had been replaced by one headed by General Sławoj-Składkowski, the fifty-one-year-old former Army doctor who had served for many years as the minister of the interior in a number of cabinets during the Piłsudski days. Składkowski was particularly close to Rydz-Śmigły and thus his appointment as prime minister was a distinct display of deference to the inspector general. In addition, Rydz-Śmigły had been allowed to name five of the twelve cabinet members. These persons were known as "Rydz's ministers." Beck continued as foreign minister and was considered as nonaligned, although he clearly favored Mościcki over Rydz-Śmigły, whom he disliked. Mościcki had contented himself with naming six cabinet members—"the president's ministers." The unfortunate Składkowski had complained that he, the prime minister, had been allowed to name none of his cabinet members and was thereupon permitted to retain for himself the post of minister of the interior. No great effort was made to soothe Składkowski's feelings, because it was not intended that his government should last for long. He was generally regarded as a rather simple soul, whose major interests were maintaining public order and improving municipal sanitation. (Ironically, the Składkowski government endured for more than three years, making it the longest-lived government in the history of independent Poland.)

In addition to giving Rydz-Śmigły an important voice in the selection of a prime minister and his cabinet, Mościcki had done even more for the new Marshal. In July 1936 the government had published an executive order stating that "General Rydz-Śmigły . . . is to be regarded and respected as the first person in Poland after the President of the Republic. All state functionaries, with the Prime Minister at the head, are obliged to show him respect and obedience."[3] This was a remarkable directive. Under the Polish constitution the Inspector General of the Army was entitled to no special hierarchical consideration—he certainly did not rank above the prime minister. Even Piłsudski had always been careful to observe the correct formalities toward those prime ministers in whose cabinets he sat. Yet Mościcki had mandated this deference, and Prime Minister Składkowski had found it acceptable. From this point on, there was little doubt as to Rydz-Śmigły's influence in Polish affairs. Mościcki's campaign to elevate his status had been successful, perhaps more so than he had intended. The aging President now found that he could not compete with the more vigorous Marshal. Henceforth, Rydz-Śmigły's influence soon made itself felt in almost every department of government. Members of the cabinet began to feel it necessary to clear any major appointments in their ministries with Rydz-Śmigły's office. Even Beck began to submit names for proposed ambassadorial appointments for approval, as he had done with Piłsudski when he was alive. Rydz, increasingly, came to enjoy the powers he wielded and the deference that was paid him. In short order the "Supreme Commander" began, successfully, to require that no senior position in any part of the government be filled without his passing on the appointment. This was something he was really not equipped to do. He had no political or civil administrative experience. But his staff and Madame Rydz insisted that he demand these powers, and Rydz-Śmigły grew to like them. Thus the general whom Piłsudski had selected as his heir precisely because he was simply a good soldier who had no interest or any demonstrated ability in political affairs was, within little more than a year after succeeding Piłsudski, sitting at the heart of the Polish political system.

Those old Piłsudski-ites who still served in the government and had once been Rydz-Śmigły's equals, or in many cases his superiors, were alarmed and embittered at the swiftness with which Rydz had superseded them. They regarded the new "Supreme Commander" as totally unsuited for the role that he was now playing. They objected to having Rydz, who was, after all, only the inspector general, pass upon their appointments and exercise veto power over their plans. But nothing could be done about it. Piłsudski himself had set the precedent and the pattern.

Sławek's dissolution of the BBWR did not, of course, mean that its supporters drifted into political parties that opposed the government. But it did mean that the opposition parties—the PPS, the National Democrats, and the Peasant Party—began to fill the political vacuum and behave in a more forceful manner. These parties could not challenge the government's supremacy in the parliament, choked as it was with deputies and senators who had only recently been elected on a ticket pledged to support the government, but they found many opportunities to throw their weight around. The PPS, for example, called a series of strikes, which made 1936 the worst year of labor unrest in Poland's history. The PPS also gathered increased strength when the quasi-illegal Polish Communist Party temporarily decided to cease attacking other proletarian parties and, under a new policy described as "No Enemies on the Left," offered to form a united front with the PPS. Together, the two parties campaigned hard in various regional elections and scored frequent stunning triumphs. In September 1936 the Socialist-Communist bloc succeeded in electing the majority of the Łódz municipal council. The government's supporters failed to win a single seat in this bellwether election in an important city.

The Peasant Party also expanded its program and its following. In response to the desperation in the Depression-impoverished countryside, the Peasant Party became increasingly radical. Its leaders called for uncompensated expropriation of large estates. Although officially the party opposed violence and illegal actions by its members, in practice it supported a fair number of peasant demonstrations that turned into antigovernment riots in which both police and demonstrators were injured and sometimes killed.

The National Democratic Party (or National Party, as it had renamed itself) was consistent with its previous position. The party was strongly nationalist, conservative, anti-Semitic and anti-Communist. If it were not for the fact that the National Democrats were historically so anti-German, the party might have become a Nazi-type organization. As it was, though, the National Democratic Party was the original party of various groups of fascist-minded younger men who, eventually concluding that their party was incurably anti-German, struck out on their own. The most important of these off-shoots was the Oboz Narodowo-Radvkalny (or National Radical Camp—referred to as the ONR), which had splintered away from the National Democrats in early 1934. The government had suppressed it, but after Piłsudski's death the ONR had popped up again with a new name—the Falanga. It was led by Bolesław Piasecki, a young man who called himself Il Duce. Under its new title the Falanga was legal, but subject to constant police surveillance. It did, however, enjoy certain significant successes—particularly in organizing the university students.

The challenge that the opposition parties were beginning to offer was quickly perceived by the government. All of the Piłsudski-ites, particularly those who had ended up within the ruling circle, now regreted Sławek's impetuous dissolution of the BBWR. Obviously, it was necessary to re-create a pro-government party around which the Polish people could be rallied. In particular, it was evident that a great deal of work had to be done with Polish youth, who seemed increasingly disaffected and dissatisfied with the regime of the older Piłsudski-ites.

Once the need for a new party had become apparent, the only question was the form it should take. The government members considered this for several months. Eventually, it was decided that what was really wanted was much more than just a political party or a coalition on the pattern of the defunct BBWR. Instead, what they hoped to create was a broad-based movement that would unite as many Poles as possible under the government's leadership. Ideally, this new movement would rally Poles from every class, every occupation, and every political affiliation. In addition to providing the government with political support, the proposed confederation was expected to mobilize public opinion on behalf of such desirable objectives and institutions as the Army, technological advance, and the development of heavy industry. The plans that the government had in mind for this organization were endless. If it all worked out as contemplated, the organization would be of enormous size.

The first intimations of the government's intention to found such a movement came in May 1936, when Rydz-Śmigły made an important address to a meeting of the Polish Union of Legionnaires. The Marshal called for the formation of an institution that would consolidate the nation in these dangerous times. "There is no choice," he said, "one must speak plainly. You must either stand here in the ranks with us, like a brother, or you are not our brother!"[4] Similar demands for national unity were made in the government-inspired press.

To head this as yet unannounced movement, Rydz-Śmigły had already appointed a retired Army colonel named Adam Koc. As it turned out, this appointment was a mistake. Although only forty-six years old, Koc was a man who had already passed his prime. In his earlier years, Koc had been among the most dynamic of the Piłsudski-ites. His credentials could not have been improved upon—wartime service in the First Brigade of the Polish Legion, during which he had been severely wounded, followed by underground service in the P.O.W. Koc had entered the Army in 1918, and until 1926 Piłsudski had used him as a liaison officer on both official and private missions. Following the 1926 coup, Koc had been sent to Sikorski's headquarters as chief of staff, with the obvious assignment of keeping a Piłsudski-ite eye on his commander. From 1928 onward, Koc had occupied a series of the distinguished civilian posts that were open to former Army officers with strong Piłsudski connections. In 1936 he was, in fact, president of the Bank of Poland.

However, in the course of recent years, Koc's personality had suffered a slow but pronounced alteration for the worse. Some of this was probably due to aftereffects of his wartime wound. He had been shot through the liver, and he never completely recovered. In the middle 1930s Koc began to suffer constant pain from his old injury. It was debilitating, and his associates observed that Koc found increasing difficulty in arriving at decisions. He was noticeably slower in both action and reaction than he had been. He would take no action until he had made the most meticulous and time-consuming preparation. His political views hardened, and he had become intensely conservative.

Although Rydz-Śmigły had indicated, in veiled terms, the formation of a new political organization as early as May 1936, it was not until February 1937 that Koc had succeeded in putting the whole concept together. At that time, in a radio broadcast to the nation,

Koc announced the formation of an important new movement that became known as the Camp of National Unity or OZON.

The program for this new organization went considerably beyond anything that had ever been contemplated for the old BBWR. In essence, the new OZON was intended to create and maintain a sense of undivided nationalism among the Polish people. Discipline, strength and solidarity were its watchwords. As Rydz-Śmigły announced, OZON would "consolidate" the nation and "give it an organized and singly directed will."[5]

An important feature of the OZON program was to raise the level of national consciousness among the populace. This was to be accomplished by means of a propaganda campaign that would publicize great periods in Polish history, by massive rallies and parades, by patriotic organizations, and by stressing loyalty to such common denominators of "Polishness" as the Roman Catholic Church and the Army.

Koc claimed that the OZON program was nothing more than a continuation of the Piłsudski tradition. But many Piłsudski-ites, including important members of the parliament, disagreed. As OZON's policies and objective were gradually revealed, the whole movement began to appear conspicuously proto-fascist. Many of the old Piłsudski-ites pointed to this in alarm. They denied that OZON represented a continuation of the Piłsudski ideology, as Koc claimed. Piłsudski had never espoused anti-Semitism, a policy that OZON had begun to advocate. Piłsudski had opposed both communism and fascism; OZON was conspicuously anti-Communist but was silent regarding fascism. All the men who had served as prime minister during the Piłsudski years were invited to join OZON. All refused.

The whole matter of OZON, which definitely had all the makings of a fascist movement, would have become most serious had the movement succeeded in accomplishing what its organizers hoped for it. However, it did not. Only in OZON's first weeks did it have any significant organizational successes. A large combination of associations of former military men known as the Federation of Polish Associations of Defenders of the Fatherland joined OZON almost as soon as its establishment was announced. A few small rump offshoots from the Peasant Party and the National Democrats incorporated themselves into OZON, and several unions of government employees also joined, as did a great many individual government employees.

After the first month of OZON's official existence, Koc could claim with accuracy that two million Poles had joined it.

It was an impressive beginning, but there it ended. Gaining additional members proved extremely difficult. None of the major parties of the Center or the Left—notably not the PPS and the Peasant Party—cared to affiliate itself with OZON. Even the National Democrats on the Right refused to subordinate themselves to OZON. Of the various trades unions, only those consisting of government workers would join. And within the cabinet, to the intense embarrassment of Rydz-Śmigły and Mościcki, there was no unanimity of support for OZON. Several cabinet members, Beck included, refused to join OZON.

As it became evident that the movement was failing to achieve its objectives, Koc was driven to certain excesses. He persuaded Prime Minister Skladkowski that the government must support OZON in a more positive manner. The Ministry of the Interior was instructed to confiscate editions of newspapers that ridiculed or disparaged OZON. State employees were pressured into joining the organization and supporting its programs. Koc even proposed to the cabinet that any trade union that refused to align itself with OZON be dissolved and replaced with an entirely new union led by his men. But this was clearly too much, and the cabinet refused to consider Koc's proposal.

Gradually, it was seen that OZON was a failure. Its every effort became counterproductive. The opposition political parties took heart at the government's discomfiture. Refreshed and reinvigorated, the previously demoralized opposition parties renewed their criticisms of the government. In fact, they became more active than they had been before OZON was conceived. On January 10, 1938, Koc resigned as the head of OZON and was replaced by an Army general, Stanisław Skwaraznski. From then on OZON ceased to pose an authentic fascist threat. Its new leader viewed it primarily as an organization for whipping up support for the Army—which had never been a problem in Poland. It became only a political party that various opportunists and career government people joined as a matter of duty. Apart from an unhealthy anti-Semitism, which its nationalist policies had stimulated, OZON drifted into unimportance on a sea of greater events.

There is almost no element of Polish life during the post-Piłsudski period more controversial than anti-Semitism. Although, to be sure, anti-Semitism was not confined to Poland, there was no other European nation where it affected so many persons.

The Polish census of 1931 indicated that there were 3,114,000 Jews in Poland. Next to the Ukrainians, the Jews were the largest of the Polish minorities. They made up 10 percent of the Polish population, by far the largest percentage of Jews in any nation in the world. The 350,000 Jews who lived in Warsaw equaled the number of Jews in all of France. The 200,000 Jews who lived in Łódź equaled the entire Jewish population of Czechoslovakia. Poland was second only to the United States in terms of the actual number of Jewish inhabitants.

The extensive Jewish presence in Poland had certainly not come about overnight. One of the most successful of the Polish kings, Casimir the Great (reigned 1333–70), had invited Jews into his kingdom and given them certain special privileges, which were reconfirmed by subsequent Polish kings. In welcoming Jews to Poland the Polish royal house had acted entirely in its own interests. There was, in the Middle Ages and almost up to the beginning of the twentieth century, no indigenous Polish mercantile class. Enterprising and resourceful, the Jews filled this necessary economic role. They became the traders, the estate administrators, and the tax collectors. They operated the royal mint and managed the royal salt mines. At a time when the Christian Church forbade the lending of money for interest, Poland's Jews provided this important economic service. Almost all the medical doctors in Poland during the Middle Ages were Jews. Jews were the artisans, tailors, metalworkers and jewelers. In short, Jews provided a host of skills that were lacking in medieval Poland. And unlike the rebellious Polish gentry, the Jewish community faithfully and punctually paid taxes to the king. Gratified, the Polish kings placed their Jewish subjects under their personal protection. Any Christian who killed or wounded a Jew was haled before a special royal court, which severely punished such crimes. The Jewish community was permitted pretty much to regulate its own internal affairs and was allowed to have its own courts, schools and police, and to follow its own religious laws. There were sporadic outbreaks of anti-Semitism, during some of which the Jews petitioned, and were granted, the right to construct defensive walls around the Jewish quarter of the city in which they lived.[6] But until the latter part of the

eighteenth century Poland's Jews were, by and large, safe and prosperous. Poland was generally regarded as a Jewish sanctuary, and Jews
from all over Europe immigrated to Poland. In fact, during the
seventeenth century it is estimated that four-fifths of the world's Jews
lived in Poland.[7]

Poland's position as a haven for Jews began to change with the
partitions at the end of the eighteenth century. The parts of Poland
in which most Jews lived were taken by Russia, which had an official
policy of anti-Semitism. The situation worsened following the assassination of Alexander II in 1881. Imperial Russia embarked on a
campaign of the most vicious anti-Semitism. In the course of these
pogroms, followed twenty years later by the "Black Hundreds," Jews
who lived in Russia were systematically impoverished, terrorized, and
deprived of every right and privilege. These people could save themselves only by emigrating abroad or by moving westward "beyond the
Pale" into Congress Poland, which, although under Tsarist rule, did
not enforce many of the Russian anti-Semitic laws.

Hundreds of thousands of Jews moved into Poland. They were the
most impoverished, the least educated, the old and sick of Russia's
Jews. Their flight into Poland overwhelmed the capacity of the Jewish charitable organizations, which had traditionally taken care of
their own, to help them. These refugees from Russia had nowhere to
go except the cities, where they jammed into the already crowded
Jewish sectors. The proportion of the population of Polish cities that
was Jewish had always been high. Now it became higher. Thirty percent of the population of Warsaw was Jewish, a similar percentage
was reached in the other major Polish cities during the first years of
the twentieth century. Generally the inhabitants of the Jewish quarter
of the cities led lives deeply rooted in religious tradition. They formed
their own closed society and did not attempt to assimilate into the
Polish culture. They wore traditional dress and spoke their own
languages. A great many Polish Jews could not even speak Polish.

Most of these Jews, both those who were native to Poland and those
who were refugees from Russia, were poor people. They were the ill-
paid minor artisans—the tailors, hatmakers and shoemakers. Although
they continued to dominate Polish mercantile life, they were mostly
the poor peddlers, the keepers of little shops, and the proprietors of
shabby market stalls, where a few zlotys' worth of goods represented
the vendor's entire wealth.

The traditional modes of occupation inevitably led to certain tensions. In every Polish village a Jew owned the store, a Jew was the horse-and-cattle trader, and a Jew was the moneylender. When times were difficult in the Polish countryside, which occurred frequently, it was the Jew who had to collect money, refuse credit, or buy cattle cheaply. These were not occupations calculated to popularize Jews with the Polish peasantry. The peasant, who rarely comprehended the necessary function of the middleman in business transactions, tended to regard the Jew as a bloodsucker, when, in fact, the Jews were generally no better off than the peasants for whom they were scapegoats.

To be sure, there were a number of Polish Jews who had become wealthy and successful. These persons had usually assimilated themselves into the Polish society, where they were called "Poles of the Mosaic faith." Such Jews dominated the professions of law and medicine. They played major roles in banking and the insurance industry. In fact, Jews handled practically all of preindependence Poland's commerce.

The question of Jewish dominance within the commercial and professional classes had first been widely discussed in the late nineteenth century at a time when Poland's Jewish population was growing dramatically through emigration from Russia. Roman Dmowski and his associates, in planning for an independent Poland, had developed definite theories regarding the nation and its Jewish population. They advanced the argument that no nation could long exist with its commercial functions virtually monopolized by a separate ethnic group that, they claimed, had proved generally to be unassimilable. Dmowski's theories became the tenets of his National Democratic Party, which was outspokenly anti-Semitic. The National Democrats insisted that independent Poland must be industrialized and that the only way to do this was to create a commercial class of ethnic Poles who would displace the Jews. Their slogan was "On the banks of Vistula there is no room for two nationalities," and beneath the masthead of Dmowski's newspaper was the exhortation "Patronize your own."[8] In 1914 Dmowski led a boycott of Jewish enterprises. In fact, Dmowski was so forthright in expressing his anti-Semitic views that he raised great concern among the Allies at the Paris Peace Conference. It was primarily to protect the Jewish minority that the Allies demanded that Poland sign the minorities treaty, a document which most ethnic Poles found extremely offensive and which did nothing to enhance Jewish popularity in Poland.

The attitude of the Jews of independent Poland toward their nation and toward ethnic Poles was understandably complex. Under the pre-Piłsudski coup governments, which were strongly influenced by the National Democrats, most Jews believed that the rights that they had been guaranteed had been infringed upon—and most certainly they had. The government had not subsidized Hebrew schools to the degree required by the minorities treaty, and there were many other instances of official indifference or outright hostility. For example, the government announced that henceforth certain kinds of artisans had to pass examinations and become licensed to pursue their trade. The examinations, however, were conducted only in Polish, thus excluding the large number of Jewish craftsmen who spoke only Yiddish. Jews always found difficulty in obtaining civil-service jobs. And during the Polish-Soviet War many Jews conscripted into the Army were isolated in separate camps by a government that apparently did not trust their loyalty.[9]

But then, in 1926, came Piłsudski's coup, which was regarded by almost all Jews as a most welcome development. Piłsudski had long been identified with opposition to anti-Semitism in any form. It was known that he regarded anti-Semitism as a sentiment unworthy of an important nation and inconsistent with Poland's historic attitudes. Piłsudski seems to have viewed himself as a sort of successor to the Polish kings in their role as protectors of the nation's Jewish population. The Bartel governments repealed much of the residue of old Tsarist laws that had been designed to harass Jews. The government announced its opposition to the *numerus clausus*, a quota system by which Polish universities attempted to reduce the percentages of Jewish students to a level equal to their population within the nation. In 1927 Bartel succeeded in having a law passed that gave official recognition to the formal Jewish communal organizations, the kehilloth, and established them as the conduit through which the government subsidized Jewish schools. Certain laws that had the effect of being economic sanctions against Polish Jews, such as the compulsory Sunday-closing laws, were no longer enforced.

To be sure, Poland's Jews continued to suffer in certain ways. As a group they were very poor—but Poland itself was a poor country. There was always a certain amount of anti-Semitic harassment in Poland, particularly in the countryside, which the government could do nothing about. However, the police and the courts were always on hand to protect Jews against any physical assault. Poland's Jews continued to lead separate lives, mostly in separate places, and following separate occupations from ethnic Poles. But as long as Piłsudski lived, Poland's Jews could consider themselves personally, economically and culturally safe.

All of this ended with the Marshal's death in 1935. Without Piłsudski's restraining hand, anti-Semitism began to take on a quasi-official character. A government-approved boycott of Jewish merchants began to develop. And combined with this were various physical attacks that were not curbed by the police until, in 1936, a number of Jews had been killed and several hundred injured.[10] This was the worst period of anti-Semitic violence that independent Poland had ever experienced. Prime Minister Sławoj-Składkowski publicly deplored it, but only modestly. He told the Sejm that "my government considers that nobody in Poland should be injured. An honest host does not allow anybody to be harmed in his house. An economic struggle? That's different, of course."[11]

Shortly afterward, Boguslaw Miedzinski, a prominent government spokesman, attempted to make clear to parliament the character of the government's anti-Semitism. It had nothing to do with racism, he claimed. As a matter of fact, it was well-known that Miedzinski's wife was Jewish. The problem was numbers. "Personally, I love Danes very much, but if we had three million of them in Poland, I would implore God to take them away as soon as possible," Miedzinski told the Sejm.[12]

With the formation of OZON in early 1937 the government's involvement in anti-Semitism became more direct. The highly nationalistic OZON program with its emphasis on Polish culture made anti-Semitism a natural corollary. Also, OZON was attempting to draw the National Democrats into its fold, and this party had, of course, a highly developed and long-standing anti-Semitic ideology.

Adam Koc, when first outlining OZON's policy regarding the Jewish question, announced that "the promulgation of racial hatred is foreign to the Polish Spirit" and that his movement could not approve "of any arbitrary action and brutal anti-Jewish outbursts." Nonetheless, "the instinct of cultural self-preservation is understandable, and the desire of the Polish community for economic self-sufficiency is natural."[13]

The National Democrats instantly attacked the half-heartedness of OZON's anti-Semitism and challenged it as not being well thought out. Indeed, it was not—as was the case with many of Koc's programs. OZON had a lot of difficulty with its ideological policy toward Jews. On April 20, 1937, an OZON official announced that "All Poles are permitted to join [OZON], irrespective of their religious origins or race—but only Poles." This was interpreted as meaning that membership was open to the relatively small number of Jews who had assimilated themselves into the general Polish culture.

The next day it was announced that there had been a misunderstanding. "The principles of Christianity, on which the declarations of Colonel Koc rest, will be the decisive factor in selecting members."[14]

Even this correction failed to satisfy the National Democrats. And, of course, it was violently attacked by the Falanga, who preached that Jews "should be deprived of their political rights, eliminated from all social associations, and denied the right to serve in the Polish Army. They should be forbidden to participate in Polish enterprises, to employ Poles, or to work for Poles . . . a radical elimination of the Jews from Poland is the ultimate solution of the Jewish problem."[15]

With this type of thinking circulating unchecked throughout the nation, anti-Semitism spread with formidable speed. OZON produced a series of posters featuring such slogans as "Buy only in Polish shops!" and "Each new Polish Shop is an Outpost in This Struggle," or "A Poland Free from Jews Is a Free Poland."[16] These were plastered up in prominent locations all over Poland.

The Roman Catholic hierarchy had already contributed a pastoral letter from Cardinal Hlond advising Catholics that "one does well to prefer his own kind in commercial dealings and to avoid Jewish stores and Jewish stalls in the market, but it is not permissible to demolish Jewish businesses."[17] Although condemning any form of violence, the Cardinal stated that "it is a fact that Jews fight against the Catholic Church . . . constituting the advance guard of a godless life, of the Bolshevik movement, and of subversive action. . . . It is a fact that the Jews are embezzlers and usurers and that they engage in the white-slave traffic."[18]

Government spokesman Miedzinski wrote a series of articles on the Jewish question for the semiofficial newspaper *Gazeta Polska* in which he attacked the "hopeless dirt and slovenliness" allegedly found in the Jewish section of Polish cities. He claimed that this "lowered the level of our culture in our own eyes and those of foreigners."[19] In subsequent articles he pointed out the large number of Jews who had played prominent roles in the Russian Revolution. Miedzinski claimed that 90 percent of the membership of the Central Committee of the Polish Communist Party was Jewish.

Some of the most persistent anti-Semitism was practiced in the Polish universities. In these institutions the gentile students, as was then the case throughout Continental Europe, were mostly conservative and Rightist. The large number of Jews who attended Polish universities, at times exceeding 20 percent of the general student body, was a long-standing irritant. Now, with the emergence of open anti-Semitism in Poland, the conservative students began to demand that a quota be placed on the number of Jewish students. They also demanded that Jews be compelled to sit in separate classroom sections known as ghetto benches.

Many university professors declined to enforce either a quota or the ghetto-bench system, but a substantially larger percentage did permit such practices. The result was that the number of Jews attending Polish universities declined rapidly, and even though some Jewish students remained standing throughout their classes rather than sit on the ghetto benches, separate seating areas came to be common practice.

Probably the most effective aspect of Polish anti-Semitism was the professional and economic boycotts that the government either encouraged or, sometimes, actually initiated. These sanctions were enforced in a number of ways. For example, in 1937 the government abruptly terminated all the long-standing licenses to sell tobacco at retail. Almost all tobacco vendors had been Jews. When the licenses were reissued they were given almost exclusively to gentiles. Thus at one stroke, an estimated 30,000 Jews were deprived of their livelihood. The government initiated a campaign to replace Jewish shopkeepers with ethnic Poles. To encourage Poles to "patronize their own," a law was passed requiring every shop owner to post his name outside his store. The government encouraged "Markets without Jews," which were village market days on which Jewish stallkeepers were excluded. A law was passed that limited the production of kosher meat on the grounds that kosher slaughtering techniques were "inhumane."[20] Very few Jews were permitted to purchase land under the land-reform program, and the percentage of Jews in government service was kept extremely low. Various professional organizations—

including medical doctors, lawyers and engineers—began to restrict new members to "Aryans," which made it impossible for new Jewish professionals to practice in Poland.

Polish anti-Semitism was rarely accompanied by physical violence —the police would usually move with vigor to put an end to that— and a great many distinguished Poles found the government's campaign disgusting. Janusz Jedrzejewicz, once the prime minister of a Piłsudski government, was asked to a meeting of the Marshal's old supporters to hear Koc reveal OZON's anti-Semitic program. Jedrzejewicz later wrote, "I cannot recall a more tragic meeting. . . . Koc presented us with the political organization's policy, which departed so drastically from the principles we had professed for so many years. . . . We were devastated with what we heard from Koc."[21] Many old Piłsudski-ites objected violently, and their influence helped to blunt some of the worst excesses. But even if the Polish government refrained from direct physical action against Jews, it was indirectly responsible for one of the early Nazi atrocities on Germany's Jewish population. In October 1938, the Polish government suddenly announced a plan for the "control of foreign passports." This scheme required Poles living abroad to bring their Polish passports to a Polish consul prior to November 15, 1938, for revalidation. If the consul refused to revalidate the passport, then the document became void, and its holder could not reenter Poland. It was known that this measure was directed at Polish Jews who were living in Germany. The consuls were expected to refuse to revalidate their passports on some specious grounds, whereupon these people would become stateless persons.

The Nazi government found this Polish plan to be unacceptable. Deprived of their Polish citizenship, these Jews would be forced to remain in Germany, which did not want them. So to forestall the Polish scheme, the German government abruptly swept up seventeen thousand Polish Jews, all that it could find on its soil, threw them into cattle cars, and transported them across the Polish border. Involved in this forced repatriation, which was accompanied by severe suffering, was a couple named Grynszpan. They wrote to their seventeen-year-old son, who was living in France, telling him of their ordeal. On November 7 the young man bought a pistol and went to the German embassy in Paris and asked for the ambassador. A third secretary named Ernst vom Rath (ironically, a man who was slated to lose his job because of his anti-Nazi attitude) was sent out to deal with him. Hershel Grynszpan shot and killed him.

Two nights later the Nazi SS and the German police retaliated for the assassination by initiating the infamous "Week of Broken Glass" at the end of which more than seven thousand German-Jewish shops had been smashed and looted, a hundred and nineteen synagogues set on fire, twenty thousand Jews arrested, and thirty-five killed. This event signaled the beginning of more-or-less open Nazi atrocities against Germany's Jews.

Although it is certain that such a German pogrom would eventually have occurred no matter what the level of Polish anti-Semitism, it is also certain that an official Polish action indirectly triggered it off. In foreign eyes, rightly or wrongly, Polish anti-Semitism was equated with the much more violent type being practiced in Germany. This, of course, did nothing good for Poland's image abroad. As a *New York Times* editorial stated on June 12, 1937, "The spread of racial intolerance alienates from Poland the world sympathy which more than anything else won the Poles their independence."

Even after Koc's departure from OZON in 1938 the quasi-official anti-Semitism continued. However, it was now accompanied by far-fetched government schemes for emigration of Jews from Poland. Various government departments were instructed to investigate how this should be done, and they came up with various plans. All, however, were either impractical or impossible. Polish Jews could not emigrate in any substantial numbers to Palestine, because the British were restricting entry into this mandated territory. And almost every other European nation was either itself practicing anti-Semitism or else was already flooded with Jewish refugees. There was literally nowhere for Poland's Jews to go. Even if they had been able to leave in large numbers, their departure might have caused the Polish economy to collapse. Although Poland's Jews comprised 10 percent of the population, they paid between 35 and 40 percent of Poland's taxes. And because they owned a substantial amount of Poland's wealth, their mass emigration would have seriously drained the nation of capital. Finally, while the official campaign to replace Jewish shopkeepers with Christians in the countryside had been fairly successful, it had not resulted in the development of mercantile expertise in these gentile replacements. It was quite noticeable that gentile shopowners frequently failed where Jews had survived.

So the net result of the Polish anti-Semitism of the late 1930s was not that it drove Jews from Poland or even that it significantly reduced their dominant role in Polish mercantile life. All it did was to cause great suffering and to pauperize an enormous number of small Jewish shopkeepers and artisans. It is estimated that by 1939 one third of Poland's Jews were totally dependent upon relief payments contributed mostly by Jewish charities in the United States.

In the end, the government's program of anti-Semitism stood revealed as a complete disaster. It had accomplished none of its objectives, and it had alienated many of the government's friends, both at home and abroad.

From about the beginning of 1938 onward, the level of political controversy within Poland sharply declined. There was a simple reason for this: Every Pole was increasingly frightened by the threat of a general European war, and this drew them together politically as OZON had never been able to do.

Even Rydz, as mediocre a symbolic replacement for Piłsudski as he was proving to be, came generally to be accepted as the nation's leader. A great deal of official propaganda effort had gone into building up the "Supreme Commander's" image, but it is unclear just how much actual influence this had. Probably Rydz-Śmigły's popularity was due more to the fact that most Poles simply hoped that the new Marshal was all he was claimed to be.

By 1938, Rydz-Śmigły was indisputably in command of most aspects of the Polish government. Mościcki, now seventy-one years old, remained influential, but his energy was flagging. In order to maintain his position as president, he was content to defer to Rydz-Śmigły in most matters. Prime Minister Sławoj-Składkowski was similarly willing to subordinate himself to the "Supreme Commander." Only in the field of foreign affairs, where deference was generally paid to Beck's expertise and his recommendations almost always were adopted, was there any significant resistance to intrusion from Rydz-Śmigły. But however much Rydz-Śmigły controlled the government, his power did not extend to the parliament in the same degree. In the Senate and the Sejm, the *outright* opposition did not amount to much; the opposition parties had pretty well excluded themselves from these bodies by their boycott of the 1935 elections. Curiously, the real "opposition" was now the large bloc of disgruntled Piłsudski-ites who had been shunted aside by Mościcki or Rydz-Śmigły in the course of the struggle that had followed Piłsudski's death. These men had other grievances, too. Some were opposed to OZON; others were repelled by the government's role in the promotion of anti-Semitism or by the "radical" economic policies being pursued by Mościcki's protégé, Finance Minister Kwiatkowski. At any rate, many of these men, who had once been important *sanacja* figures and who, as recently as 1935, had been elected as BBWR candidates, were now in the peculiar position of being either in covert opposition to (or else very reluctant supporters of) the government. The first open defiance from this source came after Stanislaw Car's death in June 1938. As his successor to the important position of marshal of the Sejm, the deputies immediately selected Piłsudski's old friend, Walery Sławek. This was a definite slap in the face for the government. Sławek was very popular among most of the old Piłsudski-ites, who felt that "Faithful Walery" had been dealt with unfairly by Mościcki and Rydz-Śmigły. The government retaliated in September 1938, when Mościcki, with Rydz-Śmigły's approval, suddenly dissolved parliament and set new elections for November 6 and 13.

When the new elections took place, it developed that the government had much stronger popular support than it had ever dared to hope. One thing that helped was the effectiveness of the government's economic policies. Industrial production had increased by 40 percent since 1935 and now stood at its highest point in Polish history. The government's electoral campaign had been based upon an appeal for national solidarity in a dangerous hour. It was completely successful. As in 1935, the opposition parties boycotted the elections, and the dissident Piłsudski-ites gave the government no support. Nonetheless, more than 67 percent of the voters turned out. The election was notable for the government's "hands-off" attitude toward tampering with the vote. It was regarded as an extremely clean election—at least in comparison with those of years past. OZON, amazingly, elected 161 of the 208 deputies to the Sejm—a higher percentage of support than any Polish government had ever enjoyed. The government's percentage in the Senate was much higher; in fact, it was nearly a clean sweep. In addition, the government was able to punish the disgruntled Piłsudski-ites by denying many of them places on the OZON ticket— Walery Sławek being one of those who was forced to run on his own and therefore failed to be elected. A few months later, on April 2,

1939, at 8:45 P.M., the precise hour of Piłsudski's death, Sławek shot himself. The suicide weapon was the pistol that he had carried in 1908 in Piłsudski's raid on Bezdany.

The new parliament was filled with men who had been virtual nonentities only three years before. Their support for the government was utterly unquestioned. Much more than at any time during the Piłsudski years, the cabinet could do whatever it wished, without any fear of parliamentary obstruction.

This, then, was the political system that Poland carried into World War II. It had been shaped by and for Piłsudski; but now he was gone, and the mechanism was operated by a few of his heirs who were considerably less talented than their onetime leader. It was a government that was neither totalitarian nor fascist, but it was certainly authoritarian. It was not notably efficient, but it did enjoy the general support of the Polish people, who had never known any better system.

17

"The Bones of a British Grenadier"

AMID THE VARIOUS ALTERATIONS in official method and objective that followed upon the death of Piłsudski, there was one feature of Polish government that remained constant—the direction of foreign policy. There was never any real question but that Józef Beck would continue as Polish foreign minister. No one doubted that this was Piłsudski's wish and intention. Nor was there any question but that Beck would carry on the foreign policy that he and the Marshal had developed together. Poland's objectives would continue to be the maintenance of the friendliest possible relations with both Germany and the Soviet Union. Poland would endeavor always to keep its friendships with its two neighbors at the same level of warmth. At no time would Poland consider entering into any kind of alliance with one of its powerful neighbors against the other. In fact, Poland would not even discuss the subject with the Soviet Union or Germany. The only alliances that Poland would maintain were its 1921 treaties and military conventions with France and Rumania which Poland continued to regard as the cornerstone of its foreign policy.

It was this Piłsudski-ite continuity that enabled Beck to operate in his own unique style. Beck was given no instructions from anyone—not from President Mościcki, whom he only tolerated, nor from Rydz-Śmigły, whom he disliked, nor from Prime Ministers Koscialkowski or Sławój-Składkowski, whom Beck regarded (probably with justice) as very much his intellectual inferiors. All these persons were content to let Beck set his own objectives, use his own methods, and generally conduct Polish foreign affairs as he wished. Mościcki, Rydz-Śmigły, and the prime minister of the time seem to have asked only that Beck keep them informed of what he was doing and what he intended to do.

While such a manner of conducting foreign policy would seem on the face of it to be fraught with the greatest perils, it often seemed at the time to be highly successful. Even though Beck was widely disliked in various other European foreign ministries, notably of course in the Quai d'Orsay, he was at least a known quantity amid the post-Piłsudski political turmoil in Poland. It was understood that, as Piłsudski's protégé, Beck was continuing the policies established during the Marshal's regime. Beck might sometimes be abrupt or unpleasant to deal with and was often accused of being devious. But, it was observed, this trait was apparent only when he wished to stall for time or avoid an issue. Otherwise he would be extremely direct and candid. At least one could get a decision from Beck and other foreign ministries appreciated this.

Even a diplomatic opponent of sorts, the French ambassador to Poland, Léon Noël, had to confess considerable respect for Beck.

His [Beck's] ability could not be denied. Extremely intelligent, he could master skillfully and very rapidly any concept he was exposed to. Blessed with a remarkable memory, he could recall without effort and without recourse to notes any information given to him or the proposed version of a text.

Colonel Beck had undeniable talent for diplomacy: a mind always alert, inventive, and resourceful, great self-control, an inclination to secrecy . . . one can understand and appreciate—after one had to do business with him—why Piłsudski directed this young officer into foreign affairs.[1]

In 1937 the new United States ambassador to Poland, A. J. Drexel Biddle, wrote President Roosevelt about his early impressions of Beck. "From my own observation," Biddle reported, "Beck is steadily becoming the leading force in the Polish government, due mainly to his initiative, his willingness to make decisions, and to shoulder responsibility. I find him a man of courage and intelligence."[2]

Like Piłsudski, Beck did not believe in a passive approach to diplomacy. He was restless, aggressive and inventive. He had endless ideas for Polish foreign policy—some of which, like his "third Europe" scheme, involved Polish leadership of a number of East-Central European nations. Beck thought in terms of large concepts, and if he had a fault in this regard, it was that he sometimes overplayed his hand and ignored the reality that Poland could not truly be classed as a "great power" in Europe.

There is no question but that Józef Beck thoroughly *enjoyed* being Poland's foreign minister. A handsome and rather vain man, he liked dressing elegantly. Beck and his family lived in considerable style in the official apartments constructed in the Foreign Ministry building on Wierzbowa Street in Warsaw. Although other men in Poland might hold positions that were technically superior to that of the Foreign Minister, it is certain that Beck regarded himself as Poland's most important personality. He was probably right.

By late 1935 the eyes of every European foreign ministry were focused, of course, on Adolf Hitler. With each day that passed, German diplomacy became bolder and more aggressive. It was structured around a series of limited objectives, each of which was to be tackled in its turn. Poland's time had not yet come, so relationships between the two nations remained relatively cordial. In July 1935, Beck visited Berlin for two days of conversations, including his first extended meeting with Hitler. All went well, and these talks led directly to the conclusion of the important Polish-German Trade Agreement later in the year.

But it was evident to the Poles that a major German move was in the wind. They suspected that it would be the remilitarization of the Rhineland, that section of Germany which lay west of the Rhine and which, under the terms of both the Treaty of Versailles and the Locarno Pact, Germany was forbidden to fortify or garrison.

If Germany sent its troops into the Rhineland, the German military frontier would be advanced as much as seventy-five miles in some areas. France would be denied easy access into unfortified German territory, a circumstance of crucial importance in the event that the Franco-Polish military convention had to be implemented. The remilitarization of the Rhineland, if successful and unopposed by France, would establish a sort of German moral ascendancy over their old World War enemies.

The German General Staff was practically paralyzed with fright at the prospect of this operation. They considered it an extremely dangerous undertaking at this time. German rearmament was progressing rapidly, but its army had not come near to reaching parity with the French. If France should decide to riposte, it could easily crush any German unit sent across the Rhine. The German generals were terrified of the risk involved. Nonetheless, at Hitler's demand, three battalions of German troops crossed the bridges into the Rhineland at dawn on March 7, 1936. Simultaneously, Hitler announced the abrogation of the Locarno agreements.

It is now known, of course, that had the French retaliated with almost any kind of armed counterinvasion of the Rhineland, the German high command would instantly have withdrawn its troops. The hurried retreat would have been so humiliating that it might well have led Hitler's overthrow by a military junta. But none of this occurred. The French government, advised by its cautious General Staff that any move into the Rhineland would require the complete mobilization of the French Army, backed down. Hitler had guessed correctly. The French were afraid to go to war.

The Poles, of course, had not known what the French reaction would be. Beck had strongly suspected that the French would not move against the Germans in the Rhineland. However, Lipski, the Polish ambassador in Berlin, had recently been given the most positive assurances by André François-Poncet, the French ambassador to Germany, that if the Rhineland were to be reoccupied by Germany, "this will mean [French] general mobilization, and it will mean war."[3] François-Poncet had invited Lipski to pass these categoric assurances back to Warsaw. Similar declarations had been made by other senior French officials to various important Poles. Under these circumstances, the Polish government, whatever Beck's suspicions to the contrary, could only assume that the remilitarization of the Rhineland might well mean war and that Poland would be called upon to make good its treaty obligations to France. The Poles now established their *bona fides* as faithful allies. They regarded their 1934 Declaration of Nonaggression with Germany as having no force in this situation. They had advised Germany at the time of its signing that Poland would continue to honor prior treaty obligations. Almost instantly upon receiving news of the German incursion, Beck summoned Ambassador Noël to his offices in the Raczynski Palace. He formally requested that Noël inform his government that "Poland is anxious under the circumstances to assure France that she will be true, in case of emergency, to the engagements binding her to your country."[4]

But the French, for their part, were much less forthright with the Poles. Even before Beck's message of support had reached Paris, French Foreign Minister Pierre Etienne Flandin had summoned the Polish ambassador in Paris to the Quai d'Orsay and demanded to know what the Polish reaction would be. The Polish ambassador protested that diplomatic protocol required the French to reveal their plans and then to request Poland to conform. Flandin refused at that time to disclose French intentions although the question shortly became academic when Beck's message reached Paris.

The whole affair revealed a lot. To the French, whatever their view of Beck himself might be, the fidelity of Poland could not be in doubt. The Poles, on the other hand, suspected that the French Foreign Office had actually tried to entice Poland into declaring that its army would *not* march—thus giving the French government an excuse for its own inaction. Under these circumstances, the demonstration of Polish loyalty was almost unwelcome in certain French circles. The Quai d'Orsay suspected that Beck had expected that France would not respond to the German incursion and that he had made his offer in the belief that the French would not take it up. The Poles subsequently discovered that the French Foreign Ministry had made an effort to conceal the fact of Beck's unsolicited message of support. Polish diplomats in Paris retaliated by leaking their account of the affair to a wide circle of influential French contacts.

A new government under Léon Blum very soon took office in France. This new cabinet put a greater value on the Polish alliance. Blum and his Foreign Minister Yvon Delbos felt it obligatory that France display a sense of appreciation to its staunch ally. Steps were promptly taken. In August 1936, General Maurice Gamelin, chief of the French General Staff, was sent on an official visit to Warsaw. He was most cordially received and professed himself to be extremely impressed with what he saw of the Polish Army.

The next month Rydz-Śmigły visited Paris. Typically, the French invitation had been extended directly to Rydz-Śmigły at a time when Beck was away from Poland. In fact, the French ambassador to Poland suggested to his government that Rydz-Śmigły might be told that Beck's continuation as foreign minister was a distinct damper on relations between the two nations and that Beck should be dismissed.

In any event, Rydz-Śmigły's visit to France was a distinct success. The French did not follow their ambassador's suggestion to demand Beck's ouster. In fact, after protracted negotiation they agreed to make a loan of goods and cash worth two billion six hundred francs (equal to approximately $500 million at that time) to help finance the modernization of the Polish Army.

The French loan, together with various other visits that followed between Warsaw and Paris, considerably revitalized the Franco-Polish alliance. But at the same time Beck never allowed Poland's relations with Germany to be anything less than strictly correct. Polish diplomats were always available to give explanations and reassurances to the German Foreign Office regarding Poland's connections with France. From time to time Beck visited Berlin and on various occasions senior Nazi officials visited Warsaw. The talks were always cordial. Germany was given little to complain about in terms of the Polish attitude.

On the German side, Hitler's disposition toward Poland fluctuated with the needs of the moment. Immediately after the Rhineland adventure, Hitler was in a euphoric mood. The Poles seemed less important, and he temporarily lifted the restraints on the Nazi stormtroopers in Danzig. The result was a series of violent anti-Polish rows in the Free City, culminating with a visit from the German cruiser *Leipzig* on June 25, 1936. The captain of the *Leipzig* let it be known that he was under orders *not* to pay the customary courtesy call upon the League of Nations' High Commissioner. This was considered such a gross offense that the Commissioner brought the matter to the Council of the League, together with his complaints regarding the violence directed against Poles in Danzig. For a time it was rumored that the Council was considering withdrawing the League from Danzig rather than have its prestige subjected to further humiliations. In the end, however, Beck suggested that Poland negotiate the *Leipzig* matter with Germany directly. This was done. Hitler reimposed some curbs on his Danzig followers and gave assurances that the *Leipzig* incident was not a prelude to a German occupation of the Free City. A certain calm was restored to Danzig.

Soon afterward, various German sources commenced to sound out their Polish contacts on a variety of proposals concerning an eventual joint anti-Bolshevik crusade. The most important of these overtures was made by Hermann Göring during a visit to Warsaw in February

1937. Göring first assured Marshal Rydz-Śmigły that Hitler "was more than ever determined to continue the policy of *rapprochement* with Poland."[5] There was a strictly practical reason for this. "It should always be remembered," Göring said, "that there was one great danger coming through Russia from the East and menacing both Germany and Poland alike. . . . In Berlin, they had no illusions that Stalin was not planning to let loose world revolution."[6]

Göring suggested collaboration between Germany and Poland in developing a common anti-Communist front. The first step was to be a program of anti-Soviet propaganda designed to "influence the public opinion of both countries."[7] Once this had been accomplished, the two nations could move on to a closer "aligning" of German and Polish policies.

There was nothing new in this proposal, of course. Germany had frequently made off-the-record suggestions that some sort of joint military crusade against Soviet Russia could result in rich rewards for Poland in terms of Ukrainian territory. The Poles had always turned a deaf ear to these proposals. But now, in late 1936, the German pressure became somewhat more difficult to resist. On November 25, 1936, Germany signed the Anti-Comintern Pact with Japan. In this treaty the two nations agreed not to support Soviet Russia in any manner in the event of conflict between Russia and either of the two signatories. Both nations also undertook not to conclude any treaties with Soviet Russia that would violate the spirit of anti-Communism. Having signed this pact, the Germans and Japanese were now anxious to enlarge upon it and draw in additional signatories. It was a foregone conclusion that Italy would eventually join. But how about other nations? Poland was an obvious candidate. The activities of Colonel Adam Koc and OZON were viewed with approval as having created a suitably anti-Communist climate in Poland. But it was recognized that Poland would not join unless Beck was convinced that it should. And he remained absolutely steadfast in his refusal to align Poland with Germany against Soviet Russia. He would not even discuss the possibility of Polish enlistment in the Anti-Comintern Pact.

However, the Soviet Russians were as usual extremely suspicious of Poland's integrity in this matter. They found it very hard to believe that any capitalist nation would not, given an opportunity, join an anti-Communist crusade. Additionally, the great Soviet purge trials had just begun. Millions of Soviet citizens were being haled before courts to be found guilty. Obviously, they had to be tried on some sort of charge, and one of the most convenient and plausible-sounding was that they were agents or saboteurs in the pay of Polish intelligence organizations. Fairly quickly, the officials who had created these trumped-up charges were themselves purged, and the Soviet government could no longer separate fact from fancy. The Soviet leaders began to believe that a large percentage of the horde of people convicted for treasonous activities truly *were* Polish agents.

In short order, the hysteria that produced the purge trials also destroyed the Communist Party of Poland. The Soviet distrust of the CPP went back to the "May Errors" of 1926, and even before. Polish Communism had subsequently done little to repair its reputation with Moscow. The CPP was thought to be controlled by Trotskyites and thoroughly infiltrated by Polish police spies. Whatever the truth of the former charge, it is certain that the latter allegation was very real. Even though the CPP had been an illegal party since 1919, the Polish government had always been very tolerant of the various "front" parties through which the Communists worked. Usually only those Communists who operated in a blatant fashion or who were clearly functioning as Soviet intelligence agents were put into jail. The CPP's total membership in Warsaw probably never exceeded a thousand persons, and the government's secret police apparently preferred to have the party alive and infiltratable, rather than dead. The Polish government never denied that its security agents had penetrated the CPP most extensively.

However, it was scarcely necessary for the government to expend much energy in repressing Poland's Communist Party. Stalin and the Comintern in Moscow did a much better job than the Poles could possibly have done. Beginning in the early thirties, and culminating in the purge trials in 1937–38, Stalin succeeded in annihilating the Polish Communist Party. In successive waves, the party's leaders were called to Moscow for "consultations," given a Comintern "trial," and shot. The next group of Polish leaders who replaced them was similarly dealt with—and so it went.

The only Polish Communists who were safe were the lucky few who were imprisoned in Polish jails. One of these persons later told how he was one of a group of seventeen Communists who were arrested by the Poles and shuffled around, rather loosely guarded, from prison to prison. Eleven of the group escaped and after making their way to "safety" in the Soviet Union, were promptly executed as Polish spies. The balance of prisoners, the most intelligent one suspects, huddled thankfully in their Polish prisons. Nothing could have induced them to escape.

Eventually, at some time during 1938, Stalin put a temporary end to Polish Communism. No one in the West knows who signed the decree or exactly when it was promulgated, but the Comintern officially dissolved the CPP.

In the paranoid climate produced in the Soviet Union by the purge trials, the cordial atmosphere that had followed the signing of the Polish-Soviet Nonagression Pact of 1932 began rapidly to dissipate. *Pravda* began to print attacks on Polish foreign policy in general and on Beck in particular—"Everywhere Mr. Beck is carrying out the same task: he is preparing the ground for the subversive work of Fascist warmongers."[8] The Soviets recommenced the border raids that had been suspended since 1932. They began a program of radio broadcasts directed toward dissaffected minorities within Poland. They abruptly closed down Polish consulates in many parts of the Soviet Union. It seemed as if no Polish official of note could visit any other nation, or receive a visit from a senior foreign diplomat, without the Moscow press citing this as a fresh instance of anti-Soviet intrigue. The Soviet Foreign Office went out of its way to make trouble for the Poles by warning the French government that Poland's real loyalties lay with the Germans.

To all of this hostility, Beck responded calmly and with diplomatic correctness. Moscow was repeatedly assured that Poland had no intention of joining the Anti-Comintern Pact. The Polish press was encouraged not to respond to the Soviet attacks. In time, things smoothed out—but the atmosphere between the two nations was never to return to its previous cordiality.

In the meantime, Poland's relations with Germany appeared to be going along agreeably. On November 5, 1937, the two countries announced their agreement on "guiding principles" for the treatment of each other's minorities. The agreement took the form of a detailed listing of the identical privileges that the German minority would have in Poland and the Polish minority would have in Germany. At the same time, it was recognized that the members of the minority groups had the obligation "to give complete loyalty to the State to which they belong." The Polish ambassador was personally received by Hitler to signify the importance of this German-Polish understanding. In the course of the reception Hitler twice stated reassuringly that *"Danzig ist mit Polen verbünden"* ("Danzig is bound to Poland.)"[9]

Anschluss with Austria was now Hitler's most immediate and most obvious objective. The Polish position regarding this was fairly simple. Inasmuch as none of the great Western powers—France, Britain, Italy—was prepared to use military force to prevent Germany's taking over Austria, Poland could do nothing about it. Throughout the first months of 1938 the German Foreign Office repeatedly sounded out the Poles for their views regarding German annexation of Austria. In mid-January Beck visited Berlin for two days of talks with German leaders. He met with Foreign Minister Konstantin von Neurath on the morning of January 13, 1938; with Göring for luncheon on the same day; and finally with Hitler himself on the following afternoon. Each time he was told that Germany regarded the solution of the "Austrian problem" as being exclusively a German internal matter. Each time he replied, in effect, that his nation was disinterested in the matter—"Poland has only economic relations with Austria; we have no special political interest there."[10]

In the following weeks the Germans continued to seek assurance that the Polish position had not changed. Göring visited Warsaw in late February and brought up the matter again with Beck. He was given the same reply as previously. In compensation for this understanding attitude on the part of Poland, the Germans made categoric assurances that they would never infringe on Polish rights in Danzig. Hitler went so far as to tell the Yugoslav prime minister that the existence of the Polish Corridor was "a bitter pill for Germany to swallow but it had to be accepted."[11] The observation was meant to be repeated to the Poles and it was.

The details of the German *Anschluss* with Austria are well known. On February 12, 1938, Austrian Chancellor Kurt von Schuschnigg was summoned to Hitler's spectacular mountain retreat at Berchtesgaden. There, Schuschnigg was harassed and intimidated and given an ultimatum. Either Schuschnigg signed an "agreement" that required that various Austrian Nazis be given key cabinet posts in the Austrian government or, Hitler stated, the German Army would march into Austria at once. Schuschnigg signed the agreement. Hitler anticipated, of course, that his Austrian nominees would soon be able to assume full powers and invite Germany to annex Austria on the pretext that the majority of Austrians desired *Anschluss*.

However, once back in Austria, Schuschnigg announced that a plebiscite in which the Austrian people would vote upon whether they desired a "free, independent, social, Christian and united Austria" would be held on March 13. They had only to vote yes or no, and it was obvious that the majority of Austrians would vote yes, signifying that they desired to retain their independence. Hitler could not permit such a vote to be held, and so, on March 12, the day before the plebiscite, the German Army invaded and annexed Austria.

While all European eyes were fixed on the situation in Austria, the Poles took the opportunity to exert some power diplomacy of their own on one of their neighbors.

Polish diplomatic relations with Lithuania had, of course, been nonexistent since 1919, when the Polish Army had occupied Wilno and the surrounding area. Lithuania closed its borders with Poland and stopped all rail and road traffic across the Polish frontier. Lithuania refused to exchange diplomatic envoys with Poland and generally refused to sign any international treaties that Poland had signed. Lithuania tore down the telegraph and telephone wires that crossed into Poland, and there was no mail service between the two nations.

This situation had continued for nearly twenty years, and there is no question but that the Polish government found it profoundly irritating and inconvenient. From time to time, Warsaw had attempted to put together some sort of alliance of the Baltic states. Generally there was no difficulty in obtaining the preliminary agreement of Latvia and Estonia. But the various plans had always fallen apart because Lithuania would not discuss anything with Poland, much less conclude an alliance with it. Without Lithuania, any "Baltic alliance" was pointless. Beck regarded the Lithuanian intransigence as one of the principal obstacles to a defensive alliance of Baltic states led by Poland—an alliance that Beck had long desired. It became a major objective of Polish foreign policy that diplomatic relations be restored with Lithuania. Following that, pressure could be exerted to compel the Kaunas government to fall into line with Polish objectives. But the first step had to be the reestablishment of diplomatic relations—and the Poles were not prepared to be very fussy about how this was accomplished.

In March 1938, an event that took place on the Polish-Lithuanian border near Wilno provided the opportunity for which Poland had been waiting. Both Polish and Lithuanian intelligence services were constantly passing agents across the frontier in this area. On the night of March 10–11 a Polish Army detachment intercepted two Lithuanian agents crossing the border. In the process, and under circumstances that are still unclear, a Polish soldier named Stanisław Serafin was shot and killed.

Beck instantly saw that this affair provided a superb opportunity to issue an ultimatum to Lithuania. At the moment, Beck was on an official visit to Rome. He terminated it at once and rushed back to Warsaw. He explained to his colleagues that with the attention of the world directed toward Austria, any Polish pressure upon Lithuania would go almost unnoticed. And, of course, the climate of the times in Europe seemed to favor coerced negotiations.

An ultimatum demanding that Lithuania open its borders to traffic and commence diplomatic relations with Poland was quickly prepared in Warsaw. (This was surely a unique event in diplomatic history. One cannot recall any other ultimatum that demanded nothing more than the *opening* of diplomatic relations.) It was telegraphed to Tallin in Estonia, where the Polish legation handed it to the Lithuanian envoy there on March 17. An affirmative reply was demanded by March 19. The date was selected by Beck as one of special significance—it was the Feast of Saint Joseph, Piłsudski's name day. The Polish Army was mobilized along the Lithuanian frontier.

The Lithuanian government immediately turned to various of the great powers for advice. They were absorbed by the *Anschluss* events, and it was hard for them to see how Lithuania's interests would be harmed by an exchange of envoys with Poland. Their general counsel was that the Lithuanians ought to yield. It was widely, although incorrectly, assumed that the frontier incident was contrived and that Poland had created the situation with the blessing of Germany.

On the morning of March 19, Lithuania, isolated and frightened, capitulated to the Polish ultimatum. Diplomatic relations commenced within the month, the frontiers were opened, and various trade agreements were concluded. On the face of it, the event seemed to have been a distinct Polish diplomatic victory.

By the early summer of 1938, Czechoslovakia was clearly Hitler's next objective. "Case Green," the German code name for a surprise attack upon Czechoslovakia had been drawn up a year before, in June 1937, but Hitler had vetoed it as being too crude. He was not necessarily opposed to military action against Czechoslovakia, but he insisted that it be prefaced by a period of diplomatic activity and political tension which would confuse France and Britain.

Czechoslovakia was particularly vulnerable to political attack. No European nation possessed a minorities problem as acute as that of Czechoslovakia. Fifteen million persons lived in Czechoslovakia, but of these fewer than half were Czechs—the politically dominant nationality. There were two million Slovaks, a million Hungarians, a half million Ruthenians, a quarter million Poles in the Teschen region, and three and a quarter million "Sudeten Germans." These last were Austrians who had become Czechoslovakian citizens when the Sudetenland, a region mostly located in northern Bohemia, had been made part of Czechoslovakia upon its creation at the Peace Conference of Paris.

Beginning in 1935, the German government began secretly to subsidize the creation of a Nazi movement in the Sudetenland. This movement grew with great rapidity under the leadership of a physical education teacher named Konrad Henlein. Acting on the instructions of the German Foreign Office, Henlein whipped the Sudetenland Germans into a baleful sense of outrage against the Czech government. No grievance, however slight, went unprotested. No concession from Prague, and there were many, was sufficient. Every possible source of tension between Prague and the Sudeten Germans was fully exploited. The German *Anschluss* with Austria aggravated the situation because it gave Germany additional borders with Czechoslovakia, the bulk of which was now encompassed on three sides by German territory.

In May 1938, the Sudetenland question almost came to a crisis. Certain German troop concentrations on the Czechoslovak borders convinced Prague that an attack was imminent. The Czech army was partly mobilized. Britain and France were induced to give the strongest warnings to Berlin about the consequences of an invasion of Czechoslovakia. The Soviet Union, which had in 1935 concluded a pact of mutual assistance with Czechoslovakia, sent word to Prague that "if requested, the U.S.S.R. is prepared—in agreement with France and Czechoslovakia—to take all necessary measures relating to the security of Czechoslovakia. She disposes of all necessary means for doing so."[12]

Actually, the Czechs had been premature in their assessment of German intentions. The German troop movements on the Czech frontiers had only been the result of spring maneuvers. It was not Hitler's intention to invade Czechoslovakia at this time. His anti-Czech propaganda campaign was not completed. Considerable publicity remained to be released regarding alleged Czech atrocities against the Sudeten Germans. But Hitler could now foresee the date on which he would be ready to attack. On May 28, 1938, he convened a meeting of his military leaders and announced that it was his "unshakable will that Czechoslovakia shall be wiped off the map."[13] Hitler ordered that "Case Green" for the invasion of Czechoslovakia be revised and planning for its implementation begun. The date for the invasion was set as October 1, 1938. Word of Hitler's intentions was soon leaked out to the British and French by a disaffected German diplomat.

The French and British reaction to the May 1938 war scare had, however, proved significant. For the first time, Germany's probable opponents had shown a determined and more or less united attitude. Their stern warnings had frightened the leaders of the German Army, who believed that Hitler was courting disaster by accepting the risk that Britain and France might intervene to support the Czechs. For a time there was a good chance that the German generals might revolt against Hitler and, in fact, General Ludwig Beck, chief of the Army general staff, resigned his post. It now seems likely that had the French and British preserved their unanimity and had the Poles and Czechs made a common front, Czechoslovakia might have been saved. But, of course, this did not occur.

One reason why it did not was Józef Beck's conviction, inherited from Piłsudski, that Czechoslovakia was a hybrid state, which was bound to collapse at any moment of great tension. Twenty years of acrimony had precluded any Polish sympathy toward its menaced neighbor. In 1937, foreseeing the possibility of a Czech-German conflict, Poland had allowed its Treaty of Arbitration and Conciliation with Czechoslovakia to lapse. The Poles had refused to join in the May 1938 warnings to Hitler against invading Czechoslovakia. In fact, Poland and Rumania had let it be known that they would not permit Soviet troops to cross their soil to assist Czechoslovakia. This, of course, made valueless any Soviet assurance of aid, because the Red Army had no way to reach Czechoslovakia except through Poland or Rumania. In May 1938, at the height of the war scare between Germany and Czechoslovakia, Poland issued a note to the Prague government. It demanded that the Polish minority in Czechoslovakia be given the same benefits that might be awarded to the German minority in the Sudetenland. The Czechs accepted this demand on May 24.

On the face of it, the Polish demand was not excessive—or at least Warsaw did not regard it as such. Beck subsequently explained that "we demanded simply that, if the government of Prague decided to make concessions to other countries, our interests should be treated in exactly the same fashion."[14] The French government supported the Poles, and on June 11 the Polish ambassador to Paris reported that he had been officially advised that "the French government fully concurs with the position of the Polish government on the matter of the Polish minority in Czechoslovakia."[15]

As the fall of 1938 approached, and with it the date that Hitler was known to have set for his army to march, tension rose to an almost unendurable point. The determination of France and Britain now weakened. They were no longer prepared to give stern warnings to Berlin, and back them up, as they had done the previous May. The sequel to the whole affair is, of course, common knowledge. The French cabinet appealed to British Prime Minister Neville Chamberlain to intervene with Hitler and make some sort of deal. On September 15 Chamberlain flew to Munich and was taken by train to Berchtesgaden. After the customary harangue by Hitler, Chamberlain was told that the only way to avoid war was to have a plebiscite conducted in the Sudetenland and, following the expected outcome, the cession of the region to Germany. Would the British and French agree to this?

Chamberlain replied that he would attempt to gain the approval of both cabinets. He flew back to London, consulted with his associates and with the French. They decided that the Führer's demands must be agreed to and promptly put pressure on the Czechs to accept a plebiscite and eventual cession of the Sudetenland, which meant the loss of Czechoslovakia's entire fortification defenses against Germany. After being subjected to the most brutal form of diplomatic intimidation from France and Britain, the Czechs agreed. They had

already appealed to the Soviet Union for help, but were reminded by
Moscow that under the Czech-Soviet pact of 1935 the Russians were
obligated to come to Czechoslovakia's defense only if France did likewise. France was obviously not doing so, and consequently the Soviets
regarded themselves as absolved of responsibility. And, in fact, what
could they do? Poland and Rumania barred the way to Czechoslovakia. Chamberlain flew back to Germany on September 22 to inform Hitler that his demands would be met. The next day he met
with Hitler at Godesburg, where he was told that the Czech concessions were now not enough. It was too late for plebiscites and
negotiations. The entire Sudetenland must be occupied by German
troops within two days. Hitler handed over a map on which, marked
in red, was the area that he demanded to occupy without plebiscite
or further discussion. Chamberlain replied that this was an ultimatum, not negotiation, but he offered to return to London and see
what could be done. Hitler agreed to defer military action until
October 1 and made the promise that this was his last territorial
demand in Europe.

   In the following days it appeared almost certain that a world war
would break out. Hitler became frightened that he had overplayed
his hand, particularly since he had committed himself to march on
October 1. At the eleventh hour, the British induced Mussolini to
propose a meeting of France, Britain, Italy, and Germany to be held
in Munich on September 29 to resolve the crisis. Hitler jumped at
the opportunity. With Mussolini's backing, and without any significant protests from Chamberlain or the French Premier Édouard
Daladier, the Germans got all they wanted at Munich. The Czechs
were summoned in and instructed to hand over the Sudetenland to
Germany without delay. Additionally, the four powers at Munich
agreed that any claims that Hungary and Poland had against Czechoslovakia should be reserved for settlement at a later date.

   During all of the developments that led to Munich, Poland had
been active. Although denied any participation in the actual negotiation, the Poles had managed to keep themselves well informed.
The Poles were determined that they should obtain concessions from
Czechoslovakia identical to those extracted by the Germans. Polish
demands upon the Czechs had kept careful pace with the constantly
escalating demands of the Germans. On September 21, having learned
of the Czech concessions that Chamberlain would present to Hitler
on the following day at Godesburg, the Poles handed the Czechs a

note demanding that the Prague government also make concessions "immediately and similar to those which the Czechoslovakian government has made in regard to its German [minorities] problem."[16] In other words, if the Czechs were ceding their German-inhabited territory to Germany, the Poles demanded a similar cession of the Polish-inhabited regions. Simultaneously, the Warsaw newspapers announced that the Polish Army had moved six divisions of troops close to the Teschen border.

The desperate Czechs, who at that time believed themselves about to be attacked by Germany, answered the Poles evasively on September 25. Warsaw responded with an even stronger note on September 27, virtually demanding "the immediate ceding [to Poland] of the territory inhabited by a Polish majority."[17]

While this exchange of notes was taking place, the Poles were subjected to a certain amount of diplomatic pressure from France and Britain, who had been asked by the Czechs to intervene on their behalf. The French and British ambassadors in Warsaw handed Beck a joint note from their governments urging Poland to negotiate its differences with Czechoslovakia and cautioning the Poles against any military action. The French approached Rydz-Śmigły with the reminder that in 1936 he had promised that he would never use the Polish army to attack the Czechs. But the Franco-British pressure on the Poles was never intense. They were distracted by the larger problems of Munich. In the end the British advised the Czechs "to abandon without delay all diplomatic maneuvering"[18] and simply agree to give up any of its territory which was inhabited by a Polish majority. Soviet Russia, again appealed to by Prague, was a little more helpful. On September 23 the Polish envoy in Moscow was given a note stating that the Soviet government regarded the Polish troop movements reported in the Warsaw press as "alarming." The Soviets threatened to repudiate their nonaggression treaty with Poland. Warsaw instantly responded that Polish troop movements were Poland's "exclusive concern" about which it was not obliged "to give explanations to anyone."[19] The Soviets let the matter rest there.

The Munich conference was now underway, and the Poles felt obliged not to be left behind. The British ambassador to Warsaw had informed the Polish foreign ministry that he had seen a copy of the map that Hitler had given Chamberlain (on September 23) and that indicated his territorial demands on Czechoslovakia. Within the region that Hitler demanded was the important railway junction city of Bohumin (in German, "Oderberg"). This city was at the northwest corner of the Duchy of Teschen, and the Poles regarded it as of crucial economic importance to the duchy. Beck believed that he must act rapidly to forestall the German occupation of the city. At noon on September 30 Poland gave an ultimatum to the Czech government. It demanded the immediate evacuation of Czech troops and police from Teschen and its environs and gave Prague until noon the following day to evacuate the region. At 11:45 A.M. on October 1 the Czech foreign ministry telephoned the Polish ambassador in Prague and told him that Poland could have what it wanted. The Polish Army occupied the region at once.

The Germans were delighted with this outcome. Intoxicated by the enormous triumph of the Sudetenland seizure, they were happy to give up a provincial rail center to the Poles. It was a small sacrifice indeed, compared to the advantage of having another nation share in the obloquy of the dismemberment of Czechoslovakia. It spread the blame and confused the issue; Poland was accused of being an accomplice of Germany—a charge that Warsaw was hard put to deny. Göring made a point of congratulating the Polish ambassador on "a very bold action performed in excellent style."[20] The Polish press was unanimous in its support of the government's action. Amid the general euphoria in Poland—the acquisition of Teschen was a very popular development—no one paid much attention to the bitter comment of the Czech general who handed the region over to the incoming Poles. He predicted that it would not be long before the Poles would themselves be handing Teschen over to the Germans.

Regarding the Polish action against the Czechs, and Colonel Beck who directed it, it has been rightly observed that "this was not the Colonel's finest hour."[21] Beck subsequently professed not to understand why Poland was regarded by Western diplomats as having given "an undignified imitation of the small fish that seek their meat in the wake of a shark."[22] After all, he protested, Poland would never actually have gone to war with Czechoslovakia over Teschen. In fact, had the Czechs stood firm against the Germans (and drawn in the French and British), the Poles would probably have gone to war with Germany. Perhaps this is true—but the Czechs didn't know it.

About the best that can be said for Beck at this juncture is that he was consistent. Like Piłsudski, he had always predicted that Czechoslovakia would collapse in a moment of great pressure—and it did.

But Beck himself had done much to bring his prophecy to fulfillment. He had always opposed "four power directorates," such as the one that convened at Munich. He had always held that Poland must signal its displeasure whenever it was snubbed by the great powers of Europe by means of some sharp, direct action. In wresting Teschen from the Czechs, Beck had done this. He had always made a riposte to any unwelcome German thrust. In demanding Bohumin from the Germans, Beck had shown that he had not deviated from his previous policy.

But what had been gained by this Polish consistency? Only a few hundred square miles of territory and 230,000 persons (of whom about 80,000 were Poles). By the Munich Pact, however, the Germans gained about 10,000 square miles, three and a half million persons, and the entire Czech fortification system. Soon they would have even more of Czechoslovakia and would then encompass Poland on the north, south, and west.

Unquestionably the Munich Pact was as significant a defeat for Poland as it was for France and Britain. And for all these nations there were still more humiliations to come out of the Czech crisis. Poland experienced them earlier than others in the German sabotage of Beck's "Third Europe" scheme. This was a grandiose project that the Polish Foreign Minister had contemplated for years. In essence, it consisted of putting together an alliance of East Central European nations stretching from the Baltic southward deep into the Balkans. If this could be developed—under Polish leadership—these states might find collective safety against Hitlerite Germany and Soviet Russia.

Nothing had ever come of this elaborate scheme, because in the past neither Lithuania nor Czechoslovakia would join Poland's "Third Europe." But now, in the fall of 1938, it seemed to Beck that the time was more favorable. Lithuania had been coerced into diplomatic relations with Poland, and Czechoslovakia seemed about to disintegrate. To get the plan moving all that was required was to put together a coalition of Rumania, Hungary and Poland. But although both Rumania and Hungary were historically friendly to Poland, they were historic enemies of each other. In addition, Poland had no common frontier with Hungary, a condition that was thought strategically necessary for the plan to function.

In the aftermath of Munich, Beck quickly developed a scheme to overcome these obstacles. The first step was to convince the Slovaks that they should secede from Czechoslovakia and form an independent nation under the protection of Poland and Hungary. Once this was done, then Ruthenia, a region in the extreme eastern part of Czechoslovakia, would be detached and awarded to Hungary, thus giving Poland and Hungary a common frontier. Naturally, neither the Czech government nor the inhabitants of Ruthenia were consulted about this plan. The Germans were given an inkling of it, but were told that the "Third Europe" was just an anti-Bolshevik alliance.

The whole scheme collapsed almost as soon as it was proposed. The Rumanians declared that they wanted nothing to do with enlarging Hungary. The Slovaks settled for autonomy within a Czechoslovak federation instead of opting for outright independence. Then the Germans stepped in. It did not suit them to have the Poles enjoy a common border with Hungary—not just now at any rate. So on November 1, 1938, the Italian and German foreign ministers, Galeazzo Ciano and Joachim von Ribbentrop met in Vienna. Germany and Italy had been asked by Hungary to act as the arbitrators of its claims on Slovakian territory. The Germans and Italians were happy to oblige. They cut an enormous slice out of southern Slovakia and simply gave it to Hungary, an act known as the "Vienna Award." The hapless Czechs could not resist. Hungary, satisfied by this German beneficence, promptly lost all interest in "Third Europe." Beck's whole scheme fell apart, and Polish foreign policy had to be redirected toward the maintenance of the now traditional goal of equilibrium between Germany and Soviet Russia.

As has previously been recounted, relations between Poland and Soviet Russia had cooled markedly during the years before Munich. The Russians had been suspicious of Warsaw's involvement with Germany; and the Poles had been too preoccupied with German matters to pay sufficient attention to Moscow. But now, in the immediate aftermath of Munich, fear of Germany drew the two nations closer together.

In October 1938, the Polish ambassador in Moscow indicated that his government would like to establish closer ties with Soviet Russia. He was granted an interview with Soviet Foreign Minister Litvinov for fuller discussion. A number of irritants had recently crept into Russo-Polish relationships. Among them was the Soviet government's destruction of an old Polish military cemetery in Kiev, the canceling of some railroad service between the two nations, and miscellaneous frontier incidents. It was quickly agreed that these should all be rectified or forgotten. The Poles proposed a sizable increase in trade between the two nations, so that both would be less dependent upon Germany. The Russians agreed and also proposed a joint declaration of the changes in Russo-Polish relations. The Poles were in accord, and on November 26 the two governments announced their plans for increasing mutual trade and "disposing" of frontier incidents. They pledged that relations between the two nations "are and will continue to be based to the fullest extent on all existing Agreements, including the Polish-Soviet Pact of Non-Aggression."[23]

This declaration, as bland as it seems, was not without importance in the climate of the times. In fact, while the Russo-Polish talks were going on in Moscow, the Poles were being presented with German pressure of a type that they had not previously experienced.

In the late fall of 1938 no one knew where Hitler would turn next. It was hoped that he might be satiated by the Sudetenland seizure. He had, after all, made the positive promise that this was his "last territorial claim." But it was widely feared that this would not be enough.

As a matter of fact, at this period even Hitler was not certain what his next move should be–apart from the eventual seizure of what remained of Czechoslovakia, which was regarded by him as a foregone conclusion. At present he was willing that Poland should survive as a nation and that Germany should maintain tolerable relations with it. But Hitler did not intend that this state of affairs should continue indefinitely. Eventually Poland was to be isolated and reduced to the position of a vassal state. Work began at once on this project. On October 24, 1938, the Polish ambassador to Germany, Józef Lipski, was asked to meet Ribbentrop for luncheon in a private room at the Grand Hotel at Berchtesgaden.

The luncheon lasted for nearly three hours. Although a German Foreign Office memorandum describes the meeting as taking place "in a very friendly atmosphere,"[24] it is doubtful that Lipski found the luncheon pleasant. After certain preliminaries, Ribbentrop suddenly announced that he had proposals for "a general settlement of issues between Poland and Germany."[25] In brief, Ribbentrop's proposals included the return of Danzig to Germany and an agreement by Poland that an extraterritorial highway and railroad, both subject to joint German-Polish control, should be built across the Polish

Corridor to connect Germany with East Prussia. (The highway project had been casually suggested by the Germans at various times since 1935, but always previously in such a manner that it was easy for the Poles to ignore it.) In return for these Polish concessions, the Germans would extend the Polish-German Nonaggression Treaty for twenty-five years (it was due to expire in 1944) and Germany would guarantee Poland's present borders. Ribbentrop also indicated to Lipski that Poland would be expected to join the Anti-Comintern Pact. He told Lipski that he would like to discuss these matters with Beck personally, and with that the Polish ambassador was dismissed.

A half-hour later Lipski was summoned back to the Grand Hotel. Ribbentrop had had an afterthought. If the Poles were seriously interested in having a common frontier with Hungary, then Germany would agree to the detachment of Ruthenia from Czechoslovakia and its annexation by Hungary. But this approval was contingent upon Poland's meeting the other German demands. Ribbentrop was genial now. He encouraged Lipski to report the German proposals to Beck in confidence. Expansive and reassuring, Ribbentrop told the Poles to take their time with their answer. These were important issues, and the Poles should not be overhasty in making their decisions.

No one had to tell Lipski of the gravity of these German proposals. He was an experienced diplomat. In these times, no European nation could fail to be attentive, and alarmed, by any sudden German proposal for a "general settlement of issues." Lipski immediately got on a train for Warsaw to seek instructions.

On October 31 Beck prepared for Lipski a detailed memorandum on the matter. In essence it rejected the turnover of Danzig to Germany and said that any German "attempt to incorporate the Free City into the Reich must inevitably lead to a conflict"[26] that would not be localized. No mention was made of the proposed extraterritorial highway and railroad across the Polish Corridor or of Polish membership in the Anti-Comintern Pact. Beck, however, did state that he was willing to have personal discussions with Ribbentrop. Lipski returned to Berlin on November 1 and immediately indicated his availability for discussions with the German Foreign Minister.

It was not until November 19 that Lipski was given an audience with Ribbentrop. The Germans had had considerable experience in the intimidation of smaller adjacent nations and were letting the

Poles stew for a while—a technique that had proved rewarding in the past.

Lipski read Beck's memorandum to Ribbentrop. The German Foreign Minister listened attentively and answered in a conciliatory tone. He claimed that the idea of Danzig's restoration to Germany had been his own, not Hitler's—a statement that was patently untrue and said that he "would gladly have a talk [with Beck]."[27] Lipski returned to Warsaw to report.

A few weeks passed, and the Poles became anxious. They were acutely conscious of the fact that they had not responded directly to the German proposals of October 24. Observation had shown them that this was dangerous when dealing with Hitlerite Germany. After considerable discussion, it was decided to extend an invitation to Ribbentrop to visit Warsaw toward the end of January. Ribbentrop accepted, but it was indicated that a preliminary meeting between Beck and Hitler himself might be in order. Since Beck would be passing through Germany after a Christmas vacation at Monte Carlo, it was agreed that he would meet with Hitler at Berchtesgaden on January 5 and with Ribbentrop in Munich on the following day.

There was nothing overtly new in these conversations. The Germans presented no additional requests. Hitler was almost genial. He opened his talk with Beck by inviting the Polish Foreign Minister to ask any questions he had regarding German policies. If he had any, Hitler was at his service to reply to them. Beck, of course, inquired about the matters that Ribbentrop had brought up with Lipski—the construction of a highway and railroad between East Prussia and Germany; the restoration of Danzig to Germany; and Polish commitment to the Anti-Comintern Pact. The Führer spoke at length on this last point. He emphasized the Russian menace and assured Beck that "a strong Poland was absolutely necessary for Germany . . . every Polish division engaged against Russia was a corresponding saving of a German division."[28]

The talk turned to Danzig. Hitler emphasized that Danzig "was a German city [and] sooner or later it must return to the Reich."[29] Beck indicated that this was an extremely difficult problem, for which he could not imagine any solution. Hitler replied that it would be necessary to try something "quite new." Just what this would be was left unsaid, except that Hitler promised there would be no German *fait accompli* in Danzig.

The meeting ended in an atmosphere of general cordiality. Hitler had made no threats nor had he pressed for immediate Polish replies to the German requests. He had even promised that there would be no unilateral German action against Danzig. Despite all this there was an undertone to the interview that alarmed Beck. It was evident to him that the Germans were offering an anti-Bolshevik alliance in an attempt to draw Poland into a satellite status. Beck had no intention of permitting this to happen, and he was concerned about the German reaction when Polish refusal of the German offer eventually became clear. At his meeting with Ribbentrop the next day, Beck was quite frank. So was Ribbentrop. The German Foreign Minister pressed for definite answers to the various German requests. Beck was evasive regarding these demands but was otherwise candid. He said that whereas in the past every meeting he had had with German officials had left him feeling optimistic, he was now, for the first time, pessimistic. There was nothing theatrical about this declaration. Just as soon as he returned to Warsaw, Beck says in his memoirs, "I considered it my duty to warn the President of the Republic and Marshal Rydz-Śmigły of these alarming symptoms, which could result in war."[30]

Ribbentrop's official visit to Warsaw took place on January 25–27, 1939. Although every effort was made by the Poles to make things go off pleasantly, it was obviously an occasion that required much plain speaking. Ribbentrop had interviews with President Mościcki and Marshal Rydz-Śmigły that were mainly devoted to pleasantries and generalities. His talks with Beck were much more specific. Ribbentrop was made to understand that Poland would not join the Anti-Comintern Pact, would not permit an extraterritorial highway to be constructed across the Corridor, and would not give up any of its Danzig rights without some sort of major and positive German compensation. Beck warned Ribbentrop, if any warning was necessary, that the German Foreign Minister should not report to Hitler on his visit to Warsaw in "too optimistic a light."[31]

The official communiqué regarding Ribbentrop's Warsaw visit reported the customary "atmosphere of friendly understanding,"[32] but this was only window dressing. From this point on the Germans understood that Poland would not become their satellite and would not join them in any undertaking directed at Soviet Russia.

By the early spring of 1939, significant events in Europe were occurring with staggering multiplicity and speed. On March 14 aged and senile President Emil Hácha of Czecho-Slovakia, the successor to Beneš, who had resigned the previous October, arrived in Berlin at Hitler's invitation. At 1:15 A.M. on March 15 he was conducted into the Führer's presence. By five minutes to four, Hácha had been terrorized, humiliated, abused, had physically collapsed (and been revived by Hitler's physician), and had then signed a document requesting that the Czech section of Czecho-Slovakia—Bohemia and Moravia—become a German "protectorate." Within two hours, German troops marched into this region and occupied it without resistance. That night Hitler himself made his own triumphal entrance into Prague. The next day he announced German recognition of an independent Slovakia detached from the Czech nation and proclaimed a German protectorate over this state. Hungary was permitted to occupy Ruthenia, the easternmost of the old Czecho-Slovak provinces.

Although the Poles welcomed the fact that the Hungarian seizure of Ruthenia now gave them a common border with a presumed ally, it was very difficult to put a good face on the German seizure of Czecho-Slovakia. The German Army now controlled lands that bordered Poland on three sides. And particularly ominous was the fact that, despite Poland's historic interest in Slovakia, Hitler had not troubled to inform Warsaw in advance of his planned takeover.

It was obvious that Germany no longer cared much about Polish sensitivities. In Danzig German university students were harassing Polish students. Signs reading "Entrance is forbidden to dogs and Polish students" began to appear in Danzig cafés. The German government had always been able to control this sort of thing in the past, but it seemed that it no longer cared to do so. Fights broke out, and there were counterdemonstrations by Poles against German students in Poznań, Lwów and Kraków.

On March 21 Ribbentrop summoned Polish Ambassador Lipski to the German Foreign Office. In a curt and abrasive tone he reminded Lipski that Poland had never favored the German government with a formal and definite answer to Germany's questions of some months before regarding an extraterritorial highway across the Corridor and the return of Danzig to Germany. Ribbentrop also recited a long litany of German complaints, new and old, against

Poland. He pointed out a number of past evidences of alleged German favors toward Poland and stated that Hitler had begun to question the sincerity of Poland's friendship. Ribbentrop warned that Hitler might "come to the conclusion that Poland was rejecting all his offers."[33]

Lipski responded by reminding the German Foreign Minister of Poland's acquiescence at the times of the *Anschluss* and the Sudetenland crisis and generally rebutting the German complaints. In conclusion, he asked about German intentions toward Lithuania. Since the previous year Poland had regarded Lithuania as definitely within its sphere of influence, but now rumors had begun to float that Germany intended to seize the Lithuanian seaport of Memel. More precisely, it was said that the Germans intended to retake Memel, which Lithuania had seized in 1923. Lipski said that the Poles were very much concerned over the rumors of possible German action against Memel, Lithuania's only seaport. Ribbentrop grew evasive and replied only that the Memel matter "called for a solution."[34] With this, Lipski was dismissed.

Actually, the German "solution" to the Memel problem was practically at hand. Following a technique that had by now become classic, the Germanic inhabitants of Memel had been organized into a strident group that demanded the city's return to the Fatherland. On March 21, the very day that Ribbentrop was avoiding discussion of Memel with Lipski, the German Foreign Office had, by ultimatum, notified the Lithuanian government that it must send ministers plenipotentiary to Berlin by special airplane on the following day. When these dignitaries arrived they were routinely intimidated by German officials, and the immediate cession of Memel was demanded. This procedure was, by now, so practiced that it could be left to Hitler's subordinates. In fact, the Führer was already aboard the battleship *Deutschland* steaming toward Memel. By 1:30 A.M. on March 23, the Lithuanians had capitulated, the German Navy had entered the Memel harbor, and Hitler had disembarked to survey his latest seizure.

The Polish response was the partial mobilization of its army, which began on March 23. Traditionally an announcement by a European nation of the mobilization of its army had been regarded as the ultimate provocation or threat by its neighbors. To prevent this, the Poles had developed a scheme for secret mobilization. Instead of the usual announcements by press, radio and placards, the Polish Army had prepared envelopes addressed to a great many of the Army's reservists. When it was decided to mobilize secretly, a printed card stating where and when the reservist was to report to his mobilized unit was simply put into the envelope bearing his name. The envelopes were delivered as routine letters by the Polish postal service. The press was forbidden to discuss the mobilization, and indeed the reservists themselves were warned against any comment.

This secret mobilization system was expensive and imperfect and was used to mobilize only the cavalry brigades and certain infantry divisions on the frontiers. But it more than doubled the size of the active Polish army, and it had the advantage of leaving the Germans in the dark as to how many reservists had actually been called up. It was not until March 25 that German intelligence noted the partial Polish mobilization, and even then they believed that the call-up was confined to a few divisions in the north and was limited to parts of three age groups.

The German capture of Memel dealt a final blow to Polish hopes for a negotiated diplomatic settlement with Germany. The Memel event told Colonel Beck that there was no acceptable way for Poland to placate or appease Germany. It was clear that Hitler planned to convert Poland into a German dependency or, failing this, to invade Poland. Realizing this, Beck began to display a stature far more impressive than that he had previously shown. In the past he may have been devious, evasive, too cunning, or overly persistent in pursuing outdated tactics. But now, he became straightforward, resourceful and extremely determined.

On March 24 Beck convened a meeting of senior Polish diplomatic officials at the Foreign Ministry in Warsaw. It was apparent that the events of the past ten days had shaken them. Lipski, the Polish ambassador to Germany, had offered to resign his post in the hope that someone else could deal more successfully with the Germans. Beck had refused Lipski's resignation, but it was obvious that all of Poland's senior diplomats needed guidance and assurance. Beck gave it to them. He opened the meeting by conceding that the present situation was extremely serious and that it was complicated by Hitler's unpredictability. "Germany has lost its calculability," he said. Hitler had become unbalanced by his stunning successes—"the mighty have been humble to him, the weak have capitulated in advance." But Poland would not be among the nations that gave up their inde-

pendence without a struggle. "We will fight," Beck assured his
listeners. Poland had drawn a line. It would give up none of its
territory and none of its rights at Danzig. It would not "join that
category of eastern states that allow rules to be dictated to them."
Poland would not capitulate—it would go to war first. Beck encouraged those present to behave in a manner commensurate with
Poland's determination. They should express their firm resolve to
their subordinates. Beck was not overly pessimistic. They might well
find that everything would turn out all right. "We have arrived at
this difficult moment in our politics with all the trump cards in our
hand. This does not speak too badly for us," he claimed. "On this
basis we shall start our international action."[35] At that moment it
was not clear what Beck meant by "trump cards," but it would
within a week.

The historic policy of Great Britain toward Continental nations
was one of strict noninvolvement. For generations, Britain's policy
had been to retain for itself the role of mediator or makeweight
between contending European states. It was always unencumbered
and free to act as served its best interests in any given situation. This
policy was historic, invariable, and well known and understood by
every European government.

It was therefore astonishing when, at 3 P.M. on March 31, 1939,
Prime Minister Neville Chamberlain rose in the House of Commons
to inform the British Parliament that his government had decided
that

> in the event of any action which clearly threatened Polish independ-
> ence, and which the Polish government accordingly considered it vital
> to resist with their national forces, His Majesty's Government would
> feel themselves bound at once to lend the Polish Government all sup-
> port in their power. They have given the Polish Government an
> assurance to this effect.
>
> I may add that the French Government have authorized me to make
> it plain that they stand in the same position in this matter as do His
> Majesty's Government.[36]

There was nothing casual or spontaneous in this guarantee. Every
single word, with all its implications and ramifications, had been

studied at great length by the British Foreign Office and the full cabinet. This enormously broad guarantee virtually left to the Poles the decision whether or not Britain would go to war. For Britain to give such a blank check to a Central European nation, particularly to Poland—a nation that Britain had generally regarded as irresponsible and greedy—was mind-boggling.

There were, of course, important reasons for this awesome British departure from its historic policy. One was that Adolf Hitler had overplayed his hand. The German seizure of Bohemia and Moravia was his first major miscalculation in international affairs. Hitler had thought that the British, having caved in so easily in the Sudetenland matter, would as readily acquiesce to a German takeover of the balance of the Czech lands. Hitler, not being himself a gentleman, could not understand the reaction of a British gentleman, Neville Chamberlain, to the German seizure. Chamberlain's government regarded itself as having guaranteed Czech independence. The Führer had promised Chamberlain that the Sudetenland was his "last territorial claim," the "last problem to be solved"; he had even said that "we don't want any more Czechs."[37] Chamberlain had actually believed him. Now he felt that he had been made the fool and nothing could induce Chamberlain to trust Adolf Hitler again.

From mid-March of 1939 onward the British government believed that it had analyzed the purpose and technique of Hitler's foreign policy. The German objective was the domination of Europe, and the German tactic was to penetrate a smaller nation, confuse the major powers with a propaganda effort designed to convince them that the present German objective was not worth fighting for, and then gobble up the terrified prey. With this realization, British policy abruptly hardened. Britain still longed for peace, but the Chamberlain cabinet decided that the only way to obtain it was to risk war. Although no one knew what Hitler's next move would be, all indications led the British to conclude that the Germans would proceed to the south or east. Poland and Rumania appeared to be the likely German targets. The new British policy was to give the broadest guarantees to the threatened nations to prevent their being terrorized, subverted, and gobbled up by Germany.

On March 24 the Polish ambassador to Great Britain, Count Edward Raczyński, had called on British Foreign Secretary Lord Halifax. Acting on the instructions of his government, Raczyński proposed a "confidential bilateral understanding" between Poland and Great Britain. The Poles had in mind a simple agreement that the two nations would consult with one another in the event of some new threat from Germany. To the surprise of the Poles the British agreed and then went much further, with their spectacular guarantee of March 31. They also invited Colonel Beck to come to London immediately in order to formalize the British unilateral guarantee into an alliance in which the Poles would undertake to come to Britain's assistance under the same terms as Britain had committed itself to Poland.

On April 2, Beck set out on his journey. His train stopped briefly in Berlin, where Ambassador Lipski came on board to consult with him. Lipski cautioned Beck that relations between Poland and Germany were deteriorating rapidly. The previous week, on March 26, Lipski had given Ribbentrop the Polish reply to the German demands of March 21. Although it offered to negotiate to improve transit facilities across the Corridor, Poland completely rejected the concept of an extraterritorial highway, and its position regarding Danzig remained unaltered. Lipski had been given what he had described in his report as "a distinctly cold reception" by Ribbentrop, and this important interview had not gone well. The Germans showed no interest at all in any further discussion. Ribbentrop warned that Hitler "might come to the conclusion that it is impossible to reach an understanding with Poland."[38] A British-Polish mutual alliance coming on top of this would certainly make things more critical. Lipski warned Beck that the Germans might well use it as an excuse to abrogate the German-Polish Nonaggression Declaration of 1934.

Beck's visit to London was reasonably successful. Certainly it was more successful than his previous visit in 1936. Beck was not a good drinker, and he had been very tired at that time. As his ambassador in London had noted, "The few glasses he had to drink made him arrogant and aggressive."[39] There was none of this behavior now, although the British Foreign Office found Beck a tough negotiator. It had been hoped that Poland would participate in a large anti-German coalition that France and Britain would put together. It would include Soviet Russia, Rumania, Hungary, and perhaps Greece and Turkey. Beck flatly refused. Poland would gladly accept the British guarantee and, in turn and at some risk to itself, would make the guarantee reciprocal. But Beck was interested only in a defensive alliance with the British. Poland would not join an anti-German coalition—especially one that included Soviet Russia. The British had to be satisfied with the reciprocal guarantee—and generally they were. Lord Halifax told the cabinet that, although the talks with Beck had not been unsatisfactory, "they had not turned out quite as we had expected."[40]

In the end, Beck and Halifax agreed to issue a communiqué that announced that they were in the process of drafting a treaty of defensive alliance. (The Treaty was signed on August 25, 1939, and in the interim, both nations regarded themselves as being bound reciprocally under the terms of the British guarantee of March 31.)

It was tacitly understood by both parties that this announcement would invite some sort of German retaliation. The British even thought that Germany might invade Poland at once. Winston Churchill was a guest at a Foreign Office luncheon for Beck. He asked, "Will you get back all right in your special train through Germany to Poland?" Beck was optimistic and replied, "I think that we shall have time for that."[41]

In fact, the Germans were not prepared for an invasion of Poland. It was not until April 6, three days after Beck arrived in London, that secret instructions were issued to the German armed forces to prepare for the invasion of Poland. The operation was given the code name "Case White," and its objectives were the destruction of Polish military strength and the occupation of Poland and Danzig. Preparations were to be made so that the operation could be carried out at any time after September 1, 1939.

On April 28, Hitler appeared before the Reichstag to deliver a speech which was broadcast throughout the world. In turn he denounced President Roosevelt for meddling in European affairs. (Roosevelt had issued a "peace appeal" to Hitler and Mussolini several weeks before.) Hitler next attacked Great Britain for its "policy of encirclement" and announced that Germany would no longer be bound by the Anglo-German Naval Treaty of 1935. He then moved on to discuss Poland. Hitler began with an analysis of the events that had led to the German-Polish Declaration of Non-aggression of 1934. But, subsequently, he claimed, problems had arisen. Portraying himself as the world's most reasonable statesman, Hitler described the necessity of reaching agreement with Poland regarding an extraterritorial highway across the Corridor and the return of Danzig to Germany. In return for these concessions Hitler

listed a series of pacts and guarantees that he said he had offered to
the Poles. But the Poles had displayed an "incomprehensible attitude" and had refused these generous German offers. Moreover, they
had partly mobilized their army and had concluded a mutual assistance pact with Britain. To roars of approval, Hitler pronounced
the German-Polish Declaration of Nonaggression to have "been unilaterally infringed by Poland and thereby no longer in existence!"[42]

Hitler's announcement was not unexpected by the Poles. As early
as April 6, Ambassador Lipski had been summoned to the German
Foreign Office, where he had been told that the German "offers" for
a settlement of outstanding differences had been withdrawn.

The Poles, of course, gave the most detailed study to Hitler's
speech, and to a German note that had been received at Warsaw on
the same day. Their conclusion was that this was just the opening
salvo of a German campaign to isolate Poland and, eventually, destroy its alliances. The Germans had indicated that notwithstanding
their abrogation of the nonaggression declaration, they were still
open to negotiation. The Poles generally viewed this as an effort to
frighten them into a split with the British and French. They refused
to be intimidated or terrorized. Beck replied to the Germans with
a courageous speech on May 5 before the Polish parliament. He rejected Hitler's contention that Poland was the unreasonable partner
in their negotiation. Why, Beck asked, should Poland be asked to
give up its rights in Danzig and to open an extraterritorial highway
across its Corridor? These rights and lands were legally Poland's.
And what was Poland being offered in exchange for these proposed
cessions? Only some airy assurances from Adolf Hitler, including his
"recognition" of Polish frontiers. It would indeed be a weak nation
that felt these promises to be any sort of compensation. Poland regarded its frontiers as indisputably settled. It required no German
assurances, and it would defend its frontiers if need be. "Peace is a
valuable and desirable thing," Beck concluded. "But peace, like
almost everything in this world, has its price, high but definable.
We in Poland do not recognize the conception of peace at any price.
There is only one thing in the life of men, nations and states that is
without price, and this is honor."[43]

There was not the slightest doubt that Beck meant what he said.
The entire Polish parliament cheered him, and the Polish press
endorsed his statements. The speech had been reported in detail by
the foreign press, and it was widely praised by Poland's allies. Even

in Paris, where Beck was unpopular, the Polish ambassador spent an entire day taking telephone calls from French ministers, senators, deputies, and the press, all congratulating him on Beck's speech.

By the late spring of 1939 practically all diplomatic negotiation between Poland and Germany had come to a halt. Unlike any of the other nations that had been the target of German intimidation, Poland simply refused to be frightened. For a nation that had suffered from war so much and so recently in its history, Poland displayed a remarkable *sang-froid* in the face of war. Of course, as events were to prove, they were distinctly overconfident. The Poles believed themselves to be militarily stronger than they actually were. And they believed the Germans to be weaker than they proved to be. There is little question that the Poles underestimated the quality and sophistication of German armaments and overestimated the effectiveness of an infantryman armed only with a bolt-action rifle and a capacity for suffering. This simple combination had stood them well in the past—and they saw no reason to doubt it now.

For many months the Polish government had foreseen the probability of war with Germany. Naturally, they regretted this and were apprehensive. But they were not terrified. If war came, the Poles anticipated that Germany would be able to thrust its army deep into Poland, but that France and Britain would quickly join the conflict. The war would become general. Only the Soviet Union, exhausted by its purges and distracted by its undeclared war in the east with Japan, would stand aside. The Polish government expected that its army would be forced slowly into the southeast quadrant of the nation, where it might eventually be overrun, but more probably would be able to hold on. Supplies from France and Britain would reach the Polish defenders through friendly Rumania, or perhaps even through the Soviet Union which, although neutral, would be glad to assist any enemy of Germany.

In the end, the Poles believed the combination of their forces and those of Britain and France, would prevail. To be sure, the Poles expected to experience awful losses and terrible suffering. But their grateful allies would admire the courageous Polish resistance that would contribute greatly to the eventual victory. France and Britain would see to it that Poland was restored, compensated and honored. They would take steps to ensure that Germany would never again become a menace to them or to any other nation. Poland would probably become larger, stronger and more durable as the Allies made it a sort of warden of the eastern marches. From defeat would come victory. These were the Polish hopes as the fall of 1939 approached.

With the outbreak of war believed imminent, the Poles bent every effort to improving the last-minute readiness of their armed forces and to working out exact war plans with their allies. In particular, Poland was anxious to obtain the strongest possible commitment of French support during the first days of warfare. It was thought that the war would begin with a concentration of the German Army in the east followed by an invasion of Poland. To field a force large enough to overwhelm Poland before French mobilization was complete, the Germans would be forced to leave their western frontier with France temporarily undermanned. Poland hoped that British and French assistance would enable it to withstand the larger German army. A rapid and forceful French attack on the weakened German western front, combined with strong bombing attacks by the French and British air forces, was expected to draw a lot of the pressure off Poland.

To present this plan, and to obtain categoric acceptance of it by the French, the Polish government sent its Minister of War, General Tadeusz Kasprzycki, to Paris in mid-May. The French General Staff offered no objection to the Polish plan, and within three days, Kasprzycki had signed a formal agreement with the French General Staff that, on the outbreak of war between Germany and Poland, the French would immediately undertake air action against Germany. It was also agreed that on the third day of French mobilization its army would launch a local diversionary offensive into German territory, which would be followed by a major military offensive of the full French army to take place no later than fifteen days after mobilization.

Military negotiation with the British seemed equally straightforward and took the form of a visit to Warsaw in July by British General Sir Edmund Ironside and a small staff. There was, of course, not very much that the British could offer to do for the Poles upon the outbreak of war. In fact, Ironside made it clear that the Royal Navy would not attempt to contest control of the Baltic. The small Polish navy would have to flee to British waters as soon as war began.

On the other hand, the British had promised to make bomber attacks on Germany in the early days of the war, and Ironside was optimistic regarding the result to be expected from this offensive. He implied that the RAF could do a lot to tie down the German forces. Ironside did not even exclude the possibility of British infantry fighting on the Polish front. The Imperial War Plan called for the concentration of sixty battalions of troops in Egypt. "Perhaps they would join you over the Black Sea," Ironside told the Poles.[44]

One important nation had been excluded from all the conferences, alliances, treaties and understandings that had been exchanged among the European states that felt themselves menaced by Germany. That was Soviet Russia. There were a number of reasons why the British, who were now virtually directing the affairs of the embryonic anti-German alliance, had not chosen to approach the Soviet government. One, of course, was that they believed Moscow already to be safely in their bag. The ideological conflict between Communism and Fascism was considered so fundamental that the British were convinced that the Soviets must inevitably be on their side when it came to war. At worst, Russia would be neutral. A second reason was uncertainty about what a formal treaty should demand of the Russians in the event of war with Germany. At no point did Germany make geographical contact with the Soviet Union. The only way that Russia could assist in any military alliance was for the Red Army to cross into Poland, Rumania, or the Baltic States. But these nations, especially Poland, had made it very clear that they absolutely refused to have the Red Army on their soil. They did not know what they feared most—a German attack or a Soviet rescue. They made it known to the British, and the French as well, that if the Red Army came to their "rescue" they would fight it off. They were certain that the Soviets, once established on their soil, would never leave. This was, indeed, a most formidable obstacle to the negotiation of an alliance with Russia.

Finally, the British government itself was beset with a profound anti-Soviet bias. The Foreign Secretary, Lord Halifax, believed that negotiating with the Russians simply "meant our acquiescing in Soviet blackmail and bluff."[45] Prime Minister Neville Chamberlain found such negotiation even more distasteful. A close friend observed that Chamberlain was "a man of prejudices which were not easily eradicated . . . [his] instinctive contempt for the Americans was matched by what amounted to a hatred of the Russians. . . . He was, in a sense, a man of one-track mind."[46]

Despite all of these problems, the prospect of concluding an anti-fascist alliance with Soviet Russia had so many obvious advantages that the British government was compelled to give it constant consideration. An alliance between France, Britain, Poland and Soviet Russia would obviously present Hitler with an enormous accumulation of deterrent forces. It might very well prevent the outbreak of war. So when, in April 1939, the Soviet government proposed a series of conversations in Moscow between British Ambassador Sir William Seeds and Soviet Foreign Commissar Litvinov, the British agreed. Talks began on April 15, and, to the intense surprise of the British, the very next day Litvinov produced a draft of a treaty of mutual assistance between Russia, Britain and France that would bring them all to one another's support in the event of German attack. It would also guarantee the safety against German aggression of various states, Poland included, in Eastern Europe. Poland would even be invited to join the major powers as a signatory nation.

The sweeping character of Litvinov's proposals left the British rather breathless. For a period of several weeks they procrastinated, consulted the French, consulted the Poles (who would have nothing to do with the treaty on the grounds that if they joined such an alliance it would be regarded as a direct provocation by Germany), and consulted their Ambassador in Moscow. Various half-hearted counterproposals were put by the British to the Russians through Ambassador Seeds. The Soviet government declined these. What they had offered was clear-cut and straightforward. Were the British interested or not?

More time went by. In early June it was decided to send a special envoy to Moscow to handle discussions. Anthony Eden, who had been British foreign secretary until his relatively recent resignation in February 1938, volunteered to be the envoy. But his offer was refused by Chamberlain, who was jealous of Eden. William Strang, a career official in the Foreign Office, was selected instead and arrived in Moscow on June 14, along with a French delegation.

By this time, two months after the original Soviet proposal had been made, there was definite alteration in the Soviet attitude. Indeed, foreign affairs in Russia were now being conducted by different people. On May 3, 1938, Maxim Litvinov had been dismissed as foreign commissar and replaced by Vyacheslav M. Molotov. Although the Soviet government publicly said that this had no special significance, it ought to have been a sharp warning to the British. Litvinov was a Jew who had for years been associated with a strong antifascist policy. His wife was English. His replacement by a relatively uncommitted personality should have alerted the British to the possibility of momentous changes.

But it did not. Nor were the British sensitive to the fact that they had repeatedly offended the Soviets. They had not consulted them prior to the Polish guarantee. They were procrastinating on the Soviet alliance offer. And they had sent to Moscow only Strang, a relatively minor official whose dispatch as special envoy was regarded by the Russians as a positive snub.

None of these difficulties and resentments seems to have been perceived by the British or their French colleagues. Negotiation was continued at a leisurely pace. Molotov pressed for a positive response to the original Soviet proposal. The Franco-British delegation had constantly to refer to their capitals for instructions, which were delayed in coming. The Soviet government insisted that any alliance must include guarantees for a number of Germany's neighbors, including Rumania, Poland, Latvia, Estonia and Finland. Most of these nations did not want guarantees of their safety from the Soviet government. The whole thing dragged on and on, as the British attempted to water down the Soviet demands.

In all of this it is now evident that the British were laboring under a serious misapprehension. They believed that Soviet Russia had no one else to turn to for security but the Western powers. As Sir Ivone Kirkpatrick later explained,

> Our Government thought they were inviting the Russians to join the Turf Club and that they would fall over themselves with delight. The Russians, on the other hand, thought that they had a valuable oriental carpet to sell and were dissatisfied with the price offered.[47]

Moreover, the British and French did not really understand that however suspicious they may have been of the Soviets, the Soviets were even more suspicious of them. The Western powers had backed down before, in the face of German aggression. Nothing the Russians had yet seen had convinced them that the Western powers would not back down again. Before the Soviets threw in with the French and

British, they wanted to be very sure that their potential allies would stand firm.

On July 23, with negotiations still dragging on in Moscow, Molotov proposed that military talks begin at once and run simultaneously with the main political discussions. The British and French objected that this was not the proper procedure. The Soviets replied that time was of the essence and pointed out that they were, in fact, attempting to conclude a *military* alliance. The British and French reluctantly agreed to the Soviet proposal and assembled in London a joint military mission headed, on the British side, by Admiral Sir Reginald Aylmer Ranfurly Plunkett-Ernle-Erle-Drax—a man whose name the Russians found unpronounceable or ludicrous, or perhaps both.

Various technical problems arose in transporting the military mission to Moscow. There were no airplanes of sufficient size to fly from London to Russia without overflying German territory—and Germany was expected to be sensitive to such a mission flying over its soil. Similarly, it was considered provocative to dispatch the mission by train through Germany or to send it aboard warships through the Baltic. Finally, a merchant ship was chartered for the trip, but once the members of the mission were on board it was found that the boilers were defective and the vessel could proceed only at thirteen knots. The French and British officers did not reach Moscow until August 11.

Military negotiations commenced the following day. The Soviets were represented by Marshal Kliment E. Voroshilov assisted by the chiefs of staff of the Soviet army, navy, and air force. By comparison the Franco-British representation was distinctly junior. Moreover, they had not been given full powers to negotiate. Their governments were reluctant to divulge their military plans to the Russians. The mission was supposed to try to find out what the Russians were prepared to do.

It took Voroshilov and his colleagues only three days to establish that the Western allies had little that was concrete to discuss. Voroshilov asked the obvious question—"Do the French and British general staffs think that Soviet land forces will be admitted to Polish territory in order to make direct contact with the enemy in case Poland is attacked?"[48] (This was a delicate area, and the head of the French delegation, General Joseph Doumenc, had been instructed by his government to "try to avoid letting that question be put by the Russians."[49]) Voroshilov then asked the same question about Rumania.

Admiral Plunkett and his French colleagues had to reply that the Red Army could enter these nations only on the invitation of their governments. Moreover, the British and French were driven to admit that if the Red Army was not permitted to help Poland and Rumania, these nations would probably be overrun by the Germans. The Soviet negotiators virtually threw up their hands at this. Was Russia to refrain from action until the German Army had beaten their neighbors and was firmly installed on the Soviet border?

The British and French, without much hope or conviction, agreed to try to get the Poles and Rumanians to consent to allow the Red Army to enter their territories. This, however, would take time, and in the meanwhile all the talks in Moscow were deadlocked and formally suspended.

Colonel Beck was approached by both French and British ambassadors in Warsaw. Poland was told that its allies considered it very important that Soviet Russia should be allowed to enter Poland to assist in fighting Germany should war break out. Colonel Beck was, at first, evasive. He promised to reconsider his position. The French government pressed very hard to get the Poles to acquiesce and were strongly supported by the British. But in the end Beck proved intransigent. Despite the obvious anger and irritation of their allies at their "folly" and "recalcitrance,"[50] the Poles would not make any commitment to permit the Red Army on their soil. Beck made it clear that he believed the Russian demand to enter Poland was only an attempt to obtain by diplomatic means what it had failed to accomplish by war in 1920. On August 19 Beck gave what was described as *"un non catégorique,"* and not even the greatest pressure from the French and British could make him change his mind.

By now it was the third week in August 1939. Nothing concrete had been accomplished between the Allies and the Soviets. But suddenly there were rumors of definite developments elsewhere. Reliable sources reported that the Soviets were simultaneously negotiating with the Germans. The French and British foreign offices found this impossible to believe. When the French ambassador in Berlin had reported stories of secret meetings between German Foreign Minister Ribbentrop (the architect of the Anti-Comintern Pact) and the Soviet ambassador, the French Foreign Office cautioned its ambassador "to refrain in the future from sending such unlikely dispatches."[51]

But suddenly, on August 22, it was announced in Moscow that Ribbentrop was flying to the Soviet capital on the following morning. He arrived in Moscow at noon on August 23 and had two lengthy meetings with Stalin that very day. Late that night Ribbentrop and Molotov signed the Soviet-German Nonaggression Pact. This agreement consisted of a pledge that each party would "desist from any act of violence, any aggressive action, and any attack on each other."

There was, in addition, a secret protocol to the pact. In this, the Germans and Soviets agreed to split up eastern Europe into spheres of influence for each to do with what it wished. The Russians got Finland, Estonia, Latvia, part of Rumania, and the eastern half of Poland up to the line formed by the Vistula, Narew, and San rivers. The Germans got everything west of that, along with Lithuania. (On September 28, 1939, the Soviets and Germans amended this protocol. The Russians got Lithuania, and in compensation the Germans got the Polish territory that lay between the Vistula and the Bug rivers.) It was agreed that whether or not Poland was to continue to exist as a state would be "determined in the course of further political developments."[52]

It is almost impossible to describe the worldwide astonishment at the news of the Soviet-German Nonaggression Pact. The British and French military missions left Moscow at once. Their members were dazed by the event. The Poles could scarcely believe it had happened. The entire premise of the Polish foreign policy of equilibrium had been overturned.

The last week of peace in Europe was marked by a frantic series of diplomatic exchanges between Britain and Germany over the subject of a solution to the "Polish problem." In all of this, Poland itself was permitted to play only the most minor role.

Hitler was determined upon war with Poland, and he seems to have been half convinced that the French and British would stand aside. In any event, he was not deterred by the possibility that the Western allies might honor their pledge and that the war would then become general.

By the day after the German-Soviet Nonaggression Pact was signed, most of Europe had mobilized in large degree. The British Royal Navy and important segments of its air defense were all at war strength. The French Army had called up 600,000 specialist troops—a major step, not far short of full mobilization. The Poles also took every step short of complete mobilization. The Germans were already on a complete war footing, with their army concentrated on the Polish frontiers.

The British government, although now giving every evidence of being thoroughly determined, resolved to make one more attempt to prevent war. On August 22 Neville Chamberlain dispatched a personal letter to Hitler giving his solemn warning that there should be no misunderstanding—if Hitler attacked Poland, the British government was "resolved, and prepared, to employ without delay all the forces at their command, and it is impossible to foresee the end of hostilities once engaged."[53]

On the day when this letter was sent, Hitler addressed his senior military staff and announced his immediate intention to go to war with Poland. His only fear, he said, was that "at the last minute some *Schweinhund* will make a proposal for mediation."[54] The next morning, on August 23, Hitler established "Y-Day," the date for the invasion of Poland. This action was to begin at 4:15 A.M. on August 26, subject to final reconfirmation from him on August 25.

But later, on August 23, Hitler was handed Chamberlain's letter by British Ambassador Sir Neville Henderson. A virtual shouting match ensued with Hitler screaming a tirade of complaints and recriminations against the British and Poles. He charged that the British guarantee to Poland had encouraged Poland to perpetrate "atrocities" on its German minorities. He swore that his armies would march with the next "Polish provocation" at Danzig or the Corridor. As soon as Henderson left the room, Hitler turned to an aide, slapped his thigh, laughed, and said "Chamberlain won't survive that conversation; his Cabinet will fall this evening."[55]

But Chamberlain's government did *not* fall, and two days later, on August 25, Hitler again summoned Henderson to the Chancellery. This time he was calm. There was no shouting. Hitler had a proposition. If Britain stepped aside and allowed him to solve the Polish question as he wished, then Hitler was prepared personally to guarantee the continued existence of the British Empire. The effrontery of this offer was so astounding that Henderson declared it no offer at all. It was only because Hitler insisted, that Henderson agreed to fly to London to present the plan to his superiors. In the meantime, he assured Hitler that Britain would always stand by Poland.

This day, August 25, saw a number of temporary reverses for Hitler. The British ambassador had shown not the slightest interest in his "large comprehensive offer."[56] Then came news that the British and Poles had that day formalized their mutual guarantees into an actual treaty. This indicated that the British were truly serious. In the evening a letter arrived from Mussolini. Hitler had asked for his support in a war on Poland. Now the Duce announced that Italy was not presently in a condition to engage in a general European war. This was all too much to digest at once. Hitler issued instructions to postpone the invasion of Poland, scheduled for the next morning, until he could sort things out.

On August 28, the British government had come up with one final idea. Various third parties, including a meddlesome Swedish businessman named Birger Dahlerus, who was apparently close to Göring, had encouraged the British to put together a conference of Polish and German negotiators to see if German demands were reasonable and might be met. The Poles agreed to participate in such a conference. Ambassador Neville Henderson flew back to Berlin to present the plan to Hitler that same evening. Hitler said that he would study it and would summon Henderson back.

The next day, at 7:15 P.M. Henderson was again in the presence of the Führer. Hitler virtually screamed at him. Henderson lost his temper and shouted back. Finally, Hitler allowed that he might negotiate with Poland but made the unreasonable demand that the Poles must have a delegate with "full powers" in Berlin the next day. Henderson said that this sounded like an ultimatum and His Majesty's Government did not transmit ultimatums to its friends. Hitler said that his demand wasn't an ultimatum, and the meeting ended with the Germans agreeing to put their demands on paper for transmission to the Poles by the British.

At midnight on August 30, Henderson was received by Ribbentrop at the foreign ministry. Henderson asked whether the German proposals for a Polish settlement were available, as promised. Ribbentrop announced that they were—but inasmuch as no Polish emissary had shown up that day, the German proposals were no longer valid. For the record, Ribbentrop read off the proposals at top speed. They apparently consisted of sixteen points, very few of which were clear to the British, because Ribbentrop refused to give them to Henderson in writing.

Henderson returned to his embassy deeply depressed. It was obvious that Hitler wanted only war. Henderson telephoned Polish Ambassador Lipski and, despite the late hour, asked Lipski to come to his offices immediately. When Lipski arrived, Henderson asked the Polish Ambassador to telephone Beck in Warsaw and obtain his permission to request that Ribbentrop give Poland the German sixteen-point proposal. Lipski went away to see what could be done. There were exchanges of messages between Lipski and Beck during the day of August 31. The Poles had before them the examples of the German treatment of plenipotentiaries from Austria, Czecho-Slovakia and Lithuania in the last moments before Hitler moved. Beck had no intention of sending emissaries simply to receive an ultimatum. All that he would permit Lipski to do was to announce to Ribbentrop that Poland had learned of the "possibility of direct negotiation between the Polish and German governments," and "the Polish government . . . will make a formal reply on the subject within the next few hours."[57]

It was, of course, foreseen that the Germans would find this answer to be completely unacceptable. At 6:30 P.M. on August 31, Lipski was received by Ribbentrop in the Foreign Ministry. It was the first time that he had been in the building since April 6. As he walked toward Ribbentrop's office, Lipski paused briefly before the elegant Empire table at which he had signed the German-Polish nonaggression declaration in 1934. Then he went in to Ribbentrop. He was asked if he possessed full plenipotentiary powers to negotiate with Germany. Lipski said that he did not. The interview ended at once. That night the German radio service broadcast the German sixteen-point proposal with the statement that Poland had rejected it.

At 4:45 A.M. the following morning, September 1, 1939, the German army invaded Poland.

INVASION OF POLAND
SEPTEMBER 1939

0 — MILES — 100
0 — KM — 100

BALTIC SEA

BOCK
A.G.NORTH

LITHUANIA

Memel

NIEMEN R.

Kaunas

Wilno

Krzemierz

Minsk

HEL PENINSULA

Gdynia • Danzig • Königsberg

POMERANIA

POLISH CORRIDOR

EAST PRUSSIA

Grodno

NIEMEN R.

U.S.S.R.

4TH ARMY

3RD ARMY

Krojanty

A

F

Białystok

PRIPET MARSHES

Toruń

G

NAREW R.

POZNANIA

VISTULA R.

BUG R.

Pinsk

Poznań

B

Kutno

SZURA

Warsaw

Brest-Litovsk

PRIPET R.

8TH ARMY

Łódź

C

Kock

Naleczow

Breslau

10TH ARMY

Radom

H

Lublin

Włodzimierz

EAST GALICIA

RUNDSTEDT
A.G.SOUTH

Czestochowa

Kielce

VISTULA R.

WIEPRZ R.

Krzemieniec

GERMANY

Katowice

D

Kraków

E

Lwów

Tarnopol

U.S.S.R.

14TH ARMY

DNIESTR R.

Zaleszyki

DNIESTR R.

SLOVAKIA

CARPATHIAN MOUNTAINS

Kolomyja

Snyatyn

Cernauti

Kuty

CZEREMOSZ RIVER & BRIDGE

Vienna • Bratislava

HUNGARY

Budapest

RUMANIA

POLISH ARMIES

N

A   Pomorze

Initial deployment of Polish Armies

B   Poznań

Final position of Polish Forces

W   E

C   Łódź

German advance Sept. 1-5

D   Kraków

German advance Sept. 6-17

S

E   Carpathian

✗   Counterattack by the Poznan Army & remnants of Pomorze

F   Narew Group

G   Modlin

Russian advances   Molotov-Ribbentrop Line

H   Reserve Forces

18

The Fourth
Partition of Poland

THE TIME-WORN AXIOM that every general staff is preparing for the last war it fought certainly held true for the Polish Army during the years before World War II.

To the leaders of the Polish Army, their victory in the Polish-Soviet War represented the epitome of modern military experience. They believed that any future war would be more or less identical with that of 1920. It would consist of a series of rapidly developing infantry battles spread out over a broad area, without time for concentrations of heavy artillery to be brought up. This would not be a static war. The Polish General Staff foresaw very little trench warfare, but a lot of marching as the armies maneuvered. Tanks would be used primarily to accompany the infantry and reduce enemy strong points. The principal function of aircraft would be reconnaissance and artillery observation. A major role would be played by the cavalry, which would, as in 1920, slash deep behind enemy lines in knifelike thrusts, to rupture an enemy's supply lines and convert its retreat into a rout. The Polish Army had a lot of cavalry. But the essential force of the Army would be brave, tough and devoted infantry—sturdy soldiers who could march long distances, were thoroughly trained in the skills of the infantryman, and were prepared to sell their lives dearly. Poland had plenty of such troops. They would be commanded by officers and noncommissioned officers who had had practical experience in

war during 1919–1920 and whose additional virtues were ruthlessness, bravery, and complete competence in the basics of infantry
leadership. Poland had plenty of these too. Relatively little emphasis
was placed on specialized officer training at higher levels. Piłsudski
had not thought it necessary. He had not cared much for staff officers.
In the years from 1920 to the Marshal's death in 1935, only 1,136
officers had been graduated from the Polish Military Staff College.
And during this time fewer than fifty officers had been sent to the
École Supérieure de Guerre in Paris, which was open to Polish students. Apparently Piłsudski's successors thought even less of staff
training. They cut enrollment in the staff college by one half. In 1939
fewer than 5 percent of the Polish Army officer corps had had higher-
level training. But for morale, élan, toughness, and competence up to
the regimental level, the Polish officer corps was probably equal to
any in the world.

Piłsudski had, of course, been "the founder and the father of the
Polish Army." He loved his army and insisted upon retaining the
power of decision on any matter concerning it. But in certain respects
Piłsudski was the Polish Army's worst enemy—particularly during
the last years of his life, when it had been almost impossible to get
him to give sustained attention to the problems of reorganization and
modernization of the Army. No change in doctrine or armaments
could be made without Piłsudski's approval, but as the Marshal grew
increasingly ill, he became withdrawn and uncommunicative.

Upon Piłsudski's death in 1935, it was at last possible for a new
look to be taken at the Polish defense system. In early 1936 the Polish General Staff produced a detailed study that compared its army
with those of France, Germany and Russia. The rudimentary character of the Polish Army, as well as the obsolescence of its equipment,
was glaringly presented.

A six-year program was immediately started to rectify the Army's
worst weaknesses. Although modest by the standards of other European nations, the plan was very extensive for Poland. Its objectives
included improving the artillery; providing the Army with a radio-
communication network so that it would not be totally dependent on
the civil telephone and telegraph system; increasing the fire power of
a standard infantry division; and improving antiaircraft defenses.

Almost as soon as the program was started, it was realized that it
was much too ambitious. There simply was not enough money to

maintain the Army at its present active strength while implementing the costly improvements proposed by the general staff. Poland was already allocating a third of its national budget to military expenditures. It was impossible to go beyond this. Sharp cutbacks in the new program were made, and the modernization program was extended from six years to ten (that is, it was to be completed in 1946 rather than 1942). The Polish military leadership consoled itself on this setback with various comforting theories, which it did not hesitate to make public. After all, the argument ran, they had won the Polish-Soviet War without anything at all in the way of sophisticated equipment. All that had been required then—and just about all that would be required in the future—were the bare essentials: tough infantry, hard-riding cavalry, simple weapons, brave officers. Poland's leaders were authentically optimistic about their army's ability to deal with any enemy. They were not at all frightened. Great store was set by the extensive practical experience in war that the Polish officer corps was considered to possess. If it was pointed out that there was a lot of cavalry in the Polish Army at a time when other armies were phasing out the horse, the leaders replied that the cavalry was traditionally an arm at which Poles excelled. And no one could deny the very important role that the cavalry had played in the Polish-Soviet War less than twenty years before. In fact, some foreign observers agreed that the Poles were right to have a large proportion of cavalry. The United States Ambassador Drexel Biddle, was greatly impressed by the fact that in any sort of wet weather much of Poland turns into a huge muddy marsh. He wrote to President Roosevelt that "I can now more readily understand why the Polish military authorities have maintained an exceptionally large cavalry establishment."[1]

It was more difficult to speak well of the Polish air force. It was recognized as being technologically deficient. The standard Polish fighter aircraft was the PZL-11. The PZL-11 was a high-wing, gull-winged craft with nonretractable wheels. When it was introduced in 1931, the PZL-11 was one of the world's best fighter planes. But by 1936 it was clearly obsolete, and its top speed of 243 miles per hour was greatly exceeded by the new low-wing, retractable-wheeled fighters that were coming into production in other nations. A great deal of money was spent on the development of prototypes, but by 1939 the Polish air fighter force still consisted mostly of the obsolete PZL-11's.

For whatever reasons—lack of money, Piłsudski's obstinacy, poor planning, or simple overconfidence—Poland entered World War II with a numerically large but comparatively primitive military force.

By late August 1939, the German Army was fully prepared for the invasion of Poland. Leaving a screen of second-line divisions to man the Siegfried Line against the French, the Germans had massed the bulk of their army on the Polish western frontier and in East Prussia. The first-line German forces committed to this offensive consisted of thirty-one conventional infantry divisions, five Panzer divisions, four motorized infantry divisions, and four "light divsions," which consisted of a battalion of tanks, two or three infantry regiments in trucks, and motor-drawn artillery. Supplementing this total of forty-four divisions were second-line formations, frontier guards, et cetera, which probably added the equivalent of another eleven divisions.

The German Panzer divisions and light divisions possessed a total complement of 2,700 tanks of varying sizes. Opposing them were only 800 Polish tanks, practically all of which were old French models, scattered about among infantry formations. It is probable that a German infantry division disposed of at least twice the fire power of its Polish equivalent.

The German ground forces were supported by an entirely modern air force of 1,150 bombers and dive bombers, 250 transports, and nearly 400 fighters. The Poles countered this with an air force consisting of 935 airplanes of all types. About half of these were obsolete.

However, it would be incorrect to think of the German Army as stunningly modern, completely equipped, and faultless in all respects. German rearmament had been going on for only five years, and many of the junior officers and noncommissioned officers lacked training. The conventional German infantry divisions were unmotorized and therefore were as dependent on horse transport as their Polish opposites. The German reserves of gasoline and ammunition were insufficient to support a war of great duration or intensity, and a large part of the German panzer divisions consisted of Mark I and Mark II tanks, which had been developed as training vehicles and were much too light for warfare against a strongly armored opponent.

The Polish scheme for opposing a German attack was known as Plan Z. It was, of course, entirely defensive and based on the expectation that the main German attack would consist of a direct drive on Warsaw from Silesia and Slovakia in the southwest. A secondary assault was expected in the form of a pincers attack coming simultaneously from East Prussia and German Pomerania, with the objective of cutting off the Polish Corridor. Another German thrust was expected south and east from East Prussia toward the Narew River.

The Polish plan for countering such an invasion was simple and rather artless. Seven separate "armies"—typically consisting of two to four infantry divisions plus two cavalry brigades— were created and stationed at intervals along the northern, western, and southern borders of the nation. Clockwise from the south these armies were known as the Carpathian army (a smallish force charged with blocking the Carpathian mountain passes against invasion from Slovakia); the Kraków army (based in that city and given the task of defending it against attack from Silesia); the Łódź army and the Poznań army (both defending the center of the border with Germany); the Pomorze army (stationed in the throat of the Polish Corridor); the Modlin army and the Narew group (respectively on the south and east borders of East Prussia). Additionally, there was a brigade of marines and several army battalions based at the seaport of Gdynia and charged with defending the Westerplatte depot and the Polish fortifications on the Hel Peninsula. And in the center of Poland, just south of Warsaw, there was a general reserve of fourteen divisions. Under the Polish command structure, each of these nine separate commands reported directly to the commander in chief, Rydz-Śmigły. There were no army group commands to handle broad sections of the front.

No Polish forces of any strength were stationed on the eastern border with Soviet Russia because there were no troops to spare and because Germany posed the greatest immediate danger.

In general the Polish Plan Z called for as much resistance as possible at the frontiers followed if necessary by a slow retreat eastward to the center of Poland. During this retreat, advantage would be taken of the defensive barriers offered by the major rivers. Eventually, according to the general staff plan, the French and British attacks in the west would draw the German strength in that direction. Winter and wet weather would come. The mechanized Germans would be stalled, and the Polish Army would go over to a general offensive.

Under Plan Z the Polish Army was dispersed along a frontier with Germany that was about 1,250 miles long. The Slovakian border added another 500 miles to defend. The Poles had built practically no fortifications anywhere, except to a limited extent on the Narew River in the northeast. Permanent fortifications would have cost **too** much money. No nation could have fortified frontiers of the length of Poland's. So the whole fortifications problem had been left up to the commanders of the individual armies who were instructed to build field defenses and antitank ditches at the points of greatest danger, or not build them, as they chose. During the summer of 1939 very few were built. The Army commanders were reluctant to dig up the farmland before the peasants had gotten in their crops. When the British military attaché in Warsaw, Colonel Roland Sword, was asked by London for a report on the Polish frontier defenses, he told his friends, "I've done my report. It consists of three words 'there aren't any.' "[2]

The French, who had been apprised of Plan Z, were openly critical of it. French Chief of Staff General Maurice Gamelin had advised the Poles to keep their army concentrated away from the frontiers. He suggested that the Polish Army create a fortified line along certain river barriers in the Polish interior and thus reduce the line to be defended to 420 miles.

The Poles answered the French criticism of Plan Z with the observation that to station their armies in the central or eastern parts of Poland would mean the instant sacrifice of most of the nation's largest cities and important manufacturing centers. Silesia, Kraków, Lódź, Poznań and Gdynia would all fall instantly to the Germans if there were no armies to defend them. It was the obligation of the Polish government and its army to make an effort to defend their citizens who lived in the west, the most populous region of the nation.

The German plan for the attack on Poland was novel and had a definite risk attached to it. It is difficult now to recall how very original, indeed experimental, was the blitzkrieg offensive that the Germans were preparing to unleash on Poland. This is because within no more than a few years every nation's army had copied the Germans, and the blitzkrieg became a "conventional" tactic. But before 1939 the Poles (and the British and the French) envisaged the coming conflict as being a war of artillery and infantry battles in which a defender would have considerable advantages. However, the German plan for the Polish invasion was startlingly innovative. The German military objective was to crush the Polish Army—this much was obvious. In 1939, however, Germany did not have the resources to fight a prolonged war with Poland while simultaneously defending itself against a determined attack by the Western Allies. In order to

eliminate Poland quickly, a novel type of campaign had to be conducted—the blitzkrieg. This offensive was to consist of a series of
swift, relatively slender penetrations into the crust of the enemy
defenses by highly mobile columns of armor and motorized infantry.
These columns were to pay little attention to their flanks. They were
to bypass enemy strong points, leaving them to be reduced by slower
infantry divisions, which would move in the conventional manner.
The objectives were to completely disrupt the enemy's rear, to cut
the front off from its supply lines, to harass and confuse the defender
at every point, and to offer battle only on terms that were advantageous to the attacker.

The new German Army was uniquely suited for this type of warfare. Alone among European armies, it had developed the ability to
put into the field masses of tanks able to fight as armored divisions
rather than dispersed as support for infantry divisions. Only the Germans possessed quantities of armored and motorized infantry, armored artillery, armored engineer and signal troops, and motorized
service forces—all combined into single divisions and trained to work
in the closest coordination. Two or three of these divisions together
constituted a mobile and flexible corps, capable of extended independent operations. And only the Germans possessed a substantial
number of dive bombers that were designed to function as a sort of
super-long-range artillery in support of the fast-moving motorized
divisions.

Poland was an ideal testing ground for this new kind of war. The
whole nation was essentially an open plain. It was almost impossible
for defenders to block roads or hold junctions against a motorized
invader who could, in dry weather at least, simply leave the roads
and drive through the fields.

In 1939 the blitzkrieg had never been tried out. No one knew
whether or not the knife-edged armored columns could be cut off and
destroyed piecemeal. No one knew how far the armored columns
could move in a day. No one knew whether the Stuka dive bombers
could deliver accurate support under actual field conditions. It was
all rather dicey.

Strategically, the German plan was based on two enormous pincers.
One German force striking upward from Silesia in the south was to
converge on Warsaw, meeting forces coming down from East Prussia
and German Pomerania in the north. A second pincers, an outer set,
was later added to the plan at Hitler's insistence. It was to stem from

the same bases but meet much farther to the east—approximately in the region of Brest Litovsk.

In terms of command, the German invading forces were divided into two groups—Army Group North and Army Group South. The northern force was commanded by General Fedor von Bock and was made up of the German Fourth Army in Pomerania and the Third Army in East Prussia. Army Group South was commanded by General Gerd von Rundstedt and consisted of the German Eighth, Tenth and Fourteenth Armies. The wide area between these two army groups was filled up with a mixed bag of German reserve formations, frontier guards, mobilized police, et cetera, who were under instructions to make only local attacks intended to deceive and pin down the opposing Polish Poznań army.

Careful preparations were made for the employment of the German Luftwaffe, whose initial mission was to crush the Polish air force. Only after that was it to turn its full attention to the support of ground troops. The German navy was to patrol the Baltic and the Bay of Danzig, ready to do battle with the Polish navy. An old German battleship, the *Schleswig-Holstein*, had been dispatched to Danzig, ostensibly to participate in ceremonies honoring the German naval dead of World War I. From its berth it could fire point-blank at the small Polish force of marines still stationed at Westerplatte.

Precisely at 4:45 A.M. on September 1 the *Schleswig-Holstein* trained out its eleven-inch guns and commenced firing at the Polish bunkers on the Westerplatte. There was no German declaration of war, and there would be none until ten that morning, when Hitler addressed the Reichstag.

The German irregular forces within Danzig had jumped the gun and surrounded the Polish post office at 4:17 A.M. They called upon the fifty-one Polish postal workers inside to surrender. These workers were armed, and when they refused to surrender, a battle began that would last all day.

At first light the German planes began to bomb Polish airfields, and bombers flew low over Warsaw dropping sticks of bombs. At all the designated points of invasion the German Army machine-gunned the Polish frontier police huts and drove across the border.

The Germans achieved tactical surprise in their assault. In fact, the Polish Army had only just begun full mobilization, despite the warning evident in the utterly deteriorated diplomatic situation. The reason for the late mobilization was that the French and British governments had repeatedly pressed the Poles not to take the dread step of outright, publicized mobilization for fear it might antagonize Hitler. They did not know that the German Army had itself secretly mobilized in mid-August. Finally, on August 29 the Poles decided to announce their intention to mobilize. The British and French ambassadors immediately called on the Polish foreign office and persuaded the government to delay the announcement. This was done, and the "first day" of mobilization was rescheduled for August 31. It was most unfortunate for Poland that the German invasion struck at a time when roads and railroads were suddenly choked with reservists finding their way to their units and reserve divisions in the process of formation.

All did not go completely well for the German Army on the first day of the invasion. The attacking troops displayed some of the initial confusion that is to be expected of soldiers coming under fire for the first time. In the north the Germans were hampered by a heavy fog that prevented artillery observation. A battery of German guns firing blindly into the haze nearly killed General Heinz Guderian, the panzer specialist. In the north, too, German tank columns of the Third Army ran into one of the few Polish fortification systems and were stopped with serious losses from Polish antitank fire. At one point in East Prussia, the Polish Podlaska Cavalry Brigade counterattacked, crossed the border, and actually captured a few small German villages.

But, in general, the invaders' first-day objectives were achieved. The German pincer attacks were launched, and any initial confusion was quickly straightened out. The Luftwaffe had been extremely successful. It had concentrated upon bombing the major Polish airfields, and it had destroyed a large part of the Polish air force on the ground. The remaining Polish planes were dispersed to small dirt landing strips in the east of Poland from which they could not operate effectively. Long-range German fighters, ME-110s, were kept on standing patrols to engage any enemy aircraft that appeared. By the end of the first day it was evident that the Polish air force had been virtually eliminated as a threat.

On only the third day of the war the Germans began to earn authentic dividends. Their Third Army (attacking eastward out of German Pomerania) met up with the Fourth Army (attacking westward out of East Prussia). With this linkage the Germans had cut through the Polish Corridor at its base. At the "top" of the corridor, just below Danzig and Gydnia, other German armored units joined hands. The Corridor was now controlled by the invaders, who had cut in two the defending Polish Pomorze army, fifteen thousand members of which were captured in a single day. The remnants of the Pomorze army commenced a retreat. The entire German Third and Fourth armies were now free for their drive to the south.

There had been hard fighting, of course, in this three-day battle for the Corridor. The Poles had counterattacked whenever they could and had been very difficult to dislodge whenever they could hole up in a forest or behind some other natural defense that defied tank assault. But these pockets of resistance could safely be left for reduction by the German infantry divisions, which toiled after their armored comrades.

It was during this battle for the Polish Corridor that the legendary charges of Polish cavalry against German tanks took place. These accounts apparently create a vivid and dramatic mental picture because they are events which come instantly to the mind of almost everyone who knows anything at all about this war. Actually, the "charges" of Polish lancers upon German tanks occurred in only a very few instances and were not really charges in a technical sense. In one case, on September 1, two squadrons of the Polish 18th Uhlans attacked a battalion of German infantry near Krojanty in the Corridor. At this precise moment German tanks and armored cars appeared. Before the Uhlans could get away, they were very roughly handled. There were a few other instances of inadvertent contact between German armor and Polish cavalry. But almost always the Polish "charge" was simply an attempt to break out of a German encirclement. The Polish cavalrymen well realized their inability to attack German armor.

In the south the German progress was even more rapid than in the north. By September 5, each of the three German armies that made up Army Group South had made very good headway. On an average, they occupied a line about sixty miles within Polish territory. The German Eighth Army was approaching Lódź. The Fourteenth Army had captured all of the Silesian industrial basin and was now before Kraków, which would surrender the next day. The Tenth Army was driving rapidly on Warsaw and was, in fact, only seventy miles away. After only the fifth day of the war General Franz Halder, chief of the German general staff, wrote in his diary, "The enemy is practically beaten."[3]

The Germans could scarcely believe the extent of their own successes. On September 5 Hitler visited his troops in the field. General Guderian took the Führer for a brief tour of the battlefield. Hitler was amazed at the slight German losses. Only a few thousand casualties had been suffered in the entire process of capturing the Corridor. Hitler compared this with the enormous toll suffered by his own regiment in World War I. He found the speed and power of the panzer formations to be equally astounding. He was shown the wreckage of an entire Polish artillery regiment that had been destroyed and asked Guderian, "Our dive bombers did that?" Guderian replied "No, our panzers!" Hitler was plainly astonished.[4]

The blitzkrieg tactic was indeed yielding spectacular results. The panzer columns, rumbling across the Polish plains in spear-shaped wedges about three miles wide, were doing everything that had been expected of them and more. Plunging through or around the Polish infantry divisions, they kept their enemy constantly off balance. The Polish Army was given no breathing space. There was no time to sort things out. No one knew exactly where the battle line was. Polish artillery regiments, thought to be securely behind the front, were surprised by panzers and destroyed before the gunners could man their weapons.

Almost everything was working for the Germans. The summer had been exceptionally dry, and there was no rain in September. The rivers were low and therefore fordable by the panzers wherever bridges had been blown up by the defenders. The ground was hard and firm, perfect for tank operations and difficult for digging anti-tank ditches. The German tanks could easily leave an obstructed road, swing out through the fields, and bypass the roadblock—leaving it to be dealt with by their infantry. At any given time there were probably hundreds of these small isolated pockets where Polish troops were waging a heroic but vain struggle with surrounding German infantry or were being pounded to death by the overwhelming German artillery. Not only did the Germans have great superiority in conventional artillery, but also each infantry regiment was accompanied by a dozen 88mm antiaircraft guns mounted on mobile platforms. Since there were few Polish airplanes to fire at, these "88's" were driven up close to the front and used for direct fire support with spectacular effect.

Well behind the front, the German dive bombers were constantly at work. From the first day of the war they had been systematically attacking the Polish railroad system. Within a few days they had knocked out so many bridges and destroyed so much important trackage that railroad activity had practically come to a stop. This meant that much of the Polish mobilization stopped, because the railroads were the only means by which most reservists could get to their divisions. This simple technique of dive bombing the railroads yielded the Germans the benefit of facing a Polish Army that was perhaps only half the size it would have been had the Polish mobilization been unobstructed.*

As early as September 5, the entire battlefield situation had become very confusing for the Polish Army as well as for its supreme commander, Marshal Rydz-Śmigły, at his general headquarters in Warsaw. The worst problem was communication. The telegraph and telephone system upon which the Polish Army had mainly relied was largely broken down in western Poland; the German armored columns routinely pulled down the wires as they drove across the country.

The Polish command system was also now seen to be faulty. There is a rough rule of thumb in military affairs that one commander can competently direct only three or four subordinate commands. Rydz-Śmigły had made the mistake of attempting to personally control nine separate armies. The communications breakdown and the overcentralized command structure resulted in a situation whereby Polish general headquarters had no clear idea of the location of many of its own divisions or what they were doing. The problem was further complicated when, on the night of September 6, with the Germans driving hard on Warsaw, Rydz-Śmigły left the capital to set up new headquarters at Brest Litovsk, some 115 miles to the east. Before leaving, he dispatched orders to his armies to retreat eastward to form a

---

* Upon complete mobilization the Polish army would have disposed of 1,700,000 well-trained men with about another 1,000,000 older trained men still in reserve. In peacetime the active army consisted of 280,000 men, but various preliminary mobilizations had increased it to about 700,000 at the outbreak of war. During the full mobilization which began on August 31 probably only 150,000 to 200,000 men actually reached their assigned units. Therefore a Polish army of slightly under 900,000 had to face an invader employing over one and one half million men.

defensive line behind the Vistula River. It was becoming increasingly clear that Poland could not hold out much longer. Three things must soon occur—the promised French offensive, the promised British bombing attack on Germany, and the fall rains to bog down the German armor. None of these seemed imminent.

Poland's Western allies had certainly not come to its aid with alacrity. In fact, it had taken some time for France and Britain to declare war on Germany. On the day that Poland was invaded, the British and French governments had contented themselves with mobilizing and making appeals. The British cabinet met at 11:30 A.M.; and its members adopted the view that the news from Poland was too confusing to make a judgment. The German chargé d'affaires in London had informed the British Foreign Office that the fighting amounted only to a Polish-initiated exchange of gunfire across the border. He flatly denied that Warsaw was being bombed. It was easier for the cabinet to believe the Germans than the report of their own ambassador in Poland who could hear the bombs exploding.

That afternoon the British ambassador in Berlin was instructed to deliver a "warning," not an ultimatum, to the German government. It notified the Germans that unless they "suspended all aggressive action against Poland and are prepared promptly to withdraw their forces from Polish territory, His Majesty's Government will without hesitation fulfill their obligations to Poland."[5] The French followed with a similar message. At 6 P.M. Chamberlain read the British message to the members of the House of Commons.

The British and French cabinets had consulted, of course, and it was obvious that rather than go to war they both hoped to negotiate some understanding with Hitler. The Italian government muddied the waters by declaring itself a nonbelligerent and offering to convene an international conference to prevent the outbreak of general war.

The French and the British spent the morning awaiting for a reply to their warnings to Germany. During these hours the Polish ambassadors in London and Paris were running frantically back and forth to the foreign office of their presumed allies. The Poles smelled betrayal in the air, and they buttonholed every important personage they could find to point out that France and Britain were under the most solemn obligations to declare war on Germany. In Warsaw, Beck called in the French and British ambassadors to ask when his allies would enter the war.

On the afternoon of September 2, the British House of Commons met in a session that, with a recess, lasted into the evening. There was a terrible scene. Prime Minister Chamberlain delivered what was generally regarded as an evasive speech, dwelling upon the fact that no reply had yet been received from Germany regarding the British "warning" of the previous day and indicating the British government's willingness to join in any negotiation that the Germans and Poles might undertake following Germany's withdrawal from Poland.

Most members of the House of Commons felt that the Prime Minister was avoiding the main issue. There was a bitter uproar. The House was obviously prepared for war. A recess was called while Chamberlain met with his cabinet. The cabinet members clearly felt that Britain had temporized too long. Chamberlain finally agreed to his ministers' demands that the Germans be given an ultimatum: the Germans must withdraw from Poland or a state of war would exist between Britain and Germany. Extensive telephone conversations were held with French Foreign Minister Georges Bonnet in Paris. The French were reluctant, but were carried along by the British. The only question now was the time limit to be given in the ultimatum. The French wanted forty-eight hours, but the British felt that this was too long. With no decision on a time limit, the British cabinet returned to the House of Commons, which resumed sitting, obviously expecting to be told that they were at war.

When Chamberlain confessed that no definite decision had been arrived at with the French, his government nearly fell. A group of Chamberlain's own cabinet ministers gathered in an office at the House of Commons and sent word that they would simply wait there until Chamberlain declared war—with or without the French.

At 11:30 P.M. there was another cabinet meeting. Chamberlain announced that he would accede to his colleagues' wishes. It was decided that an ultimatum would be handed to the Germans at 9 A.M. on the following morning, September 3. It would expire two hours later. No one believed that the Germans would accept the British terms, so the dispatch of this ultimatum was tantamount to a declaration of war. The French were simply informed of the British action and were thus compelled, willy-nilly, to conform. Their ultimatum to the Germans expired at 5 P.M. on September 3.

So, fifty-three hours after Poland was attacked, Britain finally went to war with Germany, and six hours later France entered the conflict.

Crowds of cheering Poles filled the Warsaw streets outside the French and British embassies. Beck visited each of the Allied ambassadors to express his deep gratitude. He stepped out onto the balcony of the British embassy and told the crowd below that "we never doubted that Great Britain and France would fight."[6] Perhaps not, but the Poles had had some anxious moments. The French ambassador visited the statue of Prince Józef Antoni Poniatowski, the Polish hero who had been one of Napoleon's marshals, and laid a wreath at its base. Buoyed by the entrance of the British and French into the war, the Poles now believed that their allies would save them.

Late on September 8, panzer elements of Army Group South arrived at the suburbs of Warsaw. Although these were only an advance guard of the principal forces following behind, the German commander immediately ordered an attack for 7 A.M. on September 9. At that time the Germans found that the defenses of the capital had been made far stronger than those of other Polish cities. A series of barricades and strong points had been created, and the populace had dug antitank ditches. There was a sufficient number of antitank guns on hand. The German attack was repelled with heavy loss and the panzers were pulled back to await the arrival of heavy artillery and enough troops to conduct a proper siege.

As it turned out, Warsaw got a respite for a number of days because early on September 10 the Polish Army launched a sudden offensive that surprised the German Army Group South and forced it to divert its forces away from the capital. In the course of its advance, Army Group South had to leave its left (northern) flank exposed. The German command had been concerned about this vulnerability, but the German advance had been so swift that there was no help for it. It was, of course, known to the Germans that the Polish Poznań army was present on the north flank of Army Group South. It was also known that the Poznań army consisted of four infantry divisions and two cavalry brigades. Alone among the Polish armies, the Poznań army had not yet been seriously engaged and its troops were fresh. The Germans assumed that the Poznań army was marching due east in order to cross the Vistula. Two German divisions were ordered from reserve to form a screen against this force. The Poznań army would be pinched off by the capture of Warsaw, which seemed imminent.

But at noon on September 10, the German 30th Infantry Division, which was on the extreme north flank of Army Group South, reported itself to be under heavy attack by several Polish divisions supported by two cavalry brigades. The attackers were all quickly identified as part of the Poznań army.

This was indeed a surprise. The German 30th Infantry Division was strung out in an advancing column more than twenty miles long. This division's situation was similar to that of its parent corps, the Eighth Army. Indeed all of Army Group South had been deployed in extended marching columns on the assumption that the Poznań army was retreating parallel to it. Now, suddenly, it transpired that the Poznań army had halted and concentrated. It had gathered up the battered remnants of the Pomorze army to make a group of about eight divisions. This very sizable force had now abruptly turned due south and was launching an attack twenty miles wide across the Bzura River. All the Polish preparations had been missed by German aerial reconnaissance. If this Polish attack was successful, it might saw through the German forces well west of Warsaw. Alternatively, this Polish army might turn back east, enter Warsaw, and reinforce the city's already sizable garrison. This would make the Germans' planned siege of the capital extremely difficult.

Faced by this unexpected assault, the Germans displayed amazing resourcefulness. The most easterly German divisions were turned around and directed back to the northwest. Only a few regiments of troops were left around Warsaw to sustain the illusion of a siege. The most northerly German corps formed a front to its left flank. Army Group South committed its reserves to the battle and stripped subordinate commands of motorized divisions, which drove to the fighting at top speed.

The battle developed rapidly on a narrow front. The Polish infantry, as usual, fought very well. Their flanks were protected by cavalry brigades, which proved very useful in reconnaissance of the German flanks. For almost two days the battle teetered in the Polish favor. But the rapidly arriving German reinforcements eventually stemmed the Polish southward attack. The Polish commander, General Tadeusz Kutrzeba, now saw that he could not hope to cut through the entire German Army Group South, and on September 12 he redirected his attack eastward in an attempt to break into Warsaw and either relieve the capital or join its garrison.

General Gerd von Rundstedt, commanding Army Group South, now saw the crucial opportunity. The divisions of the Poznań army constituted the last Polish force capable of large-scale action. If they were destroyed, the German army could easily force the line of the Vistula (which the Poles were now attempting to defend) and could also besiege and capture Warsaw at leisure.

On September 13 Rundstedt's divisions turned from defense to attack. The German Eighth Army, heavily reinforced, assaulted the Poles from the west and south. The German Tenth Army attacked from the south and east. The Fourth Army, part of Army Group North, closed the ring from the north. The fighting was awesome. The center of the Polish force was the small city of Kutno, and the struggle became known as the Battle of the Kutno Pocket. The Polish divisions attempted to break out to the east and were generally ground down and exhausted in the process. The Battle of the Kutno Pocket lasted until September 17, when, following a concentrated air attack on the compact targets offered by the Polish forces which had been compressed by the concentric German assault, the Polish defenses broke down. That day the German Eighth Army took 40,000 prisoners. The Tenth Army took 12,000. Only about two divisions of Poles escaped to join the defenders of Warsaw.

This completed the destruction of the last of the major Polish field armies. With the exception of the garrisons of Warsaw and Modlin, a fortress city about twenty miles north of Warsaw, and the tiny group of defenders on the Hel Peninsula, the Germans now had only to deal with stragglers, isolated pockets of defenders, and a few improvised forces the size of a division or two. The inner pincers of the German strategic plan had met at Warsaw. The outer pincers was making excellent headway. The German panzers were dashing at top speed across the Polish countryside. The only significant problems they faced were a shortage of gasoline in the south and a number of worn-out tank treads as the result of two and one half weeks of hard driving. General Guderian's XIX Panzer Corps had entered Brest Litovsk deep in the east of Poland on September 14. The city's Citadel had been strongly defended, but it was captured on the seventeenth. Meanwhile two of Guderian's divisions had advanced farther south and had established radio contact, although not actual physical link-up, with advanced units of Army Group South.

All surviving Polish field forces were now trying to escape to the southwest corner of Poland in a forlorn attempt to establish a sort of bridgehead against the Rumanian border.

September 17 was a milestone date for Poland. A flood of events occurred on that day. It was a date that was also significant for an event that was supposed to occur but did not—the full-scale French offensive in the West. Under the terms of the Military Protocol of May 19, the French were obliged to commence a major military offensive against Germany by the fifteenth day after mobilization. Since the "first day" of French mobilization had been September 2, their offensive should have begun no later than the seventeeth. In addition, under the protocol, the French had been required to conduct diversionary assaults on the German lines as early as the third day of mobilization. Bombing attacks on targets in Germany were also to be conducted by the French and British from the outbreak of war.

Virtually none of these promises had yet been kept, nor was it likely that they would be. To be sure, on September 7 the French army had launched a "diversionary attack." The site of this offensive was on the Saar River on the Franco-German frontier. Nine French infantry divisions moved cautiously into a small wood called the Warndt Forest, from which the Germans had retreated. After advancing about seven miles on a front approximately 25 miles wide, the French ran up against the Siegfried Line, which was still unfinished. At this point they simply stopped and sniped at the German fortifications with rifles. For the benefit of Polish morale, much was made by the French of this capture of a few square miles of no-man's-land. But this negligible "offensive," if it can be called that, caused the Germans not the slightest inconvenience and certainly resulted in no forces being withdrawn from Poland.

The projected Allied bombing offensive against Germany was conducted with equal timidity. In 1939 it was widely believed that aerial bombing could pulverize enormous cities almost overnight. Of course, in 1939 neither side had enough heavy bombers (or technical experience in their use) to destroy a major enemy city. But the French and British did not know this. Their governments were extremely apprehensive that, if provoked, Germany might launch huge raids against London or Paris, and that these raids would kill hundreds of thousands of civilians.

At the beginning of the war, the British government decided to attack only very isolated and easily identifiable military objectives within Germany—such as the German Fleet as it lay at anchor in a roadstead. The hope was that Hitler would deal with Britain in the same fashion. The British feared to bomb almost any target in Germany because they might inadvertently kill some civilians and thus provoke Hitler into attacking British civilian targets. The French were more than pleased to align their bombing policy with that of the British. The result was that virtually the only enemy air activity over Germany during the Polish campaign consisted of RAF planes dropping propaganda leaflets.

The Poles could not understand this inactivity by its allies. And, of course, the Poles had no reason to be understanding. The Polish ambassadors and military attachés in London and Paris ceaselessly harassed their allies at every level of contact. They pleaded, suggested, badgered, and remonstrated with their allies. When General Stanisław Burhardt, head of the Polish military mission to France, arrived in Paris on September 10, he immediately sought an interview with General Gamelin, commander in chief of the Allied forces on the western front. Gamelin assured the Polish general that the full-scale offensive would take place by September 17 as promised. As for the air attacks on Germany, Gamelin would make no promise, as this was essentially a British operation. Gamelin professed to realize the increasingly desperate situation in which the Polish Army found itself. He was truly sympathetic. He suggested that they fight their way into the southeast corner of the nation, where, protected on three sides by neutral Rumania, Hungary and Soviet Russia, the Poles might hold out until the eventual victory.

In the end, the Western Allies did nothing to aid the Poles militarily. There were no bombing raids, and there was no massive assault on the Siegfried Line. The pitifully small offensive that the French had conducted on the Saar River was exaggerated by the French and used to salve their own consciences. Gamelin wrote to the Polish military attaché, "More than half our active divisions in the North-East are engaged in combat . . . the Germans have offered vigorous resistance . . . we can claim with justice to be keeping on front a large part of the German Air Force." None of this was true. In a postscript Gamelin added, "With all my heart, I share your anguish and have faith in the tenacity of your resistance."[7]

This was all that Poland's allies were prepared to do for it, although even if they had scrupulously observed every one of their commitments it would have been too late to save Poland.

At 6 A.M. on September 17, the Soviet Union invaded Poland in a simultaneous offensive along the entire Polish eastern frontier. The blow came as a surprise to the Poles, although it should not have. The only strange thing about it was that Russia had not entered the war sooner. As early as September 4, the Germans had invited Soviet Russia to join in the war and occupy the extensive areas that it had been allotted under the secret protocol to the Soviet-German Pact of August 23.

Molotov had replied, "We agree with you that at a suitable time it will be absolutely necessary for us to start concrete action. We are of the view, however, that this time has not yet come . . . it seems to us that through excessive haste we might injure our cause and promote unity among our opponents."[8] Actually, the reasons for Russia's delaying its entry into the war were a little more complex. The Soviet government had only just ordered the mobilization of the Red Army, and it would be several weeks before it was ready to move. The Soviets also had to develop the propaganda that would justify its invasion of Poland. The signing of the Soviet-German Nonaggression Pact only two weeks before had already created enormous problems as the Soviets strove to explain to their own people and to the world at large how it had come about that the only Communist state in the world had entered into a form of alliance with the world's leading fascist nation. And now Moscow had to work out an explanation for its joining forces with Germany in the destruction of a small neighbor.

Finally, a complicated propaganda line was developed and began to be disclosed in *Pravda*. On September 10 this official journal printed an in-depth "survey" of the war, in which the great German superiority was stressed and the general impression given that the war was coming rapidly to an end. Two days later *Pravda* ran an editorial which claimed that the Polish Army was scarcely fighting at all. Why? Because incorporated into the Polish state were, allegedly, eleven million Ukrainians and Belorussians who were "living in a state of national oppression."[9] (According to the 1931 Polish census these particular Polish minorities totaled fewer than six million persons.) It was explained that no state which oppressed so many people could fight a successful war. The Polish nation was disintegrating, and it was incumbent on the Red Army to go to the protection of the Polish Ukrainian and Belorussians, who were blood brothers to major nationalities within the Soviet Union.

This propaganda line was sketchy and weak, because it was developed in great haste. The Germans were making surprisingly rapid progress, and the Soviet government soon recognized that unless the Red Army invaded Poland quickly, they might find that the Germans had occupied all of Poland—which would be an embarrassment to both Russia and Germany. So, although the Red Army was only partially mobilized and the propaganda justification for an invasion only partly developed, the Soviet Union invaded Poland on September 17.

Fortunately for the Russians, there were practically no Polish troops on the Soviet-Polish border. The Red Army poured over the 800-mile-long frontier as a semiorganized horde, many of whom were riding in horse-drawn peasant carts. The only troops who were in a position to oppose this invasion were a few battalions of the Polish Frontier Area Protection Corps. And they were confused by the fact that, before attacking, the Russian soldiers frequently waved white flags and shouted "Don't shoot, we're come to help you against the Germans."[10] The situation was chaotic, and the few Polish troops present on the Soviet frontier were quickly routed or captured. Senior Polish officers taken prisoner by the Red Army frequently were shot on the spot. It appears that in certain locations invaded by the Red Army its soldiers actually were welcomed as liberators by some Belorussians and Ukrainians.

At 3 A.M. on the morning of the Red Army's invasion the Soviet foreign ministry summoned Polish Ambassador Waclaw Grzybowski to receive a note. Grzybowski arrived at the ministry offices to be greeted by Vladimir Potemkin, deputy foreign minister. Potemkin read him a note that began, "The Polish-German War has revealed the internal bankruptcy of the Polish State . . . the Polish government has disintegrated and no longer shows any sign of life." The document then stated that the Soviet Union was obliged to intervene in order to protect "the kindred Ukrainian and White Russian people who live on Polish territory." In addition, the Soviet government announced that it intended to "take all measures to extricate the Polish people from the unfortunate war into which they were dragged by their unwise leaders."[11]

Grzybowski made the only protest available to him. He refused to accept the Soviet note and left the foreign ministry. A rather farcical playlet ensued. The Soviet foreign ministry rushed the note to the Polish embassy so that it arrived ahead of the returning Grzybowski. The Polish ambassador thereupon sent a messenger back to the Soviet foreign ministry with the note. The foreign ministry porters, alerted to this possibility, slammed the doors and refused to touch the note. Finally, Grzybowski simply mailed it back.

But all of this, of course, had no effect on the truly desperate situation in Poland.

By the end of September 17 the Red Army had advanced deep into eastern Poland. Since there were practically no Polish forces to resist the Russians, the rate of the Red Army's advance was pretty much regulated by how rapidly its troops could march to the agreed-upon demarcation line with the Germans. Wherever the German army had moved into the Soviet sector, the Germans retreated.

In the west the Germans were mopping up the Kutno Pocket and had begun shelling Warsaw, which was now closely invested—as was the nearby city of Modlin. The Polish naval brigade defending the Hel Peninsula in the north was still holding out. Its resistance, against enormously superior German forces including fire support from two German battleships, was nothing less than heroic.

With the exception of the troops in these isolated areas of resistance, what was left of the Polish Army (now reduced to perhaps a third of its strength at the war's opening) was marching southeast to the small area of Poland that projected like a tongue into Rumania and Hungary. Here, with its back to two friendly nations, the Polish Army could make a last-ditch stand. The region, which was only about 120 miles square, was becoming known as the Rumanian Bridgehead because it was hoped that the Polish Army could receive supplies from the West through the Rumanian ports on the Black Sea. And if the Polish Army was eventually overwhelmed, then the survivors could cross over into Rumania and from there make their way to the West.

In its retreat to the southeast the Polish Army was now operating entirely on previous orders. It would receive no more instructions from its supreme commander or its general headquarters. The last orders to the Polish armies from their GHQ were issued on September 16. They consisted of a broadcast message mostly listing enemy units known to be on the southern front as of September 14. After the sixteenth no further general orders were issued. The Polish general headquarters had not, for some days, known where most of its remaining forces were, and it had ceased trying to coordinate their actions.

Polish general headquarters had indeed had a very rough time. For most of the war Rydz-Śmigły and his staff had been forced to flee from place to place in an exhausting procession that would have made effective command almost impossible even if Polish Army communications were very good—which they certainly were not.

On September 6 Rydz-Śmigły had left Warsaw, arriving after midnight on September 7 at Brest Litovsk. On September 11 Polish GHQ was again forced to change location as German panzers approached Brest Litovsk from the north. Rydz-Śmigły and his staff drove a hundred miles south and reestablished themselves in the small city of Włodzimierz. Two days later they moved to Mlynow, and only two days after that they moved to Kołomyja, deep in the Rumanian Bridgehead and close to the Rumanian border.

In the course of all this movement, the Polish GHQ had lost touch almost completely with the battle. Rydz-Śmigły's staff received only sporadic reports, and not all of these reports could be trusted. Very soon after the war began, the Germans had destroyed the Polish Seventh Infantry Division. In the course of this action, they had seized enough material on Polish codes so that they could decipher messages from the Polish GHQ and send misleading coded replies to them. Each time that Polish GHQ moved, the German code breakers soon knew the new location, and the Luftwaffe began constant bombing of the area.

The Polish government had been as completely overwhelmed by events as the Army had. Like the staff of the Army general headquarters, the principal figures of the Polish government had been forced to flee from place to place during the war. As early as September 4 most of the Polish government offices and the Polish parliament were ordered to leave Warsaw and establish themselves in various cities to the south and east. The gold reserves of the Bank of Poland and various important archives were sent south to the Rumanian border. Almost at once, the orderly processes of government began to crumble. Although the Polish cabinet and President

Mościcki had remained in Warsaw, the foreign embassies and legations accredited to the Polish government were told to be ready to move at a few hours' notice.

On the morning of September 7 the foreign office advised all foreign diplomats that Mościcki and his ministers were leaving at once for Nałeczów, a resort town about eighty-five miles to the southeast. In a large convoy of cars and trucks, the Polish cabinet left Warsaw, dutifully followed by various foreign ambassadors, missions, staffs, press corps, etcetera.

Nałeczów proved to be utterly unsuitable as a temporary capital. The town was virtually without electricity; there were no communication systems; and the German army was reported to be only ten miles away. On the morning of September 8, Beck announced that the government would continue its flight, this time to Krzemieniec, which was two hundred miles to the southeast but unfortunately only twenty-five miles from the border of then-neutral Russia. The journey was difficult in the extreme. German fighters continually strafed the column. The United States Ambassador Biddle, reported being bombed fifteen times and machine-gunned four times. Even making allowances for the fact that anyone in a car in this convoy would think that any bomb falling nearby had been directed at him, this was quite a lot of attention from the Luftwaffe. It does seem evident that the Germans knew of the Polish government's movements and made every effort to kill off its officials.

After six days in Krzemieniec under constant bombing, the Polish government was in increasing danger of being engulfed by the German southern advance. Although the Soviet Union was still neutral, no one in the Polish government would consider crossing over into Russia to ask for asylum. It was evident that the cabinet must move still farther south to the Rumanian border. If they were driven from Poland, they could then at least get to the West by crossing through a friendly nation. In the early morning of September 14 the Polish cabinet, together with President Mościcki, traveled a hundred miles south to the little town of Zaleszczyki on the banks of the Dniester River, which separated Poland and Rumania. The town was promptly bombed by the Luftwaffe. This was too much for most of the diplomatic corps accompanying the Polish government. They had been bombed constantly and had been shunted for two weeks willy-nilly across the Polish countryside, without news and with practically no way to communicate with their governments. Most of the ambassadors and ministers of legation crossed the bridge between Poland and Rumania, and made their way to Bucharest from which they could at least send reports to their capitals. But some of the ambassadors remained close to the Polish government. There was no room for them in Zaleszczyki, so they moved into a little town called Kuty, also on the Rumanian border but on the Czeremosz River about ten miles from Zaleszczyki and about the same distance from Koło-myja where Rydz-Śmigły and the Polish GHQ had come to rest. In due course, the Polish government also moved to Kuty, although Beck and Prime Minister Składkowski spent most of their time at GHQ in Kołomyja.

The Polish government had not, in general, displayed itself to good advantage during the two and one half weeks that had brought them from peace in Warsaw to disaster at Kuty. The government had gone into the war with an attitude of optimism. When delegations from the opposition political parties had approached the government with a proposal that a wartime "all-party" cabinet be formed, they were told, "Ah, yes! Now you have come to cooperate! But it's already too late, now there will be only commands!"[12]

The principal slogan of the government had been *"Silni, Zwarci, qotowi"* ("Strong, United, Ready"). But to the Polish people exposed to the horrors of the blitzkrieg there seemed to be nothing strong, united, or ready about the Polish government. The government, out of communication in its retreat across the country, seemed to have evaporated. In their flight the government officials seemed to have abandoned the Polish people.

By the time the caravan of automobiles bearing Prime Minister Sławój-Składkowski, President Mościcki, the cabinet, staff, foreign diplomats, and military missions reached Kuty on September 17, the Polish government was thoroughly discredited. They were desperate as well. That afternoon the mayor of Śniatyn, which was only twenty miles away, telephoned to report that Red Army tanks were just out-side his town. At 4 P.M. there was a cabinet meeting. It was very in-formal, and no minutes were kept. Rydz-Śmigły and President Mościcki were present. It was concluded that the Polish government must leave Poland, cross over into Rumania, and from there go on to France, where it would continue the fight. There seemed no time for delay. The Russians might appear at almost any moment, and the government's only defensive force was the few score soldiers that made up the presidential guard.

Beck informed the cabinet that he had discussed the matter of flight through Rumania with the Rumanian government. In view of the historic friendship between the two nations—and particularly because Rumania had been bound by treaty to come to Poland's aid, but had not done so—the Rumanian government was expected to permit the civil members of the Polish government the right of passage through its nation. Concerning the passage of Polish soldiers, from Rydz-Śmigły downward, through Rumania, it was anticipated that "there would probably be some formal difficulty, but they would all be able to proceed to France."[13]

Early that evening the members of the Polish government got into their automobiles and joined the long line of fleeing Poles at the bridge that crossed the Czeremosz River into Rumania.

Rydz-Śmigły had attended the cabinet meeting, and although he urged the government to flee Poland, he had not given the slightest indication that he too intended to go. He had not asked the government's permission to leave Polish soil. It was known that he was considering flying into Warsaw to personally direct the struggle in the besieged capital.

But during the night of September 17 after the government had departed, Rydz-Śmigły came to the conclusion that the war against Germany was lost—within Poland at any rate. He decided to leave Poland and continue the battle from France. Early in the morning of September 18 the marshal and his staff drove to the Rumanian border and crossed over. The members of the Polish government, Beck in particular, were astonished to learn of this action. Rydz-Śmigły issued no final orders to the fighting forces, which then probably totaled 250,000 men, many of whom were still resisting heroically. No orders for a general surrender of the Polish Army were ever given and no general surrender ever took place.

The fact that the Polish Army had been, in a sense, abandoned by its commander and headquarters staff actually made little difference in the outcome of the struggle. The fighting soon wound down as the various pockets of Polish resistance were crushed by either the German or the Soviet army. German sources claim that the Polish campaign can be considered to have been concluded on September 20. But, in fact, the Polish agony continued for nearly two more weeks. Warsaw resisted heroically until September 27, by which time German artillery and bombers had destroyed the water-supply system, the city was in flames, and the food supply had been exhausted. Modlin surrendered on September 28, and the marine and navy defenders of the Hel Peninsula held out until October 2.

In the south, the Rumanian Bridgehead, commanded by General Sosnkowski, rapidly crumbled under the combined pressure of the German panzers and the Red Army. The Polish defenders, cornered in this little tongue of territory, either died on the spot, were taken prisoner, or made their way into Hungary and Rumania. Nearly a hundred thousand Polish soldiers escaped from Poland to fight again. They had suffered enormous hardships—not the least of which were endured while they were making their way to Rumania. The section of Poland through which they had to pass was mostly populated by peasants of Ukrainian origin. Their long-standing resentment toward the Poles now displayed itself in horrifying form. The peasants rose up and murdered Polish soldiers who, in small groups or individually, were trying to escape southward. The Polish soldiers responded by burning villages and shooting or hanging any peasants who behaved suspiciously.

The last real battle in which organized forces of the Polish Army took part in the homeland was on October 4–6 at Kock in central Poland. After it was lost, remnants of the Polish Army commenced an underground war that continued with increasing intensity until the end of World War II.

The overwhelming German victory in Poland astonished the world. In only thirty-six days of battle the Germans, with relatively minor assistance from Soviet forces, had destroyed a major European army at a cost to the Germans of about 14,000 killed and 30,000 wounded. They had killed 66,500 Poles and made prisoners of about 700,000 more. This victory convinced Adolf Hitler, who had had some hand in the planning of the campaign, that he was a military genius. And the totality of the German victory made it possible for the Red Army to capture more than 200,000 Polish soldiers while sustaining only seven hundred casualties.

Afterword

THE HISTORY OF independent Poland came to an end, for all practical purposes, on the night of September 17–18, 1939, with the departure of the Polish government to Rumania and the subsequent internment of its senior members. Beck's expectation that the Polish president, prime minister, and cabinet would be permitted to transit Rumania on their way to France proved wrong. The Rumanians, under extreme pressure from the German government, were compelled to intern the most important of the Polish government leaders. For a short period of time the Rumanians kept this handful of Poles under careful watch. But as months passed the Rumanians permitted the internees either to leave with their blessing or else to "escape," providing they did it discreetly. President Mościcki, who had once been a Swiss citizen, took advantage of the fact that Swiss citizenship cannot be lost or renounced. The Rumanians allowed Mościcki to depart for Switzerland, where he died in 1946. Prime Minister Sławoj-Składkowski eventually escaped from Rumania and made his way to the Near East. From there he went to Great Britain, where he died in 1962. Marshal Rydz-Śmigły also fled from Rumania. In December 1940 he crossed into Hungary, and in disguise he slipped into Poland during the autumn of 1941. Rydz-Śmigły died of a heart attack in Warsaw in December 1941, after having failed to make contact with the underground Polish Home Army in which he had hoped to play a role. Józef Beck was interned at a hotel in a small village near Bucharest. He made one attempt to escape, but it was so poorly arranged that the Rumanian authorities were compelled to apprehend him. His place of residence was changed to another small village, where he lived in a peasant cottage and occupied himself with dictating his memoirs. He developed tuberculosis and died in Rumania in June 1944.

On September 17, 1939, Poland ceased to be an authentically sovereign state. The most important decisions affecting the nation have subsequently been made by, or at least been subject to the veto of, one or several of the great powers that were victorious in World War II.

During the course of the war the leaders of the Polish government-in-exile, which was established first in France and then in Great Britain, learned that in the end they must defer to their allies in matters great and small. No longer masters of their own house, they lived the inevitably subservient lives of reluctant guests of frequently reluctant hosts.

The first of such submissions came only a week after the flight of the Polish government into Rumania. Under the Polish constitution, the president had the right during wartime to designate his successor. Since he was interned in Rumania, President Mościcki decided to resign his office and choose his successor from among those Poles who were at liberty in the West. The new president would make his place of office in Paris, where a government-in-exile could be formed from among the many Poles who were at the moment escaping to France through Rumania, Hungary, and the Scandinavian states. As his successor, Mościcki designated General Bolesław Wieniawa-Długoszowski who was then Polish ambassador to Italy. Almost certainly there was a secret understanding that Wieniawa-Długoszowski would, in turn, yield the presidency to General Kasimierz Sosnkowski, who was at this point still fighting in Poland and whose exact whereabouts were unknown to Mościcki. It was assumed that eventually Sosnkowski would leave Poland and make his way to Paris. It was apparently agreed that, when this happened, he would assume the office of president. Only a handful of Poles knew anything of this secret and risky arrangement.

The Quai d'Orsay regarded Wieniawa-Długoszowski as nothing more than a playboy cavalryman who was a pliable friend of all of the interned Polish government figures. In addition it was well known that the General had once had a drinking problem, and it was not certain that he had overcome it. The French indicated that they considered the appointment of Wieniawa-Długoszowski unsuitable and that they would refuse to recognize any government headed by him, no matter how legally constituted it might be under Polish law.

The humiliated Poles found themselves compelled to bend to the wishes of the French. They inquired whether Władysław Raczkiewicz, a well-known Polish politician who was then in London, would be acceptable. They were informed that he was satisfactory, but only on the understanding that Raczkiewicz would appoint General Władysław Sikorski as prime minister and commander in chief. Sikorski had been for many years in opposition to Piłsudski and his successors, but the French liked him very much and considered him "France's foremost friend among the Poles."[1] (Sikorski had escaped from Poland into Rumania, and the French had arranged for his immediate transit from there to Paris.)

As the prime minister of the Polish government-in-exile, Sikorski put together a cabinet that contained mostly members of the prewar opposition. For the first time in nearly fifteen years it was not an advantage for a Polish leader to have been an old Piłsudski-ite. In fact, all things being equal, the Piłsudski-ites were at a political disadvantage in the government-in-exile, although it was not possible to exclude them entirely. Only three old *Sanacja* personalities—Koc, Sosnkowski, and Zaleski—were given ministerial positions.

The turnover of the Polish government to the prewar opposition was not simply the result of the Quai d'Orsay's preference for Sikorski. At that point no government made up of old Piłsudski-ites could have commanded much loyalty from among the Poles abroad or within Poland. The Piłsudski-ites were associated with the September defeat—which was regarded as a national disgrace. Actually, it was not the defeat itself that was so humiliating. It had been foreseen that Poland might not be able to withstand a full onslaught by the German army, and no one had expected Poland to survive a joint attack by both Germany and Soviet Russia. But what had *not* been foreseen was the swiftness and ease of the German triumph. The Polish Army and government appeared simply to have collapsed, and the prewar leadership was generally blamed for it. Later, when most of the rest of Europe was overwhelmed by the German blitzkrieg, the Polish people would feel somewhat better disposed toward their former leaders. But this lay in the future, and at the time of its formation the Sikorski government-in-exile commanded substantial support. It proved capable of building up in France a significant army, which fought extremely well during the German invasion in May 1940. When France was defeated, the Polish government-in-exile moved to London, where it rebuilt the Polish Army into an important and distinguished fighting force that eventually totaled some 200,000 men.

In the meantime, within Poland there was appalling suffering. Under the Molotov-Ribbentrop agreements of August 23 and September 28, 1939, the Germans and Soviets had partitioned Poland between them. The Russians were anxious to eliminate all ethnic Poles from their sector of Poland and thus make it difficult for any future Polish state to demand the territory's restoration. The Soviets, therefore, adopted the policy of either deporting all ethnic Poles to the German part of Poland or arresting them and transporting them to work camps within the Soviet Union. The best estimates indicate that 1.5 million Poles were sent to these camps, where many of them died.

The Germans, on the other hand, treated Poland as a sort of economic resource center and systematically plundered it of its foodstuffs, factory equipment, cattle and horses. And eventually, of course, the Germans made Poland into a vast killing ground for their annihilation of Europe's Jewish population.

There can be no doubt that the Poles, no matter which regime they lived under, suffered more than any other nation subjugated during World War II. As Winston Churchill observed in 1941, "Every day Hitler's firing parties are busy in a dozen lands. Monday he shoots Dutchmen, Tuesday, Norwegians, Wednesday, French and Belgians stand against the wall, Thursday, it is the Czechs who must suffer . . . But always, all of the days, there are the Poles."[2] Actually, something quite similar could be said about the slaughter of Poles by the Soviet NKVD on the Russian side of the Molotov-Ribbentrop Line. The Poles found little difference between the Germans and the Soviets when it came to savagery worked upon a conquered people.

In June 1941, Hitler invaded Russia. At that time the Polish government-in-exile had, of course, no diplomatic relations with the Soviet Union and had had none since the Soviets attacked Poland in September 1939. During the first desperate weeks of the German invasion, the Russian government cast about for any form of support it could get from any source whatever. The British, who had taken over the role of Poland's mentor from the defeated French, encouraged the Polish government to enter an agreement with the Soviet Union under which the two governments would recognize each other diplomatically and exchange ambassadors and the Polish government would undertake to raise an army within the Soviet Union from among the Polish prisoners there. But prior to signing these agreements, the Polish government attempted to pin the Russians down to a commitment regarding the postwar frontier between the two nations. Certainly, the Poles observed, the Soviet Union would agree to the old Treaty of Riga frontiers. Surely the Soviet Union did not expect to keep that portion of Polish soil that it had gotten by agreement with the Nazis? But the Russians were evasive on this issue. They would not commit themselves, and the British, anxious to see relations restored between their Polish wards and their Soviet allies, pressed the Poles to sign anyway. As Churchill put it, "We had the invidious responsibility of recommending General Sikorski to rely on Soviet good faith in the future settlement of Russian-Polish relations and not to insist at this moment on any written guarantees for the future."[3] The Poles reluctantly accepted the British advice and signed the agreement on July 30, 1941. Later, in December 1941, again at the urging of the British, Sikorski flew to Moscow to conclude a treaty of friendship and mutual assistance with Stalin. The British again prevailed upon the Poles to sign without receiving a Russian commitment on postwar frontiers.

But now there was a second matter on which the Poles were obtaining only evasive responses from the Soviets. Approximately ten thousand Polish army officers had been captured by the Red Army in 1939 and taken to prison camps in western Russia. Polish intelligence sources could find no trace of them. It was known only that at some time about April 1940 most of this large body of men seemed to have disappeared from the face of the earth. The Soviet government claimed that these officers must now be prisoners of the Germans, who had, it was alleged, captured them from the Russians in mid-1941.

Dragged down by the burden of unresolved issues, the Soviet-Polish relationships languished. There was certainly little trust or good will displayed by either side. Eventually, in March 1943 after the Polish government-in-exile flatly demanded that the Russians agree to the postwar restoration of the pre–September-1939 frontiers, the Soviets finally announced their intention to continue to hold all territory up to the Molotov-Ribbentrop Line. (It is certain that there was more than simple territorial greed involved in the Soviet determination to hold onto this previously Polish territory. The activities of the NKVD in this region before the German invasion had been so horrifying that it was unthinkable that the area should be restored to an independent postwar Poland. The Poles would surely conduct a public inquiry into the Soviet atrocities, and the findings would have serious propaganda consequences for the Soviet Union.)

Hard on the heels of this statement came a shattering announcement by the Germans on April 13, 1943. They claimed that their occupying forces in Russia had come across huge mass graves in the Katyn Forest near Smolensk. There the Germans had discovered more than four thousand bodies, which were identified as those of some of the missing Polish officers. All had been shot through the back of the head. The Germans announced that all evidence indicated that they had been killed in April 1940, at which time they had been Russian prisoners. The Soviet government protested that the Germans must have killed these Poles. The Germans denied this and asked for an investigation by the International Red Cross. The Polish government-in-exile also asked the Red Cross to investigate. At this, the Soviet government broke off all diplomatic relations with the Polish government in London and refused to recognize it as the legitimate government of Poland. Soon afterward, General Sikorski was killed in an airplane crash at Gibraltar. His place as Polish prime minister was taken by Stanisław Mikolajczyk, a leader of the Polish Peasant Party, but a man with absolutely no international reputation and only modest powers of command over his colleagues in the government.

At the end of November 1943 the Tehran Conference commenced. The Western Allies were profoundly conscious that at that moment they had in action against Germany only thirteen or fourteen divisions, which were inching their way up Italy. The Soviets, on the other hand, were employing 178 divisions in a ferocious struggle with the German army. Stalin expressed to Churchill his desire to reach an agreement with Britain and the United States regarding the future of Poland. Churchill was anxious to be accommodating. In meetings over a period of days a sort of deal was developed under which the Russians would hold onto their Polish gains of September 1939 (but now they called the western border of their Polish territory the *Curzon* Line, rather than the Molotov-Ribbentrop Line, and indeed the two "lines" did not differ much in location). Poland would be compensated for its loss of 55,000 square miles of territory by the award of most of East Prussia and the enlargement of Poland westward into Germany for a then-unspecified distance. The British left Tehran determined to get the Polish government-in-exile to accept this plan on the basis of which diplomatic relations would be restored between Moscow and the Poles in London. As Churchill cabled to Anthony Eden, "If they [the Poles] cast it all aside, I do not see how His Majesty's Government can do anything more for them. The Russian armies may in a few months be crossing the frontiers of prewar Poland, and it seems of the utmost consequence to have friendly recognition by Russia of the Polish Government."[4]

Despite the pressures imposed by Britain, and they were considerable, the Polish government strongly resisted the Tehran plan. The Poles would not agree to give up a third of their territory which included five million persons and the cities of Lwów and Wilno. They did not wish to acquire huge chunks of German territory containing large German populations which would forever constitute an intractable and dangerous minority. And, in any event, the Polish government-in-exile utterly distrusted the Soviets. They could not forget the invasion of September 1939. They could not forgive the subsequent brutalization of Polish citizenry by the Russians. The members of the Polish government did not see how they could possibly tell those Poles who lived in the eastern marches of the nation that their homelands were being abandoned to the Russians. Nor could they envision giving such news to the soldiers in the Polish armies fighting in Europe, most of whom had come from eastern Poland. And always before them was the massacre of the Katyn Forest in which every member of the government had lost relatives and friends.

To the British, the Polish government-in-exile seemed both unreasonable and unrealistic. The British believed that the advancement of the Soviet frontiers to the Curzon Line was not altogether unfair. It had, after all, been drawn by expert demographers, who had considered it to represent the authentic eastern boundary of ethnic Poland. And, anyhow, Poland was being compensated for its eastern losses.

No one was more anxious than Winston Churchill to see the development of a strong, non-Communist Polish nation in postwar Europe. He thought it a matter of the greatest importance. At the same time Churchill believed that many of Mikolajczyk's cabinet ministers were so excessively anti-Soviet as to have lost their powers of objective judgment. He regarded the entire Polish government-in-exile as crippled by the historic Polish vice of thinking that the affairs of the world revolved around Poland. As 1944 began, Churchill warned the Poles that there was "not much room for negotiation."[5] He could not seem to convey the sense of urgency that the British felt in this matter. That year would surely see the Red Army enter Poland, and since the government-in-exile had no relationship with the Soviets, there was little that could prevent the Russians from setting up a Communist regime in Warsaw. The government-in-exile would, as Churchill warned Mikolajczyk, then "be powerless to do anything but make its protests to the world."[6] Regardless of the rights or wrongs of the situation, the Polish government must come to terms with Stalin.

For many months this argument continued. The Polish government was adamant in its refusal to accept the Tehran arrangement and, consequently, they remained without diplomatic recognition by the Soviet Union. Churchill, exasperated by the Polish attitude, constantly warned that time was running out. Concessions to the Russians were mandatory. The British prime minister bluntly cautioned the Poles that it was "unthinkable" and "useless to imagine" that Great Britain and the United States would ever go to war with Russia over the matter of Poland's eastern frontier.[7]

On July 17, 1944, the first units of the Red Army crossed the Bug River and entered into territory that even the Soviets conceded was Polish. They had not arrived politically unprepared. The Soviet government had scraped together enough Polish Communists to be able to announce in January 1942, the formation of a "Polish Workers' Party." This had been a very difficult task because of the almost unanimous hatred of the Poles for anything connected with the Soviet Union. It was a feeble beginning, but it provided the nucleus around which a "National Polish Council for the Homeland" could be formed in Moscow. A few days after the Soviets entered

Poland, the National Council was brought to Lublin, the first large Polish city to have been freed from the Germans. This group was renamed the Lublin Committee and was obviously the Soviets' shadow government for Poland, available to be trotted on stage when required.

The only authority which the Polish government-in-exile possessed within its homeland was the underground Home Army. This was an extremely well-organized secret force of several hundred thousand men and women. It had been built up over a period of nearly five years, and its leaders were appointed by the government in London, which provided political direction, money and supplies. There was regular courier service between London and Warsaw as well as constant coded radio traffic. It was a very substantial operation—in fact, it was the largest resistance army in any occupied nation in Europe.

The plan of the Polish government-in-exile had been that as the Red Army gradually fought its way into Poland, the Home Army would rise up in the German rear. The Home Army would make a significant contribution to the German defeat and would thereupon take over the administration of liberated Polish territory in the name of the government-in-exile. But it did not happen that way. The Red Army refused to accept the cooperation of the Home Army. As soon as the Soviets succeeded in clearing any section of Poland, they promptly disarmed the Home Army, drafted the enlisted men into a Communist-directed military organization called the People's Guard, and usually arrested and imprisoned the Home Army officers.

At the end of July 1944, the Red Army thrust out an assault force on a narrow front. This attack broke through a fault in the German defense, and suddenly, to general surprise, the Russians found themselves with an armored column practically in the suburbs of Warsaw. On July 29 Moscow radio broadcast an appeal for the Warsaw population to rise up against the Germans. The Polish Home Army within Warsaw consisted at that time of about 50,000 trained men and women. To their commander, General Tadeuz Komorowski, whose cover name was "Bor," it seemed that the Germans were at the point of collapse. His political advisers agreed that it was crucial for the Home Army itself to liberate Warsaw. Immediately following this, the designated representatives of the Polish government-in-exile would assume the administration of the Polish capital. The London government would then be flown into Warsaw, and once this government was sitting in the capital which its army had liberated, its legitimacy could not be disputed. On August 1, 1944, acting on his own initiative, Bor ordered the Polish Home Army in Warsaw to commence an uprising. The Russians, it appears, were kept completely ignorant of this Polish plan.

Within only a few hours of the start of the uprising the Polish forces were in possession of two thirds of Warsaw. Almost the entire population of the city threw itself into the fight. All went well for a few days—but only for a few days. The Germans brought in massive reinforcements to reconquer the city. They commenced an offensive that drove back the slender, overextended Russian force outside Warsaw. In the end the Warsaw uprising became a prolonged massacre of the Home Army and the heroic population that supported it. When the remnants of the Home Army surrendered on October 4, sixty-four days after the rising had started, 90 percent of the city was destroyed.

In retrospect, it is certain that the Warsaw uprising was premature. Even if the Soviets had wanted to assist the Home Army, it is probable that they could not have intervened in time against the heavily reinforced Germans. In fact, the Soviets did not themselves capture Warsaw until January 1945. However, the refusal of the Russians even to permit British or American aircraft to land in its territory for refueling after making air supply drops over Warsaw (a refusal which, given the distance involved, effectively prevented such flights) and the passive stance of the Red Army on the Warsaw front are clear indications of the Russians' desire that the Home Army should be liquidated.

As the British had predicted, with every territorial gain that the Russians made in Poland, their price for recognition of the government-in-exile increased. By the middle of 1944 it would no longer have been enough for the London Poles to agree to the Curzon Line frontier with the Soviet Union. Now they would also have to apologize publicly for believing the Russians guilty of the Katyn Forest massacre. As time went by, the Russians added the requirement that the government-in-exile cleanse itself of "anti-Soviet elements" which included Minister of War Sosnkowski and President Raczkiewicz. Shortly afterward, even this was not enough. By October 1944, Stalin was telling Churchill that a condition for Soviet recognition of the London government was that it amalgamate itself with the Lublin Committee which the Soviets had informally recognized as the administrative apparatus for liberated Poland.

At each stage Churchill counseled the Polish government-in-exile to accept the Soviet offer. The Poles consistently refused. Churchill's interviews with them assumed the most formidable character. He pointed out that while they once could have been recognized by Russia as *the* Polish government, a year later they were reduced to discussing whether the Russians would accept them as *part* of a Polish government. If they waited any longer, they might find that even this opportunity had vanished. The Red Army and the Lublin Committee were on Polish soil. The Western Allies and the London Poles were not. On January 4, 1945, Churchill's fears were realized. Disregarding the frantic appeals of Britain and the United States, the Soviets formally recognized the Lublin Committee as the government of Poland.

In February 1945 the Allied leaders met at Yalta. At that time the Red Army was engaged in clearing the German army from Poland. Warsaw had been "liberated," and the Lublin Committee, having renamed itself the Polish Provisional Government, had immediately gone to the capital, where, under Russian protection, it was performing all the functions of the Polish administration. Despite the *de facto* situation in Poland, the Western Allies had not ceased to contest the issue. In fact, at Yalta the subject of Poland figured prominently in seven of the eight meetings of the three powers.

The Western position regarding Poland had again been eroded by events. Now there was no longer any talk whatever of the Polish government-in-exile's returning to Poland to direct its nation's affairs. The objective of the Western Allies was now reduced to attempting to persuade the Russians to broaden the Communist Provisional Government into an "all-new" government that would include a number of Poles from other parties, including certain prominent figures like Mikolajczyk. Should this be done and should the reorganized government be found palatable enough, the Western Allies would recognize it. Following this, if free elections were held, it was expected that the non-Communist parties would show such strength that they would assume an increasingly important role in the Polish government. This was certainly a long way from what the Western Allies would have found acceptable only twelve months before—and it was not certain that Stalin would agree to even these modest requests.

But before anything else could be discussed, boundaries had to be settled. In fairly short order it was agreed that the Curzon Line should be Russia's western frontier. As compensation, Poland would get part of East Prussia and would reach to the Oder in the west. Stalin also proposed that, in the southwest, Poland should be extended to the Western Neisse River. Churchill and Roosevelt were dubious about this last, believing that it gave Poland more German territory than it could digest. The Russians agreed to defer the Western Neisse matter until some later date.

There was much inconclusive haggling. At the end of the Yalta Conference it was agreed only that the Provisional Government in Warsaw was to be broadened by "the inclusion of democratic leaders from Poland itself and from Poles abroad." A Commission of Three, consisting of Molotov and the British and American ambassadors to the Soviet Union, was to meet in Moscow to supervise the Polish governmental reorganization. When this had been accomplished, the Western Allies agreed to recognize the new government. Western ambassadors and observers would enter the country, and free elections would be held within a month.

Clearly, this agreement represented very little in the way of concessions by the Soviets. And whether that which had been agreed to would ever be carried out was largely dependent on the good will of the Soviet government. But, as Churchill observed, "This was the best I could get."[8]

There was not much time left for the government-in-exile in London. The Polish affair was played out in its predictable sequence. The Commission of Three in Moscow found itself deadlocked by the Soviets. The Western observers whom the Russians had promised to admit to Poland were not admitted. The elections which were to have taken place "within a month" were not to be held for two years. And when they did take place they were obviously rigged and were strongly denounced by the United States and British governments. The Communist Provisional Government, which the Soviets at Yalta had agreed to enlarge and reorganize, remained virtually unaltered. Practically every non-Communist name suggested by the

American Ambassador Averell Harriman and the British Ambassador Sir Archibald Clark-Kerr was vetoed by Molotov on the grounds that the nominee was "hostile to the Soviet Union."

In the meantime, the Communist government in Warsaw continued to consolidate its position. Controlling, as it did, every organ of administration and propaganda, the Provisional Government clamped a vise on the entire nation. The only opposition it found difficult to suppress was that posed by the remnants of the Home Army. In January 1945, the commander of that underground force had publicly announced its disbandment. Actually, though, the staffs of the Home Army and its various cadres had simply gone back underground. They kept in communication with the London government-in-exile, which sent them political instructions. This permitted the Warsaw government to brand these Home Army remnants as "fascist guerrillas." An authentic civil war broke out within Poland, as the Provisional Government suppressed these diehard troops. The Russians made their own contribution by inviting to Moscow sixteen well-known Home Army leaders. The pretext was that they were to consult on the makeup of a broadened Polish government. Written guarantees of personal safety were given to the Poles, but when they arrived in Moscow, they were all arrested and tried for "diversionary activity in the rear of the Red Army."[9]

The Western Allies, worn down by the intransigence of the Soviets, finally made a settlement. Since Yalta, the Allies had had very little to do with the Polish government-in-exile. In November 1944 Mikołajczyk had resigned as Polish prime minister and had been replaced by Tomasz Arciszewski, a Socialist leader and a forthright anti-Communist, who had been spirited out of Poland to take this post. However, the Western Allies had continued to do business with Mikołajczyk, who, although he held no office, was considered by the British and American governments to be the most moderate Polish leader of standing who was accessible to them. Mikołajczyk and two associates were induced to go to Moscow, where in June 1945 they met with the leaders of the Provisional Government. The Communists made only one offer—Mikołajczyk could come back to Warsaw, where he would become vice premier and have the privilege of naming a few cabinet ministers. It was evident that they would be only window-dressing. It was take it or leave it. Mikołajczyk was assured that even if he refused the Communist offer, the Western

Allies would recognize the Polish Provisional Government. Mikołajczyk accepted. On June 21 the governments of Britain and the
United States were notified that the Poles had reached an agreement.
Choosing to make no further inquiries, the two nations recognized
the Warsaw government on July 5 and 6, 1945. With this, the Polish
government-in-exile disappeared from the stage of world events.*

Two weeks later the Potsdam Conference took place. The most
important outcome as regards Poland was that in the east the Curzon
Line border was awarded to Russia, while in the west the territory
extending to the Oder and Western Neisse rivers was placed "temporarily" under Polish administration. The exact determination of
the Polish frontier with Germany was to be left to a general peace
conference—which, of course, never took place. The Polish government instantly proceeded to expel practically all of the millions of
Germans living within its borders and to regard the Oder–Western-
Neisse line as being a resolved issue. Poland now comprises a territory of 120,000 square miles, which is about four fifths of the size
of the prewar nation. Poland no longer has a minorities problem.
The combination of the Curzon Line and the ruthless expulsion of
the Germans has produced a nation that consists almost entirely of
ethnic Poles.

The majority of those Poles who escaped from Poland in 1939
and spent the war years abroad refused to return to Poland. Only
about a fifth of the members of the wartime Polish Army who served
abroad ever went back to their homeland. To all those émigrés the
British government offered a kind of protection in the form of
"traveling documents" issued in lieu of passports. These people,
among whom are the members of what could technically still be
considered the "legitimate" government of Poland, have generally
not ceased to reproach Britain and the United States for the series of

---

* Stanisław Mikołajczyk served in the Polish government for about two years during
which time he attempted to rebuild an independent peasant party that could resist the
Communists. But gradually the Communist vise tightened in Poland. By 1947 the opposition parties were largely disenfranchised. A program of terror began, and the
opposition leadership was clearly in great physical danger. On the night of October 21,
1947, Mikołajczyk appeared at the British embassy in Warsaw and asked for assistance
in fleeing the country. The British secret service was able to spirit this man, the Polish
vice premier, to Danzig, where he was smuggled aboard a British vessel and taken to
London. Most of Mikołajczyk's associates whom he left behind in Poland were imprisoned or killed during a period of Communist consolidation that commenced in
1949. Mikołajczyk himself, rejected as an appeaser and a coward by most of the anti-
Communist Polish community abroad, died in the United States in 1966.

events that resulted in the control of their nation by a Communist government.

It is now quite common, and it serves the purposes of the present Communist government, to dismiss the independent Poland of 1918–1939 as nothing more than a shabby and inefficient pseudofascist regime. As this argument runs, Piłsudski and his henchmen played a silly, imperialistic charade. They were anti-Semitic and pro-German. They oppressed both the Polish people and the minority groups that they had greedily and shortsightedly absorbed. Poland of those years is described as a nation run by power-mad colonels, foolish cavalrymen, and rich landowners all of whom acquiesced in the implementation of a predatory and opportunistic foreign policy. In the end, these wretched persons were duped by Hitler, who swiftly snuffed out their wicked reign. The rapid collapse of Poland in 1939 is considered to prove this assessment of Poland between the two World Wars.

On the other hand, it pleases many of the defenders of the Poland of 1918–1939 to regard that period as entirely one of great accomplishments. These persons do not concede that any significant errors were made in the governing of Poland, and they regard its foreign policy as generally being very cleverly conducted. At the very least, they regard Poland's diplomacy as having been handled fully as well as circumstances permitted. The defeat of 1939 is ascribed entirely to lack of support by Poland's allies. The subsequent demise of the government-in-exile is looked upon as purely the result of Allied "treachery at Yalta."

The truth, of course, lies somewhere between these two extremes. There can be no doubt that Poland between the two great wars can be credited with many remarkable achievements. Heading the list of these is the fact that Poland was re-created and survived for as long as it did. That Poland came eventually to be regarded almost as one of Europe's major powers was more remarkable. In 1919 even Poland's friends had been dubious of the nation's ability to survive. For more than a hundred years the Polish people had been the second-class citizens among alien powers. They had had little experience in the art of self-government, and that experience had been mostly bad. The new nation possessed practically none of the prerequisites for national survival. Poland was too poor, had too many unproductive mouths to feed, too few national resources, too many minorities, too many political parties, too many indefensible frontiers and, above all, too many powerful neighbors that were determined to have Poland destroyed. But even after being defeated and occupied by its great neighbors, the Polish nation continued to fight. Poland was the only Nazi-occupied nation in which the Germans were not able to put together even the barest beginnings of a Quisling-type government. The Polish people behaved with such heroism, honor and patriotism that the postwar continuation of the nation—albeit displaced and under a different form of government—was never in doubt.

The defenders of Poland between the wars can make other valid claims. The general standard of education in Poland was enormously increased. Illiteracy, once almost the norm in rural areas, was cut by almost two thirds. All sorts of specialized educational institutions were established to teach agricultural, commercial and technical subjects. The Polish Army, in which every young man had to serve, was used as an enormous compulsory-schooling project in which technical subjects of all kinds were taught.

Not the least of the Polish accomplishments was the development, starting from nothing, of a class of trained and reasonably efficient civil servants and administrators. Similarly, Poland succeeded in the Herculean task of integrating into one whole a host of institutions and enterprises that had previously been separated by the preindependence partitioning powers. Among these were the railroads, the legal system, the highways, and the commercial structure.

The Polish industrial worker was the beneficiary of a very extensive social-welfare plan incorporating protection against sickness and unemployment. A separate compulsory pension scheme covered all workers at retirement.

For the peasant, significant strides were made in land redistribution. About 750,000 new farms were created as the result of land reform. Nearly a million dwarf holdings were bought up by the government and consolidated for resale. This process did not solve Poland's persistent problem of excess population living on the land—in fact, it probably retarded any solution to this problem—but it was an honest effort to satisfy the demands of the peasants for land of their own.

After using overly orthodox measures to deal with the Depression, the Polish government developed more imaginative economic methods. Industrial activity increased, and by 1938 the standard of living in Poland as represented by consumption in most categories was higher than it had ever been.

The level of national consciousness, among ethnic Poles at least, was raised enormously—as proved by the exceptional dedication with which they fought during World War II.

The defects of the Polish government in the 1918–1939 period are quite evident. In part, they were attributable to various characteristics that had historic roots. For example, the leaders of Poland rarely adopted a truly *humanistic* attitude toward its populace. Most Polish governments were much more interested in the welfare of the Polish *nation* as an abstract political entity than in the welfare of the Polish *people*. Probably this is attributable to the fact that the persons who made up the governing class of Poland (Piłsudski, of course, in the forefront) had struggled so hard and so long for Polish independence that the survival of the Polish nation took precedence over anything else. Interestingly, the mass of the Polish people did not for a long time resent this; they knew nothing better. The pre-independence rulers of Poland had shown no interest whatever in the people's welfare. Without question, a great deal was asked of the Polish people by its government, and the Polish people were by and large willing to give a great deal. Only toward the very end of the interwar era did they begin to sense that they were being dealt with a trifle too indifferently, and the political makeup of the government-in-exile, from which old Piłsudski-ites were largely excluded, reflected this feeling.

There were various other "character flaws" common among the governments of independent Poland. Among these was a tendency toward obstinacy, resistance to compromise, and a basic lack of political acumen. These were serious defects. Poland was never able to establish a workable parliamentary democracy. The Polish Constitution of 1935 was probably as badly flawed as the Constitution of 1921. The politicians of the *sanacja* did not seem significantly better or worse than those who preceeded them or, indeed, those who would follow them in the post-Piłsudski years.

Generally speaking, it is hard to hold the interwar Polish governments responsible for the Polish defeat in September 1939. No combination of foreign policy and military preparedness could have saved Poland from destruction at the hands of a rearmed Germany. Once Adolf Hitler had determined to crush Poland, and had developed the means to do so, there was nothing that Poland could do to save itself. Adequate preparation of Poland for a defense against blitzkrieg warfare was simply beyond the taxing or borrowing power of the nation. And for Poland to have resisted a combined assault by Germany and the Soviet Union was beyond imagining. In the end, for all the enormous effort that went into interwar foreign relations, it was a totally fruitless exercise.

The one possible exception to the hopelessness of the Polish situation vis-à-vis a rearmed and determined Germany *might* have been a pre-Munich alliance between Czechoslovakia and Poland. If at some inspired moment, possibly in the spring of 1938, the leaders of these two countries had recognized the supreme advantages of such an understanding and had dismissed the problems and hatreds of the past, then an alliance could have been put together that would have produced a formidable combination of manpower, arms and fortifications that might well have insured the safety of both these Eastern European states. Certainly it would have prolonged their independent existence. The conclusion of such a pact would have established its creators as great statesmen and would have elevated Poland to authentic great-power status.

But if it is not possible to condemn the Poles for the end result of their pre–World War II diplomacy, it is surely fair to criticize the *manner* in which Polish foreign affairs were conducted. Under Piłsudski and Beck, Poland's relations with its neighbors were handled in a fashion that was abrasive and overly aggressive. Its diplomacy was characterized by serious tactical errors and miscalculations. The policy of pursuing "equilibrium" between its great neighbors proved a failure. The Nonaggression Declaration with Germany undermined the resolution of the French government to resist Hitler. Poland's renunciation of the Minorities Treaty further weakened the League of Nations at a critical time. And, of course, the Polish 1938 ultimatum to Czechoslovakia and its point-of-the-bayonet acquisition of Teschen were gross tactical errors. Whatever justice there might have been to the Polish claim upon Teschen, its seizure in 1939 was an enormous mistake in terms of the damage done to Poland's reputation among the democratic powers of the world. The Polish ultimatum made it appear that Poland was either in league with Germany or, at least, had a sense of international morality that was not much different from that of Nazi Germany. It was an action that coming at the time and in the manner that it did, was not exactly *wrong*, but it was *insensitive*. It was the capstone to a foreign policy that was conducted in a manner "too clever by half."

An additional failure of interwar Poland was the inability of the nation to reconcile its national minorities, in particular the Ukrainians and Belorussians. These groups believed that they had been deprived of various rights guaranteed to them under the Minorities Treaty. They were certain that they were discriminated against in matters of public employment, land redistribution, and schooling. Their pot of grievances was stirred by the Soviet Union, which had a far greater population of Ukrainians and Belorussians. In the end, the best relationship that the Polish government seemed able to achieve with these two groups, totaling about five and one half million citizens, was a guarded truce between a suspicious government on one hand and a sullen minority on the other. In fact, what is remarkable is that the Polish government never seemed to realize just how profoundly alienated these people were—until September 1939.

The basis of this minority problem was the never-resolved conflict between Piłsudski's Federalism and his opponents "assimilationism." This led to a situation in which Poland was both too small and too large. If Poland was to become the leader of a federal system, then it should have continued the 1920 struggle with Russia to the point where enough of the Ukraine and Belorussia were free to enable these peoples to put together their own semiautonomous states. But clearly this was impossible. Poland was exhausted. Therefore it had to be conceded that the federalist issue was dead. The very highest statecraft would then have been to recognize the probable permanence of Soviet Russia and to have refused to incorporate into Poland any sizable minority upon which the Soviets would always have a claim. This would have involved Poland taking less territory at Riga than it did, but it would have had many future advantages. An ethnically homogeneous Poland would have had a lot fewer problems to solve.

The government-sponsored anti-Semitism of the post-Piłsudski period is, of course, a squalid tale. Poland's apologists point out that like fascism, anti-Semitism was rampant in Europe during the late thirties and that Poland's anti-Semitism was mild indeed compared to that of Nazi Germany. This is probably true, but it is no justification for the systematic harassment by the Polish state of three million of its citizens. It is frequently alleged that anti-Semitism is somehow an inherent part of the Polish character and that the Poles' systematic persecution of Jews has been stayed from time to time only by a strong ruler. On the other hand, it has been held that the enormous numbers of Jews who lived in Poland are evidence that Poland was historically a Jewish sanctuary. Therefore any anti-Semitism in Poland is only an occasional and spontaneous aberration in the national character. It is for the reader to decide which is the correct view.

Any analysis of the Polish nation in the interwar years obviously must include an assessment of Józef Piłsudski. It does not seem excessive to say that, at his best, the man was a genius. He had remarkable vision and steadfastness of purpose. It is difficult to believe that independent Poland without Piłsudski could have continued to exist for any period of time. For a politically immature, newly established nation like Poland, a figure of prestige and authority like Piłsudski was absolutely indispensable. And, of course, he won the Polish-Soviet War. His coup of May 1926 can be defended on the grounds that Poland was drifting into a chaotic state. No one else could have saved the republic. But as Piłsudski aged, his emotional health declined along with his physical health. While continuing to hold important offices, he went into semiretirement and isolated himself from much of the business with which he ought to have dealt. He continued to ignore, or more precisely *failed to comprehend*, the importance of political matters. He failed to develop a workable ideology. What he brought to Poland was his personality, his integrity, and his romantic view of the Polish nation. As a result he failed to insure that he would be followed by a competent successor or that the system that he had directed would be capable of producing gifted leaders.

It is, of course, fair to criticize Piłsudski for indulging in cronyism. Without doubt, much too great a proportion of the nation's affairs were directed by Piłsudski's old followers from the First Brigade, the intelligence section of the P.O.W., or the prewar Riflemen's Associations. Even making allowance for the fact these organizations drew an elite group of volunteers, it is obvious that these ten thousand or so veterans could not represent all of the best talent available to the Polish state. A large number of able Poles were excluded from public service as a consequence of the preference always shown to men with old Piłsudski credentials.

The Poland of these years is often incorrectly described as a fascist state. Piłsudski and his followers established what was certainly an authoritarian state, but not one that could accurately be described as fascist. Interwar Poland was not a totalitarian state, nor were its leaders avowedly antidemocratic. At no time did Piłsudski or any of his successors refer to their regimes as "dictatorships." In fact in 1934 a crypto-fascist political party (the ONR) was broken up by the police, and its leaders were put briefly into the Brest Litovsk prison camp.

The Piłsudski regime and its successors behaved toward their political opposition in a manner that was unpleasantly authoritarian. The opposition parties were the victims of unfair electoral practices, and there were sporadic instances of illegal persecution of the opposition leadership. The opposition was denied the use of the state-owned radio during political campaigns and at times the authorities made it difficult for the opposition to use public facilities to hold political rallies. But despite this harassment, the opposition remained vigorous and vociferous right up to the end. It can even be argued that by September 1939 the opposition parties were in a sturdier condition than they had ever been. The only exception was the Communist Party, which, although legally proscribed, had been allowed to function politically under various subterfuges. And the reason that the party did not continue to exist until September 1939 was that the Comintern, not the Polish government, destroyed it.

There was occasional press censorship in Poland, but it was only intermittently and half-heartedly enforced. The newspapers mostly printed whatever they wanted, and the government found it almost impossible to suppress any determined criticism. Opponents of the regime continued to teach in universities and to make their opposition known in very forthright terms. The judiciary preserved its independence and enforced a generally impartial standard of justice. Foreign newspapers and publications were freely sold at all times in Poland. Polish citizens never experienced any difficulties in leaving or reentering their country. Interwar Poland was as democratic as any of the "successor states," and much more than most. In a period when many much larger European nations, like Italy, Germany and Spain, all became authentically fascist, it is incorrect to imply that the Polish political system even modestly resembled theirs.

If the world's view of interwar Poland was frequently less than sympathetic, much of this disapproval was the result of Piłsudski's cavalier disdain for what would now be called public relations. This set the style for the successive Polish governments that devoted little time or effort to the cultivation of a favorable international image of Poland. This indifference to world opinion was an astonishing deviation from the Polish character. For a century and a half before independence Poles had demonstrated that they ranked among the world's greatest publicists. Poles were visible and articulate in espousing attractive causes throughout the world. Polish soldiers, scientists and artists were glamorous international figures. But strangely the independent Poland of 1918–39 produced no attractive international personalities, nor, more importantly, did the nation's leaders even do an adequate job of explaining their own objectives and actions. Compared to, say, Czechoslovakia, which operated a superb public-relations apparatus, the Polish national image is flat and unattractive. This careless attitude toward its own image is responsible for a good many of the critical misconceptions regarding interwar Poland which exist to this day. And, of course, there are not now many persons interested in or capable of correcting the record.

The Poles are a much misunderstood people who inhabit a very poor nation but who have a past, and indeed a present, that is in many ways rich in cultural and scientific achievement. Brave, devout and determined, the Polish people have demonstrated an extraordinary capacity for endurance under suffering. No disaster, and their nation has seen many, seems to blunt their patriotism or stifle their thirst for a national independence.

Source Notes

PREFACE

The bulk of material for these pages is taken from United States Ambassador A. J. Drexel Biddle's personal account, Cannistraro *et al* (eds.), *Poland and the Coming of the Second World War.*

CHAPTER 1

For general background on Poland and its early history I used such accepted sources as Reddaway *et al*, *The Cambridge History of Poland*, Vol. 1; O. Halecki, *A History of Poland*; P. Wandycz, *The Lands of Partitioned Poland, 1795–1918*; and V. L. Beneš and N. J. G. Pounds, *Poland*. For background on the formation of the PPS and the conflict between the various socialist factions I used J. P. Nettl, *Rosa Luxemburg* Vol. 1; and M. K. Dziewanowski, *The Communist Party of Poland.*

1. J. Piłsudski, *Joseph Piłsudski: The Memories of a Polish Revolutionary and Soldier*, p. 13.
2. *Ibid.*, p. 161.
3. *Ibid.*, p. 15.
4. G. Humphrey, *Piłsudski: Builder of Poland*, p. 98.
5. A. Piłsudska, *Piłsudski: A Biography by His Wife*, pp 189–90.

CHAPTER 2

The U.S. preparation for the Paris Peace Conference is best covered in L.E. Gelfand, *The Inquiry*; R. Landau, *Piłsudski and Poland*; and Harry Kessler, *Tagebücher.*

1. J. Piłsudski, *Pisma Zbiorwe* (henceforth *PZ*), Vol. IV, p. 8.
2. T. Komarnicki, *Rebirth of the Polish Republic*, p. 94.
3. Reddaway *et al*, *The Cambridge History of Poland*, Vol. II, p. 485.
4. Haskins and Lord, *Some Problems of the Peace Conference*, p. 171.
5. F. Czernin, *Versailles 1919*, p. 218.
6. *Ibid.*, p. 201.
7. N. Davies, *White Eagle, Red Star*, p. 63.

CHAPTER 3

For background on the conflict surrounding Polish "Federalism" see M. K. Dziewanowski, *Josef Piłsudski: A European Federalist 1918–1922*.

1. David Lloyd George, *Memoirs of the Peace Conference*, Vol. I, p. 201.
2. H. I. Nelson, *Land and Power*, p. 98.
3. P. Wandycz, *France and Her Eastern Allies*, p. 7.
4. *Ibid.*, p. 22.
5. F. Czernin, *Versailles 1919*, p. 202.
6. U.S. Dept. of State, *Papers Relating to the Foreign Relations of the United States: The Paris Peace Conference, 1919*, Vol. III, p. 778.
7. *Ibid.*
8. David Hunter Miller, *My Diary at the Peace Conference of Paris*, Vol. VI, p. 351.
9. U.S. Dept. of State, *Papers Relating to the Foreign Relations of the United States, op. cit.*, Vol. IV, p. 316.
10. Lloyd George, *op. cit.*, Vol. II, p. 631.
11. See Miller, *op. cit.*, Vol. VI, pp 350–68, for this report *in extenso*.
12. U.S. Dept. of State *Papers Relating to the Foreign Relations of the United States, op. cit.*, Vol. IV, p. 417.
13. *Ibid.*
14. *Ibid.*, p. 454.
15. *Ibid.*
16. C. Seymour, *Letters from the Paris Peace Conference*, pp. 222–23.
17. *Ibid.*
17. *Times* (of London) February 8, 1919.
19. Stephen Bonsal, *Suitors and Suppliants*, p. 124.
20. Lloyd George, *op. cit.*, Vol. II, p. 646.
21. *Ibid.*, p. 647.
22. *Ibid.*, p. 648.
23. Wandycz, *op. cit.*, p. 47.

CHAPTER 4

1. R. Gorecki, *Poland and Her Economic Development*, pp. 20–22.
2. Nancy Hooker (ed.), *The Moffat Papers: Selections from the Diplomatic Journals of Jay Pierrepont Moffat, 1919–1943*, p. 13.
3. J. Piłsudski, *PZ*, Vol. IX, p. 90.
4. *Ibid.* Vol. V, p. 205.
5. *Ibid.*
6. W. Baranowski, *Rozmowy z Piłsudskim*, pp. 104–7.
7. K. Kumaniecki, *Odbudowa Panstwowosci Polskiej*, p. 135.
8. B. Schmitt (ed.), *Poland* pp. 91–92.

CHAPTER 5

1. E. H. Carr, *The Bolshevik Revolution* Vol. III, p. 152.
2. M. K. Dziewanowski, *The Communist Party of Poland*, p. 78.
3. P. Wandycz, *Soviet-Polish Relations 1917–1921*, p. 76.
4. *Ibid.*, p. 52.
5. *Ibid.*, p. 77.
6. *Ibid.*
7. *Ibid.*, p. 159.
8. *Ibid.*, p. 82.
9. *Ibid.*, p. 134.
10. *Ibid.*, p. 131.
11. J. S. Reshetar, *The Ukrainian Revolution*, p. 267.
12. U.S. Dept. of State, *Papers Relating to the Foreign Relations of the United States: Paris Peace Conference, 1919*, Vol. VIII, p. 219.
13. *Ibid.*, p. 221.
14. N. Hooker (ed), *The Moffat Papers*, p. 17.
15. R. Debicki, *The Foreign Policy of Poland: 1919–1939*, p. 28.
16. Carr, *op. cit.* Vol III, p. 159.
17. Wandycz, *op. cit.* p. 155.
18. Woodward and Butler (eds), *Documents on British Foreign Policy 1919–1939* First Series, Vol. III, p. 804. (Henceforth "DBFP.")
19. Wandycz, *op. cit.*, p. 162.
20. U.S. Dept. of State, *Papers Relating to the Foreign Relations of the United States, 1920,* Vol. III, p. 382.
21. Quoted in Dziewanowski, *op. cit.*, p. 195.

CHAPTER 6

Of value in the research for this chapter, although unreferenced below, was A. Seaton, *Stalin As Military Commander* and also T. Kutzreba, *Wyprawa Kijowski: Roku 1920.* For an alternate view of the Soviet position at the height of the war see T. Fiddick, "The Miracle of the Vistula," in *Journal of Modern History*, December 1973.

1. L. Trotsky, *My Life* pp. 457–58.
2. G. Bailey, *The Conspirators*, p. 181.
3. N. Davies, *White Eagle, Red Star: The Polish-Soviet War 1919–1920*, p. 132.
4. J. Piłsudski, *1920*, p. 15.
5. N. Davies, *op. cit.*, p. 111.
6. *Ibid.*, p. 119.
7. R. Luckett, *The White Generals*, p. 324.
8. K. M. Murray, *Wings over Poland*, p. 193.
9. J. Piłsudski, *op. cit.*, p. 64.
10. Isaac Babel, *Red Cavalry* "Berestechko"

11. N. Davies, *op. cit.*, p. 105.

12. J. Piłsudski, *op. cit.*, p. 33.

13. *Ibid.*, p. 77.

14. *Ibid.*, p. 142.

15. *Ibid.*, p. 137.

16. N. Davies, *op. cit.*, p. 183.

17. P. Wandycz, *Soviet-Polish Relations*, p. 211.

18. Woodward and Butler, *"DBFP,"* First Series, Vol. VIII, p. 442.

19. *Ibid.*, p. 506.

20. *Ibid.*, p. 502.

21. *Ibid.*, p. 503.

22. *Ibid.*, p. 505.

23. *Ibid.*, p. 505.

24. *Ibid.*, p. 502.

25. *Ibid.*, p. 505.

26. *Ibid.*, p. 530.

27. *Ibid.*, p. 526.

28. I. Deutscher, *Trotsky: The Prophet Armed*, p. 466.

29. J. Korbel, *Poland Between East and West*, p. 49.

30. All quotations from Soviet note of July 17, 1920, are from J. Degras, *Soviet Documents on Foreign Policy 1917–1924*, pp. 194–97.

31. G. Riddell, *Lord Riddell's Intimate Diary of the Peace Conference*, p. 221.

32. D'Abernon, *The Eighteenth Decisive Battle of the World*, p. 18.

33. *Ibid.*, pp. 33–34.

34. N. Davies, *op. cit.*, p. 174.

35. *Ibid.*, p. 220.

36. D'Abernon, *op. cit.*, p. 74.

37. *Ibid.*, p. 71.

38. J. Piłsudski, *"PZ,"* Vol. VII, pp. 152–53.

39. *Ibid.*

40. J. F. C. Fuller, *Decisive Battles: Their Influence upon History and Civilization*, p. 954.

41. P. Wandycz, *Soviet–Polish Relations*, p. 230.

42. Fuller, *op. cit.*, p. 956.

43. Fuller, *op. cit.*, pp. 956–57.

44. J. Piłsudski, *1920*, p. 173.

45. *Ibid.*, p. 176.

46. *Ibid.*, p. 177.

47. *Ibid.*, pp. 177–78.

48. *Ibid.*, pp. 189–90.

49. M. Weygand, *Mémoires: Vol. II, Mirages et Réalité*, p. 166.

CHAPTER 7

For general data on Upper Silesia see R. Machray, *The Problem of Upper Silesia*. For information on the *Freikorps* in Upper Silesia I used R. G. L. Waite,

Vanguard of Naziism, the standard work on the German independent armies. The account of Danzig in its early years as an independent port was drawn from C. Kimmich, *The Free City*. Data on the Polish minorities was drawn principally from S. Horak, *Poland and Her National Minorities*, and R. Buell, *Poland: Key to Europe*. For background on Lithuania I used G. von Rauch, *The Baltic States*.

1. W. Rose, *The Drama of Upper Silesia*, p. 23.
2. *Ibid.*, p. 187.
3. J. Benoist-Méchin, *Histoire de l'armée allemande*, Vol. II, p. 199.
4. Rose, *op. cit.*, p. 69.
5. P. Wandycz, *Czechoslovak–Polish Confederation and the Great Powers 1940–43*, p. 9.
6. W. Jedrzejewicz (ed), *Diplomat in Paris*, p. 57.
7. G. M. Gathorne-Hardy, *A Short History of International Affairs 1920–1939*, p. 96.
8. M. K. Dziewanowski, *Josef Piłsudski: A European Federalist, 1918–1922*, p. 127.
9. *Ibid.*, p. 317.
10. *Ibid.*, p. 345.
11. F. Carsten, *Reichswehr and Politics: 1918–1933*, p. 140.

CHAPTER 8

For political matters discussed in the chapter, and in subsequent chapters, I have drawn most heavily on A. Polonsky, *Politics in Independent Poland 1921–1939*, which is definitive in its field.

1. P. Wandycz, *France and Her Eastern Allies*, p. 235.
2. *Ibid.*, p. 395.
3. R. Machray, *Poland: 1914–1931*, p. 180.
4. J. Piłsudski, *"PZ"* Vol. V, p. 293.
5. A. Polonsky, *Politics in Independent Poland 1921–1939*, p. 111.
6. S. Segal, *The New Poland and the Jews*, p. 35.
7. R. Machray, *op. cit.*, p. 242.
8. For this account of the assassination of Narutowicz, I am indebted to the late Dr. Jan Fryling, of New York City, who was present at the Warsaw Palace of Fine Arts and witnessed Narutowicz's murder at close hand.
9. A. Polonsky, *op. cit.*, p. 112.
10. R. Machray, *op. cit.*, p. 249.
11. R. Landau, *Piłsudski and Poland*.

CHAPTER 9

Because agriculture and economic matters relating to the peasantry were so important in Poland there are numerous books and scholarly articles on these subjects. Among these which were used in the preparation of this chapter were R. Redfield, *Peasant Society and Culture*; T. Mincer, *The Agrarian Problem in Poland*; W. Staniewicz, "The Agrarian Problem in Poland Between Two Wars," *Slavonic and East European Review* No. 100, Dec. 1964; and Sir John Russell, "Reconstruction and Development in Eastern Poland," *"Geographic Journal,* November–December, 1941.

For Polish economic history in the period I found Charles F. Dewey, *The Report of the Financial Adviser to the Bank of Poland: 1930*, to be of great value. Also useful were R. Gorecki, *Poland and Her Economic Development*, and F. Zweig, cited below.

1. Republic of Poland, Ministry of Information, *Concise Statistical Year-Book of Poland, September, 1939–June, 1941*, p. 18.

2. G. Jackson, *Comintern and Peasant in East Europe, 1919–1930* p. 13.

3. B. Schmitt (ed.), *Poland*, p. 222.

4. F. Zweig, *Poland Between Two Wars: A Critical Study of Social and Economic Changes*, p. 38.

5. A. Polonsky, *Politics in Independent Poland*, p. 119.

CHAPTER 10

This chapter has been drawn very heavily from J. Rothschild, *Piłsudski's Coup d'Etat*, which is the definitive work on its subject.

1. H. Roos, *A History of Modern Poland*, p. 114.

2. R. Machray, *Poland 1914–1931*, p. 254.

3. *Ibid.*

4. J. Piłsudski, *PZ*, Vol. VIII, pp. 248–49.

5. *Ibid.*, p. 334.

6. *Ibid.*, p. 336.

7. W. Witos, *Moje Wspomnienia*, Vol. III, p. 83.

8. A. Piłsudska, *Piłsudski: A Biography by His Wife*, p. 330.

9. A. Polonsky, *The Politics of Independent Poland 1921–1939*,

10. *Ibid.*

11. *Ibid.*

12. Colonel Sawicki to Prof. W. Jedrzejewicz of New York City, and from Prof. Jedrzejewicz to this author.

13. Roos, *op. cit.*, p. 114.

14. J. Rothschild, *J. Piłsudski's Coup d'État*, p. 337.

15. Polonsky, *op. cit.*, p. 172.

16. Rothschild, *op. cit.*, p. 152.

17. Piłsudska, *op. cit.*, p. 331.

18. Piłsudski, *PZ*, Vol. IX, pp. 30–33.

19. *Ibid.*, p. 33.

20. Machray, *op. cit.*, p. 324.

21. W. Baranowski, *Rozmowy z Piłsudskim*, p. 198.

22. Piłsudski, *PZ*, Vol. IX, pp. 10–11.

23. General Anders to Prof. Jedrzejewicz of New York City, and from Prof. Jedrzejewicz to this author.

24. Rothschild, *op. cit.*, p. 228.

25. Dewey, C. F. *The Report of the Financial Adviser to the Bank of Poland*, p. 3.

CHAPTER 11

Helpful in the preparation of this chapter, although unreferenced below, were J. Jacobson, *Locarno Diplomacy*; H. Levine, *Hitler's Free City*; C. Kimmich, *The Free City*; and R. Debicki, *The Foreign Policy of Poland 1919–1939*.

1. H. Von Riekhoff, *German-Polish Relations 1918–1933*, p. 134.
2. Józef Beck, *Final Report*, p. 5.
3. J. Laroche, *La Pologne de Piłsudski*.
4. J. Piłsudski, *PZ*, Vol. VII, p. 293.
5. Craig & Gilbert (eds.), *The Diplomats 1919–1939*, pp. 587–88.
6. P. Wandycz, *France and her Eastern Allies*, p. 342.
7. G. von Rauch, *The Baltic States*, p. 105.
8. J. Korbel, *Poland Between East and West*, p. 218.
9. R. Machray, *Poland 1914–1931*, p. 341.

CHAPTER 12

1. W. Baranowski, *Rozmowy z Piłsudskim*, p. 205.
2. *Le Matin*, May 26, 1926.
3. A. Polonsky, *Politics in Independent Poland, 1921–1939*, p. 252.
4. A. Piłsudska, *Piłsudski: A Biography by His Wife*, p. 334.
5. J. Piłsudski, *PZ*, Vol. IX, p. 117.
6. Polonsky, *op. cit.*, p. 276.
7. Piłsudski, *PZ.*, Vol. IX, p. 190.
8. *Ibid.*
9. J. Rothschild, *Piłsudski's Coup d'État*, p. 342.
10. Polonsky, *op. cit.*, p. 311.
11. Pobóg-Malinowski, *op cit.*, Vol. II, p. 717.

CHAPTER 13

For background and economic data on the Depression in Poland I drew on F. Zweig, *Poland Between Two Wars*; R. Gorecki, *Poland and Her Economic Development*; C. S. Dewey, *Report of the Financial Adviser of the Bank of Poland*; R. Buell, *Poland: Key to Europe*; and The Polish Ministry of Information's *Concise Statistical Year-Book of Poland* for 1937 and 1939–41 respectively.

CHAPTER 14

For the section on the Polish-Soviet Non-Aggression Pact and related matters I drew heavily upon B. Budurowycz, *Polish-Soviet Relations 1932–1939.*

1. A. Polonsky, *Politics in Independent Poland: 1921–1939* p. 328.
2. *Ibid.,* p. 329.
3. *Ibid.*
4. A. Vaghts, *A History of Militarism,* pp. 412–13.
5. Polonsky, *op. cit.,* p. 334.
6. *Ibid.,* p. 335.
7. Laroche, *op. cit.,* p. 106.
8. Korbel, *op cit.,* p. 273.
9. J. Beck, *Dernier rapport,* p. XIX.
10. L. Noël, *L'Agression allemande contre la Pologne,* p. 22, Note 1.
11. Galeazzo Ciano, *The Ciano Diaries.*
12. J. Beck, *Final Report,* p. 22.
13. E. Beneš, *Memoirs of Dr. Eduard Beneš: From Munich to New War and New Victory,* pp. 7, 44–45.
14. Woodward and Butler (eds.), *"DBFP,"* Second Series, Vol. IV, No. 298.
15. Republic of France, *Documents diplomatiques français,* I Serie, Vol III, No. 82.
16. Beck, *op. cit.,* p. 39.
17. W. Jedrzejewicz (ed.), *Diplomat in Berlin,* p. 21.
18. *Ibid.,* p. 73.
19. *Ibid.,* p. 74.
20. Republic of Poland, Ministry for Foreign Affairs, *Official Documents Concerning Polish–German and Polish–Soviet Relations 1933–1939 (The Polish White Book,* hereinafter White Book), p. 13.
21. H. Levine, *Hitler's Free City,* p. 61.
22. See Craig and Gilbert (eds), *The Diplomats,* pp. 612–14, for extended listing.
23. W. Jedrzejewicz, "The Polish Plan for a Preventive War Against Germany," *Polish Review,* Vol. XI, No. 1, Winter 1966, pp. 26–27.
24. J. Beck, *op. cit.,* p. 27.
25. Jedrzejewicz (ed), *Diplomat in Berlin,* p. 97.
26. Jedrzejewicz, *Polish Plan,* p. 27.
27. Jedrzejewicz (ed), *Diplomat in Berlin,* p. 96.
28. Republic of Poland, "White Book," p. 18.
29. *Ibid.*
30. *Ibid.,* p. 19.
31. *Ibid.,* p. 21.
32. Beck, *op cit.,* p. 54.
33. Republic of Poland, "White Book," p. 26.
34. *Ibid.*
35. *Ibid.,* p. 28.

36. Craig and Gilbert (eds), *op. cit.*, pp. 585–86.
37. Jedrzejewicz, *Diplomat in Berlin*, p. 180.
38. Beck, *op. cit.*, p. 53.

CHAPTER 15

1. A. Polonsky, *Politics in Independent Poland: 1921–1939*, p. 387.
2. Beck, *Final Report*, p. 87.
3. *Ibid.*, pp. 88–89.
4. W. Jedrzejewicz (ed.), *Kronika Życia Jozefa Piłsudskiego*, vol. II, p. 517.

CHAPTER 16

1. E. Wynot, *Polish Politics in Transition*, p. 48.
2. *Ibid.*, p. 65.
3. A. Polonsky, *Politics in Independent Poland: 1921–1939*, p. 412.
4. *Ibid.*, pp. 419–20.
5. R. Buell, *Poland: Key to Europe*, p. 111.
6. L. Dawidowicz, *The War Against the Jews 1939–1945*, p. 206.
7. S. Segal, *The New Poland and the Jews*, p. 177.
8. C. Heller, *On the Edge of Destruction*, pp. 44–45.
9. *Ibid.* p. 51.
10. E. Wynot, " 'A Necessary Cruelty': The Emergence of Official Anti-Semitism in Poland: 1936–1939," *The American Historical Review*, Vol. 76, No. 4, October 1971, p. 1037 (hereinafter "A Necessary Cruelty").
11. Polonsky, *op. cit.*, p. 466.
12. Wynot, "A Necessary Cruelty," *loc. cit.*, p. 1039.
13. *Ibid.*, pp. 1039–40.
14. *Ibid.*, p. 1042.
15. Buell, *op. cit.*, p. 301.
16. Wynot, "A Necessary Cruelty," *loc. cit.*, p. 1048.
17. Heller, *op. cit.*, p. 113.
18. *Ibid.*, p. 131.
19. Wynot, "A Necessary Cruelty," *loc. cit.*, p. 1049.
20. Heller, *op. cit.*, p. 107.
21. *Ibid.*, p. 93.

CHAPTER 17

Unreferenced below, but of great value in the preparation of this chapter, was A. Cienciala, *Poland and the Western Powers, 1938–1939.*
1. L. Noël, *L'Agression allemande contre la Pologne*, p. 21.
2. Cannistraro *et al., Poland and the Coming of the Second World War*, p. 206.

3. W. Jedrzejewicz (ed.), *Diplomat in Berlin*, p. 253.

4. Noël, *op. cit.*, p. 125.

5. Republic of Poland, *"White Book,"* p. 36.

6. *Ibid.*, pp. 37–38.

7. *Ibid.* p. 38.

8. B. Budurowycz, *Polish–Soviet Relations 1932–1939*, p. 98.

9. W. Jedrzejewicz, (ed.), *Diplomat in Berlin*, p. 309.

10. *Ibid.*, p. 328.

11. U.S. Dept. of State, *Documents on German Foreign Policy*, Series D, Vol. V, No. 163, p. 224.

12. Budurowycz, *op. cit.*, p. 111.

13. W. Shirer, *The Rise and Fall of the Third Reich*, p. 365.

14. J. Beck, *Dernier rapport*, p. 159.

15. W. Jedrzejewicz (ed.), *Diplomat in Paris*, p. 109.

16. L. Namier, *Europe in Decay*, p. 287.

17. A. J. P. Taylor, *The Origins of the Second World War*, p. 159.

18. R. Debicki, *The Foreign Policy of Poland 1919–1939*, p. 119.

19. Budurowycz, *op. cit.*, p. 123.

20. Jedrzejewicz, *Diplomat in Berlin*, p. 437.

21. Craig and Gilbert (eds.), *The Diplomats*, p. 605.

22. *Ibid.*

23. Republic of Poland, *White Book*, p. 182.

24. W. Shirer, *op. cit.*, p. 455.

25. Republic of Poland, *White Book*, p. 47.

26. *Ibid.*, p. 50.

27. Jedrzejewicz (ed.), *Diplomat in Berlin*, p. 468.

28. Republic of Poland, *White Book*, p. 52.

29. *Ibid.*, p. 53.

30. Beck, *Final Report*, p. 172.

31. Republic of Poland, *White Book*, p. 57.

32. *Ibid.*

33. *Ibid.*, p. 63.

34. *Ibid.*, p. 57.

35. All quotes from Jedrzejewicz, *Diplomat in Berlin*, pp. 503–4.

36. Republic of Poland, *White Book*, p. 72.

37. *Ibid.*

38. *Ibid.*, p. 68.

39. S. Aster, *1939: The Making of the Second World War*, p. 123.

40. *Ibid.*, p. 126.

41. W. Churchill, *The Gathering Storm*, p. 350.

42. Republic of Poland, *White Book*, p. 80.

43. *Ibid.*, p. 88.

44. Beck, *op. cit.*, p. 199.

45. Aster, *op. cit.*, p. 179.

46. *Ibid.*, p. 184.

47. *Ibid.*, p. 172.

48. *Ibid.*, p. 303.

49. Noël, *op. cit.*, p. 423.

50. Woodward and Butler (eds.), *Documents on British Foreign Policy*, 3rd Series, Vol. VII, p. 102.

51. P. Reynaud, *In the Thick of the Fight*, p. 229.

52. Aster, *op. cit.*, p. 313.

53. Britain, H. M. Stationery Office, *Documents Concerning* . . . , p. 97.

54. Shirer, *op. cit.*, p. 531.

55. Aster, *op. cit.*, p. 334.

56. *Ibid.*, p. 337.

57. Republic of Poland, *White Book*, p. 119.

CHAPTER 18

For general background on the Polish-German war of September 1939, I found the most helpful works to be R. Kennedy, *The German Campaign in Poland (1939)*, Norwid-Neugebauer, *The Defense of Poland*, and V. Esposito, *The West Point Atlas of American Wars*, Vol. II. The procrastination of the British and French in declaring war on Germany is well told in S. Aster, *1939: The Making of the Second World War*.

1. Cannistraro *et. al.*, *Poland and Coming of the Second World War*, p. 243.

2. Nicholas Bethell, *The War Hitler Won: The Fall of Poland, 1939*, p. 32.

3. W. Shirer, *The Rise and Fall of the Third Reich*, p. 625.

4. H. Guderian, *Panzer Leader*, p. 84.

5. Great Britain, H. M. Stationery Office, *Documents Concerning* . . . , p. 168.

6. Bethell, *op. cit.*, p. 83.

7. *Ibid.*, pp. 119–20.

8. U.S. Department of State, *Documents on German Foreign Policy*, series D, Vol. VIII, No. 5.

9. A. Werth, *Russia at War*, p. 57.

10. Bethell, *op. cit.*, p. 311.

11. Republic of Poland, *White Book*, pp. 189–90.

12. Wynot, *Polish Politics in Transition*, p. 257.

13. Bethell, *op. cit.*, p. 318.

AFTERWORD

The literature on the relations between the Soviet Union and the Polish government-in-exile is almost endless. A valuable supplement to any study of the extended controversy between the Polish government in London and the Soviets, and the British attempts to support and mediate, is F. Loewenheim *et. al.* (eds.), *Roosevelt and Churchill: Their Secret Wartime Correspondence*. The source for the Warsaw Uprising and the Polish Home Army in general is Tadeus Bor-Komorowski, *The Secret Army*.

1. W. Jedrzejewicz (ed.), *Diplomat in Paris*, p. 357.

2. B. Schmitt (ed.), *Poland*, p. 429.

3. W. Churchill, *The Grand Alliance*, p. 391.

4. W. Churchill, *Closing the Ring*, p. 45.

5. Gen. Sikorski Historical Institute, *Documents on Polish-Soviet Relations 1939–1945*, Vol. II, p. 146.

6. *Ibid.*, pp. 168–69.

7. *Ibid.*, p. 145.

8. W. Churchill, *Triumph and Tragedy*, p. 385.

9. N. Bethell, *Gomulka*, p. 91.

Bibliography

Aster, Sidney, *1939: The Making of the Second World War.* London, 1973.

Babel, Isaac, "Red Cavalry," *Collected Stories.* London, 1957.

Bailey, Geoffrey, *The Conspirators.* New York, 1960.

Baranowski, W., *Rozmowy z Piłsudskim: 1916–1931.* Warsaw, 1938.

Beck, Józef, *Dernier rapport.* Neuchâtel, 1951. (Translated as *Final Report,* New York, 1957.)

Beneš, Eduard, *Memoirs of Dr. Eduard Beneš: From Munich to New War and New Victory.* London, 1954.

Beneš, V. L., and Pounds, N.J.G., *Poland.* London, 1970.

Benoist-Méchin, J., *Histoire de l'armée allemande* (2 vols.). Paris, 1938.

Bethell, Nicholas, *The War Hitler Won: The Fall of Poland, 1939.* New York, 1972.

Bonsal, Stephen, *Suitors and Suppliants: The Little Nations at Versailles.* New York, 1946.

Bor-Komorowski, T., *The Secret Army.* London, 1950.

Budurowycz, Bohdan, *Polish–Soviet Relations 1932–1939.* New York, 1963.

Buell, Raymond Leslie, *Poland: Key to Europe.* New York, 1939.

Cannistraro, P. V., Wynot, E. D., and Kovaleff, T. P. (eds.), *Poland and the Coming of the Second World War: The Diplomatic Papers of A.J. Drexel Biddle, Jr., United States Ambassador to Poland 1937–1939.* Columbus, Ohio, 1976.

Carr, E. H. *The Bolshevik Revolution* (3 vols.). New York, 1953.

Carsten, F. L., *Reichswehr and Politics: 1918–1933.* Oxford, 1966.

Churchill, Winston S., *Closing the Ring.* Boston, 1951.

———, *The Gathering Storm.* Boston, 1948.

———, *The Grand Alliance.* Boston, 1951.

———, *Triumph and Tragedy.* Boston, 1953.

Ciano, Galeazzo, *The Ciano Diaries.* Garden City, N.Y., 1946.

Cienciala, Anna M., *Poland and the Western Powers 1938–1939.* London, 1968.

Concise Statistical Yearbook of Poland, 1937. Warsaw: (Polish) Ministry for Foreign Affairs, 1938.

Concise Statistical Yearbook of Poland, September 1939–June 1942. London: (Polish) Ministry for Foreign Affairs, 1942.

Craig, G.A., and Gilbert, F., (eds.), *The Diplomats 1919–1939.* Princeton, N.J., 1953.

Czernin, Ferdinand, *Versailles 1919.* New York, 1964.

D'Abernon, Lord, *The Eighteenth Decisive Battle of World History*. London, 1931.

Davies, Norman, *White Eagle, Red Star: The Polish Soviet War 1919–1920*. London, 1972.

Dawidowicz, Lucy S., *The War Against the Jews 1933–1945*. New York, 1975.

Debicki, Roman, *The Foreign Policy of Poland 1919–1939*. New York, 1962.

———, "The Remilitarization of the Rhineland and the Impact on the French-Polish Alliance," in Gromada, T. V. (ed.), *Essays on Poland's Foreign Policy*. New York, 1970.

Degras, Jane (ed.), *Soviet Documents on Foreign Policy 1917–1924*. London, 1951.

Deutscher, Isaac, *The Prophet Armed: Trotsky 1879–1921*. New York: Random House (Vintage edition), 1965.

Dewey, Charles S., *Report of the Financial Adviser to the Bank of Poland*. Warsaw, 1930.

Documents Concerning German-Polish Relations and the Outbreak of Hostilities Between Great Britain and Germany on September 3, 1939. London: H.M. Stationery Office, 1939.

Documents diplomatiques Français, I Série, Vol. III, No. 82. Paris: Ministry of Foreign Affairs, 1964–66.

Documents on German Foreign Policy, 1918–1945. Series D, 1937–45. Washington, D.C.: U.S. Dept. of State, 1947.

Dziewanowski, M.K., *The Communist Party of Poland*. Cambridge, Mass., 1959.

———, *Josef Piłsudski: A European Federalist, 1918–1922*. Stanford, Cal., 1969.

Esposito V. J. (ed.), *The West Point Atlas of American Wars* (2 vols.). New York, 1957.

Fiddick, Thomas, "The 'Miracle of the Vistula': Soviet Policy versus Red Army Strategy," *The Journal of Modern History*, Vol. 45, Number 4 (December 1973).

Fuller, J. F. C., *Decisive Battles: Their Influence upon History and Civilization*. New York, 1940.

Gathorne-Hardy, G. M., *A Short History of International Affairs 1920–1939; Fourth Edition*. London, 1955.

Gelfand, Lawrence E., *The Inquiry*. New Haven, Conn., 1963.

Gorecki, Roman, *Poland and Her Economic Development*. London, 1935.

Guderian, Heinz, *Panzer Leader*. New York, 1952.

Halecki, O., *A History of Poland*. Chicago, 1956.

Haskins, C. H. and Lord, R. H., *Some Problems of the Peace Conference*. Cambridge, Mass., 1922.

Heller, Celia S., *On the Edge of Destruction: Jews of Poland Between the Two World Wars*. New York, 1977.

Horak, Stephan, *Poland and Her National Minorities: 1919–1939*. New York, 1961.

Humphrey, Grace, *Piłsudski: Builder of Poland*. New York, 1936.

Jackson, George D., Jr., *Comintern and Peasant in East Europe, 1919–1930*. New York, 1966.

Jacobson, Jon, *Locarno Diplomacy*. Princeton, N.J., 1972.

Jedrzejewicz, Waclaw, "The Polish Plan for a 'Preventive War' Against Germany in 1933," in *The Polish Review*, Vol. XI, No. 1 (Winter 1966).

———, ed., *Diplomat in Berlin 1933–1939: Papers and Memoirs of Jozef Lipski, Ambassador of Poland*. New York, 1968.

———, ed., *Diplomat in Paris 1936–1939: Memoirs of Julius Lukasiewicz, Ambassador of Poland*. New York, 1970.

———, ed., *Kronica Życia Jozefa Piłsudskiego* (2 vols.). London, 1978.

Jurgela, Constantine R., *History of the Lithuanian People*. New York, 1948.

Kennedy, Robert M. *The German Campaign in Poland (1939)*, U.S. Dept. of Army Pamphlet 20–255, 1956.

Kessler, Harry, *Tagebücher: 1918–1937*. Frankfurt, 1961.

Kimmich, Christopher M., *The Free City: Danzig and German Foreign Policy*. New Haven, Conn., 1968.

Komarnicki, Titus, *Rebirth of the Polish Republic*. London, 1957.

Korbel, Josef, *Poland Between East and West*. Princeton, N.J., 1963.

Kumaniecki, Kazimierz, *Odbudowa Państwowości Polskiej*. Warsaw, 1924.

Kutrzeba, T., *Wyprawa Kijowska: Roku 1920*. Warsaw, 1936.

Landau, Rom, *Piłsudski and Poland*. New York, 1929.

Laroche, Jules, *La Pologne de Piłsudski: Souvenirs d'une ambassade 1926–1935*. Paris, 1935.

Lawton, Mary, *The Paderewski Memoirs*. New York, 1938.

Levine, Herbert, *Hitler's Free City*. Chicago, 1973.

Lloyd George, David, *Memoirs of the Peace Conference* (2 vols.). New Haven, Conn., 1939.

Loewenheim, F. L., Langley, H. D., and Jonas, M., eds. *Roosevelt and Churchhill: Their Secret Wartime Correspondence*. New York, 1975.

Luckett, Richard, *The White Generals*. New York, 1971.

Machray, Robert, *Poland 1914–1931*. New York, 1932.

———, *The Poland of Piłsudski: 1914–1936*. London, 1936.

———, *The Problem of Upper Silesia*. London, 1945.

Miller, David Hunter, *My Diary at the Peace Conference of Paris* (21 vols.). New York, 1925.

Mincer, Tadeus, *The Agrarian Problem in Poland*. London, 1944.

Moffat, Jay Pierrepont, *The Moffat Papers: Selections from the Diplomatic Journals of Jay Pierrepont Moffat, 1919–1943*, ed. Nancy Hooker. Cambridge, Mass., 1956.

Murray, K. M., *Wings over Poland: The Story of the 7th (Kosciuszko) Squadron of the Polish Air Service 1919, 1920, 1921*. New York, 1932.

Namier, Louis B., *Europe in Decay*. Gloucester, Mass., 1963.

Nelson, Harold I., *Land and Power*. London, 1963.

Nettl, J. P., *Rosa Luxemburg* (2 vols.). Oxford, 1966.

Noël, Léon, *L'Agression allemande contre la Pologne*. Paris, 1946.

Norwid-Neugebauer, M., *The Defence of Poland*. London, 1942.

Papers Relating to the Foreign Relations of the United States.

Piłsudska, Alexandra, *Piłsudski: A Biography by His Wife*. New York, 1941.

Piłsudski, Józef, *Jozef Piłsudski: The Memories of a Polish Revolutionary and Soldier*. ed. D. R. Gillie. London, 1931.

———, *Pisma Zbiorowe* (10 vols.). Warsaw, 1937.

———, *Year 1920*. New York, 1972.

Pobóg-Malinowski, W., *Najinowsza historia polityczna Polski, 1864–1945,* 2nd ed., revised (2 vols.). London, 1963, 1967.

Ministry for Foreign Affairs, *Official Documents Concerning Polish–German and Polish–Soviet Relations 1933–1939 (Polish White Book)*. London: (Polish) Ministry for Foreign Affairs, 1940.

Polonsky, Antony, *Politics in Independent Poland 1921–1939*. Oxford, 1972.

Rauch, Georg von, *The Baltic States: The Years of Independence 1917–1940*. Berkeley, Calif., 1974.

Reddaway, W. F., ed., *The Cambridge History of Poland to 1696*. Cambridge, 1950.

Redfield, R., *Peasant Society and Culture*. Cambridge, 1950.

Reshetar, John S., *The Ukrainian Revolution*. Princeton, N.J., 1952.

Reynaud, Paul, *In the Thick of the Fight*. New York, 1955.

Riddell, George, *Lord Riddell's Intimate Diary of the Peace Conference and After*. New York, 1934.

Riekhoff, Harald von, *German-Polish Relations 1918–1933*. Baltimore, 1971.

Roos, Hans, *A History of Modern Poland*. New York, 1966.

Rose, William J., *The Drama of Upper Silesia*. Brattleboro, Vt., 1935.

Rothschild, Joseph, *Piłsudski's Coup d'État*. New York, 1966.

Russell, John, "Reconstruction and Development in Eastern Poland," *Geographic Journal*, November–December 1941.

Schmitt, Bernadotte E., ed., *Poland*. Berkeley, Calif., 1945.

Seaton, Albert, *Stalin As Military Commander*. New York, 1976.

Segal, Simon, *The New Poland and the Jews*. New York, 1938.

Seymour, Charles, *Letters from the Paris Peace Conference*. New Haven, Conn., 1965.

Shirer, William L., *The Rise and Fall of the Third Reich*. New York, 1960.

Sikorski, General, Historical Institute, *Documents on Polish-Soviet Relations 1939–1945* (2 vols.). London, 1967.

Staniewicz, Witold, "The Agrarian Problem in Poland Between Two Wars," *Slavonic and East European Review*, Vol. XLIII, No. 100 (December 1964).

Taylor, A. J. P., *Origins of the Second World War*. London, 1961.

Trotsky, Leon, *My Life*. New York, 1930.

Vaghts, Alfred, *A History of Militarism* (revised). New York, 1959.

Waite, R. G. L., *Vanguard of Naziism*. Cambridge, Mass., 1952.

Wandycz, Piotr S., *Czechoslovak–Polish Confederation and the Great Powers 1940–1943*. Bloomington, Indiana, 1956.

———, *France and Her Eastern Allies 1919–1925*. Minneapolis, Minn., 1962.

———, *The Lands of Partitioned Poland, 1795–1918*. Seattle, Wash., 1974.

———, *Soviet–Polish Relations 1917–1921*. Cambridge, Mass., 1969.

Werth, Alexander, *Russia at War 1941–1945*. New York, 1964.

Weygand, Maxime, *Mémoires: Mirages et Réalité*. Paris, 1957.

Woodward, E. L. and Butler, R., eds, *Documents on British Foreign Policy 1918–1945.* Ist Series, London, 1947–

Wynot, Edward D., Jr., " 'A Necessary Cruelty': The Emergence of Anti-Semitism in Poland: 1936–1939," *American Historical Review,* Vol. 76, No. 4 (October 1971).

———, *Polish Politics in Transition.* Athens, Ga., 1974.

Zweig, Ferdynand, *Poland Between Two Wars: A Critical Study of Social and Economic Changes.* London, 1944.

Acknowledgments

In the course of the more than ten years that it took me to write this book I was assisted by a great many persons who are authorities on Poland during the period between the two World Wars. Of those, I am most deeply indebted to Professor Waclaw Jedrzejewicz, of New York City, whose long career spans membership in Piłsudski's Riflemen's Brigades, service in the First Brigade of the Polish Legion and the P.O.W. Intelligence Branch, and an interwar career as a general staff officer, diplomat, and cabinet minister. Professor Jedrzejewicz is also professor emeritus of Wellesley College and Ripon College, and the author of a number of distinguished scholarly works. Currently the president of the Jozef Piłsudski Institute of America, his exceptional assistance to historians working in the field of interwar Poland has been acknowledged in scores of doctoral dissertations, scholarly papers and books. All testify to his objectivity, although he was indubitably a prominent *Sanacja* personality. I am pleased to be able to add my deep appreciation to this remarkable man.

Among those who were of additional assistance to me in specific fields and to whom I wish to express my indebtedness is Professor Kay Lundgreen-Nielson of Odense University, Odense, Denmark, an authority on the activities of the Polish delegation at the Peace Conference of Paris, who was kind enough to review the sections of my manuscript that deal with that subject. Wieslaw Domaniewski, of New York City, formerly a director of the Bank of Poland, was good enough to give valuable comments on those parts of my work that discuss the Polish economy. General Kasimierz Glabisz, of London, who in September 1939 was emergency assignments officer of the staff of Marshal Rydz-Śmigły, reviewed my chapter on the September War in Poland and provided considerable insight on the course of the fighting. As he did with my earlier works, Colonel John Elting, U.S.A., retired, of Cornwall, New York, a military scholar and historian and formerly a member of the Department of Military Art and Engineering at the U.S. Military Academy, assisted me in military matters. I wish also to thank Dr. Antony Polonsky, of the Department of International History, London School of Economics, for friendly encouragement and advice.

I am very grateful to my editor Michael V. Korda for his unfailing support. I also wish to thank Barbara Crincoli, who with endless patience typed and retyped this manuscript. Finally, I record my gratitude to my wife, Nancy, who endured uncomplainingly the years of my absorption with this project.

Index

483

DANZIG & ENVIRONS

Baltic Sea

HEL PENINSULA

Gdynia

BAY OF DANZIG

WESTERPLATTE

FREE CITY OF DANZIG

Braunsberg

Danzig

Elbing

Dirschau

EAST PRUSSIA

POLISH CORRIDOR

POLAND

VISTULA R.

MARIEN WERDER

Allenstein

Marienwerder

Osterode

Tannenberg

ALLENSTEIN

SWEDEN

DENMARK

Copenhagen

NORTH SEA

Hamburg

Stettin

ELBE R.

Bremen

Berlin

ODER R.

NETHERLANDS

Hannover

GERMANY

Amsterdam

Antwerp

RHINE R.

Kassel

Leipzig

BELGIUM

Cologne

Dresden

FRANCE

Spa

Weimar

LUX.

Frankfurt

MAIN R.

Prague

UPPER SILESIA & THE DUCHY OF TESCHEN

Nuremberg

Breslau

ODER R.

Kreuzburg

Częstochowa

DANUBE R.

GERMANY

UPPER SILESIA

POLAND

Munich

Neisse

Linz

Neustadt

Oppeln

Bytoń

Ratibor

Katowice

Kraków

AUSTRIAN SILESIA

Rybnik

Oświęcim

AUSTRIA

Troppau

Karyna

Biała

Teschen

DUCHY OF TESCHEN

ITALY

CZECHOSLOVAKIA